MIDLOTHIAN
PUBLIC LIBRARY

FREUD

Also by Louis Breger

Clinical Cognitive Psychology
(editor)

The Effect of Stress on Dreams
(with I. Hunter and R. W. Lane)

From Instinct to Identity:
The Development of Personality

Freud's Unfinished Journey: Conventional and Critical
Perspectives in Psychoanalytic Theory

Dostoevsky: The Author as Psychoanalyst

FREUD
Darkness in the Midst of Vision

Louis Breger

John Wiley & Sons, Inc.
New York • Chichester • Weinheim • Brisbane • Singapore • Toronto

FOR OUR GRANDCHILDREN
Peter, John, and Benjamin
Katherine, Jack, and Annie
Dylan, Jack, and Annie
Gregory and Thomas

This book is printed on acid-free paper. ∞

Copyright © 2000 by Louis Breger. All rights reserved

Published by John Wiley & Sons, Inc.
Published simultaneously in Canada

This publication is designed to provide accurate and authoritative information in regard to the subject matter covered. It is sold with the understanding that the publisher is not engaged in rendering professional services. If professional advice or other expert assistance is required, the services of a competent professional person should be sought.

Library of Congress Cataloging-in-Publication Data:

Breger, Louis.
   Freud: darkness in the midst of vision / Louis Breger.
      p.   cm.
   Includes bibliographical references and index.
   ISBN 0-471-31628-8 (hardcover : alk. paper)
   1. Freud, Sigmund, 1856–1939. 2. Psychoanalysis.
   3. Psychoanalysts—Austria—Biography. I. Title.

BF109.F74 B74   2000
150.19'52'092—dc21
[B]   99-059994

Printed in the United States of America
10 9 8 7 6 5 4 3 2 1

Contents

Acknowledgments

IN ALL WAYS, this book has been a collaboration with my wife, Barbara. It took shape over the course of our many conversations; she edited the manuscript through seemingly endless permutations, introducing a number of original ideas. Many of the chapter headings with their quotations from nonpsychoanalytic sources came from her broad reading. The principal ideas concerning militarism in the nineteenth century, the women's movement in Europe, the First World War, and the history of the treatment of war neuroses were the result of her independent scholarship. My understanding of Freud's attitudes toward women, and the influence of his military identifications, were significantly shaped in our dialogues. She was the primary author of the chapter on the First World War and coauthor of the chapter *Trauma Revisited.*

My agent, John W. Wright, believed in me and the book at an early stage, gave helpful editorial advice, and was, and remains, everything that a good agent should be. I also thank my colleague Robert Dallek for recommending me to John. Hana Umlauf Lane, my editor at John Wiley, is that all-too-rare find, an editor who has been deeply involved in bringing out the best in the manuscript at every stage of its development. She has given generously of her time and fine editorial skills.

I want to give special thanks to my colleague David Markel, who gave important suggestions with early drafts, and was supportive in many other ways. Judith Viorst shared her enthusiasm, critical comments, and friendship, for all of which I thank her. Polly Young-Eisendrath gave helpful comments on the Jung chapter and put me in contact with Dierdre Bair, who took time to read that same chapter and share her reactions. Jim Lieberman read the chapter on Otto Rank and gave helpful comments and suggestions. Kitty Moore gave encouragement at an early stage and also put me in touch with Freud's granddaughter, Dr. Sophie Freud, who was extremely generous with her time. She read material on the Freud family, commented on its accuracy, and went over the manuscript in its final form, offering many valuable suggestions.

Other colleagues and friends who read different parts of the book as it was taking shape, and gave generously of their time and efforts, include: George Atwood, Arthur Barron, Philip Bromberg, Leslie Brothers, Kristi Clark, Christopher Gelber, Victoria Hamilton, Deborah Lott, and Murray Schwartz. My understanding of the mind of the traumatized child was enhanced by Carl Utsinger. I thank my Caltech secretary Helga Galvan for all her help.

Barbara wishes to thank Jonnie Hargis of the UCLA Research Library, Linda Gerstein for her good advice, and her teachers: Temma Kaplan, Rose Glickman, and Debora Silverman. But, most of all, she thanks Hans Rogger for his support, his scholarship, and for assigning her the topic of "war and culture" without even asking if the subject would be of interest to a woman.

I express my gratitude to all those scholars and translators whose work forms the foundation on which this book stands. My own understanding of psychotherapy and psychoanalysis has grown deeper over many years of immersion in the lives and struggles of my patients, and I take this opportunity to thank them.

"The Development of the Hero"

The General always insisted that, if you bring off adequate preservation of your personal myth, nothing much else in life matters. It is not what happens to people that is significant, but what they think happens to them.

—Anthony Powell, *A Dance to the Music of Time*

FREUD'S FACE is instantly recognizable: the wise, gray-haired genius with his cigar, neatly trimmed beard, and finely tailored suit; the psychoanalyst whose gaze seems to penetrate the depths of the human soul. The picture on the next page shows Freud in his sixties, the icon the world has come to know. What the world does *not* know is that Freud worked hard to create this image; it is an integral part of a personal myth that he embellished over the years, a vision of his life that is part truth and part pseudohistory, a mix of fact and fantasy. Even the penetrating gaze is something he appropriated from two of the heroes of his university days: his mentors Ernst Brücke and Jean-Martin Charcot.

As early as 1885, when Freud was twenty-eight years old, just completing his medical training, and before he had done any work of real significance, he was already concerned with obscuring the details of his life. He wrote to his fiancée, Martha Bernays: "I have destroyed all my notes of the past fourteen years, as well as letters, scientific excerpts, and the manuscripts of my papers. . . . As for the biographers, let them worry, we have no desire to make it too easy for them. Each one of them will be right in his opinion of 'The Development of the Hero,' and I am already looking forward to seeing them go astray." He conducted several later purges of his papers—one in 1907—and, toward the end of his life, attempted to destroy important letters written in the years of his self-analysis.

Freud in his midsixties.

Freud's letter to his fiancée reveals that even before he had done the work that would make him famous, he envisioned himself as a hero, a man whose life would be chronicled by biographers. There is nothing intrinsically wrong with such a grand ambition; many who make significant contributions are buoyed up by faith in their eventual success. But to understand Freud fully, it is necessary to know what drove him toward the kind of heroic role he craved. He was not primarily motivated by scientific curiosity, though this played some role. The scientists he admired were not Louis Pasteur or Robert Koch—whose work did so much to control the spread of disease—but Kepler and Darwin, men whose theories turned the world upside down. Nor did he wish to alleviate human suffering, to become a doctor devoted to healing. His passionate desire was to become a great man, to achieve fame, to be, in his own words, a "hero."

Freud suffered a very traumatic, impoverished, and difficult childhood that left a legacy of fear, insecurity, and unhappiness. Like many bright children in similar circumstances, he escaped into the world of his imagination. Romantic novels, accounts of life in ancient Egypt, Greece, and Rome, tales of generals and their military exploits, were the worlds where the young Sigmund found solace and consolation, where he could imagine himself in a variety of guises. The heroic figure that most appealed to him was the conqueror, the general who led his army in victorious combat. Alexander the Great, Napoléon, and the Carthaginian Hannibal who crossed the Alps to attack the power of Rome were the men who aroused his ardor. He was also drawn to another figure, one out of the dramas of ancient Greece: Oedipus, who bested his own father in comabt, solved the riddle of the Sphinx, and became king of Thebes. For the young Freud, it was far better to live in his mind as one of these powerful men than to feel himself a poor Jewish boy, living in a crowded ghetto in anti-Semitic Vienna.

As an adult, Freud sought fame, created theories that he hoped would surpass all others and secure his stature in the world as a great man. This drive arose from the same source as the heroic identifications of his childhood: the longing to overcome the poverty, failures, and losses that suffused his early life. The creation of a new, heroic self required the obliteration of his origins, and so he destroyed documents and later falsified much of his personal history.

In creating a new heroic self, Freud relied on his impressive literary skills. The young boy who had lived in the world of books and his imagination became a masterful stylist, capable of presenting his ideas in compelling prose, of shaping arguments with persuasive metaphors and rhetoric. He lived most intensely—his most powerful emotions were at play—when he was writing. His complete works fill twenty-three volumes and his correspondence was enormous, running to over twenty thousand letters. Freud used his literary and rhetorical skills to control and shape his personal legend as well as the history of the psychoanalytic movement. He was so good at this that many today, both friend and foe, are still engaged in either defending or attacking his ideas within the context that he created. The power of his writing is such that he continues to define the terms of these debates.

Freud created psychoanalysis in part from his observations of neurotic patients, but an even more potent source for his theories was the self-analysis that he carried out in his late thirties and early forties, confided in letters to his close friend, the Berlin physician Wilhelm Fliess. He analyzed himself using his own dreams, many of which he recorded in the book he always considered his most significant: *The Interpretation of Dreams.* Most of his biographers—and a great many others—describe the self-analysis as a uniquely heroic act. It was here, they feel, that Freud, the honest and courageous explorer, descended into the dark regions of his own mind and confronted those sides of human nature that his timorous contemporaries dared not face. On this inward journey, as the legend has it, Freud came face to face with his forbidden desires, exposed them, and, as a result, unmasked the sexual hypocrisy of the Victorian age. And he also discovered—or invented—his Oedipus complex, which he instantly promoted to a universal law: All boys lust after their mothers, which brings them into rivalrous combat with their fathers. The conflict, fear, and guilt of this situation became his principal explanation for the symptoms and anxieties of adult neuroses, both his own and those of his patients.

Freud's early psychoanalytic work, along with the self-analysis, culminated in profound discoveries and brilliant insights. He exposed sexual conflicts of many kinds and cast new light on the emotional events of infancy and childhood; dreams and a method of interpreting them were developed, and he described the many manifestations of the unconscious—from neurotic symptoms to the phenomena of everyday life—in persuasive terms. In addition to these theories, Freud developed a method of treatment that became the forerunner of modern psychotherapy, which has flowered forth in a great variety of forms. He wove all these ideas and methods together in an encompassing system, modeled after the great scientific theories of the nineteenth century.

Along with these brilliant contributions came the overblown theories, sweeping generalizations, and personal biases that have plagued psychoanalysis since its inception: the *universal* Oedipus complex, sexuality as the driving force for *all* human action, the belief that all women desire the maleness they lack—the theory of penis envy—and that the greatest fear of men is their inner femininity—the theory of unconscious homosexuality. These sweeping generalizations and imperial theories were fueled by Freud's desire for greatness; they were his attempt to be a powerful scientist-hero. There was never any convincing evidence for these ideas; they arose primarily from his needs and personal blind spots. The version of Freud's own childhood that emerged from his self-analysis—that he was a young oedipal warrior lusting after his mother and at war with his powerful father, that sexuality was at the root of his fears and symptoms—and that he later extrapolated into psychoanalytic orthodoxy—was an invention, a self-interpretation that served to cover up the unbearable traumas and losses of his own life.

In demythologizing Freud—penetrating to the truth beneath the heroic image he created and that passes for the gospel in psychoanalytic lore—the real person will emerge in all his human complexity. He was a man of great accomplishments along with significant failures and weaknesses; someone whose startling originality coexisted with a rigid adherence to dogma; a person who spent his life immersed in the most intimate details of other people's lives, yet remained wrapped up in himself and curiously remote from others; a man capable of penetrating insights who was also blind to the effect he had on other people.

PART ONE

Freud's Life:
The First Thirty Years

CHAPTER 1

A Traumatic Infancy

Freud has emerged as a person stranger and less explicable by his own theories than he himself realized.

—Charles Rycroft

SIGMUND FREUD was born in 1856 in Freiberg, Moravia (today Příbor, in the Czech Republic), a small market town one hundred fifty miles north of Vienna, the first child of the newly married Jacob and Amalia Nathanson Freud. Freiberg was then part of the Austro-Hungarian or Hapsburg Empire, a vast region that included parts of what later became Czechoslovakia, Hungary, Poland, Romania, the Ukraine, Yugoslavia, and present-day Austria. Of the 4,500 inhabitants of Freiberg at that time, only 130—about 3 percent—were Jews like the Freuds; there were an equally small number of Protestants. The rest of the townsfolk—over 4,000—were Czech Catholics. The new baby was named Sigismund Schlomo. Sigismund was a German name from the word *Sieg,* or victory. Schlomo—Solomon in English—was a Hebrew name bestowed in honor of Jacob's recently deceased father. The two names reflected the historical and cultural milieu of Jacob and his family, positioned between traditional Jewish life and the new path of emancipation and assimilation that was just opening to them in the middle of the nineteenth century.

Jews had been a persecuted minority in Europe for centuries, their fortunes waxing and waning at different times and in different countries. Under some progressive regimes, they prospered as merchants, traders, and advisers to kings, while at other times they were subject to oppression, legal restrictions, banishment, and pogroms in which they were slaughtered by the thousands. Such persecution forced families to move from one country to another, and the father of Kallamon Jacob Freud—to give him his full name—had settled in what was then the Austro-Hungarian region of Galicia (now part of the Ukraine), in the village of Tysmenitz. During Jacob's youth, half the population of Tysmenitz

7

was Jewish; many were traders and merchants, and the town was also a center of Jewish learning and scholarship. Jews in the village, or *shtetl,* of Tysmenitz followed centuries-old Orthodox traditions: they celebrated their own holidays, studied the Talmud, adhered to dietary laws, and spoke Yiddish among themselves, all of which isolated them from their gentile neighbors. Forbidden from owning land, they served as merchants, shopkeepers, and traders. As in many of the shtetls of eastern Europe, the Jews interacted with their gentile neighbors, yet constituted a world unto themselves with their separate religious practices, customs, and language.

Jacob's maternal grandfather, Siskind Hofmann, traveled between Galicia and Moravia, trading in wool, linen, honey, and tallow; Jacob became his junior partner and would work as a merchant and salesman for the rest of his life. His travels took Jacob away from the narrow confines of the shtetl and introduced him to a somewhat wider world. These journeys took him to Freiberg, where he became a permanent resident in 1852. Sally Kanner, whom he had married as a very young man, did not join him on his travels; she died in Tysmenitz before he moved to Freiberg. His two sons from this first marriage—Emanuel and Philipp—joined their father in Freiberg to work in his business there.

As the nineteenth century progressed, discrimination toward Jews gradually lessened. The rise of the Enlightenment—particularly in Germany—brought about increased religious tolerance. The Austrian emperor Joseph II issued a Tolerance Ordinance in 1781 that did away with many restrictions on the Jews in his realm, and Prussia officially emancipated its Jewish population in 1812. The revolution that shook western Europe in 1848 had, as one benefit, greater religious freedom. Franz Joseph, emperor of Austria-Hungary throughout much of Freud's lifetime, granted full rights to Austrian Jews in 1849. When Jacob set up in Freiberg as a trader in wool, he was the beneficiary of these new freedoms. The old prejudices did not disappear, of course; Jacob was still a "tolerated Jew" who had to apply to the authorities every year for permission to pursue his business. Nevertheless, full political and civic rights and the abolition of many restrictions meant that Jews were in a far better position then they had been for centuries.

The new freedoms, along with contact with the world outside the shtetl, encouraged Jacob to shed many of the traditions of Jewish life. He was part of a generation in transition, people who were beginning to think of themselves as Austrians or Germans as much as Jews, who moved away from Orthodox religious practices and adopted the customs, mores, and languages of their new countries. Where his ancestors spoke Yiddish and wrote in Hebrew, Jacob—who knew these languages—conducted his business in German. By the time he married Amalia, his new family was set on this assimilated path: they continued to celebrate the traditional Jewish holidays of Purim and Passover, but more as festive events; the Orthodox practices of their forebears were gone and the new family was raised as culturally but not religiously Jewish. Still, with all the new freedom and assimilation, memories of persecution hovered in the air: there were many reminders in daily life of their position as Jews; the effect of centuries of mistreatment, and the possibility of new violence, could not be erased from their minds. They were, after all, a tiny minority in Freiberg, surrounded by people who did not share their history or religion.

Following the death of his first wife, Jacob may have married a woman named Rebecca, who apparently also died. It is not known for certain whether this woman even existed but, if she did, Freud as an adult showed no awareness of her, though she would have been known to his older half brothers and, no doubt, his mother. Jacob and Amalia Nathanson were married in 1855, when he was forty and she twenty. Jacob has been described as fair and, in the later words of his grandson Martin, tall and broad-shouldered. Photographs of him around the age of fifty reveal a handsome and distinguished-looking man. He was a person of pleasant manners, easygoing, with a sense of humor—he was, after all, a salesman—and, at the time of his marriage to Amalia, somewhat successful in business.

Little is known about Amalia Nathanson's background. She was born in the town of Brody in eastern Galicia and lived for a time in Odessa, where her older brothers settled. With her parents, and her younger brother Julius, she moved to Vienna when she was a child, and it was here that she and Jacob met. Her father was a merchant and the family, at least in later years, was not poor. She was an attractive young woman, slender and dark, and possessed of great vitality and a powerful personality. Jacob and Amalia were married by a rabbi affiliated with the Reform movement, a further sign of their move away from the Orthodox traditions of their ancestors.

Sigismund Schlomo Freud was the firstborn son of the new marriage between Jacob and Amalia. He was known as "Sigi" throughout his childhood and his mother still called him this when he was in his seventies, though he used the name Sigismund throughout adolescence, shortening it to Sigmund around the time he entered the university. Jacob, Amalia, and their infant son were soon joined by two additional babies. While Jacob's business seemed sufficient to support his family, they could afford no more than a single rented room above the locksmith shop of a Czech family named Zajic in a building that still stands in Příbor. The family's living conditions were cramped, and which continued for a number of years after they moved to Vienna, a situation that exposed little Sigi to many intimate details of his parents' lives; at this time, babies were born at home and nursed in the conjugal bed. And they died at home as well.

The young Freud was part of an extended family in Freiberg that made up a small world unto itself. Jacob's two grown sons from his first marriage—Emanuel, age twenty-four at the time of Sigmund's birth in 1856, and Philipp, age twenty—had moved to Freiberg to work with their father. Emanuel was married to a woman named Marie and they had two children of their own: a son John—Sigmund's nephew, though one year older—and a daughter Pauline, about seven months younger than Sigi, infants who would soon become his first playmates. Philipp, his unmarried half brother, lived across the street from Jacob and Amalia, while Emanuel, his wife, and his children occupied an apartment a few blocks away.

All of the adult Freuds worked together in the family business, buying wool woven by the local peasants, dyeing and finishing it, and selling it to manufacturers in other locations. Jacob was, in other words, a middleman whose business depended on contacts and trade with customers in other cities. Since the business required the participation of many of the family members, including Amalia, the infant Sigi was left with a nursemaid, a Czech woman who served as an important substitute mother in Amalia's absence. If we imagine things from the point of view of the very young Freud, his was a world of big people and small children: his parents and half brothers—who were uncle figures—his nephew and niece—who were really like cousins—and the three women who mothered him in various ways—his mother, his nursemaid, and Emanuel's wife, Marie. Interestingly, several of Freud's adult dreams, analyzed in *The Interpretation of Dreams,* depict him with three mothers.

Although Jacob, his older sons, and his new wife were relatively recent arrivals in Freiberg, he probably had some contacts from his earlier business dealings there. Nevertheless, their status as members of a tiny minority must have given them a sense of isolation, a state that would have turned them toward each other for social and emotional support. They did know at least one local Jewish family, the Flusses, whose father, Ignaz, also came from Tysmenitz and was in the same business as Jacob, and whose son, Emil, was the same age as Sigmund. Emil remained a friend after the family moved to Vienna, and other members of the Fluss clan played significant roles in Freud's adolescence.

Within the extended family, Sigmund had two playmates: the older John and the younger Pauline. Family members told how he and John played and scrapped together and described their misdeeds and teasing of the younger Pauline. As Freud himself later wrote to his confidant Wilhelm Fliess at the time of his self-analysis: "I have also long known the companion of my misdeeds between the ages of one and two years; it is my nephew, a year older than myself. . . . The two of us seem occasionally to have behaved cruelly to my niece, who was a year younger."

In a rare published account of his earliest years, Freud recalled playing in the fields of Freiberg with two other children and painted an idyllic pastoral scene. But whatever happiness there may have been was soon overtaken by a host of calamities. Even before Sigmund's birth, the family had been marked by death. Jacob lost his first wife, Sally, his second, Rebecca, and his father,

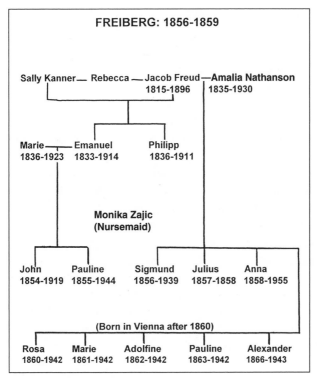

FREIBERG: 1856-1859

Sally Kanner—— Rebecca — Jacob Freud—Amalia Nathanson
1815-1896 | 1835-1930

Marie———Emanuel   Philipp
1836-1923 1833-1914   1836-1911

Monika Zajic
(Nursemaid)

John   Pauline   Sigmund   Julius   Anna
1854-1919 1855-1944   1856-1939 1857-1858 1858-1955

(Born in Vienna after 1860)

Rosa   Marie   Adolfine   Pauline   Alexander
1860-1942 1861-1942 1862-1942   1863-1942 1866-1943

The Freud family tree.

Schlomo, the last just six months before his son was born. Emanuel and Philipp had lost their mother, their first stepmother, and their grandfather. These deaths were followed during the next years by a series of losses that would have powerful traumatic effects on the young boy.

The losses began when Amalia, quickly pregnant after she had Sigmund, gave birth to a second son, Julius. This new brother was Freud's first rival, a competitor who took his mother away from him when he was just eleven months old. She named the new baby after her own younger brother Julius, who had died of tuberculosis at the age of twenty, just a month before she gave birth to her second child. The infant Sigmund's first exposure to death followed close at hand; his baby brother died of an intestinal infection about six or eight months after he was born, when Sigmund was close to two. It is almost certain that the death occurred in the one-room apartment and that Freud was exposed to it. He certainly witnessed his parents' and older half brothers' reaction to this death.

Amalia was, in all probability, depressed following the death of her brother and his namesake, her half-year-old son. Although there is no direct account of her grief, it is an almost universal occurrence when a mother suffers the death of an infant. Not only did the very young Freud lose his mother to a rival, but she became unavailable in her unhappy state following her losses. Because the deaths of Jacob's first and second wives a few years earlier, and grandfather Schlomo's death shortly before Sigmund's birth, had been assimilated by the family, the acute periods of mourning would have passed. But the deaths of Amalia's brother and her new baby were fresh. It is a good guess that the loss of this baby, in the context of the other deaths, created a family atmosphere of mourning and depression. The infant Sigmund would have been immersed in this atmosphere at a very young age and, with only a limited understanding of death, must have felt vulnerable and fearful that he too might die, become sick, or disappear. The death of Julius and his mother's grief could be expected to set off highly threatening reactions in a child that small—fears that he would lose those he most needed—reactions that the bereaved parents would be little able to respond to, if they were even aware of them.

The losses of Freud's first two years produced long-lasting fears associated with maternal absence and death, fears illustrated by a terrifying dream he had at the age of eight or nine, which he recorded in his forties in *The Interpretation of Dreams*. The dream occurred at a time in his middle childhood when new babies were still being born and his mother was occasionally absent from home due to tuberculosis, the terrible disease of the nineteenth century. In the dream he saw his "beloved mother, with a peculiarly peaceful, sleeping expression on her features, being carried into the room by two or three people with bird's beaks and laid upon the bed." He associated the figures with funerals and "awoke in tears and screaming, and interrupted my parents' sleep." He wrote:

> The expression on my mother's features in the dream was copied from the view I had of my grandfather [mother's father] a few days before his death as he lay snoring in a coma. The interpretation carried out in the dream . . . must therefore have been that my mother was dying; the funerary relief fitted in with this. I awoke in anxiety, which did not cease till I had woken my parents up. I remember that I suddenly grew calm when I saw my mother's face, as though I needed to be reassured that she was not dead.

This anxiety dream was a clear example of the continuing power of Freud's fear of the death/loss of his mother. He "awoke in tears and screaming," his terror directly felt. The immediate trigger for the dream was the death of another parental figure, his maternal grandfather, which, combined with Amalia's preoccupation with new babies and absence due to tuberculosis, set off the deeper fear that he might lose her forever.

This long-lasting connection between Freud's mother and the theme of death was again illustrated in a dream from his adult years, reported in *Interpretation of Dreams*, in which he found himself in a kitchen in search of food. This led to associations of "the three Fates who spin the destiny of man, and I knew that one of the three women—the inn-hostess in the dream—was the mother who gives life, and furthermore—as in my own case—gives the living creature its first nourishment. Love and hunger, I reflected, meet at a woman's breast."

This stimulated a childhood memory:

> When I was six years old and was given my first lessons by my mother, I was expected to believe that we were all made of earth and must therefore return to earth. This did not suit me and I expressed doubts of the doctrine. My mother thereupon rubbed the palms of her hands together—just as she did in making dumplings, except that there was no dough between them—and showed me the blackish scales of *epidermis* produced by the friction as a proof that we were made of earth. My astonishment at this ocular demonstration knew no bounds and I acquiesced in the belief which I was later to hear expressed in the words: "Thou owest Nature a death."

The death of his baby brother Julius, and the loss of his mother's attention and care, were the sources of the infant Freud's own anxiety and grief. However, as an adult, he was never able to sort out these experiences or relate them to his own fear and unhappiness. He was able to reconstruct his feelings of guilt in relation to the death of Julius because, like almost every young child who is replaced by a new infant, he had wished to get rid of his rival, and it was this guilt that he emphasized in his later accounts of these events. In the midst of his self-analysis he wrote to Fliess: "I greeted my one-year-younger brother, who died after a few months, with adverse wishes and genuine childhood jealousy; and . . . his death left the germ of self-reproaches in me."

But he was never able to see his own reactions to the loss of Amalia to new babies, the sense that she had betrayed him, and the yearning for her love. He clearly felt these things as a young child and, in his later writings, could describe them, but he always attributed the reactions to others—never himself. Even at the age of seventy-five, in his essay *Femininity,* he wrote:

> The turning away from the mother is accompanied by hostility; the attachment to the mother ends in hate. A hate of that kind may become very striking and last all through life. The reproach against the mother which goes back furthest is that she gave the child too little milk—which is construed against her as lack of love. The next accusation against the child's mother flares up when the next baby appears in the nursery. If possible the connection with oral frustration is preserved: the mother could not or would not give the child any more milk because she needed the nourishment for the new arrival. In cases in which the two children are so close in age that lactation is prejudiced by the second pregnancy, this reproach acquires a real basis, and it is a remarkable fact that a child, even with an age difference of only 11 months, is not too young to take notice of what

is happening. But what the child grudges the unwanted intruder and rival is not only the suckling but all the other signs of maternal care. It feels that it has been dethroned, despoiled, damaged in its rights; it casts a jealous hatred upon the new baby and develops a grievance against the faithless mother. . . . we rarely form a correct idea of the strength of these jealous impulses, of the tenacity with which they persist, and of the magnitude of their influence upon later development. Especially as this jealousy is constantly receiving fresh nourishment in the later years of childhood and the whole shock is repeated with the birth of each new brother or sister.

This passage captured the powerful emotions Freud still felt over seventy years later in regard to his mother and the many later babies that displaced him. Amalia gave birth to Julius when Sigi was eleven months old; significantly, this was exactly the age he chose in his example. And the new arrival did deprive him of her milk and "all the other signs of maternal care." And Julius was followed by six more babies before he reached the age of ten, repeating the "whole shock" and reinforcing the sense of being "dethroned, despoiled" and "damaged." This passage gave an accurate account of Freud's early experience of his mother, including his anger at her and the babies who displaced him. But he did not connect any of this to himself, or even to male babies as a group; in his essay *Femininity,* only little girls were presumed to have such feelings.

Following the death of Julius, Amalia became pregnant again, giving birth to a daughter, Anna, when Freud was two and a half. While his wish to get rid of Julius was a reconstruction that he later made—he had no direct memory of it—he did recall his dislike of this sister, which persisted throughout his life. Anna was followed by four more sisters, two of whom, Rosa and Adolfine, he was rather fond of; the final sibling, Alexander, was born when he was ten. It was a repetitive pattern: throughout his childhood, his mother was pregnant and he was constantly losing her to new babies. The combination of his mother's grief, following the deaths of her brother and second son, and her seemingly endless pregnancies and the demands of new infants, meant that the young Freud had very little of her time, attention, and care. But it was not only his mother's ministrations that he lost in these first years; the trauma was compounded by further losses, including that of an important substitute mother.

Freud was cared for during his first two-and-a-half years by a nursemaid, a Czech Catholic woman—scholars disagree about whether her name was Monika Zajic or Resi Willek—who told him pious stories, took him to church, and shaped his early education and sense of himself. While he later described her with the words he heard from his mother—"elderly, ugly and clever"—his own memories, unearthed in the self-analysis, struck a different note. In the midst of his recollection of scenes from the Freiberg years, he wrote to Fliess that his nursemaid "told me a great deal about God Almighty and hell and . . . instilled in me a high opinion of my own capacities." She was a vital maternal figure who supported his early sense of importance and precocious intelligence. His mother later told him that he would come home from the Catholic church with his nursemaid and tell the family "how God carried on." The bright little boy thought the priest was God, and the Catholic rituals made a vivid impression on him. His memory of the nursemaid, as reported to Fliess, was most significant: "I shall be grateful to the memory of the old woman who provided me at such an early age with the means for living and going on living. As you see, the old liking is breaking through again today."

This memory, from the time when death and death fears permeated the family, shows the nursemaid's importance in sustaining his will to live and also demonstrates his direct affection for her, a feeling that came back to him almost forty years later. This kind of open love—"the old liking is breaking through again today"—was almost never voiced in relation to Amalia. And then he lost the nursemaid, too. She was caught stealing by his half brother Philipp, arrested for petty theft, and sent to prison. He never saw her again.

That the young Freud blended together the traumatic losses of both his mother and nursemaid is evident in an important memory that he unearthed during his self-analysis. He recalled a scene in which "my mother was nowhere to be found; I was crying in despair." His older half brother Philipp "unlocked a closet (*Kasten*) for me, and when I did not find my mother inside it either, I cried even more until, slender and beautiful, she came in through the door." Puzzling through this memory, he hit upon a solution: "When I missed my mother, I was afraid she had vanished from me, just as the old woman had a short time before. So I must have heard that the old woman had been locked up and therefore must have believed that my mother had been locked up too—or rather, had been 'boxed up': *eingekastelt*."

This memory turns on the double meaning of the German word *Kasten*— box or closet—also used colloquially for jail, as in "put in the box." The very young Freud took his brother's words that the nursemaid had been put in a *Kasten* concretely, as children are wont to do, and, in his despair, hoped to find her—and the mother that he had also lost—in the closet. The disturbing power of both losses is seen in his crying and the persistence of the memory over the years. The *Kasten* vignette also shows one way that Freud adapted to his losses; he remembered his mother in ideal terms—"slender and beautiful," not pregnant as she in fact was for most of his childhood—while he referred to the nurse-maid—a woman of around forty—as "old" and associated her with stealing and guilt. In fact, the words he used to characterize her—"elderly, ugly and clever"— make her sound like a witch in a fairy tale.

Freud was two and a half when his nursemaid suddenly vanished from his life; this was also the time when he lost his mother to another baby, his sister Anna. Current understanding of the psychological capacities of children this age makes clear that he would have been little able to understand these events, and even less able to deal with them effectively. They were traumas that overwhelmed the capacities of the young boy. Following soon after these losses, Jacob Freud's business collapsed. Earlier accounts attributed the business failure to an economic crisis that swept the Moravian textile industry in the 1850s and to anti-Semitism, but more recent research has revealed that there is no foundation to these explanations; the local economy was, in fact, booming, and there was no more prejudice against Jews than there had been in previous years. Jacob's compatriot Ignaz Fluss, who was also a wool merchant, became the successful owner of a textile mill in Freiberg at this time. Clearly, the business failure was a result of Jacob's own incompetence, an explanation supported by his later work history; he was never again successful in business, never able to earn much of a living.

The collapse of Jacob's business forced the family to leave Freiberg; Freud, in a rare later reference to this time, described it as the "original catastrophe that involved my whole existence." The departure broke up the close-knit, extended family that had provided Sigmund with what security he enjoyed during his first three years. His adult half brothers Emanuel and Philipp, Emanuel's wife Marie, his playmate and best friend John, and John's sister Pauline, all vanished from his life. Emanuel and his family, along with Philipp, moved to England, where they pursued their trade in Manchester, the great textile center. Children without reliable maternal attachments typically gain security from other relationships and their familiar surroundings; losing the other members of the extended family, his playmates, and his home added weight to the traumas he had already suffered. Jacob, Amalia, Sigmund, and baby Anna left Freiberg for Leipzig, Germany, where they remained for about a year, but Jacob was not able to establish his business there and they were forced to move again, this time to Vienna, where Amalia's family lived, and there they settled permanently.

Upon their departure from Freiberg, when Freud was three and a half, his fear of train travel made its first appearance. At the railway station, the gas jets used for illumination made him think of "souls burning in hell," an association with his lost nursemaid, who had told him "a great deal about God almighty and hell." Interestingly, the little boy was not frightened by the other strange things he encountered at the station, including the large steam locomotive, which might have seemed overpowering to a small child. His phobia was quite specific; he was afraid that the train would leave without him, that he would be left behind, that he would lose his mother and father, just as he had lost his nursemaid a year before. This travel fear would reverberate throughout his life and reach phobic dimensions during the time of his self-analysis; as he wrote to Fliess, "You yourself have seen my travel anxiety at its height." As in his infancy, his fear was that the train would leave without him: as an adult, he was always anxious to get to the railway station well ahead of time. The travel phobia persisted for many years, as illustrated by his difficulty visiting Rome. For years he longed to see the Italian capital, yet kept inventing obstacles that interfered with the trip. Similarly, his famous voyage to the United States in 1909 was accompanied by a fainting incident just before departure, as well as a number of other anxiety symptoms—stomachaches, diarrhea—that he complained about for years afterward.

The traumatic experiences of Freud's first four years vanished from his awareness. In contemporary terms, the events and images were stored as physical and emotional sensations, but the memories were not available to consciousness; they were dissociated, not integrated into a coherent sense of self. They existed in a separate compartment of his personality, protecting him from their disruptive effects. When he did look back on his early years, he cast them in pleasant imagery, smoothing out and reconfiguring the traumatic events of his infancy. He remembered Freiberg, the scene of his early fear and misery, in ideal terms, as he did his mother; Vienna, where the family eventually fared better, was the object of both love and hate. His nursemaid, who he only referred to in the Fliess letters, was recalled with a mixture of love and distaste. The dissociation of his traumatic losses was supported by a happy fantasy of Freiberg; the negative emotions came out elsewhere. For the rest of his life he would find a variety of targets for his fears, unhappiness, disappointments, and hatreds.

By the age of three, Freud had lost his two most important caretakers—his mother and his nursemaid—the first in an atmosphere of illness, death, and grief, and the second in one of crime and guilt. His lifelong preoccupation with illness and death—both his own and of others close to him—had its origin here. Then the collapse of his father's business dispersed the extended family, causing the loss of his "uncles" and "aunt," his playmates, and the only home he knew. Jacob, Amalia, and their two infants were forced to move twice; these were years of financial insecurity and the births of five more children. If the three-year-old Freud felt deprived and frightened, so did his parents as they faced poverty and an uncertain future. It is unlikely that they would have been able to give him reassurance and emotional support when they were overcome with their own troubles.

As a very young child, Freud could do nothing about the painful realities that engulfed him; he almost certainly felt frightened, helpless, shunted aside, and overcome with longing for love and care. As Charlotte Brontë put it in her novel *Jane Eyre*, he experienced "such dread as children only can feel." There was no one to comfort or understand him. The adults controlled everything: they were present or absent, Philipp had his nursemaid sent away, the extended family members disappeared, his father lost his business and was likely preoccupied—if not despairing—over their plight. Although Jacob later appears as a kindly and well-meaning, if somewhat hapless, father, he was certainly not able to protect his son during these early years.

This account of Freud's life, emphasizing the traumatic losses and disruptions he suffered as a little boy, has been drawn from all the available biographical and historical evidence. His own version of his childhood makes reference to some of these events but, ultimately, gave major weight to his sexual desire for his mother and fear of his rival-father as the most important sources of his conflicts and fears. Years later, in his self-analysis, Freud remembered some of the events of the Freiberg period: the birth and death of Julius, his play with John and Pauline, his love for his old nursemaid and her disappearance. Reexperiencing his losses set off potentially overwhelming anxiety and sadness, feelings that he was not able to tolerate or contain on his own, and he turned away from them to what seemed like a great discovery. He wrote to Fliess:

> A single idea of general value dawned on me. I have found, in my own case too, the phenomena of being in love with my mother and jealous of my father, and I now consider it a universal event in early childhood. . . . Later between two and two and a half years—my libido toward *matrem* was awakened, namely, on the occasion of a journey with her from Leipzig to Vienna, during which we must have spent the night together and there must have been an opportunity of seeing her *nudam*. . . . You yourself have seen my travel anxiety at its height.

In these passages, Freud asserted that seeing his mother naked was the primary source of his travel phobia and other manifestations of anxiety. (Interestingly, he misremembered his age, his first train journey having occurred at age three and a half, not two and a half, though the earlier time was when he lost the nursemaid.) According to this explanation, fear was aroused because his sexual wishes for his mother brought him into conflict with his powerful father. These ideas, of course, were elaborated over the years into his theory of the Oedipus complex and used to explain Sophocles' *Oedipus Rex* and Shakespeare's *Hamlet,* as early as the Fliess letters, as well as his own troubling emotional states. Eventually, this interpretation became the centerpiece of the psychoanalytic theory of neurosis, a theory which located the boy's anxiety in fear of castration at the hands of the father as punishment for his sexual desire for the mother. The details of the discovery of the Oedipus complex—or, more accurately, its invention—in the self-analysis are critical given the great importance Freud gave to it.

The contrast between Freud's memories of his nursemaid—or his anxiety dream about his mother's death from age eight or nine—and his "memory" of his oedipal feelings is significant. In the first, he felt "the old liking" for the nursemaid and, in the *Kasten* incident, directly recalled his crying and despair. The same was true of the terrifying nightmare of his mother's death. In the case of the "memory" of his oedipal arousal, the distancing Latinisms—libido, *matrem, nudam*—were employed, and he guessed "we must have spent the night together and there must have been an opportunity of seeing her *nudam*." In other words, he had no direct image or feeling for this oedipal event; it was a reconstruction, an invention.

Freud spent his first three and a half years in the one-room apartment in Freiberg, and most of his subsequent childhood in small quarters in the Jewish ghetto of Vienna. The precocious little boy witnessed many distressing events, including the births and nursing of the seven babies born in his first ten years, deaths, illnesses, and his parents' reactions to their poverty and business failures. Exposure to all this was no doubt far more disturbing than seeing his mother unclothed. In other words, Freud created his oedipal theory because his traumatic losses aroused overwhelming emotions that were impossible to manage alone, in a *self*-analysis. By turning to the oedipal story, he created a comforting myth, one which allowed him to think that what most disturbed him was his adultlike sexual desire for his mother, and also promoted his weak father to a position of kingly power.

The distorting effects of Freud's substitution of the less threatening oedipal explanation was paralleled by his reworking of other childhood events. In the essay *Femininity*, for example, he stated that it is only the little girl who feels "dethroned, despoiled, damaged [and who] casts jealous hatred upon the new baby and develops a grievance against the faithless mother." He continued, "A mother is only brought unlimited satisfaction by her relation to a son; this is altogether the most perfect, the most free from ambivalence of all human relationships." This expressed his wishful fantasy—but certainly not the reality—of his early years. A related distortion appeared in his interpretation of the nightmare from age eight or nine. After describing his terror and sobbing over the sight of his dead mother, he constructed a complicated and strained interpretation in which the dream was supposed to be driven by his sexual desires: "I was not anxious because I had dreamt that my mother was dying; but I interpreted the dream in that sense in my preconscious revision of it because I was already under the influence of the anxiety. The anxiety can be traced back, when repression is taken into account, to an obscure and evidently sexual craving that had found expression in the visual content of the dream."

Rivalrous feelings between a boy and his father are central to Freud's theory of the Oedipus complex, and he convinced himself that this aggressive conflict was the origin of his own symptoms. In reality, there were many rivals for his mother's love, though it is not likely that Jacob, who was probably away from home on business trips for long periods, was a significant one in this early period; two-year-olds don't have oedipal fantasies, nor was his father connected to the very painful loss of the nurse. There were no direct memories of such rivalry and fear between the young Sigmund and his father, nor did they appear in later writings about himself, though he saw such conflicts everywhere else: in his patients, his disciples, characters in literature—indeed, in almost everyone.

What is apparent in the emotion-laden memories from the self-analysis—in contrast to theory-based reconstructions—is how the anger and rivalry aroused in the young Freud by the birth of Julius was retrospectively described as the source of his guilt feelings after the baby died. In addition, in his own recollections he did not locate rivalry and guilt in relation to his father but, rather, in his competitive play with his nephew John, who he described as the first of many ambivalent figures in his life. As he put it in 1925: "An intimate friend and a hated enemy have always been indispensable to my emotional life; I have always been able to create them anew, and not infrequently my childish ideal [his nephew John] has been so closely approached that friend and enemy have coincided in the same person; but not simultaneously, of course, as was the case in my early childhood."

Speaking of John and the death of Julius he said, "This nephew and this younger brother have determined, then, what is neurotic, but also what is intense in all my friendships." Freud's attribution of guilt feelings following the death of Julius was not in keeping with the psychology of a two-year-old. The same is true with regard to his rivalrous play with his one year older nephew. Freud described the "misdeeds" he and John committed and their "cruel" behavior towards his niece—John's sister—Pauline, which he framed in sexual terms, imagining himself and John attempting to rape or "deflower" the little girl. Once again, this does not fit with the capacities of a two-year-old. The little boys no doubt misbehaved and treated Pauline roughly, but it is unlikely that their actions, or his aggressive play with John, were the basis for a lifelong pattern of love and hate in intimate relationships. Children that age don't have rape fantasies that they feel guilty about years later, nor is it likely that his aggressive-competitive play with John could have had the long-lasting effects that he attributed to it.

The powerful and lasting ambivalence that Freud described—his need for "an intimate friend and a hated enemy"—must be based on a firmer foundation than this innocuous sibling play and fighting. Knowing what transpired with his mother at this time, it seems likely that the "memories" of his feelings about Julius, John, and Pauline symbolized the more threatening reactions of love and hate he felt toward Amalia, reactions which continued throughout his childhood. The loss of her to new babies, her later absences due to illness, and his frustrated longing for her care continued for many years. The emotional reactions that remained with him after the births of Julius and Anna were reinforced by the arrivals of the next five infants. These losses and frustrations, repeated over and over, were a much firmer basis for the lifelong pattern of ambivalence than the reactions to the playmates of his infancy, a picture that he reconstructed in his forties. But while he felt love and hate toward his mother, his desperate need for her made it impossible to consciously acknowledge these feelings. To the end of his long life he remained unaware of the full range of his feelings for Amalia.

There is a common thread running through all Freud's reconstructions of his infancy. He continually pictured himself as more able, more competent, more powerful than he could have been at the ages described. He emphasized his competitiveness, his rivalry, his anger, and the guilt occasioned by his death wishes. While these are certainly observable reactions in young children, they are found at later ages than those Freud sets forth. An infant under two, exposed to the death of a baby and his parents' grief, would feel frightened, bewildered, lost, and helpless. As additional losses occurred—as they did—the anxiety would be reinforced: who will disappear/die next? His mother? Himself? In fact, anxiety about her death, and his own, continued well into his adult years. The psychoanalyst-scholar Seigfried Bernfeld has done a careful analysis and noted: "In the self-confessions scattered throughout his writings, Freud figures at times as a villain, a parricide, ambitious, petty, revengeful, but never as a lover—save for a few very superficial allusions to his wife."

While the infant Freud's anger was part of his reaction to the early traumatic events, his stress on it, and the corresponding neglect of his fear and helplessness, was a way of protecting himself against these more overwhelming emotions. His reconstruction of his early years created a picture in which he had greater control, was not the helpless little infant he in fact was. Little boys certainly have rivalrous feelings toward their fathers, and two-year-olds commonly feel angry and competitive with new babies, and even wish them dead—within their limited understanding of death—but such competitive feelings are not necessarily a source of serious conflict. But it was safer for the adult Freud to focus on them than on his terror and helplessness. The interpretation he created to explain his own childhood became the prototype for his understanding of everyone, a foundation that he relied on throughout his life.

CHAPTER 2

Childhood and Adolescence

*When I was three, the branch of industry in which my father was concerned
met with a catastrophe. He lost all his means and we were forced to leave
[Freiberg] and move to [Vienna]. Long and difficult years followed, of which,
as it seems to me, nothing was worth remembering.*

—Freud, *Screen Memories* (1899)

WHEN THE Freud family arrived in Vienna in 1860, the Hapsburg capital was
undergoing a period of rapid economic and social growth. The new religious
freedom that followed the German revolution of 1848 was accompanied by the
lifting of restrictions and special taxes that Jews had suffered for many years.
Now, they enjoyed the rights of full citizens; the professions were open to them,
they could employ Christian servants, own real estate, and live outside the ghet-
tos. These new opportunities had stimulated a flood of Jewish immigrants from
the provinces during the second half of the nineteenth century. In 1860, there
were 6,000 Jews in Vienna; by 1900, the number was 147,000, the largest Jewish community of any country in Western Europe. In the capital, they found
expanding economic, educational, and cultural avenues; by the turn of the century, they were a powerful presence in banking and industry, in medicine, law,
journalism, literature, and music. This did not happen all at once, of course,
and, while Emperor Franz Josef had officially abolished discrimination, a large
number of Viennese—including much of the Catholic clergy—remained anti-
Semitic. Many of the immigrants arrived with little money and struggled in this
strange, unfamiliar, urban environment. Some were able to adapt and better
their lot, while others did not rise very far above their origins. But, with the traditional Jewish commitment to education, they pushed their sons to take advantage of the new opportunities. The Freuds were typical in this respect.

When the family first arrived in Vienna, they took up residence in Leopoldstadt, a district that had contained a Jewish ghetto since the Middle Ages. The

largest concentration of Jews in the city was housed in this district, and the Freuds were among the many families who settled, until they could afford something better, in this slum. The apartments were poor and overcrowded, and many families were forced to share their quarters with subrenters, sometimes with no more than a chalk line drawn on the floor to separate the spaces. Because of the poverty and close living conditions, disease was easily spread; tuberculosis was particularly rampant. The Freud family, like many others, moved frequently, and, for at least part of this time, shared space with Jacob's relatives.

Life in the Leopoldstadt slum had many sides to it. There were hardships: poverty and the struggle to earn a living, along with widespread disease, and psychological stresses, for, while the Jews flocked to Vienna because of new and promising opportunities, life in the city was far different than it had been in the provincial shtetls. The second half of the nineteenth century was a period of rapid industrialization and modernization; the new arrivals confronted an unsettling environment, which caused a great deal of culture shock. Since many of them, like Jacob and his family, were giving up the old Jewish ways in their drive to assimilate, they lacked the security of the ancient traditions—both religious and cultural—that had characterized shtetl life. In spite of all these difficulties, life in Leopoldstadt had its consolations; the emancipated immigrant-Jews shared a common plight as they struggled to succeed in this new—still anti-Semitic—world. While the Freud family had shed its Orthodox religion, almost all their social and business acquaintances and friends remained Jewish, a pattern that continued throughout Freud's own life. These were the people with whom they felt most comfortable.

Amalia continued to give birth nearly every year during this early period in Vienna; four more sisters and a brother were added by the time Freud was ten. The family was now complete: Jacob and Amalia, Sigmund and Anna, the next four sisters—Rosa, Marie, Adolfine, and Pauline—and the last child, his brother Alexander. It is likely that these births took place in the small, crowded apartments, along with the care and nursing of the babies, all with little privacy for the young Sigmund or his parents. One can picture the small boy escaping into his books as soon as he learned to read, in an apartment filled with little—mainly female—babies. Later, when Freud developed his theories of infancy, he did not avail himself of the opportunity to observe his own children, claiming that his theories were based on what his adult patients reported in their analyses. Yet, his entire childhood was spent in crowded rooms filled with growing babies and, while he may have tried to ignore all their clamor, these scenes surely left traces in his memory.

The young Sigmund was taught to read by his parents, and his precocious intelligence was soon recognized. One of his earliest memories was of his father giving him and his sister Anna a book and suggesting they amuse themselves by tearing out the colored pictures, an event that Freud connected to his lifelong

*Freud at about age nine with his mother and sisters
Rosa and Adolfine.*

passion for reading and book collecting. Jacob later gave him a Bible with the inscription, "It was in the seventh year of your age that the spirit of God began to move you to learning." In describing Freud's childhood, his biographer Ernest Jones wrote, "Reading and studying seem to have filled the greater part of his life." His intellectual and verbal gifts were specially valued by both parents; Jacob seemed a bit in awe of his brilliant child, and Amalia made him her "Golden Sigi." For both of them, he was the firstborn son whose achievements and success would compensate the family for its struggles and hardships.

When Sigmund was nine or ten years old, his uncle Josef Freud—Jacob's younger brother—was caught in a scandal involving counterfeit money, a scandal that may have also involved Emanuel and Philipp, since the false notes originated in England, where the brothers lived. While some accounts minimized this event, recent evidence has shown that Josef was convicted and sentenced to ten years in prison. Jacob's reaction was severe; Freud remembered that his father's hair "turned grey from grief in a few days." The shame of this family scandal weighed on Jacob, already a failure in his own business, and, in the years that followed, he never got back on his feet financially.

Emanuel, his family, and his brother Philipp had emigrated in 1859 directly from Freiberg to Manchester, England. Arriving there as poor Jewish immigrants, both brothers eventually established themselves as successful businessmen. Emanuel achieved sufficient prosperity to raise five children and acquire a second home in the country where Freud's son Martin visited him some fifty years later and found him to be a perfect gentleman, more English in his manners and speech than the natives. He had come a great distance from his beginnings as a poor Jew in a Galician shtetl. Freud kept in contact with his half brother, who was twenty-four years older, and there seems to have been a real bond of affection and respect between them. It is likely that Freud's later admiration for England was partly based on the fact that it was the home of this stable and successful father figure. Both Emanuel and Philipp were able to send money to support their father and the family that was left behind, which was supplemented by money from Amalia's relatives. This need for financial support continued to the end of Jacob's life; in 1884, when his father was sixty-nine years old, Freud—himself still at the university and not earning any money—wrote to his fiancée: "Yesterday I met Father in the street, still full of projects, still hoping. I took it upon myself to write Emanuel and Philipp urging them to help Father out of his present predicament. He doesn't want to do it himself since he considers himself badly treated. So I sat down last night and wrote Emanuel a very sharp letter."

All these harsh experiences—Jacob's lifelong inability to provide for the family, the disgrace connected to the family scandal, poverty, anti-Semitism—characterized Freud's childhood and reinforced the traumatic events of his infancy. While his public statements about his father were always respectful, in a rare moment of revelation in his self-analysis, he wrote to Fliess: "I know from my youth that once the wild horses of the pampas have been lassoed, they retain a certain anxiousness for life. Thus, I came to know the helplessness of poverty and continually fear it."

Freud's public references to Jacob emphasized his power as a father, his loving nature, and made no mention of his failures. By all accounts, he was easygoing with his children, as the example of letting them tear pictures out of a book illustrates. He was also the model for Freud's most pleasurable adult indulgence: smoking. The relationship between father and son was predominantly a caring and supportive one, but there was also, from the earliest years, a striking reversal of the father and son roles; Sigmund was the premature adult who would achieve great things in the world, while Jacob, as the years progressed, became ever more childlike and helpless.

The picture of Jacob as a gentle and loving man is supported by the description of Freud's son Martin in his memoir, *Sigmund Freud: Man and Father*. Martin recalled his grandfather's frequent visits to the family apartment when he was a boy: "Every member of my family loved Jacob and treated him with great

Freud at about age nine with his father.

respect. He was tall and broad-shouldered, very much the size to which I reached when I grew up myself. He was terribly nice with us children. He brought us small presents and he used to tell us stories, mostly with a little twinkle in his great brown eyes, as if he wanted to say, 'Isn't everything we are doing and saying here a great joke?'" Judith Bernays Heller, the daughter of Freud's oldest sister Anna, described Jacob as "tall and broad with a long beard . . . very kind and gentle, and humorous in the bargain."

This picture of a kind and loving Jacob only captures part of the truth; the difficulties of his life had taken their toll, and he was not happy all the time. As his son put it in a letter to his fiancée, "When he isn't exactly grouchy, which also is very often the case, he is the greatest optimist of all us young people." Freud likened his father to Charles Dickens' Mr. Micawber, the eternal optimist who, in the face of life's miseries, always believes "something will turn up." This cast Jacob's failures in a somewhat humorous light; in fact, his incompetence was a serious burden for the entire family.

In his seventies, Freud wrote in *Civilization and Its Discontents,* "I cannot think of any need in childhood as strong as the need for a father's protection."

Jacob's inability to fulfill this need was illustrated by a most important memory from the age of ten or twelve that Freud reported in *The Interpretation of Dreams*. Father and son were on a walk when Jacob told a story to illustrate how much better things were in the present, compared to the time of his own youth:

"When I was a young man," he said, "I went for a walk one Saturday in the streets of your birthplace; I was well dressed, and had a new fur cap on my head. A Christian came up to me and with a single blow knocked off my cap into the mud and shouted: 'Jew! Get off the pavement!'" "And what did you do?" I asked. "I went into the roadway and picked up my cap," was his quiet reply. This struck me as unheroic conduct on the part of the big, strong man who was holding the little boy by the hand. I contrasted this situation with another which fitted my feelings better: the scene in which Hannibal's father, Hamilcar Barca, made his boy swear before the household altar to take vengeance on the Romans. Ever since that time Hannibal had a place in my phantasies.

This memory illustrates, quite clearly, Freud turning from his weak father to an identification with a heroic military figure.

While Freud never referred to it, the memory of his father's humiliation also reverberated with the exploits of another of his childhood heroes: Oedipus. In Sophocles' play, Oedipus encountered King Laius on the road and was ordered out of the way and struck with a staff. Unlike the passive Jacob in an analogous situation, he became enraged, overturned the king's carriage, and killed him. Freud knew the play intimately, having translated it from the Greek for his final examination at the *Gymnasium* (high school); later, of course, he made the story central to his theories.

Jacob's lack of authority within the family was evident when the name of the last-born child was chosen, a decision that was made in a "Family Council." The ten-year-old Sigmund proposed the name of Alexander, after the great general of the ancient world, and supported his choice with a long account of Alexander the Great's triumphs. His view prevailed. The naming of his brother was the beginning of an enduring habit: Freud selected the names for all his children; his wife had no say in what should have been, for her, a continuation of the Jewish custom of naming children in honor of deceased relatives. His sons were named after his heroes—including the English general Oliver Cromwell—and his daughters after women who were important to him; he even dictated the names of some of his grandchildren.

Sigmund was deeply troubled by Jacob's weakness and failure; he loved him but could not take him as a model and began, very early, to identify with powerful, dominating men—Hannibal, Oedipus, Alexander the Great, Napoléon, Moses—a pattern that continued throughout his life. There was, in all likelihood, an earlier time when the small boy revered and perhaps even feared his father as a large and powerful character, but it was precisely because of this early veneration that he suffered a crushing disappointment when he became aware of his father's inadequacies in the world. For a boy who had suffered repeated losses of his mother's care, this was still another loss. However much affection the young Sigmund felt for his father, he turned away from him and sought out other, more powerful, male figures. In Freud's mythological version of his childhood, he pictured his father as Laius, king of Thebes, the sire of Oedipus. In fact, Jacob was more a Willy Loman, the central character in Arthur Miller's *Death of a Salesman*: a failed salesman who was a terrible disappointment to his son.

While Freud never spoke openly of his disaffection with Jacob, he revealed his feelings indirectly in his evocative 1914 essay, *Some Reflections on Schoolboy Psychology*:

> From his nursery the boy begins to cast his eyes upon the world outside. And he cannot fail now to make discoveries which undermine his original high opinion of his father and which expedite his detachment from his first ideal. He finds that his father is no longer the mightiest, wisest and richest of beings; he grows dissatisfied with him, he learns to criticize him and to estimate his place in society; and then, as a rule, he makes him pay heavily for the disappointment that has been caused by him.

While Sigmund's relationship with Jacob was marked by both love and disappointment, his mother presented him with a whole other set of conflicts and problems, in their way much more difficult than those associated with his father. Amalia Freud went through hard times in the early years of her marriage; a poor Jewish woman, burdened with seven young children and an uncertain financial situation, she lived at a time when there were no opportunities open to her outside of home and family. Unlike Jacob, who was easygoing, pleasure-loving, and, ultimately, ineffective, she was a driving force. Freud's son Martin, who knew his grandmother for many years, gave a telling description of her in his memoir. He depicted her as a woman of indomitable will: aggressive, insensitive to the feelings of others—she conscripted her sweet daughter Adolfine (Dolphie) and made her a nurse-companion for life—and determined to have her own way. Martin described the Jews of East Galicia as a "peculiar race [with] little grace and no manners [whose] women were certainly not what we would call 'ladies.'" He continued:

> They were highly emotional and easily carried away by their feelings. . . . whenever you hear of Jews showing violence or belligerence, instead of that meekness and what seems poor-spirited acceptance of a hard fate sometimes associated with Jewish peoples, you may safely suspect the presence of men and women of Amalia's race. These people are not easy to live with, and grandmother, a true representative of her race, was no exception. She had

great vitality and much impatience; she had a hunger for life and an indomitable spirit. Nobody envied Aunt Dolfie, whose destiny it was to dedicate her life to the care of an old mother who was a tornado. Aunt Dolfie once took Amalia to buy a new hat—and she was not perhaps wise to recommend what seemed to her "something suitable." Studying carefully her image crowned by the hat she had agreed to try on, Amalia, who was on the wrong side of ninety, finally shouted, "I won't take this one; it makes me look old."

Martin's description of Amalia is supported by that of Freud's niece Judith Bernays Heller, who spent time as a child living in the household of the older Freuds. She felt affection for Jacob but "really feared" her grandmother, despite her admiration for her "stateliness and the nice clothes she wore."

[Jacob] remained quiet and imperturbable, not indifferent, but not disturbed, never out of temper and never raising his voice. My grandmother, on the other hand, had a volatile temperament, would scold the maid as well as her daughters, and rush about the house . . . I hated to go back to my grandparents', where there were only grown-ups, among them my somewhat shrill and domineering grandmother. . . . She was charming and smiling when strangers were about, but I, at least, always felt that with familiars she was a tyrant, and a selfish one. Quite definitely, she had a strong personality and knew what she wanted . . . When there was a special invitation, as for instance to the celebration of my uncle Sigmund's seventieth birthday in 1926—when she was already ninety—she insisted that she be bought a new dress and hat to go . . . to his house . . . so she could be honored and feted as the mother of her "golden son," as she called her Sigmund. . . . I think that one of the circumstances that helped reinforce my impression of my grandmother's selfishness was the fact that she so successfully used her increasing deafness in order to avoid hearing what she did not want to hear—principally the report of any event that might require her to bestow an extra measure of sympathy or consolation upon some member of the family.

Amalia's domination was primarily directed at her daughters; while suffering her society's antifemale prejudices, she herself valued males over females and gave preference to her sons, especially her firstborn. She would achieve power through her connection with his success. Like Jacob's veneration of his intellect, this gave the growing boy a special place in the family, particularly in comparison to his many baby sisters who, ironically, received some of the maternal care he had missed. It was gratifying to be his mother's golden child, yet Amalia, with her insensitive and dominating ways, was not a safe person to become intimate with. She was still tied, at some place within him, to the traumatic losses of the earlier years, making her doubly dangerous. Sigmund dealt with all this by assuming an outwardly dutiful stance in relation to his mother and exerting extreme control over his emotions. This control was his outstanding characteristic as a boy; he took up the mantle of the special achieving child, burying himself in his books and schoolwork and avoiding emotional entanglements— particularly with girls. He was "moral"—prudish, unexpressive, censorious—to an extreme degree.

Freud's only public account of his childhood appeared in the *Autobiographical Study* that he published in 1925, though there are disguised memories of his early years in his 1899 essay *Screen Memories*. He began the *Autobiographical Study* with an account of the migration of his father's family into German Austria, but, significantly, said nothing of the years in Freiberg; they were missing from his autobiography just as they were largely blotted out of his awareness. He continued: "When I was a child of four I came to Vienna, and I went through the whole of my education there. At the 'Gymnasium' [grammar and high school] I was at the top of my class for seven years; I enjoyed special privileges there, and had scarcely ever to be examined in class. Although we lived in very limited circumstances, my father insisted that, in my choice of a profession, I should follow my own inclinations alone."

Freud enrolled at the newly established Sperl Gymnasium in Leopoldstadt in 1865, when he was nine years old, one year ahead of the normal entrance age, indicating that he must have already acquired a solid educational foundation, probably from lessons given by his father and study on his own. While the Jews were a minority in Vienna, constituting about 10 percent of the population, their traditional emphasis on education led to much higher representation in the schools and university. Over half the students of the Sperl Gymnasium were Jewish when Freud went there.

At the Gymnasium, Freud was commended for outstanding academic work as well as for his exemplary conduct. In some of his later letters to his fiancée, he depicted himself as a boy who stood "in opposition" and protested against one of the unpopular teachers, but more recent evidence indicates just the opposite. Sigmund seems to have sided with the authorities against a group of troublemaking students. This is certainly consistent with his overall demeanor as a schoolboy, as well as his later actions in the university; he prided himself on the rewards he received for being at the top of his class, was enormously diligent, worked hard at pleasing his teachers, and was not the least rebellious.

While an excellent general student, Freud's greatest talent was for language and literature, which would, as the years progressed, provide some of his most profound satisfactions. He was a voracious reader and early mastered Latin, Greek, French, English, and, later, Italian and Spanish. Jacob read Hebrew as well as German and his son took instruction in this language. Freud's teacher was Samuel Hammerschlag, who became an important alternative father figure, loaning money to his bright but impoverished young student. Significantly, with all his brilliance in languages, Freud later claimed to have forgotten what little Hebrew he once knew. He could not read it as an adult. It seems likely that he purposely avoided Hebrew, just as he did Yiddish, which Amalia spoke all her life, because both these languages were associated with the ghetto life of poor Jews. Like many boys, he lost himself in romantic fiction—Schiller's *The Robbers* was a favorite—where he could imagine himself performing heroic deeds. He began reading Shakespeare at eight—or so it has been said—and committed many quotations to memory; he always loved Goethe.

The idealization of the past played a significant role in Freud's childhood. He was, very early in his reading, drawn to the ancient world: Egypt, Athenian Greece, the Roman Empire. As he put it in his *Reflections on Schoolboy Psychology*: "I used to find, the present time seemed to sink into obscurity and the years between ten and eighteen would rise from the corners of my memory, with all their guesses and illusions, their painful distortions and heartening successes— my first glimpses of an extinct civilization, which in my case was to bring me as much consolation as anything else in the struggles of life."

His interest in ancient history and culture, like his immersion in literature, brought him a kind of esthetic-intellectual pleasure, but it was pleasure of a safe kind, far removed from the family's difficult circumstances, and under his own control. This consoling activity persisted to the end of his life, as the collection of ancient artifacts that filled his office bore witness.

While many bright children who find themselves in difficult or unhappy families escape into reading and study, in Freud's case this choice set a pattern for the remainder of his life. To the outside world, he was the compliant student, a boy lost in his books, someone who did not reveal his feelings; in short, a premature adult, cut off from emotion and his early memories. All his blocked desires and longings—unmet needs for affection and comfort, terror and helplessness, the wish for a heroic father, anger and the drive for power—were forced into the narrow channel of books, reading, and, later, writing. This was where his emotional self came to life: here he could be Hannibal, a hero out of Schiller or Shakespeare; here he could imagine romantic love.

Freud's life in the world of imagination and language served another important purpose. Not only was he powerful in this realm, but his talent and self-control set him apart and made him superior to all those female babies who lacked his verbal skills. They were the ones who could not control themselves; they were infantile creatures who gave way to their impulses, females incapable of the renunciation of pleasure in comparison to their civilized older brother. As his brother Alexander remembered it: "When I was a boy of six, and my brother Sigmund was sixteen, he said to me: 'Look Alexander, our family is like a book. You and I are the first and the last of the children, so we are like the

Ancient artifacts in Freud's office.

strong covers that have to support and protect the weak girls who were born after me and before you.'"

Freud's sister Anna revealed his censorious attitude toward all the girls in her brief sketch, "My Brother, Sigmund Freud": "Not only did he read a great deal himself, but he exercised definite control over my reading. If I had a book that seemed to him improper for a girl my age, he would say, 'Anna, it is too early to read that book now.' When I was fifteen, I remember, he felt that I should not read Balzac and Dumas."

When he was twenty, he wrote to his sister Rosa, four years younger than he, and warned her against having her head turned by a slight social success. She had given a performance on the zither, an instrument on which she was not terribly accomplished. Freud went on about how unscrupulous people give too much praise to young girls, which was bad for their characters and could end in their "becoming vain, coquettish, and insufferable!"

Sigmund imposed his control, not only on his sisters' reading and play, but also used his position as favored oldest son to abolish music from the household. As his sister Anna recalled:

In spite of his youth, Sigmund's word and wish were respected by everyone in the family. When I was eight years old, my mother, who was very musical, wanted me to study the piano, and I began practicing by the hour. Though Sigmund's room was not near the piano, the sound disturbed him. He appealed to my mother to remove the piano if she did not wish him to leave the house altogether. The piano disappeared and with it all opportunities for his sisters to become musicians. Nor did any of my brother's children ever receive musical instructions where he would have to hear it.

Ernest Jones says that Freud's aversion to music was well known to his colleagues and recalled "the pained expression on his face on entering a restaurant or beer garden where there was a band and how quickly his hands would go over his ears to drown the sound."

Music was at the very heart of Viennese cultural life, so this aversion was extreme and atypical. Traditionally, musical education was highly valued in Jewish families, yet the Freuds were one of the few without a piano. Freud's avoidance of music was part of his wider need to control emotion, for music has the power to evoke a range of feelings in the listener, to carry one away on a tide of romantic passion or bring on sadness and grief, and these were reactions that he had to suppress at all costs. Because Amalia was never one to inhibit her feelings, the piano incident gave him an opportunity to put a lid on her musical interest as well. In later years, he did enjoy a few operas—Mozart's *Don Giovanni* and *The Marriage of Figaro,* Bizet's *Carmen,* and Wagner's *Meistersinger*—but mainly for their dramatic content; his interest and appreciation of music itself remained very circumscribed.

These incidents within the family reveal a boy whose morality was based on the control of pleasure and the commands of duty and work. Many have traced these prudish attitudes to the social and historical climate, the oft-mentioned Victorian morality. But this is not a satisfactory explanation, since the Victorian Age was never so one-dimensional. True, the era was defined by the bourgeois values of control, thrift, orderliness, propriety, and the work ethic. And some people lived in accord with these standards. But more did so in Berlin, or even London, than in Vienna, which had its own unique climate.

Vienna, capital of the Austro-Hungarian Empire, had been ruled—since he ascended the throne as a young man in 1848—by Franz Josef, who, among other things, was decidedly pro-Jewish. The empire was highly stratified into royalty, the middle and upper-middle classes of merchants, doctors, lawyers, journalists, and civil servants—there was a vast and creaky bureaucracy, the model for Franz Kafka's *The Trial*—and a lower class of workers and peasants. The society was also segregated along gender lines with a long-standing, antifeminine bias. For a single woman, especially a single Jewish woman, of the middle and upper-middle class, strict sexual prohibitions and taboos were enforced. Lower-class women, on the other hand, frequently sought a way out of their plight through affairs with men of higher station, and prostitution was widespread in the poorer neighborhoods. Men, in contrast, were not held to such strict standards and premarital affairs, mistresses, liaisons, and traffic with prostitutes were common.

The contradictory standards applied to men and women existed in a city noted for its casual attitude toward the enforcement of rules. Those who knew Vienna well spoke of two attributes: *Schlamperei*—defined as sloppiness—and duplicity. Everyone knew what the rules were, but they also knew they could be winked at, that official prohibitions could be ignored in practice. The Viennese were also noted for their outward charm and manners, which served as façades to conceal real intentions and motives that were frequently self-serving. In short, to characterize Vienna as a rigid and sexually repressive society is far too simple. In addition to its relaxed and contradictory ways, the city was in love with its pleasures: it was famous for its music, being the home, at one time or another, of Beethoven, Brahms, Schubert, Mahler, and Johann Strauss; its love of food, especially sweets and pastry; and café life.

The life of the writer Arthur Schnitzler—who was just a few years younger than Freud, came from a middle-class Jewish family, and also attended medical school at the University of Vienna—provides an illuminating contrast. From adolescence on, Schnitzler, along with many of his friends, was engaged in one love affair after another. He paid so little attention to his studies, preferring to sketch out plays and stories during class, that he was surprised when his professors allowed him to graduate from medical school. Like many Viennese men, he spent hours talking with friends in cafés. His fiction gives a good picture of the sexual freedom—and sexual duplicity—characteristic of Vienna at the turn of the century.

Like Schnitzler, Freud came from a freethinking, emancipated Jewish family; Jacob was certainly no model of Victorian sternness. His own extreme sexual inhibitions and prudishness, as well as his powerful work ethic, were by no means universal in men from his background. His avoidance of sexual contact with women—he would be a virgin at the time of his marriage at age thirty, and, by his own admission, his sexual activity after marriage was minimal—the need to block music out of his life, and his driven work habits, already well entrenched as a school boy, stemmed from personal sources.

The adolescent Freud continued on the same path he had traveled as a child. He lived in a world of study, beloved books, and imagination; play and fun existed in the realm of ideas. He was not isolated from social contact and seemed always to have made friends with boys his own age, particularly if they shared his intellectual and literary interests. This was the beginning of a pattern of meaningful attachments to men with whom he could achieve some degree of intimacy.

Heinrich Braun was one of the first boys Freud was drawn to during the *Gymnasium* years. Braun, who grew up to be a prominent Social Democratic politician and editor, was an early ideal, someone who served as a model for the young Sigmund, though the friendship waned after they entered the university. As Freud put it in a letter to Braun's widow in 1927:

> We soon became inseparable friends. I spent every hour not taken up by school with him, mostly at his place . . . he aroused a number of revolutionary feelings within me, and we encouraged each other in overestimating our critical powers and superior judgement . . . I admired him, his energetic behavior, his independent judgement, compared him secretly with a young lion and was deeply convinced that one day he would fill a leading position in the world . . . Under his influence I also decided at that time to study law at the university.

Another friend from the adolescent years, his closest in fact, was Eduard Silberstein, also a classmate at the *Gymnasium.* Silberstein was more a peer, less of an admired ideal, than Braun. Freud described their relationship in a letter to his fiancée Martha Bernays in 1884: "We used to be together literally every hour of the day that was not spent on the school bench. We learned Spanish together, had our own mythology and secret names which we took from some dialogue of the great Cervantes. Together we founded a strange scholarly society, the *Academia Castellana,* compiled a great mass of humorous work which must still exist somewhere among my old papers; we shared our frugal suppers and were never bored in each other's company."

Freud's letters to his friend, written between the ages of fifteen and twenty-five, were preserved by Silberstein and provide a revealing glimpse of Sigmund as an adolescent. The young friends were learning Spanish together and invented a "Spanish Academy" with themselves as the only members, conducting their correspondence in their budding Spanish. They addressed each other with the names of dogs taken from Cervantes: Freud was "Cipion"—the critical, pedagogic and clever one—and Silberstein "Berganza," his talkative and adventurous friend. In these playful letters, Freud the young moralist emerges, lecturing Silberstein on the dangers of rash behavior. As in his later correspondence with Fliess, Freud expressed fear concerning his friend's health, along with open affection, albeit by letter and in a foreign language. When Silberstein did not reply promptly, Freud's anxiety was aroused, just as it would be with many of the intimate correspondents of his later years. The letters range across the interests of these precocious boys: schoolwork, books they were reading, philosophy, family matters, and, of course, girls and romance.

Freud experienced his first infatuation at the age of sixteen when he made a trip back to the place of his birth, Freiberg. The girl was Gisela Fluss, the daughter of the family the Freuds knew from their earlier time in Freiberg. Sigmund had remained friends with her brother, Emil, and the Fluss family later moved to Vienna, where Gisela and her sister knew Freud's sisters. Significantly, two versions of the incident exist: Freud's retrospective account, published in

1899, and the one described in letters to Silberstein in 1872, when the events occurred. Freud's later version, written when he was forty-three, made the incident seem like a typical adolescent crush, complete with shyness and unrequited yearning: "I was seventeen, and in the family where I was staying there was a daughter of fifteen, with whom I immediately fell in love. It was my first calf-love and sufficiently intense, but I kept it completely secret. After a few days the girl went off to her school . . . and it was this separation after such a short acquaintance that brought my longings to a really high pitch. I passed many hours in solitary walks through the lovely woods that I had found once more and spent my time building castles in the air."

This account, written many years after the events, contained references to the underlying feelings: it was a fantasy of love—he could not speak to the girl—there was frustrated longing, and an escape into an idealized version of nature. The letters written to Silberstein show that Freud's memory was quite faulty. The actual events in Freiberg in 1872, as they were reported at the time, provide striking evidence that it was a longing for maternal love that was aroused in the adolescent Freud on his return to his first home. It was Gisela's *mother* and not the young girl that he was taken with.

The facts are these: at the time of the visit he was sixteen, not seventeen, and, of greater importance, Gisela was eleven, not fifteen. She may have been a pretty eleven-year-old, but she was a child and not a possible partner for the sixteen-year-old boy. While his comments to Silberstein referred to his interest in her—"Gisela's image refused to budge from my mind, Caramba!"—the greater passion was directed to her mother. Freud wrote to Silberstein at the time of the Fluss incident:

> It would seem that I have transferred my esteem for the mother to friend-ship for the daughter . . . and I am full of admiration for this woman whom none of her children can fully match. Would you believe that this woman from a middle-class background, who once lived in fairly straitened circumstances, has acquired education of which a nineteen-year-old salon-bred young thing need not be ashamed? She has read a great deal, includ-ing the classics, and what she has not read she is conversant with. Hardly a branch of knowledge not too remote from the middle classes is foreign to her, and though she cannot, of course, have a solid grounding in every-thing, she has sound judgment . . . She is even knowledgeable about poli-tics, participates fully in the affairs of the little town, and, I think, it is she above all who is guiding the household into the modern mainstream. . . . None of the children has a horizon beyond her own. I have never seen *such* superiority before. Other mothers—and why disguise the fact that our own are among them? we shan't love them the less for it—care only for the physical well-being of their sons; when it comes to their intellectual devel-opment the control is out of their hands. Frau Fluss knows no sphere that

is beyond her influence . . . I have never seen her in a bad mood, or rather, vent her mood on the innocent.

She was certainly a contrast to Amalia; Freud had found the ideal mother, one who was not volatile and given to anger, one who could share his deepest intellectual and literary interests. And there was more; Freud described how a terrible toothache led him to drink too much alcohol, whereupon he passed out. Frau Fluss cared for him "as for her own child." When he awoke the next day, as he told it to Silberstein: "She asked me how I had slept. Badly, I replied, I didn't sleep a wink. Or so it had seemed to me. Smiling, she said, I came to see you twice during the night, and you never noticed. I felt ashamed. I cannot possibly deserve all the kindness and goodness she has been showing me. She fully appreciates that I need encouragement before I speak or bestir myself, and she never fails to give it. That's how her superiority shows itself: as she directs so I speak and come out of my shell."

If a patient had told this tale to Freud in later years, he might have wondered if the toothache and drinking were unconsciously created to obtain the secret gratification of motherly attention. Whether this was so or not, it is clear that Freud had found a loving and understanding mother in Freiberg, the very place where he suffered his original losses.

Freud's friendship and correspondence with Silberstein continued until he was twenty-five. His letters reveal a striking absence of relationships with girls and women; in fact there were no actual women in his life for the next ten years, although the fantasy of Gisela Fluss continued for a while, with Freud writing to Silberstein that no one can take her place, "indeed, that place can remain empty."

Freud was comfortable with—indeed, he seemed to require—emotional distance from women. The Gisela–Frau Fluss incident was not typical for a young man of this time and place. Silberstein himself, as well as the writer Arthur Schnitzler and his many friends, provide interesting comparisons, since all of them came from similar backgrounds. Schnitzler's autobiography chronicles many flirtations and affairs, and the Silberstein correspondence refers to several of Eduard's romantic entanglements. Significantly, the nineteen-year-old Freud took the same moralistic stand with his friend as he did with his sisters:

A thinking man is his own legislator, confessor, and absolver. But a woman, let alone a girl, has no inherent ethical standard; she can act correctly only if she keeps within the bounds of convention . . . Therefore do not become the cause of the first transgression of a young girl—one who has barely outgrown childhood—against a justified moral precept, by arranging meetings and exchanging letters against her parents' wishes. For what else can you write or tell her but that you love her, etc., and what purpose will it serve when you lie yourself into a passion and she dreams herself into one?

Even assuming that you are too honorable to act in that way, you have nevertheless taken the first step along a path that cannot possibly add to her dignity, you have taught her to anticipate a dangerous and wanton freedom which she can exercise to her detriment, if not now, then at some future time.

In his written accounts, Freud liked to give the impression that he had his own room as a child, but, in fact, it was not until he was nineteen that the family moved to a larger apartment and he finally acquired a long, narrow, private space, called a "cabinet." Freud worked and slept in this room, which he crammed with more and more books as time passed, and frequently ate his meals there as well, so he could continue studying, and, no doubt, escape from his mother and sisters. This was his self-created world; he remained there until he left for his medical internship eight years later.

Later, as an adult looking back, Freud seemed remarkably unaware of the most salient emotional dimensions of his childhood. He did not recognize his craving for a strong and successful father, his painful disappointment in Jacob, and the pervasive effects this had on his life. He was equally unaware of the longing for maternal love that resulted from his repeated losses of Amalia's care. The distortion in his memory of the Fluss incident—the way he remembered love for the daughter when he really yearned for the mother—revealed his lack of awareness of his longing for mother love. Nor did he ever seem to recognize how Amalia's dominating and self-centered personality affected him, though he would become very much like her in his later years.

CHAPTER 3

The Early Adult Years: Searching for an Identity

If his inmost heart could have been laid open, there would have been discovered that dream of undying fame; which dream as it is, is more powerful than a thousand realities.

—Nathaniel Hawthorne, *Fanshawe*

FREUD ATTENDED the University of Vienna from 1873 to 1882, a time when it had become a world famous institution of higher learning. During these years, Vienna was a rapidly modernizing city that was also riddled with vestiges of the past. It was not a democracy, but a mix of nobility, rising bourgeoisie, fusty bureaucrats, workers, peasants, and recent émigrés. Significant prejudices and restrictions against women were still prevalent—their public education ended at age fourteen and they were barred from the university. And, of personal relevance to Freud, anti-Semitism still existed, despite the emperor's pro-Jewish policies.

It is widely known that Freud was a Jew in German-speaking Austria and that anti-Semitism played a significant role in his life. While some people assume that he lived in a society like that of Nazi Germany, this was not the case. While the roots of the Nazi horrors can be found in nineteenth-century Europe, the specific situation of Jews during Freud's youth was quite different from what it eventually became in the 1930s. At the time he entered the university, many educated individuals associated Germany with the Enlightenment of the eighteenth century, with the revolution of 1848 which brought greater religious tolerance, with an orderly and reasoned way of life, and with faith in science as the path of progress beyond the outmoded beliefs associated with religion. All these ideas and values were more strongly linked, at this time, with Germany than

Austria-Hungary, which was still a backward empire, largely Catholic, and more anti-Semitic than its northern neighbor. German was the language of science, and of the writers and poets that Freud loved: Schiller and Goethe.

If Germany appeared to be the land of progress, Austria was an empire encrusted with vestiges of the past. Members of the Austrian nobility considered it beneath their station to engage in trade, finance, and the professions, leaving these fields open to enterprising and educated Jews who were able to rise up and achieve positions of security, wealth, and prominence. By the latter half of the nineteenth century, they dominated a number of fields. The Rothschild banking empire is well known, yet it was but one of several Viennese banks owned by Jews. In industry, there was Karl Wittgenstein—father of the philosopher Ludwig Wittgenstein—Austria's largest steel magnate, with interests in other industrial concerns as well. By the 1880s, 12 percent of the population of Vienna was Jewish, yet they made up one-third of the student body of the university, with even higher numbers in certain fields: 50 percent in medicine and almost 60 percent in law. All the liberal daily newspapers were owned by Jews and a large proportion of the journalists were Jewish. As the turn of the century approached, the majority of the liberal, educated, intellectual elite of Vienna was Jewish. The politicians Victor Adler—brother-in-law of Freud's school friend Heinrich Braun—and Otto Bauer—older brother of the woman who became his famous case, "Dora"; the journalist Karl Kraus; the writers Arthur Schnitzler, Hugo von Hofmannsthal, and Stefan Zweig; the composers Gustav Mahler, Arnold Schoenberg, and Alban Berg—all came from Jewish families. Even that most Viennese of musicians, Johann Strauss, was, it is now believed, part Jewish.

An important difference between the nineteenth- and twentieth-century treatment of Jews was the distinction between *religious* and *racial* anti-Semitism. All the laws and discriminatory practices in the nineteenth century were directed against members of the Jewish religion; if one wanted to escape these constraints, one could convert to Christianity. The idea of the Jews as a race—bearers of a hereditary taint that remained whether they changed their religion or not—arose toward the end of the century and gained increasing power in the following years, culminating in the Holocaust. Before this, most successful Viennese Jews thought of themselves as Austrians, identified with German culture, and assimilated to the dominant society, ridding themselves of their heritage in the process; many intermarried and some converted. The Wittgenstein family became Protestant. Victor Adler, the politician, and Alfred Adler, the psychoanalyst, both converted to Protestantism, as did Freud's later disciple Otto Rank. The composers Mahler and Schoenberg also converted, as did Kraus. The motivation for such conversions varied with different individuals, though many wished to distance themselves from the poverty, low status and mistreatment suffered by their ancestors; by converting and assimilating they were able to identify with the upper classes. Not only did many successful Viennese Jews renounce their religion and history, a number turned on those who displayed too much "Jewishness." Baron Maurice de Hirsch—a railroad builder and banker and, after Rothschild, Vienna's second-richest Jew—gave millions for the resettlement of Jews in Argentina so he would not have them around his city; as he put it, "All our misery comes from Jews who want to climb too high." Kraus—who converted first to Catholicism and than to Protestantism—was described as "an exquisitely Jewish anti-Semite" who urged all Jews to jettison their beliefs, rituals, and mannerisms. He had many admiring readers from the sophisticated upper reaches of Vienna's Jewish community.

Not all successful Jews attempted to escape their heritage; Theodor Herzl founded the Zionist movement in Vienna during these years, and attracted a small group of followers. Nevertheless, the movement toward assimilation—toward renunciation of any signs of Jewishness—was powerful. Freud himself never converted—never hid the fact that he was Jewish—yet, as early as adolescence, he looked down on poor Jews from the shtetls. Writing to his friend Emil Fluss as a sixteen-year-old, he described his repulsion at the sight of an eastern European Jewish family that he saw on a train. The father, he wrote, was a "swindler . . . crafty . . . mendacious, encouraged by his dear relatives in the belief that he has talent, but without principles or a view of life." In the years after his marriage, Freud banished all signs of religion from his home; the family celebrated Christmas with a candlelit tree and Easter with painted eggs. When his son Martin got married in a synagogue, it was the first time the young man had ever set foot in one. Still, like many Viennese Jews, the family associated primarily with others who shared their cultural background and assimilated-emancipated present; their doctors, their lawyer, all their friends, and almost all the psychoanalysts who initially joined the movement were Jewish.

Leopoldstadt, during the years Freud grew up there, had the largest Jewish population in Vienna; the Sperl Gymnasium was 60 percent Jewish. Although Jewish children were sometimes taunted in the streets, and boys drawn into fights, there is no evidence that Freud encountered this himself as a child. During his years at the University of Vienna, there was a heavy concentration of Jewish students, especially in medicine. When he began his medical practice in the 1880s, 60 percent of the doctors in Vienna were Jewish; by 1900, Jewish doctors held the majority of chairs at the Medical School and most of the directorships of the city's hospitals. The emperor's personal physician, the obstetrician to the women in the imperial family, and the surgeon general of the Army were all Jewish. Within the university and his chosen field, the fact that Freud came from a Jewish background, far from being a handicap in advancing his career, may well have been an advantage, since he would have fit in with this group of like-minded, assimilated physicians.

Still, the place of Jews in nineteenth-century Vienna was complex. Jacob Freud's family was part of the wave of immigrants that flooded into the city, and Sigmund was not unlike many first-generation children who took advantage of the new freedoms and educational opportunities to reach positions higher than their parents. At the same time, anti-Semitism was a centuries-old reality, and many signs kept a sense of persecution alive in Freud. His knowledge that he was a member of a group that had been subjected to harsh and unfair treatment reinforced the other ways he felt ill-used, and embattled. The oft-repeated tale of his vow to model himself on Hannibal, rather than his father, who passively submitted to anti-Semitism, was an early instance of the assumption of the combative stance that became such a central part of his personality. His later accounts of his youth contained few if any references to direct anti-Semitic attacks, but he let the impression stand that he had suffered this, that he was a Jew, an outsider, fighting against the "compact majority," as he later termed it, a picture that was partly true but also played down other causes of his sense of persecution, such as his poverty and his mother's difficult personality.

Freud graduated from the *Gymnasium* in 1873, passing his *Matura*, or final examination, with outstanding marks. He did well in all areas: Latin, Greek, mathematics, and German, where he was specially commended for his distinctive writing style. He was seventeen years old, five feet seven inches tall, thin, handsome, well-groomed, with a shock of dark hair and small mustache, and neatly dressed. He enrolled in the University of Vienna, and here he remained for the next nine years, first taking courses in philosophy and science, and then working in physiological research.

Freud's school achievements, literary passions, fantasies of the ancient world, friends, and relations with father, mother, and siblings gave an initial direction to his life; now he moved into the larger world and began to consolidate his adult identity. He had long been a brilliant student with a wide range of interests; at the university, he continued to submerge himself in his intellectual-scholarly endeavors, pursuing his studies with great thoroughness. This period of his life can best be thought of as an extended *adolescent moratorium,* to use Erik Erikson's concept, a time when certain adult goals—sexuality, the assumption of full adult responsibilities—are held in abeyance until one is ready to move to the next developmental level. During this moratorium period, Freud was most comfortable in his role as diligent student, absorbed in his ideas and schoolwork. While ambitious for fame and recognition, he directed little attention to earning a living, despite his family's lack of means. In this, he followed his father: like Jacob, he earned little and depended on "loans" from friends.

During his first six years at the university, Freud continued to live in his parents' apartment, along with his five sisters and younger brother. His life was made up of study, reading, and his preoccupation with the products of his mind, balanced with friendship with a select group of young men. As he wrote to Eduard Silberstein, "There is the pleasant prospect of every month enlarging my beloved small library, which gives me infinite pleasure." Silberstein remained

Freud at age sixteen with his mother.

the closest during these years, and Freud's letters to him give a clear picture of his passions, ideas, and way of life. Heinrich Braun—the friend who had been a model in the *Gymnasium* years—is mentioned from time to time in the letters to Silberstein, but, within a few years, the relationship was over: "Braun is here but have not seen him. This is an example of how old attachments can evaporate." Emil Fluss remained a friend and correspondent, and Joseph Paneth was a fellow student with whom he took courses, discussed philosophy, and, later, worked in the physiology laboratory of Ernst Brücke. But Silberstein was the recipient of Freud's deepest affection.

Eduard Silberstein came from the town of Braila, Romania, where his father was a successful businessman with enough money to send his son to school in Vienna. Amalia Freud's illnesses took her to a spa in the town of Roznau, where she met Frau Silberstein, and there are references in the correspondence to the fact that their mothers were acquainted. Eduard attended the Sperl Gymnasium, where he and Sigmund met, became friends, and began their "Spanish Academy." After graduation, he returned to his home, and later studied law at the

University of Leipzig. From what can be pieced together, Silberstein was a young intellectual who shared Freud's interests in language—their correspondence was conducted in Spanish, as well as other tongues—philosophy, literature, poetry, society, and the questions of the day. According to his granddaughter, in a brief sketch written many years later:

> He was an intellectual, totally unsuited for the business world, [though he was forced to take over the family grain trade.] He was a socialist in the sense that he was for worker's rights and the common man . . . He liked the Yiddish language and had a correspondence with Shalom Aleichem . . . He had a special admiration for Saint Francis of Assisi . . . [He] was a modest, learned, practical, aristocratic, dear man. I have childhood memories of him which I cherish. I remember his love for me, the charming ditties he composed for me in Spanish, and the stories he used to tell me.

Silberstein seems to have been a lovable and unambitious person, far different than his driven friend Sigmund. His love of Yiddish indicates that he felt no need to disavow his Jewish heritage—nor did he need to distance himself from the common man as Freud did—while the composition of Spanish ditties shows that even as a grandfather, he was still taken up with the playful language games of the adolescent letters. When he traveled to England he loved to stay with Quakers and attend their meetings; he had a great admiration for the gentle Saint Francis of Assisi. Quakers and Saint Francis are ideals that stand at the opposite end of the spectrum from Freud's generals and conquerors.

Freud's letters to Silberstein show him struggling between two extremes: on the one side, the possibility of emotional expression and intimacy, and, on the other, the well-ordered world of work and science. The intimacy is clearest in the affection Sigmund expressed for his friend Eduard: "Come to Vienna, where I await you with longing . . . I am much more anxious . . . why you do not write? . . . This explains why I have not had time to reply to you for four of five days, something that would horrify me were you to do it to me . . . I dragged [your] letter about again because I was loath to be separated from it for another whole day." And, in another passage, Freud revealed even more of his emotions: "I have your melancholy mood to thank for allowing me to hear once more affectionate words such as I rarely heard from you in Vienna . . . The gap your absence has opened in my social life has remained unfilled, nor have I ever looked for anyone to fill it. I should be unable to muster a dozen friends, although I have enemies by the dozen and of all shapes and sizes—a veritable pattern book."

Freud's affection and need for Silberstein's letters are apparent. It is also significant that even as an eighteen-year-old, he felt himself surrounded by "enemies." Who were the enemies of this bookish, quiet, young man? Since he did not mention any, this was likely a reflection of his general sense that the world was a hostile place and other people potential combatants. In addition to these direct expressions of longing and affection—and anxiety when the object of his love did not respond to him immediately—the letters included warnings to stay away from women, typically couched in moralistic terms. Sigmund needed to keep Eduard for himself.

The warm friendship between the two young men rested on their shared intellectual interests, love of language and word games, and their playful sense of humor. Freud was passionate about the novels and poems he discussed, as well as the debates over the great questions of the day: Was it possible to reconcile a belief in God with new scientific findings? What was the basis of morality when one abandoned religion? Along with these serious discussions, there was gossip about mutual acquaintances and glimpses of Freud's life at home. Freud mentioned his sisters, but he almost never referred to his father and spoke occasionally of Amalia, referring several times to her illnesses and recoveries, and cautioning Eduard to keep information from her. Regarding a proposed trip to England, Sigmund said, "My mother would be the last person I would want to know until it is definitely settled." And, about a cholera epidemic, "please do not mention it to my mother." There were no negative comments about Amalia, save for the indirect one when he implied that she, unlike Frau Fluss, "cares only for the physical well-being of her son." These references to his mother were small signs that Freud was not aware of his ambivalence toward her, especially as it was set off by her illnesses and absences. The need to protect himself from her anxious intrusiveness was also apparent.

Girls and romance were on the minds of these young men, and it was in his letters to Silberstein that Freud described his return to Freiberg and love for the Fluss women. As part of their literary play, Freud gave Gisela Fluss the name of "Ichthyosaura," an extinct river creature—*Fluss* means "river" in German—and jokingly called her this at several points in the correspondence. The real Gisela was around—the Flusses had moved to Vienna and the families were close—but Freud showed no real interest in her. Calling her an ichthyosaur revealed his underlying feeling about women, an attitude which came forth in starker form in several other comments. Warning Eduard away from "feminine creatures whose innocence shines forth from their eyes," he referred—one assumes in jest—to young girls who "degenerate into reptiles with venomous fangs, scaly armor, and Mephistophelian ideas." In another letter, he spoke of the "deleterious effect flattery has on people, especially on those who are unstable, incapable of grasping their own unimportance and whom nature has, moreover, inclined to be vain, a combination especially found in girls." Finally, he wrote: "Young ladies are boring, ergo they are a cure for boredom, poison being the best antidote. But if one is healthy to start with, isn't poison just poison, and if one is not bored by oneself, aren't young ladies crystallized poison of boredom and not an antidote against it?" Extinct water creatures, reptiles, vain young things, and poison—not a particularly pleasant set of images to associate with the female sex.

Freud was quite shy and afraid of women; as he put it in another letter: "I am going to continue feeling awkward in the company of ladies." When he was twenty and doing research in the city of Trieste, he was aware of the attractive Italian women, but, in his letters, he lapsed into mocking, quasi-scientific references; he saw the "Italian goddesses" on his walks around the town, but did not speak to them, they were "specimens," and he wrote to Silberstein that "since it is not allowed to dissect human beings, I really have nothing to do with them." His underlying suspicions and distaste for woman persisted throughout his life; there is a direct line from his adolescent attitudes to his later theories in which women are described as morally inferior and suffering from penis envy. These beliefs cannot be explained as typically Victorian; some men held such notions, but many others, including his friend Silberstein, who came from similar emancipated, well-educated backgrounds, did not see women the way Freud did.

Freud's relationship with Eduard Silberstein lasted for over ten years and was as close as he came to love during this period of his life. The friendship contained the components that were essential for Freud to permit himself emotional intimacy: the other person was a man, he lived in a distant city, and most of the communication was by letter, where he could control the interchange with his command of language. This pattern was to be repeated with Fliess within a few years, and, still later, with other male intimates such as Carl Jung and Sándor Ferenczi.

Not a great deal is known about the later life of Eduard Silberstein. He lived and worked for many years in his native Braila, where he was financially successful and active in Jewish cultural, but not religious, affairs. Among other things, he gave shelter and money to Jewish refugees from the east on their way to the United States. He was aware of his companion Sigmund's work as a psychoanalyst, and, when his first wife was depressed in 1891, he sent her to be treated by his old friend. She committed suicide by jumping out a window on the fourth floor of the building where Freud had his office. According to Silberstein's granddaughter, she had been "treated unsuccessfully by . . . Freud," though Walter Boehlich, editor of the correspondence, said she "threw herself to her death . . . without having seen Freud." Whichever was the case, Freud never referred to this shocking event. Silberstein remarried, had one daughter, and died in 1925.

Freud's friendship with Eduard Silberstein reveals the kind of personal intimacy he permitted himself during his early years at the university, but such interactions were brief respites in a demanding work schedule. For the most part, he lived the life of the dutiful student, driven to do well, please his professors, and gain admiration for his academic excellence. He made great demands on

Eduard Silberstein with his first wife, Pauline, about 1890.

himself; his way of life was, as he put it, "semi-nocturnal, I usually study from ten to two o'clock, quite often over-stretching my energies until four or five."

Freud's choice of medicine as a career was not what one would have expected from a boy with his gifts. By his own account, he had no great desire to be a healer, to alleviate human suffering, nor did he have the interests that often lead to work in science; he was not especially gifted in mathematics and did not have the mechanical or practical genius that one frequently sees in physical scientists. And, while he had an appreciation of nature, he was not one of those children who immerse themselves in the world of animals or nature as a prelude to biology. His talents were linguistic and literary, which could have led him to be a writer or a philosopher. In fact, he initially moved in these directions. Freud gave his own account of why he chose medicine in his *Autobiographical Study* of 1925:

> Under the powerful influence of a school friendship with a boy rather my senior who grew up to be a well-known politician [Heinrich Braun], I

developed a wish to study law like him and to engage in social activities. At the same time, the theories of Darwin, which were then of topical interest, strongly attracted me, for they held out hopes of an extraordinary advance in our understanding of the world; and it was hearing Goethe's beautiful essay on Nature read aloud at a popular lecture . . . just before I left school [the *Gymnasium*] that decided me to become a medical student.

Like many of Freud's autobiographical comments, this was a mixture of truth and myth. He mentioned two components in his attraction to medicine: the promise of great scientific achievements and the appeal of the essay on nature. The late nineteenth century was a time when optimism about science was at its height; the "extraordinary advance in our understanding of the world" that he referred to was an expression of these hopes. Such widespread beliefs appealed to his desire to be involved in a great or heroic endeavor. The second factor—hearing the essay on nature—is of special interest. Freud heard a popular lecture in which a passage attributed to Goethe was read by the anatomist Carl Brühl. It was a romantic ode to nature as an ever-giving mother, an essay replete with images of loving protection, embracing warmth, and inexhaustible nourishment. Nature was the lovely, nurturing mother who allows her favored children the privilege of exploring her mysteries, images which no doubt reverberated with Freud's own deepest longings.

The choice of medicine brought together hopes for fame—the promise of extraordinary discoveries—with the underlying longing for maternal love. Freud himself said he had "no particular partiality for the position and activity of a physician in those early years, nor, by the way, later. Rather, I was moved by a sort of greed for knowledge." While declaring himself in favor of science and medicine, he still wavered, as he wrote to Silberstein: "Of the next, my first university year, I can give you the news that I shall devote all of it to purely humanistic studies, which have nothing to do with my later field but will not be unprofitable for all that . . . To this end, I shall be attending the philosophy faculty during my first year."

And so he did; he and another friend, Joseph Paneth, took courses from the philosopher Franz Brentano where they debated whether it was possible to retain a belief in God—as Brentano maintained—in the face of the discoveries of modern science. Freud was particularly taken with Ludwig Feuerbach, "whom I revere and admire above all other philosophers," being drawn to his pugnacious, critical style and his attempt to unmask the "utterly pernicious illusions" of religion. By Freud's second year, however, science gained the upper hand; philosophy and the humanities—with their focus on human, moral, and emotional questions—were left behind as he became a "godless medical man and empiricist." In addition to the promise of great achievements—the chance to become the next Newton, Kepler, or Darwin—science promised the order and control that Freud needed to counter his emotionally chaotic childhood. His overweening conscience—he often commented on his "laziness" when he was obviously working extremely hard—not only brought praise for work well done, but helped control his potentially disruptive emotional states. Despite his choice of a scientific career, he remained, in the letters to Silberstein, most passionate when discussing poems, novels, moral questions, and people; his interest in science was mentioned, but he was not driven by the burning curiosity that one typically finds in great scientists. Rather, scientific work seemed to be a refuge, a safe haven to which he could retreat from the turmoil of the world.

When he began his studies, the University of Vienna had a world-renowned faculty in science and medicine. A number of professors had come from Germany: the Berlin-trained Ernst Brücke, in whose Physiological Institute Freud would eventually work; Carl Claus—from the University of Göttingen—head of the Institute of Comparative Anatomy; Hermann Nothnagel, head of the Division of Internal Medicine, like Brücke, trained in Berlin; and the accomplished surgeon Theodor Billroth, brought to Vienna after holding positions in Germany and Switzerland. In addition to their scientific accomplishments, these men were cultured and active in other fields: Brücke was an amateur painter; Nothnagel was involved in a number of liberal causes and, in 1891, founded the Society for Combating Anti-Semitism; and Billroth was a musician and close friend of the composer Johannes Brahms. Freud pursued a full scientific curriculum: anatomy, botany, chemistry, microscopy, physics, physiology, and zoology; he studied with and was influenced, to one degree or another, by all these distinguished, German-trained professors.

In 1875 the family could finally afford to send Sigmund on a delayed trip to Manchester, England, to celebrate his graduation from the Gymnasium. He visited his half brothers Emanuel and Philipp and reencountered John and Pauline, the playmates from his infancy in Freiberg, along with Emanuel's new children, Bertha and Samuel. Freud had a most favorable impression of Emanuel; here was a man from his own family who, starting from impoverished beginnings, had achieved success and a respectable position in society. He was also taken with England: "Many peculiarities of the English character and country that other Continentals might find intolerable agree very well with my own makeup," he wrote to Silberstein. He was probably taken with the English reserve and emotional control, such a contrast to Mediterranean—not to mention Galician—volatility.

In his third year at the university, Freud began to work in the Institute of Comparative Anatomy of Carl Claus. Claus had set up a marine biology research station in Trieste and it was here that Freud carried out careful anatomical work, dissecting more than four hundred eels, searching for their gonadal structures, work that led to his first publications. Microscopic research was a "school of scientific asceticism and self-denial," which required long and arduous training. Students could spend years bent over their microscopes before making original discoveries. Freud acquired these research skills in Claus's institute, but he did

The Freud family in 1876. Back row: *Pauline, Anna, Sigmund, half brother Emanuel, Rosa, Marie, and Amalia's cousin Simon Nathanson;* front row: *Adolfine, unknown girl, Amalia, and Jacob.* Seeated in front: *unknown boy and Alexander.*

not take to his professor and was unhappy under his direction, for reasons that are not clear, and he moved on in his search for a man to whom he could apprentice himself.

As he continued his education at the university, Freud left his childhood heroes behind, along with adolescent ideals such as Braun, and took his scientist-professors as his models. After leaving Claus's group, he apprenticed himself to Ernst Brücke, where he continued his microscopic research. As he put it: "At length, in Ernst Brücke's physiological laboratory, I found rest and full satisfaction—and men, too, whom I could respect and take as my models: the great Brücke himself, and his assistants, Sigmund Exner and Ernst Fleischl von Marxow."

The identification with Brücke supported the ideals of work, scientific achievement, and emotional control; his professor became the powerful and protective father that he longed for. Brücke's influence was pervasive, and Freud stayed on in his Physiological Institute for several extra years. He received his professor's stern form of "love": approval for meeting the highest standards of performance, which was of great value, though it still left his deeper longings for care and intimacy untouched.

Freud always referred to his teacher as "the great Brücke" and described him as "the greatest authority I ever met," an opinion that he never revised. He named his third son Ernst in honor of him, and later referred to the six years doing research in the Physiological Institute as "the happiest years of my youth." It is a great irony that after being drawn to medicine by the maternal-romantic images of the nature essay, he should have found his home in this laboratory, for Brücke had devoted his life to ridding biology of just such notions. It is clear that Brücke came to embody one side of Freud's need for a strong father. The language—"great," "the greatest authority," "Master Brücke"—all point to the intensity of his feelings.

During these years Freud was exposed to many areas of science and a number of excellent teachers; out of all this he was drawn to Brücke and settled comfortably into work within his sphere. Brücke, who was forty years older than Freud—almost exactly Jacob's age—was a well-established and famous scientist when Freud encountered him. His approach to science, the specific form of the work in his laboratory, and his personality all exerted forceful influences on his young apprentice; they appealed to that side of Freud that craved a model who was strong and certain in his aims, and who avoided—or seemed to banish—the emotions that might interfere with these goals.

Ernst Brücke was one of a group of outstanding German scientists known as the Helmholtz School of Medicine. Impressed with the achievements of physics, the members of this school were committed to applying its methods to the study of living organisms, including man. They saw themselves as crusaders for the new scientific approach, and opposed the vestiges of superstition and mysticism they saw in biology: nature worship, romanticism, "Vitalism." As Emil Du Bois-Reymond, a member of the Helmholtz group, put it: "Brücke and I pledged a solemn oath to put into effect this truth: no other forces than the common physical-chemical ones are active within the organism. In those cases which cannot at the time be explained by these forces one has either to find the specific way or form of their action by means of the physical-mathematical method or to assume new forces equal in dignity to the chemical-physical forces inherent in matter, reducible to the force of attraction and repulsion."

The Helmholtz program—positivism as we have come to know it—espoused the methods of physics and mathematics as the only acceptable way to study human life. Objectivity rather than subjectivity, "the chemical-physical forces inherent in matter" rather than sentiments or emotions, work with precise and replicable measurements rather than unquantifiable ideas and feelings—all these defined an approach that promised great achievements.

Freud's research in the Physiological Institute was far different from his later work as a psychoanalyst, where he plunged into the emotional chaos of his patients' lives. Brücke initially set him to work studying the nerve cells of an ancient species of fish, where he would be wedded to his microscope for many hours a day, as he had been in Claus's institute. This was followed by related forms of research: tracing nerve fibers, developing methods of staining, close and painstaking observation, careful literature reviews, and cautious conclusions. The titles of his papers give the flavor: "The Posterior Roots in Petromyzon," "The Nerve Cells in Crayfish," "A New Method for Anatomical Preparations of the Central Nervous System," "A Histological Method for the Study of Brain Tracts," and "A Case of Cerebral Hemorrhage." In his master's eyes he was an excellent researcher, wrote fine papers, and became an outstanding teacher. Clearly, he worked hard and successfully to meet Brücke's demanding standards.

Along with the appeal of positivist science and the work itself, Brücke's personality strongly attracted Freud. His stature, his fame, his certainty, and his dedication to a field that was rationality incarnate, all made him a hero, along with certain personal elements that struck deeper notes. Ernest Jones described the great man as follows:

> He was a small man with a large and impressive head, a balanced gait, and quiet, controlled movements; small-lipped, with the famous "terrifying blue eyes," rather shy, but stern and exceedingly silent. A Protestant, with his Prussian speech, he must have seemed out of place in easygoing Catholic Vienna, an emissary from another and more austere world—as indeed he was. A conscientious and indefatigable worker himself, he exacted the same standard from his assistants and students . . . The general opinion had him labeled as a cold, purely rational man. What degree of violent force against himself and his emotions he needed to build up this front is revealed by his reaction to the death of his beloved son in 1873. He forbade his family and friends to mention his son's name, put all pictures of him out of sight, and worked even harder than before. But this man was completely free of vanity, intrigue, and lust for power. To the student who proved his ability he was a most benevolent father, extending counsel and protection far beyond scientific matters. He respected the student's own ideas, encouraged original work, and sponsored talents even if they deviated considerably from his own opinions.

There is much in this description that accounts for Freud's attraction to Brücke: his scientific stature, his confidence, and his "benevolent" and "protective" fatherly qualities. Brücke's firmness and emotional control also set him apart from Freud's volatile mother, who rarely held her feelings back. What is more, Brücke was not all science and rationality; he had an interest in painting and considered himself an ambassador of culture to his students, a sort of permissible, aesthetic pleasure that fit well with Freud's attraction to the classical world.

Brücke's great capacity for emotional control was evident in the way he crushed all feelings about his son who died in 1873, and this, too, made him a

Ernst Brücke.

desirable model for Freud, who entered the university that same year. It is not known if Freud was aware of the death of Brücke's son, but he could certainly see that his professor was a man who kept his feelings tightly bound. Brücke's way of dealing with death and his reliance on a severe conscience and demanding work ethic to control potentially overwhelming emotional states appealed to the side of Freud that needed to banish his own fear of death and loss. By identifying with his professor—Brücke's "terrifying blue eyes" were one model for the penetrating gaze that Freud later made his own—he found support for the disavowal of his own yearnings and fears. As long as he followed this model, he received his professor's praise and support, identified with his greatness, and avoided his own unruly passions. Fifteen years after Freud left the Physiological Institute, he had a dream—which he called *Non vixit*—in which Brücke's gaze had the power to banish death.

Freud's apprenticeship in the Physiological Institute, and his personal identification with Brücke, left many traces on his personality and on psychoanalysis. This can be seen in all those ways in which he attempted to formulate his theories in positivist terms and his attraction to the concepts of "force," "energy," and "drive." The early manuscript *The Project for a Scientific Psychology*—written in draft form and sent to Fliess but never published—was an attempt to frame his emerging psychoanalytic ideas in a language that would have met with Brücke's approval. In his essay *Beyond the Pleasure Principle*—written many years later when he was struggling with the specter of the First World War and the problems of aggression, loss, and death—he took flight into "far-fetched speculation" of a quasi-biological nature: "Biology is truly a land of unlimited possibilities. We may expect it to give us the most surprising information and we cannot guess what answers it will return in a few dozen years to the questions we have put to it."

This was a nostalgic glance back at the time of his physiological research in the safe haven of Brücke's laboratory. If only he could still feel and believe as he did in those fondly remembered days, his life, he imagined, would be serene.

CHAPTER 4

Opening Up:
Martha, Cocaine, Fleischl

*His inner man gave him other evidences of a revolution in the sphere of
thought and feeling. In truth, nothing short of a total change of dynasty and
moral code, in that interior kingdom.*

—Nathaniel Hawthorne, *The Scarlet Letter*

THERE IS an enormous gulf between Freud in Brücke's laboratory and the man
who invented psychoanalysis ten years later. The first is a careful positivist-
scientist, immersed in neurological research, the second someone who works in
radical ways with disturbed human beings, who plunges into tumultuous emotions and dreams, including his own. During his years in the laboratory he had
no contact with women; then, in 1882, he fell passionately in love. The time
when he left the Physiological Institute and began his medical training was the
transition between these two extremes. From the diligent student, glued to his
microscope, he moved from a state of celibacy to his love for Martha Bernays,
began to experiment on himself with cocaine—a drug with powerful psychological effects—and developed a special intimacy with the older, attractive, Ernst
Fleischl von Marxow. Within the crucible of these new relationships, he was able
to experiment with new, less orderly and controlled, ways of being. More and
more, the submerged side of him came to life.

In 1882, Freud was a twenty-six-year-old medical student, working hard at
physiological research, buried in his books, and spending his free time with
a group of male friends who shared his intellectual interests. To all outward
appearances, he showed no signs of romantic interest in women. His adolescent
passion for Gisela Fluss had been, in reality, a longing for her mother. He lived
in his parents' small apartment with five younger sisters whose friends were

frequent visitors, yet Sigmund and his comrades never seemed to notice them. As his oldest sister Anna later recalled: "One would have imagined that the presence in the house of five young women would have had some attraction for these young men, but they seemed less interested in entertainment than in scientific discussion with our learned brother, and disappeared into his room with scarcely a glance at any of us!"

The pattern was broken one evening when, upon arriving home, he noticed a petite young woman, twenty-one-year-old Martha Bernays, chatting with his sisters. He joined the conversation and was instantly taken with her. It was love at first sight, and, in a matter of weeks, he was pressing her to marry him; within two months, they were secretly engaged. Speaking of such events much later, he said: "When making a decision of minor importance I have always found it advantageous to consider all the pros and cons. In vital matters, however, such as the choice of a mate or a profession, the decision should come from the unconscious, from somewhere within ourselves. In the important decisions of our personal life, we should be governed, I think, by the deep inner needs of our nature." These deep inner needs had been held in abeyance until this point; now, they began to assert themselves.

Martha Bernays came from a distinguished German-Jewish family; her grandfather, Isaac Bernays, had been the chief rabbi of Hamburg, a staunch defender of Jewish Orthodoxy in the face of the Reform movement. He was related to the great poet Heinrich Heine and was mentioned in Heine's letters as a man of high intelligence. Isaac had three sons; the first two became language professors at the Universities of Munich and Heidelberg, while the third—Martha's father, Berman Bernays—became a merchant. Berman married Emmeline Phillip, an intelligent, educated woman whose family originally came from Scandinavia, and both of them adhered to the strict rules of Orthodox Judaism. They had three children: a son Eli, Martha, the middle daughter, one year younger, and Minna, four years younger than her sister. Berman moved his family to Vienna in 1869, when Martha was eight years old, to assume a position with a well-known economist, but the move never sat well with his wife, who pined for the family she left behind in Germany. He died suddenly of heart failure ten years later when Martha was eighteen, leaving his wife and three children in a difficult financial situation. His son Eli was able to take over his position, so the Bernayses were not as destitute as the family of Jacob Freud; nevertheless, Martha and Minna would have little financial backing when it came time to find husbands.

With the death of Berman Bernays, control of the family passed into the hands of Emmeline, a woman of strong will who was firm in her Orthodox beliefs and protective of the welfare of her two daughters. The younger Minna was outspoken and independent, while Martha's attitude toward her mother was always one of devotion and strict obedience. The Bernays daughters were young women of gentility and education whose family lacked money, a type frequently encountered in the novels of Jane Austen, Charles Dickens, and Charlotte Brontë; Raskolnikov's sister Dunia, in Dostoevsky's *Crime and Punishment*, is such a case, while Arthur Schnitzler's novella *Fräulein Else* describes, with much insight and sympathy, the plight of such a girl in turn-of-the-century Vienna. These women were in precarious positions; available employment meant working as servants, nannies or governesses, which would imperil their chances of marriage, yet there was barely enough family money to keep up required middle-class appearances. The Bernays girls—thanks to their brother Eli's job—had sufficient funds to maintain a respectable front, though Minna, later, had to take work as a "lady's companion." Freud's sisters, on the other hand, were continually in danger of falling out of their class; Marie took a job as a governess, and the marital prospects of the others remained under a cloud. Before she met Freud, Martha almost became engaged to a much older businessman, which would have been a typical marriage of financial convenience, but Eli talked her out of it, insisting that it was foolish to marry someone she did not love. This was one of several considerate acts on his part that secured her affection for him.

Eli Bernays and Freud knew each other before Sigmund met Martha; the two young men were part of a close-knit group that included the Fluss brothers, the Sanskrit scholar Ignaz Schönberg, and three brothers named Wahle. Freud was closest to Schönberg, who was engaged to Minna Bernays before Sigmund became engaged to Martha. Sadly, Schönberg contracted tuberculosis and died before the marriage could take place, and Minna never found another suitor. Eli became engaged to Anna, the oldest Freud sister, shortly after Sigmund and Martha's engagement, and, since he was in a better financial position, he and Anna were able to marry in 1883. They emigrated to New York nine years later, and it was their daughter, Judith Bernays Heller, Freud's niece, who returned to Vienna as a young girl and later wrote about her time with Jacob and Amalia. Eli was a good friend of Freud's in the years before the engagement, a fact that must be kept in mind in light of the intense jealousy and anger that Freud later directed toward him.

When they met in 1882, Martha was five years younger than Sigmund, a slim, pale young woman from a family on the financial edge. Freud, and Martha kept their engagement secret, afraid that Martha's mother would object because of his lack of means. For the first nine months they were in Vienna together and were able to see each other for walks and occasional meetings where they exchanged kisses and embraces. But then Emmeline, who never liked living in Vienna, took her two daughters back to Wandsbek, a city close to her native Hamburg, much to the dismay of Freud and Schönberg, who were then separated from their fiancées. Since Freud was too poor to get married, he and Martha remained engaged for the next three-and-a-half years, spending just a few months of this time in each other's physical presence. He was only able to visit her in Wandsbek a few times, since he could not afford the train fare. Their relationship during this lengthy engagement was conducted by letters written almost daily. Unfortunately for biographers, Martha's letters have not been preserved, but Freud's are available—though only one-tenth of the more than nine hundred have been released from censorship by the Freud Archives—and provide a rich account of his personality during this time, including his complex feelings for Martha.

The picture of Martha that Freud held in his mind was powerfully colored by his fantasies. His lack of experience with women, and the paucity of direct contact with his beloved fiancée, no doubt facilitated this; but the perception of other people through his private lens was an enduring characteristic: when his passions were aroused, others were cast as players in a drama of his creation.

Martha was the recipient of his longings, hopes, fears, disappointments, and rages; there was a real young woman somewhere in all this, but she was difficult to discern. There were several dimensions to his image of her: the romanticized love object, his "Little Princess"; the desperately needed one that he might lose, to illness or a rival; and the independent woman who must be mastered, conquered, and bent to his will. Freud's romanticized image of Martha was striking: "My precious, most beloved girl . . . Fair mistress, sweet love . . . My sweet little woman . . . My dearest treasure," were the common greetings with which his letters began. Such sentiments ran through the correspondence:

> Today is the sixteenth monthly memorial of our engagement and an especially affectionate greeting is due to the sweet girl whose letters have continually grown better and cleverer and nobler, although she herself has always possessed these qualities.

> Heavens above, little woman, how innocent and good-natured you are!

> Do you still remember the first compliment I paid to you, the unsuspecting girl, more than 3½ years ago? I said that roses and pearls fall from your lips as with the princess in the fairy tale and that one is left wondering only whether it is goodness or intelligence that has the upper hand with you. That is how you acquired the name of Little Princess.

This romanticized image was, in some ways, typical of a first love, for, while Freud was over twenty-six when they became engaged, his lack of experience made him more like a sixteen-year-old. His ideas about women were also shaped by novels, dramas, and poetry; he knew about romance from fiction, but real women were a mystery to him. There was, as well, an individual twist to his image; he had to see Martha as a particular kind of woman: "sweet," and "innocent," a "girl," someone who fit his ideal of the passive female, obedient to her man and, above all, not aggressive or domineering, not "masculine," as he later termed it. Part of this stemmed from the attitudes toward women typical of this society and historical era. But not all. Literature was available that challenged these stereotypes; the roots of feminism went back to the preceding century. Freud was not the least bit religious, and his intelligence and wide reading brought him into contact with these alternative views. In fact, he had translated some essays by John Stuart Mill—an early spokesman for the rights of women—and his comments to Martha on Mill's ideas revealed his attitudes on "the woman question":

> He [Mill] lacked the sense of the absurd, on several points, for instance in the emancipation of women and the question of women altogether. I remember that a main argument in the pamphlet I translated was that the married woman can earn as much as the husband . . . In all his writings it never appears that the woman is different from the man, which is not to say she is something less, if anything the opposite. For example he finds an analogy for the oppression of women in that of the Negro. Any girl, even without a vote and legal rights, whose hand is kissed by a man willing to risk his all for her love, could have put him right on this.

> It seems a completely unrealistic notion to send women into the struggle for existence in the same way as men. Am I to think of my delicate sweet girl as a competitor? After all, the encounter could only end by my telling her, as I did seventeen months ago, that I love her, and that I will make every effort to get her out of the competitive role into the quiet, undisturbed activity of my home. It is possible that a different education could suppress all women's delicate qualities—which are so much in need of protection and yet so powerful—with the result that they could earn their living like men. It is also possible that in this case it would not be justifiable to deplore the disappearance of the most lovely thing the world has to offer us: our ideal of womanhood. But I believe that all reforming activity, legislation and education, will founder on the fact that long before the age at which a profession can be established in our society, nature will have appointed woman by her beauty, charm, and goodness, to do something else.

> No, in this respect I adhere to the old ways, to my longing for my Martha as she is, and she herself will not want it different; legislation and custom have to grant to women many rights kept from them, but the position of woman cannot be other than what it is: to be an adored sweetheart in youth, and a beloved wife in maturity.

Freud's belief that Martha was a fragile female creature that he, the strong man, had to shelter and protect was one side of his image of her, but it contrasted sharply with another side: his desperate need for her love and reassurance. Throughout the engagement, he would become anxious if she did not respond to his letters immediately, a reaction that was present in his teenage correspondence with Silberstein and that continued throughout his life with his intimate male friends. When someone was promoted to the role of loved one, fear of loss, and the urgent longing for contact, were powerfully activated. His letters to Martha throughout their engagement revealed how distraught he became without her, and how her loving words could lift him out of his melancholy.

Freud's dependence on Martha, and his fear of losing her, made him exquisitely sensitive to any sign of illness; as Jones noted, "Freud was throughout unnecessarily concerned about her health, and would often say that she had only two duties in life, to keep well and to love him." When Schönberg was dying of tuberculosis, Freud wrote that the blue rings under Martha's eyes agitated him more than his friend's illness. He also believed that contact with his sexuality could damage her. As Jones put it: "Freud had been disturbed lest Martha's poor health, with pale cheeks and blue rings under her eyes, might have proceeded from his ardent embraces . . . the first hint of what he was later to describe as the anxiety neurosis of engaged couples."

This was an odd idea: that sexual expression, even embraces and kisses, had the power to cause illness. When encountered during an engagement made difficult by long separations, one can see it for what it is: an expression of Freud's long-standing anxiety over the absence or loss of the woman he needed, along with the fear that his longing—for which "sexuality" later became the code word—was connected to sickness and death. He was moving out of the protective shell of his emotionally and sexually inhibited existence at the time of his engagement and, as he did so, his ancient fears of illness, loss, and death bubbled up from the depths.

Another reaction—one which took Freud over with great force—was his concern that he might lose Martha to a rival, a fear that set off jealous rage and a fierce possessiveness. One of the first competitors for her love was Fritz Wahle, a friend of Freud's and a member of the circle that included Eli, Schönberg, and the Fluss brothers. Fritz was engaged to a cousin of Martha's and was affectionate in a brotherly way; he seemed genuinely fond of her and concerned for her welfare. There may have been something more on his side—what he actually said at the time was that he was worried that Freud might make Martha unhappy—but the situation made Freud wild with jealousy. He vowed that he would treat Wahle ruthlessly and demanded that Martha, who insisted that Fritz was no more than an old friend, take his side against him. Fritz was a possible suitor, so Freud's jealousy was understandable, but this was not true with the other two "rivals" who most agitated him: Eli and Emmeline Bernays.

Eli was quite young when the conflict erupted with Freud, his friend and future brother-in-law. He was a successful businessman who had taken over his father's job at the age of nineteen, and was the sole support of his mother and two sisters, to whom he was devoted. After he married Freud's sister Anna in 1883, he contributed to the support of Jacob, Amalia, and their children, showing his generosity and responsibility. In the period before their conflict, Freud was impressed that Eli would choose to marry Anna, a penniless girl, when he could easily have found someone with more money. Those who knew him—including Freud during the earlier period—found him openhearted, easygoing, friendly, and charming. In spite of their friendship and Eli's admirable qualities, two weeks after his engagement to Martha, Freud remarked that Eli was going to be his "most dangerous rival," and, a few weeks later, his former friend had become "unbearable" to him.

Freud's hostility toward Eli stemmed from his fear that Martha's love for her brother threatened his exclusive claim to her. Eli also had money to support the various family members, which set off Freud's resentment at being in a dependent position; he was looking for an excuse to pick a quarrel and, when Eli supported his mother's plan to move back to Wandsbek, he became enraged, broke off relations, refused to attend Eli's wedding to Anna, and did not speak to his former friend for two years. Later, when Freud was desperately trying to raise enough money for his own marriage, he claimed Eli had mishandled some funds of Martha's that he held in trust, though this turned out not to be true. Freud again became enraged and demanded that Martha take his side, telling her that "she was not to write to him again until she promised to break off all relations with Eli." Clearly, these incidents were driven by Freud's belief that his connection to Martha was endangered by rivals—"enemies"—and that he needed to defeat them and claim her for himself. His animus toward his brother-in-law continued for several years, eventually fading, though never completely disappearing, after Eli and Anna moved to America.

Martha, a dutiful and obedient girl, was very attached to her mother and was, to some degree, under her influence. From the very beginning, this made Emmeline a dangerous rival in Freud's mind. He wrote to Martha, early in the engagement: "She is fascinating, but alien, and will always remain so to me. I seek for similarities with you, but find hardly any. Her very warm-heartedness has an air of condescension, and she exacts admiration. I can foresee more than one opportunity for making myself disagreeable to her and I don't intend to avoid them. One is that she is beginning to treat my young brother, of whom I am very fond, badly; another is my determination that my Martha's health shall not suffer by yielding to a crazy piety and fasting."

Emmeline was initially cool to her daughter's suitor, who had little in the way of financial prospects and was, in addition, hostile to her deeply held religious beliefs. Freud urged Minna to take his and Schönberg's side in opposition to Emmeline, claiming that he did not "feel hostile to her" and that he saw her as "a person of great mental and moral power standing in our midst, capable of high accomplishments, without a trace of the absurd weaknesses of old women."

Nevertheless, he felt she was "taking a line against us all. Because her charm and vitality have lasted so long, she still demands in return her full share of life—not the share of old age—and expects to be the center, the ruler, an end in herself. Every *man* who has grown old honorably wants the same, only in a woman one is not used to it."

Freud was, of course, only too used to a woman who "expects to be the center, the ruler, an end in herself": Amalia. Having lived with a tyrannical mother for many years, he would not allow himself to be in that position again; this time he would be the victor, he would take control and push his future mother-in-law aside. He saw the pull of loyalties between the various family members, so common at the time of a marriage, as a war; Eli and Emmeline were enemies who had to be defeated. No compromise was permitted; he demanded that Martha share all his loves and hatreds. As Jones noted, Freud's goal "was fusion rather than union."

Freud's concern that "Martha's health . . . not suffer by yielding to crazy piety and fasting" revealed his tenacious opposition to the Bernays' Orthodox Judaism. Of course, it was precisely this Orthodoxy that prescribed the subservient position of women that Freud required of Martha; he could, after all, have sought out an emancipated, freethinking partner. But he was never attracted to any woman who might be his equal. He needed someone like Martha who would serve him and, to that end, he had to tear her away from her religion—he spoke of the time when he would "make a heathen of her"—just as he had to destroy the bonds with her mother and brother.

Freud and Martha clashed sharply over her loyalty to Eli, Emmeline, and Judaism; one suspects that the letters in which these conflicts raged were censored from the published correspondence. Jones, who had access to the complete correspondence, suggested as much. Martha fought back initially but, in the end, the combination of his expressed love and need—which were certainly strong and genuine—his forceful personality, and his eloquence were enough to carry her along. She acceded to his wishes; her devotion and obedience to her mother, the fact that she was "good," someone who did not question conventional values, predisposed her to go along with his program for their life together, and she eventually capitulated and assumed the position of subordinate wife.

The sudden outbreak of love that Freud felt for Martha was an important indication that he was opening up, emerging from his emotionally constricted state. Once he was engaged and planning marriage, he needed to earn a living sufficient to support his wife-to-be and the family they desired. His salary in the Physiological Institute was minuscule and his chances of getting a higher position, say as one of the assistants, seemed remote. Brücke spoke directly to his young student and advised him to leave research and take the training necessary to open a medical practice. Following his professor's advice, Freud left home for the first time, moved into quarters at the Vienna General Hospital, and spent the next three years acquiring medical experience.

Sigmund and Martha at the time of their engagement.

In his *Autobiographical Study*, Freud told how he left physiological research for medical practice: "The turning-point came in 1882, when my teacher, for whom I felt the highest possible esteem, corrected my father's generous improvidence by strongly advising me, in view of my bad financial position, to abandon my theoretical career. I followed his advice, left the physiological laboratory and entered the General Hospital." While Freud's version is true to the external events, it left his deeper motives unexplored. It did not account for why he fell in love so suddenly, when there had been no women in his life until this time, nor did it explain why, if he was so happy in the Physiological Institute, he did he not find some way to remain with that kind of research. His need for money was very real, yet it had been so for the preceding ten years: there was another reason why leaving became such a pressing issue.

Freud's work in Brücke's laboratory was a very one-sided solution to the threat posed by his disavowed longings, with their attendant fears and miseries. His neurological research was not taking him any closer to understanding, much less alleviating, his psychological distress, nor were the laborious microscopic studies likely to bring him the fame and glory he desired. His description of the time with Brücke as "the happiest years of my student days" sounds like an ideal fantasy, as do his many references to his "great master." The scientific work led to a sense of accomplishment, earned praise, and gave order and structure to his life—the identification with Brücke provided strength and peace—but, in the end, his deeper emotional needs were neglected.

Although Freud liked to remember his years with Brücke as happy ones, a time free from "plaguing desires," this was hardly the case. His letters to Martha, as well as later accounts, reveal the fairly severe psychological symptoms from which he suffered, plagued by his travel phobia and many other manifestations of anxiety, including gastric distress and "migraine" headaches. He was also prey to shifts of mood that moved between periods of elation, excitement, and self-confidence, and depression, doubt, and low self-worth. During the depressed periods he could not work, and would move in and out of twilight states of mind. It was this emotional distress, more than anything else, that drove Freud away from his constricted life as a research scientist and toward new relationships and activities.

Freud's training at the General Hospital was the equivalent of what today would be called a medical internship and residency. He rotated through the various departments—surgery, internal medicine, dermatology, ophthalmology, psychiatry, and nervous diseases—acquiring familiarity with different conditions and treatment methods. This brought him into contact with a wide range of sick people, something that had not occurred during the preceding years of his scientific training. He worked in Hermann Nothnagel's Division of Internal Medicine and spent more than six months in Theodor Meynert's Psychiatry Clinic, but was unimpressed with what he saw there. Psychiatry, at this point in history, dealt with the manifestly insane, with an emphasis on physical causes and treatments. While outwardly the obedient student, his letters to Martha revealed his competitiveness and drive for fame: "I could achieve more than Nothnagel, to whom I consider myself superior, and might possibly reach the level of Charcot."

One of the most important people that Freud encountered at Brücke's laboratory was Josef Breuer, a brilliant research scientist and accomplished general physician, fourteen years older than the fledgling doctor. They first met in the late 1870s and quickly developed a close and mutually gratifying relationship. On his side, Breuer saw great promise in the bright young man and more or less adopted him as a son-colleague. Breuer was someone who, far from envying the talent of others, took pleasure in nurturing it. When they were later working together on the treatment of hysterics, Breuer commented: "Freud's intellect is soaring at its highest. I gaze after him as a hen at a hawk." For his part, Freud was searching for an older male ideal and he was more than pleased with what Breuer offered him: financial help, the sharing of personal information, and scientific and professional collaboration. For over six years, beginning in 1881, Breuer gave him a monthly stipend, a "loan" of money that the impoverished Freud was not expected to repay. When the younger man from time to time expressed discomfort over accepting the money, Breuer told him he could easily afford it and that Freud, rather than losing self-respect, should take the gift as an indication of his value in the world.

Through these years as Freud struggled to establish himself, he remained uncertain of his skill as a physician, filled with grand ambitions that had yet to bear fruit, and subject to mood swings, anxiety, and physical symptoms. Breuer was generous with the praise, support, and openness that the young doctor desperately needed. In a letter to Martha, written a few years after meeting Breuer, Freud said: "You know what Breuer told me one evening . . . he had discovered that hidden under the surface of timidity there lay in me an extremely daring and fearless human being." A fuller picture of their intimacy is provided in a letter to Martha, written in 1883:

> Realizing that I was badly in need of refreshment, I went to see Breuer, from whom I have just returned, rather late . . . The first thing he did was to chase me into the bathtub, which I left rejuvenated . . . then came a lengthy medical conversation on moral insanity and nervous diseases and strange case histories—your friend Bertha Pappenheim also cropped up— and then we became rather personal and very intimate and he told me a number of things about his wife and children and asked me to repeat what he had said only "after you are married to Martha." And then I opened up and said: "This same Martha . . . is in reality a sweet Cordelia, and we are already on terms of the closest intimacy and can say anything to each other." Whereupon he said he too always calls his wife by that name . . . and the ears of both Cordelias, the one of thirty-seven and the other of twenty-two, must have been ringing while we were thinking of them with serious tenderness.

Bertha Pappenheim—later famous as "Anna O.," the first case in Breuer and Freud's *Studies on Hysteria*—was treated by Breuer in 1880–1882, before Freud had even finished his medical training. He described his work with this young woman, who was also a friend of Martha's, to his young colleague-in-training, and Freud would return to this material in a few years when he began seeing similar patients in his own practice. Breuer's work with Bertha revealed the same care, sensitivity, and humanity that was evident in his relationship with Freud. Where other physicians at the time treated their hysterical patients as objects of scientific study, Breuer became involved with Bertha as a person. Of all the gifts that Breuer gave to Freud, the most significant, in the long run, was the method of treating and understanding hysteria that he first evolved in his work with Bertha Pappenheim.

Breuer's warm, empathic, and understanding nature was of tremendous value to Freud. The older man never played the part of distant authority; rather, he related to his colleague as friend, helper, and confidant. He did not give advice, but encouraged Freud to find his own way, to bring out his own proclivities. To talk with Breuer, Freud commented, was "like sitting in the sun . . . he radiates light and warmth . . . he is such a sunny person, and I don't know what he sees in me to be so kind . . . He is a man who always understands one."

Breuer helped Freud expand his knowledge of philosophy, literature, and art as well as science and medicine. He took the young doctor-in-training on his medical rounds, sometimes to distant cities where they spent the night together. On one of these occasions, Breuer signed Freud into the hotel as his brother, so that the young man would not have to leave his own tip, showing both his generosity and his sensitivity to Freud's potential shame about his poverty. In addition to the intimacy between the two men, Freud became a semiadopted member of the Breuer family. Breuer's wife Mathilde became an affectionate friend, and he later named his first child for her. In their home, Freud found the loving family setting and the successful, intellectually compatible parents that he longed for.

Brücke provided support for Freud's research and praise for his academic and scientific accomplishments, but the connection to him was relatively distant and impersonal; he was a "great man" to admire and emulate. Freud and Breuer related in a far different manner. There was praise, but also a sharing of feelings, confidences, and daily concerns. They had a good deal in common. Where Brücke was a German Protestant, Breuer was an emancipated Viennese Jew, with his own exposure to anti-Semitism, who moved in the same circles as Freud. In fact, his apartment was next door to that of Samuel Hammerschlag, Freud's old Hebrew teacher and benefactor, and Breuer's daughter later married Hammerschlag's son Paul. In addition to these personal connections, the two men worked together as physicians, treating sick and suffering patients; when their mutual friend and colleague Ernst Fleischl von Marxow was at the worst stage of his drug addiction, Breuer, who was his personal physician, "again behaved magnificently in the Fleischl affair," according to Freud.

Falling in love with Martha and shifting careers from physiological research to medical practice were ways in which Freud broke free of his emotional constrictions during these years, as was the growing intimacy with Breuer. Another was his experimentation with the drug cocaine, where he had one foot in the laboratory and the other in the world of emotion and psychology. There is an oft-repeated version of these events, based on his own later account, which obscured a central reason for his fascination with cocaine. His later account stressed his desire to make a name for himself as a scientist, a story that fit with the driving ambition that was to become increasingly apparent. But it did not explain why he selected a drug with powerful psychological effects. His letters to

Josef and Mathilde Breuer.

Martha at the time indicated, quite clearly, that he was drawn to cocaine because he believed it could alleviate his depression and anxiety, as indeed it did.

Freud's papers on cocaine showed that he was familiar with the use of coca leaves by the Indians of Peru, and with the work of a German army doctor who gave the drug to soldiers to improve their energy and endurance. The Indians knew "this divine plant . . . satiates the hungry, strengthens the weak, and causes them to forget their misfortunes." In other words, he knew it was a mood elevator that might alleviate the apathy and low energy from which he suffered. He obtained samples of the drug, began taking it, and found that it removed his depression, made him cheerful, and left him feeling that he had "dined well so that there is nothing at all one need bother about," while, at the same time, filling him with energy for work and exercise.

In his letters to Martha, he became more and more enthusiastic: "[It is a] magical drug . . . I take very small doses of it regularly against depression and against indigestion, and with the most brilliant success." He sent some to his fiancée "to make her strong and give her cheeks a red color," gave it to patients and friends, and even to his sisters. He wrote to Martha: "Woe to you, my princess, when I come. I will kiss you quite red and feed you till you are plump. And . . . you shall see who is the stronger, a gentle little girl who doesn't eat enough or a big wild man *who has cocaine in his body*. In my last severe depression I took coca again and a small dose lifted me to the heights in a wonderful fashion."

It seems clear that Freud was attracted to the drug because it alleviated his unhappiness, yet, in his retrospective *Autobiographical Study* of 1925, he made no mention of his psychological distress, focusing, instead, on how he supposedly did not become famous as the discoverer of the drug's use as a local anesthetic. As he put it:

> I may here go back a little and explain how it was the fault of my *fiancee* that I was not already famous at that youthful age. A side interest, though a deep one, had led me in 1884 to obtain . . . cocaine and to study its physiological action. While I was in the middle of this work, an opportunity arose for making a journey to visit my *fiancee,* from whom I had been parted for two years. I hastily wound up my investigation of cocaine and contented myself in my monograph on the subject [*Über Coca*] with prophesying that further uses for it would soon be found. [He recounted how he told an ophthalmologist friend about the drug and how another friend, Karl Koller, discovered its use as a local anesthetic for eye surgery.] Koller is therefore rightly regarded as the discoverer of local anaesthesia by cocaine . . . but I bore my *fiancee* no grudge for the interruption.

In his enthusiasm for cocaine, Freud prescribed his new wonder drug for his friend Fleischl, who had become addicted to morphine, which he initially took for intractable pain. Freud began giving him cocaine, believing it would cure the addiction. Unfortunately, this did not work, and Fleischl became as addicted to the new drug as he had been to the old. This was the first of several negative consequences that came to Freud's attention. One of the things he learned was the individual variation in response to cocaine. As he put it: "The subjective phenomena after ingestion of coca differ from person to person, and only few persons experience, like myself, a pure euphoria without alteration. Others already experience slight intoxication, hyperkinesia, and talkativeness after the same amount of cocaine."

Fleischl became more than "slightly intoxicated"; as he took higher and higher doses, he went into states of deliria with hallucinations of white snakes creeping over his skin. Freud had begun by giving his friend cocaine in the hope that it would cure his addiction only to find that, if anything, it made him worse. Cocaine then came under attack from the medical authorities and was condemned as a new scourge, in a class with opium. Because of the public outcry against the drug, and his unfortunate experience with Fleischl, Freud toned down his own drug use and backed away from his public enthusiasm so as not to be tainted by association. Far from gaining the fame he sought, he could have been branded a corruptor of public morals. Nevertheless, he was still using the drug ten years later on prescription from his friend Fliess, who was a great believer in its curative properties.

Together with his love for Martha and his use of cocaine, Freud's special closeness with Fleischl was another sign that he was breaking out of his blocked emotional state. The adolescent friendship with Silberstein had been one of the first in the series of male intimacies that would run through Freud's life; now came Fleischl. They worked together in Brücke's laboratory and Fleischl, who came from a wealthy family, gave his poor, younger colleague financial support, as several other friends did. But their closeness had more to do with the pain they shared; they were both men who turned to narcotic drugs with the hope of alleviating their suffering. Freud described his friend to Martha in 1882 and 1883:

> He is a thoroughly excellent person in whom nature and education have combined to do their best. Wealthy, skilled in all games and sports, with the stamp of genius in his manly features, good-looking, refined, endowed with many talents and capable of forming an original judgment about most things, he has always been my ideal, and I was not satisfied until we became friends and I could properly enjoy his value and abilities.

> I admire and love him with an intellectual passion, if you will allow such a phrase. His destruction will move me as the destruction of a sacred and famous temple would have affected an ancient Greek. I love him not so much as a human being, but as one of Creation's precious achievements. And you [Martha] needn't be at all jealous.

While he reassured Martha that his love was "intellectual," he was alive to his friend's physical attractiveness. And he was well aware of the wide range of permissible love between men and boys in ancient Greece. Fleischl bore a striking physical resemblance to Heinrich Braun, the older boy that Freud took as a model in his school days. He had a special and long-lasting love for Fleischl. Pictures of Freud's consulting room taken in 1938—over forty-five years after Fleischl's death—reveal that his was the only photograph in this space where Freud spent so many hours. It hangs over his couch, next to an engraving of Oedipus, surrounded by antiquities and pictures of ancient Greece and Rome.

The "destruction" that Freud mentioned in his letter to Martha referred to Fleischl's physical state; he suffered continuous pain caused by neuromas, tumors that sometimes grow on nerve endings when the nerves are damaged. Some years earlier, he had contracted an infection in his hand while doing research on a cadaver, necessitating the amputation of his thumb. Unfortunately, neuromas formed, requiring repeated operations. According to Jones, "His life became an

Heinrich Braun

"I admired him, his energetic behavior, his independent judgment, compared him secretly with a young lion. . . . Under his influence I also decided to study law at the university."

unending torture of pain and slowly approaching death. This mutilated and aching hand performed experimental work of technical perfection. His sleepless nights he used for studying physics and mathematics (and later) Sanskrit." This was his state—physical pain and suffering, dependent on morphine—when he and Freud became close. As Freud wrote to Martha: "I believe he has been engaged for ten or twelve years to a girl of his own age, who was prepared to wait for him indefinitely, but with whom he has now fallen out, for reasons unknown to me."

Jones described the time with Fleischl:

[Freud] asked him quite disconsolately where all this was going to lead to. He said that his parents regarded him a great *savant* and he would try to keep at his work as long as they lived. Once they were dead he would shoot

Ernst Fleischl von Marxow

"He is a thoroughly excellent person . . . with the stamp
of genius in his manly features, good-looking, refined. . . .
He has always been my ideal."

himself, for he thought it was quite impossible to hold out for long. It
would be senseless to try to console a man who sees his situation so clearly
. . . "I can't bear," he said, "to have to do everything with three times the
effort others use, when I was so accustomed to doings things more easily
then they. No one else would endure what I do."

As their friendship grew, Freud and Fleischl moved to deeper levels of intimacy as they sat up all night, Fleischl spending the whole time in a warm bath.
Freud (in an unpublished letter to Martha, quoted by Jones) wrote that he had
never experienced anything like it: "Every note of the profoundest despair was
sounded. [It was the first of many such nights over several months.] Every time
I ask myself if I shall ever in my life experience anything so agitating or exciting
as these nights . . . His talk, his explanations of all possible obscure things, his

Freud's office with couch and Fleischl picture in 1938.

judgments on persons in our circle, his manifold activity interrupted by states of the completest exhaustion relieved by morphia and cocaine: all that makes an ensemble that cannot be described."

This was a most powerful, emotion-laden experience. Here were two brilliant men, their fiancées absent or distant, sharing the depths of their pain. In his role as doctor, Freud had intimate contact with his friend's body, giving him injections, sitting by while Fleischl was in a bath, one assumes naked. And talking through the night. They had certain important features in common: both were involved in long engagements—Fleischl apparently never got married—and both were driven to satisfy the high expectations of their parents: Fleischl the "savant" was a match for the "Golden Sigi." For all the intellectual and aesthetic satisfaction they obtained from their work, there remained deep areas of unhappiness; they both struggled with depression. Freud had been using cocaine to treat his apathy and agitation and Fleischl morphine for his pain. All this contributed to the intimacy they experienced during their nights together.

Until this time—apart from infancy and the playful intellectual correspondence with Silberstein—there had been little in Freud's life that was openly emotional. Brücke was his model and he was rewarded for rigorous research and emotional control. The contrast between the days in the Physiological Institute and the nights with Fleischl was dramatic, with the two friends immersed in suffering, with suicide in the air, talking the night through under the influence of powerful drugs. For all the ultimate tragedy, it was an experience of great vitalization, another bridge from the constrained laboratory years to a new world of personal excitement.

The tragedy was that Fleischl could only obtain care in this dangerous manner. He lived on another six years, dying in 1891. Freud later told his follower Marie Bonaparte that he had never kissed the hand of any woman, the exception being Fleischl's mother, when she was at her son's death-bed.

The long nights with Fleischl, when "every note of the profoundest despair was sounded," which were full of "explanations of all possible obscure things," were, for Freud, part of the plunge into the world of his emotions, so blocked during the moratorium years with Brücke. It was an experience of tremendous enlivenment, a precursor to the methods of catharsis and the "talking cure" that he would soon adopt from his older colleague Breuer. He was moving into the next phase of his life, a move that would lead to new ways of working with patients and, a few years later, the self-analysis.

CHAPTER 5

Jean-Martin Charcot:
"The Napoléon of Neuroses"

There are laws governing even frenzy.

—Leo Tolstoy, *The Kreutzer Sonata*

IN 1885, when Freud had been engaged to Martha Bernays for over three years, was completing his medical residency, and was still working at physiological research in Brücke's laboratory, he decided to apply for a traveling grant to study in Paris with Jean-Martin Charcot, the most renowned neurologist of the time. The grant would provide up to six months of leave and a small stipend, but the award depended on Brücke's support, and Freud was dubious whether his mentor would help him; as he wrote to his fiancée, Brücke was a "very honorable but hardly energetic advocate." He underestimated how much his professor valued him, for Fleischl wrote to him that Brücke strongly supported the petition to the university committee and described his "downright championship of you, which has made a great stir."

The official purpose of Freud's stay in Paris was to continue his studies of brain anatomy, but the exposure to Charcot, both as a scientist and a man, reinforced the changes already taking place in him. He went to Paris as a student of neuroanatomy and returned to open his practice as a neurologist, treating disturbed human beings. The groundwork for this transition had been laid by the fervent courtship of Martha, the move from Brücke's Physiological Institute to medical training, the experimentation with cocaine, and his intimacy with Fleischl. The time with Charcot was another important step on this journey.

Freud left Vienna at the end of August and stopped to see Martha in Wandsbek, where she was living with her mother and sister Minna. This was their first meeting in over a year. After six weeks in Wandsbek, he went on to Paris,

74

where he continued to write to his beloved girl almost daily, letters which provide a detailed account of his experience during the next four-and-a-half months.

Freud arrived in Paris an unworldly young man and, for much of his time there, he was lonely—"melancholy" in his own words—and longing for friendly contact. His initial plan, the one that Brücke so warmly supported, was to study infant brain tissue. While the many years in Brücke's laboratory had exhausted the satisfactions of painstaking neuroanatomical research, he had not found anything with which to replace it. When not at his microscope, he filled the time wandering about the city and taking in the sights. He was impressed with much that he saw there, especially the Notre Dame cathedral, which he visited several times, and the Louvre, where the antiquities aroused his ardor: "An incredible number of Greek and Roman statues, gravestones, inscriptions, and relics . . . wonderful things, ancient gods represented over and over again, as well as the famous armless Venus de Milo . . . What attracted me most was the large number of emperors' busts . . . Assyrian kings tall as trees and holding lions for lapdogs in their arms, winged human animals . . . veritable colossi of kings, real sphinxes, a dreamlike world."

There were also outings to the theater for plays by Molière, Beaumarchais's *Le Mariage de Figaro,* and a chance to see the great Sarah Bernhardt, who enchanted him with her "intimate, endearing voice . . . every inch of this little figure was alive and bewitching . . . her caressing and pleading and embracing, the postures she assumes, the way she wraps herself around a man." But his enjoyment was not without its cost: "I again had to pay for this pleasure with an attack of migraine," he wrote to his fiancée.

Freud's feelings about Paris and Parisians were mixed; the city was "magic," and he took pleasure in many of its artistic treasures, yet it also struck him as "a vast overdressed Sphinx who gobbles up every foreigner unable to solve her riddles." While he was able to enjoy the art and architecture, the French people— especially the women—were a threat. He found them "arrogant . . . inaccessible . . . polite but hostile"; they left him feeling "isolated." The inhabitants, he wrote, "strike me as uncanny; the people seem to me of a different species from ourselves; I feel they are all possessed of a thousand demons . . . I don't think they know the meaning of shame or fear; the women no less than the men crowd round nudities as much as they do round corpses in the Morgue . . . [they are] given to psychical epidemics, historical mass convulsions." Because his spoken French was halting he did not actually talk with any of these demonic creatures, certainly not with any females, who provoked the following comment: "The ugliness of Paris women can hardly be exaggerated: not a decent pretty face." Needless to say, not every visitor to Paris saw French women in this way. These impressions seemed to come more from the imagination of the insecure, prudish, and lonely young man than from contact with actual people.

While the time in Paris eventually proved significant in shaping the later direction of Freud's work, he was very unhappy at first, and, after two months, was on the verge of going home. The stipend provided by the university was meager, and he was compelled to ask his friends in Vienna for money. The independently wealthy Joseph Paneth, fellow undergraduate and colleague in Brücke's Institute, set up a "fund" that Freud could draw on; Breuer sent 300 francs in response to a request; he also wrote to Fleischl, but his friend was too far gone in drug addiction to reply. His letters to Martha were filled with concerns over the cost of all the small items of daily life: "I had to pay 3.5 francs [for some toilet articles] and then one is expected to economize! . . . My new shoes arrived today, with laces and English soles, but twenty-two francs!" At one point, he bought a fine nibbed pen so that he could cram more words into each page of his letters and save on the cost of paper.

In addition to his own tight financial situation, Freud was worried about the desperate state of the family back in Vienna. Jacob was still not able to earn anything and suitable work for the sisters was difficult to obtain without compromising their marital prospects. The situation was miserable; there was not enough money for fuel or food, and Freud wrote to Martha that once, when invited out to lunch by a friend, he found it hard to eat roast meat, knowing how hungry his sisters were. The problem was eventually alleviated as others took over the support that Jacob was unable to provide. Emanuel sent money from England, Anna and her husband Eli were able to help, a room was rented to a lodger, and Freud himself, even with his meager funds in Paris, sent small sums home to his mother. The family poverty was a continuing reminder of the larger impoverishment—financial and emotional—of his childhood.

Freud's unhappiness and dissatisfaction were expressed in mood fluctuations, "migraine" headaches, bouts of "melancholy," physical complaints of a variety of kinds, and what he termed "neurasthenia"—what today would be called anxious depression. While he had his lofty aspirations, he was convinced that no one loved him for himself. He wrote to Martha: "The idea that you were not thinking of me as affectionately as usual gave me a strange feeling of forlornness, a feeling I couldn't have stood for long . . . I consider it a great misfortune that nature has not granted me that indefinite something which attracts people. I believe it is this lack more than any other which has deprived me of a rosy existence."

Freud was able to counter his unhappiness and symptoms in several ways. One was the intimate correspondence with Martha; he depended on letters affirming her love: "You write so charmingly and sensibly and every time you speak your mind about something I feel soothed." Then, after the first two months, he made contact with several male colleagues; one, a Russian of "melancholy disposition" named Darkschewitsch, helped offset the loneliness as they dined together, drank tea, talked of their mutual research interests, and eventually collaborated on a neurological paper. Freud "began to feel less isolated." Two of Martha's male cousins visited; they went to the theater together, had a late dinner, and "drank beer, and didn't get to bed till 2 A.M. No migraine today." And, there was cocaine. Before a visit to Charcot's house he took "a little cocaine, to untie my tongue," and remained "quite calm with the help of a small dose of cocaine . . . These were my achievements or rather the achievements of cocaine." A month later he wrote, "The bit of cocaine I have just taken is making me talkative, my little woman," and, about an evening at Charcot's: "It was so boring I nearly burst; only the bit of cocaine prevented me from doing so." Clearly, he was able to counter his fear of new and stressful situations—as well as manage his depression—with this potent drug.

The letters from Martha, aesthetic pleasures, male companionship, and cocaine all provided some solace, as did that old standby: reading; in the midst of his desperate financial situation he splurged and spent 80 francs for a set of Charcot's complete works. But the larger dissatisfaction—the need to move his life and career in new directions—remained. He longed for a great man to connect with, a new hero, and was about to find one: "Charcot lets fall quite casually any number of the most brilliant remarks, is constantly asking questions and always good enough to correct my wretched French. As long as he is present I try to keep near him, and already feel quite at home."

In the early months in Paris, Freud had been lost in the crowd of foreign students who had come to study with the famous neurologist. Then he hit upon the idea of translating some of Charcot's works into German; he wrote a deferential letter outlining his plan, was granted permission, and joined the inner circle. Having secured a place with the great man, the time in Paris came alive. He wrote to Martha:

> I think I am changing a great deal . . . Charcot, who is one of the greatest of physicians and a man whose common sense is touched by genius, is simply uprooting my aims and opinions. I sometimes come out of his lectures as though I were coming out of Notre Dame, with a new idea of perfection. But he exhausts me; when I come away from him I no longer have any desire to work at my own silly things; it is three whole days since I have done any work, and I have no feelings of guilt . . . no one else has ever affected me in the same way.

Jean-Martin Charcot was at the height of his fame and power when Freud encountered him in 1885. He had labored slowly for many years as a physician, carrying out research and building his reputation, eventually taking over the direction of a large section of the Salpêtrière Hospital in Paris, a medical poorhouse for several thousand women. The Salpêtrière was a small society unto itself, a vast and ancient complex of buildings, streets, gardens—there was even an old church on the grounds—that had, at one time or another, been an asylum for prostitutes, beggars, and the insane, at another the site of massacres during the French Revolution, as well as the setting for poems and novels. Charcot realized that many of the women in the Salpêtrière were suffering from unknown neurological conditions and saw the research potential in this population. With great energy and an iron will he established laboratories, clinics, and teaching facilities, attracted a group of devoted students and assistants, and carried out the research that established his reputation. Before turning to neurology, he had done significant work with pulmonary and kidney diseases and what would now be called geriatrics. In neurology, he delineated several classic conditions—amyotrophic lateral sclerosis, locomotor ataxia, aphasia—and did significant work on the functions of the cerebellum and medulla. All of France's best neurologists trained under Charcot, who was a spellbinding lecturer with a comprehensive grasp of neurology and the skill to present his ideas with creativity and flare. His reputation rested on both his solid research contributions and his charisma as a teacher.

Charcot was as impressive a personality as he was a scientist and physician. As Freud wrote after his first encounter: "Charcot arrived, a tall man of fifty-eight, wearing a top hat, with dark, strangely soft eyes—or rather, one is; the other is expressionless and has an inward cast—long wisps of hair stuck behind his ears, clean shaven, very expressive features with full protruding lips—in short, like a worldly priest from whom one expects a ready wit and an appreciation of good living."

Freud overestimated his height; Charcot was short, stout, and bullish with a resemblance to Napoléon that he liked to cultivate. He was, indeed, worldly, knew English, German, Spanish and Italian, in addition to his native French, was fond of quoting Dante and Shakespeare in their own languages, and had a keen appreciation of art and literature. He was married to an immensely wealthy widow, charged high fees for his private services, and was called as a consultant to the nobility all over Europe. He lived in lavish style in a mansion he had designed and decorated with Renaissance furniture, tapestries, fine works of art, and rare books, where he entertained leading figures from the worlds of politics, science, and the arts at weekly soirees. Charcot had become what the French called a *prince de la science;* he was something of a national treasure—though not without his enemies—and his countrymen were immensely proud of his accomplishments which, along with those of Louis Pasteur, were used as evidence that France had its geniuses to challenge the alleged scientific superiority of Germany, a competition of particular significance in the aftermath of France's humiliating defeat in the Franco-Prussian War fourteen years earlier.

Charcot's accomplishments and fame went hand in hand with his complete control of the Salpêtrière School; there was an iron-fisted character beneath the outward charm and worldly sophistication. Léon Daudet, a medical student at the Salpêtrière and the son of Charcot's intimate friend, the novelist Alphonse

Jean-Martin Charcot.

Daudet, said: "A more authoritarian man I have never known, nor one who could put such a despotic yoke on people around him . . . one only had to see how he could, from his pulpit, throw a sweeping and suspicious glance at his students and hear him interrupt them with a brief, imperative word . . . He could not stand contradiction, however small. If someone dared contradict his theories, he became ferocious and mean and did all he could to wreck the career of the imprudent man unless he retracted and apologized." The Goncourt brothers, whose well-known *Diary* chronicled many events of the period, described him as "an ambitious man, envious of any superiority, showing a ferocious resentment against those who declined invitations to his receptions, a despot at the university, hard with his patients . . . As a scientist, Charcot was a mixture of genius and charlatan."

Part of Charcot's charisma rested on his acute powers of observation, which had served him well in his earlier work, based, as it was, on the fine-grained differentiation of neurological symptoms and brain tissue during autopsies. Earlier in his life he had shown talent as an artist—he continued to sketch as a hobby—and he seemed to place great faith in the power of his eyes. As Freud noted: "He was not a reflective man, not a thinker: he had the nature of an artist—he was, as he himself said, a *'visuel'*, a man who sees. Here is what he himself told us about his method of working. He used to look again and again at the things he did not understand, to deepen his impression of them day by day, till suddenly an understanding of them dawned on him."

This approach had been productive in his medical research, but had become mixed with charlatanism when applied to so-called hysterical patients. Here he did make important contributions, but his visual powers were also used to mount impressive demonstrations that were, in the end, of little scientific value. Patients were brought to his office by his assistants for examinations; the walls and ceiling of the room, as well as all furniture, were painted black for dramatic effect. In this setting, Charcot would stare at the patient and then pronounce his diagnosis. This made an impression of profundity on many who witnessed it; as one of the young doctors later put it: "He was almost uncanny in the way he went straight to the root of the evil, often apparently after a rapid glance at the patient from his cold eagle eyes." In fact, these feats were of little value in understanding the patients or helping them. While some who witnessed these demonstrations were skeptical, Freud remained impressed with the power of his new mentor's penetrating gaze.

By the 1880s, Charcot had turned his attention to hysteria, and it was here that his need for power and control most interfered with his scientific aims. Hysteria—from the Greek word for "womb"—was a little-understood condition, sometimes believed to be no more than malingering. It was stigmatized by the medical establishment and associated with witchcraft and medieval states of possession. Hysterical patients displayed a variety of symptoms including amnesias, paralyses, spasms, involuntary movements, and anesthesias. Closely related were cases of so-called neurasthenia, characterized by weakness and lassitude. Unlike the neurological conditions that Charcot had previously studied, no anatomical basis could be found for these syndromes. Looking back from today's vantage point, it is doubtful if there ever was a single entity that could be described as hysteria. The diagnosis was, rather, a grab bag for a variety of conditions whose common feature was that they were "psychological," that no discernible physical causes could be found for them. From a modern standpoint, the so-called hysterics comprised a diverse group; some probably had medical conditions that were undiagnosable at the time, others psychotic and borderline disorders, and many— it seems clear from the descriptions—suffered from severe anxiety, depression, the effects of a variety of traumas, and dissociated states.

Charcot made crucial contributions to the understanding of hysteria, clarifying the psychological-traumatic nature of symptoms and conducting convincing hypnotic demonstrations. In addition to the so-called hysterical women on the wards of the Salpêtrière, there were a number of persons of both sexes who had been involved in accidents—for example, train wrecks—who displayed symptoms such as paralyses after the accident. Some of them were classified as cases of "railway spine" and "railway brain" because their symptoms mimicked those found after spinal cord or brain injuries. Physicians debated, with much fervor, whether these conditions had a physical basis. Charcot studied several such patients and was able to demonstrate the absence of damage to the nervous system, hence proving the psychological nature of the symptoms. His most convincing demonstrations relied on the use of hypnosis, a procedure which he had rehabilitated and made scientifically respectable. He was able to hypnotize subjects and suggest that when they awoke from their trances their limbs would be paralyzed. These hypnotically induced symptoms were exactly the same as those of both hysterical patients and the victims of accidents. He was also able to remove such symptoms with hypnotic suggestion. In a related demonstration, he was able to distinguish between hysterical and organic amnesia, using hypnosis to help patients recover lost memories, which was not possible, of course, when the amnesia was based on the destruction of brain tissue. While these demonstrations established the psychological nature of hysterical symptoms, it was a psychology without awareness. The patients were not conscious, either of the origin and nature of their symptoms—they were not malingering or deliberately faking—or of their reactions to the hypnotic suggestions. Charcot spoke of a post-traumatic "hypnoid state"—what today would be called dissociation—the blotting out of consciousness of events and emotions associated with traumatic events.

Charcot's genuine contributions were several. He made hysteria a respectable subject of scientific study, described and classified syndromes on the basis of symptoms, and differentiated the condition from known neurological diseases. By documenting a number of cases of male hysteria, he disproved the old link between the condition and the organs of female sexuality. He reestablished hypnotism as a research tool and showed how it could be employed to induce and remove hysterical and post-traumatic symptoms. Finally, and perhaps most significant in terms of its long-range importance for Freud, all these findings and demonstrations gave evidence of an unconscious mind. As Freud put it much later:

> What impressed me most of all while I was with Charcot were his latest investigations upon hysteria, some of which were carried out under my own eyes. He had proved, for instance, the genuineness of hysterical phenomena and their conformity to laws . . . the frequent occurrence of hysteria in men, the production of hysterical paralyses and contracture by hypnotic suggestion and the fact that such artificial products showed, down to their

smallest details, the same features as spontaneous attacks which were often brought on traumatically.

With his solid background in neurology, Freud was well prepared to understand the import of these hypnotic demonstrations; he knew that what he observed could not be explained in terms of physical damage to the nervous system, and that it also required a conception of psychological function without conscious awareness.

Alongside of Charcot the scientist was the implacable authority and showman. He was identified with hypnotism, split personality, somnambulism, and acquired the title "the Napoléon of Neuroses," the seer whose searching gaze penetrated the depths of the human mind. In this guise, he interpreted works of art, giving neurological diagnoses to cripples in old paintings, thus extending his genius into the past. He held weekly teaching seminars on hysteria and hypnosis which drew many sophisticated Parisians; writers and artists, interested in fantasy, dreams, and the imagination, came to his demonstrations of the unconscious mind, and based novels, plays, and paintings on what they witnessed at the Salpêtrière. The adulation he received during his performances reinforced his sense that he was a sage, a scientist whose findings were beyond question. His assistants—fearing his wrath if his theories were contradicted—provided him with patients who, without his knowledge, were prehypnotized on the hospital wards. They were then ready material on which to demonstrate the specific types of hysteria and stages of hypnosis that he believed he had discovered.

Charcot treated the patients during his well-attended demonstrations as if they were nerve tissue under a microscope. He was not interested in them as persons or in the social conditions in which they lived, nor did he concern himself—as Freud and Breuer were soon to do—with the details of their lives. For him, they were examples of this or that hysterical pathology. He never saw them on the hospital wards, but only when they were presented in his teaching clinic, where he would lecture about the stages of hysterical "crises" they were supposed to manifest—and the steps in the hypnotic process they were to undergo—in their presence, as if hearing all this had no effect on them. These patients were not disease specimens, of course, but persons with their own goals and interests, women who lived in the particular minisociety of the Salpêtrière, spoke with each other, and were aware of their roles in his shows. The most famous, Blanche Wittmann, became known as "the queen of hysterics" because of the ease with which she displayed the "classic" grande hysteria. She is the woman with her blouse falling off her shoulders, swooning into the arms of an assistant, in Pierre Brouillet's famous painting of Charcot in his clinic. She later revealed that she was at least partly conscious throughout these demonstrations; like the other patients, she sensed the opportunity to become a star attraction in the weekly demonstrations by displaying the required symptoms and reactions. If

Charcot giving a demonstration in his clinic.

some patients were all too ready to comply, Charcot's assistants also knew what he wanted and provided it. This led to a tacit three-way collaboration between the great doctor, the patients, and his assistants, in which genuine traumatic and unconscious phenomena were turned into oversimplified cases that were used to prove his theories and aggrandize his stature. Charcot had immense power within the world of the Salpêtrière and it was this, more than anything else, that corrupted him as a scientist.

Charcot's work with hysteria made him famous during his lifetime, but his theories did not survive without the force of his personality and his control over the Salpêtrière. Indeed, within a few years after his death in 1893 no one took him seriously. What is more, he did not develop any useful forms of treatment. Not only were his attempts to treat hysterics with electricity, the ingestion of iron, and suspending them from the ceiling in iron harnesses ineffective, there were also no satisfactory explanations for the conditions he described. While he recognized the role of trauma, when he turned to the patients who were labeled hysteric, he asserted that their conditions were explained by heredity. As Freud later put it: "He put forward a simple formula: heredity was to be regarded as the sole cause. Accordingly, hysteria was a form of degeneracy . . . All other aetiological factors played the part of incidental causes, of *agents provocateurs.*"

The connection between trauma and hysterical symptoms was lost in Charcot's need to impress his audience. No doubt his inability to empathize with the human plight of his women patients played a role, for, to appreciate the helplessness, fear, and personal disorganization that follows severe trauma, one must feel something of it oneself. This was not compatible with playing the role of Napoléon. At the time he observed Charcot's demonstrations, Freud was clearly aware of the role of trauma in hysteria. At one point he spoke of "the proposal to regard neuroses arising from trauma—'railway spine'—as hysteria," and, at another, said "[when] we enter into the history of the patient's life and find some occasion, some trauma, which would appropriately evoke precisely those expressions of feeling."

Freud left Paris early in 1886, spent a month in Berlin studying pediatrics with Adolf Baginsky, a well-known German specialist on childhood disease, and returned to Vienna in April, where he presented a report of the activities supported by his traveling grant to the professors at the university. He opened his private practice, and received an appointment at the Kassowitz Institute, a private hospital specializing in children's diseases, where he worked part-time as a consultant for the next ten years. In the fall, he presented a paper, "Male Hysteria," to the prestigious Viennese Society of Physicians, in which he enthusiastically championed Charcot's views. In his *Autobiographical Study* of 1925, written almost forty years after this event, he told of the cold and uncomprehending reactions of his medical colleagues; this incident—or Freud's retrospective version of it—has passed into psychoanalytic lore and is the first of many in which he described the misunderstanding and hostility he encountered when presenting his ideas: "I met with a bad reception. Persons of authority, such as the chairman . . . declared that what I said was incredible . . . The impression that the high authorities had rejected my innovations remained unshaken; and, with my hysteria in men and my production of hysterical paralyses by suggestion, I found myself forced into the Opposition."

The historical record shows that there is no truth to this account. Cases of male hysteria were well known to the Viennese physicians and, far from being incredulous, they felt that Freud was not telling them anything new. While open to some of Charcot's ideas about hysteria, they remained skeptical about others—with good reason, as later experience showed. What seemed to have happened is that Freud, caught up in his admiration for a new hero—and identified with Charcot's power—hoped for adulation from his medical colleagues, similar to what he observed the master receiving in Paris. When he met with a balanced, skeptical reception, it was a blow to these aspirations. His later account turned things around: he was the genius-innovator and the Viennese doctors were the narrow-minded, conservative ones, resistant to his exciting new ideas.

Charcot had a very important influence on Freud, who was, during his months in Paris, freeing himself from the constricted world of Brücke's laboratory and searching for a new direction that would engage his energies. The famous neurologist possesed a number of qualities that led Freud to adopt him as an idol. For one, Charcot immersed himself in clinical work and had little sympathy for theory. When one of his students objected that a clinical innovation "contradicts the Young-Helmholtz theory" he replied, "Theory is good; but it doesn't prevent things from existing." Helmholtz was Brücke's progenitor; in this respect, Charcot was a great man who was much different than Freud's earlier mentor, someone who operated more from his intuitive-artistic side. In addition, he was immersed in work with hysterical women who were a far cry from the dead nerve tissue that Freud originally came to study in Paris. In his demonstrations of hysteria and hypnosis, he displayed himself to the public with flair, again a contrast with the tightly contained Brücke. Finally, Charcot made the most disruptive emotional states safe to study; they could be "subject to laws." As Freud put it in the obituary he wrote about Charcot in 1893, "If I find someone in a state which bears all the signs of a painful affect—weeping, screaming and raging—the conclusion seems probable that a mental process is going on in him of which those physical phenomena are the appropriate expression." This was subject matter that reverberated with his own emerging emotional life.

In addition to opening up the possibility of dealing scientifically with tumultuous emotional states, Charcot was a grandiose figure who fit perfectly with Freud's preexisting dreams. The French doctor was a renowned scientist and a wealthy and powerful man. Imagine the contrast Freud must have felt when he attended the soirees at Charcot's mansion—amid wealthy guests in formal dress, dining on fine cuisine—and the miserable plight of his parents and sisters back in Vienna, at times on the verge of starvation. Charcot was also a commanding authority with his patients and colleagues, someone who could manipulate persons in the most extreme emotional states while retaining his scientific calm. He even bore the title of a military conqueror: "the Napoléon of Neuroses." No one could have been a greater contrast to Jacob Freud. As was the case with Brücke, Freud attributed uncanny visual powers to his new hero. While he dreamt of Brücke as someone whose burning stare could banish death, Charcot, with his hypnotic eyes, could make hysterical symptoms come and go, as if by magic. Freud always spoke of him in reverential terms, named his first son for him— Jean Martin, later known as Martin—kept his picture in his office for the rest of his life, and never questioned this idealized image, even though Charcot's work came into disrepute and Freud's own treatment of hysteria moved in radically new directions.

CHAPTER 6

Martha: "The Loss of an Illusion"

Marriage was a subject upon which it was hard to obtain accurate information. Its secrets, naturally, are those most jealously guarded; never more deeply concealed than when apparently most profusely exhibited in public.

—Anthony Powell, *A Dance to the Music of Time*

FREUD RETURNED from his time with Charcot and announced the opening of his new practice in the daily newspapers and medical journals on Easter Sunday in 1886: "Dr. Sigmund Freud, Docent in Neuropathology at the University of Vienna, has returned from spending six months in Paris and now resides at Rathausstrasse 7." Josef Breuer's wife Mathilde helped him decorate his new quarters, located in an area where the best doctors had their offices. Success now depended on patients who could pay his fees.

Freud was driven by the urgent need to establish himself in his new profession and achieve recognition—if not yet fame—along with the desire to overcome the years of poverty and raise enough money so that he and Martha could finally get married. Hopes that his cocaine research would bring his name to the attention of the world had come to naught, for, far from gaining recognition, his association with the drug could have sullied his reputation. He continued his anatomical research in laboratory facilities that his old professor Meynert made available and, for a time, hoped that a method he developed for staining tissue samples would establish his position, but this, too, led nowhere. And he struggled with his new medical practice. Breuer provided the most referrals, other patients came from Fleischl, Meynert, and another former professor, Nothnagel. But the practice grew slowly; if he had to depend on it alone, it would be years before he could marry. He made some money from his German translation of Charcot's books, and his part-time position at the Kassowitz Institute provided a small and stable sum, but he saw little prospect of fame tending to sick children. With all this, funds were tight well into the 1890s, leaving him dependent on donations and loans from his wealthier friends—Breuer, Paneth, Fleischl; even his old Hebrew teacher Samuel Hammerschlag, who was far from rich, gave what he could. As the months passed in 1886, Freud worked desperately to gather enough money to get married. His practice was interrupted for a month of required service as a doctor in the Austrian army, which prompted Martha's mother Emmeline to write and urge him to put the wedding off, a suggestion he pointedly ignored. Finally, he and Martha were able to scrape enough together from his small earnings, gifts from her relatives, and an additional donation from Paneth. The long engagement was at an end, the wedding could take place. It was to be—at his insistence—a small, private, civil ceremony in Wandsbek. As it turned out, the civil marriage, while legal in Germany, would not count in Austria so, much against his will, he took a quick course in the necessary Hebrew prayers from Martha's uncle and went through a Jewish wedding two days later, on September 15. They took a brief honeymoon from which Freud wrote to his mother-in-law—jokingly, one assumes—that this was "the first day of what we hope will prove a Thirty Years War between Sigmund and Martha."

The newly wed Freuds returned to Vienna from their honeymoon and took up quarters in a four-room apartment on Maria Theresienstrasse. Their apartment was in a building known as the House of Atonement, built on the site where many people had died in a fire that burned down the Ring Theater in 1881. Freud, the rational scientist, was not bothered by superstitions that the building was ill-fated—the stigma associated with the fire may have also made the rents lower than normal—and they were among the first tenants. This was not the only area where his antimystical, antireligious views were in force; he insisted on banishing all Jewish customs from his home and Martha—the granddaughter of a famous rabbi, raised in strict Orthodoxy—reported "how not being allowed to light the Sabbath lights on the first Friday night after her marriage was one of the more upsetting experiences of her life."

Within a year their first child, a daughter named Mathilde in honor of Breuer's wife, was born. Freud wrote to his mother-in-law that she was "terribly ugly, has sucked on her right hand from her first moment, otherwise seems very good-humored and behaves as though she is really at home." A few days later he was writing that everyone was saying that she "looks strikingly like *me* [and] has already grown much prettier." Martha nursed her new baby for only a few days before employing a wet nurse. Like many new fathers, he came to enjoy the smiles and playfulness of his baby girl.

Oscar Rie, an acquaintance of Freud's from medical school and a coworker at the Kassowitz Institute, became the family pediatrician and affectionate friend to the children, a role he continued to play for many years. Rie also remained one of Freud's few long-term friends outside of psychoanalysis, a bond cemented by other connections: Rie's wife was the sister of Ida Bondy, who later married Wilhelm Fliess. Rie, Freud, their colleague the ophthalmologist Leopold König- stein, and a few others would gather every Saturday night to play the popular Viennese card game Tarok. These evening diversions with his male friends, along with obligatory Sunday meals at Amalia's, were among the very few breaks in his concentrated work schedule.

It was in 1887, just one year after the wedding, that Freud met Wilhelm Fliess. Breuer had suggested that Fliess attend a lecture by the young neurologist, where they were introduced. They exchanged a few letters during these first years, but it was not until the early 1890s that the relationship expanded, and Fliess became Freud's most intimate friend.

In most Jewish families, even those where the parents are casual about reli- gion, children were named in honor of recently deceased relatives; Freud himself had been named after his paternal grandfather. It would have been natural for the Freuds to name their first son "Berman" after Martha's father, who died just three years before she met Sigmund. But this was not to be. Mathilde had been named after Breuer's wife and the next child, a son born in 1889, was named Jean Martin after the revered Charcot. Their second son was born fourteen months after Martin, and Freud named him Oliver after the English general Oliver Cromwell, an unusual choice for a poor Jewish boy from Vienna, but one that fit with his military-heroic identifications. Freud chose the names of all his children and, later, some of his grandchildren, playing out a pattern that began as a ten-year-old, when he named his younger brother Alexander. This practice, like his banishment of religion, exemplified his dominance within his new family.

Freud's control was also apparent in the selection of their new apartment. With three infants, they needed more space. Sigmund and Martha decided to find larger quarters and had drawn up a list of requirements: number of rooms, access for patients, closeness to schools, and so on. Then one day, when Freud was out walking, he found himself outside a building with an apartment for rent. Jones reported:

> He suddenly felt a great attraction toward the house, went in; inspected the available apartment, decided that it suited the family's needs and without more ado signed the lease. He returned home and told Martha that he had found their ideal quarters, Berggasse 19, and that evening took her there. Martha was apparently appalled. The neighborhood was a poor one, the stairs inside the building were dark, steep and of stone, and the accommo- dation was barely sufficient. But she did not protest. She realized that her husband had not only signed the lease but had set his heart on the place.

Freud chose this apartment because he had visited his friend Heinrich Braun there when they were university students. Braun, whom he had not seen in years, had been one of the first men—apart from his literary heros—that Freud sought as a male ideal. Even with the passage of time, the memory of his old friend was intensely alive, and Freud, regardless of the needs of Martha and the children, had to live in an apartment associated with him, just as he needed to keep a picture of Fleischl—who bore a striking resemblance to Braun—next to his couch through the many years of his residence at Berggasse 19.

Oliver was followed in 1892 by a third boy, named Ernst after the great Brücke. Sophie, the second daughter, was born a year after Ernst, and named for the wife of Freud's friend and benefactor, Paneth. She became her mother's favorite, and a special love of her father's as well. The last child, born in 1895, was named Anna, after Anna Hammerschlag Lichtheim, one of Freud's favorite patients and the daughter of his affectionate and generous old Hebrew teacher Samuel Hammerschlag. (Sophie Paneth was also Hammerschlag's niece.) All three sons had been named after powerful men who had been Freud's idols and mentors, while his three daughters were named after women from the families that gave him financial support during the years of poverty. Martha, while responsible for their care, apparently had no say in this; not one of the six children bore names related to her or her family.

Martha's younger sister Minna Bernays had been engaged to Freud's friend Schönberg, who died in 1886 before they could marry. Freud had struck up a friendship with her during his own engagement, signing his letters, "Your brother Sigmund." She never found another suitor after the death of her fiancé, and was in danger of falling out of her class into the life of a governess or maid—she did work for a time as a "lady's companion"—when Sigmund and Martha rescued her. She came to live with them after Anna was born in 1895 and stayed for the rest of her life. She was the more intellectual and less compliant of the Bernays sisters, witty and known for her sharp remarks, and, in the years before he began to attract outside attention, Freud would discuss his plans and theories with her. They sometimes visited Italian cities and Swiss resorts together, though it is quite unlikely that they had an affair—as has been rumored recently—which would have been much out of character for both of them. Tante Minna had a severe appearance and put on weight; in photographs, she looks older than her sister Martha though she was, in fact, four years younger. As her nephew Martin later wrote, even on the hottest summer days when the family was on holiday, Minna would remain fully clothed: "I knew Aunt Minna for the best part of my life . . . but I have never had any realization that she had legs." As the psychoanalytic movement grew after 1900, Freud's friendship with Minna faded, and her life became centered on her sister, the children, and the management of the household; she and Martha, who came to be called "Siamese twins," would do all the shopping together. The bond

Family picture, about 1898. Back row: *Martin and Sigmund;* middle row: *Oliver, Martha, and Minna;* front row: *Sophie, Anna, and Ernst.*

between the two sisters—one without a family of her own and the other with a husband married to his work—was a strong one.

The Freud family lived in the most conventional manner. And the household grew to be a large one, with Minna, the children and their nannies, and various other servants who took care of cooking and cleaning. Martha was an efficient supervisor of all that went on, and—outwardly—did not complain. To the world they presented a picture of calm bourgeois respectability; the marriage appeared to be a harmonious one, characterized by love and respect. But that was on the outside; there was another drama within. While Freud never spoke about it publicly, the most revealing picture of his own marriage appeared in the form of general remarks in his 1908 essay *"Civilized" Sexual Morality and Modern Nervous Illness*:

> This brings us to the question whether sexual intercourse in legal marriage can offer full compensation for the restriction imposed before marriage. There is such an abundance of material supporting a reply in the negative that we can give only the briefest summary of it. It must above all be borne in mind that our cultural sexual morality restricts sexual intercourse even in marriage itself, since it imposes on married couples the necessity of contenting themselves, as a rule, with a very few procreative acts. As a consequence of this consideration, satisfying sexual intercourse in marriage takes

place only for a few years; and we must subtract from this, of course, the intervals of abstention necessitated by regard for the wife's health. After these three, four or five years, the marriage becomes a failure in so far as it has promised the satisfaction of sexual needs. For all the devices hitherto invented for preventing conception impair sexual enjoyment, hurt the fine susceptibilities of both partners and even actually cause illness. Fear of the consequences of sexual intercourse first brings the married couple's physical affection to an end; and then, as a remoter result, it usually puts a stop as well to the mental sympathy between them, which should have been the succession to their original passionate love. The spiritual disillusionment and bodily deprivation to which most marriages are thus doomed puts both partners back in the state they were in before their marriage, except for being the poorer by the loss of an illusion, and they must once more have recourse to their fortitude in mastering and deflecting their sexual instinct.

These comments have been taken as Freud's doleful insights on the difficulties of finding happiness in marriage, but not as a disguised account of his own relationship with Martha. The assumption is often made that these insights are based on work with his patients, yet there is nothing in any of his case reports to support the specific picture he paints. There is, on the other hand, much in his own marriage that fits it quite closely.

Freud's sexual interest in Martha declined in the early years of the marriage; even the ardent embraces and kisses disappeared. In several of his letters to friends, he alluded to his lack of sexual activity, impotence, or inability to obtain pleasure. In 1897, at the age of forty-one, he wrote to Fliess, "Sexual excitement, too, is no longer of use for someone like me." Thirteen years later he wrote to Jung, "My Indian summer of eroticism that we spoke of on our trip has withered lamentably under the pressure of work," and, later still, to his American colleague, the neurologist James Jackson Putnam, "I stand for an infinitely freer sexual life, although I myself have made very little use of such freedom." One cause of his loss of sexual interest after the first few years may have been the pregnancies and new babies that arrived with such rapidity. When the slim, petite girl of the courtship became a pregnant mother-to-be, it may have set off the unconscious fear of loss associated with his own mother's pregnancies, as well as his anger at being displaced by rivals for her love and attention. As he wrote to Martha two years before their wedding: "I always think that once one is married one no longer—in most cases—lives for each other as one used to. One lives rather with each other for some third thing, and for the husband dangerous rivals soon appear: household and nursery."

It was also clear that the shared intimacies and confidences of the engagement faded away once Sigmund and Martha were married; this was the end of the "mental sympathy" that he referred to. He became increasingly engrossed with his work and communicated primarily with his male colleagues, and, as he developed psychoanalysis, it became his "tyrant": the recipient of his passion, time, and energy. While he discussed some of his interests with Martha in the early years, it was not long before they drew apart; she was not interested, or not capable of understanding, or preoccupied with home and children, or—perhaps—drawn to the household world free from his domination. Whatever the reasons, in all their remaining years together, she had no understanding of and little sympathy for the work that lay at the core of his being. As she once remarked: "Do you really think one can employ psychoanalysis with children? I must admit that if I did not realize how seriously my husband takes his treatments, I should think that psychoanalysis is a form of pornography!" Their daughter Anna, speaking of Martha some years later, said: "So far as psychoanalysis was concerned, my mother never cooperated . . . My mother believed in my father, not in psychoanalysis."

For all his psychoanalytic insight, Freud never saw the disappointments of his marriage as due to the qualities that he and Martha brought to the relationship. In the *"Civilized" Sexual Morality* essay, he attributed the failure of intimacy to outside factors such as "cultural sexual morality." There certainly were, and are, social taboos that interfere with sexual pleasure: feelings of shame, or a sense of guilt arising from a punitive conscience. Freud's insights into these factors were liberating for many people, including some of his patients, though not for him personally, as his remarks to Putnam reveal. But not everyone in his society was held back by such restrictions and, by framing his discussion in terms of general taboos, he avoided an examination of the powerful emotional inhibitions that he and Martha both suffered.

While sexual constrictions were characteristic of some segments of Victorian society, many men of Freud's background, education, and antireligious views were not held back by them. He, however, was terribly shy with women and confessed to Martha how once, when they were out walking during their engagement, he saw her pulling up her stockings: "It is bold of me to mention it, but I hope you don't mind." Later, she told him she wished to stay with an old friend, recently married, who had "married before her wedding," that is, had engaged in premarital intercourse. As Jones noted, "Contact with such a source of moral contamination, however, was sternly forbidden by him." His letters to her mentioned many of the novels he was reading, including Henry Fielding's ribald *Tom Jones,* but he "did not think it suitable for her chaste mind."

His inhibitions were not confined to sexuality, but extended to other emotions as well. As a boy and adolescent, he had needed to control his excitement and the joy or sadness aroused by music, not only in himself, but in those close to him, such as his sisters. He wrote to Martha, after seeing the opera *Carmen,* about the way they differed from the common people: "The mob gives vent to its appetites, and we deprive ourselves. We deprive ourselves in order to maintain our integrity, we economize in our health, our capacity for enjoyment, our emotions; we save ourselves for something, not knowing what. And this habit of constant suppression of natural instincts gives us the quality of refinement."

As an obedient young woman from an Orthodox Jewish family, Martha was as sexually and emotionally inhibited as Sigmund; her purity, chastity, and "goodness"—as he called it—were qualities that drew him to her. After the marriage, she was able to establish a separate arena for herself with home, children, and sister; she remained single-mindedly committed to her duties, and never openly challenged her husband's authority. Though living in Vienna since childhood, she never adopted the easygoing manners of the Viennese, and retained her precise Hamburg speech to the end. All this is evidence of the severity of her own conscience, for a prudishness and control that matched his. Within the home, she was an efficient manager, extremely reserved, punctual, and orderly, which provided a stable environment for her husband and children. She was also guilt-ridden and compulsive, substituting duty and work for the intimacy that was missing in her marriage. She was extremely self-denying, would not spend money on herself, and, while she enjoyed reading, imposed severe restrictions on this "pleasure." She was so committed to maintaining a spotless house that she would come to the dinner table with a pitcher of hot water and special napkin so that she could immediately remove any stains that were made on the tablecloth. She once told a young analyst how important it was to water flowers every day at exactly the same time. When she was an old woman in London, she spoke of reading as her only "diversion," but quickly added, at once apologetic and amused, "however, only at night in bed." She would begrudge herself this pleasure during the day, held back by her "good upbringing."

The most striking passage in the *"Civilized" Sexual Morality* essay is Freud's idiosyncratic belief that all known methods of birth control impair sexual enjoyment, and that contraceptive devices can "even actually cause illness." Modern readers—who can enjoy sex with contraception—may mistakenly assume that this was due to the lack of adequate methods of birth control in the nineteenth century. In fact, a number of relatively effective devices existed as early as the 1850s that allowed men and women to enjoy themselves while controlling conception. By the time of Freud's marriage in the 1880s, these methods were available, certainly to an educated physician living in a cosmopolitan city such as Vienna. There were "protective sheaths"—condoms—made of animal intestines, silk, or rubber; "womb veils" or "womb guards"—early versions of the diaphragm; and contraceptive sponges that could be soaked with spermicide and inserted in the vagina. While not as effective as their modern counterparts, all these devices did control pregnancies; as did timing intercourse to less fertile times of the menstrual cycle, mutual masturbation, and withdrawal before ejaculation, what Freud termed "coitus interruptus." The fact that he was aware of these methods is evident from his prescription, in 1909, of vaginal sponges for his patient Albert Hirst so that the young man could enjoy sex with his lover.

While contraceptive methods were available, they remained the subject of controversy and attack by Catholics and some other religious groups. They were also associated in the minds of some people with debauchery and sinfulness. Condoms had been in use for over a hundred years in Europe, originally employed for protection against syphilis by men having contact with prostitutes. Because of this history, they were associated with brothels and were offensive to the "fine susceptibilities" of those like Sigmund and Martha. The same was true, to one degree or another, with the other devices: the use of diaphragms, douches, and vaginal sponges required an openness to mutual sexual enjoyment that is hard to imagine in these two shy, inhibited individuals. Martha's inability or unwillingness to suckle her infants also deprived her of the natural contraceptive effect provided by nursing and accounts, in part, for the short spaces between her pregnancies. But it is Freud's odd idea that contraception can cause illness that is most puzzling.

Freud's belief that sexual gratification is harmful already appeared in his letters to Martha during their engagement, where he worried whether his passionate embraces would make her ill. He later had a "scientific" theory in which anxiety purportedly resulted from improperly expressed libido; sexual energy, in this view, was somehow "dammed up" and "converted" to anxiety. His ideas were not consistent; sometimes it was lack of sexual "discharge" that produced anxiety, at other times it was masturbation, the "interference" of contraceptive devices, or ejaculation outside the woman, and, at others, too much, too little, or the "wrong" kind of intercourse. While these beliefs about the pathological nature of sex originated with nineteenth-century religious and quasi-medical authorities, Freud was reluctant to part with them, even after they were shown to be without substance. With some patients—and in his later writing—he could argue that sexuality was not harmful—indeed, that symptoms could result from excessive guilt and a punitive conscience—he simultaneously held on to his beliefs that many sexual practices were damaging, warning his children about the ill-effects of masturbation, and believing that "too much" cuddling of babies was a form of dangerous sexual stimulation. In the 1890s he proposed a theory of "actual neurosis," a condition in which "harmful" sex was supposedly directly converted into anxiety and symptoms. In other words, he thought this was a form of neurosis without psychological conflict, where therapy was not possible because blocked or misdirected sexual energy was directly converted into illness. While he never gave any examples of this—and, when writing his *Autobiographical Study,* could not even remember the cases where he supposedly observed it—he clung to this belief as late as 1925.

While Freud's ideas on the connection between sex and anxiety took a number of contradictory forms—some liberating and some constricting—the idea that contraception can cause illness, with its later theoretical elaboration in the theory of libido converted into anxiety, has a simple, personal explanation.

Freud desperately longed for physical intimacy and his letters to Martha are replete with this passionate yearning, but he was also terrified about what would happen if he gave way to this desire, especially with a woman. While Martha—small, shy, obedient—was as safe as a woman could be, the danger was still present. But he was unaware of this conflict and so needed to attribute the sexual failure of his marriage to outside sources: cultural taboos and contraception. He could then think that it was not his own longing for love that made him anxious, but, rather, contraception or the wrong kind of sexual activity. In the end, these unrecognized conflicts caused a personal tragedy: he "lost the illusion" of a sexually pleasurable marriage and did not gain a vital and intimate partnership.

Sigmund and Martha's engagement years had been filled with romantic excitement and great hopes, along with their shared interests in people, literature—Cervantes, Dickens, Shakespeare—and their mutual aspirations for home and family. There had also been stormy times brought about by his jealousy, possessiveness, and drive to impose all his preferences and hates on her. The relationship had almost foundered over his insistence that she break away from her mother and reject her brother and her religion. They had weathered these tempestuous times, but then, once married, living—and sleeping—together, his passion quickly faded. He was able to express a range of emotions during the engagement when their primary contact was by letter. With a protective distance between them, and his literary skill at play, he could give free reign to his powerful yearnings for love. But the courtship and engagement, conducted in literary form, had been filled with his fantasies, and the romance of the letters could not withstand the reality of life—especially sexual life—together.

In the years that followed, Freud and Martha, while outwardly compatible, followed very different roads. He became ever more focused on his work, she increasingly involved with her children and the running of the house. There were six pregnancies and births in nine years; he really was opposed to contraception and seemed oblivious to the impact of so many children on her. The slim young girl of the engagement is unrecognizable in pictures of the matronly woman ten years later. He worked long hours to support the rapidly growing family—Jacob, Amalia, and his four unmarried sisters also needed financial help—and in his striving after the fame and recognition that he desired above all else.

Martha had been very inexperienced when they first met and his subsequent dominance prevented her from developing much beyond the compliant girl she had been. Whether she could have become a more independent person is difficult to say. A higher education or a profession were not available to someone from her background and, without a father or dowry, her opportunities were severely limited. She was in a precarious social position, as the fate of her sister Minna demonstrated. Martha eventually had the security and money to raise her children and take in her sister, and was, in later years, the "Frau Professor," with servants and time for vacations. All in all, she lived a life of some comfort and privilege, though the cost was a certain obliteration of her independent, emotionally alive self.

In the end, Freud's marriage provided him with a safe haven; he effaced Martha's individuality and made her into the woman who attended to all his outer needs. She was the mother of his large brood, efficient housekeeper-manager, and uncomplaining wife-companion. Still, his inner turmoil did not abate and, in fact, his anxiety, depression, and physical complaints got worse in the years after he was married. His deeper yearnings remained and he was impelled to look elsewhere for relief. One was in the partnership with Fliess that began just one year after his wedding. Another was in his friendship with Josef Breuer. They had met some years earlier, but the relationship came to assume great importance in the early years of the marriage as Freud began his practice. Breuer's work pointed the way to what would eventually become psychoanalysis, and, from the late 1880s on, they worked together on the development of new methods for treating neurosis, culminating in the jointly authored *Studies on Hysteria* of 1895.

PART TWO

The Birth
of Psychoanalysis

CHAPTER 7

Josef Breuer and the Invention of Psychotherapy

Each individual hysterical symptom immediately and permanently disappeared when we had succeeded in bringing clearly to light the memory of the event by which it was provoked and in arousing its accompanying affect, and when the patient had described that event in the greatest possible detail and had put the affect into words.

—Breuer and Freud in the *Studies on Hysteria,* 1895

ONE OF THE first people to greet Freud when he returned to Vienna in 1886 had been Josef Breuer, who welcomed him with a warm kiss and embrace. They had remained in touch during Freud's sojourn in Paris, and he now turned to his older colleague for help with his new medical practice. Freud had received the title of *Privatdozent*—unpaid lecturer—at the University of Vienna Medical School on the basis of his earlier research, which allowed him to give lectures— a practice he continued for a number of years—and conferred a certain prestige that enhanced his chances of establishing himself as a neurologist. But the title did little to guarantee that patients would come to him.

During these uncertain early years Freud was very dependent on Breuer, who gave him money, was the most reliable source of referrals, and was also the person to whom he turned for advice about the bewildering variety of patients who, with their terrors, depressions, and strange physical maladies, consulted a specialist in neurology. Some of the patients who came to see the fledgling doctor had genuine neurological conditions, but a great many others suffered from neuroses, "hysteria," "neurasthenia," and other conditions for which there was no clear physiological basis. During the first two years of his practice, Freud treated these patients with two methods: Erb's electrotherapy, a method originated by the German neurologist Heinrich Erb, and the Weir Mitchell system, developed by the American physician after whom it was named. In the first, a mild electrical current was applied to afflicted parts of the body, producing tingling sensations and muscle spasms. The Weir Mitchell system consisted of a regulated regime of bed rest, isolation, feeding, massage, and electrotherapy. Whatever benefits came from these two techniques were, no doubt, due to placebo effects and the relationship with a confident, authoritative doctor. The treatments were also brief; sending someone off to a spa for a rest cure did not provide much in the way of continuing income.

Freud was discouraged with both electrotherapy and rest cures; by the end of 1887, he began to experiment with hypnosis, which he knew from Charcot's demonstrations, as well as the work of the French physician Hippolyte Bernheim. The following year, he translated Bernheim's book *On Suggestion and Its Applications to Therapy* into German and visited him in Nancy, where he learned more about the use of hypnotic suggestion. In the beginning, he used hypnotism to remove symptoms, putting patients in a trance and telling them that when they regained consciousness, their vision or hearing would be restored or they would be able to move their paralyzed limbs. While such hypnotic suggestion initially seemed to produce better results than electrotherapy and rest cures, it still left much to be desired. Not every patient could be hypnotized, and the symptoms that were eliminated with this technique frequently reappeared. Freud soon realized that hypnosis did not reveal anything about the cause of hysteria; it was not a method that would lead to new discoveries.

In his search for more effective treatments, Freud began to use the cathartic method that he had known of since Breuer first told him the story of his work with Bertha Pappenheim ("Anna O.") in the years before he had gone to Paris. In the cathartic method, patients would be hypnotized and, while in a trance, instructed to remember and express as much as possible about the circumstances when their symptoms first appeared. Freud noted in the lectures he gave at Clark University in 1909: "If it is a merit to have brought psycho-analysis into being, that merit is not mine. I had no share in its earliest beginnings. I was a student and working for my final examinations at the time when another Viennese physician, Dr. Josef Breuer, first—in 1880–2—made use of this procedure on a girl who was suffering from hysteria." While Freud later downplayed Breuer's contribution in his *History of the Psychoanalytic Movement* (1914), his older colleague had in fact invented a treatment method and worked out a number of ideas that were the real beginnings of psychoanalysis.

Josef Breuer was intellectually gifted, financially comfortable, and, at the time Freud first met him in the late 1870s, devoting most of his energy to the direct care of patients. He combined up-to-date scientific knowledge with personal warmth, a combination of qualities that had made him one of the most sought-after physicians in Vienna.

Very little is known about Breuer's childhood and background. He was born in 1842 into a family at the opposite end of the social and economic spectrum from Freud's. His father began life as a poor rabbinical student but married into a prosperous family of merchants, adopted modern values, and became a well-known teacher of religion. Both parents, and other relatives, were part of the established, affluent, Viennese-Jewish community; they were well educated and involved with high culture and the arts.

Breuer's mother Bertha died when he was two, following the birth of his brother. In his own words, "[Mother, age 22] died, as the inscription on her grave tells us, 'in the flower of her youth and beauty' following the birth of her second son, my brother. Some time later her mother, a brilliant and witty woman, came to live with us. She was to manage the household and act as mother to the two motherless boys." Although Breuer claimed to have no memory of his mother, and described his childhood as a happy one, his earliest years, like Freud's, were marked by maternal loss. A two-year-old child is deeply attached to its mother, and her death is a profoundly traumatic event.

Like Freud, Breuer showed precocious intelligence, reading at age four, and doing excellent work in school. Breuer's father was a successful and educated man who taught his son at home until he entered the *Gymnasium* at age eight. He was a stable and admirable figure and, unlike Freud, Breuer was not driven to identify with "great men" to compensate for his father's failures and inadequacies. The grandmother served as a mother substitute and, in contrast to Sigmund's childhood, Josef was not replaced in her affections by a string of new babies.

Although he had broad scientific and philosophical interests and a genuine talent for original research, Breuer knew early in life that he wanted to be a physician. A full-time position at the university was difficult to obtain, but, even if one had been available, his caretaking nature would have led him to medical practice. He became an internist and general practitioner, and developed a wide circle of friends, scientific colleagues, and patients, who valued his kindness, unselfishness, warmth, understanding, and breadth of interests, as well as his supreme skill as a doctor. It was this combination of qualities that led many distinguished members of the Medical School faculty—including Brücke and Fleischl—to select him as their personal physician.

Breuer married Mathilde Altmann—who also came from an established and affluent family—when he was twenty-six; they eventually had five children. By his own account, his marriage and family were sources of joy and contentment. But beneath Breuer's sunny surface there lay other emotions, as his feelings about the anti-Semitism he encountered at the university revealed:

> None of you realizes how badly people such as ourselves are affected by these matters. Nevertheless I prefer not to "bother" my friends with the problem.

In all the years my indignation has "boiled over" only twice, over the bloody vileness of the "ritual murders" [a reference to an anti-Semitically motivated trial of Jews in Hungary in 1883]. Yet my friends are astonished at my "fanaticism"! So in future I shall keep my feelings to myself. But I cannot deny that the general silence on matters which afflict me, and which everyone can see afflict me, the trouble everyone takes to avoid discussing them, all this comes to have a seriously oppressive effect.

Breuer was a man of strong moral convictions and deep feeling; like Freud, he felt the pain of anti-Semitic persecution, even if his own career was not hindered by it.

In addition to his medical practice, Breuer was able to pursue his research interests and made significant scientific contributions in several areas. He did work on the origins of fever, the regulation of respiration—the "Hering-Breuer reflex" is a term still in use—and the role of the semicircular canals (the vestibulum, or inner ear) in balance. His qualities as a scientist were apparent in each of these areas. He selected a problem for which an important question needed to be answered, devised and carried out incisive experiments, and interpreted his findings in creative and sophisticated ways. His biological views were ahead of their time, and he was careful, committed to observation and evidence, and not given to sweeping speculations. His scientific work revealed someone who thought for himself; Breuer did not venerate authority and was not bound by received doctrines.

As a general physician with a large practice, Breuer no doubt saw a number of cases of hysteria, along with a variety of other psychological disorders. At that time, there were no effective treatments for these conditions; psychiatry, just emerging as a specialty, dealt with the manifestly insane, largely from a neurological perspective. Everyone else in psychological distress went, if they went to anyone, to a physician, perhaps one with a specialty in neurology. The understanding of hysteria and related conditions was extremely limited, although there were various theories about abnormalities of the nervous system—hence the term "neurosis"— and speculations about inherited degenerative tendencies.

The situation with treatment was no better. A variety of methods were recommended, including special diets and the use of a variety of drugs, some relatively harmless and some, such as morphine, chloral hydrate, and chloroform, quite powerful. Patients were treated with electrical stimulation, hydrotherapy, and rest cures at spas and sanitariums. Charcot had his patients ingest iron and hung them from the ceiling in iron harnesses.

With his extensive experience as a research scientist, his capacity for independent thought, and his desire to cure, Breuer could see that the existing theories and treatment methods were inadequate. Something new was needed, both to help suffering individuals and to better understand what was afflicting them. This was his state of thinking when he undertook the treatment of Bertha Pappenheim in 1880.

Breuer was probably the Pappenheim family physician when he was called in to see Bertha, a woman of twenty-one, who was suffering with a variety of serious symptoms. He saw her intensively; typically every day and sometimes twice a day. He used hypnosis and also listened to her semicoherent talk and fantasies, and gradually began to understand her many symptoms and moods in relation to the events of her life, particularly the illness and death of her father. He also, with her cooperation, developed the "cathartic method"—what she referred to as "the talking cure" or "chimney sweeping"—in which the doctor attempts to free the patient of symptoms by encouraging the expression of the memories and emotions connected to them.

It was Breuer's scientific curiosity—hysteria was a great mystery and he was interested in developing a better understanding of it—and his wish to cure that drew him to Bertha Pappenheim and led to his unique approach. None of the many intelligent, well-trained physicians in Vienna who attempted to treat hysterical patients came near the understanding that Breuer achieved because they lacked his strong personal motivation. It is likely that Breuer was personally driven to help Bertha because she aroused the long-dormant feelings associated with his mother's death. Both of these women were named Bertha and, at the time she was first seen for treatment, Bertha Pappenheim was almost exactly the age as his mother had been when she died. In addition, her breakdown was precipitated by the impending death of a parent, and her illness was replete with thoughts of death. Breuer's encounter with this second, young Bertha probably reverberated with memories of the death of his mother when he was two years old. His involvement with his patient went far beyond the usual; Breuer's biographer Albrecht Hirschmüller noted that "Breuer had a very special relationship with his patient. His commitment to the case . . . had been of an unusually high degree . . . [his] report is ten or twenty times longer than is usual for that period . . . [he had] an extraordinary degree of empathy."

Breuer described his patient as a "markedly intelligent [woman with] an astonishingly quick grasp of things and penetrating intuition . . . a powerful intellect [and] great poetic and imaginative gifts." He noted at the outset that her willpower was "energetic, tenacious and persistent; sometimes it reached the pitch of an obstinacy which only gave way out of kindness and regard for other people." Along with these qualities was a "sympathetic kindness. Even during her illness she herself was greatly assisted by being able to look after a number of poor, sick people, for she was thus able to satisfy a powerful instinct." Finally, and most telling in terms of later developments in psychoanalysis, Breuer noted that "the element of sexuality was astonishingly undeveloped in her." Bertha had

Bertha Pappenheim (Anna O.)

never been in love and seemed to have no thoughts or fantasies of a sexual nature. She was, however, "passionately fond" of her father, who was dying of a lung disease at the time her hysteria broke out.

Her illness or hysteria was characterized by striking physical symptoms, shifting states of consciousness, and emotional storms. Among the myriad of bodily symptoms were partial paralyses ("contractures") of arm, leg, and neck muscles, so that she could not rotate her head, or use one of her arms; a pronounced squint and related disturbances of vision; a nervous cough, leading to hoarseness and difficulty talking; and severe headaches. She suffered from a loss of language and was not able to use her native German, instead making garbled sounds from a mixture of four other languages. For some time, she could only speak in English.

Alterations in consciousness were most striking, as Breuer described: "Two entirely distinct states of consciousness . . . which alternated frequently and without warning . . . in one of these states she recognized her surroundings; she was melancholy and anxious, but relatively normal. In the other state she hallucinated and was 'naughty'—that is to say, she was abusive, used to throw the cushions at people, so far as her contractures . . . allowed, tore buttons off her bedclothes and linen with those of her fingers which she could move, and so on." She spoke of "having two selves, a real one and an evil one which forced her to behave badly," and there were periods of "absence"—amnesias—of short or longer duration.

Shifts in her emotional states were equally striking: "There were extremely rapid changes of mood leading to excessive but quite temporary high spirits, and at other times severe anxiety, stubborn opposition to every therapeutic effort and frightening hallucinations of black snakes, which was how she saw her hair, ribbons and similar things." Powerful anxiety, in various guises, was a constant feature of her illness, as were suicidal urges and depression.

This was the bewildering mass of symptoms and psychological states that Breuer encountered and which he needed to make sense of if he was to help his patient. There were two possible points from which to begin: trauma and hypnosis. It was known—Freud mentioned it from his time with Charcot—that some cases of hysteria were set off by traumatic events such as being in a train crash. And it was also known that patients could be induced, while under hypnosis, to forget and remember things, and that hysterical-like symptoms could be implanted and removed. With these guiding facts in mind, Breuer began to visit Bertha every day, encouraging her to talk about the events related to her symptoms, searching for the possible traumas that could have set them off. He would take her "mutterings," repeat them back, and encourage her to talk, tell a story, or make up a fantasy. He also tried to hypnotize her, suggesting that she recall the events related to the onset of her illness. A cooperative relationship developed; as he noted, "she was *completely unsuggestible;* she was only influenced by arguments, never by mere assertions." He could not play the magical hypnotist with her, suggesting her symptoms away; rather, they worked together at discovering the cause of her illness and alleviating the symptoms. Bertha was a woman of great intelligence and creativity, and she was a genuine collaborator in the invention of psychotherapy; the "talking cure" and "chimney sweeping" were her terms. Breuer, who had no taste for the role of authority, was open to this collaboration and he gave her credit as coinventor of the cathartic method.

Out of this work came the two central features that were the starting place for both psychoanalytic theory and therapy. In connecting symptoms to past events, Breuer came to see them as *symbols* that gave expression to traumatic memories. For example, one night, at the outset of her illness, Bertha was sitting by the bedside of her gravely ill father, awaiting the arrival of his doctor:

> Her right arm [was] over the back of her chair. She fell into a waking dream and saw a black snake coming towards the sick man from the wall to bite him. . . . She tried to keep the snake off, but it was as though she was paralyzed. Her right arm, over the back of the chair, had gone to sleep

and had become anaesthetic and paretic; and when she looked at it the fingers turned into little snakes with death's heads. . . . When the snake vanished, in her terror, she tried to pray. But language failed her: she could find no tongue in which to speak, till at last she thought of some children's verses in English and then found herself able to think and pray in that language.

The paralysis of her arm, and her inability to think or speak in any language but English, first occurred in this context of fear and death. These symptoms then took on a life of their own, spreading out to related motor and language disturbances, though Bertha herself was not conscious of this process and did not associate her symptoms with her original terror and death imagery. This is what Breuer was able to understand at the time. The course of his work with Bertha over a two-year period consisted in tracing each symptom back to its traumatic origin and encouraging the expression of the emotions and memories that had been blocked. When this was accomplished the symptoms seemed to disappear. Toward the end of her treatment, they arranged her room as it was at the time of her father's death and she went through, on a day-by-day basis, the major events of the previous year.

In the course of this work Breuer described Bertha's different states of consciousness, especially what he called her "absences," "double conscience," and "the unconscious." He understood her hysteria as the result of the breakthrough of dammed-up, unconscious traumatic memories and emotions. In other words, Bertha dealt with her fear—as in the incident when she was sitting by her father's bedside—by automatically banishing the frightening images, leaving her mind split into conscious and unconscious parts. But the banished material continued to intrude in the form of symptoms, altered mental states, and mood swings. These concepts would become central to the psychoanalytic theory of neurosis, to be elaborated by Freud in the years to come.

Breuer's work was not without its limitations. While he could see that Bertha's role in nursing her dying father, and his eventual death, were traumatic, he did not have an explanation for why she had such a disturbed reaction to these events. Other young women go through similar experiences without developing a near-psychotic illness. The closest he came to an explanation was his suggestion that "this girl, who was bubbling over with intellectual vitality, led an extremely monotonous existence in her puritanically-minded family." This caused her to spend much time daydreaming, which was the precursor to her divided consciousness. This explanation points to the family atmosphere, but is only suggestive. In fact, there was a particular background of oppression, suppressed anger, and guilt—along with death and loss—in the Pappenheim family that helps explain why the death of her father was such an overwhelming event.

Breuer also did not understand the impact he had on Bertha as her ever-attentive physician and therapist. He became intimately involved in her treatment and described how her condition became worse—how her symptoms returned and she became anxious and depressed—whenever he left her or missed their regular sessions. But he did not pursue the implications of these observations. From today's perspective, it appears that the feeling she had for her father was reexperienced with her doctor. The pain of her abandonment, so central in her reaction to her father's death, was alleviated when Breuer was with her, only to return when he was gone. Freud would later recognize the significance of such a reaction and name it "transference."

Breuer ended his case report on Bertha Pappenheim with the implication that she was largely cured. Given the severity of her illness, it is not surprising that this was not the case. While there was improvement, later evidence has revealed that her illness continued for at least six years. Breuer, in fact, placed her in a sanatorium and gave her chloral hydrate for sleep as well as morphine for her distress. She became addicted, and it was some time before she could be weaned from these drugs. Her mother, who had just lost her husband, later became involved with her daughter's care and with this help, a large and supportive group of relatives, and meaningful work, Bertha gradually recovered from the worst features of her disturbance. The imaginative gifts that Breuer noted led her to write poetry as well as a series of fairy tales and children's stories.

In the subsequent years, Bertha Pappenheim lived a long and productive life. She was a pioneer feminist and social worker in Germany, activities which, like her writing, were foreshadowed during the period of her illness by the satisfaction she took in helping the sick and less fortunate. She never married, nor did she have any close relations with men. Moral severity, dedication to her work, and an iron will were characteristic of her until the end of her life. A poem she wrote in 1911 captured these qualities:

Love did not come to me—
So I live like the plants,
In the cellar, without light.

Love did not come to me—
So I sound like a violin
With a broken bow.

Love did not come to me—
So I bury myself in work
And, chastened, live for duty.

Love did not come to me—
So I like to think of death
As a friendly face.

Bertha Pappenheim must be seen as a unique individual: intelligent to the point of brilliance, creative, imaginative, and very strong willed, certainly not someone who could be lumped into the category of "hysterical Victorian women." While there has been much written about the role of Victorian sexual repression as a cause of hysteria, Bertha was not a typical woman of her time—nor perhaps typical of any time—and sexuality, in the narrow sense, was not a significant factor in her illness.

The intensity of her disruptive emotions, the terror, debilitating physical symptoms, and depression, the extreme shifts of mood, and the presence of two or more selves, all point to a severe dissociative disorder. Much about her is similar to what one sees today in patients who have been traumatized or abused, and who suffer from a variety of post-traumatic stress conditions: syndromes that existed in the nineteenth century just as they do today.

George Eliot's *Daniel Deronda*—a novel that Freud knew and admired, by the way—captured the essence of Bertha's situation: "You are not a woman, you may try but you can never imagine what it is to have a man's force of genius in you, and yet to suffer the slavery of being a girl. To have a pattern cut out—'this is the Jewish woman'—this is what you must be; this is what you are wanted for; a woman's heart must be of such a size and no larger or it must be pressed small, like Chinese feet; her happiness is to be made as cakes are, by a fixed receipt."

Looking at Bertha's life from a modern perspective, one can gain a deeper appreciation of her plight. The Pappenheims were wealthy on both the father's and mother's sides and the young girl led a materially comfortable existence. Her father was an Orthodox Jew who founded a shul, or synagogue, in Vienna. He required his daughter to adhere to the demanding rules of that religion and, as a woman, dedicate herself to the role of dutiful Jewish wife. As Breuer noted, "Her excessively regimented lessons offered no outlet for her natural vitality, and a wholly uneventful life gave no real content to her intellectual activities." She outwardly complied with these demands, while inwardly rebelling by living a lonely existence in the "private theater" of her imagination.

Bertha was not only subjected to an oppressive upbringing, but was also scarred by the deaths and losses that befell the family. She was the third of four children, having been preceded by two sisters, the second of whom died two years before she was born and the oldest at age eighteen, when she was eight. The fourth child, a boy, survived. Both of these sisters died of tuberculosis, and her father was dying of lung disease, probably tuberculosis, at the time of her breakdown.

Breuer noted that Bertha's "gaiety had displeased her mother, who was a very solemn person." In other words, it sounds as if the mother was understandably depressed by the deaths of her two other children and was unavailable to her surviving daughter, who turned to her father as the only possible source of love. Because of her passionate nature, and, in spite of his controlling demands, she focused her desires on him to the exclusion of other adult relationships. But this left her trapped in a childhood love-hate struggle with her father and the identity he imposed on her. Outwardly she complied with his rules, inwardly she rebelled. All this was brought to a state of crisis with his illness. The family was about to lose still another member to tuberculosis and Bertha to lose the person she most loved.

Her family did not know, much less respond to, her inner life—her most significant hopes, longings, and disappointments. For several months after her illness began, no one even noticed her symptoms and moods. Her mother and brother prevented her from seeing her father as he was dying, an exclusion that she experienced as a betrayal, the neglect of her most important feelings, as intolerable "lies." It seems that throughout the earlier years, she went about her duties with an entirely separate, secret self, and no one noticed. In short, she was emotionally isolated—abandoned—in this death-ridden family. Well before her breakdown, she was a divided person, with a false outward self—compliant, dutiful, but unemotional—and an inner self where her genuine feelings were kept alive in fantasy. These emerged as the "good" and "evil" selves of her illness. In her breakdown, she fragmented; the pieces of her personality came apart.

Bertha's writing and work were major factors in her eventual recovery. The "private theater" of her childhood was the precursor to the literary compositions of the adult years. In addition to her poetry and fairy tales, she wrote plays, a translation and a preface to Mary Wollstonecraft's *Vindication of the Rights of Women*, newspaper articles, and polemical pieces. She sought out female models, first in Mary Wollstonecraft, the pioneer of the feminist movement, and then in an ancestor, Gluckel von Hameln, who exemplified these same qualities. She had her portrait painted, dressed in this woman's clothes, entitled "Bertha Pappenheim as Gluckel." These identifications enabled her to construct a new self out of the fragments of her old life.

Following her feminist models, she forged a National Association of Jewish Women in Germany, worked with teenagers, as well as unwed mothers and their babies, and eventually established a home for abandoned and abused girls in a town near Frankfurt, which she ran for many years. She was devoted to the cause of "girls at risk" and unmarried mothers, care of the homeless, concern about tuberculosis, and combating "white slavery" (the procuring of girls from eastern Europe for prostitution). In both her writing and career, she was preoccupied with the themes that had precipitated her breakdown: abused and mistreated girls and women whose rights were denied. The collaboration with Breuer in her cathartic treatment foreshadowed the productive, creative life that followed her recovery. Her later life was an adaptive, productive mastery of the conflicts that were earlier apparent in her hysterical illness.

Yet Bertha never married, never became intimate with men, and was very controlled; her emotions were all channeled into her writing and the care of young girls. By her own account—see the poem quoted earlier—she never found love. This does not mean she was without sexual feeling; rather, that emotional intimacy, sexual or otherwise, was so compromised by the impossible conflicts of her earlier life—the anger and guilt, the loss and terror—that she would not go near it. Often, a person who has been through the years of horrific pain and fear that constituted her hysterical illness is determined to never feel such things again. She needed her emotional control; the satisfactions of work and writing were achievements enough.

Breuer saw Bertha Pappenheim from 1880 to 1882, and continued to treat her, in and out of a sanatorium, for a few more years. He saw other psychiatric cases in his practice, but never again attempted a full cathartic treatment. His young colleague Freud, however, with a new practice and desperately in need of money, was only too happy to accept such patients. As Breuer put it: "When cases now came my way which promised good results from treatment by analysis . . . I showed them to Dr. Freud. . . . We shared a most intimate relationship as friends and scientists. The cases, their development, treatment, and anything that emerged from this concerning theory, were naturally always dealt with between us."

CHAPTER 8

Breuer, Freud, and the
Studies on Hysteria: 1886–1895

*If any one faculty may be called more wonderful than the rest, I do think
it is memory. There seems something more speakingly incomprehensible in
the powers, the failures, the inequalities of memory, than in any other of
our intelligences. The memory is sometimes so retentive, so serviceable, so
obedient—at others, so bewildered and so weak—and at others again so
tyrannic, so beyond control! We are to be sure a miracle every way, but our
powers of recollecting and forgetting, do seem peculiarly past finding out.*

—Jane Austen, *Mansfield Park*

In HIS WORK with the hysterical patients that Breuer sent his way, Freud gradually shifted from the use of hypnosis and suggestion to the cathartic method;
by 1889, it had become his primary therapeutic tool. Treating these patients,
whose symptoms and emotional states resonated with his own inner disturbance,
he finally had a reliable source of income and a path to the important new discoveries he had sought for so long. Over the next few years, he worked with a
series of women and, by 1892, he was pressing Breuer to join him in publishing
their findings. This they did, first in the form of a journal article, *Preliminary
Communication: On the Psychical Mechanism of Hysterical Phenomena,* in 1893,
and then in the *Studies on Hysteria,* of 1895. The *Preliminary Communication*
appeared as the first chapter in the *Studies,* and Breuer's case of Bertha Pappenheim—now called "Anna O."—was the second chapter; it was followed by four
of Freud's cases—Emmy von N., Lucy R., Katharina, and Elisabeth von R.—
along with brief comments on several other patients. These cases were followed
by a theoretical chapter, authored by Breuer alone, and a final chapter on theory
and treatment, authored solely by Freud.

Freud's first case in the *Studies* was the woman he called Frau Emmy von N., a forty-year-old widow who was, in reality, Baroness Fanny Moser. He employed the cathartic method with her in an effort to bring buried memories to consciousness, along with hypnotic suggestion and what he termed the "pressure technique," a variant of suggestion in which he pressed his hand on her forehead and instructed her to recall memories and emotional states. Frau Emmy suffered from a number of severe hysterical symptoms much like Bertha Pappenheim's. There were convulsive movements, a "curious clacking sound," insomnia, a variety of physical pains, anxiety, frightening hallucinations, depression with death imagery, and vocal outbursts: "Keep still!—Don't say anything!—Don't touch me!" As was the case with Bertha, many contemporary therapists would see these symptoms as characteristic of a severely traumatized individual, a view confirmed by her history.

Frau Emmy was the thirteenth of fourteen children, of whom only four survived. She was brought up, as Freud put it, "carefully, but under strict discipline by an over-energetic and severe mother" who died when she was nineteen. She married at twenty-three to an older, wealthy industrialist who died suddenly in her presence within a few years. Her husband's death precipitated the symptoms that brought her to Freud fourteen years later. Memories that emerged in the treatment included: "'When I was five years old . . . my brother and sister often threw dead animals at me. . . . I was frightened again when I was seven and I unexpectedly saw my sister in a coffin . . . and again when I was nine and I saw my aunt in her coffin and her jaw suddenly dropped . . .' She continued her list of terrifying memories. One, at fifteen, of how she found her mother, who had had a stroke, lying on the floor . . . again, at nineteen, how she came home one day and found her mother dead, with a distorted face."

Her husband's death was equally sudden and frightening. She was in bed after giving birth to her second daughter; he was sitting beside her, reading a newspaper, when he "got up all at once, looked at her so strangely, took a few paces forward and then fell down dead." In the aftermath, his family turned on her and blamed her for the death, and her relations with her daughters became clouded. Given the large number of deaths and losses in her childhood, and her hostile treatment at the hands of her husband's relatives, it is hardly a mystery why his death precipitated a state of extreme anxiety and depression. Freud saw her for seven weeks and, with a combination of hypnotic suggestion and catharsis, claimed to have relieved her fear and pain. Subsequent reports indicated that her "cure," not surprisingly, did not last. The brevity of this treatment is significant, since Freud was well aware that Breuer had treated Bertha Pappenheim for over two years.

Freud's use of this case material in the development of his theory of neurosis revealed the two sides that would characterize his psychoanalytic work for years to come. On the one hand, he described the relationship between her symptoms and the traumatic deaths and losses in her life. Such a connection may seem obvious now, but was not apparent to many doctors at that time. One could proceed quite logically from these observations to a "trauma, death and loss theory of neurosis." Freud presented the evidence for such an explanation but, even here, he placed greater emphasis on the role of sexuality. In other words, while some of his interpretations were close to the traumas of Frau Emmy's life, toward the end of his case history he reformulated the material to fit his theory of sexual causation, speaking of the patient as

> living for years in a state of sexual abstinence. Such circumstances are among the most frequent causes of a tendency to anxiety. . . . It has also struck me that amongst all the intimate information given me by the patient there was a complete absence of the sexual element, which is, after all, more liable than any other to provide occasion for traumas. . . . I cannot help suspecting that this woman who was so passionate and so capable of strong feelings had not won her victory over her sexual needs without severe struggles, and that at times her attempts at suppressing this most powerful of all instincts had exposed her to severe mental exhaustion.

In this passage, Freud played down Frau Emmy's traumatic losses and substituted speculations about her sexuality. He had to "adduce the sexual element" to account for the persistence of her symptoms, as if the deaths and terrors that she suffered were not enough. He guessed that sex was important because it was absent, though there was no confirmation of this interpretation from the patient herself. Most important, he introduced the theory that it was the undischarged sexuality—"abstinence"—that produced her anxiety, which reversed cause and effect. In fact, Frau Emmy was overcome with fear set off by the losses in her life, along with feelings of guilt and shame, which were made worse by the ill-treatment she received from her husband's family. To become intimate with someone once more, sexually or otherwise, was to risk a repetition of further loss, further attack. Understanding her situation in this way, it seems clear that it was her fear of repeated trauma that caused her to avoid sex, and not "abstinence" that produced the anxiety.

Freud's second case in the *Studies* was Miss Lucy R., an English governess employed by a wealthy widower to care for his children. Compared to Bertha Pappenheim and Frau Emmy, her symptoms were relatively mild: some depression, fatigue, and disturbance in the sense of smell; she could not rid herself of the odor of "burnt pudding." Freud was able to successfully explain these symptoms in relation to the events and emotions in her life. She was secretly in love with her employer, and her hopes that he would return her affection were aroused by some remarks he made. This put her into conflict with the other servants, who thought she was aspiring above her station. She subsequently discovered that her love for him was not reciprocated and decided to leave his employ, though this meant she would lose contact with his two young daughters, whom she loved. The specific symptom of the burned pudding smell came from an incident in which the prospect of losing her connection to the children occurred simultaneously with some actual burning of pudding.

Freud used a combination of catharsis, suggestion, and the pressure technique to discover the distressing events and feelings symbolized by Miss Lucy's symptoms. His explanation was clearly stated in terms of trauma, emotional conflict, and a "splitting of consciousness." While the patient's conflict—her unrequited love for her employer—could be called "sexual," she herself, in response to Freud's question, "Were you ashamed of loving a man?" said, "Oh no, I'm not unreasonably prudish. We're not responsible for our feelings, anyhow. It was distressing to me only because he is my employer and I am in his service and live in his house." Today, her symptoms would be attributed to the tangled web of master-servant relations, loyalties to the other servants, and love for the children in her care, along with the disappointment of her hopes and longings.

The next case study was Katharina, a young woman who Freud encountered on one of his vacations in the mountains, and whose "hysteria" he interpreted in a single meeting. She approached him, knowing he was a doctor, and described her symptoms: shortness of breath, pains in the head, a crushing feeling in her chest, and a frightening image of an angry male face. Freud pursued the memories connected to the onset of these symptoms and traced them to certain traumatic sexual experiences. Her symptoms had first appeared when she discovered her "uncle" and "cousin" (in reality her father and older sister, as Freud later revealed) engaged in sexual intercourse. This incident was frightening because it reminded her of sexual advances made by her father two years previously, when she was fourteen. The fear engendered by these incestuous attacks appeared in her symptoms: shortness of breath, hammering in the head, and the crushing feeling in her chest representing her father's body pressing on her. She subsequently told her mother of his advances, which led to angry quarrels, a divorce, and the father turning his "senseless rage against her." This last accounted for the image of the angry male face.

In his explanation, Freud made a clear connection between the sexual attacks and Katharina's symptoms. He did not, however, appreciate the full traumatic effect of such a sexual molestation on a fourteen-year-old girl, rather, claiming that "a mere suspicion of sexual relations calls up the affect of anxiety in virginal individuals." This was no "mere suspicion," however, but an attempted rape by a drunken father who had also sexually abused her sister.

Freud's fourth case in the *Studies* was Fraulein Elisabeth von R.—in reality Ilona Weiss—whose life circumstances and symptoms were similar to those of Bertha Pappenheim. She struggled against the limitations imposed on her because she was a woman, nursed her father during a fatal illness, and suffered the death of a sister. When she first came to Freud, her main symptoms were pains in the legs and difficulty walking, along with fatigue and depression. Freud noted that "first the patient's father had died, then her mother had had to undergo a serious eye-operation and soon afterwards a married sister had succumbed to a heart-affliction of long standing after a confinement. In all these troubles and in all the sick-nursing involved, the largest share had fallen to our patient."

During an earlier period, when her mother was ill and unavailable, Elisabeth had drawn close to her father; she was a bright young woman who sought intellectual stimulation and freedom from the constrictions imposed on women through involvement and identification with him. He alternately encouraged her and, as Freud wrote, "jokingly called her 'cheeky' and 'cock-sure,' and warned her against being too positive in her judgements and against her habit of regardlessly telling people the truth, and he often said she would find it hard to get a husband."

In spite of his teasing, Elisabeth was very close to her father and, when his heart disease struck, she nursed him for eighteen months until his death. This death brought hard times to the family—social isolation, the loss of other connections—all made more difficult by the mother's increasing ill health. Elisabeth worked hard to remedy the situation but, as Freud commented, "felt acutely her helplessness, her inability to afford her mother a substitute for the happiness she had lost and the impossibility of carrying out the intention [to return the family to its former state] she had formed at her father's death."

Following these distressing deaths and illnesses, her married sister—like her father before her—died of heart disease. It was from this time that Elisabeth developed the symptoms that made her the family invalid. The sister's death was doubly difficult for Elisabeth because of her conflicting emotions. She loved her and, at the same time, was a rival for the affections of her sister's husband, her brother-in-law. It was this love, and the guilt that she felt after her sister's death, that Freud focused on as the cause of her hysteria. He pressed her to confess that at the moment of her sister's death the thought had shot through her mind, "Now he is free again and I can be his wife." As he put it, "This girl felt towards her brother-in-law a tenderness whose acceptance into consciousness was resisted by her whole moral being."

As was true for all these cases, there were many factors at play in Elisabeth's situation: death and loss of loved ones, "strangulated affect"—the inability to adequately mourn these deaths—and the struggle to find a meaningful female identity in a society that imposed great restrictions on women. She had partially resolved her situation by becoming a dutiful nurse and caretaker; but the deaths of her father and sister, and her helplessness to do anything about the family's plight, undermined the strength and sense of worth she derived from this solution. And there was the conflict between her sense of duty and her desire for her brother-in-law, leading to guilt. Although Freud described all these factors, in the end, he gave special weight to the conflict between erotic desire and conscience.

In addition to Anna O. and Freud's four cases, six other patients were very briefly described in the *Studies*. They displayed a variety of symptoms, including "outbursts of weeping," paralyses, a "choking feeling and constriction of the throat," and a "nervous cough." Three of the six had suffered deaths or the loss of loved ones, and the three others sexual assaults and molestations. Freud also alluded to twelve other cases "whose analysis provides a confirmation of the psychical mechanism of hysterical phenomena [termed] sexual neuroses." He gave no other information about this group, so one assumes they were similar to the ten cases that were described. "Psychical mechanisms" were consistently supported, and some of the patients were sexually abused, but, overall, Freud's case material does not support his budding theory that the root of hysteria was always to be found in sexual factors.

From a contemporary perspective, the cases presented in the *Studies*—Anna O., Frau Emmy, Miss Lucy, Katharina, Fräulein Elisabeth, and the six that were briefly described—demonstrate the variety of factors involved in hysterical-emotional breakdowns. These women suffered sexual molestations, betrayals by intimates and family members, disappointed hopes, loss of love, deaths, disturbed relationships of a variety of kinds, and difficult identity struggles. In many of these families, communication about emotions was absent, minimal, or forbidden. Specific sexual traumas were present in the case of Katharina, who was molested by her father, and in three of the case vignettes. Sexuality as part of love in a larger sense was present in the case of Miss Lucy, whose longing for her employer was not reciprocated. In the case of Fräulein Elisabeth, the desire for her dead sister's husband was connected to guilt. Three of the vignettes involved death and the loss of love. And, finally, in the cases of Anna O., Frau Emmy, and some of the vignettes, Freud assumed sexuality was significant because the patients never mentioned it.

The case material in the *Studies on Hysteria* simply does not support the sweeping theory of sexuality that Freud was increasingly promoting. Deaths and losses were more prominent in these cases than disturbance of what Freud termed "the sexual function." Anna O.'s symptoms made their first appearance as she was nursing her dying father, while two of her three siblings died in childhood. Frau Emmy's family history was filled with the deaths of siblings, her mother, and other relatives, and her hysteria appeared following the sudden death of her husband. Miss Lucy's disappointed longing for love was connected with the threatened loss of her friends and young wards, with whom there were strong bonds of affection. And Fräulein Elisabeth's breakdown, much like Anna O.'s, occurred in reaction to the death of her father, her sister, and her mother's illness. Three of the short cases involved these factors. If one had to posit a single cause underlying the symptoms of these patients, a much stronger case could be made for death and loss than for sexuality.

But, as early as the *Studies,* Freud was ignoring his own case material—which was replete with the complex emotional states, histories, and identity struggles of his patients—and insisting that sexuality was *the* underlying cause of neurosis. By 1898, in his paper *Sexuality in the Aetiology of the Neurosis,* this had hardened into doctrine:

> Exhaustive researches during the last few years have led me to recognize that the most immediate and, for practical purposes, the most significant causes of every case of neurotic illness are to be found in factors arising from sexual life. . . . We must not be led astray by initial denials. If we keep firmly to what we have inferred, we shall in the end conquer every resistance by emphasizing the unshakeable nature of our convictions. . . . If one proceeds in this manner with one's patients, one also gains the conviction that, so far as the theory of the sexual aetiology of neurasthenia is concerned, there are no negative cases. In my mind, at least, the conviction has become so certain that where an interrogation has shown a negative result, I have turned this to account too for diagnostic purposes.

This statement shows how Freud collapsed the complex histories and life situations of these women into a single, sweeping principle that cannot be contradicted. It is, "every case of neurotic illness . . . no negative cases . . . the unshakable nature of our convictions." He also put forth the resistance argument, which he would continue to rely on for the rest of his career, as seen in his conviction that when a patient does not confirm his theory—"where interrogation has shown a negative result"—it is further evidence that he is right.

The search for a single cause for hysteria was a mistake. It is not a unitary disease, to begin with, and, what is more, every one of these patients had a unique life in which many factors converged at a particular time to produce a psychological breakdown. The deaths and losses in these women's lives cannot be understood apart from their childhood histories of attachments, separations, and losses, just as their adult sexuality cannot be comprehended apart from their childhood experiences of love, affection, and physical care, as well as the status of women in society at the time. All of this was lost as Freud pursued his search for a single theoretical principle that would make him famous.

Throughout the writing of the *Studies,* Freud had been drawing away from Breuer; now, with his claim to have found the universal sexual cause of neurosis, they were headed for a collision that would destroy their relationship.

CHAPTER 9

The Break with Breuer

*You know what Breuer told me one evening? I was so moved by what he said
that in return I disclosed to him the secret of our engagement. He told me he
had discovered that hidden under the surface of timidity there lay in me an
extremely daring and fearless human being.*

—Freud, in a letter to Martha in 1886

*I think of the underhandedness with which he doled out praise . . . and the
consideration which led him to express his picky objections to the essentials to
other people from whom I then heard about them. Again and again I am
glad to be rid of him.*

—Freud, in a letter to Wilhelm Fliess in 1898

AFTER MANY YEARS of intimacy, support, and creative collaboration Freud
turned vehemently against Breuer and, once the *Studies on Hysteria* was published in 1895, cut him out of his life. The contrast between their relationship
in the early and later years is striking. The dropping of Breuer occurred simultaneously with Freud's growing closeness with Wilhelm Fliess; his Berlin colleague became the one he loved and depended on, and his older friend the
object of his hatred. He stopped speaking to Breuer, paid him back the money
he had been given, though not asked to do so, and severed the bond that had
been essential for so many years.

Freud's attempt to explain all of hysteria with his sweeping principle of sexuality was the crucial point where he and Breuer parted company. In their
jointly authored *Preliminary Communication*, they began with a recognition of
the importance of trauma and discussed the variety of reactions they observed in
their patients: "Painful emotion, moral disgust, fright, anxiety, shame, physical
pain, suffering, mortification, tormenting secrets and confessions, unreparable

loss of a loved person, severely paralyzing affects such as fright, strangulated affect, [reactions from] tears to acts of revenge, crying oneself out." In his own chapter in the *Studies,* Breuer noted that sexuality was one among these many factors and described two case examples. In one, he traced a twelve-year-old boy's symptoms of refusal to eat, vomiting, and disgust to an attempted molestation in which a man in a public urinal had tried to make him suck his penis, causing the boy to run away in terror. The other case was a seventeen-year-old girl suffering from anxiety. A "number of brutal [sexual] attempts" had been made on her, including an attempted rape by a young man. Breuer also discussed the conflicts that can arise between sexual desire and conscience, though he did not see these as universal. Then, after voicing opinions congruent with Freud's on the important role of "defense" against sexuality, he added: "Along side sexual hysteria we must at this point recall hysteria due to fright—traumatic hysteria proper—which constitutes one of the best known and recognized forms of hysteria."

In a presentation to their medical colleagues in November of 1895, Breuer gave Freud credit for their work together and praised most of his discoveries and accomplishments. He did sound one note of dissent, however: "One point on which the speaker does not agree with Freud is the overvaluation of sexuality; Freud probably did not want to say that every hysterical symptom has a sexual background, but rather that the original root of hysteria is sexual. We do not yet see clearly; it remains only for the future, the masses of observations, to bring full clarification to this question; in any event, one must be grateful to Freud for the theoretical hints he has given us." Freud would later view this as intolerable opposition, "picky objections."

Another crucial difference between the two men was Breuer's belief in the importance of dissociation—what he called "hypnoid states"—in contrast to Freud's emphasis on "defense neurosis," later to become the psychoanalytic theory of resistance and repression. Scholars have noted that this was one of several disagreements that agitated Freud, but few have looked closely at what it was about. It is of great significance, for what Breuer termed a "hypnoid state" is what today would be called a dissociative reaction to severe trauma.

In his chapter in the *Studies,* Breuer distinguished two ways in which ideas that are charged with emotion can become unconscious: the first was Freud's defense theory, in which "distressing ideas" posed a threat to "happiness or self-esteem," leading to their repression from awareness. The second was what he termed a "hypnoid state," in which the ideas never were conscious because a "splitting of the mind" occurred at the time of an overwhelming or traumatic experience. In this second case, the memory registers emotionally and bodily, but not consciously; it does not become part of one's continuous sense of self. Breuer emphasized that these hypnoid states were characteristic of "severe hysteria." The cases presented in the *Studies* reveal that many of these patients suffered the abuse, molestation, sudden deaths, and losses that are now known to precipitate a dissociative splitting of the personality.

Freud was clearly aware of these two theories—Breuer's hypnoid state and his own repression-defense theory—as his comments in the *Studies* showed:

> Breuer has put forward for such cases of hypnoid hysteria a psychical mechanism which is substantially different from that of defense. . . . In his view what happens in hypnoid hysteria is that an idea becomes pathogenic because it has been received during a special psychical state and has from the first remained outside the ego. . . . I regard this distinction as so important that, on the strength of it, I willingly adhere to this hypothesis of there being a hypnoid hysteria. Strangely enough, I have never in my own experience met with a genuine hypnoid hysteria. Any that I took in hand has turned into defense hysteria. . . . In short, I am unable to suppress a suspicion that somewhere or other the roots of hypnoid and defense hysteria come together, and that there the primary factor is defense.

Although he initially gave credit to Breuer's idea of a hypnoid state, he then discounted it and claimed that his theory of defense was the more encompassing.

Another important difference between Freud and Breuer lay in their method of treatment. Breuer's work as a therapist is only known from the case of Bertha Pappenheim, of course, yet even there one sees an approach far different than Freud's. There was the cathartic technique itself, with its emphasis on facilitating the full expression of feelings and thoughts. Given what is known of Breuer's warm and understanding personality, it is reasonable to assume that he created a relationship that made such cathartic expression possible. He gave Bertha credit for inventing the method that she called "the talking cure," pointing to the collaborative nature of the treatment. Far from an all-knowing authority—one who forced his ideas on her—he was open to learning from his patient.

Freud's psychotherapeutic method, as early as 1889, had a different flavor: he was more the forceful authority, less the sympathetic collaborator. In the *Studies* he stated, "I decided to start from the assumption that my patients knew everything that was of any pathogenic significance and that it was only a question of obliging them to communicate it." He went on to speak of "penetrating into deeper layers of memory," using "the weapons in the therapeutic armoury"; of "forcing our way into the internal strata, overcoming resistances all the time"; and of psychotherapy as a "surgical intervention" akin to "the opening up of a cavity filled with pus, the scraping out of a carious region." These images and metaphors give a flavor of how Freud approached his patients, who were, of course, almost all women. He viewed what was inside them as sick, infected material—pus, dead tissue—which he must remove. The need to control and dominate, which characterized his marriage and his later relations with colleagues, was evident.

Freud's aggressive approach characterized his approach to therapy for the rest of his career and fits well with his theories on the cause and form of neurosis. For if neurosis was driven by guilt over secret forms of sexual gratification, it followed that patients should be pushed to confess. When they did, they would feel relieved. If, however, they were not conscious of the source of their distress because their symptoms were tied to overwhelming states of fear, pain, and unhappiness, forcing the material into consciousness would be a retraumatization. It came down to whether the therapist was capable of feeling empathy for the patient. While there was much that Breuer did not understand about Bertha Pappenheim, he seemed in tune with her painful states and emotions. Freud, in contrast, became increasingly convinced of the correctness of his theories and was insistent that when patients did not confirm his view of things, it was their resistance; it was proof that he was right. As he put it in his 1898 paper: "We shall in the end conquer every resistance by emphasizing the unshakeable nature of our convictions."

A final point of difference between Breuer and Freud was the length of time they treated their patients. Breuer saw Bertha Pappenheim daily for over two years and, while progress was made, she did not fully recover until several more years had passed. Freud saw Emmy von N. for seven weeks—and Katharina for one session—and claimed that they were cured. Today, it is clear that it takes a great deal of time and dedication on the part of the therapist to help such patients, that effective therapy is much closer to Breuer's approach than to Freud's. Freud did not have the benefit of current knowledge, of course, yet he knew about Breuer's work with Bertha Pappenheim in detail—and also heard about her from her friend, his wife, Martha—including the length of time required for her treatment. He knew that Breuer had worked with her for over two years, yet he thought he could achieve results in a drastically shorter time. His concurrent letters to Fliess make clear that what drove him was the quest for fame, for a striking new discovery and powerful treatment method. He needed to produce "cures" to prove his theories, and this overrode both the welfare of his patients and a careful assessment of the results of his treatment. These severely disturbed and traumatized women were not cured by Freud with his relatively brief interpretive therapy; his claims that they recovered are not supported by what evidence is available about their later lives, nor is it consistent with current knowledge regarding the treatment of such conditions.

Working with Breuer's cathartic method had brought Freud too close to his own dissociated core of loss, anxiety, and helplessness. He needed to repudiate this way of working because it set loose his own threatening memories and emotions. Though initially drawn to Breuer's cathartic method, he rejected it in favor of his theory of sexuality and his stance as the all-knowing therapist-authority because listening to the agonizing memories of loss and pain related by these patients rekindled his own perturbing memories. To empathize with them, to feel their losses and fears, was not a safe place for Freud; interpreting their sexual instincts and fantasies, and minimizing their traumas, was much more comfortable.

In addition to the emotions that his patients stirred up, Freud also needed to break out of the relationship with Breuer, whose love and generosity aroused a threatening dependency. The fact that the referral of patients, like the money that Breuer gave him in the preceding years, reminded Freud of the time when he was poor and needy was reason to reject his older friend. In addition, in 1894, the year before the *Studies* was published, Freud had a serious heart condition which, again, put him in a potentially frightened and helpless position. With his medical background, he knew his life was at risk; in fact, he predicted that he would die within four or five years. In such a state, he turned to Breuer, one of the most respected diagnosticians in Vienna, putting him in a further position of dependency on his older colleague. He became the sick person who must look to his expert physician for help.

Freud's dire view of his life span was justified since the symptoms of heart disease were well known in the 1890s and there was little in the way of effective treatment. Breuer, after a careful assessment of Freud's coronary symptoms— pain in the region of the heart, rapid and irregular heartbeats, pain radiating down the left arm, shortness of breath—told his young friend that he was, indeed, in danger of a heart attack. Knowing that this was true, yet not wanting to know it, Freud then turned to Fliess, where he received advice that was more hopeful. Fliess told him his symptoms were caused by smoking—they certainly could have been aggravated by nicotine, but the acute coronary blockage was not caused by it—and that there was an effective treatment. The treatment, Fliess told Freud, was to "abstain" from his gratifying but harmful habit. This fit with one part of Freud's theory of the role of sexuality in neurosis—his belief that patients became ill from too much gratification—and he struggled to comply with Fliess's advice. While Freud knew in some part of himself that Breuer was right about his heart condition, he could not let himself take in this depressing knowledge and grasped at the unscientific but more hopeful ideas of Fliess, since this took him further from his dependence on Breuer. Freud's heart symptoms passed within a year or two—apparently he had an unusual blockage of a minor coronary artery—and he suffered no more symptoms for a number of years.

Many years after he turned away from Breuer, Freud, in his 1914 *On the History of the Psycho-Analytic Movement*, reconstructed history and explained the rejection of his friend in terms favorable to himself. This version was elaborated by Ernest Jones in his biography and has passed into psychoanalytic lore. The Freud-Jones tale has it that toward the end of his treatment of Bertha Pappenheim, Breuer was called to her house and found her in the midst of a hysterical pregnancy, calling out that she was "giving birth to Dr. Breuer's baby." This manifestation of an erotic transference supposedly caused Breuer to flee from her and from work with neurotic patients entirely. Freud, so the tale goes, was not frightened away when his patients displayed their sexual feelings for him; he had the courage to persevere and went on to make sexuality and transference central to his theories. This version of events has been frequently repeated, but it is far from what actually happened.

The reality is that Freud could not tolerate it when Breuer did not completely support his ideas, particularly the theory of sexuality. At the time he turned on his friend, his anger, as revealed in his letters to Fliess, was aroused by Breuer's expressing the least doubt about his theories; he made no mention of Bertha Pappenheim's erotic feelings or any frightened reaction of Breuer's. In the Clark lectures of 1909, Freud was still giving Breuer credit for the early discoveries of psychoanalysis, though he changed his story in 1914, and his account of Bertha's treatment in the first of these lectures did not differ from that in the *Studies on Hysteria*. It was only much later that he explained their differences with reference to Breuer's fear of sex. In his *History* essay of 1914, he stated: "Now I have strong reasons for suspecting that after all her [Bertha's] symptoms had been relieved Breuer must have discovered from further indications the sexual motivation of this transference, but that the universal nature of this unexpected phenomenon escaped him, with the result that, as though confronted by an 'untoward event', he broke off all further investigation. He never said this to me in so many words, but he told me enough at different times to justify this reconstruction of what happened." He gave a similar account in his *Autobiographical Study* of 1925.

Finally, in a 1932 letter to Stefan Zweig, Freud told the same story and added that Bertha's erotic transference manifested itself in a hysterical birth fantasy. Jones accepted Freud's story without question and embellished it. In his version, not only did Breuer stop treating Bertha when her sexual transference appeared, but his wife was jealous, causing him to feel guilt. He fled from his patient "in horror" and went to Venice for a second honeymoon, where his daughter Dora was conceived. This daughter then committed suicide in New York years later, giving some sort of fitting end to Breuer's failure to deal successfully with Bertha Pappenheim.

There is no factual support for this tale. Even in Freud's own account, he "suspects," "interprets," and "reconstructs," implying that the events must have occurred in the way he imagined because his theories of sexuality and transference required them to. And, clearly, the story became embellished as the years passed. Freud's *History* was written in 1914, thirty-two years after Breuer's treatment of Bertha, while 1932, when Freud told Zweig about the supposed birth fantasy, was fifty years after the event.

Nor does the evidence support Jones's elaboration of Freud's story. The Breuers did not vacation in Venice at the time Jones suggested; their daughter Dora was conceived before the end of Bertha Pappenheim's treatment. Dora did not commit suicide in New York, but took poison when the Gestapo came for her in 1936 and died in a Viennese hospital. Both the Freud and Jones version of the end of Breuer's work with Bertha are reconstructions that support their theories; they make Freud the hero at Breuer's expense.

What happened between Breuer and Bertha Pappenheim is actually much different. First, he did not flee from her, but continued as her physician for several years after the conclusion of the cathartic treatment. Breuer's biographer Hirschmüller has documented his involvement with her, as well as with a number of other psychiatric cases, in the years that followed. What is more, a careful review of her case reveals that sexuality did not play a central role: personal and intellectual suffocation, neglect, oppression, death, loss, and abandonment were at the core of her disturbance. Indeed, Breuer's failure to give total support to Freud's sexual theory came from his direct observations rather than his fear of an erotic transference.

While Breuer did continue to treat Bertha Pappenheim and other neurotic patients in succeeding years, he did not take on any further cases in a full cathartic treatment after the early 1880s. But the reasons for this are different than those put forth by Freud. If Breuer were to flee from anything that was personally threatening in his work with Bertha it would have been the feelings aroused by death and loss. There is no direct evidence for this, however. There is a much simpler explanation for why he gave up working intensively with hysterical patients: it was too emotionally draining. As he wrote to the Swiss psychiatrist Auguste Forel in 1907: "I learned many things, things valuable from a scientific view, but also . . . that it is impossible for a physician . . . to treat such a case without having his practice and private life completely ruined by it. At the time, I swore *never again* to submit to such an ordeal."

Treating patients who are undergoing the breakthrough of dissociated material related to severe trauma is extremely difficult. They display a wide range of disruptive emotions, including terror and suicidal depression, as well as bizarre symptoms, fragmentation of the self, and loss of the sense of reality, and require a great deal of the therapist's time and attention. Even with the current understanding of these conditions, it is very difficult for many therapists to work effectively with such threatening material, and Breuer did not have the benefit of current experience. As a busy and successful physician, it is not surprising that he decided to pass these patients on to Freud.

Freud's theory of sexuality was the half-truth with which he reconfigured his own traumas and anxiety, as well as his attempt at a world-shaking discovery, his move to be a Newton of the mind. Breuer's withholding of complete agreement with this theory was a blow to these grandiose aspirations and aroused Freud's intense enmity. The tale of Breuer's flight from sexuality and the erotic transference shows Freud turning the tables on his friend, reversing the relationship of power and dependence. One typically thinks of Freud as a secure and world-famous figure, but during these years he was a young doctor just beginning his practice, and was worried about his career, financial future, and health. The fact that Breuer was kind and giving, that he had played the role of the loving parent during the time of uncertainty, poverty, and struggle, made it all the more necessary for Freud to reject him as he moved to establish his independent stature in the world. And there was, too, Breuer's opinion with regard to Freud's heart symptoms. As a physician, he confronted Freud with a frightening truth that he did not want to know about, which he tried to reject just as he rejected Breuer's emphasis on trauma in the hysterical patients.

Freud also needed to get rid of Breuer because he was not, in his mind, a charismatic "great man." Despite the years of collaboration and friendship, Freud never referred to him with such words. Breuer's scientific contributions were equal if not superior to Brücke's or Charcot's, yet he was not, in Freud's eyes, a "master," not a famous authority, nor were there references to the power of his gaze. He was, rather, a careful scientist, a modest person without driving ambition; he did not invent theories with an eye to his place in history, but was more concerned with the care and welfare of his patients, all of which made it difficult for Freud to make him into an idol as he did with his other mentors, and as he was in the process of doing with Fliess.

The turn against Breuer was a critical juncture in the unfolding of Freud's adult personality. Until this time, he had lived on two levels: outwardly, he was the obedient, deferential apprentice with Brücke, Charcot and—to some degree—Breuer, while inwardly he harbored dreams of power and fame. By the time of the *Studies on Hysteria,* however, the latent, heroic Freud was bursting forth; he could no longer remain within the easy, give-and-take relationship with Breuer and he moved to a new stance in which one partner had to dominate and the other submit.

Many years later, Hanna Breuer, Breuer's daughter-in-law, wrote to Jones shortly after the publication of the first volume of his Freud biography: "May I mention that I have never heard a word from my father-in-law concerning his relationship with Freud. True, when I became a member of the family in 1906 it had long been a thing of the past. But how deeply the break must have wounded Breuer can be guessed from a significant little incident that happened when he was already an old man: he walked in the street in Vienna when, suddenly, he saw Freud coming head on towards him. Instinctively, he opened his arms. Freud passed professing not to see him."

The shift from Breuer to Fliess would prove fateful for the later direction of Freud's work as both theorist and therapist, for it was here that he moved from the open and mutifaceted approach, as seen in the *Preliminary Communication* which he coauthored with Breuer, to the doctrinaire stance that has characterized so much of later psychoanalysis.

CHAPTER 10

Self-Analysis and the Invention of the Oedipus Complex

A single idea of general value dawned on me. I have found, in my own case too, the phenomena of being in love with my mother and jealous of my father, and I now consider it a universal event in early childhood.

—Freud to Wilhelm Fliess

VIENNA DURING the last decade of the nineteenth century was a city of contradictions. Austro-Hungary, a concatenation of nationalities, languages, and cultures, had been eclipsed as an empire by England, France, and Germany, yet the government and bureaucracy lumbered on under the rule of the aged Franz Josef, in tandem with the conservative Catholic Church. It was a many-sided society: the decaying empire that still put on sumptuous court balls coexisted with both a flourishing middle class and groups of intellectuals who questioned both imperial and bourgeois values. Anti-Semitism was widespread alongside a small new Zionist movement. Emerging Socialism challenged the prevailing economic and class system, and active feminists struggled against the stifling restrictions imposed on women.

Progress in science and industrialization was transforming much of Europe at this time, which brought economic and social upheavals and new forms in the arts that came to life on all fronts, nowhere more prominently than in Vienna. Long a great musical center, it was now the home of experimental works such as the symphonies of Gustav Mahler. Similar innovations occurred in literature, in the poems and novels of Hugo von Hofmannsthal and the dramas and novels of Arthur Schnitzler; in architecture, where Otto Wagner was a forerunner of the modernist movement; and in painting, in the works of Gustav Klimt and, later, Oskar Kokoschka and Egon Schiele. Artists in all these media knew of and were

126

influenced by each other. Klimt, whose sensual-sexual murals were commissioned at the end of the century for the Burgtheater and the university, both public buildings, said that Mahler's Third Symphony of 1896 was an inspiration for him.

Some historians have argued that turn-of-the-century Vienna was the birthplace of modernism in its many guises, more so than Paris, Berlin, or London. In the midst of these exciting new developments, Freud was largely preoccupied with science, archaeology, and ancient artifacts; the revolutionary arts of his own time hardly touched him, if he was even aware of their existence. The irony is that his ideas would eventually become central to modern consciousness even though he, personally, was largely cut off from all its other manifestations. His mind was concentrated on work with patients and, increasingly, on attempts to come to terms with his own demons. When he needed distraction, he turned to ancient Greece and Rome; music never aroused him; his architectural and artistic tastes were decidedly bourgeois; and, while he did read some contemporary literature, there is little evidence of its influence on his thinking. The vibrant cultural life of Vienna passed him by; as he wrote to Fliess in 1895, "Of the world I see nothing and hear little."

For over ten years, Freud's closest friend and confidant was the Berlin nose and throat physician Wilhelm Fliess. They had met when Fliess attended one of Freud's lectures a year after his marriage to Martha, and as the breach with Breuer widened, the frequency and emotional intensity of their correspondence built up. At the height of their intimacy through the 1890s, Freud confided the details of his personal life to Fliess and relied on his advice about the drafts and preliminary versions of his developing theories. His Berlin friend was the only person who knew about the self-analysis, in which Freud revealed a good deal about his childhood. He confessed his symptoms and fears, reported dreams, associations, and interpretations, and turned to Fliess as a trusted physician with his medical problems. Fliess was a great believer in the medicinal power of cocaine, further strengthening Freud's dependence on both his friend and the drug he prescribed.

Freud shared the details of his daily life with Fliess, speaking with pride of his growing brood. "Annerl produced her first tooth today, without discomfort, Mathilda is feeling incomparably better since she has been taken out of school. Oliver, on a recent spring excursion, asked quite seriously why the cuckoo is always calling its own name," he wrote in the spring of 1896. On a vacation in May of 1897, he observed that Martin was a budding poet—he later sent several of his oldest son's poems to his Berlin friend—commented on Oli's precocious intelligence, and expressed pleasure when Mathilda became enraptured with Greek mythology. Concern about the health of his "rascals"—they contracted all the usual childhood diseases—was a continuing refrain in the correspondence: "Much joy could be had from the little ones if there were not also so much fright."

Fishblood *by Gustav Klimt, 1898.*

Freud, aged forty-one, initiated the correspondence after meeting Fliess and, while it is not known what transpired between them at this encounter, Freud's first letter already contained the flattery that would become characteristic: "Esteemed friend and colleague: My letter of today admittedly is occasioned by business; but I must introduce it by confessing that I entertain hopes of continuing the relationship with you and that you have left a deep impression on me which could easily lead me to tell you outright in what category of men I place you."

One month later, Freud wrote: "Your cordial letter and your magnificent gift awakened the most pleasant memories for me, and the sentiment I discern behind both Christmas presents fills me with the expectation of a lively and mutually gratifying relationship between us in the future. I still do not know how I won you; the bit of speculative anatomy of the brain [the topic of Freud's 1887 lecture] cannot have impressed your rigorous judgment for long."

Freud wrote only three letters to Fliess in 1888, none in 1889, and three each in 1890 and 1891. But, by 1892, the pace quickened to more than one a month and, until the end of the century, they averaged almost three per month. In addition to the over three hundred letters—including drafts of theories and projects—there were meetings, or "congresses," as Freud called them, some in Vienna, where Fliess's wife's family lived, and occasional get-togethers without their families for two or three days in other cities. They met in Salzburg in August of 1890, in Munich in 1894, in Dresden in April of 1896, and their final meeting took place in Achensee near Innsbruck in the fall of 1900. In his letters, Freud spoke of his great desire to see his friend: "I am looking forward to our congress as to the slaking of hunger and thirst . . . the congress . . . brought me pleasure and renewal. Since then I have been in a continual euphoria and have been working like a young man." Yet, despite his great longing to be with his "only other," Freud often found excuses to delay the meetings or put them off; in the more than thirteen years of their relationship, there were only seventeen or so congresses, a little over one per year.

Over the years, Freud's expressions of affection for Fliess increased: "Esteemed friend and colleague" became "Dear friend," then "Dearest friend," and finally "Dearest Wilhelm" and "My beloved friend." The more formal *Sie* (German has two forms for the English "you") changed to the intimate *du*, and the letters expanded to include a range of personal as well as intellectual matters. In June of 1892 Freud wrote, "I have had no opportunity other than in memory to refer back to the beautiful evening on which I saw you *[du]*." In September of 1893 he wrote, "You altogether ruin my critical faculties and I really believe you in everything." In May of 1894: "And you are the only other, the *alter*." In March of 1895: "Altogether, I miss you very much. Am I really the same person who was overflowing with ideas and projects as long as you were within reach?"

Freud's love reached a peak in January of 1896:

> Your kind should not die out, my dear friend; the rest of us need people like you too much. How much I owe you: solace, understanding, stimulation in my loneliness, meaning to my life that I gained through you, and finally even health that no one else could have given back to me. It is primarily through your example that intellectually I gained the strength to trust my judgment, even when I am left alone—though not by you—and, like you, to face with lofty humility all the difficulties that the future may bring. For all that, accept my humble thanks! I know that you do not need me as much as I need you, but I also know that I have a secure place in your affection.

The overvaluation, the need for contact—and unhappiness when his *only other* was not available—and the way his sense of worth depended on complete acceptance and praise from Fliess—are all signs of someone in love. As the correspondence evolved, Freud was increasingly intimate. He discussed the state of his marriage and sex life—"we are now living in abstinence; and you know the reasons for this as well"—and there was an inordinate preoccupation with the state of each other's health that allowed these two respectable men to focus on each other's physical and emotional states. Fliess twice operated on Freud's nose, and there is much in the letters about their pains and mood swings; both of them suffered from migraine headaches. While it is not known what Fliess wrote about his own health, from comments in Freud's letters one senses that they used their roles as physicians to express a caring interest in each other's bodies. On Freud's side, this reached a peak during his coronary episode, where he desperately wished to make Fliess into his "magical healer." In April of 1894, when he thought he would die of a heart attack, he wrote, "[the children] and wife are well; the latter is not a confidante of my death deliria." At this critical time, he told his beloved friend about the most important fear in his life, but did not discuss it with Martha.

In part, it was the intelligence and charisma of the man that aroused Freud's admiration and love. Wilhelm Fliess, two years younger than Freud, had broad interests and was described as "fascinating" by many who knew him. In addition to his work as a doctor, he put forth wide-ranging biological theories; some physicians and scientists saw these as great discoveries while others viewed them as quackery. The novelty of his ideas, their skeptical reception by the medical establishment, and the fact that he was a Jew were all features that he and Freud shared. Fliess's theories were based on two suppositions, one involving the nose and the other what he termed "male and female periods." He began with the fact that there is an anatomical similarity between nasal and genital tissue and then expanded this to what he called "the nasal reflex neurosis." Problems with the nasal membranes and bones were held responsible for symptoms and diseases throughout the body: migraine headaches; pains in the abdomen, arms, and legs; coronary symptoms; asthma; gastrointestinal problems; and, of special interest to Freud, disturbances in sexuality—miscarriages, dysmenorrhea, cramping, and so on. The theory prescribed simple treatments; sexual difficulties or heart symptoms could be cured by applying cocaine to the nasal membranes or treated with surgery on the nose.

The second of Fliess's ideas also began from a fact, the twenty-eight-day menstrual cycle. From there, he postulated a "male cycle" of twenty-three days, and developed a theory of "critical dates." The twenty-eight- and twenty-three-day periods were part of his conception of "bisexuality"; the first defined the "female period" and the second the "male." According to his theory, these sexual periods determined the stages of human growth, illnesses, and death; they operated throughout the animal kingdom and connected biological phenomena to the movements of the sun, the moon, and the stars. Armed with knowledge of a person's birthday and other critical dates, a great deal could be predicted with seeming mathematical certainty, using the numbers twenty-eight and twenty-

Sigmund Freud and Wilhelm Fleiss in the early 1890s.

three, with the later addition of the number five—twenty-eight minus twenty-three—which could be added or subtracted as needed to make the calculations fit.

Fliess's theories began with small possibilities—similarities between nasal and genital tissue, the periodicity of some biological phenomena—and then wildly expanded them. The state of scientific medicine at the time made his ideas more plausible than they seem today, but not much. The problem was his grandiosity, his need to move from some minor observation to the most wide-ranging claims. Many patients with medical and psychological problems are only too ready to grasp at such ideas, and the treatments associated with them, especially when they are espoused with conviction by a charismatic physician. Perhaps some of the patients whose noses he treated surgically felt better as a result of their association with a powerful doctor; certainly the "local application" of cocaine, which Fliess frequently prescribed, would relieve pain and lift their moods. However, at least one patient developed a serious infection from Fliess's less-than-competent operation on her nose.

Freud's need to see his friend in ideal terms was strikingly illustrated in their mutual treatment of a young woman named Emma Eckstein. Emma was a patient of Freud's in late 1894, the time when his fear of dying from a heart attack was at its worst. Fliess came to Vienna in January or February of 1895 and operated on both of their noses—on Freud for his cardiac symptoms, and on

Emma for her sexual-hysterical problems. The operation on Emma led to a serious infection and bleeding that had not healed by March. Other doctors were called in, and it was discovered that the cause of the infection was a strip of gauze Fliess had left in her nose. Here is Freud's own description of what transpired, from a letter to his friend:

> There still was moderate bleeding from the nose and mouth; the fetid odor was very bad. [The doctor] suddenly pulled at something like a thread, kept on pulling. Before either of us had time to think, at least half a meter of gauze had been removed from the cavity. The next moment came a flood of blood. The patient turned white, her eyes bulged, and she had no pulse. [She is revived] . . . At the moment the foreign body came out and everything became clear to me—and I immediately afterward was confronted by the sight of the patient—I felt sick. After she had been packed, I fled to the next room, drank a bottle of water, and felt miserable. . . . I do not believe it was the blood that overwhelmed me—at that moment strong emotions were welling up in me. So we had done her an injustice; she was not at all abnormal, rather, a piece of iodoform gauze had gotten torn off as you were removing it and stayed in for fourteen days, preventing healing; at the end it tore off and provoked the bleeding. That this mishap should have happened to you; how you will react to it when you hear about it; what others could make of it; how wrong I was to urge you to operate in a foreign city where you could not follow through on the case, how my intention to do my best for this poor girl was insidiously thwarted and resulted in endangering her life—all this came to me simultaneously.

Freud showed some feeling for the unfortunate Emma, but his concern quickly shifted to Fliess: he was mainly worried about his friend's reputation. The letter continued with his attempt to exculpate his idol: "You did it as well as one can do it. . . . Of course, no one is blaming you, nor would I know why they should. And I only hope that you will arrive as quickly as I did at feeling sympathy and rest assured that it was not necessary for me to reaffirm my trust in you once again."

Over the next months, Emma's condition remained serious. There were times when she was close to death, yet Freud continued to express his faith in Fliess: "For me you remain the physician, the type of man into whose hands one confidently puts one's life and that of one's family. . . . I wanted to pour forth my tale of woe and perhaps obtain your advice concerning Emma, not reproach you with anything. That would have been stupid, unjustified, and in clear contradiction to all my feelings."

In the ensuing months, Freud's love and trust in Fliess did not abate. Emma eventually recovered and, a year later, he wrote the following remarkable letter to

Emma Eckstein in 1895 before the operation by Fliess.

his friend in Berlin: "First of all, Eckstein. I shall be able to prove to you that you were right, that her episodes of bleeding were hysterical, were occasioned by *longing,* and probably occurred at the sexually relevant times [a reference to Fliess's theory of male and female periods]. The woman, out of resistance, has not yet supplied me with the dates."

The Eckstein episode shows how Freud, with his need to see Fliess as an exalted being, seriously distorted reality. The botched operation on Emma—the infection and life-threatening bleeding—were not distant childhood traumas; they occurred before his own eyes. Yet a year later he was calling them "hysterical" and accusing her of "resistance." This was psychoanalytic interpretation at its most grotesque.

Looked at now, Fliess appears to be one in the long line of therapist-charlatans whose need for fame leads them to create totalistic theories and treatments. And he was seen as such by perceptive critics in his own time. Ry, the pseudonym of a reviewer of Fliess's 1897 *The Relationship between the Nose and the Female Sexual Organs,* noted only one worthwhile finding in the entire book:

that labor pains could be treated with the application of cocaine to the nose. Even this finding does not support Fliess's theory, for it is not the nose per se that is important; cocaine would be effective however it got into the blood-stream, as Freud, who used to take it orally, should have known. Ry went on to characterize the book as "mystical nonsense" and "disgusting gobbledygook" that "has nothing to do with medicine or natural science." Out of loyalty to his friend, Freud withdrew in protest from the editorial board of the journal that published the review.

This appraisal of Fliess's theories reveal them for what they were: overblown speculations, without foundation in observation and therapeutically worthless, if not harmful. Yet, in spite of their failings, Freud saw these ideas as bold and rev-olutionary. Fliess's theories seemed to provide a bridge between Freud's old neu-roanatomical research and his new involvement in psychology; they dealt with tissues, bones, drugs, numbers, and surgery, rather than ephemeral thoughts, memories, feelings, and psychological therapy. Struggling with the uncertainty of his new psychoanalytic approach, Freud took comfort in the seemingly scientific solidity of Fliess's theories. As he put it in a letter of June 1896: "With regard to the repression theory, I have run into doubts that could be dispelled by a few words from you, in particular about male and female menstruation in the same individual. Anxiety, chemical factors, and so forth—perhaps with your help I shall find the solid ground on which I can cease to give psychological explana-tions and begin to find a physiological foundation."

Another attraction was Fliess's concern with two topics close to Freud's heart—sexuality and bisexuality. There was a great deal in their letters concern-ing these matters, ostensibly as areas of scientific research. Freud saw his col-league as someone who was not afraid to engage these topics at a time when they were still shrouded in taboos, making him into a courageous ally. In addi-tion, the idea of "universal biological bisexuality" legitimized his attraction to Fliess. But the principal appeal of Fliess's theories was their ostensible scope and power; his friend seemed to be a great man whose discoveries would shake the world.

Fliess's sweeping speculations can best be termed *theoretical imperialism,* an approach in which a small number of ideas are put forth to explain an extremely wide range of phenomena—the many diseases he traced to the nose, or the host of predictions that could be made from the male and female periods. When facts and observations did not conform with the theory, they were ignored or forced to fit. What was important was proving the breadth of the theory, not getting at the truth, for this affirmed the stature of the theorist. As Freud wrote to him: "I hope the path you have taken will lead you even farther and even deeper, and that as the new Kepler you will unveil the ironclad rules of the biological mech-anism to us. Indeed you have your calling in life."

Fliess's theoretical imperialism was the principal reason Freud took up with him and dropped the cautious and scientific Breuer. Fliess seemed like a bold scientific conquistador, a "new Kepler," which made him a model for Freud, who would be, in his turn, the new Darwin or Newton of the mind. It was a twinship in which one would be the great biologist and the other the great psychologist. Thus, Fliess became another in the long string of male idols; Freud overinflated his accomplishments and blinded himself to obvious shortcomings because he needed to be attached to a man who exuded confidence and power. Where before he was associated with Brücke and Charcot as an acolyte, now he and Fliess would travel on to fame together. With his attachment to Fliess firmly in place, Freud was ready to plunge into his self-analysis.

Freud's heart condition, with its attendant fear of death, had passed by 1895. In 1896, his father Jacob died at the age of eighty-two. He wrote to Fliess: "By the time he died, his life had long been over, but in my inner self the whole past has been reawakened by this event. I now feel quite uprooted." Some years later, in a preface to the second edition of *The Interpretation of Dreams,* he referred to his father's death as "the most important event, the most poignant loss, of a man's life." Freud claimed that Jacob's death was the event that precipitated his self-analysis—and most biographers and commentators have gone along with this idea—but, as his own words indicate, Jacob's life "had long been over" and Freud had little to do with him by 1896. The death did have a powerful impact, however, since it was one of many during this time that awoke the past.

The years immediately preceding had seen the deaths of several men who had been extremely important to Freud. Joseph Paneth, his friend since their first year in the university, his colleague in Brücke's laboratory, and financial benefactor, died a young man in 1890. Ernst Fleischl von Marxow, financial supporter and companion during the nights of drug-inspired philosophizing in the early 1880s, died, after many years of physical and mental decline, in 1891. Brücke himself died in 1892, and Charcot, Freud's other most influential older mentor, in 1893. Perhaps most disruptive was the loss of Breuer, who did not die but was turned away by Freud in the early 1890s. Breuer was the most supportive and nurturing figure in Freud's adult life, and while Freud claimed he was glad to be rid of him, the loss was a profound one.

The losses of all these men did reawaken the whole past of his inner self. The deaths of Paneth, Fleischl, Brücke, Charcot, and his father—along with the loss of Breuer—intensified the anxieties and depressing feelings that had lived on in an isolated compartment of his mind since earliest childhood. Ancient terrors and symptoms now came back with new vigor. According to Ernest Jones:

> There is ample evidence that for ten years or so—roughly comprising the
> nineties—he suffered from a very considerable psychoneurosis. . . . his suf-
> ferings were at times very intense, and for those ten years there could have
> been only occasional intervals when life seemed much worth living . . . It
> consisted essentially in extreme changes of mood, and the only respects in

which the anxiety got localized were occasional attacks of dread of dying
. . . and anxiety about traveling by rail. . . . The alternations of mood were
between periods of elation, excitement, and self-confidence on the one
hand and periods of severe depression, doubt, and inhibition on the other.
In the depressed moods he could neither write nor concentrate his
thoughts. . . . He would spend leisure hours of extreme boredom, turning
from one thing to another, cutting open books, looking at maps of ancient
Pompeii, playing patience or chess, but being unable to continue at anything for long—a state of restless paralysis. Sometimes there were spells
where consciousness would be greatly narrowed: states, difficult to describe,
with a veil that produced almost a twilight condition of mind.

Freud suffered from fairly severe anxiety and depression with the specific symptoms of fear of dying and the travel phobia, both connected with the traumatic
losses of his earliest years. It was at this time, and in this state, that he would
attempt to understand and treat his inner turmoil with the same method he used
on his hysterical patients; he began to analyze himself, with his dreams as the
vehicle and Fliess as his sounding board.

The letters to Fliess, beginning in late 1896, detail Freud's discoveries in his
self-analysis, including the events of his infancy: the death of his brother Julius,
the loss of his mother's care and attention, his love for his nursemaid and her
sudden disappearance, his ambivalence—his need for someone to love and
hate—which he located in his relationship with his childhood playmate John,
and the origin of his travel phobia when the extended family was torn apart as
they were forced to leave Freiberg. He was also, at this same time, treating hysterical patients, and there he gave primary importance to real sexual events:
seductions of children by nursemaids, governesses, older siblings and, frequently,
girls by their fathers.

As he pursued his self-analysis in 1896 and 1897, he would have had to
apply his theory of sexual seductions to account for his own neurosis, which
would have implicated his own father. In September of 1897, he wrote to Fliess,
"I no longer believe in my *neurotica* [the theory of sexual seduction]," giving, as
his reasons, his inability to cure his patients with interpretations based on the
theory, the belief that "there are no indications of reality in the unconscious,"
and that too many respectable fathers—"not excluding my own"—would have
to be accused of being perverse. In the letters over the next weeks he disclosed
the most important events of his early years, including his many traumatic
losses. And it was at precisely this time, when he was reexperiencing the loss of
his nurse and mother, that he turned away from the unbearable emotions associated with these events and substituted his theory of the Oedipus complex. This
was the pivotal event in his abandonment not just of the seduction theory, but
of the reality of childhood trauma in all its many forms. As he wrote to Fliess:
"A single idea of general value dawned on me. I have found, in my own case

too, the phenomena of being in love with my mother and jealous of my father, and I now consider it a universal event in early childhood."

Freud was driven by two contradictory forces. On the one side, he wanted to discover the truth of his own past, yet, as the self-analysis proceeded, he was exposed to the threatening memories and emotions of his early years; not seductions, in his case, but overwhelming losses. On the other side, he could counter these traumatic emotions with a discovery that would affirm his strength. As he put it in the same letter: "The expectation of eternal fame was so beautiful, as was that of certain wealth, complete independence, travels, and lifting the children above the severe worries that robbed me of my youth. Everything depended upon whether or not hysteria would come out right."

Freud's substitution of his universal Oedipal theory was a compromise: it revealed his wish for his mother's love and her loss to a rival. At the same time, it made him into a warrior, a young Oedipus, in combat with a powerful king-like father. It also did away with actual traumas, sexual or any other kind, and gave primary emphasis to drives and fantasies. In this new theory, it was not what actually happened to the child that was the source of fear, depression, and symptoms, but masturbation, infantile pleasures, Oedipal fantasies, and sexual wishes that conflicted with moral standards. And the theory itself, immediately promoted to "universal" status, became his bid for "eternal fame"; it would make him a great and powerful scientist.

The seduction theory was only partly true in the first place and the reasons given for abandoning it do not hold water. The fact that his patients did not get well when he interpreted their seductions did not prove that the theory of childhood trauma was wrong but, rather, that he had not found an effective form of treatment. His belief that "there are no indications of reality in the unconscious" was also mistaken; the unconscious world of dreams and fantasies extends in many imaginative directions, but there is always a starting place in reality. And, finally, while it may have been hard for Freud to believe in the prevalence of sexual abuse within the families of his neurotic patients, even his own cases in the *Studies on Hysteria* revealed that it was fairly widespread.

Modern research has shown that child abuse is much more prevalent than many people like to think. Interestingly, there was evidence for this in Vienna just two years after Freud substituted his theory of sexual drives and fantasies for the real traumas of childhood. In November of 1899, the newspapers were filled with reports of two sensational trials involving child abuse. In the first, a poor family named Hummel had tortured their five-year-old daughter to death; in the other, the wife of a civil servant named Kutschera had tortured and mutilated seven of her stepchildren, murdering one of them. While the abuse in these sensational cases was not specifically sexual, they certainly might have led Freud to rethink his turn away from the importance of childhood traumas. He was poring over the newspapers for reviews of his just published *Interpretation of Dreams* at this time, yet he seemed completely unaware of these events; his letters made no reference to them. Nor did he ever modify his drive-fantasy theory of neurosis.

Freud's account of the supposed failure of his seduction theory was retold in his 1914 *On the History of the Psycho-Analytic Movement,* where he turned his disappointment into a victory: "If hysterical subjects trace back their symptoms to traumas that are fictitious, then the new fact which emerges is precisely that they create such scenes in *phantasy,* and this psychical reality requires to be taken into account alongside practical reality. This reflection was soon followed by the discovery that these phantasies were intended to cover up the autoerotic activity of the first years of childhood, to embellish it and raise it to a higher plane."

There is an important truth here, though it is mixed together with a serious distortion. Freud's retreat from the reality of trauma went hand in hand with his discovery of the significance of fantasy and "psychic reality," soon to be elaborated in *The Interpretation of Dreams.* A world of dreams and imagination exists in which a great deal of experience is worked over, and highlighting its psychological significance was one of Freud's most original contributions. The fantasy-imaginative world of children is where they work out their understanding of reality, where they experiment with solutions to all the puzzling-exciting-frightening events that confront them. But the existence of this realm should not negate the disturbing effects of actual events. Posing the issue in either/or terms—either children have actually been seduced *or* their memories of such events spring from fantasy fueled by sexual instincts—is a misleading way to pose the problem. Fantasy is a crucial area of human experience, but it is always fantasy about something. In fact, it is precisely those events that arouse fear and helplessness, the ones that children are least able to control by action in the world, that they attempt to master in their play and imagination.

One important dream from the self-analysis, later used in *The Interpretation of Dreams,* will illustrate the overriding theme of death that appears in the self-analysis, along with Freud's characteristic means of dealing with it. He titled the dream *Non vixit,* a Latin phrase meaning "he did not live." The dream was precipitated by Freud's fear that Fliess, who had to undergo an operation, might die, and connected this fear to the losses of the series of men that Freud had loved and depended on, and who had died in the immediately preceding years. There were also connections to the playmates he lost in infancy—John and Pauline. Here is the dream:

> I had gone to Brücke's laboratory at night, and, in response to a gentle knock on the door, I opened it to the late Professor Fleischl, who came in with a number of strangers and, after exchanging a few words, sat down at his table. . . . My friend Fliess had come to Vienna unobtrusively in July. I met him in the street in conversation with my deceased friend Paneth. . . . Fliess spoke about his sister [named Pauline] and said that in three quarters of an hour she was dead, and added some such words as "that was

the threshold." As Paneth failed to understand him, Fliess turned to me and asked me how much I had told Paneth about his affairs. Whereupon, overcome by strange emotions, I tried to explain to Fliess that Paneth could not understand anything at all, of course, because he was not alive. But what I actually said—and I myself noticed the mistake—was "Non vixit." I then gave Paneth a piercing look. Under my gaze he turned pale; his form grew indistinct and his eyes a sickly blue—and finally he melted away. I was highly delighted at this and I now realized that Ernst Fleischl, too, had been no more than an apparition, a "revenant"—a ghost or "one who returns"—and it seemed to me quite possible that people of that kind only existed as long as one liked and could be got rid of if someone else wished.

Freud's associations led him to an "emotional storm [which] raged in this region of the dream thoughts"; it was related to the deaths of Paneth and Fleischl and his fear of losing Fliess. The "piercing look" with which he magically did away with Paneth—with which he turned him into a ghost, a revenant, one who never lived, who was *Non vixit*—he connected to the "terrible blue eyes" of his powerful mentor Brücke, who would punish ill-prepared students with his withering glare.

Freud saw the source of the dream in the "hostile current" of feeling that coexisted with his affection for Paneth and Fleischl, who, in addition to being his friends, were rivals for an academic position in Brücke's laboratory. He located this hostility and guilt at the center; rivalrous wishes, in his view, were the main source of his emotional turmoil. This interpretation was not wrong; Freud was, indeed, intensely competitive, and it took courage for him to admit that he wished for the deaths of his close friends. Clinical experience continues to provide evidence for guilt feelings connected with hostility towards parents, siblings, and others, especially when they actually die. But, this was a partial truth, an interpretation that captured one level of experience while concealing the greater threat of death and loss.

At the time of the *Non vixit* dream, Fliess had become Freud's most intimate friend, his desperately needed other. Freud had made him into the object of his longings for love, understanding, and power, while, at the same time, there was a fair share of terror and rage that he could not openly experience. The threat to Fliess's health was the stimulus for the dream; it set off Freud's deep fear that he might lose the person he most needed. The dream then brought in other men that he loved, was close to, depended on, and competed with. For all these reasons, the deaths of these benefactors, and the possible death of Fliess, were terribly threatening to him.

The *Non vixit* dream showed Freud mastering his death fears with the prototypical solution he developed to deal with the losses of his infancy. He constructed an interpretation—guilt over rivalry, a version of the Oedipus complex—that made him, and his young child-self, a powerful actor, one who fought with his rivals, who gave as good as he got with his bigger playmate John, who felt triumphant at the deaths of Paneth and Fleischl. Along with this was his identification with the powerful figure of Brücke. The dead friends who appeared in the dream were "revenants," literally "ones who return"; ghosts who represented the frightening feelings within Freud. In the dream he magically banished them, he made them disappear; they were *Non vixit*, ones who never lived, rather than *Non vivit*, persons who lived and were now dead. Since they were never alive he did not need to feel grief. And he accomplished this magical disappearance by turning Brücke's piercing eyes on them, the same glare that was used to discipline him when he had "sinned" as a student. The tightly controlled Brücke, in other words, had the power to banish death, as he did with the loss of his own son. If Freud was like him, he, too, could rid himself of these frightening revenants; he could be Brücke of the powerful eyes.

Freud's invention of the Oedipus complex, along with his belief that people are driven by fantasies fueled by sexual instincts, both de-emphasized trauma and the role of actual experience. This was a crucial turn in his thinking, one that came out of the self-analysis and his close association with Wilhelm Fliess. It was a trend that continued in the book that emerged from these years: *The Interpretation of Dreams*.

CHAPTER 11

The Interpretation of Dreams and the End of the Fliess Affair

An autobiography is the truest of all books, for while it inevitably consists of extinctions of the truth, shirkings of the truth, partial revealments of the truth, with hardly an instance of plain straight truth, the remorseless truth is there, between the lines.

—Mark Twain

FREUD WAS self-revealing in many of his works, more "between the lines"—as Mark Twain put it—than when he seemed to be writing about himself in such essays as *The History of the Psycho-Analytic Movement* and *An Autobiographical Study*. While he never openly referred to the mixture of love and hate that he felt towards his mother, he gave an accurate account of these feelings in his lecture on *Femininity* when discussing the reactions of little *girls* to their mothers. His most touching remarks on his childhood disappointment with his father came in his general comments on sons and fathers in *Some Reflections on Schoolboy Psychology*, though he did not link these to Jacob Freud. And the most telling account of his relationship with Martha can be found in *"Civilized" Sexual Morality and Modern Nervous Illness*, again without reference to his own marriage. Of all Freud's work, however, *The Interpretation of Dreams*—and the short version, *On Dreams*, which he published one year later—were the most self-revealing, since they contained a large number of his own dreams, along with his associations and interpretations. *Interpretation* is the window into Freud's unconscious mind, a work rich on many levels. Yet it, too, was characterized by "extinctions . . . shirkings . . . and . . . partial revealments of the truth."

Early in their work with hysterical patients, Freud and Breuer had become aware of the connection between symptoms and dreams: the way both gave symbolic expression to unconscious conflicts. Freud was also interested in his own dreams and, even before he began the formal self-analysis following the deaths of men important to him in the 1890s, he was writing them down, along with related thoughts, memories, and interpretations of their meanings. He carried out the self-analysis largely with his own dreams and associations, with some attention to slips, errors, and misrememberings—what he later called "the psychopathology of everyday life." The analysis was not a completely self-contained enterprise, however, though Freud liked to give this impression in later years. In truth, he was only able to plunge into the depths of his mind in the haven of his relationship with Wilhelm Fliess, who supplied vital support, encouragement, praise, and commentary. *The Interpretation of Dreams* was sent, dream by dream and chapter by chapter, to his friend for suggestions, criticism, and editing.

Freud had begun the self-analysis in October of 1896; by May of the next year, he wrote to Fliess that "he felt impelled to start working on the dream, where I feel so very certain—and in your judgment am entitled to." By February of 1898, he reported that he was "deep in the dream book, am writing it fluently, and enjoy the thought of all the 'head shaking' over the indiscretions and audacities it contains." Writing to his friend in May of the same year, he said: "I shall change whatever you want and gratefully accept contributions. I am so immensely glad that you are giving me the gift of the Other, a critic and reader— and one of your quality at that. I cannot write entirely without an audience, but do not at all mind writing only for you."

Fliess was a character in several of the dreams in *Interpretation,* either directly or by association. In the *Non vixit* dream, as we have seen, he was one of several rival-competitors who Freud wished to banish to advance his own interests, an unconscious desire—in stark contrast to his professed love and need for Fliess—that he confessed to his friend. But of all the dreams in the book, Fliess figured most prominently in the dream presented in chapter 2, "The Method of Interpreting Dreams: An Analysis of a Specimen Dream." Here, Freud subjected one of his own "specimens"—which has come to be known as "the dream of Irma's injection"—to a long and thorough analysis. The dream of Irma's injection, with its copious associations, was the subject of the longest analysis in the book—sixteen pages were given over to it—and it has been analyzed and reinterpreted by many later authors.

The Irma dream was preceded by a series of emotionally arousing events that provided the cast of characters for the night's drama. "Irma" was, in fact, Emma Eckstein, the victim of Fliess's botched nasal surgery, who was continuing in analysis with Freud at this time. Freud's medical colleagues who appeared in the dream, "Otto" and "Dr. M.," were his friend and family pediatrician Oscar Rie and Josef Breuer, respectively. On the night before the dream, Rie had seen Emma and, when later discussing her condition with Freud, said she was "better, but not quite well." Taking this as a rebuke—a criticism of his psychoanalytic work—Freud wrote out a long case history to send to Breuer in an attempt to justify his psychoanalytic treatment. In the dream itself, he met Irma/ Emma in a social setting, took her aside, and reproached her for not accepting his "solution"—his interpretation of her neurosis. When she complained of continuing pain, he became alarmed that he might have missed some organic disease, and looked down her throat, where he saw "a big white patch . . . [and] extensive whitish grey scabs . . . modeled on the turbinal bones of the nose." The dream continued with Breuer saying something that made no medical sense, and an awareness that Rie had given Emma an injection of "trimethylamin" with a syringe that was not clean.

After sorting through his many associations, Freud reached his interpretation. The dream was "a plea" for his innocence of medical mismanagement; it exonerated him and proved that he, in contrast to all the other doctors, was conscientious. The dream showed that he was not at fault for Emma's continuing pains while a whole series of other culprits were blamed: the patient herself for not accepting his interpretation, Rie for giving her an injection with a dirty needle, Breuer for being a medical ignoramus, as well as others. The dream also took revenge on Rie and Breuer for not supporting him. Fliess hovered in Freud's associations as the true friend, in contrast to all the others, who took his side and did not make him feel guilty. Freud concluded by stating that the dream "was the fulfillment of a wish and its motive was a wish," which became, in the next chapter, the overarching principle "all dreams are wish fulfillments" and, at the conclusion of chapter 4, *a dream is the (disguised) fulfillment of a (suppressed or repressed) wish.*" He felt he had discovered the key to interpreting *all* dreams—akin to his belief that the Oedipus complex was "universal"—a single principle that would make him famous. He wrote to Fliess: "Do you suppose that someday one will read on a marble tablet on this house [where he dreamt the Irma dream]:

> Here, on July 24, 1895,
> The secret of the dream
> revealed itself to Dr. Sigm. Freud"

The publication of Freud's complete letters to Fliess revealed that the principal impetus for the Irma dream was Fliess's botched operation on the turbinal bones of Emma Eckstein's nose. Thus, it was Fliess, more than Freud, that the dream attempted to exculpate. When Freud looked down Irma/Emma's throat in the dream, he saw turbinal bonelike structures, just like the bones that Fliess operated on. The injection that caused her infection was of "trimethylamin," a substance that he and Fliess had discussed shortly before in relation to the "sexual processes." Thus, the real stimulus for the dream was not so much Rie's questioning of Freud's psychoanalytic treatment as it was Fliess's bungled operation. At the moment when the gauze was removed from Emma's nose, and Freud saw what his friend had done, his need to retain Fliess as his magical healer and fellow genius was endangered. He quickly began to blame others, including Emma herself, a process that continued in the Irma dream. In other words, there was a wish operating in the dream, but it was, first and foremost, the wish to hold on to his faith in his desperately needed other.

While Freud gave the impression that his theory of dreams was based on evidence and observations of himself and his patients, it was, in fact, completely entangled with his self-analysis—with what he could see and not see about himself—and with his complex bond to Fliess. His pronouncement that "all dreams are wish fulfillments," or, more precisely, that they serve to gratify unconscious wishes in disguised form, was a Fliess-like attempt at a universal principle. It paralleled Freud's theory of hysteria-neurosis, in which *all* symptoms were attributed to the patient's unconscious sexual conflicts. While dreams can serve a variety of purposes, his focus on wish fulfillment shifted attention away from one of the most important functions of dreaming—attempting to master the disruptive emotions associated with traumatic and other threatening and distressing events. Freud, in his interpretation of the Irma dream, did not mention the terrible trauma Emma had suffered—her face was marked for life by a cavity in her cheek. A year after the surgery, he was calling her bleeding "hysterical" and attributing it to her "longing." The Irma dream was set in motion by real guilt—both Freud's and Fliess's—for a real crime, and Freud's interpretation of it was his attempt to master his conflicting feelings for Fliess, stirred up in him by witnessing the trauma inflicted on Emma.

Ironically, *The Interpretation of Dreams,* a work famous for its revelations of the truth of the unconscious, began with the cover-up of what Freud and Fliess did to Emma Eckstein. In spite of this, it—and the more accessible *On Dreams*—remains an enormously fruitful book. The Irma dream, even though it leaves out a great deal, makes a powerful impression on the reader. It is rich in symbolism, and demonstrates how much meaning can be extracted from what at first appears to be a piece of imaginative nonsense. Freud's first sentence in *Interpretation* states: "In the pages that follow I shall bring forward proof that there is a psychological technique which makes it possible to interpret dreams, and that, if that procedure is employed, every dream reveals itself as a psychical structure which has a meaning and which can be inserted at an assignable point in the mental activities of waking life."

This was the great achievement of *Interpretation*; Freud was very persuasive in showing how dreams have meaning and how they are related to the events of daily life, including the life of ordinary people. The book suggests that everyone has their unconscious motives, not only hysterics and neurotics. It opened up a world of hidden personal meaning—the realm of the unconscious, of symbolism, of warded-off experience, of personal truth denied—captured in Freud's famous dictum: "Dreams are the royal road to the unconscious." Many ideas presented in the *Studies on Hysteria* and the papers that followed it were expanded and elaborated here, and new theories were developed.

Freud stated that dreams were set in motion by "day residues"—strongly felt events from the presleep period—which were then symbolically transformed into a private, visual form. His interpretations, his translations of these pictorial dramas into accessible language, occupied a great deal of the book and were, in large part, responsible for its appeal and influence. Through a host of examples, he made dreams understandable to the reader, including many familiar dreams: those of being embarrassed in public, of feeling anxious before an examination or performance, or of feeling "rooted to the spot"—unable to move in the face of danger.

In discussing the common dream of taking an examination for which one has not studied, Freud guessed that one does not dream about past examinations one has failed but only about those one has passed, with the purpose of countering anxiety about a current test. He traced dreams of being unable to move when confronted with danger to a conflict of wills, to being caught between two opposing motives. In *On Dreams,* he noted that children frequently have dreams that symbolize their wish "to be big," to be able to have the power of older siblings and adults. He also made the astute observation that because all dreams are "egoistic," other people sometimes stand for parts of the dreamer's self. While in many of his other interpretations he ferreted out underlying sexual drives, these examples showed that he was also aware of nonsexual motives such as the need to master fear and the longing for power. *Interpretation* opened up many new topics for exploration and presented a method that later investigators have used to expand the theory beyond the narrow sexual focus that Freud put forth in the final chapter of the book.

There were other compelling qualities to *The Interpretation of Dreams.* Freud showed how the actors in a dream are often composite figures, persons from the dreamer's life who are blended together because they have some emotional connection. Equally interesting was the way in which the dream "language" could move between words and visual images, and how it made use of the same principles as puns and jokes. Many of Freud's examples of this depended on plays on German words that do not survive translation into English, though some do, such as the woman who dreamed of being kissed in a car, which turned out to represent "auto-eroticism"—that is, masturbation—or Freud's dream that brought in his acquaintance "Dr. Gärtner" (gardener) and his daughter "Flora," connected to a series of botanical associations.

Freud decoded many of his own dreams in terms of their individual meaning, coming to understand them in relation to specific life circumstances and unique associations. As he put it in the second chapter: "My procedure is not so convenient as the popular decoding method which translates any given piece of a dream's content by a fixed key. I, on the contrary, am prepared to find that the same piece of content may conceal a different meaning when it occurs in various people or in various contexts."

But this individualized approach to dream interpretation was supplemented in the lengthy chapter 6, "The Dream Work," by his elaboration of the well-known Freudian symbols: "All elongated objects, such as sticks, tree trunks and umbrellas . . . may stand for the male organ, as well as all long sharp weapons, such as knives, daggers and pikes. . . . Boxes, cases, chest, cupboards and ovens represent the uterus, and also hollow objects, ships, and vessels of all kinds. . . . Steps, ladders or staircases . . . walking up or down them, are representations of the sexual act."

At times, Freud took the position that these symbols were to be used as guidelines, not as a codebook of fixed meanings: "I should like to utter an express warning against over-estimating the importance of symbols in dream-interpretation, against restricting the work of translating dreams merely to trans-lating symbols and against abandoning the technique of making use of the dreamer's associations."

Unfortunately, Freud's suggestion that one should interpret dreams in terms of the dreamer's unique experience is difficult to follow. The ease with which Freudian symbols can be recognized, and the small titillation of rooting out hid-den sexual meanings, have made dream interpretation an irresistible parlor game. And Freud himself, despite his argument in favor of individual associations, fre-quently could not resist treating sexual symbols as if they were universal. In con-trast to his warning in *Interpretation,* in *The Introductory Lectures* of 1915 he would write, "Symbols allow us in certain circumstances to interpret a dream without questioning the dreamer, who indeed would in any case have nothing to tell us about the symbol." And, in his late essay *Moses and Monotheism* he stated: "Moreover, symbolism disregards differences of language; investigation would probably show that it is ubiquitous—the same for all peoples."

The Interpretation of Dreams also presented new theory and elaborations of ideas hinted at in earlier publications. He discussed the Oedipus complex and extended it to Shakespeare's *Hamlet,* explored ideas connecting childhood expe-riences with adult personality, and made many suggestive speculations and brief comments that branched out from the dream material and pointed to future psychoanalytic developments. While he would not work out his full theory of id-ego-superego for more than twenty years, *Interpretation* contained an early version of the way in which relationships with important people become part of the self: how the ego grew by identifying with others. It was also in *Interpre-tation* that Freud first set forth his theory of the two modes of psychological functioning: the "primary" and "secondary processes," the first associated with fantasy, visual imagery, and the unconscious, and the second with consciousness, reality, and language.

By and large, Freud saw dreams as similar to neurotic symptoms, a view which he extended to fantasy, imagination, and the primary process. In much of his later work, this sphere of mental life was defined as "infantile," driven by the quest for pleasure; it was a repository of antisocial instincts. Since Freud developed his first ideas about dreams from his work with hysterical symptoms, seeing dreams and the imagination as pathological was a natural direction for the theory to take. His exposure to positivist science, and the value attributed to rationality that he absorbed in his medical and research training, also led him to equate "normality" with reason and fantasy with illness.

From a contemporary perspective, one sees that dreams and fantasies can be suffused with emotion that is missing or muted in waking thought; they touch on powerful, often threatening, experiences, and stir up a variety of memories. The dreamer, like the artist during the phase of creative inspiration, is in a passive state; images and feelings simply come to him, he must give up control and let his mind and feelings go where they will. Freud was both drawn to such states and threatened by them. By giving himself over to his unconscious, he could eventually master his traumas and disruptive emotions. Yet, to do so, he had to give up control and dominance. Some of his comments to Fliess showed that he knew that the unconscious was the fount of his own creativity. For example, in 1899 he wrote:

> Oddly enough, something is at work on the lowest floor. A theory of sexuality may be the immediate successor to the dream book. Today several very strange things occurred to me, which I do not yet properly understand at all. As far as I am concerned, there is no question of deliberation. This method of working moves along by fits and starts. God alone knows the date for the next thrust. . . . Wild things, by the way, some of which I already surmised during the stormy first epoch of productivity. [He quotes Goethe:] "Again ye come, ye hovering forms."

Freud, who identified with writers and poets in many ways, was aware of the unconscious roots of his own creativity. The unconscious mind—what he called the primary process—is essential to creative activity in literature, the arts, science—indeed, to a variety of areas, and Freud, at different times, did see this, but then, in his general theory of the primary and secondary process, retreated to a conception of dreams and the imagination as neurotic and infantile.

Even as Freud was writing *The Interpretation of Dreams,* he anticipated that his dream child would be greeted with hostility. In the fall of 1899, when the book was completed but not yet published, he wrote to Fliess: "The psychologists will in any case find enough to rail at . . . And then they'll really let me have it! When the storm breaks over me, I shall escape to your guest room. You will find something to praise in it in any event, because you are as much on *my* side as the others are *against* me."

Once the book was published, Freud followed its sales and reviews closely. While the response was, in fact, a mixed one, he interpreted the comments of reviewers as damning. Shortly after its publication, he wrote to Fliess: "The reception it has had so far has certainly not given me any joy. Understanding for it is meager; praise is doled out like alms; to most people it is evidently distasteful. I have not yet seen a trace of anyone who has an inkling of what is significant in it."

Some years later, describing the reception of the dream book in his *On the History of the Psycho-Analytic Movement,* he wrote:

> My writings were not reviewed in the medical journals or, if as an exception they *were* reviewed, they were dismissed with expressions of scornful or pitying superiority. Occasionally a colleague would make some reference to me in one of his publications; it would be very short and not at all flattering—words such as "eccentric", "extreme", or "very peculiar" would be used . . . [a student at a clinic] had indeed enquired . . . whether he had not better first read *The Interpretation of Dreams,* but had been advised against doing so—it was not worth the trouble.

These sentiments were echoed in the *Autobiographical Study* of 1925: "For more than ten years after my separation from Breuer I had no followers. I was completely isolated. In Vienna I was shunned; abroad no notice was taken of me. My *Interpretation of Dreams,* published in 1900, was scarcely reviewed in the technical journals."

These statements are typical examples of Freud's mythmaking, which were taken as factual by many later, uncritical, biographers. Jones wrote that "for some years there was no sale at all [of *The Interpretation of Dreams*] . . . Seldom has [such] an important book produced no echo whatever." In these accounts, Freud made himself out to be the misunderstood genius-hero who persevered against a world of enemies and ultimately triumphed. But none of this was true. He was not isolated because he was shunned by the medical establishment; in fact, his early work on hysteria had been received by his medical colleagues with a mixture of interest, praise, and skepticism. But he had turned away from them, and even drove the supportive Breuer away, because they did not completely affirm his theories. Instead of working within a scientific community of peers, he had chosen to link up with Fliess in a partnership where each reinforced the other's sense of grandeur.

It is true that the dream book sold modestly at first: only 351 copies during the first two years. It took another six years for the first printing of 600 copies to sell out, though the shorter *On Dreams,* which was accessible to the general reader, sold more copies when published in 1901. This contrasts with Darwin's

Origin of Species of 1859, for example, which sold out its first printing of 1,250 copies in a single day. But the comparison is inappropriate; Darwin's *Origin* was at the center of a stormy debate in England about the nature of man and the relationship of science to religion. In 1900, Freud was a neurologist whose work was known only to a small group of medical specialists; while he dreamed of fame, he had not achieved recognition outside a narrow circle. The sales of *Interpretation* were not small for the time it was published, and, given the topic and Freud's position, it reached a fairly wide audience within two or three years.

Nor was *The Interpretation of Dreams* dismissed with scorn or ignored by the technical journals. The truth is that *Interpretation* and *On Dreams* received at least thirty reviews in the two years following their publication, a number of them quite long. Many were highly complimentary; an 1899 review in Berlin called the book "epoch-making," while Paul Näcke, a well-known psychiatrist, said, "The book is psychologically the most profound that dream psychology has produced thus far." Like many of the other reviewers, Näcke disagreed with some of Freud's interpretations, yet concluded that "in its entirety the work is forged as a unified whole and thought through with genius."

There were negative reviews, to be sure—Freud did not wholly fabricate this idea—some of them voicing what, with hindsight, were legitimate criticisms, while others were unfairly dismissive. But the majority of the reviews were complimentary, balanced, and fair. Yet Freud felt that he was scorned, isolated, and harshly attacked. One senses that this was not so much a deliberate distortion of the truth as an expression of his own experience. In his twinship with Fliess, he imagined himself as the author of a great scientific discovery; in his mind, *The Interpretation of Dreams* should have been greeted as a work of genius, and anything less felt like rejection. The book was also an expression of the products of his unconscious and this, too, heightened his sensitivity to the smallest criticism. As he put it: "No other work of mine has been so completely my own, my own dung heap, my own seedling." The exposure of intimate aspects of his psyche left Freud in a vulnerable state that required a completely accepting and affirming response. He wanted his book to be a great event. He was used to being the Golden Sigi, and was anticipating being the "new Kepler." He expected "followers." Anything short of these aspirations felt like "scornful or pitying superiority."

With *The Interpretation of Dreams* published, and the self-analysis largely completed, Freud's letters to Fliess began to hint at difficulties between them. In February of 1900 he wrote, "Thus we are becoming estranged from each other through what is most our own," presumably referring to the differences in their theories. Fliess, for his part, was becoming ever more grandiose; he was now explaining a host of medical-biological phenomena in terms of right- and left-handedness, though this did not seen to trouble Freud. Something else was brewing in him that would lead to their ultimate break. He continued to be enormously sensitive if Fliess did not respond to him immediately: "Remember that I regularly develop the gloomiest expectations when your letters fail to arrive." In March of the same year he wrote, "There has never been a six-month period in which I so constantly and so ardently longed to be living in the same place with you," but went on to speak of "a deep inner crisis," of feeling "inwardly deeply impoverished," and having "to demolish all my castles in the air." In the face of his longing and depressed state, he responded to Fliess's proposal that they meet by saying "it is more likely that I shall avoid you." In this same letter, Freud made a veiled reference to loving and hating somebody at the same time, suggesting that, in his "inner crisis," Fliess was becoming the recipient of the intense ambivalence that Freud harbored toward his mother.

The correspondence then resumed in a friendly tone for a few months. In early August, the two men met in Achensee for what turned out to be the last of their congresses—in fact, the last time they ever met. What transpired between them at this meeting is not certain, and Freud left no account of it. Fliess later gave his version of the encounter:

> On that occasion Freud showed a violence towards me which was at first unintelligible to me. The reason was that in a discussion of Freud's observations of his patients I claimed that periodic processes were unquestionably at work in the psyche, as elsewhere; and maintained in particular that they had an effect on those psychopathic phenomena on the analysis of which Freud was engaged for therapeutic purposes. Hence neither sudden deteriorations nor sudden improvements were to be attributed to the analysis and its influence alone . . . During the rest of the discussion I thought I detected a personal animosity against me on Freud's part that sprang from envy. . . . The result of the situation at Achensee . . . was that I quietly withdrew from Freud and dropped our regular correspondence. Since that time Freud has heard no more from me about my scientific findings.

Fliess was shocked because, after many years of deference and adulation on Freud's part, he was suddenly confronted by an angry man who dismissed his ideas. It seems likely that Freud was now openly displaying his ambivalence— the hatred that accompanied his excessively proclaimed love for his friend— hinted at earlier in dreams and slips. Fliess's account of their last meeting seems believable, since it fits a repetitive pattern in Freud's relations with men; he had turned on Breuer in precisely the same way a few years earlier. As the latent, "heroic" Freud came forth, there could only be *one* great man.

The fact that their theories were in conflict should have been no surprise; it was only Freud's need for an idol that had blinded him to their differences for so long. Freud had been explaining neuroses in terms of unconscious conflicts, and basing his therapy on this, while Fliess attributed "deteriorations" and "sudden improvements" to "periodic processes," to dates, birthdays, and the twenty-three- and twenty-eight-day male and female periods. The two theories were incompatible, and had been all along. From the beginning of the correspondence, Freud's comments had contained a great deal of flattery, with occasional attempts to apply his friend's theories, along with admissions that the mathematics were too much for him to follow and deference to the other's expertise. With his great personal need for Fliess, he had deluded himself about the incompatibility of their views. But with the self-analysis finished and the dream book published, he was feeling his strength and independence and could no longer ignore their differences. They burst into the open at the Achensee meeting. Fliess, for his part, was every bit as touchy as Freud when it came to criticisms of his theories; the upshot was, as he put it, that he "quietly withdrew" from the relationship.

Freud was reluctant to admit that things had changed between them and the correspondence continued for another year, though the gaps between letters became longer and discussion of their work gave way to comments on patients and chat about family matters. Freud was completing both *The Psychopathology of Everyday Life* and the Dora case during this time, and while he mentioned them to Fliess, referring to how several of the slips and mistakes in *Everyday Life* involved him, he did not send any of this material to his friend for comments as he had with *Interpretation*. It does seem that Fliess was the one who withdrew from the relationship first and that Freud had great difficulty accepting this, even though he had set the rupture in motion.

In August of the following year, Freud wrote a long letter in which he told Fliess: "There is no concealing the fact that the two of us have drawn apart to some extent. . . . You too have come to the limit of your perspicacity; you take sides against me and tell me that 'the reader of thoughts merely reads his own thoughts into other people' which renders all my efforts worthless. If that is what you think of me, just throw my *Everyday Life* into the wastepaper basket." The letter also referred to Freud's willingness to welcome Breuer back as a friend—though this did not last—and to the fact that he did not "share [Fliess's] contempt for friendship between men, probably because I am to a high degree party to it. In my life, as you know, woman has never replaced the comrade, the friend." A few months earlier he had written that "no one can replace for me the relationship with the friend which a special—possibly feminine—side demands." Breuer had told Fliess's wife Ida that she was lucky Freud did not live in Berlin since he would have interfered with their marriage. Freud's antipathy to Ida was revealed in a 1911 letter to his disciple Karl Abraham: "I particularly warn you against his wife, clever-stupid, malicious, positive hysteric; in short: perversion not neurosis."

The correspondence dwindled over the next years, ending with a final angry interchange over the ownership of the concept of bisexuality. Fliess had introduced the idea to Freud, who was skeptical at first and then embraced it as central to his own doctrines. In these early discussions, Freud had given his friend full credit. But then he "forgot" and acted as if the idea was his own. There was an exchange of charges and countercharges, with Freud finally admitting that Fliess had priority and confessing that due to his own ambition, he had suffered a lapse of memory. This did not mollify his former friend, and the argument over who had first claim to the term raged on. The dispute was not about facts or the validity of the theory, but over priority—who had used the concept first, who owned it. How ironic that their friendship should end in an argument over bisexuality when Freud's love for Fliess—bisexual or "homosexual" in his own words—was so central to it all along.

Looking back over the entire Fliess affair, one can see that the deprived and unhappy Freud—not finding what he craved in his marriage to Martha, and unwilling to remain in a collaborative relationship with the modest and scientific Breuer—turned to the charismatic Berlin doctor with his deepest longings and aspirations. In his mind, Fliess became the loving-caring mother, the powerful father-model, and the source of unquestioning praise and support who validated his claim to greatness. He loved and needed him with an intensity that would later frighten him. Fleischl had been a precursor to Fliess, but he had become too sick, too drug addicted, to be responsive to his younger colleague. Fliess was the great love of Freud's adult life; as late as 1920, in his essay *Beyond the Pleasure Principle,* he was still writing about "the large conception of Wilhelm Fliess, [in which] all the phenomena of life exhibited by organisms—and also, no doubt, their death—are linked with the completion of fixed periods, which express the dependence of two kinds of living substance—one male and the other female— upon the solar year."

While they would break off contact in 1902, Freud continued to dream about his lost "only other" for years afterward.

CHAPTER 12

The Great Freud Emerges: 1899–1905

The world owes all its onward impulses to men ill at ease; the happy man inevitably confines himself within ancient limits.

—Nathaniel Hawthorne, *The House of the Seven Gables*

So MANY OF Freud's contributions are taken for granted now that it is hard to conceive of a world without them. There was a poor understanding of neurosis and almost no useful treatment to help a large number of suffering individuals. While writers, poets, and artists valued dreams and the imagination, there was no general framework within which to understand these phenomena. Many people knew that "the child is father to the man," but there was no specific theory for how this occurred. Before Freud, there was hardly any interpretation of a wide array of phenomena—everyday slips and errors, dreams, fantasies, symptoms, neuroses—that penetrated beneath the surface of consciousness.

Freud first mentioned his interest in the mistakes of everyday life in a letter to Fliess in August of 1898: "You know how one can forget a name and substitute part of another one for it; you could swear it was correct, although invariably it turns out to be wrong." He went on to describe an incident where he could not remember the last name of the poet Julius Mosen, incorrectly substituting several other names: "Julius had not slipped my memory. Now, I was able to prove (1) that I had repressed the name Mosen because of certain connections; (2) that infantile material played a part in this repression [no doubt a reference to the death of his brother Julius]; (3) that the substitute names that were pushed into the foreground were formed, like symptoms, from both groups of material." A month later he mentioned another example to Fliess, his misremembering the name of the renaissance painter Signorelli, which, like the forgetting of Mosen, was intimately connected with the material emerging in his self-analysis. He published a version of the Signorelli episode in a journal that same year and it later became the first example in his book *The Psychopathology of Everyday Life.*

Throughout the self-analysis, Freud had been attending to his own slips and mistakes, analyzing them as if they were symptoms or dreams. He interpreted the errors of his patients in the same way, and, with *The Interpretation of Dreams* completed, he began to gather all this material together into a book. In September of 1900 he wrote, "I am slowly writing the 'Psychology of Everyday Life,'" and, by January of the next year, commented that "'Everyday Life,' half finished, has been taking a rest but will soon be continued." The German word that Freud used for the examples in the book was *Fehlleistung*—literally, "failed performance"—best translated into English as "mistake" or "blunder," though James Strachey, in the *Standard Edition,* used the more scientific sounding "parapraxes." Freud wrote: "By mistakes I understand the occurrence in healthy and normal people of such events as forgetting words and names that are normally familiar to one, forgetting what one intends to do, making slips of the tongue and pen, misreading, mislaying things, and being unable to find them, losing things, making mistakes against one's better knowledge, and certain habitual gestures and movements."

All these mistakes, in Freud's view, were motivated; they were not accidental, but arose from unconscious conflicts to which they gave disguised expression in the same manner as neurotic symptoms and dreams. *The Psychopathology of Everyday Life,* which was published in a Berlin journal in 1901, provided a great number of examples to illustrate this thesis. A man "Y" was in love with a young lady who did not return his affection, instead marrying another man "X," who was a friend and business associate of Y. Despite their long acquaintance and continuing business dealings, Y forgot X's name over and over, the obvious motivation being his "antipathy to his more fortunate rival," whose existence he wished to eradicate. A young woman could not recall the name of an English novel, despite the fact that she clearly remembered its content and was even able to visualize the book's cover and the lettering of the title. Upon analysis, the book turned out to be *Ben Hur,* words that were too close to the German *bin Hure*—"I am a whore"—an expression that she "like any other girl did not care to use, especially in the company of young men." An amusing example of a slip was provided by the president of the Austrian parliament, who *opened* a session with the announcement, "Gentlemen: I take notice that a full quorum of members is present and herewith declare the sitting *closed.*" Clearly, he wished that the meeting was over and done with. A man "without patriotic feelings" referred to his brother, who was more nationalistic, as an *idiot,* adding apologetically, "I meant to say *patriot,* of course," revealing his underlying antipathy to his brother and his beliefs.

In a more complicated example, a Jewish man had married a Christian woman with whom he had two sons who were raised as Christians but were told by their father, when they were old enough, about their Jewish background. One day at a summer resort, their hostess, who was unaware of the family's Jewish ancestry, "launched some very sharp attacks on the Jews." The father, not wanting to cause any problems, but fearing that his sons "in their candid and ingenuous way would betray the momentous truth if they heard any more of the conversation . . . tried to get them to leave the company . . . [he] said 'Go into the garden, *Juden* (Jews),' quickly correcting it to *Jungen* (youngsters)." Here, the slip betrayed the father's conflicting emotions: loyalty to his Jewish heritage, believing he should have "the courage of his convictions," while, at the same time, wishing to pass as a non-Jew and avoid trouble.

The Psychopathology of Everyday Life contained a great number of examples such as these that illustrated, in a very convincing manner, the way motives and intentions—some close to consciousness and others more deeply buried—made their presence known as everyday mistakes. Freud also made reference to important areas of his personal life—as, for example, when he described the time he "forgot" that Fliess was the first to tell him about bisexuality, saying, "It is painful to be requested in this way to surrender one's originality." He passed lightly over this incident, which, in fact, set off the painful rupture of their relationship. But of all the examples in *Everyday Life,* none is both so self-revealing and self-concealing as the long *Signorelli* example.

Freud was on a train with a stranger, discussing travel in Italy, when he asked his companion if he had seen the famous frescoes of the "Four Last Things"—Death, Judgment, Heaven, and Hell—in the town of Orvieto, painted by . . . when he could not remember the name of the artist *Signorelli*. In place of the correct name he thought of *Botticelli* and *Boltraffio*, though knowing, as he did so, that they were wrong. Freud unraveled his mistake by tracing the names of the artists to a series of thoughts, one of a patient who had recently committed suicide, and another of certain Turks who "place a higher value on sexual enjoyment than on anything else, and in the event of sexual disorders . . . are plunged into despair which contrasts strangely with their resignation towards the threat of death." These thoughts came to him during the conversation about the Signorelli frescoes, but he suppressed them, "since I did not want to allude to this delicate topic [sexuality] in a conversation with a stranger." Each of the thoughts was linked with the names of the three Renaissance artists. Freud explained that he could not think of Signorelli, and thought of the substitute names, because of associations with the topic "death and sexuality." He presented the example to show that the misremembering was motivated—was not random or inexplicable—but, like dreams and symptoms, was based on an unconscious conflict.

Freud wrote no more about his conflict regarding "death and sexuality" in the Signorelli example, though one can assume, from his many other writings, that it concerned his sexual rivalry and death wishes toward his father. What he did not comment on—what one suspects he could not let himself know—was the association of the forgetting of *Signorelli* with the traumas of his earliest years. The missing connections can be derived from the material that he himself provided.

Freud was in the midst of his self-analysis when the *Signorelli* incident occurred; he had recovered some of the memories of fear and loss from his infancy just a year previously. Riding on a train activated his travel phobia, producing a state of anxious arousal that led him to think of a fresco that depicts death, judgment, heaven, and hell. Why this, out of all the great art in Italy, if not for its association with his anxious state? And, finally, he had recently received word that "a patient over whom I had taken a great deal of trouble had put an end to his life on account of an incurable sexual disorder." For a therapist, the suicide of a patient can be a terrible disappointment and loss.

All of these factors can be correlated with the events and traumas of Freud's infancy. His fear of travel by train first appeared when the family left Freiberg, amid the many losses of these years. He became frightened when he saw gas jets for the first time and thought they were "souls burning in hell." Death, judgment, heaven, and hell were all associated with his lost nursemaid who, as he remembered in his self-analysis, took him to a Catholic church with her. And what about the associations with sexuality? People, even "Turks," don't fall into hopeless despair, don't kill themselves as his patient did, over "sexual disorders" unless sexuality has a particular meaning for them. And it did carry such a load of extra meaning for Freud, symbolizing his powerful longing for love and the dangers associated with it. Because of this, to lose the possibility of sexual pleasure was to reexperience the devastating losses of his first years, which, indeed, could plunge him into deep despair.

While Freud began *Everyday Life* with the complex *Signorelli* example, the rest of the book was filled with numerous examples of slips, errors, forgetting, and misremembering of a less complicated sort which, cumulatively, made a very convincing case for his general thesis that seemingly unintentional acts were unconsciously motivated. Such motives included "egoistic, jealous and hostile feelings and impulses, on which the pressure of moral education weighs heavily," anger toward siblings, shameful secrets, laziness, hidden competition, fear of failure, and guilt over a variety of transgressions. The fact that Freud did not, in *Everyday Life,* engage in abstract theory building, that his examples encompassed a wide range of motives from normal life, and that he did not, as was true in many other works, reduce every example to sexuality, gave the book a wide appeal. Indeed, it became one of his most accessible works and had much to do with convincing the nonspecialist audience of the prevalence of unconscious motivation. Following its publication in 1901, Freud began to expand the book by adding examples provided by his psychoanalytic colleagues, though he made no substantive changes. A second edition was brought out in 1904, to be followed by nine more, with translations into twelve foreign languages during his lifetime. The "Freudian slip" passed into the common domain.

Even before he had completed *Everyday Life,* Freud was at work on the first of his long case studies. In the fall of 1900, he wrote Fliess that "it has been a lively time and has brought a new patient, an eighteen-year-old girl, a case that has smoothly opened to the existing collection of picklocks." This was Ida Bauer, best known by Freud's pseudonym *Dora.* His original title was "Dreams and Hysteria: Fragment of an Analysis"; the case would illustrate both his dream theory and the role of sexuality—and bisexuality—in neurosis. As he wrote to Fliess, with whom he was still on good terms: "It is a hysteria with tussis nervosa and aphonia, which can be traced back to the character of the child's sucking, and the principal issue in the conflicting thought processes is the contrast between an inclination toward men and an inclination toward women." The case revolved around two of Dora's dreams and gave a good sense of how Freud worked as a therapist, with his insistent interpretations of his young patient's unconscious sexual intentions. But it is most significant, in retrospect, as the first place where he elaborated the concept of *transference,* one of his most original and enduring contributions.

Dora, a girl "in the first bloom of youth of intelligent and engaging looks," was sent to treatment at her father's insistence. She suffered from a number of "hysterical" symptoms: headaches, shortness of breath, a nervous cough that sometimes led to loss of voice, and depression with suicidal ideas. She was involved in a tangled set of relationships with her father and a married couple: Herr and Frau K. She was hostile and estranged from her mother, a woman whose near-psychotic cleaning compulsions made life in the family home impossible. Dora was, at an earlier time, close to her father, a wealthy manufacturer with a history of medical problems, but was now angry with him. The father was having an affair with Frau K. Herr K., a man close to her parents' age, made two sexual advances to Dora, the first when she was thirteen and the second when she was fifteen, though Freud, in his case history, consistently made her a year older than she was. In the second instance, Herr K. grabbed her and pressed a kiss on her mouth to which she responded with "a violent feeling of disgust," a reaction that Freud described as typically "hysterical." Freud's analysis traced Dora's neurosis to her conflicted sexual wishes, which, in his view, had their origin in her childhood sensual gratifications: she was a "little suck-a-thumbs," a bed wetter, and a masturbator. He assumed that a normal—nonneurotic, nonhysterical—girl would have responded with pleasure to Herr K.'s advances.

Freud's analysis of Dora's symptoms, memories, and dreams was meant to demonstrate the correctness of his theory of hysteria, particularly the role of unconscious oedipal-sexual conflicts. He saw her symptoms as the compromised outcome of her excessive sexual desires and the repressive forces of disgust and shame that opposed them. He ferreted out her purported oedipal wishes for her father and their manifestation in her love for Herr K.; her homosexual desire for Frau K., and the infantile roots of these desires. As one example, he interpreted her nervous cough—the tickle in her throat—as an expression of her "perverse" fantasy of oral sex with Herr K. Dora's two dreams were interpreted along the same lines, that is, as disguised expressions of her forbidden sexual desires.

The case gives a clear picture of Freud the therapist at work, of his Sherlock Holmes approach in which he played the part of a detective using clues to unravel a mystery. He saw Dora's neurosis as a puzzle to be solved; the solution lay in tracing her symptoms through associations to the precipitating events in her life and, beyond this, to antecedents in childhood. He interpreted the meaning of these symptoms in a direct and insistent manner, and, when she did not agree with his ideas about her sexual wishes, further interpreted this as her resistance. He had little empathy or understanding for her reactions when unwanted sexual advances were forced on her by an older married man whose wife, once Dora's friend and confidante, was her father's mistress.

It is clear that Freud's treatment of Dora was quite damaging, and it is painful to read the case today, to witness his unsympathetic and aggressive treatment of this young woman, already a pawn in the selfish games of her father and the other significant adults in her life. His technique, as well as his whole understanding of Dora and her life situation, is open to criticism and the case has been fully discussed by a number of later authors. Despite its failure as treatment, it was in this case that Freud formulated his theory of *transference,* as a way of understanding Dora's breaking off the treatment after three months, angry with him and claiming that he had not cured her. Earlier, when interpreting what he believed to be her pleasure at Herr K.'s kiss, he assumed that "indications . . . seemed to point to there having been a transference on to me . . . the idea had probably occurred to her one day during a sitting that she would like to have a kiss from me." When she stopped the treatment, he believed she was taking revenge on him, just as she wished to do with her father and Herr K. He also admitted that by not recognizing and dealing with this transference, he had allowed her to act out her feelings. While he was no doubt wrong about what Dora was experiencing, he was nevertheless able to use the case material to develop his first extensive definition of this important new concept:

> What are transferences? They are new editions or facsimiles of the tendencies and phantasies which are aroused and made conscious during the progress of the analysis; but they have this peculiarity, which is characteristic for their species, that they replace some earlier person by the person of the physician. To put it another way: a whole series of psychological experiences are revived, not as belonging to the past, but as applying to the person of the physician at the present moment. . . . transference cannot be evaded, since use is made of it in setting up all the obstacles that make the

material inaccessible to treatment, and since it is only after the transference has been resolved that a patient arrives at a sense of conviction of the validity of the connections which have been constructed during the analysis.

Freud completed his write-up of the Dora case in January of 1901, but did not publish it then. He had shown it to his friend Oscar Rie a month after it was finished, but Rie, a pediatrician who had a good deal of experience with the diseases of children and adolescents, did not like it. In a letter to Fliess, written when their intimacy was clearly over, Freud wrote, "I withdrew my last work [Dora] from publication because just a little earlier I had lost my last audience in you." Perhaps he was also reluctant to publish a case that had failed, though he did add a postscript in which he put a positive gloss on the outcome. Whatever the reason, or reasons, he put the manuscript away and did not publish it until 1905 as *Fragments of an Analysis of a Case of Hysteria*.

The concept of transference ultimately came to have great value in psychoanalytic psychotherapy. Unconscious motives are not only found in neuroses, dreams, sexual preferences, slips, and errors, but they determine the patterning of relationships more widely. In the course of an analysis, the analyst becomes the recipient of the patient's transference; the emotions and reactions of other key relationships are experienced live in the therapy. This has the potential to give the patient a sense of conviction beyond that conveyed by interpretations of memories, dreams, or associations. Transference brings the neurosis live into the room, where therapist and patient can work with it as it occurs.

While almost all of Freud's attention was concentrated on his work, he did keep abreast of events in his extended family, attending the wedding of his favorite sister Rosa in 1896 and commenting with approval on her new husband. The births of Rosa's son and daughter in the next two years were duly noted. He mentioned the marriage of his youngest sister Pauline, and the death of her husband in 1900. In June of 1900, his half brother Emanuel, along with his son Sam, visited from England. Freud wrote that "he brought with him a real air of refreshment because he is a marvelous man, vigorous and mentally indefatigable despite his sixty-eight or sixty-nine years, who has always meant a great deal to me." Emanuel, twenty-four years older than Sigmund, remained the admirable father figure that Jacob never was. Freud followed the career of his younger brother Alexander with interest—he became a transportation expert for the Austrian government—and they often went on vacations together, including his much discussed visit to Rome.

The *Interpretation of Dreams* was published, *Everyday Life* and Dora were completed, and the Fliess relationship was breaking apart. It was at this time that Freud was finally able to overcome what he called his "Rome neurosis." For many years, he had longed to visit the Eternal City, representative of the ancient world that had been so prominent in his youthful fantasies. His wish to go there was a "yearning . . . which becomes evermore tormenting." He had, by the turn of the century, traveled a good deal, yet still found himself blocked from going to the city of his dreams. As the self-analysis progressed, he began to understand what lay behind his inhibition. In December of 1897 he had written, "My longing for Rome is, by the way, deeply neurotic. It is connected with my high school hero worship of the Semitic Hannibal, and this year in fact I did not reach Rome any more than he did from Lake Trasimeno," the place where Hannibal, in his war against the Roman Empire, had stopped short. Freud had stopped short also, on his trip to Orvieto, less than fifty miles north of Rome, where he saw the Signorelli frescoes, stimulating the misremembering incident described in *Everyday Life.* He provided a fuller account of his Rome neurosis in *The Interpretation of Dreams,* describing Hannibal as "the favourite hero of my later school days" and explaining that "Hannibal and Rome symbolized the conflict between the tenacity of Jewry and the organization of the Catholic church." It was in this same passage that he described his childhood memory of Jacob Freud's humiliation by an anti-Semite, the time when he vowed to model himself after Hannibal rather than his father.

In the preceding years, Freud had written several times of longing to visit the Italian capital in the company of Fliess, yet he repeatedly found excuses that prevented them from meeting there. In the summer of 1900, he traveled in northern Italy for six weeks with Martha, Minna, his brother Alexander, and his sister Rosa and her husband, yet he could not bring himself to go the short extra distance to Rome. Then, in September of the following year, he finally overcame his fear and made the trip, which he described as "a high point of my life." Significantly, the letter to Fliess describing his visit to Rome followed directly upon the letter of August 7, 1901, in which he pronounced the end of their intimacy.

Freud and his younger brother Alexander spent twelve days in Rome, and the postcards he sent home to Martha captured his mood of exhilaration. He found it a "divine city"; his time there was "splendid for work and pleasure, in which one forgets oneself and other things. . . . This afternoon a few impressions off which one will live for years." While his time in Rome was spent like that of any other tourist—visiting the Vatican museum, throwing a coin in the Trevi Fountain, gazing at the paintings of Raphael and—of special importance to him—seeing Michelangelo's statue of Moses, about which he would later write an essay, the trip produced a rush of pleasure associated with the overcoming of a long-standing fear. Freud's previous biographers took up his language, transforming this ordinary bit of tourism into a momentous feat: Jones told how Freud "conquered those resistances and triumphantly entered Rome," and Gay wrote of his "conquest of Rome."

A number of interpretations have been offered to account for why Freud's phobia prevented him, for such a long a time, from fulfilling his deep longing to see Rome. His own account traced it to his childhood identification with Hannibal, with the suggestion that the fear had an oedipal root; presumably, to sur-

pass Hannibal was to possess the "Mother of Cities"—as Freud referred to it—
so that the fear was of the father's retaliation. There is no supporting evidence
in any of Freud's own associations that he feared his father in this way, however.
What is clear is that Rome was associated with one of the principal means with
which he consoled himself during his childhood years of poverty and deprivation: his escape into fantasies of the ancient world. His idealization of this world,
and his reliance on such fantasies for solace, continued throughout his life. He
was entranced with the excavations of ancient civilizations; imagined himself as
Heinrich Schliemann, a scientist-hero whose discovery of Troy was much in the
news, and spoke, in his preface to the Dora case, of "those discoverers whose
good fortune it is to bring to the light of day after their long burial the priceless
though mutilated relics of antiquity." He loved these wonders from the past, and
his offices at Berggasse 19 became crammed with his collection of artifacts from
ancient Egypt, Greece, China, and Rome.

Central to Freud's fantasies was his identification with powerful military
heroes. In analyzing his Rome neurosis in *The Interpretation of Dreams* he had
suggested that he chose Hannibal because he was a "Semite." Certainly, being a
Jew in anti-Semitic Austria was related to the misery Freud felt as a boy. But
many of his other heros—Alexander the Great, Oedipus, Napoléon, Oliver
Cromwell—had no connection with Judaism: the purpose of all these identifications was to *not* be a Jewish boy from an impoverished family with a weak and
failed father. What was important was the fact that all these men went to war
against superior forces: Alexander was a Macedonian prince who challenged the
Persian Empire; Hannibal a Carthaginian who attacked mighty Rome; Napoléon
a Corsican corporal who became emperor of all Europe; and Cromwell a farmer
who led an army to victory and became Lord Protector of England. Freud's
identification with them was only marginally connected to his Jewishness—that
is, being a Jew made him an outsider like them—but the more potent attraction
was their status as members of smaller, outside groups who defeated larger, dominant powers.

By overcoming his fear of traveling to Rome, Freud, in his mind, surpassed
his childhood idol Hannibal, who had stopped short of the capital of the
empire. This "triumph" was part of the new persona that he was constructing at
the turn of the century. All through the Fliess relationship, he had displayed a
mixture of grand ambition coupled with slavish dependence on his exalted
friend. He needed Fliess's constant support, reassurance, and love during the
self-analysis and the writing of *The Interpretation of Dreams,* but this dependence
was also threatening; it was, in Freud's own words, "homosexual." He felt it as
a menacing inner femininity, lacking in masculine power. As he completed
Everyday Life and Dora, written with little help from his Berlin supporter, he
experienced the painful loss of his fantasy of encompassing love, but he also felt
less needy and afraid, less weak, and he was able to pull away from the man he

had relied on for so long, to feel his own power, and to "conquer" Rome. Freud referred to Hannibal as the "Commander-in-Chief" of an army, and he was now on his way to becoming such a commander himself.

In his mood of triumph upon returning from Rome, Freud set about securing his promotion at the university. He had been a *Privatdozent* (lecturer) since 1885 and, despite the recommendations of Professors Nothnagel and Richard von Krafft-Ebing, his promotion to *Professor Extraordinarius* had been passed over for several years. Earlier accounts have attributed this to anti-Semitism, which, while a factor, was by no means sufficient; other Jews, including his friend, the ophthalmologist Leopold Königstein, had been promoted during these years. What was required was "Protektion": the influence of someone with connections to those in power. With his newfound confidence, Freud enlisted the help of two of his female patients; one of these, the baroness Ferstel, was able to bribe the minister of education with a painting, and the promotion was secured in 1902. Freud could now rightly call himself *Herr Professor* and, in the years to come, his followers and disciples always referred to him as "the Professor."

At several places in *The Interpretation of Dreams,* Freud had remarked on the fact that dreams contain jokes, puns, and plays on words. In the late 1890s he had begun to collect Jewish stories and other jokes, but it was not until several years later that he brought these together in the volume *Jokes and Their Relation to the Unconscious.* He wrote the book simultaneously with the *Three Essays on the Theory of Sexuality* in the early 1900s; in fact, he kept the two manuscripts on adjoining tables and worked on one or the other according to his mood. Both were published in 1905.

Freud explained jokes and humor as having the same roots as slips and mistakes. They were symbolic creations that gave disguised expression to unacceptable wishes and impulses. As was true for the examples in *Everyday Life,* the jokes that Freud analyzed expressed a wide array of motives; some were sexual, but many others involved attacks on authority, disguised competitiveness, grandiosity, absurdities, and simple playfulness. Freud also attempted to work out a complicated category system for different forms of humor, but nothing further ever came of this. In fact, unlike the other books of this period, Freud did little in the way of revisions and rarely made reference to *Jokes* in his later writings. Nevertheless, the book was important as an early effort to extend the psychoanalytic method to creative-aesthetic products. Its larger significance was to open up new areas for exploration: literature, art, and creative work more generally. It was, in its way, a forerunner of his essays on Dostoevsky, Michelangelo, Leonardo de Vinci, and the entire field of what is now called applied psychoanalysis.

Freud's ideas for the book that would eventually be titled *Three Essays on the Theory of Sexuality* had begun to rumble in his creative unconscious as he finished *The Interpretation of Dreams.* As he wrote to Fliess, "*Sexual Theory and Anxiety* is the title of my next work, which deep down must have progressed further than I know because I feel so very confident." The ideas continued to germinate; he wrote *Everyday Life* and Dora first, and did not finish the *Three Essays* until mid-1904, with publication in 1905.

There is a widely held view that Freud exposed the sexual repressions and hypocrisy of his age; that his discoveries, most clearly expressed in the *Three Essays,* freed the twentieth century from the oppression and strictures of the Victorian age. According to this view, he laid bare the pathological effects of sexual repression and discovered infantile sexuality. As the literary critic and Freud scholar Steven Marcus put it: "In its disclosure to the world of the universality and normality of infantile and childhood sexuality in all its polymorphously perverse impulsiveness, the *Three Essays* was bringing to a close that epoch of cultural innocence in which infancy and childhood were regarded as themselves innocent. . . . In the name of truth and reality, he undertook to deprive Western culture of one of its sanctified myths."

This view is partly true, and partly myth, yet it only scratches the surface of Freud's rich contributions to the understanding of sexuality. His theories were complex, extended into many related areas, and established the foundation for the work of many later investigators. But the many creative accomplishments went hand in hand with his continuing blindness regarding anxiety and his distorted view of women.

By the late 1890s, Freud's theory of sexual conflict was firmly in place. Neuroses resulted, he asserted, from unconscious conflicts between sexually driven fantasies and the repressive forces of shame, guilt, and morality. The *Three Essays* of 1905 exploded out of this early theory in a variety of creative directions. It is a complex and multilayered book that examined beliefs that others assumed were true, took them apart, and put them together in new ways. It was as if Freud had landed in a new world and was mapping out unexplored territory. Some of his maps were accurate, some were partly right, and others led in false directions, but all were enormously suggestive. Even when he was wrong, he pointed the way for later investigators who refined and corrected his theories.

The major areas that were explored in the *Three Essays* included a reexamination of a great variety of sexual practices, preferences, and roles; hypotheses regarding the development of masculine and feminine gender and identity; a theory of the development of infantile and childhood sexuality; and ideas about ambivalence, bisexuality, masochism, and sadism. The general theory used to understand neurosis and dreams was extended to personality and character more broadly as he explained the choice of a love object, the preferred means of obtaining sexual pleasure, and many specific practices and patterns in terms of symbolic meaning and the transformation of early experience.

Central to the *Three Essays* was a developmental or evolutionary approach; Darwin's influence was clearest here. Like Darwin, Freud examined a phenomenon in its current state and presented a new way of understanding it by tracing its development through time, its growth and transformation out of earlier forms. Before Darwin, it was assumed that humans simply appeared or were created in their present state. He showed, in contrast, that species as we know them were the end result of a process of evolution and change over millions of years. Freud did the same with his conceptions of the development of sexuality and the human personality. Whereas sexuality had been thought to simply appear at puberty, he showed it to be the result of growth and transformation through the years of infancy and childhood. And not just sexuality, but all of adult personality was seen in terms of its evolution from earlier stages. Before Freud, the sexual identity of adults, or preferences for different sexual practices or type of partner, were seen as moral—or immoral—choices, or as "degenerate" tendencies, fixed at birth. Freud, in contrast, described them as the result of an interaction between inborn predispositions and life events, developing and changing over the years. He had already written in *The Interpretation of Dreams*: "Child psychology, in my opinion, is destined to perform the same useful services for adult psychology that the investigation of the structure or development of the lower animals has performed for research into the structure of the higher classes of animals. Few deliberate efforts have hitherto been made to make use of child psychology for this purpose."

The developmental approach pervades the *Three Essays*. He showed that what he called the "sexual instinct" underwent a series of "transformations," and could be shaped by experience into many different forms. Freud, by the way, was no naive environmentalist; he was aware that the phenomena he described always involved an interaction of hereditary and environmental factors.

Freud's focus on development throughout childhood allowed him to explain the many directions taken by adult personality. Why does a man fall in love with a certain type of woman? Why is one person sexually aroused by members of the opposite sex, another by undergarments, and a third by members of the same sex? Why are some individuals hypersexual and others relatively unresponsive? The answers to such questions, he argued, were to be found in the person's history, in childhood sexual and personal experiences of which the adult forms were the end result. The idea of "prototypes" was central here. Early experience laid down the images, emotional predispositions, and expectations that determined adult choice and action. As Freud observed:

> It often happens that a young man falls in love seriously for the first time with a mature woman, or a girl with an elderly man in a position of authority; this is clearly an echo of the phase of development that we have been discussing, since these figures are able to re-animate pictures of their mother or father. There can be no doubt that every object-choice whatever is based, though less closely, on these prototypes. . . . In view of the importance of a child's relations to his parents in determining his later choice of a sexual object, it can easily be understood that any disturbance of those

relations will produce the gravest effects upon his adult sexual life. Jealousy in a lover is never without an infantile root or at least an infantile reinforcement. If there are quarrels between the parents or if their marriage is unhappy, the ground will be prepared in their children for the severest predisposition to a disturbance of sexual development or to a neurotic illness.

These ideas about childhood prototypes are examples of psychoanalytic theory that has passed into the common domain; it is important to remember that they were not known before Freud.

The *Three Essays* began with a discussion of homosexuality—what Freud called "inversion"—and proceeded to a consideration of a wide variety of sexual preferences and practices: bisexuality, fetishism, fixations on particular body parts or practices, sadism and masochism, and the sexual life of neurotics. In contrast to many of his contemporaries who simply labeled such conditions as "perverse," he saw them as understandable outcomes of psychological development. While, in other places, Freud thought that "homosexual libido" was an inner danger to men, his treatment of the topic in the *Three Essays* was balanced and accepting. He noted that homosexuality was a valued practice in the high civilization of Athenian Greece and reviewed the many different forms and practices that fall under this label, as well as working out a model that traced adult sexual identity to the complex course of childhood relationships.

The general idea that sexuality appears in infancy and runs through childhood was one of Freud's most creative achievements. His understanding of the role of personal history and prototypes naturally led him to an elaboration of infantile sexuality, which was presented in the second of the *Three Essays*. He began with a discussion of "infantile amnesia," explaining how almost no one remembers the sexual experiences of their early years. He continued with an exposition of his well-known theory of the stages of "psycho-sexual" development: oral, anal, oedipal, and latency. He pointed to the sensual-sexual nature of nursing and sucking and connected it with adult orality: kissing, drinking, smoking, and hysterical vomiting. He discussed anality and connected the conflicts of this stage with compliance and disobedience. Throughout these accounts, great stress was laid on early bodily and physical sensations and on experiences of pleasure and pain. There was, here, the important recognition of a language of the body, a dialect of physical and emotional symbols.

Freud's theories of infantile sexuality have been enormously significant: few modern parents see or treat their children without some influence from his ideas. At the same time, many of his specific concepts were only partly true or incorrect. His focus on "erotogenic zones"—the mouth, anus, and genitals—was far too restrictive. Babies encounter the world through sucking, but also through looking, touching, clinging, and relating. A great deal of modern research has expanded the components of this first stage far beyond Freud's idea of "orality." The same is true of his conception of "anality"; the conflicts of this stage are not so much the pleasures and frustrations of an "erotogenic zone" as they are battles that pit the young child's emerging autonomy against adult authority. Still, these later ideas rest on the platform of Freud's initial contributions.

Freud's discussion of the different forms of infantile sexuality was interlaced with his theory of unconscious conflict. Sexual desire from nursing onward, in his view, was opposed by the requirements of civilization, the imposition of restrictions that associate sexual pleasure with disgust, shame, and morality. This supposedly reached its peak in the Oedipus complex, where the boy confronted "castration anxiety" and the girl "penis envy." In a footnote added to the *Three Essays* in 1920, he wrote:

> It has justly been said that the Oedipus complex is the nuclear complex of the neuroses, and constitutes the essential part of their content. It represents the peak of infantile sexuality, which, through its after-effects, exercises a decisive influence on the sexuality of adults. Every new arrival on this planet is faced by the task of mastering the Oedipus complex; anyone who fails to do so falls a victim to neurosis. With the progress of psychoanalytic studies the importance of the Oedipus complex has become more and more clearly evident; its recognition has become the shibboleth that distinguishes the adherents of psychoanalysis from its opponents.

Note the grand sweep of the theory. It is "every new arrival on this planet" who must master the Oedipus complex: every person, in all societies, throughout history, regardless of their individual experience. The Oedipus complex became, as he put it, the, "shibboleth that distinguishes psychoanalysis from its opponents." Shibboleth is an Old Testament term meaning a criterion or test that is used to distinguish religious believers from heretics, and this is precisely what Freud had in mind; anyone who questioned this dogma could not remain within the psychoanalytic fold.

Because Freud's invention of the Oedipus complex, and his promotion of it to a universal law, were strategies for overcoming his early traumatic losses, it is no surprise that in his theory of anxiety, he placed the greatest emphasis on the threat of castration. Although he was aware of other forms of childhood anxiety, he retreated from this knowledge, and reformulated anxiety in purely sexual terms: "Anxiety in children is originally nothing other than an expression of the fact that they are feeling the loss of the person they love. It is for this reason that they are frightened of every stranger. They are afraid in the dark because in the dark they cannot see the person they love; and their fear is soothed if they can take hold of that person's hand in the dark." This statement is consistent with a contemporary understanding of attachment and separation anxiety. But Freud could not leave it in this form; he had to reverse the relationship of anxiety and sexuality in the next passage: "It is only children with a sexual instinct that is excessive or has developed prematurely or has become vociferous owing to too much petting who are inclined to be timid. In this respect a child, by turning his libido into anxiety when he cannot satisfy it, behaves like an adult." The second passage has things backward, since what constituted "too much petting" in Freud's day would now be seen as the necessary contact between infant and caretaker to produce a secure attachment. It is deprivation of such contact that produces anxiety—fear of loss of the loved person—not an excessive amount of sexuality.

There are a number of related problems in the *Three Essays*. Freud mentioned real traumas—like anxiety caused by the loss of love—at various points, but pushed them aside in the final theoretical formulations, where sexuality as overarching explanation took center stage. In certain passages Freud reduced a variety of activities to their sexual foundation, attempting to explain looking, touching, an "instinct for knowledge," sleep disturbances, and a variety of other childhood symptoms as transformations of the sexual instinct. For example, he wrote: "It is easy to establish . . . that all comparatively intense affective processes, including even terrifying ones, trench upon sexuality—a fact which may incidentally help to explain the pathogenic effect of emotions of that kind. In schoolchildren dread of going in for an examination or tension over a difficult piece of work can be important not only in affecting the child's relations at school but also in bringing about an irruption of sexual manifestations."

No evidence supports these ideas. While the emergence of sexuality in adolescence can be disruptive for some, "terrifying" experiences and "dread" of school cannot be accounted for in terms of the strength of the sexual instinct. The person who has been sexually molested or otherwise traumatized in childhood might certainly experience terror and dread in adolescence, but this is not what Freud claimed.

In addition to his sweeping oedipal theory and mishandling of anxiety, the *Three Essays* is marred by Freud's biases against women. He unequivocally equated femininity with "passivity"—and connected this to "masochism"—and masculinity with "activity" and "sadism." This led to his assumption that women were biologically predisposed to masochism. He also assumed that all women experienced "penis envy" when they discover the anatomical difference between the sexes. Speaking of the erotic life of women, he wrote:

> It is an instructive fact that under the influence of seduction children can become polymorphously perverse, and can be led into all possible kinds of sexual irregularities. . . . In this respect children behave in the same kind of way as an average uncultivated woman in whom the same polymorphously perverse disposition persists. Under ordinary conditions she may remain normal sexually, but if she is led on by a clever seducer she will find every sort of perversion to her taste, and will retain them as part of her own sexual activities.

Freud's ideas about anxiety, sexuality, and women were the most striking areas where his disavowed traumas and conflicts intruded into his theories. The underlying meaning of sexuality for Freud becomes clear if the words *longing for early love* are substituted for *sexual instinct.* Sexuality and love are not unconnected, of course, and this accounts, in part, for the appeal of these ideas; the sexual instinct theory contains a partial or disguised truth, since the experiences of the earliest attachments involve physical contact, nursing, pleasurable sensations, and intimacy with the mother. The traumatic losses of Freud's infancy left him with a powerful longing for these early, pleasurable, "infantile-sexual" experiences, along with a dread of reexperiencing the helplessness and terror associated with them. It was this fear that he mastered by becoming such a moralistic, dutiful, and hardworking young boy. The wish for pleasure was projected onto his sisters and, later, onto women in general; he remained "civilized" and in control of his impulses. And it was this same intense conflict between longing and fear that stood behind his conception of sexuality as the most powerful—the most dangerous and disruptive—of drives. In short, his dread of giving in to his infantile yearnings was transformed, in his theories, into the image of a menacing sexual instinct.

Sexuality, for Freud, had the lure of an addictive substance. It was always tempting; because giving in to it could take one over, it had to be controlled, mastered, sublimated, and channeled into socially acceptable activities. This view reflects Freud's individual experience; an alluring and dangerous sexuality is the fantasy of someone who has been, and continues to be, deprived. Freud's view of sexuality went hand in hand with his use of addictive substances to cope with his anxiety and deprivation. He was still taking cocaine—his anti-anxiety, anti-depressant drug—in the 1890s and was, by his own admission, addicted to nicotine, smoking about twenty cigars a day, for the rest of his life. In *Sexuality in the Aetiology of the Neuroses,* published in 1898, he noted the connection between addiction and sexuality:

> Left to himself, the masturbator is accustomed, whenever something happens that depresses him, to return to his convenient form of satisfaction. . . . For sexual need, when once it has been aroused and has been satisfied for any length of time, can no longer be silenced; it can only be displaced along another path . . . Not everyone who has occasion to take morphia, cocaine, chloral-hydrate . . . acquires in this way an "addiction" to them. Closer inquiry usually shows that these narcotics are meant to serve— directly or indirectly—as a substitute for a lack of sexual satisfaction.

Substituting early longing, or love in the wider sense, for sexuality gives the ideas expressed in this statement a clearer meaning. Masturbation can be a way to deal with feelings of deprivation, a form of "self-soothing," as it would be described today. But Freud could not allow himself this pleasure, certainly not by late childhood when he was lecturing his sisters and friends on the need to control their forbidden satisfactions. Cocaine and nicotine were also substitute forms of satisfaction, ways of alleviating pain and deprivation.

By 1905, Freud had formulated the core psychoanalytic ideas on which his fame rests. He had gotten rid of his first collaborator Josef Breuer, was done with Wilhelm Fliess, had broken through his phobia and traveled to Rome, and taken the steps to become a professor. As his seminal publications began to attract attention after the turn of the century, he was ready to put his dream of empire into practice, ready to welcome the "followers" that he had long coveted.

PART THREE

The Psychoanalytic Movement: 1902–1939

CHAPTER 13

The Psychoanalytic Movement: Images of War

*Potent men digest hardly anything that sets up a power to bridle their
affections, and learned men anything that discovers their errors and thereby
lessens their authority*

—Thomas Hobbes, *The Leviathan*

BEGINNING IN the early years of the century, Freud's books and lectures at the
university began to attract the attention of a small group of physicians and intellectuals. Wilhelm Stekel, a general medical practitioner with a flair for journalism, had read *The Interpretation of Dreams* and written a favorable review in a
Viennese newspaper; in 1902, he sought out Freud and suggested that they form
a small group to discuss psychoanalysis. Freud invited two physicians who had
been attending his lectures, Max Kahane and Rudolf Reitler, as well as another
general practitioner, Alfred Adler, to come to his office on Wednesday evenings
for discussions of psychoanalysis; the "Wednesday Society" was born.

The excitement of the early meetings is easy to imagine. As Stekel put it:
"These first evenings were inspiring. We found some random themes to talk
about and everybody participated in a real discussion. On the first night we
spoke about the psychological implications of smoking. There was complete har-
mony among the five, no dissonances; we were like pioneers in a newly discovered land, and Freud was the leader. A spark seemed to jump from one mind to
the other, and every evening was like a revelation." Stekel wrote popular pieces
for several Viennese newspapers, including a regular Sunday column in the *Neue
Weiner Tagblatt*, in which he brought psychoanalytic ideas to the attention of the
wider public. He even gave an account of the first meeting of the Wednesday
Society in the *Prager Tagblatt* in January of 1903, with the participants disguised:

Freud was "the Master," Adler "the Socialist," Kahane "the Relaxed," Reitler "the Reticent," and Stekel himself "the Restless."

New members were soon added to the small society: the musicologist Max Graf, father of the boy who would become Freud's famous case of "Little Hans," and the publisher Hugo Heller both joined in 1902. Paul Federn, a general practitioner from a family of Viennese physicians, joined in 1903 and remained a faithful colleague of Freud's to the very end. The next year he recommended another doctor, Eduard Hitschmann, who, like Federn, would remain with the movement through all the subsequent years. Hitschmann published the first popular exposition of psychoanalysis in 1911, titled *Freud's Theories of the Neuroses*, which endeared him to the professor. Fritz Wittels, later Freud's first biographer, joined in 1906, the same year that Adler recommended a poor, self-educated, factory worker named Otto Rank, who became the group's first secretary and, as the years progressed, Freud's right-hand man and writing collaborator.

The society met at Freud's apartment; black coffee and cakes were served, along with cigarettes and cigars, which were consumed in great quantities. Freud's son Martin later commented that when he went into the room after the meetings, he wondered how the men had been able to breathe, the smoke was so dense. From the outset, the atmosphere of the meetings was one in which the original contributions of others were encouraged, but only up to a point. As Graf put it:

> The gatherings followed a definite ritual. First, one of the members would present a paper. . . . After a social quarter of an hour, the discussion would begin. The last and decisive word was always spoken by Freud himself. There was an atmosphere of the foundation of a religion in that room. Freud himself was its new prophet who made the heretofore prevailing methods of psychological investigation appear superficial . . . Freud's pupils—he was always addressed as "The Professor"—were his apostles. . . . Good-hearted and considerate though he was in private life, Freud was hard and relentless in the presentation of his ideas. . . . I was unable and unwilling to submit to Freud's "do" or "don't"—with which he confronted me—and nothing was left for me but to withdraw from his circle.

Graf's words were echoed years later by Helene Deutsch, one of Freud's most loyal adherents: "[His] pupils were to be above all passive understanding listeners . . . projection objects through whom he reviewed—sometimes to correct or to retract them—his own ideas."

Freud celebrated his fiftieth birthday in 1906, and his pupils gave him a medal with an engraving of Oedipus to commemorate the event. The Wednesday Society had grown to almost twenty members by this time, almost all of them Jewish, about twelve of whom attended on any given evening. It included physicians interested in applying Freud's new methods to their patients, as well as a scattering of intellectuals from art, music, literature, and publishing. Visitors from other cities were also beginning to seek Freud out.

One of them was Carl Jung, a young psychiatrist on the staff of the world-famous Burghölzli Mental Hospital in Zurich, Switzerland, where he was assistant to the director, the renowned expert on schizophrenia, Eugen Bleuler. Bleuler had directed his young colleague to *The Interpretation of Dreams,* which Jung studied with great interest. In several of his early works he gave credit to Freud; in his third book, *The Psychology of Dementia Praecox,* he spoke of "the ingenious conceptions of Freud . . . [who] in his works on hysteria, compulsion neurosis, and dreams . . . has, after all, given all the essentials." The field of psychiatry, as he found it, had little to offer regarding the lives or minds of his patients; but in Freud's writings, particularly the dream book, he encountered ideas that connected with his principal interests. In addition, Jung longed for a male ideal, which he had not found in the reserved and abstemious Bleuler. Freud, in contrast, promised a relationship that was professionally stimulating and emotionally intimate; his theories connected to Jung's deepest personal concerns, arousing his hopes for an older man who would serve as mentor and model.

They began to exchange letters in April of 1906 and Jung came to Vienna to meet Freud the next year, bringing his psychiatrist colleague Ludwig Binswanger with him. During this first encounter, he was greatly impressed with Freud's stature and brilliance. Freud, determined to spread psychoanalysis beyond Vienna, set about courting Jung and, through him, Bleuler. Bringing in "the Swiss" was of great significance since Jung, Bleuler, Binswanger, and others in Zurich were gentiles—Freud was concerned that his psychoanalytic child not be branded as purely Jewish—and also carried the prestige of official psychiatry.

Jung's attraction to Freud had both personal and professional elements, and the relationship was a complex one on Freud's side, too: a mixture of political interests and personal fascination. Jung was another in the series—Braun, Fleischl, Fliess—to whom Freud was physically and emotionally drawn. There were, with each of these men, what he would later call reverberations of "unruly homosexual libido."

In 1907, Ernest Jones, then working as a physician in Toronto, came to Europe. Freud's first remark when they were introduced was that he knew, from the shape of Jones' head, that he could not be English, but must be Welsh. The young man was astonished, knowing that it was rare for someone from Central Europe to know that Wales even existed, and he was bound to Freud as a magical mind reader from this first encounter. It was only many years later that he learned that Jung had told Freud in advance of his nationality.

Another early adherent was Max Eitingon, who came from a wealthy Russian-Jewish family and had taken medical training in Germany. He, too, met Freud in 1907 and underwent an "analysis" on a few brisk walks around Vienna that made a powerful impression on the young man and converted him into a faithful follower. Also, this same year, Abraham A. Brill, a young American psychiatrist (a Jew from Hungary, he had emigrated at the age of fifteen), was put in touch with Freud through Jung. He would eventually become Freud's first English translator, as well as the leader of the psychoanalytic movement in New York.

Karl Abraham, who came from an old German-Jewish family, traveled from Berlin to Vienna and met Freud in 1907. He had talent and an interest in languages and philology, but had chosen to follow a medical career with a specialization in psychiatry. Earlier, he had taken psychiatric training in Zurich and it was during this time that Jung and Bleuler aroused his interest in psychoanalysis. He returned from his meeting with Freud greatly impressed and, by the end of the year, opened his psychiatric practice. He seems to have been unquestioningly committed to psychoanalysis from his very first contact and began a Freudian Association in 1907, which eventually grew into the Berlin Psychoanalytic Society, the most structured and organized of the early training institutes.

The first Hungarian to join the circle was Sándor Ferenczi, a physician practicing in Budapest when he discovered Freud's publications. He arranged to be introduced to the Professor on a trip to Vienna in 1908, and an instant bond developed. Freud invited the younger man to join his family on their summer vacation and, the next year, to accompany him and Jung on their trip to the United States. Ferenczi remained a close confidant and loyal member of the movement for many years.

The majority of Freud's followers were physicians, though individuals from other fields were also attracted. Hanns Sachs, like many of the early psychoanalysts, was a great reader and lover of literature. An owlish man, with thick glasses, he came from a cultured Viennese-Jewish family and was forced by his father and uncles to become a lawyer. This was an uncongenial career and, when he read *The Interpretation of Dreams,* he saw the possibility of a different path. In 1909, what he described as the most important event of his life occurred: he met Freud and joined the group of early psychoanalysts. He had found his mentor and a calling that suited his personality, and, like many of the others, would remain a loyal follower for the remainder of his life.

Oskar Pfister, a Protestant pastor from Zurich, was another nonphysician who became engrossed in psychoanalysis at this time. Pfister had long been occupied with the study of psychology in his attempts to "cure the souls" of his parishioners. Like all the other early analysts, his discovery of Freud's work was a revelation; he initiated a correspondence in 1909, became one of the first pastor-psychoanalysts, and he and the Professor remained friends and correspondents for many years to come.

From the outset, the psychoanalytic movement that grew up around Freud was a group with unique features. While it had some things in common with other scientific and intellectual endeavors, it was distinguished by the play of powerful personal forces. This was a time in European history when old societal ties were waning; Freud's early adherents did not find answers to life's larger questions in religion. While science and medicine offered professional and career gratifications, the deeper yearnings of these intelligent men remained unsatisfied. Psychoanalysis, with its focus on submerged emotions and the uncovering of secret meaning, offered a special communal experience. As the movement became increasingly defined as an embattled in-group, the members came to feel like comrades in arms in a crusade for a noble cause, men who shared special knowledge and their own private language. Karl Furtmüller, who joined the Vienna Society in 1909, described it as "a sort of catacomb of romanticism, a small and daring group, persecuted now but bound to conquer the world." The excitement produced by Freud's early discoveries gave the participants a sense that they possessed arcane secrets that set them apart and above others in their society: only they understood the unconscious meaning of neurosis and dreams, only they could trace all sorts of personal traits to their hidden roots.

Strong emotional ties bound the followers to their charismatic leader, who was much more than the first member of the Wednesday Society. As Stekel put it: "I was the apostle of Freud who was my Christ!" Freud's preeminence rested on a foundation with several interlocking components. Most important were his genius and real accomplishments. The early psychoanalysts were drawn to him after reading his published works with their revelations of unconscious conflict, neurosis, therapy, dreams, symbolism, and sexual development. They took up these theories and extended them in a variety of directions. While many of the members of the early group were bright and creative, Freud had been working on these problems longer and had a greater command of the material. Along with his brilliance and accomplishments, several other factors—his personality and the conflicts and neuroses of many of the members—bound them to him as their leader.

For these men who encountered him in the early years of the century, Freud was impressive both as a person and an intellect. He was not physically imposing—at the age of fifty, five feet seven and 126 pounds—nor was he a big-voiced orator. But he was a fine lecturer and extemporaneous speaker, had a sense of humor and a store of Jewish jokes, illustrated his points with striking images and examples, and could take up the strands of a discussion and impose order and clarity on it. He delivered all his lectures without notes. The American radical Emma Goldman, who had heard him at the university in the late 1890s, remarked: "His simplicity and earnestness and the brilliance of his mind combined to give one the feeling of being let out of a dark cellar into broad daylight. For the first time I grasped the full significance of sex repression and its effect on human thought and action. He helped me to understand myself, my own needs; and I also realized that only people of depraved minds could impugn the motives or find 'impure' so great and fine a personality as Freud." One has the impression that he spoke as he wrote: clearly, persuasively, and with great self-confidence. What he had to say fascinated his audience, and they could listen to him for hours at a time. He also seemed to be a good listener, though he always had to have the last word.

Freud possessed an air of disciplined power, of tremendous energy harnessed to a single purpose: psychoanalysis. As the devoted Hanns Sachs put it, "He was dominated by one despotic idea." Many who knew him commented on his penetrating gaze, a look that seemed to peer into the depths. Fritz Wittels described Freud's eyes as "brown and lustrous" with a "scrutinizing expression," while Joan Riviere, an English analysand and, later, translator and analyst, spoke of the "critical exploring gaze of his keenly piercing eyes," and Sachs of his "deep-set and piercing eyes." The American Mark Brunswick, a patient of Freud's in the 1920s, said that his eyes were "almost melodramatic." Freud had made the magical gaze of his former mentors his own: Brücke's terrible blue eyes that could banish death, Charcot's mesmerizing visual powers. All these qualities came together with his stature as the first psychoanalyst and made him a powerful personality, a commanding figure and natural leader.

Many of the men who were initially drawn to Freud came with their own psychological troubles. In addition to searching for new ways to understand and treat their patients, and new approaches to literature, biography, and the arts, they were also seeking, to one degree or another, cures for their own fears, symptoms, and unhappiness. Herman Nunberg, editor of the *Minutes of the Vienna Psychoanalytic Society,* noted that "at the meetings of the Society they discussed not only the problems of others, but also their own difficulties; they revealed their inner conflicts, confessed their masturbation, their fantasies and reminiscences concerning their parents, friends, wives, and children."

Stekel had originally consulted Freud for a sexual problem and had an "analysis" that lasted about eight sessions. When he first met Freud, Jung, who appeared to be a successful young psychiatrist, was, in fact, a volatile and deeply divided personality. Rank came from a harsh and impoverished background, struggled with the terrors of self-dissolution, and was terribly isolated. Freud more or less adopted him, paid for his education, and gave him a new life and career. Ferenczi was one of eleven children who suffered all his life from emotional deprivation and a longing for love and acceptance. These men were in analysis with Freud, whether it was labeled as such or not. Psychoanalysis was a means of understanding themselves, as well as a method of treatment that promised to heal them. Added to this was the fact that they were all at least a generation younger than Freud; the bonds they formed with him and psychoanalysis were reinforced by their veneration for the older Professor.

Freud's outward persona converged with his ideas and methods to make him an ideal figure in the eyes of his followers. If they were looking for the strong father they never had—as Jung and Rank so clearly were—or for the love they had missed—as was the case with Ferenczi—or for a new identity, heroic model, calling, or vocation—as was true for most of them—Freud and the fledgling movement held out enormous promise. Their ties were further intensified as they continually analyzed each other, interpreting symptoms, dreams, and slips of the tongue. Freud participated in this, but also held himself aloof, letting it be known that his unconscious conflicts had been resolved in his self-analysis. He analyzed them much more than they him. In addition, as they became full-time practitioners of psychoanalysis, they received the majority of their patients on referral from Freud. According to Stekel, "The whole clique . . . were now fed at his trough. . . . A large proportion of his important followers lived off his grace. . . . He had our business cards and bestowed patients on us as he pleased." The very livelihoods of these men depended on Freud's largesse. The effect of all this was to create, on the part of almost everyone in the society, powerful emotional bonds with the Professor. For them, he was a strong and all-wise parent figure.

In 1908 the Wednesday Society was renamed the Vienna Psychoanalytic Society. With contacts in Europe and America, the stage was now set for the first international meeting, or "congress," which was held in Salzburg, halfway between Vienna and Zurich, in April. The location reflected the two major centers of psychoanalysis: the larger, and predominantly Jewish, Vienna Society, which comprised half those attending the congress, and the Swiss, among whom Jung was the most prominent. In fact, Freud put Jung in charge of arranging the meeting and was beginning to promote him as his successor, moves which were beginning to stir up animosity among his Viennese followers. Forty-two psychoanalysts came to Salzburg, the greatest number from Austria and Switzerland, but also small groups from the United States, England, Germany, and Hungary.

At the Salzburg Congress, Abraham gave a paper on the "Psychosexual Differences between Hysteria and Dementia Praecox," Jones spoke on "Rationalization in Everyday Life," Adler presented "Sadism in Life and in Neurosis," and Jung lectured on "Dementia Praecox." But it was Freud's presentation that made the most vivid impression; he spoke for three hours, as usual without notes, about his case of "The Man with the Rats." When he offered to stop, the audience urged him on for another two hours. This was the case that he would write up that summer and publish in 1909 as *Notes Upon a Case of Obsessional Neurosis,* the third of his long case studies, preceded by *Dora* and, also in 1909, *Little Hans.*

The young patient, whose real name was Ernst Lanzer, was called "the Rat Man" because of an obsession with rats that originally broke out, along with a number of other tormenting obsessive-compulsive symptoms, when he was on military training maneuvers. The precipitating event was overhearing a captain who "was obviously fond of cruelty" describe a sadistic torture involving rats.

Ernst could not rid himself of the thought that the torture would be applied to the woman he loved and to his father, and was preoccupied with a number of rituals with which he attempted to ward off these terrible thoughts.

The Rat Man was afflicted with a number of complicated compulsive rituals, obsessive ideas, and fantasies, along with fears and inhibitions, both in his work and sexual lives, which Freud labored patiently to understand. Ernst felt his thoughts had the power to harm and kill others, particularly his father, who was already dead, as well as the woman he loved. In Freud's view, the central causes of the neurosis were Ernst's divided attraction to men and women and the mixture of love and hate that he felt toward his father. While the patient consciously saw his father as an admirable and loving man, the underlying hate, which emerged symbolically in the thought that the rat torture would be applied to him, was accompanied by intense fear and guilt. This guilt was also mixed up with his sexuality, because his father had interfered with his childhood sexual play. When the thought of the rat torture being applied to his father intruded into his mind, he would then need to undo it with various private word games and prayers, which Freud used to illustrate the role of magical thinking in obsessive-compulsive neuroses.

In the course of the analysis, Freud uncovered an entire glossary of rats. They stood for the father himself, who was a gambler (in German, *Spielratte;* literally, "gambling rat"); for money; for penises; for filthy creatures that spread disease, especially syphilis with its sexual connotations; for children—Ernst had three older sisters and a younger brother and sister, several of whom were involved in his childhood sexual games—and, finally, for the patient himself who, at a key point in the analysis, recovered the memory of how he had been severely punished by his father for biting a nurse, for acting like a nasty little rat.

The audience who heard Freud's presentation at the Salzburg Congress was awed by his skillful use of psychoanalytic interpretations to untangle the mystery of the Rat Man's neurosis. The very fact that Freud was able to see meaning in the meaningless, to impose order on the patient's chaotic mental productions, was tremendously impressive. Freud, too, was very fond of this case, and he lectured about it more than any other. But, as was typical, he presented an incomplete picture of the analysis. He asserted that the treatment "led to the complete restoration of the patient's personality, and to the removal of his inhibitions," though evidence indicates that this was only partly true. Freud, as his correspondence made clear, needed a successful case to impress his international followers, so he exaggerated the degree of Ernst's improvement.

Freud did not mention a number of important factors that were prominent in the life of this deeply disturbed young man. Ernst's mother was completely left out of Freud's published report, which depicted the father as the central figure, even though the mother was frequently mentioned in Freud's daily notes (which are available for this case) and was a dominating presence in his adult life. For instance, he needed to get her permission to see Freud, and she controlled his money, even though he was a twenty-nine-year-old attorney. Freud also did not make much of the fact that Ernst suffered several traumas related to loss and abandonment, particularly the death of an older sister to whom he was very close, when he was three and a half.

While Freud attributed the successful outcome of the analysis to his interpretive reconstructions, several other factors were clearly at work. In contrast to Dora, Freud obviously liked this young man, who had read his books, and whom he described as "clear-headed and shrewd." He conveyed his respect and care, let Ernst know that he was not an evil or bad person because of the thoughts and fantasies the young man viewed as horrible and disgusting—including aggressive thoughts directed at Freud—and, on one occasion, fed him a meal. Together, they became engaged in a complex decoding of the meaning of all the obsessions and compulsions, an arena where Freud's skill could be displayed and he was most comfortable. This was the one of Freud's published cases where the patient openly expressed his conflicted feelings toward Freud—where the transference was centrally involved in the treatment. At one point, Ernst got off the couch because he was frightened that Freud would beat him for his evil thoughts, but Freud, unlike his father, who did punish him for his aggression and assertiveness, was accepting of this reaction.

Freud's blind spots caused him to leave out or misinterpret several other events implicated in his patient's symptoms. The mother's five other children probably made her unavailable to her son when he was small, forcing him to turn to his sister Camilla, six years older, for love and comfort. He also played sexual games with this sister, and her death when he was three and a half, coincident with the biting incident and his punishment, was a crucial traumatic event in the formation of his neurosis. While Freud was aware of all this, his inability to see the father clearly blinded him to the emotional impact of these factors on his patient.

Ernst's father had been a soldier and, when his son was small, would lose his temper and beat him. Freud wrote of him:

> By all accounts our patient's father was a most excellent man. Before his marriage he had been a non-commissioned officer, and, as relics of that period of his life, he had retained a straightforward soldierly manner and a *penchant* for using downright language. Apart from those virtues which are celebrated upon every tombstone, he was distinguished by a hearty sense of humour and kindly tolerance towards his fellow-men. That he could be hasty and violent was certainly not inconsistent with his other qualities, but was rather a necessary complement to them; but it occasionally brought down the most severe castigations upon the children, while they were young and naughty.

Using one of his typical rhetorical devices—calling the father's "haste" and "violence" toward his children "necessary complements" to his "humour" and "kindly tolerance"—Freud pictured him as a sympathetic figure and explained away his violence toward his son as a relic of his "straightforward" and "hearty" soldierly ways. Freud went on:

> When he was very small [between three and four]—it became possible to establish the date more exactly owing to its having coincided with the fatal illness of an elder sister [Camilla]—he had done something naughty [the biting incident], for which his father had given him a beating. The little boy had flown into a terrible rage and had hurled abuse at his father even while he was under his blows. . . . The patient believed that the scene made a permanent impression upon himself as well as upon his father. His father, he said, never beat him again; and he also attributed to this experience a part of the change which came over his own character. From that time forward he was a coward—out of fear of the violence of his own rage. His whole life long, moreover, he was terribly afraid of blows, and used to creep away and hide, filled with terror and indignation, when one of his brothers or sisters was beaten.

It was Freud's interpretation that the terror felt by a three-year-old when he was beaten came from "fear of the violence of his own rage." No doubt the young boy felt anger, along with fear, humiliation, disappointment in his father, and guilt. But research on physical abuse in childhood reveals that three-year-olds are terrified when they are beaten by grown men. However, Freud was unable to see things from the child's point of view; his unquestioning acceptance of the father's authority, and his positive view of his "soldierly" ways, blinded him to this simple explanation. In his interpretation of the patient's symptoms, he connected the "cruel captain" to the father, but made little of the physical abuse, focusing, instead, on the patient's sexual and aggressive drives. The rats of Ernst's obsession, according to Freud, represented, at the deepest level, his greed and oral aggression.

There was an additional source of Ernst's terror as a child. His father threatened him with death and/or castration if he was "naughty"—that is, sexual. He then played sexual games with Camilla, who died, giving added force to the terrible fears connected to his father's punishment. He was convinced that if he was sexual or aggressive, he would be beaten or die. In the analysis, he described "the greatest fright of his life": he was playing with a stuffed bird, shortly after the death of his sister, when he thought it moved, and was terrified that it had come back to life. Freud interpreted this as symbolizing an erection caused by the movement of his hands; that is, he moved away from the patient's death fear and interpreted this memory in sexual terms. While there was much that Freud was able to help Ernst Lanzer understand about his disabling symptoms, his neglect of the mother's role, insistence on interpretations in terms of sexuality, and avoidance of the terrors associated with death and the father's violence seriously distorted his understanding of the Rat Man.

The Salzburg Congress of 1908 was a great success and led to the establishment of the first psychoanalytic journal, the *Jahrbuch für Psychoanalytische und Psychopathologische Forschungen,* or *Yearbook,* with Jung as editor. Freud's followers returned to their native cities and set about establishing local psychoanalytic societies, outposts of the new movement: Abraham in Berlin, Brill and Jones in the United States, Ferenczi in Budapest, and Jung in Zurich.

At the conclusion of the meeting, Freud's half brother Emanuel, seventy-five years old but still vigorous, turned up unexpectedly, and they spent some time talking over family matters and taking in the local tourist attractions. In the fall, Freud made a much longed-for visit to England to see his half brothers and their families. There he renewed his acquaintance with Emanuel's daughter Pauline, though her brother John, Freud's first playmate, seemed to have disappeared. Freud had long felt a special affection for the branch of the family that emigrated to England when Jacob's business collapsed in Freiberg so many years earlier. Emanuel's son Sam, who had taken control of his father's affairs in Manchester, would become an important source of support for Freud's own family in later years.

On his return from England, Freud stopped for four days in Zurich to see Jung. They spent as much as eight hours a day walking and talking, during which Freud attempted to persuade his Swiss follower to apply psychoanalytic doctrines to the study of psychoses and promised to make him second in command of the burgeoning movement.

Freud's famous *Analysis of a Phobia in a Five-Year-Old Boy* was published in the same year as his study of the Rat Man, though the treatment took place some time earlier. This was the case of "Little Hans" (his real name was Herbert Graf; he went on to become the stage director of the New York Metropolitan Opera), which has, over the years, been cited as evidence in support of the Oedipus complex. Hans was the son of the music critic Max Graf, a member of the Wednesday Society, who later became disaffected with psychoanalysis, and his wife, who had briefly been one of Freud's patients. Freud only saw the little boy on one occasion, the rest of the time serving as adviser-consultant to the father, who carried out the treatment, which was reported back to the Professor. Freud used these reports as the basis for his published case study.

Hans suffered from a phobia of horses, a fear that they would bite him or fall down in the street and "make a row." Freud interpreted the horses as symbolizing the father and the biting as feared castration for Hans's sexual desire for his mother. Following Freud's instructions, Hans's father, acting as his son's analyst, repeatedly interpreted the little boy's sexual curiosity, his interest in where babies come from, his feelings for his parents, and his fears in these oedipal terms.

Even in Freud's own published version of the case, however, it was clear that Hans did not confirm these interpretations and that a number of other factors were active in his life that explained his conflicts and anxieties in a more convincing manner.

Hans was more frightened of his mother than his father, for she threatened him with castration, telling him at one point, "If you do that [touch your penis] I shall send you off to Dr. A. to cut off your widdler." She also threatened him with abandonment, as the following dialogue makes clear. Father: "And have I threatened you I shan't come home?" Hans: "Not you but Mummy. Mummy told me she won't come back." In fact, the parents got a divorce shortly after the incidents reported in the case, a significant event that Freud failed to mention. Hans observed his mother using physical punishment on his baby sister, and he associated the baby's screams with his fear of horses "making a row." The mother also warned him that he would be whipped with a carpet beater if he misbehaved. Shortly before his phobia appeared, he had a tonsillectomy, with the characteristic fears that such an operation sets off in a young child. And then there was the birth of his younger sister, which did, indeed, arouse rivalrous death wishes, not against the father-as-oedipal-rival but at the new baby, who further threatened his tie to his mother. Seen in retrospect, the case gives scant support for Freud's oedipal theory. Hans's phobia is much better explained in terms of the real physical harm—the tonsillectomy, actual castration threats, beatings—and fear of abandonment.

Freud had begun work on what was to be a general account of psychoanalytic technique in 1908, but then put it aside to prepare the Rat Man case for presentation at the Salzburg Congress. There were further delays, and he finally published six papers between 1911 and 1915 that defined, in unequivocal terms, what has come to be known as the standard, or "classical," psychoanalytic method. Patients contract for a fixed series of hours—originally six per week, later changed to five—for a set fee. They are instructed in "the fundamental rule" of free association: they are to communicate everything that occurs to them, without censorship, while the analyst listens with "evenly hovering attention." Resistance to such open communication immediately becomes apparent, and the analyst's principal task is to interpret it. The patient's transference reactions also become manifest; in Freud's view, these were also resistances that must be dealt with. The analyst should act like "a surgeon who puts aside all his feelings, even his human sympathy, and concentrates his mental forces on the single aim of performing the operation as skillfully as possible."

The classical analyst has become a popular icon: the bearded man, sitting behind the couch, saying almost nothing: an image consistent with the method Freud advocated. He recommended the couch because, as he once said, he did not like being stared at for eight hours a day; whether it was best for all patients, or for all therapists, was never tested, but he was more comfortable relating via language and minimizing direct emotional contact. The analyst "should be opaque to his patients and, like a mirror, should show them nothing but what is shown to him." He must be "neutral," "anonymous," and "abstinent." As Freud put it later, "*Analytic treatment should be carried through, as far as is possible, under privation—in a state of abstinence.*" Normal social intercourse, answering questions, revealing things about himself, are all potential forms of "gratification" that are assumed to contaminate the treatment. At its most extreme, this becomes the caricatured Freudian who does not even say hello or good-bye. His task, if he is a purist, is to make interpretations of the patient's unconscious productions and nothing else.

While it is clear that Freud's technical recommendations had a far-reaching influence on the later practice of psychoanalysis, his own work with patients was quite variable and frequently did not conform to his own prescriptions. Sometimes he followed his rules and, at others, departed from them in rather remarkable ways. In one case in 1910, Bruno Walter, then the conductor of the Vienna Opera, sought Freud out because of a "professional cramp" in his right arm that he feared was an incipient paralysis that could endanger his career. Expecting a long psychoanalytic treatment, he was surprised when Freud instructed him to travel to Italy for a few weeks, forget about his arm, and just use his eyes. When Walter returned, with his arm little better, Freud told him to start conducting again. The following dialogue then took place:

WALTER: "But I can't move my arm."
FREUD: "Try it, at any rate."
WALTER: "And what if I should have to stop?"
FREUD: "You won't have to stop."
WALTER: "Can I take upon myself the responsibility of possibly upsetting a performance?"
FREUD: "I'll take the responsibility."

Freud's confident suggestions were effective in removing the symptom, though the two men then engaged in a longer process of self-exploration that Walter found helpful in "finding my way back to my profession." Nevertheless, the example shows Freud playing the magical healer in a way quite at odds with his technical recommendations.

In the fall of 1909, Freud, at the height of his psychoanalytic powers, analyzed a young man named Albert Hirst. Albert's treatment, which was a great success, was never publicly referred to by Freud, nor has it been mentioned in any of the biographies; it is only known from the patient's account, given many years later. Albert was the nephew of Freud's former patient Emma Eckstein; he knew about his aunt's treatment, which, in the family's view, was a great success, and this reinforced his belief that Freud was a great man and a genius. He was first seen in 1903 when he was sixteen years old, but his parents broke off the treatment after two weeks. The analysis itself took place over ten months, beginning in the fall of 1909, when he was twenty-three.

Albert was the third child of wealthy parents, preceded by two sisters, one of whom died when he was one or two. His other sister, two years his senior, dominated and criticized him throughout his childhood. He felt that his mother was strict, cold, and opposed to pleasure, and that she did not love him. As a boy, he had difficulty with school despite high intelligence and was preoccupied with ethical dilemmas and masturbation, which he feared was making his mind and body deteriorate. At his worst, he doubted the reality of his own existence. In the Gymnasium, he developed an obsessive love for a girl who had no interest in him, and remained preoccupied with her for many years. His life seemed so hopeless that at age sixteen he made a suicide attempt, which led to his first brief treatment by Freud.

Albert returned to analysis at age twenty-three with the same feelings of worthlessness, self-hatred, severe doubts about his intellect, obsessive focus on the same young woman, who had, by this time, decisively rejected him, and concern that his masturbation was excessive and harmful. His sexual conflicts had taken the form of a specific symptom: he did not think that he could ejaculate inside a woman. Freud saw him six times a week with the family paying a very high fee, equivalent to $190 per session in today's terms. The young man was instructed to free-associate, and he experienced Freud's intense focus on everything he said. What is particularly important about this analysis is that Freud did not, in almost any way, follow his own technical recommendations.

Albert was fifteen minutes late for each of his early sessions, but Freud made light of this. Freud often praised and encouraged the young man, reassured him that his feelings were real and sincere, told him he had talent in interpreting his own dreams, and valued his discussions of novels. At one point, Freud told him that he was more intelligent than his sister, spoke of his unusually good mind, and said, "You aren't a weak person, you are very strong." Albert reported that Freud's praise was of enormous benefit to him, since he was convinced it was the word of a genius. Freud's treatment of his patient's sexual fears and inhibitions did not seem to involve any of the theory-based interpretations that were so prominent in many of his other cases, such as the women in the *Studies* or Dora. Rather, he reassured Albert that masturbation was not destructive and encouraged him to seek sexual contact with women. During the analysis, Albert met a young woman, took her to a Viennese hotel that specialized in renting rooms for liaisons, and attempted to have sex with her. He had trouble with ejaculation, but Freud, in the sessions that followed, encouraged him, assuring him that he would succeed. When he did, Freud prescribed a vaginal suppository to use as a contraceptive, so that Albert could increase his pleasure. He carried on a very active sexual relationship with this woman for some time. Later, he met another young woman, and, even though he was uncertain of his interest, Freud insisted that Albert take her to bed, which he did.

Albert had the idea that his analysis would lead to the discovery of an early trauma. While Freud did not make much of this, the young man recollected a scene from early childhood when, suffering with diarrhea, he woke his parents in the middle of the night and heard his father say, with much irritation, "I could choke the bastard." He believed that this was his trauma, and Freud agreed with him. It was shortly after discussing this incident in his analysis that he overcame his sexual block. The father broke off the analysis after ten months, and Albert emigrated to New York the next year, got married two years later, and had a son two years after that.

While one cannot know everything that went on in Albert's analysis, his own detailed account makes plain what was helpful to him. First and foremost was the relationship with a great man whom he idolized. Freud expressed keen interest in his patient, made clear that he liked and valued him, gave advice and instructions on how to handle his sexual and work difficulties—in short, he filled the role of caring and guiding parent, providing what was lacking in Albert's family. Freud's stance was a sharp contrast to the cold mother, who was opposed to her son's pleasures, and his overall concern contrasted starkly with the way Albert was treated by his insensitive father. Freud was never neutral, abstinent, or a blank screen or mirror; he took a very active and directive role. Nor was he anonymous, talking openly about his own feelings, prejudices, and experiences. There were also a number of personal entanglements of a kind that Freud advised analysts to avoid. He had analyzed Hirst's aunt and seen the young man's sister briefly in treatment.

Freud was supportive and generous with Hirst, a young man deprived of love and affirmation in his family, yet the success of the work did not lead him to modify his technical rules for how one should conduct an analysis. The case was an aberration—though there were a few others—that was probably caused by two factors. Albert provided Freud with what *he* needed—unquestioning veneration of his stature and genius—which allowed the Professor to be relaxed and open. In addition, there seems to have been an identification with the sexual struggles of this young man, and Freud was able to help him achieve greater pleasure and intimacy with women than he ever found himself. But he drew no general lessons from the experience. He never wrote or spoke publicly about this successful treatment, though he made more presentations of the Rat Man, who Freud had seen around the same time, than any other of his cases. The Rat Man case lent itself to the complex decoding of unconscious symbolism that Freud was fond of, and also could be made to confirm his theories of sexual causation. The Hirst case was much more straightforward. He was an unloved young man who needed support, praise, encouragement, and a man to idolize; but none of these factors fit with Freud's theories of neuroses nor his classical treatment method. In his publications, he continued to speak of therapy in the combative-military terms that he used in the 1890s: the patient put up "resistances" and "defenses" that the analyst must attack; therapy was like surgery, the analyst had to take his scalpel to the neurosis and cut it out; the "pure gold of analysis" should not be contaminated with "the copper of direct suggestion." The case of Albert Hirst was a time-out from the psychoanalytic wars that continued to be waged, both with other patients and on the organizational front.

In 1909, Freud and Jung were invited by the American psychologist G. Stanley Hall to lecture at Clark University in Worcester, Massachusetts. Freud's Hungarian follower Sándor Ferenczi joined them for the trip. On the eve of their departure from Bremen, Germany, as they talked after dinner, Freud suddenly fainted, the first of two such episodes in Jung's presence. At this time Freud and Jung were on intimate terms; their correspondence from this period is rich in personal revelations, particularly on Jung's side. Just before the fainting episode, Jung, who was interested in archaeology, had been talking about "peat-bog corpses," the bodies of prehistoric men that had been dug up from certain bogs in a preserved state. According to Jung, this got on Freud's nerves, who several times commented: "Why are you so concerned with these corpses?"

Freud interpreted the fainting spell as due to his conviction that Jung wished to kill him and take his place, the evidence being Jung's talk about dead bodies, which was the same oedipal interpretation he had made of the first dream Jung had described to him three years earlier. The evidence for these interpretations, however, is not convincing: far from wishing to kill Freud, Jung was enormously attached to him and needed him as the wise and protective father he had never had. A more plausible explanation connects Freud's fainting with his own early losses, associated in his mind with images of death. The fainting episode occurred on the eve of a trip, after all, and Freud suffered all his life from a phobia that inhibited his ability to travel, a phobia that began when he lost his first home. He lived in Vienna from the age of five and, though he frequently complained about the city, he never considered moving. It had taken him forever to make the long-fantasized visit to Rome. So, in the simplest terms, he was anxious as he dined with Jung and Ferenczi on the eve of their departure because his lifelong travel phobia was very much alive. There were other factors as well.

Freud's life in Vienna was highly controlled, with Martha arranging everything around his needs and requirements, with each day following the same fixed pattern. The trip to the United States took him away from the safety of this highly structured life. In addition, he was traveling with the two men he felt closest to, separated from his family and familiar routine. As Jung noted: "The trip to the United States which began in Bremen in 1909 lasted for seven weeks. We were together every day, and analyzed each other's dreams." Being with Jung and Ferenczi, analyzing each other's dreams and personalities, aroused his long-

Group at Clark University, 1909. Back row: *A. A. Brill, Ernest Jones, and Sándor Ferenczi.* Front row: *Freud, G. Stanley Hall, and C. G. Jung.*

ings for intimacy. But it also set off apprehension that such intimacy would be followed by loss and helplessness. Because the early losses were represented by images of death, Jung's talk of corpses was the specific stimulus—within the larger context of the travel phobia, the absence of the safe structure of home, and the intimacy with male friends—that caused Freud to faint, a very unusual event for a fifty-three-year-old man in good health.

The fainting episode on the eve of the departure for the United States was only one indication of Freud's anxiety during this trip. The Clark lectures were a great success; he was warmly received by many prominent Americans, including the psychologist-philosopher William James and the Harvard neurologist James Jackson Putnam. The lectures themselves still read as clear, concise, beautifully constructed presentations of psychoanalysis. He was honored, his work and ideas given the recognition he always desired. Yet this did not seem to make him happy; he gave voice to a variety of physical complaints that he associated with the trip and became a vehement anti-American. His lasting feelings about the trip were disappointment and bodily discomfort.

The physical complaints that Freud attributed to his American trip were mainly gastrointestinal: upset stomach, diarrhea, and urinary problems. Some months after his return, he went to a spa for what he described as the "colitis earned in New York." Years later he was still complaining to Ferenczi of "prostate trouble" that he blamed on "embarrassing situations [trouble finding a toilet], as for the first time 10 years ago in America." If one sees his intestinal trouble, along with his other physical complaints, as symptoms of anxiety, then Freud's comment that they were brought on by cooking "so different than what he was accustomed to" is closer to the truth. He was deprived of the security of "what he was accustomed to"—not just food, but his whole life situation in Vienna. In addition, it is worth recalling that this is the same man who got an upset stomach every Sunday when he went to his mother's for a meal, a complaint that he attributed to the food eaten the night before. Just as he was unable to openly acknowledge the fear and anger associated with his mother, so he put the blame for his digestive problems on the United States—its food, its lack of convenient toilets.

After the lectures at Clark, Freud, Ferenczi, and Jung were invited to Putnam's camp in the mountains, where they sat around a campfire and ate charcoal-grilled steaks. According to Freud's nephew Edward Bernays, this struck his uncle as a form of "savagery." The Professor also disliked being called by his first name by the informal Americans, nor was he pleased when they questioned his theories. This lack of respect for authority made his democratic hosts less controllable than his European pupils. Freud's hatred of the United States, which began at this time, lasted for the rest of his life. Typical are the following comments: "America is gigantic, but a gigantic mistake"; "America is useful for nothing else but to supply money"; "is it not sad that we are materially dependent on these savages, who are not a better class of human beings?" Despite Freud's personal displeasure with his American visit, the time there set in motion a new conquest for the movement. Brill and Jones began to plan psychoanalytic societies for the New World—Brill founded the New York and Jones the American Psychoanalytic Societies, both in 1911—and Freud continued with his plans to expand his empire beyond its beginnings in Vienna at the next International Congress, to be held in Nuremberg, Germany, in 1910. Freud had Ferenczi open the meeting by proposing that they form an International Association, to be run from Zurich, with Jung as president for life. The president would have the power to appoint analysts and would exercise complete censorship over all publications and lectures. Jung was now clearly his favorite, and he believed that the young Swiss psychiatrist was the ideal man to promote the cause. He continued to court him assiduously, both before and after the trip to the United States, and, in March of 1909, formally pronounced him his "successor and Crown Prince"—remaining the king himself, of course—and attempted to install him as leader of the International Nuremberg Congress.

The Nuremberg proposal revealed Freud the autocrat in full flower. He had long been protective of what he felt was his invention, proclaiming on several occasions that only he could determine who should call themselves a psychoanalyst and who should not, and requiring adherence to what he called the "shibboleths" of the movement. He also saw the world as a hostile place, poised to attack or misunderstand him, and felt the only way to combat this was with an army of loyal supporters, commanded by a strong leader. This was what he had in mind for the new International Association. Interestingly, Jung's chief at the Burghölzli, Eugen Bleuler, who corresponded with Freud and valued many of his psychoanalytic ideas, maintained his independence and scientific skepticism. When he saw what Freud was attempting to do with the International Association, he resigned, writing Freud a most perceptive letter: "There is a difference between us. . . . For you evidently it became the aim and interest of your whole life to establish firmly your theory and to secure its acceptance. . . . For me, the theory is only one new truth among other truths. . . . I am therefore less tempted than you to sacrifice my whole personality for the advancement of the cause. . . . the principle of 'all or nothing' is necessary for religious sects and for political parties . . . for science I consider it harmful."

Strong opposition to Freud's plan also came from another quarter: the psychoanalysts from Vienna. The largest group in the International and Freud's first supporters, they had been chafing as he ignored them in favor of Jung and the Swiss. When Stekel called a meeting of the Vienna group to discuss their opposition, Freud appeared and made an emotional plea: "Most of you are Jews, and therefore you are incompetent to win friends for the new teaching. Jews must be content with the modest role of preparing the ground. It is absolutely essential that I should form ties in the world of general science. I am getting on in years [he was fifty-four], and am weary of being perpetually attacked. We are all in danger. . . . They won't even leave me a coat on my back. The Swiss will save us—will save me, and all of you as well."

How much Freud's plea affected the Viennese is not known, though it certainly reflected his sense of personal endangerment and ambition for the movement. Eventually, a compromise was worked out. Jung would be president for two years, not for life, and he would not have censorship over publications. In addition, a new journal, the *Zentralblatt für Psychoanalyse* (the *Central Journal*) was established with Adler and Stekel as coeditors and Freud as a third reader, with each of the three having the power to veto publications. Adler was also made chairman of the Vienna Society, though here, too, Freud retained his behind-the-scenes power as chairman of the scientific sessions. These concessions calmed things down, but only temporarily.

Freud's autocratic actions were based on his conviction that he lived in a hostile world. He was convinced that psychoanalysis was a challenge to prevailing social beliefs and, because of this, his creation was scorned and attacked by the representatives of established science, medicine, psychiatry, and other fields. This version of history, including his account of his years of "splendid isolation," became the myth that was passed down by many biographers and commentators sympathetic to psychoanalysis. The truth is more complicated. There was, from the beginning, a mixed reaction to Freud's work. There were prejudicial and critical reactions, to be sure, but there were also thoughtful and appreciative reviews, as well as balanced assessments—such as those of Breuer and Bleuler—which attempted to separate those of Freud's ideas that were supported by evidence from those that were not. Certainly, by the time of the Nuremberg Congress, a great many intelligent writers in many fields saw his work as enormously original and important. But, for Freud, there could be no middle ground. You either accepted psychoanalysis in toto, or you were an enemy.

True to their origins in Freud's personality, the controlling metaphors of the movement were expressed in a language saturated with military metaphors, a language of struggle and combat. Freud felt like a small outsider, at war with a host of enemies, and this belief was legitimized and fortified by the widespread acceptance of militarist values in Europe during this time. Freud's biographer Roland Clark titled his chapter on the psychoanalytic movement "Commander in Chief"; Peter Gay called his comparable chapter "Sketch of an Embattled Founder." Similar words, images, and metaphors abounded in Freud's own writings, particularly his private correspondence. One "attacks the resistance," which is a "defense." Psychoanalysis was a movement surrounded by "enemies" and "opponents"—all those who did not accept his ideas—which the army of his adherents had to combat. His followers were "comrades-in-arms" and "partisans" who had to show their "loyalty" to the "cause." Those who disagreed were labeled "deserters" and "disloyal," and were disciplined with banishment. In January of 1911, he encouraged Jung to pursue his study of mythology, writing: I shall be very happy when you plant the flag of libido and repression in that field and return as a victorious conqueror to our medical motherland." In 1911, Stekel wrote: "We can say with pride that our teaching, which is the teaching of Freud, is daily gaining more supporters and marches forward continuously. . . . We feel in these days like brothers of an order which demands from each single one sacrifices in the service of all." The images of war, battle, and military exploits were pervasive.

While all of Freud's biographers have made much of the role of Victorian sexual repression and its influence on his theories, few have commented on the historical and cultural background for the war and battle imagery so prevalent in Freud's view of himself and the psychoanalytic movement. Yet these beliefs and attitudes, which permeated the consciousness of Europeans in the years before the First World War, were an extremely important influence on Freud's thought.

At the turn of the century, the major countries of Europe were involved in an arms race that dominated news reports; it was a time of intense national rivalries and international crises that threatened a worldwide conflict. The German socialist Eduard Bernstein had written in 1893: "This continual arming, compelling the others to keep up with Germany, is itself a kind of warfare . . . one could say it is a cold war. There is no shooting but there is bleeding." The air was also full of reports about the founding of empires and competition among the great powers to extend their rule to foreign lands. The European arms race, with its attendant glorification of war and empire, found a most receptive audience in Freud and a number of his followers.

Although the early twentieth century in Europe was a time of extraordinary dynamism and change, with new social and political movements, each of which offered vocabularies, images, and metaphors that Freud could have adopted in shaping psychoanalysis, he ignored them in favor of the system of beliefs and practices defined by the historian Alfred Vagts as militarism: "A vast array of customs, interests, prestige, actions and thought associated with armies and wars and yet transcending the true military purposes . . . its influence is unlimited in scope, it can permeate all society and become dominant over all industry and arts." While Freud did make some use of the metaphors of archaeology, images of war and military conquest were much more potent, and his commitment to these beliefs did not change, even after the First World War.

The glorification of war, conquest, and empire, along with Freud's personal drive to assume a heroic identity, came together in the psychoanalytic movement. His literary and rhetorical skills, and the subsequent control of documents and evidence by the faithful, allowed his version of the history of the movement to go largely unchallenged. Few have questioned the appropriateness of war and battle imagery for a profession that defines itself as science, medicine, or therapy. In addition, many who have written about the history of psychoanalysis have accepted Freud's characterization of those who disagreed with his theories as motivated by unresolved personal conflicts or suffering from resistance.

Freud's adversarial stance, present from the beginning of the movement, foreshadowed the great tragedy of psychoanalysis, the way Freud's creative accomplishments—which opened up a new world of understanding and therapy—were distorted by his belief that everyone who did not completely accept his ideas was an enemy. He had to win, to defeat his adversaries, and this mission was more important than understanding and incorporating new ideas and practices into an expanding and growing field. Freud's intolerance for the ideas of others was soon to erupt in the first big internal battle, that with Alfred Adler, just a year after the Nuremberg Congress.

CHAPTER 14

Alfred Adler:
The First Dissident

An association of men who will not quarrel with one another is a thing which never yet existed, from the greatest confederacy of nations down to a town meeting or vestry.

—Thomas Jefferson

FREUD'S ACTIONS at the Nuremberg Congress in 1910 set loose conflicts in the Vienna Psychoanalytic Society, with Alfred Adler and Wilhelm Stekel speaking out about unfair practices. All of the Viennese were angry because Freud devalued them as he promoted Jung and the Swiss. Added to this was Freud's intolerance for ideas that challenged his doctrines. The personal squabbling, disputes over priority, dissatisfaction with procedures, and Freud's high-handed management of the new International Psychoanalytic Association were all preludes to the larger and more important differences that soon broke loose. Freud had set up the Vienna group as a forum to discuss his ideas, but while he was open to the contributions of the other members, there was a line that could not be crossed. He was sympathetic to new ideas only if he could assimilate them into his existing theories. Adler had worked compatibly within the society from its inception, but as he increasingly developed his own ideas, as he became less a "pupil" and "follower" and more an independent theorist, a break with Freud was inevitable.

Alfred Adler, a practicing physician fourteen years younger than Freud, was drawn to psychoanalysis after reading *The Interpretation of Dreams*. His special talents and gifts were recognized and, for several years, he was comfortable within the movement. Freud said that Adler was the best of the Viennese analysts and even sent his brother Alexander's wife to him for treatment. He was not analyzed by Freud, however, or by anyone else; nor was he looking for a father,

Alfred Adler.

a hero, or a model, as so many of the others were. Nevertheless, in the first years, he was clearly a Freudian, framing his ideas largely in terms of sexual conflict.

Adler was born in 1870 into a Jewish family that lived on the outskirts of Vienna. His father was a corn merchant and, during the early years, the family lived a comfortable middle-class life. Sometime during Alfred's youth, his father suffered business reverses and the family fell on hard times. Alfred was the second of four brothers—there were also two younger sisters—and he felt he was always trying to catch up to his older brother, who was his mother's favorite. Interestingly, the firstborn son's name was Sigmund. Alfred suffered from rickets as an infant, which made walking difficult for many years, as well as attacks of laryngitis with frightening bouts of near suffocation. He almost died of pneumonia when he was five. By his own account, it was his identification with the doctors who saved his life that led to him to study medicine. This early identification with physicians stood in sharp contrast to Freud: Adler took healers as his first models, while Freud was enamored of generals and conquerors.

Adler's early illnesses and disabilities eventually led to "compensations," a concept central in his later theories. He was very physically active as an older child and, later, led an extremely full and productive life. The early isolation due to illness may have motivated his subsequent gregariousness; from college on he was a great patron of Vienna's cafés, where he would talk the night away with friends.

Adler described his childhood as an unhappy one. The illnesses of his early years left a legacy of what he would later call "inferiority feelings": low self-worth, and a striving to overcome. While both Adler and Freud experienced poverty during their youths, the younger man emerged from his deprived background identifying with the working class and the poor, with disadvantaged children, and with women who struggled with their degraded social position. One of his prepsychoanalytic publications was the 1898 *Health Book for the Tailor Trade,* a pamphlet aimed at ameliorating the miserable lives of this group. He became a Socialist—he would cite Marx in discussions in the Vienna Psychoanalytic Society—and, later, a Social Democrat, and his early medical practice was primarily devoted to middle- and working-class patients. When he became a psychoanalyst, he continued to work with these groups. An investigation of the social class of their respective psychoanalytic practices has shown that 74 percent of Freud's patients were wealthy, 33 percent middle class, and only 3 percent working class, while Adler saw a mix of 25 percent upper-, 39 percent middle- and 35 percent lower-class patients.

Two men could hardly have been more different than Freud and Adler. The Professor was formal and reserved, confining personal and emotional expression to his writing and a few confidants; Adler was gregarious, outgoing, and talkative. In contrast to Freud's aversion to music, Adler came from a musical family, was a fine tenor, and often had songs running though his head. While both men were born Jewish, Adler grew up in a Christian neighborhood in a family that was completely secular and did not encounter anti-Semitism as a child, nor did he identify himself as a Jew, converting to Christianity as an adult. He did not practice any religion, however, and thought of himself simply as a Viennese. Freud, while vehemently antireligious, never renounced his Jewish identity, which remained a part of his sense of himself as a persecuted outsider.

As meticulous as Freud was about his dress and appearance, Adler was careless and sloppy, a contrast also seen in their writing and presentation of ideas. Throughout his life, Freud was adept at shaping arguments and historical accounts for his own ends, a skill he employed in constructing his version of the break with Adler. What is more, they used very different vocabularies to express their ideas: Adler spoke and wrote with everyday words such as "inferiority," "compensation," "love," and "power," while Freud used terms such as "libidinal energy," "metapsychology," and "death instinct" that mixed together psychological observations and quasi-biological speculations, giving his theories an aura of depth and profundity.

Adler eventually became a lecturer, a popular philosopher, a man with a redeeming mission. He had little patience for writing; his works were not well-crafted, and many of his later books were assembled by students from his lectures. His lack of attention to the written presentation of his ideas is one reason why Freud's theories have been far more influential than his. Reading Adler today, one finds many valuable concepts that anticipate later directions in psychoanalysis, but they are presented as one would give them in a speech. The concepts are overstated, not well developed, and they lack complexity and subtlety. Moreover, Adler failed to present much in the way of evidence.

Adler looked to the future, took up the implements of the modern age, learned to drive, and loved the movies, while Freud was oriented to the past, often the ancient past, and could barely bring himself to use the telephone, even though it was available in Europe by 1880. Drawn to socialism and new educational methods, Adler believed in using psychoanalysis to reform society. In 1919, well after his break with Freud, he established Child Guidance Clinics in the Vienna schools; there were more than thirty of these clinics in existence by the 1930s, when they were closed by the Nazis. In contrast, Freud had almost no interest in politics, and on those rare occasions when he expressed an opinion, it was conservative—as, for example, his views on women or his attraction to military values. He was decidedly not a Socialist or even a Social Democrat, and there are hardly any references to the political issues of the day in his adolescent correspondence with Silberstein, or in his letters to Martha or Fliess.

Freud and Adler chose very different marriage partners. Martha was a most conventional bourgeois woman, devoted to her children and household, and unquestioning of her husband's authority. As a young man, Adler fell in love with a Russian woman named Raissa Timofeyevna Epstein, pursued her to Moscow, and persuaded her to marry him. Raissa came from a wealthy family, but she had rebelled against the frivolous life prescribed for young women of her station. She came to Vienna as a student and soon became involved with political causes. Her search for personal freedom was matched by an interest in helping her fellow Russians in their struggle with czarist oppression. Adler socialized with her émigré friends and knew Leon Trotsky when the future revolutionary leader was in Vienna before his return to Russia in 1914.

As the years passed, Raissa became more politically radical, in contrast to her husband, who, while drawn to social issues, was ever more the psychologist. The marriage was one of two strong personalities and had more than its share of conflict. Even Phyllis Bottome, whose biography of Adler vibrates with praise, commented on "the long and deep estrangement between them," due to differences in nationality, background, interests, and their strong temperaments.

While Adler and the other members of the Vienna Society were largely of one mind about psychoanalysis in the early years, and expressed their reverence for Freud, the meetings themselves were sometimes marred by harsh personal criticisms and squabbles over priority, along with that unique form of psychoanalytic attack, a mixture of argument and interpretation of motives. In a meeting in 1907, Rudolf Reitler described a paper of Stekel's as "a neurotic symptom—a wave of asexuality has surged up in the author." Stekel, in a discussion of a paper by Wittels, remarked that "the speaker has projected the unpleasant self-knowledge of his own insignificant hysteria onto a quite harmless class of people," while Eduard Hitschmann, discussing the same paper, said he "disapproves of the superficiality of the arguments." Seven months later, Wittels struck back; he "denounces the . . . arrogance shown by some of the gentlemen—Hitschmann, Stekel—who consistently overlook the facts and are interested only in theoretical-psychological aspects." In a later discussion of a paper by Isidor Sadger, Stekel said he was "horrified and fears that this work will harm our cause," and Paul Federn added that he "is indignant. Sadger has not said a single word about the poet's sexual development." Wittels countered that he "takes exception to the personal outbursts of rage and indignation on the part of Stekel and Federn."

Freud typically stayed above these frays, though he could wade in with a devastating theoretical onslaught when his ire was aroused. Adler typically softened his criticisms with praise and usually discussed the substance of the presentations, rather than the personality of the presenter. Things reached such a pitch that a proposal was made that the chairman be given the authority to suppress personal attacks and invectives, but Freud, the chairman, declined this role. From the beginning, the meetings had assumed a structured form: lots were drawn to see who would present each week's paper, everyone was obligated to speak in the discussion, and new members could only be added after an open discussion and by a unanimous vote. By early 1908, there had been sufficient discontent, both with the personal conflicts and the form of the meetings, that Adler had proposed a reorganization in which more sessions would be devoted to free and open discussion, the rule requiring that everyone speak would be abolished, and new members would be elected by secret ballot, with a simple majority required for admission. All of these proposals were intended to make the society more open and democratic. After a lively debate, a compromise was finally reached. The requirement that everyone speak was dropped, more meetings would be devoted to reviews and general discussion, but the requirement of unanimous vote for acceptance, which gave Freud a veto, was retained. The reason for this revealed the feelings of most of the members, as summarized by a committee composed of Adler, Hitschmann, and Wittels: "The assembly is something in between a group invited by Professor Freud and a society; therefore, whoever is acceptable to the Professor must also be acceptable to the others." Adler offered a partial dissent, suggesting additional monthly meetings in another locality to which all who were approved by a two-thirds majority would be admitted. This provoked another discussion, culminating in Adler's withdrawal of his proposal in favor of Freud's suggestion that if a larger group were formed, it would have no connection with his Psychoanalytic Society.

As early as 1906, Adler had been presenting his theory of "organ inferiority," based on the idea that persons with inferior organs or physical functions—poor eyesight, impaired locomotion, deafness, speech defects—were driven to overcome them, to compensate, and that this explained both healthy development and neurosis. The connection of this theory with Adler's own childhood is obvious. Adler stated that he was able to "demonstrate the existence of speech defects in singers, actors and orators [such as] Demosthenes, Moses. A profession is chosen upon the demand of the inferior organ; cooks, for example, frequently show abnormal palatal reflexes." While some members of the society were critical of the sweeping fashion with which Adler applied his theory—*every* actor or orator had a speech defect, *every* poet a visual disturbance—Freud was generally sympathetic, even commenting that "cooks very frequently incline to psychoneurotic disturbances, especially to paranoia, and that good cooks are always severely abnormal."

When Adler's book *Study of Organ Inferiority and Its Psychical Compensation* had been published in 1907, Freud was generally sympathetic, not joining in the criticisms of other members such as Stekel, who objected to the way in which Adler stretched his concept to explain almost everything about everybody. Within a short time, Adler had expanded his theory of organ inferiority to "inferiority feelings," a forerunner of his best-known concept, "the inferiority complex." He defined inferiority feelings as a regular feature of childhood, since children are small, weak, and relatively powerless in relation to adults. That such feelings produce strivings to overcome led Adler to posit an "aggressive drive," defined as: "Fighting, wrestling, beating, biting and cruelties show the aggressive drive in its pure form. Its refinement and specialization lead to sports, competition, dueling, war, thirst for dominance, and religious, social, national and race struggles. . . . When the aggressive drive turns upon the subject, we find traits of humility, submission and devotion, subordination, flaggelantism and masochism."

In addition to aggression, Adler had spoken in a 1908 paper of the "need for affection" as a basic drive: "Children want to be fondled, loved and praised. They have a tendency to cuddle up, always to remain close to loved persons, and to want to be taken into the bed with them. Later this desire aims at loving relationships from which originate love of relatives, friendship, social feelings, and love." Freud also had a concept of love in his system, but it was, throughout, entwined with his theory of the sexual instinct. While he sometimes defined "libido" in a narrow sexual sense or saw it as the pressure of undischarged instinctual energy, at other times he used it to refer to love between persons. Adler's concepts of love and affection were much closer to those contemporary approaches that stress attachment and a primary need to relate to others.

Shortly before the break with Freud, Adler had introduced his concept of the "masculine protest," which heightened the conflict between the two men. This was a further development of his idea of aggressive striving as compensation for inferiority, defined as the wish to be strong and powerful in reaction to things that make one feel "unmanly." Feeling unmanly was a version of inferiority: "masculinity" was imbued with power, strength, and aggression, and "femininity" with weakness. Adler framed the issue in sexual or gender terms because he was still part of the Freudian group, but he was very clear that these were not fixed biological characteristics; they arose from the particular way males and females were treated in European society. As he put it in 1910: "To this is added the arch evil of our culture, the excessive pre-eminence of manliness. All children who have been in doubt as to their sexual role exaggerate the traits which they consider masculine."

Children who feel weak and inferior due to clumsiness, sickness, small stature, or organ inferiorities experience these traits as unmanly. "All neurotics have a childhood behind them in which they were moved by doubt regarding the achievement of full masculinity. The renunciation of masculinity, however, appears to the child as synonymous with femininity, an opinion which holds not only for the child, but also for the greater part of our culture." In calling the "pre-eminence of manliness" the "arch evil of our culture" Adler revealed that, unlike Freud, he was critical of his society's glorification of masculinity and corresponding derogation of women.

In addition to the differences in theory, Adler's approach to therapy diverged from what had become, by this time, Freud's classical method. Adler would first diagnose the individual's "life plan" or "personal myth," his personal style, conflicts, and "mistaken" neurotic path, and then communicate this to produce understanding and insight. While this was to be done with kindness and gentleness, it was, overall, an approach that positioned the therapist as an authority who instructed the patient on his faulty ways, showing him how to give them up and move to a life governed by "community feeling." Treatment was brief, results were expected within three months, and anecdotes show Adler demonstrating to patients their mistaken assumptions with clever gambits, humor, and illustrative parables. While the theory contained many brilliant insights, the therapy was hasty and superficial.

Adler was a social activist, a man with a message; he wanted to reach a wide audience. Because of this, his later publications have an air of certainty, an inspirational quality. Freud's theoretical works, because they are the site of his disguised self-analysis, are more complex. The reader senses the underlying tension and conflicts in them; they are like fine literature in which the surface plot is enriched by submerged currents. This is the paradox: in a number of ways, Adler's ideas are quite modern, but they are presented in a way that does not convey the depth of personal conflict and emotion. Freud's theories are frequently wrong, but his writing evokes the richness of human experience.

Toward the end of 1910, Adler's exposition of new concepts had reached such a state that several members of the Vienna Society voiced open criticisms, suggesting that he had departed too far from the Professor's theories. Hitsch-mann proposed that Adler's ideas be thoroughly discussed to clarify how they differed from Freud's. Freud agreed, acting friendly toward Adler, and giving him the impression that he wanted an open and fair exchange of views. This public stance was belied by Freud's private letters to Jung, Jones, and Ferenczi, however, which were quite bellicose. There he repeatedly called Adler "para-noid," "neurotic," and a danger to psychoanalysis.

Four meetings devoted to discussions of Adler's theories were held in Janu-ary and February of 1911. Adler began his presentation with an outspoken dis-cussion of several of Freud's main tenets. He criticized interpretations in terms of drives that ignored the family and social context: "For our consideration, the constant factor is the culture, the society, and its institutions." He saw sexual drive interpretations as subsidiary to struggles within personal relationships, par-ticularly those involving inferiority feelings and the masculine protest. Adler stated: "The sexual references described by Freud are indeed found in neuroses. But my findings show that whatever one sees as sexual, behind it are much more important connections, namely the masculine protest disguised under sexuality." He specifically reinterpreted the Oedipus complex: "I have seen many patients who have come to know their Oedipus Complex very well, without feeling any improvement."

Freud responded with a forceful counterattack. While there were minor crit-icisms—he accused Adler of being "difficult to understand because of his abstract manner . . . Personally I take it ill of the author that he speaks of the same things without designating them by the same names which they already have"—his main attack centered on Adler's reinterpretation of sexuality and his emphasis on what would now be called the experience of one's self. In the 1911 meetings, Freud said:

> Two traits are evident in Adler's works: (1) an anti-sexual trend . . . he . . .
> already speaks of an asexual infantile history and (2) a trend against the
> value of the details of the phenomenology of neuroses . . . I do not con-
> sider these Adlerian doctrines insignificant and would like to predict that
> they will make a great impression, at first damaging psychoanalysis very
> much . . . it is obvious that a remarkable intellect with a great talent for
> writing is working on these matters . . . [but] the whole doctrine has a reac-
> tionary and retrograde character which thereby offers a larger number of
> pleasure premiums. For the most part it deals with biology instead of psy-
> chology and instead of psychology of the unconscious it concerns surface
> phenomena, that is, ego psychology. Finally, it deals with general psychol-
> ogy rather than the psychology of libido—sexuality. Thus, to attain superi-
> ority the doctrine will capitalize on the still existing latent resistances in
> every psychoanalyst.

The criticism that Adler did not deal with the "phenomenolgy of neuroses," that his theories were generally stated, not supplemented with evidence and detail, was well taken. The claim that Adler dealt "with biology instead of psychology" was without substance, for, with his focus on the influence of the family and society, he had, in fact, moved farther from biology than Freud. But Freud's main objections were to Adler's emphasis on the ego, or self, and his substitution of other motives for sexuality. Freud the rhetorician was also at work, characterizing Adler's ideas as subversive, potentially damaging to psychoanalysis as a movement, and invoking the familiar resistance argument.

Freud's same criticisms were repeated at greater length, and with more personal invective, in his 1914 *On the History of the Psycho-Analytic Movement*: "I may even speak publicly of the personal motive for his work since he himself announced it in the presence of a small circle of members of the Vienna group: 'Do you think it gives me such great pleasure to stand in your shadow my whole life long?' [This leads to the comments on] the profusion of petty outbursts of malice which disfigure his writings and by the indications they contain of an uncontrolled craving for priority." This was Freud's attempt to discredit Adler's ideas by interpreting them as symptoms of his ambition, just as in many other places he dealt with objections to his theories by interpreting them as resistance to sexuality.

Freud and his adherents, particularly Jones, who was not present at the time, controlled, until recently, the historical versions of the conflict with Adler in the Vienna Society. Freud devoted 20 percent of his 1914 *History* essay (twelve pages out of sixty) to the conflict with Adler. Here, Freud presented himself as a fair-minded and reasonable man, reluctantly dealing with the petty ambition and malice of an ungrateful colleague. Adler, and those siding with him, described the events from their vantage point, but this version has never received much of a hearing. When the conflict was in progress, Adler ascribed it to the intolerance for competing ideas, and restrictions on free expression, that characterized Freud and the movement.

Freud, and those loyal to him, described Adler as a difficult man, while Adler's colleagues, and others who were acquainted with him over the years, presented a very different picture. Jones said Adler was "a morose and cantankerous person, whose behavior oscillated between contentiousness and sulkiness. He was evidently very ambitious and constantly quarreling with the others over points of priority in his ideas." This description, like Freud's use of the diagnoses of neurosis and paranoia, is not supported by Adler's contributions to the Vienna Society, as revealed in the *Minutes,* nor by the accounts of many friends and colleagues who spoke of his friendly, outgoing nature, and his endless supply of jokes and instructive anecdotes. There does not seem to be any evidence that he was a person given to quarrels, though the history of the psychoanalytic movement is replete with Freud's fights with his colleagues.

The last point in Freud's attack on Adler concerned the priority of theoretical ideas. A number of important concepts were first enunciated by Adler: the stress on the self, or ego; the inferiority complex; sibling rivalry; the effect of one's position within the family—what it means to be an only child, a firstborn, the last infant—and the importance of aggression, power, and competitive striving. He also employed the term "safe guarding" for what Freud would eventually call "ego defense." Freud incorporated some of these ideas into his own theories, and others found their place in post-Freudian psychoanalysis. This makes it clear that Freud's assertion that Adler was "contentious" and driven by an "uncontrolled craving for priority" was without substance. Adler was ambitious, as were Freud himself and many others in the movement, but there were genuine contributions to back up his ambition, and he wanted them recognized.

There are also different accounts of the tone of the Vienna Society meetings. Freud later described himself as a calm and somewhat reluctant warrior. Hanns Sachs, who was present and whose loyalty to Freud cannot be questioned, said: "Freud took a prominent part in the discussion; he did not spare his opponent and was not afraid of using sharp words and cutting remarks, but never descended to personalities. . . . It may well be that Freud's incisive and harsh criticism had hurt softer feelings and made them [others who resigned from the society with Adler] willing to think that Adler's complaint of intolerance was justified."

Wittels heard about the meeting from Stekel, and reported: "Freud had a sheaf of notes before him, and with gloomy mien seemed prepared to annihilate his adversary. [Freud's supporters] made a mass attack on Adler, an attack almost unexampled for its ferocity even in the fiercely contested field of psychoanalytical controversy."

The reaction of the members of the Vienna Society was divided; Stekel, Federn, and some others felt that Adler's ideas were compatible with Freud's and, indeed, constituted important new contributions to psychoanalysis, but they were a minority. A motion was introduced labeling Adler's ideas "misconceived and dangerous" and suggesting that they had no place in the society, and this was passed by the majority. Adler resigned his position as president and Stekel, in support, stepped down as deputy. Freud also succeeded in forcing Adler out of his position as coeditor of the *Zentralblatt*, pressuring the publisher with the threat of his own resignation if Adler was not removed.

Adler stayed on for another four months before resigning from the society and forming a new group, originally called "the Society for Free Psychoanalytic Research," and later named "Individual Psychology." Nine members of the Vienna Society, six who were active and three who rarely attended the meetings, resigned in support of Adler and joined his new group. Stekel sided with Adler, but stayed on in the old society for another two years before he, too, was excommunicated.

At the conclusion of the skirmish, Freud wrote to Jung: "Rather tired after battle and victory, I hereby inform you that yesterday I forced the whole Adler gang to resign from the Society." He also wrote several letters to Jones in which his anger at Adler was palpable, commenting on his "morbid sensibility . . . clever views [which were] wrong and dangerous to psychoanalysis [and how] his motives . . . are all of neurotic source," and speaking of "the revolt of an abnormal individual driven mad by ambition, his influence on others depending on his strong terrorism and sadism." The bitterness between the two men lasted to the ends of their lives; Freud was still carrying on his argument with Adler in his 1937 essay *Analysis Terminable and Interminable.*

There were two components to Freud's powerful antipathy toward Adler: his need to dominate and control psychoanalysis, and the personal threat posed by Adler's ideas. Freud had to be the Professor, the one in control. He insisted that his doctrines prevail over all others, and challenges to this position always brought forth a strong counterattack. He had broken the loving relationship with Breuer some years earlier over this point; Adler was the next important colleague to be branded a heretic.

The second reason for Freud's hatred of Adler was more complicated. Adler's ideas can be seen as interpretations of Freud's unconscious, interpretations that Freud did not want to hear, and certainly could not accept from someone whom he had to keep in a subservient position. He eventually worked his way around to a partial acceptance of some of Adler's ideas, but he did so in his own way, in the guise of abstract theory. Adler's concepts of the "masculine protest" and the need for "power as compensation for feelings of inferiority" were ideas that struck close to the core of Freud's persona. The concept of masculine protest—that one exaggerates certain culturally defined masculine traits to repudiate threatening feelings of weakness and helplessness that are seen as feminine—fit Freud only too closely. According to Adler, "If we focus on the smallness and helplessness of the child which continues so long and which brings about the impression that we are hardly equal to life, then we must assume that at the beginning of every psychological life there is a more or less deep inferiority feeling." Not every child feels inferior to the same degree; this is determined by his or her specific experience. As Adler put it: "Difficult questions in life, dangers, emergencies, disappointments, worries, losses, especially those of loved persons, social pressures of all kinds, may always be seen as included within the framework of the inferiority feeling, mostly in the form of the universally recognizable emotions and states of mind which we know as anxiety, sorrow, despair, shame, shyness, embarrassment, and disgust."

Though Adler didn't know it, he could have been interpreting Freud's own life. Freud suffered traumatic "losses of loved persons," lived with the "dangers" of death and the "worries" of poverty and failure, and struggled with the "social pressure" of his controlling and demanding mother. And, it is clear, he felt his longing for love was "unmanly"; in his own words, he experienced eruptions of "unruly homosexual libido." Freud's childhood had left him with just the kind of inferiority feelings that Adler described, including "the emotions and states of mind we know as anxiety [and] sorrow." His childhood identification with hypermasculine heroes, his view of himself as a "conquistador," and his identity as the commander of a psychoanalytic army can all be seen as masculine protest reactions to the threat of his weak and helpless position as a child, a threat that he himself associated with "femininity" and "passivity."

Adler's theories were not only a personal threat to Freud but aroused similar reactions in other members of the psychoanalytic movement, which often seemed like a vast power struggle with Freud-the-Father in control, and the children vying to get close to him so that they could share in his success and fame. Adler's observations on sibling rivalry fit the disputes within the Vienna Society, as well as the later conflicts between Jones and Ferenczi, Abraham and Jung, Abraham and Rank, Jones and Rank, and many others. Just as Freud had to repudiate those of Adler's ideas that struck too close to his personal core, so some of his followers could not accept Adler's ideas because they themselves were living versions of these very concepts. They covered up their actions with rationalizations: *they* were not resistant to sexuality like those fainthearted others; *they* were protecting psychoanalysis from enemies, advancing the field as a science. To accept Adler's ideas about power seeking, along with his specific complaints that Freud and the movement were opposed to free debate, would have required an awareness of their own tactics.

A debate on the effects of masturbation took place in the Vienna Society in 1911–1912 immediately after the expulsion of Adler. A variety of views were expressed in these meetings, with Stekel at one extreme and Freud at the other. Stekel argued that masturbation was a normal activity and, by itself, not harmful. As he put it:

> All masturbatory activity is completely harmless and uninjurious; indeed, it often has a directly salutary effect. The typical image of the masturbator as mentally and physically deteriorated is a product only of outside influence, designed to frighten . . . women do not become anaesthetic because they have masturbated; it is the other way round: they have masturbated because access to an adequate act of gratification was, in their case closed off . . . Freud drew an incorrect conclusion in thinking that if infantile sexuality is harmful, masturbation, too, must be.

Stekel's position, which recognized the importance of social factors, the way sexuality and masturbation were defined by persons in the child's world, was consistent with Adler's. At the time of these debates, Freud was busy slandering both these colleagues in his private correspondence, calling them "paranoid." In the discussions of masturbation, Freud's own position remained where it had been in the 1890s: sexuality was itself the source of neurosis; masturbation, abstinence, and other forms of sex that were not "normal" produced anxiety and symptoms. He spoke of the "injuriousness of masturbation" and disagreed with Stekel, who believed that this idea was based on a cultural prejudice. Freud called masturbation a "vehicle of pathogenic effects" in the neuroses, and said it "has done damage," going on to comment, "we may describe . . . the *direct* injuries caused by masturbation . . . and those which arise *indirectly* from the ego's resistance and indignation against that sexual activity." He also thought that masturbation was especially harmful when coupled with fantasy.

The differences between Stekel and Freud in the masturbation debate further provoked Freud's anger at his colleague. Stekel, Freud's first public champion in Vienna and long an outspoken member of the Vienna Society, had also supported Adler's proposals to democratize the meetings. Moreover, at the time of the debates in 1911, he had argued that far from posing a danger to psychoanalysis, Adler's ideas would lead to its enrichment. Stekel's presentations and comments in the meetings of the society revealed an intelligent and emotional man who was both committed to Freud and capable of thinking for himself. He was a journalist, poet, and talented amateur musician, as well as a medical doctor and psychoanalyst, known for his intuitive grasp of the unconscious, and his facility with dream symbolism. Freud was late in fully appreciating the symbolic language of dreams—his chapter on the topic was not added to *The Interpretation of Dreams* until the fourth edition of 1914—and, in his *History,* he gave Stekel credit for his contributions, though he stopped mentioning him by name in later editions, simply referring to "a colleague." If people remember anything about Stekel today, it is probably the rumor, originated by Freud and spread by Jones, that he fabricated the cases he presented to the Vienna Society. The reality of his work as a psychoanalyst, as revealed in his writings and participation in the discussions of the society, does not support this tale.

Most of the other Viennese analysts took Freud's side against Stekel, or were afraid to speak out if they did not agree with the Professor, leaving Stekel increasingly isolated. But he remained as editor of the *Zentralblatt,* and Freud was determined to drive him from that position. He tried to persuade the publisher to drop Stekel as he had done with Adler; when this didn't work, he hit on another scheme. He arranged for all the other analysts associated with the journal to resign, leaving Stekel with an empty position, and then set up a new journal—the *Internationale Zeitschrift* (International Journal), which effectively took the place of the old *Zentralblatt.* In his *History,* Freud wrote that his appreciation of dream symbolism came about "partly through the influence of the works of Stekel, who at first did such very creditable work but afterwards went totally astray." In his private correspondence he was less measured, writing to Abraham about Stekel's "treason," and to Jones about "that pig Stekel."

Like Josef Breuer, Stekel lived on for many years in Vienna and never returned the hatred that Freud directed at him. He continued to work as a psychoanalytically oriented therapist and made several attempts to resume their friendship. He wrote Freud a concerned letter when he learned of the Professor's cancer in 1923, another cordial letter in 1931 in honor of Freud's seventy-fifth birthday, and a welcoming letter when the Freuds arrived in London, where Stekel had preceded them, in 1938. All of these friendly overtures were angrily rebuffed by Freud.

The debates with Adler and Stekel reveal the particular form taken by psychoanalytic politics. Political machinations go on in many fields, and personal attacks are common when different factions vie for power, but, in no other field—the sciences, medicine, the social sciences—are such attacks a part of the theory itself. Debate by interpretation and diagnosis is a unique feature of psychoanalysis; the ideas of different theorists are rarely considered on their merits, but attributed to the personal conflicts of the theorist.

The expulsion of Adler and Stekel from the Vienna Psychoanalytic Society left Freud and his adherents in control of the movement and its journals. The fate of Adler and those who sided with him was an exemplary lesson to all who remained; it was clear what would happen to them if they contested the Professor's doctrines. The movement became, more and more, a closed system, incapable of developing beyond its own beliefs.

CHAPTER 15

The King and His Knights: The Committee

The masters of science are like kings,
surrounded by courtiers, who tint the truth.

—Alfred Binet (describing Freud's idol, Charcot)

WITH THE EXPULSION of Adler and his supporters from the Vienna Society, the departure of Stekel, and the new *Internationale Zeitschrift*—with Ferenczi, Rank, and Jones as editors—set in place of the old *Zentralblatt*, Freud and his adherents had won the battle for control of psychoanalysis on their home ground. But new waves of discontent loomed on the horizon. Jung, who was ensconced as president of the International Society and editor of the *Jahrbuch*, was writing his major psychoanalytic book, *Wandlungen und Symbole der Libido* (*Symbols of Transformation*). Published in two parts in 1911 and 1912, the book would raise questions about Freud's theory of sexuality. In addition, Jung was beginning to take personal affront at Freud's treatment of him, another omen of future skirmishes.

In the wake of the split with Adler, and with signs of Jung's questionable loyalty, Jones, always a militant supporter on the lookout for heresy, proposed in 1912, with the support of Ferenczi and Rank, the formation of a secret group to protect Freud and the movement, a group that came to be known as "the Committee." Jones wanted "a tight, small organization of loyalists, a clandestine 'Committee,' to rally around Freud as his dependable palace guard. The members of the Committee would share news and ideas with one another and undertake to talk over, in the strictest privacy, any desire to depart from any of the fundamental tenets of psychoanalytical theory—repression, the unconscious, or infantile sexuality." Freud was enthusiastic and wrote back: "What took hold of

208

my imagination immediately, is your idea of a secret council composed of the best and most trustworthy among our men to take care of the further development of psychoanalysis and defend the cause against personalities and accidents when I am no more. . . . First of all: This committee had to be *strictly secret.*"

The original Committee was made up of Jones, Ferenczi, Rank, Abraham, and Sachs, all of whom Freud judged as absolutely loyal. Max Eitingon, also a devoted follower, would be added in 1919. Over the years, some would leave or die and others, including Freud's daughter Anna, would join. Freud gave all the Committee members antique Greek intaglios—stones with engraved figures, traditionally used as seals on contracts—and commented that there was "a boyish perhaps a romantic element too in this conception," while Jones spoke of "the idea of a united small body, designed, like the Paladins of Charlemagne, to guard the kingdom and policy of their master." (Charlemagne was the Holy Roman Emperor of the ninth century, and the Paladins were his knights.) Even though they recognized the romantic aura of the Committee, it is obvious that Freud and his supporters thought of themselves as militants, engaged in a holy war.

The founding of the Committee was not a harmless or boyish game, however, but a development that revealed the most intolerant side of the psychoanalytic movement. The dangers posed by Adler, Stekel, and others were, in fact, new theoretical ideas and therapeutic methods that should have been openly discussed, tested, or at least tolerated. But that did not happen. The members of Freud's inner circle were not chosen because they had the best ideas or were the most talented therapists, but because they were loyal and devoted to the cause. The purpose of the Committee was to stifle debate and impose censorship.

As Dostoevsky wrote in "The Grand Inquisitor" episode in *The Brothers Karamazov,* most men are made uncomfortable by freedom and crave "miracle, mystery and authority." Many people are drawn to belief systems and causes that have a strong leader who provides guidance and answers to the uncertainties of life. In the case of the early psychoanalysts, the attraction to what they felt was a great cause was reinforced by Freud's forceful personality and their emotional bonds to him. As loyal members of his army, they shared in his power, including the power to defeat and expel defectors.

The Committee remained active until 1936, communicating by *Rundbriefe* (circular letters) in which they kept each other informed of both theoretical and political developments. It eventually controlled membership in the International Psychoanalytic and branch societies, determined what could be published in psychoanalytic journals, and influenced the translations of Freud's work into English. The group constituted the core of Freud's most dutiful followers: the nucleus, with the exceptions, later, of Rank and Ferenczi, of what became the orthodox psychoanalytic movement.

The Committee, 1922. Back row: *Rank, Abraham, Eitingon, and Jones.* Front row: *Freud, Ferenczi, and Sachs.*

Of the true believers who made up the Committee, Ernest Jones was, in Freud's words, zealous and energetic, combative and devoted to the cause. Jones was a loyal follower, lecturing, writing, spreading Freud's word, and attacking anyone who dared to question psychoanalytic tenets. The militaristic qualities of the movement were a good fit for Jones's personality; as the historian Paul Roazen put it, he was "a fiery little man, with a staccato, military manner, and at his worst he could be spiteful, jealous, and querulous." James and Alix Strachey, colleagues and ostensible friends of Jones's in England for many years, referred to him in their private letters as "the l.b.," for "little beast." Consistent with these personal qualities, he was a rigid and by-the-book therapist; in later years, he ruled the British Psychoanalytic Society with an iron hand, expelling groups and individuals who were "eclectic"—that is, whose views departed from the Freudian canon. He maintained similar authority and control over the *International Journal of Psychoanalysis* for many years. Jones sought power by identification with Freud and enforced his will and authority on members of the British Psychoanalytic Society, those who wished to publish in the *International Journal,* trainees, and patients.

Like many of the early adherents, his personal relationship with Freud was entangled with his work as a psychoanalyst. Freud sent Jones for a brief analysis with Ferenczi, which the Englishman resented, feeling that Freud was palming him off on a student while Ferenczi was being analyzed by the master. Meanwhile, Freud was analyzing Jones's mistress, the beautiful and drug-addicted Loe Kann, further complicating matters. Jones's letters to Freud, as well as his later actions, reveal a man prone to intense rivalries; he eventually paid Ferenczi back in his biography of Freud by perpetuating lies about his former analyst and competitor. Jones was always quick to sniff out deviations and encouraged Freud to turn on those whose loyalty was suspect.

Nevertheless, Jones was intelligent and a skillful writer. While his work, such as his essay interpreting *Hamlet* in oedipal terms, almost never departed from the orthodox psychoanalytic line, there were flashes of other insights, even in his largely hagiographic biography of Freud. On balance, however, he was the archetypical disciple who worked hard to suppress the publication of anything that cast a negative light on his idol. In the autobiography, *Free Associations,* which he was working on at the end of his life, he was still rewriting history, substituting Oscar Rie for Fliess to cover up Freud's dependence on his Berlin friend, and slandering Adler, Jung, and Ferenczi.

Hanns Sachs, another loyalist and committee member, had joined the Vienna Society in 1909, and for the rest of his life remained completely devoted to Freud and psychoanalysis. His personality was much the opposite of Jones— or of Freud, for that matter. He had had an early unhappy marriage, about which he rarely spoke, and remained a perennial bachelor, in love with his pleasures: fond of good food, fine wine, women, and the café life of Vienna. He and Freud joked about his unfailing optimism, a style far different from the Professor's.

In 1911, prior to the creation of the Committee, Sachs, along with Otto Rank, had founded *Imago,* a journal devoted to the application of psychoanalysis to literature and the arts. Sachs had little interest in the political or organizational side of the movement, but Freud sensed his absolute devotion, gave him one of the intaglios, and made him an original member of the Committee. In 1920, Sachs joined Abraham and Eitingon at the new Berlin Psychoanalytic Institute, where he specialized in training future analysts. He was early aware of the rise of Nazism and emigrated to Boston in 1932, where he continued to practice. While he never openly questioned psychoanalytic orthodoxy, his optimism, interest in creative and artistic work, and stress on his patients' "positive qualities" may have made him a less severe, more sensitive and effective therapist, than a combative and controlling person such as Jones. Several of Sachs's former analysands from the Berlin days broke free from the movement and made significant original contributions: Erich Fromm, Karen Horney, and Franz Alexander.

Not a scientist or a critical thinker, Sachs had found a hero in Freud and a calling, an identity, and a belief system to which he could devote himself in psychoanalysis. Toward the end of his life, he wrote a memoir, unabashedly titled *Freud: Master and Friend*. His charm and sensibility came through in this book, along with his continued reverence for Freud, who, he wrote, "was different" than other men, even others of genius: "I simply could not believe that he was made of the same clay as others. Some special substance had been infused into him and gave the finished product a higher grade of perfection. This meant a gulf between us which I did not try to cross. Although he called me his friend, I did not feel that I was; fundamentally he remained as remote as when I first met him in the lecture hall." Sachs's veneration and identification with Freud were palpable. He kept a portrait of the Professor on a pedestal at the end of his analytic couch where he and his patients could see it, and, like many of the followers, took up cigar smoking; it is even reported that he acquired Freud's travel phobia.

While Sachs could be perceptive, the conclusions he drew from his observations were always favorable to Freud. In his memoir he described his idol as a

> fighter . . . [who] stood within a magic circle which none of the hostile spirits were allowed to enter. . . . After the kill he returned quietly to his work, paying no attention to the excited crowd. [In defending psychoanalysis] his own brain child [Freud] . . . was untiring and unbending, hard and sharp like steel, a "good hater" close to the limit of vindictiveness. [Once someone left the cause] . . . he reacted not with violent reproof, but with contempt. No appeal exists against contempt, and its silence stings worse and causes more bitterness than the most outspoken condemnation. This made any further relation impossible when the breaking point was once reached. Every rupture with a former friend in Freud's life was final. I have seen him several times go the limit of patience and indulgence for those who passed through a crisis, but I never noticed that he felt inclined to make a step towards a reconciliation.

A "good hater," a killer who is "hard and sharp like steel," "contempt," "vindictiveness," ruptures with friends with no possibility of reconciliation—these are not an attractive set of qualities. Yet, because of his veneration, Sachs saw them as essential in the commander of an embattled army. Take away the military imagery and one has a portrait, painted by one of his most devoted followers, of Freud at his most chilling.

Another of the cherished intaglios was given to Karl Abraham. Over the years, he was active in the politics of the movement, served as president of the International Association, and analyzed a number of trainees who became prominent in the next generation of psychoanalysts. Melanie Klein, perhaps his best-known student, moved to England and established her own influential school. Abraham served as a psychiatrist with the German army for four years during the First World War, and died in 1925, at the age of forty-eight.

Karl Abraham with his wife and children.

Those who knew Abraham described a common set of qualities: unremitting optimism, boyish enthusiasm, intelligence, confidence, calmness, serenity, and steadiness. Jones called him the most "normal" of the early group. Freud was impressed with his loyalty and devotion to the cause, and relied on him as a faithful lieutenant, yet, by his own account, found him a trifle boring; he preferred to spend his vacations with the more emotional and creative Ferenczi. Abraham's wife described their marriage as "happy, tranquil, perfect." A different slant on these same qualities is evident, even in accounts that praised him. Peter Gay noted that he was "perhaps a little cool" and Jones described him as "emotionally self-contained." Sachs and Theodor Reik—another of Freud's early followers—did not like his rigidity and objected to his "orderly, methodical, surgical approach to the unconscious."

In a biographical memoir, written shortly after Abraham's death, Jones described a very revealing incident. Abraham, Jones wrote, "was . . . at times curiously oblivious to the strength of hostile emotions in other people; I have seen him cheerfully reasoning with someone who was glowering with anger and resentment, apparently blandly ignoring the emotion and full of hope that a quiet exposition would change the situation."

Abraham's "normal" qualities and the sort of obliviousness demonstrated in the above incident reveal a man who is seriously out of touch with his own emotions. Whatever the personal reasons that drew him to psychoanalysis, they remained submerged beneath his relentless cheerfulness and devotion to duty. This was someone who could spend four years treating the victims of the horrors of the First World War, a shattering experience for so many people, with his optimism apparently untouched. Nor did his contact with victimized soldiers cause him to modify his belief that traumas were insignificant in the causation of neuroses.

Another side of Abraham was revealed in his work within the psychoanalytic movement, where, like Jones, he was a vigilant watchdog, always on the alert for signs of deviation. When Rank published *The Trauma of Birth* in 1924, and Freud was still wavering in his appraisal of this book by one of his oldest and closest supporters, Abraham was instrumental in ousting Rank from the International Association. As the analyst Martin Grotjahn put it in a biographical sketch of Abraham: "He had watched Rank's personal and scientific development carefully, and he detected in Otto Rank's last book, *The Trauma of Birth*, unmistakable signs of a scientific regression resembling that of Jung twelve years earlier." The Berlin Society, under his direction, was the first to rigidly codify psychoanalytic training.

Abraham had a kind of emotional impenetrability; he responded to life's fears, pains, and traumas with his intellect, with theory. These personal qualities, along with his devotion to Freud and the cause, were starkly revealed in his writings. In the form that was later to characterize many psychoanalytic publications, Abraham always began with homage to the Founder and only then expanded on some aspect of Freud's work. He never raised questions about the assumptions of the theory, Freud's authority, or "what psychoanalysis knows." Evidence consisted almost entirely of brief clinical anecdotes, and persons were lumped into characterological categories—oral-erotic personality, anal-sadist—their individual experience distorted or lost.

One of Abraham's earliest psychoanalytic contributions, *The Experiencing of Sexual Traumas as a Form of Sexual Activity,* had been published in 1907. It was one of the very few papers by another author that Freud cited with approval. In this essay, Abraham returned to the important issue of the role of sexual trauma versus drive and fantasy in causing neurosis, attempting to prove that traumas were of little significance: "I shall more particularly try to establish the view that in a great number of cases the trauma was desired by the child unconsciously, and that we have to recognize it as a form of infantile sexual activity. Anyone who is interested in the psychology of children will have observed that whereas one child will resist temptation or seduction another will easily yield to it. . . . Further, there are children who quite definitely provoke adults in a sexual manner." He added: "If there is an underlying unconscious wish for it, the experiencing of a sexual trauma in childhood is a masochistic expression of the sexual impulse. . . . I arrived at the conclusion that their sexual development was precocious and their libido itself quantitatively abnormal, and that their imagination was prematurely occupied with sexual matters to an abnormal degree."

Abraham's examples included the attempted rape of a nine-year-old girl by a grown man. If a child of this age was sexually assaulted and did not tell her parents about it, he believed it was evidence of her pleasure and unconscious wish for the molestation. He concluded that "infantile sexual traumas play no aetiological role in hysteria and dementia praecox" and that if children claim to have experienced such traumas, it is evidence that they "already had a disposition to neurosis or psychosis."

Abraham would work with many soldiers who had gone through the First World War and his understanding of their severe disturbances paralleled his view of the symptoms that resulted from child abuse: both were caused by insufficiently controlled sexual impulses. For example, he believed that the "homosexual libido," stirred up by proximity to other men in the trenches, caused the soldier's terrors and symptoms, rather than the constant exposure to death, killing, and mutilation.

As Abraham's views of both child abuse and the neuroses of war illustrate, he was an extreme spokesman for the role of sexual drives and fantasies, as opposed to actual traumas, in the causation of neurosis. For him, unconscious instincts—sexual, sadistic, masochistic, envious—explained everything.

Jones and others championed Abraham as the most "scientific" and "biological" of psychoanalysts, but the evidence indicates that he was neither. His theoretical ideas were not supported by evidence, he never considered alternative possibilities, and his "biology" consisted of an elaboration of the least valid parts of Freud's *Three Essays*. Abraham, like many of the most orthodox, was encased in his world of theory, indoctrinating his patients and numb to human suffering. In both his theoretical writings and his work as a therapist he showed an almost complete lack of empathy. He could not put himself in the place of a child who has been sexually molested, a soldier in the trenches during World War I, a woman subjected to social repression, or a depressed person mourning the loss of a loved one.

While Jones and Abraham were influential figures in the future development of psychoanalysis, both politically—they controlled training institutes and journals—and in the dissemination of ideas, another stalwart, Max Eitingon, was a shadowy figure who made minimal contributions. As Jones put it: "He was entirely devoted to Freud, whose lightest wish or opinion was decisive for him. Otherwise he was rather easily influenced, so that one could not always be sure of what his own opinion was."

Eitingon was a late addition to the Committee. After the death of Anton von Freund, a wealthy Hungarian who had supported psychoanalysis with his private funds, the movement was left with unmet financial needs. Freud then asked the independently wealthy Eitingon to join the elite group. Eitingon gave money to support psychoanalytic publications; later, when he went to Abraham's Berlin Society, he used his wealth to establish a psychoanalytic clinic there.

Eitingon seemed comfortable within the militant and authoritarian structure of the movement, as his later remarks at the 1927 Psychoanalytic Congress revealed:

> Our Congress this year is a Jubilee Congress. As the Tenth it is the last of a decade of Congresses, silent but ever-increasing mile-stones in a splendid progress, an unchecked march to the conquest of man, of humanity. If the names of Nuremberg, Weimar, Munich, Budapest, The Hague, Berlin, Salzburg, Hamburg and Innsbruck do not actually represent the battlefields of Freud and psychoanalysis, they at least bring in review before us what has been achieved and accomplished and they are a buglecall to that onward march which we must always have in mind.

The Committee held its first formal meeting in May of 1913. Jones had just returned from Toronto, Abraham came down from Berlin, Ferenczi from Budapest, and they all joined Rank and Sachs in Vienna. Freud gave these five the Greek intaglios that they would later have mounted in gold rings. Freud was the Father and they were, as he called them, his "adopted sons." The first item of business was a discussion of Ferenczi's highly critical review of Jung's new book *Symbols of Transformation,* a review that Freud had prompted him to write. The palace guard was in place none too soon for Jung, formerly Freud's favorite son and anointed heir, was about to go the way of Adler.

CHAPTER 16

Carl Gustav Jung:
The Favorite Son Expelled

Interchangeable ever were the terms of abuse with which the aggressor discredits those about to be ravaged.
                                                   —Malcolm Lowry, *Under the Volcano*

ON THE EVE of his break with Freud, Jung was still the favorite disciple, editor of a major psychoanalytic journal, president of the International Psychoanalytic Society, as well as being the recipient of the Professor's special affection. Yet despite eight years of close collaboration, when he began to publish ideas that departed from the orthodox canon, Freud—now surrounded by his palace guard—became intolerant; he set loose the forces that would destroy their friendship, and almost destroy Jung.

Carl Jung, nineteen years younger than Freud, grew up in a village in Switzerland, the only child, until he was nine, of a country pastor and his mystical wife. A key to understanding Jung is the very special nature of what, for want of a better word, can be called his temperament. He had an isolated, frightening, and emotionally impoverished childhood, and was also receptive—in fact, porous—to impressions, sensations, and emotions. The young Carl had a vivid and active imagination, and from his earliest years lived a good deal of the time in the realms of fantasy and private games.

Jung's earliest memories and experiences vacillated between intense joy and terror. He later recalled his first memory, "a fine, warm summer day, the sky blue, and golden sunlight darting through green leaves . . . I have a sense of indescribable well-being." He remembered "the pleasant taste" and "characteristic smell" of milk and the sight of Lake Constance, which brought "an inconceivable pleasure to me, an incomparable splendor." These pleasurable memories, associated with the natural world, contrasted with others that were frightening, if not terrifying, and that were linked with death:

> I also had vague fears at night. I would hear things walking about in the house. The muted roar of the Rhine Falls was always audible, and all around lay a danger zone. People drowned, bodies were swept over the rocks. In the cemetery nearby, the sexton would dig a hole—heaps of brown, upturned earth. Black solemn men in long frock coats . . . I was told that someone was being buried in this hole in the ground. Certain persons who had been around previously would suddenly no longer be there. Then I would hear that they had been buried, and that the Lord Jesus had taken them to himself.

At the time of these death-related fears, when Carl was around three years old, his mother was taken to a mental hospital. The separation produced a "general eczema" in the young boy, who "was deeply troubled by my mother's being away. From then on, I always felt mistrustful when the word 'love' was spoken. The feeling I associated with 'women' was for a long time that of innate unreliability. 'Father', on the other hand, meant reliability and—powerlessness."

Jung's father was a country pastor who went through the motions of his religious duties without deep conviction. Toward the end of his life, he lost his faith entirely and sank further into the depression that had lurked beneath the surface for many years. Being an only child for nine years, with a mother who was dissatisfied with her husband, probably made Carl the focus of her attention, and her mystical qualities had a deep impact on him. She and her relatives were involved in spiritualism, saw ghosts, and communicated with the dead. Her son found her to be an "uncanny" creature with two different personalities: by day she seemed like an ordinary village woman, while at night she became a "strange and mysterious" creature. He once saw her, or imagined her, with her head detached from her body, floating in front of her. At other times a strange voice would emanate from her mouth, making prophetic announcements.

The uncanny personality of Jung's mother, and the images of death connected to his father, religion, and Jesus, led to extremely frightening experiences, anxiety dreams, and his "first conscious trauma." He was playing on the road by his house when he saw a figure approaching that looked like a man wearing women's clothes. As it drew near, he realized it was a man in a long black robe and had the frightful thought that it was "a Jesuit." He had heard his father speak of the "nefarious activities of Jesuits," and also associated the figure with Jesus, who "took" people to him, and with death, burials, and dangers that even his father could not protect him from. He later realized that the man was a harmless Catholic priest; nevertheless, this event produced a phobia that lasted until his thirties and that prevented him from entering Catholic churches. He finally overcame this fear and entered a church in Vienna, probably after his first meeting with Freud.

As a child, Jung distrusted his mother, who was associated with his nightmares and fears of death, and could not turn to his father for help and protection. He found the family atmosphere so suffocating that he developed fits of choking. He would sit on a stone and wonder whether "he" was on top of the stone or "he" was the stone with something on top of it. He carved a manikin out of a wooden ruler that had a frock coat, top hat, and boots, blackened it with ink, and laid it to rest in a pencil box with a smooth black stone from the river. He then hid "his friend" in the attic and, when things were at their worst with his parents, he would visit this object in its hiding place and send it messages in a private code. This game was a concrete means of comforting himself, of attempting to master the fears associated with loneliness and death. In his late thirties, after the devastating break with Freud, he returned to his manikin and his private play with stones and miniature buildings.

Jung went to school with the village children and tried to fit into the world outside his odd and unhappy family. It was not easy. Albert Oeri, a longtime friend from childhood, said of him, "I had never come across such an asocial monster before." Jung played pranks and joined in the activities of the other children, but this compelled him to "be different from what I thought I was," which led to a division within himself that persisted throughout his life: "It was as if I sensed a splitting of myself, and feared it. My inner security was threatened." All of this was kept secret. There was no one the young boy could confide in, and he was extremely lonely.

His mother had evinced two personalities and now, as a schoolboy, so did Carl. As he later wrote: "Somewhere deep in the background I always knew that I was two persons. One was the son of my parents, who went to school and was less intelligent, attentive, hard-working, decent and clean than many other boys. The other was grown up—old, in fact—skeptical, mistrustful, remote from the world of men, but close to nature, the earth, the sun, the moon, the weather, all living creatures, and above all close to the night, to dreams, and to whatever 'God' worked directly in him."

Both extremes, inferiority and greatness, run through Jung's account of his childhood and adolescence. His outward or social self, what he called his "No. 1 personality," was lonely, isolated, depressed, and erratic in his academic performance. The "No. 2" personality knew there was something more, something great inside, but there was no opportunity for it to emerge. Between sixteen and nineteen, the "fog of [his] dilemma slowly lifted, and [his] depressive states of mind improved. No. 1 personality emerged more and more distinctly." He debated religious questions with his father and found him sadly lacking, a situation that led to a powerful daydream in which Carl imagined God dropping "an enormous turd" on the Basel Cathedral, smashing it. He struggled to ward off this fantasy, but finally accepted it with a feeling of relief and bliss. He would find his own way to God, outside of the organized religion of his father. While he did not mention it in his autobiography, *Memories, Dreams, Reflections,* Jung revealed in his letters to Freud that sometime in late adolescence, he had been sexually molested by "a man I once worshiped," probably a minister friend of the family. Carl's attempt to find a male ideal, both with his father and this man, ended in painful disappointments.

When Jung entered the University of Basel, he was both introspective and boisterous, forceful with others and shy. He was nicknamed "Barrel" by his friends, in reference to both his robust physique and capacity to absorb spirits— of the liquid, not mystical, kind. He was also poor. His position was typical for the child of a minister: a combination of superior education—his father taught him Latin when he was six—and economic disadvantage. Throughout his childhood, he remembered ragged clothes, holes in his shoes, being cold, and, later, the need for a stipend and help from relatives when he went to the university. While he would have liked to make a career of archaeology, his poverty required him to find a profession in which he could earn a living. He decided to study medicine.

But science and medicine did not provide the answers to Jung's quest for self-knowledge, and he became involved with spiritualist séances, along with his mother and several of her relatives. As was typical, he read everything he could on the topic and later turned this experience to use; it became the basis of his first book, a study of "occult" phenomena. He also read Krafft-Ebing's *Textbook of Insanity*, which led him to specialize in psychiatry, a field that promised to make subjective experience the object of scientific investigation. His decision to become a psychiatrist was an attempt to understand the many puzzling aspects of his life: his mother, with her shifting, frightening states, his childhood fears and fantasies, and his divided self. It was no accident that he chose to work with schizophrenic patients under Eugen Bleuler's direction.

The adult Jung was an imposing man of six feet two, highly intelligent, possessed of great energy, a large capacity for work, and hearty appetites. He was a great talker with a booming voice, always ready to poke fun at authority. Also a voracious reader, his book on dementia praecox contained one of the most extensive reviews of the literature up to its time. Jung did not suffer from the kind of sexual inhibitions that Freud did at a comparable age; women were drawn to him and, judging by his later affairs, he was quite free sexually. Coexisting with these extroverted qualities, to use one of his own later terms, were intuition and intense emotional sensitivity. He felt himself able to connect directly with the inner lives of other people.

Jung married the wealthy Emma Rauschenbach in 1903 and had five children with her. The marriage endured and Emma, a warm and caring woman, showed a keen understanding of her husband and his work. But Jung also indulged what he called his "polygamous nature"; there are two documented instances of love affairs with women who were his patients—and probably other affairs as well. Clearly, Carl was not an easy man to be married to.

C. G. Jung with his wife and children.

Jung struggled all his life with powerful terrors, phobias, and the dangers of self-dissolution, balanced with ecstatic pleasures. He was searching for a career that would engage his deepest concerns, as well as a man who embodied these interests. Freud appeared to be just what he needed. Here was someone who was dealing with the very things—dreams, fantasies, the world of the mind—that had always preoccupied him. From his reading, he thought of Freud as a brilliant older man, an ideal father with whom he could talk openly about all the inner states and emotions that had been dammed up in him since childhood.

Jung initiated the correspondence in April of 1906 by sending Freud a copy of his *Diagnostic Association Studies,* to which Freud responded with enthusiasm. Their relationship was confined to letters for almost a year, a medium in which Freud was at his most persuasive. He wrote to Jung with a combination of praise and openness. In his first letter, Freud told his new correspondent that "I am confident that you will often be in a position to back me up, but I shall also gladly accept correction."

Jung responded with thanks and defended Freud from those who were hostile to his work. Their shared disdain for those who did not understand psychoanalysis, or who criticized it, was, from the beginning, a powerful bond. Jung wrote of Bleuler's initial "vigorous resistance" to psychoanalysis, but went on to say that he was "now completely converted." He did, however, in his first letter, raise criticisms of his own that would later become points of contention: "Your therapy seems to me to depend not merely on the affects released by abreaction [emotional expression] but also on certain personal rapports, and it seems to me that though the genesis of hysteria is predominantly, it is not exclusively, sexual."

In this brief comment, Jung alluded to two of the persisting difficulties with Freud's approach: its neglect of the healing force of the therapeutic relationship—"personal rapports"—and its exclusive emphasis on sexuality. These reservations remained in the background during the early years of his involvement with Freud, but Jung never completely gave up his independent judgment and eventually reasserted his own views. But at this point in their relationship, his need to believe in Freud and psychoanalysis was paramount.

Freud responded to Jung's letter immediately, writing that he was "especially gratified to learn that you have converted Bleuler." He then took up Jung's criticisms in what seemed an open way, and also began pulling the younger man toward him: "I venture to hope that in the course of the years you will come much closer to me than you now think possible." The burgeoning correspondence covered a variety of areas. They discussed the theory of sexuality, Jung presented case material, reported one of his own dreams, and Freud continued his praise: "You see that you have not bored me in the least. I am delighted with your letters." Jung was gratified by Freud's response, yet still wondered whether psychoanalytic theory offered a sufficient explanation for what he observed with his patients, since he was working with hospitalized schizophrenics: "My material is totally different from yours. I am working under enormously difficult conditions mostly with uneducated insane patients." Freud answered Jung's questions and continued his praise:

> You are quite mistaken in supposing that I was not enthusiastic about your book on dementia praecox. . . . [you are] the ablest helper to have joined me thus far. In reality I regard your essay on dementia praecox as the richest and most significant contribution to my labors that has ever come to my attention, and among my students in Vienna, who have the perhaps questionable advantage over you of personal contact with me, I know of only one who might be regarded as your equal in understanding, and of none who is able and willing to do so much for the cause as you. . . . don't deviate too far from me when you are really so close to me, for if you do, we may one day be played off against one another. In my secret heart I am convinced that in our special circumstances the utmost frankness is the best diplomacy.

This letter shows Freud at his most seductive; he flatters the younger man, referring to their growing bond, and plants seeds about potential enemies who might interfere with their closeness. Jung was moved by this, writing in response to Freud's "exceedingly friendly and detailed letter" that he had become converted: "You may rest assured: I shall never abandon any portion of your theory that is essential to me, as I am far too committed to it." He told Freud that he looked forward to the opportunity to meet him in person for he had "an awful lot to abreact." Jung, his wife, Emma, and his young colleague Ludwig Binswanger visited Freud for the first time in March of 1907. On this occasion, Jung and Freud spoke together for thirteen hours, with the younger man doing most of the talking; as he said earlier, he had, "an awful lot to abreact." Jung and Binswanger also attended the meeting of the Wednesday Society.

All that had gone before had prepared Jung to form a tremendous attachment to Freud. Here was a man nineteen years his senior who listened to his torrential outpouring of ideas and emotions, seemed to understand them, interpreted his dreams, and welcomed him as a colleague; he had finally met "the first man of real importance I had encountered . . . in my experience up to that time, no one else could compare with him. There was nothing the least trivial in his attitude. I found him extremely intelligent, shrewd, and altogether remarkable." The encounter dispelled Jung's remaining doubts and bound him to Freud and the cause.

Now that he was converted to Freud's sexual theory, Jung attempted to apply it in his work and sought advice from his new mentor about a case: "At the moment I am treating a 6-year-old girl for excessive masturbation and lying after alleged seduction by her foster-father," he wrote. He went on to describe the blandness of her feelings, the lack of specific memories of the seduction, and how he has not been able to get her to express any emotions, concluding, "At present it looks as if the trauma were a fake. Yet where does the child get all those sexual stories from?"

Freud responded with a reference to his abandonment of the seduction theory: "In your six-year-old girl, you must surely have discovered in the meantime that the attack is a fantasy that has become conscious, something which is regularly disclosed in analysis and which misled me into assuming the existence of generalized traumas in childhood." Freud was adamant that Jung's young patient was suffering from "a fantasy" and not a sexual molestation by her foster father despite the fact that he had never seen her. Given all that is now known about the effects of sexual abuse in a girl this age, it is quite likely that he was wrong—that she was molested. She told the story, but without emotion, and was preoccupied with sexuality—"where does the child get all those sexual stories from?"—and excessive masturbation, all of which are typical in such cases.

It is not fair to expect that Freud and Jung could have known in 1907 what is now known about the effects of sexual abuse on young children. But an understanding of these conditions would have progressed much more rapidly if Freud had not insisted on imposing his drive-wish theory on the evidence. Jung was still skeptical, but, because of his idealization of Freud, he accepted the fantasy theory.

The exchange about the six-year-old patient was followed, some months later, by Jung's account of a traumatic sexual incident from his own life, an event which he directly related to his sexual feelings for Freud. In January of 1908 he wrote, "I have a sin to confess: I have had your photograph enlarged. It looks marvelous. A few of our circle have acquired copies. So, like it or not, you have stepped into many a quiet study." His admiration and love for Freud, and the awareness of his own erotic feelings, led to a confession of a sexual molestation experience of his own, which Freud accepted as an actual memory. Jung wrote: "I have a boundless admiration for you both as a man and a researcher, and I bear you no conscious grudge. . . . My veneration for you has something of the character of a 'religious' crush. Though it does not really bother me, I still feel it is disgusting and ridiculous because of its undeniable erotic undertone. This abominable feeling comes from the fact that as a boy I was the victim of a sexual assault by a man I once worshiped."

During their first meeting in March of 1907, Jung had recounted a dream in which Freud appeared. It is clear from Jung's autobiography how much of his real or secret self was invested in his dreams, so that being able to confide them to the great Freud was a momentous event for him. Binswanger referred to what had transpired during this first meeting: "The day after our arrival Freud questioned Jung and me about our dreams. I do not recall Jung's dream, but I do recall Freud's interpretation of it, namely, that Jung wished to dethrone him and take his place."

Jung came back to the dream in a letter written to Freud, following his confession of the sexual molestation "by a man I once worshiped":

> I am suffering all the agonies of a patient in analysis, riddling myself with
> every conceivable fear about the possible consequences of my confession.
> . . . You will remember my telling you a short dream I had while I was
> in Vienna. At the time I was unable to solve it. You sought the solution
> in a rivalry complex. I dreamt that I saw you walking beside me as a *very,
> very frail old man*. Ever since then the dream has been preying on my
> mind, but to no purpose. The solution came, as usual, only after I had
> confessed my worries to you. *The dream sets my mind at rest about your
> + + + dangerousness!*" [Emphasis in the original; three crosses were chalked
> on the inside of peasant houses to ward off danger.]

Jung felt that the dream revealed his fear that he would be traumatized again, that by taking Freud as his ideal, he was in danger of being sexually exploited as he had been in his youth. Jung later told his colleague Jolande Jacobi how a family friend had made a homosexual advance, and explained that it was "also the reason why I was afraid of Freud's approaches."

Freud's letter in response to Jung's confession of his "'religious' crush," with its "erotic undertone," and the dream of Freud as an old man is, unfortunately, missing. Whatever it contained was reassuring for, in response, Jung wrote, "Heartiest thanks for your letter, which worked wonders for me." The cautions that Jung had initially voiced about the sexual theory were now put aside. His powerful attachment to Freud, who made clear in his letters that he and "the cause" were one, completed his conversion. Jung was solidly in the movement, his reservations pushed to the back of his mind; in most of his articles and lectures during the years until their break, he promoted Freud's wish-fantasy theory, along with many other of the Professor's ideas.

The relationship was an intense one from Freud's side as well. It is clear in the Freud/Jung letters, and even clearer in correspondence with others such as Jones and Abraham, that Freud saw "winning the Swiss" and bringing "Zurich" into his camp as important goals for the advance of the psychoanalytic movement. In addition to these political motives, Freud was personally drawn to Jung, who appeared to embody so much that he lacked as a child and young man. There was, in other words, an "erotic undertone" from his side as well. Jung was a very attractive man, physically imposing, with a willingness to plunge into the emotional depths and explore his unconscious. With his wealthy wife, his Christian-Swiss heritage, and his connection to science and established psychiatry, he was a sharp contrast to the sexually inhibited, impoverished boy from a Viennese-Jewish ghetto. Freud's letters make clear that he felt a connection between Jung and Fliess. In speaking of his anxiety when Jung did not respond quickly to his letters, he said, "I evidently still have a traumatic hyperaesthesia [oversensitivity] toward dwindling correspondence. I remember its genesis well—Fliess—and should not like to repeat such an experience unawares." To which Jung responded, "You may rest assured, not only now but for the future, that nothing Fliess-like is going to happen."

It was this mix of personal and political motives that led Freud to promote Jung and grant him special favors. He began calling him "Dear friend" in his letters, in place of "Dear colleague," then "My dear friend and heir," and, in April of 1909, wrote of the time "when I formally adopted you as eldest son and anointed you, *in the lands of the unbelievers,* as my successor and crown prince." In a similar vein, Jones noted that "Jung was to be the Joshua destined to explore the promised land of psychiatry which Freud, like Moses, was only permitted to view from afar," and quoted Freud as saying that "when the Empire I founded is orphaned, no one but Jung must inherit the whole thing."

The Jung that one finds in the letters to Freud is a man full of emotion, someone who often went to extremes while still striving for self-awareness. He would lash out at rivals such as Abraham and Eitingon, but also confess his own wish to be the favored son. Early in the correspondence, he described his treatment of a brilliant young Russian-Jewish woman named Sabina Spielrein who had been hospitalized at the Burghölzli in a psychotic state. Jung was her therapist, and then began an affair with her. When he first told Freud about this, he blamed her for seducing him, a view which Freud seemed only too ready to accept. Yet, in his next letters, Jung assumed responsibility for the affair. He put an end to the sexual intimacy and remained helpful and supportive with Sabina, who recovered from her psychosis, completed her medical-psychiatric studies, and went on to join Freud's group in Vienna before eventually returning to her native Russia.

The way Freud and Jung worked as therapists was another difference that foreshadowed the break between them. During his early years at the Burghölzli, Jung organized dancing parties and an annual costume ball where he and other doctors waltzed with the psychotic patients. Jung later recalled an incident that illustrated their differing attitudes:

> When Freud visited me in Zurich in 1908, I demonstrated the case of Babette to him. Afterward he said to me, "You know, Jung, what you have found out about this patient is certainly interesting. But how in the world were you able to bear spending hours and days with this phenomenally ugly female?" I must have given him a rather dashed look, for this idea had never occurred to me. In a way I regarded the woman as a pleasant old creature because she had such lovely delusions and said such interesting things. And after all, even in her insanity, the human being emerged from a cloud of grotesque nonsense.

With his comment on this woman's ugliness, Freud showed how his personal likes and dislikes interfered with an open, accepting approach; how he had to keep an emotional distance between himself and the people he treated. He did not want to feel what they felt, while Jung was able to identify with and use his own reactions to understand and make contact with his patients. About work with a very difficult man, Jung said that "whenever I got stuck, he analyzed me. In this way my own psychic health has benefitted."

Jung's search for a mode of treatment that fit his individual patients had gradually led him to question some of Freud's cherished practices and beliefs, particularly the overarching importance assigned to sexuality. Freud, for his part, was committed to his universal theories and never conceived of psychoanalytic therapy in terms of empathy or dialogue. If patients did not agree with his interpretations, he considered it a sign of their resistance. Put in different terms, Jung, while initially the dutiful son, had a strong need to become his own person; he was not one who could forever remain a dutiful follower. When the theory and therapy clashed with his own observations and experience, he was impelled to express his own ideas.

In 1911, Jung wrote what he felt was a major work, eventually titled *Symbols of Transformation*. In this book he attempted to formulate his ideas about schizophrenia and work out his growing reservations about Freud's theories, especially the theory of sexuality. The book drew on his work with patients and his personal struggles with a divided self. With his typical energy, he plunged into research in religion and mythology, drawn from a variety of sources, including the classical and Eastern traditions. A number of Jung's later theories were beginning to take shape in this book, but of special importance at this time were the ideas that would set him on a collision course with Freud. Even as Jung was writing *Symbols of Transformation,* he sensed the danger to their relationship. He was right. In November of that year Freud wrote him, "I am afraid there is a misunderstanding between us, the same sort of thing as when you once said in an article that to my way of thinking libido is identical with any kind of desire, whereas in reality I hold very simply that there are two basic drives and that only the power behind the sexual drive can be termed libido."

Jung responded with a long letter in which he gave voice to "all the difficulties that have beset me throughout the years in my attempt to apply the libido theory to schizophrenia." Referring to Freud's paper on Schreber, a German judge who suffered from a paranoid schizophrenic psychosis, he wrote, "The loss of reality function in schizophrenia cannot be reduced to repression of libido—defined as sexual hunger. Not by me at any rate." This was a genuine theoretical difference; Jung had worked directly with schizophrenic patients, and had his own struggles with self-fragmentation. He did not find Freud's sexual-libido theory helpful in understanding these conditions. Freud, who never worked with such patients—his Schreber analysis was based on the patient's *Memoirs*—attempted to force schizophrenia into his theory of sexuality.

In letters written in May 1912, Freud and Jung went back and forth on the topics of incest, anxiety, and the relative power of mothers and fathers. Jung wrote that his research had convinced him of the tremendous importance of mothers, as revealed in mythology, and questioned whether all anxiety could be traced back to castration threats during the oedipal conflict. Freud disagreed, defending his theory of anxiety, and sounding the ominous note that what Jung was saying was "very similar to what was said before the days of psychoanalysis" and that it showed "a disastrous similarity to a theorem of Adler's."

Coincident with his letters to Jung, Freud was working on his own book, and racing to publish before his colleague. This was *Totem and Taboo,* in which he developed his theory of the role of man's prehistoric past. Like Jung, he drew on sources in mythology, adding material from anthropology. He attempted to show that society, religion, and morality could all be traced to the Oedipus complex, that primitive men became civilized as a result of their guilt following their slaying of the "primal father." As he wrote to Ferenczi at the time, "I am reading fat books without any real interest, since I know the conclusions already; my instinct tells me so." The contrast between the two psychoanalysts is significant; Jung seemed genuinely interested in discovering something new, in finding the answers to questions that puzzled him, whereas Freud wanted to confirm his theory. The conclusion of *Totem and Taboo* was foreordained.

As the breach between them widened—what Jung wrote in *Symbols of Transformation* was, indeed, at odds with Freud's theories—Freud turned to a personal attack and interpretation of his friend's motives. In February of 1912 he berated Jung for being a tardy correspondent, always a sign that he was not being sufficiently loved, and suggested that this revealed Jung's unconscious motives: "I awaited your letters with great impatience and answered them promptly. I disregarded your earlier signs of reluctance. This time it struck me as more serious. . . . I took myself in hand and quickly turned off my excess libido. I was sorry to do so, yet glad to see how quickly I managed it. Since then I have become undemanding and not to be feared. As we know, irresponsibility is not a concept compatible with depth psychology."

Freud withdrew his "libido" in anger. The affection he felt for his beloved son and crown prince was quickly turned off, and he took pride in being able to control his emotions. Jung responded by asserting his right to opinions that differed from Freud's and quoted Nietzsche: "One repays a teacher badly if one remains only a pupil."

In November of 1912, Freud and Jung met in the Park Hotel in Munich, Germany, in an attempt at reconciliation. There had been a quarrel over a trip Freud made to Switzerland to visit Binswanger. Jung felt slighted that Freud hadn't come to see him, while Freud said that Jung had mixed up the dates of the trip because of his unconscious "father complex." The conflict was a small incident in the larger context of their widening differences. In Munich, they had a long talk, and Freud later said, "I spared him nothing at all, told him calmly that a friendship with him couldn't be maintained, that he himself gave rise to the intimacy which he then so cruelly broke off; that things were not at all in order in his relations with men, not just with me but with others as well."

Later, still at the hotel with Jones and some others, they talked of death and the ancient world as they had on the eve of their American trip in 1909, when Freud first fainted in Jung's presence. This time they discussed an Egyptian king who had his dead father's names removed from some monuments. In the midst of this conversation, Freud again fainted. Jung picked him up and carried him to a sofa; as he came to, Freud said, "How sweet it must be to die." In a letter to Jung after this event, Freud wrote, "The dining-room of the Park Hotel seems to hold a fatality for me. Six years ago I had a first attack of the same kind there, and four years ago a second. A bit of neurosis that I ought really to look into." To Binswanger, he wrote, "Repressed feelings, this time directed against Jung, as previously against a predecessor of his, naturally play the main part." The "predecessor" was, of course, Fliess, with whom he had fainted in the same hotel, though it was sixteen years earlier and not six as he remembered it.

Freud told Jones after he fainted that a quarrel with Fliess had taken place in the same room of the Park Hotel: "I saw Munich first when I visited Fliess during his illness . . . and this town seems to have acquired a strong connection with my relation to this man. There is some piece of unruly homosexual feeling at the root of the matter." While there was no doubt rivalry in the Freud-Jung relationship, it was not, from Jung's side, the primary cause of the conflict between them. Jung wanted and needed Freud to be the strong and loving father he never had. Far from "death wishes" posing a threat, it was disappointment and loss that was soon to prove devastating when Freud rejected him. On Freud's side, too, the threat was a repeat of what had occurred with Fliess: the loss of someone who seemed to promise the fulfillment of his childhood yearnings. For both Freud and Jung, their early traumas and losses were associated with images of death. Freud's "how sweet it must be to die," as he was being carried to the sofa by Jung, expressed both his wish to be the passive recipient of love and care and the deathlike fear associated with the disappointment of this longing. In a letter to Ferenczi, written after the second fainting episode, Freud said: "I . . . have settled well analytically my dizzy spell in Munich, and even begun work on the long-delayed [*Totem and Taboo*]. All these attacks [fainting] point to the significance of cases of death experienced early in life—in my case it was a brother who died very young, when I was a little more than a year old." This was a rare instance, only revealed in a private letter to a most trusted colleague, in which Freud linked his anxiety and fainting to a memory associated with his early losses; publicly, he clung to his oedipal-sexual interpretation.

A reconciliation of sorts was effected between Freud and Jung in Munich, but it was short-lived. Just a few weeks later, Jung let loose his feelings over Freud's refusal to consider his ideas on their merits, his anger at always being diagnosed and interpreted: "This is just what I have been hearing on all sides these days, with the result that I am forced to the painful conclusion that the majority of psychoanalysts misuse psychoanalysis for the purpose of devaluing others and their progress by insinuations about complexes. . . . A particularly preposterous bit of nonsense now going the rounds is that my libido theory is the product of anal erotism. When I consider *who* cooked up this 'theory' I fear for the future of analysis."

The *who* was Abraham: "anal eroticism" was a favorite idea of his. Abraham and other members of the Committee were busy discussing Jung's apostasy in their circular letters. A short while later Freud could not resist pointing out a slip of the pen to Jung who, in response, finally exploded:

> May I say a few words to you in earnest? I admit the ambivalence of my feelings towards you . . . I would, however, point out that your technique of treating your pupils like patients is a *blunder*. In that way you produce either slavish sons or impudent puppies . . . You go around sniffing out all the symptomatic actions in your vicinity, thus reducing everyone to the

level of sons and daughters who blushingly admit the existence of their faults. Meanwhile you remain on top as the father, sitting pretty. . . . You know, of course, how far a patient gets with self-analysis: *not* out of his neurosis—just like you. If ever you should rid yourself entirely of your complexes and stop playing the father to your sons and instead of aiming continually at their weak spots took a good look at your own for a change, then I will mend my ways and at one stroke uproot the vice of being in two minds about you.

Freud's response was to break off the personal relationship entirely, with a typical diagnostic attack: "One who while behaving abnormally keeps shouting that he is normal gives ground for the suspicion that he lacks insight into his illness. Accordingly, I propose that we abandon our personal relations entirely. I shall lose nothing by it, for my only emotional tie with you has long been a thin thread—the lingering effect of past disappointments." To which Jung wrote back, "I accede to your wish that we abandon our personal relations, for I never thrust my friendship on anyone. You yourself are the best judge of what this moment means to you. 'The rest is silence.'"

Freud labeled Jung's ideas "abnormality" and "illness," and Abraham and Jones were quick to join in the attack by diagnosis. Jones wrote to Freud that they had formed the Committee "not at all too early," and said that Jung "does not react like a normal man, and that he is mentally deranged to a serious extent; he produced quite a paranoic impression on some of the psychoanalytic psychiatrists [in America]." To Abraham, Freud wrote, "Jung is crazy, but I have no desire for separation and should like to let him wreck himself first." By 1914, Jung was forced out of the presidency of the International Psychoanalytic Association and resigned as editor of the *Jahrbuch*. As had been the case with Adler, the loyal troops rallied around their commander to defeat another enemy. Freud wrote to Abraham: "So we are at last rid of them, the brutal, sanctimonious Jung and his pious parrots. I must now thank you for the vast amount of trouble, the exceptional clear-sightedness, with which you supported me and our common cause. All my life I have been looking for friends who would not exploit and then betray me, and now, not far from its natural end, I hope I have found them."

Not content to attack Jung in his correspondence, Freud devoted the last nine pages of his 1914 *History* essay to criticisms of his former intimate. In his paper *On Narcissism*, written in the same year, he again attempted to preempt Jung, as he had done with *Totem and Taboo*, with a psychoanalytic explanation of schizophrenia aimed at countering Jung's work in this area. Freud dealt with Jung's original contributions by simultaneously dismissing them as "fairy tales," "spookery," and "occultism" and appropriating other parts, writing as if they were his own. For many years thereafter—in fact, still—those within psychoanalysis dismiss Jungian ideas as "mystical" in contrast to Freudian theory, which is touted as "scientific." At the same time, those of Jung's ideas that Freud appropriated—"psychological complex," which Jung outlined as early as 1907, and his contributions on the prehistoric origins of neurosis and culture—were, like Fliess's idea of bisexuality and Adler's concepts of inferiority, aggression, and the masculine protest, taken over by Freud.

Freud's attack on Jung's work lent additional weight to the wounds inflicted by his personal dismissal. In his final letters to Freud, Jung seemed to be a strong and combative individual; but, in fact, Freud's rejection was personally devastating. Jung was a generation younger than Freud and a far more vulnerable person. *Symbols of Transformation* was a highly personal document; Jung was trying to understand not only schizophrenia, but his own divided and troubled self. While Freud was quickly back in control—"I shall lose nothing by it, for my only emotional tie with you has long been a thin thread"—Jung came unraveled and, for several years, floundered in a near-psychotic state. As he later described it, "After the break with Freud, all my friends and acquaintances dropped away. My book was declared to be rubbish; I was a mystic, and that settled the matter. . . . a period of inner uncertainty began for me. It would be no exaggeration to call it a state of disorientation."

"Inner uncertainty" and "disorientation" put it mildly; at other points, he said, "I was menaced by a psychosis . . . the ground literally gave way beneath my feet, and I plunged down into dark depths." There were feelings of panic, terror, intense guilt, suicidal impulses, many images of death and dying, and a disorienting loss of reality. This does not mean that Freud, Jones, and Abraham were right when they said Jung was "crazy" and "paranoid." His near-psychotic state was a *result* of the rejection by Freud, not an antecedent. He was not paranoid, he did not feel Freud was persecuting him; rather, he regressed to the isolated and fantasy-ridden state of his childhood. The labels of paranoia and insanity were routinely applied to all those who challenged Freud and his doctrines; the diagnosis was not specific to the individuals involved. Adler and Stekel—and Putnam when he supported Adler—were all called "paranoid." Now it was Jung's turn.

Nothing like the near-psychosis that overtook Jung happened to Adler, who quit the movement in anger and, with a group of like-minded colleagues, quickly started a rival school. In Jung's case, the relationship with Freud and psychoanalysis was of much greater importance. With Freud the person, and with psychoanalysis as a theory, therapy, and movement, Jung had attempted to express and integrate the different sides of himself. Freud was the first man since earliest childhood that he had entrusted with his dreams, emotions, and ideas; psychoanalysis was his belief system, what he later called "the myth in which you live." Freud the man and his theories had become the central structures of his life and self; without them, his reality crumbled, and he fell into a state of personal chaos.

Jung came near psychosis but never completely lost touch with reality. He barely continued to function as a husband, a father, and a therapist. In his own words, his wife, children, and work with patients kept him anchored in the world; they were places where his No.1 self could still exist. The rest of the time he was engaged in what he later called a "confrontation with the unconscious." He was overtaken by his No. 2 self, swamped by terrors, images of hallucinatory intensity, dreams, and fantasies. Gradually, he worked his way through this with a form of play therapy and self-analysis. He returned to the games of his childhood, remembered the manikin he had secreted in the attic, recovered his frightening memories and dreams, built miniature houses and villages with stones, wrote and painted in private notebooks, and strove to make sense of his disorganized and fragmented state. Toni Wolff, a woman he had successfully treated for schizophrenia, was very helpful during this time, and he began an affair with her that lasted for many years.

Like the expulsion of Adler, the demonization of Jung was a great loss for the future of psychoanalysis. Freud's version of history was accepted and, for years afterward, anything associated with Jung or his ideas was branded as mystical and taboo. Cast into limbo were religion and spiritual life, the creative potential of the unconscious, motives other than sexuality and pleasure seeking, the importance of mothers alongside of fathers, along with issues of the wholeness, cohesion, and integrity of the self. All of these concerns eventually found their way back into psychoanalysis, but the pattern of expulsion of heretics, established by Freud and the loyalists, seen most clearly in the fates of Adler and Jung, made the consideration of ideas that departed from the Freudian canon a prolonged, uphill struggle.

CHAPTER 17

The First World War

There comes a terrible moment to many souls when the great movements
of the world, the larger destinies of mankind, which have lain aloof in
newspapers and other neglected reading, enter like an earthquake into their
own lives—when the slow urgency of growing generations turns into the
tread of an invading army.

—George Eliot, *Daniel Deronda*

SUPPORTED BY his loyal lieutenants on the Committee, Freud had completed
his successful campaign to drive Jung from the psychoanalytic movement. In
June of 1914, he wrote to Karl Abraham that "the bombshell has now burst and
we shall soon discover with what effect. I think we shall have to allow the victims [Jung and his friends] two or three weeks time to collect themselves and
react." As he savored his triumph, a shocking event occurred in Sarajevo on June
28: a Bosnian Serb nationalist murdered Archduke Franz Ferdinand, the heir to
the Hapsburg throne. The assassination did not, at first, arouse great alarm
among Europeans, many of whom were enjoying their summer months of travel
and leisure; similar crises had been successfully resolved by diplomacy. But
within a month, the rumblings of international tensions took on ominous proportions as Austria-Hungary declared war on Serbia. In support of Serbia, Russia
mobilized, and the European alliance system was activated; Germany and France
declared war, and the invasion of neutral Belgium by Germany brought England
into the conflict. The real thing—the Great War—had begun, as Europe
plunged into a brutal conflict that would prove to be one of the most destructive events of the century.

The clashes that had taken place within the psychoanalytic movement,
though flavored with military values and metaphors, had not been lethal; there
were, to be sure, "bombshells" for Freud's opponents and "victims" of his successful campaigns, but, despite Adler's frustrations and Jung's anguish, they and

their allies went on with their lives. Freud, as the victor in these psychoanalytic wars, saw no reason to question his military values. He took peace for granted, but, in fact, it had taken a stable world, in which students, patients, funds, and ideas could move freely across international boundaries, to allow the spread of psychoanalysis. The declaration of war in 1914 put an end to all this.

As scenes of jubilation prevailed in the capitals of the belligerent nations, even pacifists and socialists, who had opposed war and the European arms race, joined in the widespread outpouring of patriotism. In Vienna, the British ambassador observed "a frenzy of delight, vast crowds parading the streets and singing patriotic songs till the small hours of the morning." Newspaper editors wrote of a new "Austrianness, a new Hungarianness", as divisiveness in the Hapsburg Empire was replaced with a spirit of commonality. Viennese citizens mobilized for volunteer work, ministering to the needs of refugees from the front; doctors went from door to door giving inoculations; women gave up their gold wedding bands to pay for the war effort. Despite the public celebration, Alexander, Freud's younger brother, was aware that "people are very dejected, since everyone has friends and acquaintances who are being called up." The artist Oskar Kokoschka observed a more resigned mood among the recruits from a poor district in Vienna: "These simple, starving, bewildered lads and men, who have had nothing but misery all their lives, are being driven to their deaths, or crippled, and nobody gives a tuppeny damn about it afterwards. The streets are filling with pitiful women, who are already pale and ill, but still have the strength of soul not to let their menfolk see how it affects them. . . . Yet the recruits are docile, and grateful for a friendly look."

Freud, who had always stayed aloof from politics and had shown little patriotism in previous years, was swept up in the massive expression of national unity. In a letter to Abraham, he spoke of his enthusiasm for the outbreak of hostilities: "For the first time in thirty years I feel myself to be an Austrian and feel like giving this not very hopeful Empire another chance. Morale everywhere is excellent. Also, the liberating effect of courageous action and the secure prop of Germany contributes a great deal to this." Jones noted that "Freud's immediate response to the declaration of war was an unexpected one. One would have supposed that a pacific *savant* of fifty-eight would have greeted it with simple horror, as so many did. On the contrary, his first response was rather one of youthful enthusiasm, apparently a re-awakening of the military ardors of his boyhood. . . . he was quite carried away, could not think of any work, and spent his time discussing the events of the day with his brother Alexander. As he put it: 'All my libido is given to Austro-Hungary.'"

It was a leap of faith for him to hope that his own country would prove powerful and victorious. While Freud had long identified with military heroes from the past, the faltering Austro-Hungarian Empire, which had lost its last two wars and was riven by class and nationality conflicts, had little claim on his sympathy.

Joyful German troops marching off to the First World War.

Unlike Freud and Abraham, Ferenczi did not share the patriotic fervor of the buoyant crowds. Awaiting mobilization on August 21, he wrote to Freud: "I have felt like a foreigner with respect to the war enthusiasm—anachronistic to my way of thinking." Sensitive to his colleague's more doubtful mood, Freud's comments to Ferenczi emphasized his longing for national security; he wrote that he "hoped to get a viable fatherland from which the storm of war had wafted away the worst miasmas and in which the children could live with confidence."

The initial enthusiasm for the war, which Freud shared with so many others, was based, in part, on the popular notion that it would be quickly resolved. The last European wars had been brief: the Austro-Prussian War of 1866 had lasted but seven weeks, and the Franco-Prussian War of 1870–1871 six months. These were the wars of Freud's boyhood; as a ten-year-old schoolboy he had attempted to organize a campaign to supply bandages to Austrian troops, and, as a fourteen-year-old, followed the Franco-Prussian war with great interest. Memories of these conflicts predisposed both the general public, as well as many political and military leaders, to expect a war of movement, not one in which their armies would be pinned down in trenches for months and years. The war, they believed, would be won or lost after a few decisive battles with limited casualties or disruptions to civilian life. Most people expected it all to be over by Christmas; the Hungarian minister of finance thought it would last no more than three weeks, and the Austro-Hungarian army had supplies for only a few weeks.

The great majority of European intellectuals had an unrealistic, idealized picture of war. The bloody realities of the Napoleonic Wars had long been obscured by romantic myths and symbols, and the new war, most imagined, would be a chivalric, heroic endeavor in which men revealed their bravery. Indeed, many felt that they could not achieve full manhood unless they were tested in battle; they believed that until they passed through a warlike ordeal, they were in danger of sinking into a life of pleasure and softness. In 1912, the French writer Abel Bonnard had rhapsodized, "We must embrace it in all its wild poetry. When a man throws himself into it, it is not just his own instincts that he is rediscovering, but virtues which he is recovering." Freud, believing that the war would have a "liberating effect," was relying on images that pervaded European culture.

War was seen as inevitable, necessary, even beneficial: it would sweep away the dross of old and corrupt societies, have a cleansing effect, and bring out the best in man and country—patriotism, loyalty, selfless dedication to a cause, and heroism. Freud's image of war as a "storm" that would rid Austria-Hungary of its unwholesome "miasmas" was widely shared. The German delegate to the Hague peace conference, Karl von Stengel, had praised the benefits of war with the same metaphor: "Just as storms cleanse the air and throw decayed and putrid trees to the ground while the robust and sturdy oak perseveres through the most powerful storm, so is war the test for the political, physical, and spiritual value of a people and state." On the eve of the Great War, ideas and intense emotions about masculine identity, national autonomy, security, and community intertwined, resulting in its wide acceptance.

Only a small minority expressed opposition to the war at the outset. One hundred German scientists were asked to sign a petition for peace in the first months of the war, but only four were willing to do so, one of whom was Albert Einstein. He wrote to a friend: "Europe, in her insanity, has started something unbelievable. In such times one realizes to what a sad species of animal one belongs. I quietly pursue my peaceful studies and contemplations and feel only pity and disgust." Einstein was among the few—the leader of the French Socialist Party, Jean Jaurès, the German Socialist Rosa Luxemburg, and the French novelist Romain Rolland were others—who steadfastly opposed the war and held to their internationalist and pacifist views. But narrow patriotism and enthusiasm for the war such as Freud's were the prevailing reactions of many prominent European intellectuals. Even those who eventually opposed the war were, like Freud, swept up in the initial enthusiasm: Stefan Zweig, one of Vienna's most popular authors and, later, a staunch pacifist, was one such, and the Viennese journalist Karl Kraus, who would become famous for his biting criticisms of the war, did not begin voicing them until 1915.

A few prescient thinkers foresaw the potential for devastation in the modern, industrialized war that was soon to engulf Europe. In 1890, the elder Moltke, retired chief of the Prussian General Staff, told the Reichstag of the unforeseeable severity of a future European war: "Woe to him who sets Europe alight, who first puts the fuse to the powder keg." Ivan Bloch, a Warsaw banker, published a six-volume work in 1898 predicting the stalemate and slaughter of the Western Front, and the English economist Norman Angell, in 1910, projected the financial disaster that would overtake all the participants. In his science fiction novels, H. G. Wells imagined the horrors that would be unleashed by the military applications of scientific discoveries. Earliest of all was Friedrich Engels, who, in 1887, warned:

> Eight to ten million soldiers will swallow each other up and in so doing eat all Europe more bare than any swarm of locusts. The devastation of the Thirty Years War compressed into the space of three or four years and extending over the whole continent; famine, sickness, want, brutalizing the army and the mass of the population . . . Collapse of the old states and their traditional statecraft, so that crowns will roll by dozens in the gutter and no one will be found to pick them up; it is absolutely impossible to predict where it will all end and who will emerge from the struggle as victor.

This was the kind of war Europe would get, not the illusory, brief war it was expecting, and the shock of it would reverberate through all the prewar expectations, values, and emotions, making casualties of ideas as well as young soldiers.

In August, when the Great War burst into their lives, the Freud family was preoccupied with the fates of their children and friends. Like many others in Europe, the family was caught off guard by the outbreak; nineteen-year-old Anna was visiting friends in England, and many tense days passed before her family heard from her. Making her way home through Gibraltar and Pontebba, she arrived safely on August 26. Freud's oldest son Martin was, like many young men, swept up in the early excitement and patriotism and was among the first to enlist in the Austrian army, while Freud's son-in-law Max Halberstadt, living in Frankfurt, Germany, with Sophie, was also declared fit to serve. The close circle of psychoanalytic colleagues was broken up by the mobilization; Ferenczi was called up as a physician to the Hungarian army and Abraham volunteered to serve in a German military hospital. As Freud ruefully remarked to Abraham, "Jones, is of course our enemy."

Caught up in the agitation of the times, Freud was irritable and unable to work; he noticed that he made slips of the tongue and found himself "living from one German victory to the next." Despite his intense interest in the war, he did not join in the volunteer work as so many other physicians did, but withdrew, as he had done as a boy, into his private world. For solace, he spent the first months of the war working with his faithful secretary Otto Rank cataloging his books and fondling his ancient artifacts. As he wrote to Ferenczi in August of 1914, "I have thought up a . . . little game; I take my antiquities and study and describe every piece."

In the early months Freud identified with the progress of the German and Austro-Hungarian armies, and was certain of a swift military triumph. But on the Western Front it was becoming clear that something new and monstrous had been unleashed. As early as August 20, an English captain with the French army saw the war as something alien and unexpected: "A chill of horror came over us. War seemed suddenly to have assumed a merciless, ruthless aspect that we had not realized till then. Hitherto it had been war as we had conceived it, hard blows, straight dealing, but now for the first time we felt as if some horrible Thing, utterly merciless, was advancing to grip us." Even the German chief of staff at this time, General Helmuth von Moltke, felt overwhelmed by the casualties in the initial month of fighting. He wrote to his wife on September 7, "Terror often overcomes me when I think of this and the feeling I have is that I must answer for this horror."

For many, the exposure to this unprecedented, total war would bring about a profound reexamination of beliefs. Language itself seemed to be dissolving in the face of the new warfare. In an interview in the *New York Times,* the novelist Henry James asked the reporter to think about this statistic: in a twenty-minute period, there had been five thousand casualties on the Western Front. He then observed, "One finds it in the midst of all this as hard to apply one's words as to endure one's thoughts. The war has used up words: they have weakened, they have deteriorated like motor car tires; they have, like millions of other things, been more over strained and knocked about and voided of the happy semblance during the last six months than all the long ages before."

The war had begun to work on Freud's mind, too. By September, his son Ernst was about to be called up, and he began to realize that this war would not end swiftly "by catastrophic strokes." In a letter to Abraham on September 22, he referred to the war as "unleashed brutality." In a world at peace, he had been able to deploy military metaphors for the conflicts within psychoanalysis. Now, as he recalled his "battle" with Jung, he wrote, "It is like remembering an earlier life according to the doctrine of the transmigration of souls." His new awareness kept him in a state of anxiety about the young men in his family. "In the spring," he wrote Ferenczi on December 15, "when the big bloodletting comes, I will have three or four sons in it. My trust in the future after the war is very slight."

By Christmas of 1914, the belief that the conflict would be settled with rapid victories had evaporated, replaced by the recognition that this would be a war of stalemate and attrition. The trenches of the Western Front stretched from the sea to the Alps, creating a desolate landscape: a new vision for Europeans accustomed to battle images vibrant with color and glory. Victor Fleming, a member of the British Parliament, in a letter to his friend Winston Churchill in November, described the "terrain of death":

First and most impressive, the absolutely indescribable ravages of modern artillery fire, not only upon all men, animals and buildings within its zone, but upon the very face of nature itself. Imagine a broad belt, ten miles or so in width, stretching from the Channel to the German frontier near Basle, which is positively littered with the bodies of men and scarified with their rude graves; in which farms, villages and cottages are shapeless heaps of blackened masonry; in which fields, roads and trees are pitted and torn and twisted by shells and disfigured by dead horses, cattle, sheep and goats, scattered in every attitude of repulsive distortion and dismemberment.

By the end of 1914, the losses for the embattled nations were staggering: between September and December, Germany had suffered 800,000 casualties. The Austro-Hungarian army had been depleted by nearly a million men, and was deeply compromised as a fighting force. In the first five months of fighting, the French had lost 300,000 dead and 600,000 wounded, captured, or missing, more than the total number of British war dead throughout the Second World War. But the warring states sought new allies and new fronts, not a negotiated peace. As the war came to the home front, the calamitous damage expanded: civilian targets were bombarded, and the Allied nations subjected the Central Powers to a naval blockade. In the Austro-Hungarian Empire, food shortages had appeared as early as October, and the euphoria of the early months vanished.

Although the Freud family was relatively sheltered from the hardships of the war, the disruptions to civilian life began to intrude. Freud's practice had shrunk to a quarter of its former size; he worried that psychoanalytic journals would be discontinued for lack of readers and subscribers, and that the association was dead and could no longer keep "international" in its title. The publishing industry was disrupted, and the 1914 psychoanalytic yearbook (*Jahrbuch*) was not distributed, nor was the publisher willing to put out the 1915 edition.

By year's end, despite these worries and distractions, Freud had returned to his writing, which was, as before, filled with military imagery, now modernized to include the trench warfare of the Western Front. "The work is again going well," he wrote to Ferenczi. "I am living, as my brother says, in my private trench. I speculate and write, and after hard battles have got safely through the first line of riddles and difficulties. Anxiety, hysteria, and paranoia have capitulated. We shall see how far the successes can be carried forward." Even as he felt a breakthrough in his writing, his awareness of a world at war compromised his satisfaction. Habitually fearful about the reception of psychoanalytic ideas, he worried that the fragmentation of Europe into hostile nations would affect his life's work. He complained to Ferenczi, "I may say that I have already given the world more than she has given me. I am now, and, because of the foreseeable consequences of the war, will also be later, more isolated than ever, and I know that at present I am writing for five people, you and the few others." Torn between his intellectual work and his anxiety about the effects of the war, Freud's writing began to fluctuate between creativity and emptiness. "Impotence and penury," he wrote to Abraham at the end of 1914, "have always been my bugbears and I am afraid we are now approaching both." He complained of being "often completely at a loss what to do with myself." Instead of the brief, cleansing storm he had imagined, the war had become a destructive hurricane that threatened to sweep away all he had labored to build: his practice, his publications, the international psychoanalytic organization, and the safety of his family.

The gloom and paralysis that descended on him in December of 1914 also had its source in the disarray of his internal world. His identification with military heroes, an early source of strength and solace, had coexisted with his need for order and emotional control, but now he faced a dilemma, for this profoundly brutal war was anything but controlled and orderly. While in August he had imagined that courageous action would swiftly restore order, by year's end this expectation had been overturned; the images that were so much a part of his thinking seemed less comforting.

The reality of the Great War forced Freud to begin to question his long-held, largely unexamined ideas about war. He was fifty-eight years old in 1914. In the past, using military imagery, he had imagined himself a "conquistador" savoring the defeats of his opponents, but his boyish excitement was no longer in keeping with the times. Total war had the potential to undermine a way of thinking which had invigorated him and formed a central part of his identity. For a man fearful of death and loss, the danger to his sons was unnerving. He needed to rethink the war from the vantage point of psychoanalysis.

In January of 1915, Freud saw his son Martin off at the train station as he left for the Galician theater. "I thought in all clarity," he wrote to Abraham, "about the doubt there is whether and how we shall ever see him again." However much heroic stories had stirred his imagination as a youth, he now saw the battlefield through the eyes of a father fearful for his son's safety. He did not allow himself to remain in this frightened state, however. On February 16, just weeks after Martin's departure, he gave a lecture to his B'nai B'rith lodge on the emotional impacts of the war. This lecture would later be published as *Our Attitude towards Death,* the first part of a larger essay, *Thoughts for the Times on War and Death.* In his lecture, he took an ironic stance, later describing the talk in a letter to Ferenczi as "saucy . . . inspired by gallows humor." He had moved away from his fear, and now used the losses of the war to tweak "pious souls" about their refusal to acknowledge their hidden emotions about death. He assumed a

Freud with his sons Ernst and Martin, 1916.

detached tone and did not mention the anxiety he felt about the danger facing his sons, speaking instead about the anxiety at large in society; but his fear came through obliquely as he referred to what Martha, whose life was centered on her children, might have been feeling: "We are paralyzed by the thought of who is to take the son's place with his mother." The reference to paralysis also hinted at his "bugbear"— the dread feeling of impotence he had mentioned to Abraham in December.

His lecture was directed at those on the home front who fearfully awaited word, as did the Freuds, of family members at the front. The war, he held, had caused "bewilderment" because it had uprooted established ideas about death, and new ones had not yet been found. He urged his audience to consider what psychoanalysis had revealed: that our attitudes toward death were determined by unconscious forces that remained almost the same as those of our primitive forebears. The war, like psychoanalysis, "strips us of the later accretions of civilization [and] lays bare the primal man in each of us." He claimed that "at bottom no one believes in his own death . . . in the unconscious every one of us is convinced of his own immortality." What is more, he argued, we are ambivalent toward the deaths of those we love, and we can kill strangers without guilt—we are all, in our unconscious, "a gang of murderers."

The loss of loved ones posed a special problem for Freud, who had been, throughout his life, preoccupied with death and now faced the possible loss of his sons. He approached the devastation that such losses could wreak, noting "we will not be consoled, we will not fill the lost one's place," but then moved away from such potential grief by extolling risk taking. When life is held too dear, he observed, "when the highest stake in the game of living, life itself cannot be risked," life becomes "shallow and empty." If our attachments to loved ones made us too fearful to court danger, many actions would not be undertaken; he warned that we would "dare not contemplate a great many undertakings which are dangerous but in fact indispensable, such as attempts at artificial flight, expeditions to distant countries or experiments with explosive substances." Preserving the capacity to undertake dangerous behavior was, in his view, an ideal way for everyone to deal with the fear of loss and grief; a less daring life would be constricted and lose meaning.

The war, Freud told his audience, will not allow us to deny death as had been done in peacetime. The bewilderment and anxiety of the war years would be eased, Freud advised, if people would recognize these psychoanalytic truths about their attitudes toward the terrible casualties and the constant fear of personal loss. Death must not be suppressed, it must be given its proper place in our thoughts, and this "realistic" stance would not only make life more tolerable, but make it "interesting again" and restore "its full content." Counseling stoical acceptance, he asserted that "war cannot be abolished" and repeated the old maxim, "If you want to preserve peace, arm for war," without noting that every European nation had prepared only too well for war and got war, not peace.

The personal accounts in the extensive memoirs and literature on the Great War both confirm and contradict Freud's ideas. Some men—and women, too—relished the excitement of constant danger. On both sides of No-Man's-Land, soldiers in combat wrote of discovering within themselves "a Paleolithic savage," "the beast that is inside man." But after the battles of the Somme and Verdun, testimony from the front evoked industrial images: "workers of war," "we are all screws in a machine that wallows forward." Some did, as Freud had imagined, become inured to death and killing; others resisted, fiercely preserving their peacetime values.

Most striking was Freud's neglect of fear as one of the most pervasive and intense emotions experienced in battle. The German writer Ernst Jünger wrote of a night patrol in which he felt both "the tense excitement of the hunter and the terror of the hunted." Jünger's account is a reminder that aggression could be closely linked to fear; the soldiers on the other side were not simply the enemy, they were also one's potential killers. Believing that, at the deepest level, no one believed in their own death, Freud held that the fear of death was a secondary emotion, the product of guilt. But the memoirs of a number of soldiers tell another story: the fear of death was intense and primary. As the poet Wilfred Owen put it, he was "kept alive by brandy and the fear of death."

Although Freud had been afraid of death and loss for most of his life, he seemed strangely comfortable, even indifferent, in his wartime lecture. In war, he observed, "death is no longer a chance event. To be sure, it still seems a matter of chance whether a bullet hits this man or that; but a second bullet may well hit the survivor; and the accumulation of deaths puts an end to the impression of chance. Life has, indeed, become interesting again; it has recovered its full content." But it was precisely when a soldier could no longer believe in his chances for survival that despair set in. The British historian C. R. M. F. Cruttwell, at Ypres during the first German gas attack, was psychologically damaged by his experience and suffered a breakdown after the war. He observed that "nearly every soldier is or becomes a fatalist on active service; it quietens his nerves to believe that his chance will be favourable or the reverse. But his fatalism depends on the belief that he has a chance. If the very air which he breathes is poison, his chance is gone: he is merely a destined victim for the slaughter."

Such feelings of despair and helplessness, particularly intense in the trenches of the Western Front, along with the exposure to massive casualties, were profoundly destructive to the emotional well-being of a great many soldiers. In early 1915, Freud was not yet aware of the numbers of men who were broken by their experiences, but the epidemic of mental illness had begun as early as September of 1914. On the Western Front, several men had to be evacuated from battle, disabled by nervous disorders. By the time Freud was preparing his lecture, more than a hundred British officers and eight hundred men were being treated for "severe mental disability," later called shell-shock. The testimony of the psychological damage inflicted by the war was expressed in sheer numbers; unlike the war literature written by the educated, the cases of shell-shock were a more democratic form of evidence, since they documented the mental anguish of both officers and men in the ranks. The armies of every nation in the Great War would be challenged to find explanations and treatments for this flood of disabled men.

But psychoanalysis had not predicted that lasting mental illness would be one of the results of the war. Freud, certain that the mayhem of war was consistent with the underlying, fundamental nature of *all* soldiers—even asserting that war would be life-enhancing—was blind to the immensely disruptive impact of combat experiences. In addition, his attempt at a universal interpretation ignored the great variety of combat situations that men faced as they fought at sea and in the air, in the trenches of the Western Front, or in the many other war zones.

But for Freud, words had not lost their vigor; he rescued himself from the self-doubt and confusion that the war had aroused by subjecting his turmoil to psychoanalytic scrutiny. When he gave the B'nai B'rith talk, Freud was not among the bereaved; he only feared the loss of his sons, but he assuaged his anxieties with his speculations and felt enlivened by the reinstatement of his idealized attitude toward war. He had returned to emotional control, stoical acceptance, and the solace he always found in the world of theory. But his words, particularly the notion that the dangers of the war would make life "interesting" again, offered cold comfort to those who were actually grieving.

The second part of *Thoughts for the Times on War and Death,* the essay titled *The Disillusionment of the War,* was written in the month following the speech to the B'nai B'rith. Between February and March, Freud had abandoned his stoical stance. Although he believed that attitudes toward death could be changed by *any* war, he now realized that the European conflict was not just war in general. This war of all against all was an unprecedented event. "We cannot help but feel," he wrote, "that no event has ever destroyed so much that is precious in the common possessions of humanity," and he condemned this new, total war for its immense casualties, its attacks on civilian populations, and the bitter enmity it had created among the nations of Europe.

Freud recognized that the Great War, unlike previous wars, had undermined a whole system of beliefs about human nature and Western culture, and now the industrial nature of modern war entered his vocabulary, as he described the noncombatant as "a cog in the gigantic machinery of war." In a paean to the internationalism of prewar Europe, he described its achievements in art and science, its reliance on order and law, and its high standards for individual behavior. Linked by interdependent economies, many citizens had traveled widely, experiencing the high civilization of all nations as those of a common "fatherland." The years of peace had instilled a confidence in the capacities of this culture: "We had expected the great world-dominating nations of white race upon whom the leadership of the human species has fallen . . . to succeed in discovering another way of settling misunderstandings and conflicts of interest." But even if mediation failed and a war broke out, many had believed that the conflict would be a limited war: "We pictured it as a chivalrous passage of arms, which would limit itself to establishing the superiority of one side in the struggle . . . " This vision of war as a chivalric action—even euphemistically portrayed as "a passage of arms"—had enabled Europeans to imagine themselves as culturally superior; it was the other races and nationalities who were driven by their primitive instincts. Yet the Great War did not begin in street riots in the workers' districts; it was not waged by Asians, Africans, or Americans, but by the educated male leaders of western Europe, among whom, Freud believed, the capacity for restraint was most developed. Old assumptions crumbled in the face of the war, and the European citizen, Freud wrote, had come to "stand helpless in a world that has grown strange to him."

Although he had disparaged other nations in his private correspondence, in this essay Freud's initial enthusiastic support for the Central Powers did not escalate into more intense hatred of the enemy nations; instead, he described the war as a general human failing. Evil, according to him, did not inhere in any one group or nation. While the wartime vilification of enemy nations continued to create an atmosphere of intense nationalism that helped to prolong the war, Freud's ideas countered this trend, which was a step toward renewed understanding among Europeans. As late as 1917, Einstein would write with disgust of the extreme nationalism of his German academic colleagues. Freud, in contrast, called all the belligerent states to account.

Freud took the position that if some of his old ideas had been proved wrong, at least the war confirmed his psychoanalytic theories about the irrational nature of man. The brutality of the war shook his assumptions, but did not completely overturn his ideas, as it did with so many liberal European and American thinkers. Psychoanalytic practice had revealed to Freud that the intellect—rationality—even among those living in "civilized" nations, was not firmly in command. The passions released by war had to be taken into account; they were an ineradicable part of human nature. Even while European leaders and generals continued to make arguments in favor of continuing the conflict, others began to experience the war as senseless. After the war, Freud's ideas became increasingly persuasive, and they remain important in the understanding of the First World War. A contemporary historian, James Joll, has concluded that the decisions to declare war "suggest that the motives of statesmen and generals were far less rational and well thought out than the view that they deliberately embarked on war as a way out of their insoluble domestic social and political problems."

Freud, however, did not offer his ideas as a partial explanation. His innovative insights into irrational motives were made problematic, as he leaped to a sweeping and simplistic explanation for the particularly destructive nature of this war. His theory of the timelessness of unconscious emotions did not explain why total war emerged at this moment in European history. His psychoanalytic understanding took no account of contemporary developments: the fears induced by the arms race, the constraints of military plans, and the influence of prewar values. While he attempted to stake out a psychoanalytic claim to insight into mankind's violent capacities, neither he, nor others in the psychoanalytic movement, had predicted the uniquely destructive nature of the war. With the exception of Ferenczi, Freud and his colleagues did not voice opposition to war, as had internationalists, pacifists, socialists, and some feminists. Those who had foreseen the emergence of total war were careful students of modern economics, politics, and military technology. Emphasizing the peaceful nature of Europe before 1914 ignored those aspects of the culture that embraced war and military values. Ideologies such as rampant nationalism, which demonized "enemy" nations, or imperialism, which fueled aggressive foreign policies, played their roles in the perpetuation of the war and its expansive goals. The adherents of

Social Darwinism assumed that national survival depended on struggle, stirring up aggression and setting loose anxiety about personal security and national autonomy.

Emotions other than primal aggression played a role. The historian Roland Stromberg, reviewing a wide range of sources, commented: "Much evidence belies the trite explanation of the war as a breaking forth of evil, whether Christian Original Sin or, more fashionably, Freudian inner aggression. Too many went forth joyfully to war . . . in a spirit of adventure but also a serious search for fulfillment in a worthy purpose, and for true companionship." Many men in the ranks felt that the overwhelming casualties were the product of the remoteness of the staff officers, that it was more a case of indifference than the release of primitive impulses. In his memoirs, Lloyd George wrote of the British military commanders: "Some of the assaults on impossible positions ordered by our generals would never have been decreed if they had seen beforehand with their own eyes the hopeless slaughter to which their orders doomed their men."

Despite his pessimistic appraisal of the relative power of primitive emotions, in his essays Freud expressed hope about the future, believing that the combatants would make a smooth transition to peacetime values: "We may anticipate that the ennoblement of their instincts will be restored in more peaceful times." Instilling hope in the future may have been his goal here, for his depictions of a return to normalcy are in sharp contrast to the much gloomier views he expressed in his correspondence in the winter of 1914. But his prediction was also based on a simple model in which the state, previously a bastion that contained primitive emotion, set loose those explosive feelings by declaring war. An armistice would restore civil restraints and return Europe to its previously peaceful ways. Despite his psychoanalytic experience, Freud's vision was not a guide to the future: the postwar years saw the emergence of Nazism, Fascism, and Bolshevism, political movements that perpetuated the violence of the war. The writer Jules Romains, who had served on the front, imagined a darker future. In his novel *Verdun,* he wrote: "This . . . is the one irreparable loss . . . it has taken civilization centuries of patient fumbling to teach men that life, their own and that of others, is something sacred. Well, it's been so much work thrown away. We shan't, you'll see, get back to that attitude in a hurry."

Freud's sense that his interpretation of the war affirmed the findings of psychoanalysis enabled him to overcome his paralysis, and the next few years were very productive. As the rest of the world plunged further into destructive chaos, he returned to abstract theory building, launching an ambitious project to write a book on psychoanalytic "metapsychology." Twelve essays were planned—though only five were eventually published—all written in a burst of activity in 1915: *Instincts and Their Vicissitudes, Repression, The Unconscious, A Metapsychological Supplement to the Theory of Dreams,* and *Mourning and Melancholia.* As the titles indicate, he was working on topics that had concerned him since the

Studies on Hysteria, now attempting to treat them at a general or abstract theoretical level. And, as was true for so much of his theorizing that was far removed from direct observations, this was fertile soil for his unique blend of disguised self-analysis, arguments with enemies, astute insights, and flights of theoretical fancy. As he described it to Fliess years before, the metapsychology was "my ideal and woebegone child."

The most enduring and insightful of these essays was *Mourning and Melancholia,* a brief, condensed work that traced depression, the "melancholia" of the title, to loss of love and loss of the love object. Freud described the similarity between normal mourning and depression; both involved painful dejection and sadness, loss of interest in the world, low energy, and inability to love. But in depression there was the added feature of low self-regard that in extreme cases became self-hate and self-attack. He accounted for this by describing the way vital relationships were represented within the mind. Grief and preoccupation with loss was a way of holding onto the lost person; he noted how in depression the self splits, how "one part of the ego sets itself over against the other, judges it critically, and, as it were, takes it as its object." This was an example of conscience—what he later called the superego—and illustrated how one could keep valued others alive inside oneself as punitive authority figures.

Throughout the war years, Freud continued to give his Saturday evening lectures at the University of Vienna. This was an opportunity to bring psychoanalytic ideas to a wider audience; he would talk for two hours, typically without notes, covering his basic concepts: slips and errors, dreams, the theory of neurosis, and psychoanalytic treatment. These lectures provided the basis for his next writing project, the *Introductory Lectures on Psychoanalysis,* which were published in 1916 and 1917. The *Introductory Lectures* proved to be one of his most popular works, selling more copies than any of his other books, with the exception of *The Psychopathology of Everyday Life,* and appearing in fifteen foreign language translations.

Significantly, the large body of Freud's writing during these years made little mention of the war itself. The *Introductory Lectures* contained only one substantive comment in over 450 pages of text, while the metapsychological papers did not deal with it at all. *Mourning and Melancholia,* directly concerned with the topics of death and loss, drew no examples from the death, destruction, losses, and fears that preoccupied so many people during this time.

Suffering increased among the civilian population in Austria-Hungary as the Allied naval blockade, combined with the demands of the war, caused severe food shortages in 1915. By April, ration cards for the coarse, unappetizing "war bread" had been introduced in the cities, and food riots struck in May and October. No flour, potatoes, or fat were available in Vienna in the fall, and the black market flourished. Despite his capacity to insulate himself from the stress of the relentless misery of the war, Freud continued to have breakthroughs of feeling about its impacts. In November of 1915, he wrote to his friend and col-league Lou Andreas-Salomé about Ernst and Martin: "My second warrior . . . had a stroke of luck similar to that of his elder brother. He happened to be away from the dug-out where the whole crew in charge of his gun had sought shelter during the battle on the Karst plateau and he was thus the only one to escape the fate of being buried alive by a direct hit. Do you think we can count on the regular repetition of such chances? My other [eldest] son suddenly arrived one day . . . unkempt but in good fettle, and decorated with the silver medal for bravery." The Freud sons' luck still held, but their father, remembering their two near misses, felt relief and continuing anxiety. He lived with the awareness that they were at the mercy of chance and could be killed or wounded at any moment.

On Freud's sixtieth birthday in 1916, mindful of the surrounding misery of the war, he asked for a quiet celebration. Nevertheless, the birthday was an-nounced in the newspapers in May, and he received such an abundance of flow-ers that he grumbled about all the work the fuss caused him. His birthday seemed to evoke gloom and was a reminder of advancing age. As he wrote to Lou Andreas-Salomé, "For had I known how little joy I would feel on my sixtieth birthday, my first birthday would probably not have given me pleasure either. Even in the happiest of times it would be but a melancholy event." He joked in a letter to Abraham that, in the future, he would not need any funeral wreaths.

The poor harvest of 1916 caused severe shortages of food, and fuel was also scarce. In the winter of 1916–1917, city households were allowed to heat only one room. Even the relatively well-off Freuds felt the deprivations, and his mood continued to go up and down. The family suffered without heat; "for two weeks, darkness and cold have made my usual nightly work impossible," he wrote to Ferenczi in February of 1917. In July, shortly before the family left for a vacation in Hungary, he learned that his sister Rosa had lost her only son, Hermann, a casualty on the Tyrolean front. The war losses had not, until now, hit the family directly. This was mourning at first hand; Freud wrote to Abra-ham that "her grief surpassed description." He did not comment on his own feelings, however, quickly changing the subject, and reassuring himself that there was no bad news about "his warriors." The family went on to enjoy a holiday of plenty: "The Hungarians are uncouth and noisy but obliging and hospitable and friendship and loyalty are taking the form of generosity, with the result that we are able to wallow in a superfluity of bread, butter, sausages, eggs, and cigars, rather like the chief of a primitive tribe."

At home, the Freud family received generous gifts of food and cigars from colleagues and supporters, in stark contrast to the desperation of the workers in Vienna. By September of 1917, the German ambassador noted that the "people in the suburbs of Vienna are starving." An officer in the U.S. Embassy observed "strings of poorly dressed women and children held in line by police . . . waiting for milk, vessel in hand. . . . Latecomers went home empty-handed, while lucky ones obtained only half as much as they expected." Strikes and food riots in Vienna and Budapest necessitated the recall of seven army divisions from the front. In the midst of these dire events, Freud's practice had picked up to eight psychoanalytic patients a day. He cheerfully reported to Ferenczi in November that his work was going extremely well, though he mentioned one hardship: "Yesterday I smoked away my last cigar, and since then I have been grumpy and tired. . . . Then a patient brought me fifty, I lit one, became cheerful." Protection from the surrounding misery continued for Freud. A few weeks later, a patient supplied him with more cigars. Groceries, too, were abundant compared to the year before. Even in the last months of the war, the Freuds lived on gifts, "like a doctor's family in the old days," well supplied with cigars, flour, lard, and bacon from colleagues and patients, his "quartermasters." But living so much more comfortably than others in Vienna did not dispel his depressed state of mind; he complained to Abraham that his prevailing "mood is powerless embitterment, or embitterment at my powerlessness." Being sustained by the largesse of others brought back the old feelings of helplessness he had endured in his poor, early years when he was forced to depend on handouts from Breuer and other friends.

All three of Freud's sons were safe at home in March of 1918, a welcome respite for their parents, who had lived with a constant burden of worry, undoubtedly intensified by the death of their nephew just months earlier. But they had new cause for dread in the spring, as the Austrian chief of staff decided on another offensive in Italy, even though his army was undermanned, undersupplied, and mutinous. In June, both Oli and Martin prepared to serve in this disastrous campaign.

When weeks had passed with no word of Martin, Freud confessed to Ferenczi that he suffered real dread; "this time I felt the anxiety about him with more torment than usual, indeed perhaps real torment for the first time, and I also brushed off . . . obvious assurances." The casualties suffered by the Austrian army in Italy had been horrific; the danger to Martin made real his father's worst imaginings. But Freud dealt with his anguish by interpreting away his fear: "Analysis then showed me the presumed neurotic contribution. There was also envy of the sons in it, of which I had otherwise felt nothing, and, in fact, envy on account of youth." In this piece of self-analysis, Freud turned his fear of loss into a competitive father-son struggle, as he had done ever since the 1890s. Significantly, when Martin had been cited for gallantry in 1915, his son's heroism had not stimulated feelings of anxiety or competitiveness.

In October of 1918, Freud wrote of the dreadful tension in Vienna, as everyone awaited the disintegration of the Austro-Hungarian Empire. Added to the impending political crisis, the epidemic of Spanish flu, which had begun to devastate Europe in June, gave him another fright. Anna, Ernst, Oli and Mathilde were all stricken but recovered. He wrote to Ferenczi, "The epidemic is still dominating the scene. One hears about horrendous cases and is always reassured when someone has already had it." Death seemed omnipresent at home as well as on the distant battlefield. At this anxious time, cut off from direct contact with his colleagues, besieged by fears about the war and the epidemic, he mentioned that "Annerl's analysis is getting very fine, otherwise the cases are uninteresting." He had begun the psychoanalytic treatment of his daughter that would eventually make her his most reliable caretaker and disciple.

On November 4, 1918, the armistice was signed in Austria, and the long war finally came to an end. Oli came home and so did Ernst, after spending some time in a hospital. Other members of the immediate family had survived the battlefields, the influenza epidemic, and the privations of the war years. Communication with his colleagues resumed, and Freud reestablished psychoanalytic publishing in December. But Martin's fate was still unknown. Not until February of 1919 would Freud learn that his son had survived the war and was a prisoner in Genoa. When he was released, without permanent injuries, the Freuds were finally free of anxiety.

The family had come through the war relatively unscathed, but it had been a trying time for Freud, now in his sixties and less resilient than his younger colleagues. Having hoped for a revitalized nation, he faced the future in a defeated, truncated Austria where privations continued. By 1918, he had lost his life savings—150,000 crowns invested in Austrian state bonds, and 100,000 crowns in life insurance. As a boy, he had suffered disillusionment over his father's inadequacies; now his fury at the failure of the Hapsburg dynasty carried the extra sting of these old disappointments, and his anger burst out in a final curse: "The Hapsburgs have left behind nothing but a pile of crap." The optimistic hopes for the renewal of European civilization, expressed in *Thoughts for the Times* in 1915, had faded. Attuned by his early disillusionment to the emotions of the defeated nations, he predicted to Ferenczi, "I expect there will begin to be a frightful dawning in Germany. Much worse than with you or with us. Think about the abominable tension of these four and a half years and the terrible disappointment that is now suddenly releasing this pressure." As the dark war years ended in hardship and the dissolution of his homeland, even the shelter of psychoanalysis seemed to fail him. In November of 1918, he wrote despondently, "Our analysis has actually also had trouble. No sooner does it begin to interest the world on account of the war neuroses than the war ends. . . . Our kingdom is indeed not of this world."

More soldiers were killed in the First World War than in any other known to history. Many millions more were injured and emotionally damaged and would suffer from their wounds—both physical and psychological—for the rest of their lives. The devastation in Freud's Austria could be measured in relative casualty figures; Hapsburg armies had lost 12,500 men in the war of 1859,

20,000 in 1866, and 2,000,000 in the First World War. All these deaths and injuries spread out to families and loved ones. Civilians were not spared; millions died from starvation and the influenza epidemic, an aftermath of wartime conditions, and material damage was overwhelming. Profound changes were also set in motion in the inner landscape. The French poet Paul Valéry spoke of this crisis of the mind:

> One can say that all the fundamentals of our world have been affected by the war . . . something deeper has worn away than the renewable parts of the machine. You know how greatly the general economic situation has been disturbed, and the polity of states, and the very life of the individual; you are familiar with the universal discomfort, hesitation, apprehension. But among all these injured things is the Mind. The Mind has indeed been cruelly wounded; its complaint is heard in the hearts of intellectual men; it passes a mournful judgement on itself. It doubts itself profoundly.

Many experienced the Great War as a supremely irrational event, and the postwar world would be far more open to new forms in literature, art, and systems of thought. Previously confined to small circles, psychoanalysis, with its focus on unconscious emotions, now began to find a more receptive audience. Before the war, when Ernest Jones and David Eder, the first English practitioners of psychoanalysis, had attempted to introduce Freud's ideas to British medicine, their entire audience walked out. In prewar Great Britain, mental illness was stigmatized, seen as a hereditary degeneration. After the war, when men of "good character" suffered psychotic symptoms, it became more acceptable to believe that "what had been considered abnormal might be discovered in the mind of the average man." The exposure to victims of shell-shock redefined the practice of British psychiatry.

The four years of total war had been a whirlwind, inflicting enormous disruptions in personal lives, conditioning large numbers to expect and accept change. Young soldiers and nurses had been torn from their roots by the war, and forced to live far from home, away from the control of their elders and traditional patterns of life. Increased sexual freedom, heightened by the fear of death, was one important consequence. Prophylactics had been distributed to the soldiers; there were war babies and venereal disease. The wartime sexual experiences required new attitudes and a new language. The Great War, with its global scope, long duration, and traumatic intensity, put its stamp on the minds of all who lived through it, and many men and women now searched for values, beliefs, and ideas to encompass their recent experiences. Despite Freud's pessimistic outlook, the "kingdom of psychoanalysis" would have a greatly expanded place in this new world.

CHAPTER 18

Trauma Revisited:
The Neuroses of War

Most of the neurotic diseases which had been brought about by the war disappeared on the cessation of the war conditions.

—Freud, 1921

The older I get, the sadder I feel about the uselessness of it all, but in particular the deaths of my comrades . . . I thought I had managed all right, kept the awful things out of my mind. But now I'm an old man and they come back out from where I hid them. Every night.

—A First World War veteran

A N EPIDEMIC of mental illness—variously labeled "shell-shock," "war neurosis," or "war psychosis"—was caused by the Great War, confronting psychiatry as well as psychoanalysis with a large population of seriously afflicted men. Many of these soldiers and veterans bore a striking resemblance to the hysterics Freud worked with in the 1890s—the very patients with whom he developed psychoanalysis. Here was a remarkable opportunity for psychoanalysts to demonstrate the value of their theories and therapeutic methods, since both the military and medical authorities were at a loss to understand, much less successfully treat, these men.

Soldiers suffering from shell-shock or war neuroses displayed a variety of reactions: tremors and uncontrollable shaking, paralyses of many types, blindness, deafness, hallucinations, compulsive and tic-like movements, obsessive thoughts, recurring nightmares, hypervigilance and extreme reactions to stimulation, pains, headaches, and gastric distress. A frequent symptom was fixation on some terrible event such as the mutilation or death of a comrade, which would appear in hallucinations or nightmares. Profound guilt, along with fear, ranging from anxiety to outright terror, were the underlying emotional states of most of them. The mental breakdown of these soldiers was initially thought to be caused by injuries to the brain, concussions due to the barrages of large-caliber artillery, hence "shell-shock," but this was a mistaken belief. They were not suffering from the physical effects of explosions, but were in emotional shock. There was no medical or neurological basis for their conditions, though the men themselves typically believed they had actual injuries.

Psychiatric breakdowns had begun in the very first month of the war. After the first serious fighting by the British on the Western Front in 1914, several men were evacuated from France, having collapsed in the retreat from the battle. The phenomenon continued as more and more young soldiers were sent back from the front lines with a host of symptoms. At the base hospitals in France, an expert on nervous diseases noted that many disabled men suffered from wounds that seemed relatively slight: "trivial bullet and shell wounds, or even slight contusions of the back, arms and legs." Military physicians, puzzled by the disparity between the soldiers' mental anguish and their actual injuries, believed they were dealing with an unknown malady, a new medical-military problem. None of the armies had prepared for these mental casualties; military psychiatry hardly existed, and no effective treatments were available.

The unique horrors of this war, most starkly in evidence on the Western Front, made old ideas of bravery and cowardice irrelevant, as the military and masculine virtues—honor, courage, duty—dissolved in the trench warfare. At Passchendaele, the war diary of a young officer, Edwin Vaughn, portrayed men disintegrating in a war that drove them out of their minds: "Captain Spencer . . . babbling incoherently in a shell hole . . . Wood, who could not walk or even talk but lay shuddering on a wire bed in a bunker . . . Lynch, shaking and helpless with fear, who cries that he cannot walk, but is shamed . . . into running forward, and is killed before he has gone three yards." This was an unprecedented kind of war, a battlefield of invisible armies, a war in which the soldiers inhabited a blasted landscape, huddled in trenches, unable to move or act. The weaponry—machine guns, artillery, poison gas—was preeminent. The men at the front cowered helplessly in their holes, remembering themselves as "infinitely small, running—affrighted rabbits from the upheaval of the shells, nerve-wracked, deafened; clinging to earth, hiding eyes, whispering, 'oh God!'" The passivity and helplessness, together with the death and destruction, created the greatest numbers of psychiatric casualties; men who had at least a chance to move and fight were much less likely to crack.

This was the reality of the war, which caused so many to break down, and known, only too well, to the men who were in it—the soldiers and line officers. But an awareness of the overwhelming levels of stress on the front did not penetrate the higher echelons, where military policies, as well as long-standing beliefs about mental illness and patriotism, led to punitive treatments. Men who broke down in combat were seen as degenerates or moral invalids who must be disciplined. One of General Erich von Falkenhayn's aides, in a visit to the battlefield at Verdun, said to a shivering soldier, "Are you freezing? Only masturbators, drunkards, and whoremongers freeze!" On the Somme in 1916, one of the worst of many bloody battles, a nineteen-year-old private, who had served since 1914, panicked and fled at the noise of the "gas gong." He was arrested and charged with desertion. During the trial, his commanding officer testified that the young soldier had broken down under the combination of shellfire and the threat from a grim new weapon, poison gas. This brought no mercy from the court, and he was sentenced to execution. Death sentences for mentally disabled soldiers continued throughout the war.

Such harsh attitudes toward soldiers were rooted in prevailing ideas in Europe about the nature of modern war. From the turn of the century, the military thinkers of Europe had become convinced that victory would be achieved through the most aggressive tactics. Although the new technology of war—the greater range, accuracy, and rate of modern firearms—increasingly favored defensive tactics, the preference for attack became so extreme that it has been called a cult or ideology of the offensive. Not just a method of planning and training, these tactics were also projected into idealized visions of national character: attack was held to be the only way of waging war that was consistent with the unique qualities of the nation's soldiers. For some military planners, the doctrine became a means to assuage fears about modern "degeneracy," national decline, or inferiority. The emphasis on an offensive strategy stressed, above all, the importance of morale, and preached the insignificance of material conditions; when a soldier broke down, more than the loss of manpower was at stake. Mental breakdowns struck at the linchpin of military plans as well as self-gratifying visions of national greatness. This bias contributed to large numbers of psychiatric casualties and then condemned the men who suffered from shell-shock.

A punitive approach was used by all the belligerent armies; shell-shocked soldiers were taken to hospitals and treatment centers where doctors used painful electrical currents, forcing them to renounce their symptoms. They were put on restricted diets, isolated from other people, and commands for obedience were shouted at them, with promised relief when their symptoms were relinquished. While some men were made fit to serve as a result of these regimens, some were killed by electrocution, and others were driven to suicide as the only escape from an impossible choice: medically induced pain or death on the front. Even those who were "cured" and sent back to battle frequently relapsed. This was ineffective therapy by torture, and, from the beginning of the war, at least some doctors felt conflicted about administering it. They sought other methods, including hypnosis and psychotherapy.

Electric shock used on shell-shocked soldier.

The contrast between the disciplinary and healing approaches was apparent in the debate in France between Paul Dubois and Pierre Janet. Dubois condemned hypnosis and argued that "neurotics, like the delinquents, are *antisocial* . . . unworthy soldiers who must be punished with discipline, even shot down. Neurotic people are stragglers from the army . . . we do not like them much; we are ready to throw in their faces reproaches of laxness, of simulation, or lack of energy." Janet, who had been using hypnosis as part of his therapeutic work with a variety of neurotic patients for many years before the war, believed that the soldiers had no conscious control over their conditions, and he argued forcefully against Dubois. The debate in France, which also emerged in other nations, exemplified the opposing positions for dealing with psychiatric casualties.

In England, the physician and anthropologist W. H. R. Rivers was put in charge of the Craiglockhart War Hospital outside Edinburgh, where he had about a hundred shell-shock patients under his care, including the poets Wilfred Owen and Siegfried Sassoon. Aware of psychoanalytic ideas, he could see that the soldiers' symptoms were representations of their unconscious emotional conflicts and that he could help them by encouraging the open expression of blocked feeling. As he put it: "The great merit of Freud is that he has provided us with a theory of the mechanism by which this experience, not readily and directly accessible to consciousness, produces its effects, while he and his followers have devised clinical methods by which these hidden factors in the causation of dis-ease may be brought to light."

William Brown, a British physician who had seen close to three thousand cases of war neuroses in England and France, argued that the symptoms of the shell-shock victims were similar to those of the female hysterics in Breuer and Freud's *Studies on Hysteria:* all these patients displayed bodily expressions of dammed-up emotions. Soldiers confronted with the impossible conflicts of the battlefield broke down, unable to discharge their overwhelming emotions through normal channels; their feelings were then "materialized" in physical-bodily form. Like Breuer and Freud's hysterics, the soldiers had no memory of the traumatic events that set off their disturbances; they were unconscious, amnesic, their memories existed in sealed-off compartments. Brown used light hypnosis, which allowed the men to recover their memories with emotional vividness. Such emo-tional "abreaction"—the release of the pent-up emotions and memories—helped relieve the symptoms and produced "a re-synthesis of the mind of the patient" in which he was able to integrate the traumatic experience into the continuity of his life.

The work of Rivers, Brown, and other English and French physicians was not known to Freud and his Austrian and German colleagues during the war, but they did learn of the efforts of Ernst Simmel, a physician who was in charge of a German field hospital for psychological casualties. Simmel found that he could help the soldiers in his care by bringing the traumatic events associated with the onset of their symptoms to consciousness with a combination of psy-choanalytic conversation, dream analysis, and "analytic-cathartic hypnosis." Like Josef Breuer so many years before, he described a "splitting of the personality" that occurred in situations of extreme terror and helplessness and noted the ther-apeutic value of expressing emotions—he focused on anxiety, dread of death, and rage—in the treatment setting. Simmel also described how the dreams and fantasies of these soldiers were attempts at mastery; that is, they were not aimed at the unconscious gratification of wishes, but were attempts to come to terms with the devastation they had experienced. He also noted the prevalence of guilt in these men, so many of whose comrades had been killed. While relieved to be alive, they were terribly torn over the deaths of their friends. Simmel summa-rized his findings in a book entitled *War Neuroses and Psychic Trauma,* published in 1918.

These physicians knew Freud's ideas from their reading, but none of them were psychoanalysts during the war, nor were they part of the psychoanalytic movement, so they were free to select those aspects of his theories and methods that fit their own observations and apply them in their work with soldiers suf-fering from war neuroses. It was the early theory and therapy from the *Studies on Hysteria* that were most useful: symptoms were caused by severe traumas; the traumatic experiences themselves were split off—their effects emanated from a

*Drs. William Brown, W. H. R. Rivers, and
Elliot Smith, 1915.*

part of the mind that was unconscious—and effective treatment involved catharsis, the open expression of the sealed-off memories with a full range of emotions.
Many of the men were overwhelmed by the horrendous things they had been
forced to undergo, as well as being caught up in powerful psychological conflicts. The conviction that they must be brave and not let their country or their
comrades down clashed with their desperate need to escape injury and death.
Others experienced terrible guilt over killing. Raised all their lives to believe that
murder was wrong, they were then forced to kill others who they could see were
young men like themselves, trapped on the battlefield.

   Their symptoms were attempts to resolve—to master—these impossible
dilemmas. The cathartic-psychoanalytic treatments enabled them to give open
expression to their conflicts; it became an alternative to the bodily manifestations
of their "neurotic" symptoms. Also, while none of the physicians directly wrote
about it, the doctor-patient relationship was itself central to the healing process.
Siegfried Sassoon described the qualities of his relationship with Dr. Rivers upon
leaving Craiglockhart: "Shutting the door of his room for the last time, I left
behind me someone who had helped and understood me more than anyone I
had ever known. Much as he disliked speeding me back to the trenches, he realized that it was my only way out. And the longer I live the more right I know

him to have been." Rivers, Brown, and Simmel were medical officers imbued with authority, who, in contrast to the generals who sent soldiers to their deaths with indifference, related with interest and sympathy as they attempted to heal the men's suffering.

Karl Abraham called Simmel's work to Freud's attention in a letter written in February of 1918: "This is the first time that a German physician, basing himself firmly and without patronizing condescension on psychoanalysis, speaks of its outstanding usefulness in the treatment of war neuroses. . . . I think a year's training would make a good analyst of him. His attitude is correct." But not as "correct" as Abraham would have liked, for, in October of the same year, he wrote to Freud that he had gotten to know Simmel better and that "he has not yet in any way moved beyond the Breuer-Freud point of view, has strong resistances against sexuality which he is not yet clearly aware of, and, unfortunately, actually stressed at the Berlin meeting that, according to his own experience, sexuality does not play an essential part, either in war neurosis or in analytic treatment."

Freud echoed these sentiments in a letter to Ferenczi, commenting that even though Simmel's work was essentially "cathartic," it was still on analytic ground and was evidence that "German war medicine has taken the bait." Although he noted that Simmel was not investigating the sexual drives of his patients, he felt sure that training would make an analyst of him. Freud and Abraham's comments reveal the essential features of what would soon become the official psychoanalytic position with regard to the war neuroses. As was typical, Freud's first thoughts were directed to how Simmel's findings could be used to advance the movement. This was followed by the assertion that sexual conflicts must be implicated in these conditions. In fact, while work with shell-shocked soldiers gave solid evidence for the role of unconscious emotions and memories in the formation of symptoms, it provided scant support for Freud's belief in the primacy of sexuality; instead, it highlighted the role of trauma that he had discarded when he renounced his "seduction theory" years before. Nor did it support his idea that only the experiences of early childhood could cause neuroses. In addition, Simmel's work was, as both Abraham and Freud noted, a return to the cathartic therapy first developed by Breuer in the early 1880s, and, as such, posed a challenge to classic psychoanalytic technique. The evidence from work with the war neuroses affirmed the value of psychoanalysis but also raised questions about several of Freud's most cherished doctrines.

The Fifth International Psychoanalytic Congress was held in Budapest in September of 1918, just as the war was winding down. A central topic was the application of psychoanalysis to the psychological casualties of the war. Freud was elated by the success of the congress, and, in a rare moment of joy, crowed to Ferenczi: "I am swimming in satisfaction. I am light hearted, knowing that my problem child, my life's work, is protected and preserved for the future by your participation and that of others. I will see better times approaching if only from a distance." Simmel, Ferenczi, Abraham, and Jones presented papers at the congress that were later collected together in a monograph, with a brief introduction by Freud, titled *Psychoanalysis and the War Neuroses,* published in 1921. Simmel's paper summarized the findings presented in his earlier book, and was clearly the best of the four; his work anticipated the findings on trauma survivors and their treatment that have been amassed in subsequent years. He made a bow to the importance of sexuality at the beginning of his paper—he was analyzed by Abraham in 1920 and had become a member of the Berlin Psychoanalytic Institute, so this was obligatory—but these remarks were at odds with the gist of his presentation. The papers by Ferenczi and Jones occupied a middle ground; they both had some direct experience treating soldiers, but were also committed to the Professor's theories. Abraham's paper and Freud's introduction were the most doctrinaire.

Abraham had been a psychiatrist attached to the German army, where he saw a large number of men suffering from shell-shock. He believed they were psychologically deficient if they shrank from killing: "It is a question of aggressive achievements which a soldier must be ready to undertake at every moment. Along with the willingness to die, the willingness to kill is demanded of him." His explanation for the symptoms of traumatized soldiers rested almost entirely on sexual factors. Symptoms such as "trembling, agitation, irritability, sensitiveness, sleeplessness, headaches, anxiety, depression" were somehow due to "impotence" and "frigidity." "War neurotics already before the trauma were labile . . . especially so as regards their sexuality." Being in the company of other men aroused their "homosexuality"; they had an "effeminate disposition" and were "weakly potent." He commented on the "feminine-passive surrender to suffering," the use of symptoms to get sympathy or a pension and, finally, the way "the damaged part of the body receives for them a significance as an erotogenic zone." This was psychoanalytic-sexual interpretation carried to grotesque lengths.

Freud's introduction to the *War Neuroses* monograph was closely aligned with Abraham's position and at odds with Simmel's. He reaffirmed his conviction that "the driving forces which find expression in the formation of symptoms are sexual in nature, and that the neurosis is the result of the conflict between the ego and the sexual impulses which it has repudiated." If work with war neurotics had not confirmed this belief, it was, in his opinion, because investigators had not looked hard enough. The well-worn resistance argument was brought out; "opponents of psycho-analysis, whose repugnance to sexuality has shown itself to be stronger than their logic, have hastened to proclaim that the investigation of the war neuroses has not shown that the sexual theory of the neuroses is correct, this is quite another matter from showing that this theory is incorrect." He commented on Simmel's work, saying that it "has shown what results may be obtained if the war neurotic is treated by the cathartic method, which, as is well known, was the first stage of the psycho-analytic technique." Thus, Simmel and others would supposedly have done more for their patients if they had pursued a "correct" psychoanalytic course and dug into the deeper sexual factors.

A great many Viennese doctors had devoted their services to the care of wounded soldiers. Josef Breuer, seventy-two years old when the war began, had taken over the medical treatment of men in a distant suburban hospital, commuting daily on crowded streetcars in all kinds of weather and in the face of his own fatigue. Freud, in contrast, had not seen a single one of these men, spending the war years immersed in writing his abstract theoretical papers and the *Introductory Lectures,* analyzing his daughter Anna, and seeing those private patients who could pay his fees. Lacking any direct contact with suffering soldiers, he derived his conclusions from theory. Even with the lack of direct exposure, he could have gathered evidence by talking with his sons Martin and Ernst, who had gone through terrible fighting in the Austrian campaigns on the Eastern and Italian Fronts. In a letter to his friend Oskar Pfister, written in 1919 when Martin was still a prisoner of war in Italy, he mentioned his son's "great dangers escaped and severe ordeals," but there was never a suggestion that he and Martin talked about these "ordeals," certainly not in a way to influence his theories.

Freud's lack of firsthand experience led him to several erroneous conclusions regarding the war neuroses, conclusions that unfortunately endured because they were associated with his name and prestige. In 1915, before learning that anyone had applied psychoanalysis to psychiatric casualties, he had acknowledged his limitations. "It would be most interesting, no doubt," he declared, "to study the changes in the psychology of the combatants, but I know too little about it." This did not deter him for long, and he soon propounded various theories to explain these conditions. His unswerving commitment to the theory of sexual causation did not budge in the face of the evidence supplied by the doctors who worked directly with these men. Rivers, commenting directly on this point, wrote, "We have over and over again abundant evidence that pathological nervous and mental states are due, it would seem directly, to the shocks and strains of warfare; there is, in my experience, singularly little evidence to show that, even indirectly and as a subsidiary factor, any part has been taken in the process of causation by conflicts arising out of the activity of repressed sexual complexes."

Freud also asserted that civilized man had no prohibitions against killing enemies in war. As he put it, "When the furious struggle of the present war has been decided, each one of the victorious fighters will return home joyfully to his wife and children, unchecked and undisturbed by thoughts of the enemies he has killed whether at close quarters or at long range." The war, he believed, had removed all civilized restraints, creating a cultural vacuum in which mankind's primitive aggression would run free.

The full range of the soldiers' reactions to killing was much more complicated. A number of them were so brutalized by the war that they became numb and fought as if in a trance. Others did enjoy the excitement and fighting, especially if they were not powerless and immobilized. But many veterans were haunted for years by the memories of those they killed. As the war ground on, the men became increasingly estranged from their generals and the population at home; more and more, their identification with their comrades extended to the soldiers on the other side. Otto Binswanger, uncle of the Swiss analyst Ludwig Binswanger, was treating a shell-shocked soldier with cathartic hypnosis when his patient cried out, "'Do you see, do you see the enemy there? Has he a father and a mother? Has he a wife? I'll not kill him.' At the same time he cried hard and continually made trigger movements with his right forefinger." Freud's attempt to encompass all this with a single generalization not only got things wrong but missed the rich, individual texture of these experiences.

Another of Freud's erroneous beliefs was that the combat neuroses would be short-lived, writing in 1920 that "most of the neurotic diseases which had been brought about by the war disappeared on the cessation of the war conditions." This idea was based on his conviction that all neuroses originated in early childhood, so that adult trauma could not, by definition, have long-lasting effects. While some of the men who broke down in battle were only temporarily disturbed, a great many more were permanently damaged. There were war psychoses as well as war neuroses. The total number of men officially declared mentally disabled in all the countries that participated in the First World War was 250,000, with many more suffering nightmares, flashbacks, terrors, and depressions that were not officially diagnosed. Far from ending with the cessation of fighting, men continued to break down and suffer for years afterwards. Throughout the 1920s, psychoses among veterans increased, with more pensions for mental breakdowns dispensed in Britain in 1929 than had been given in the years immediately after the war. As Wilfred Owen wrote of the inmates of the Craiglockhart War Hospital:

These are men whose minds the Dead have ravished
Memory fingers in their hair of murders,
Multitudinous murders they once witnessed.

Another group were the men who functioned well enough in the world, sometimes reaching high levels of achievement, who remained haunted by their wartime experiences. For ten years after the war, the poet, translator, and novelist Robert Graves suffered a variety of disruptive symptoms. He could not use the telephone, nor see more than two people a day, nor count on a night's sleep; train travel made him ill, and he was plagued by flashbacks from the trenches. The poet Edmund Blunden spent two years on the front, was gassed, won the

Medal of Honor, and managed to lead a long and creative life in the succeeding years. Shortly before his death at age seventy-seven, he wrote, "My experiences in the First World War have haunted me all my life and for many days I have, it seemed, lived in that world rather than this."

Many veterans described their lives as divided into segments of "before" and "after" the war, which produced feelings of estrangement from those at home, as well as from their own prewar selves. Their very identities—their core sense of who they were—seemed discontinuous. "Hard to believe. Impossible to believe. That other life, so near in time and distance, was something led by different men," recalled the British veteran Stuart Cloete. "Two lives that bore no relation to each other. That was what they felt, the bloody lot of them." The damage was passed on to family members, as wives and children sensed that the men who came home from the war would never again be whole or even recognizable. Freud, committed to a theory that explained the war neuroses in terms of forces internal to each individual—the sexual instinct, primitive aggression—had no language for the dislocations of identity and social estrangements that deeply troubled so many former soldiers.

Enduring grief was widespread after the war among both veterans and civilians. The millions of deaths from the influenza epidemic piled on more losses: Europe was a continent in mourning. The mutual dependency and comradeship of frontline soldiers created relationships of unusual intensity, and the huge casualty rates left survivors in states of profound grief. Siegfried Sassoon noted "how many a brief bombardment had its long-delayed after-effect in the minds of these survivors, many of whom had looked at their companions and laughed while inferno did its best to destroy them. Not then was their evil hour, but now; now, in the sweating suffocation of nightmare, in paralysis of limbs, in the stammering of dislocated speech." Freud did not want to know about the effects of these terrible traumas and immense losses. Lou Andreas-Salomé wrote to him in 1919 about a young woman patient who had lost her twin brother in the war, and suffered from a number of serious somatic and obsessional symptoms. Neither she nor Freud paid the least attention to the brother's death, discussing, instead, the usual sexual factors: repressed homosexuality, father fixation, phallic symbols, and the Oedipus complex.

Direct experience was necessary to gain a satisfactory and humane understanding of the war and the psychological casualties it produced, but Freud, encased in his private world of theory, could never do justice to the complexity and variety of the individual reactions. Even experience by itself was not enough; an open-minded scientific approach was also critical, as seen in the work of Rivers, Brown, and Simmel. Jones and Ferenczi saw many victims of shell-shock in English and Hungarian hospitals during and immediately after the war, but their commitment to Freud's theories interfered with a full understanding of what they saw. Abraham, clearly, was the most extreme example of the blindness brought about by doctrinal servitude.

Julius Wagner-Jauregg, head of psychiatry at the University of Vienna and a former medical school classmate of Freud's, treated cases of war neuroses with electric shock and other disciplinary methods. He and his psychiatrist colleagues saw a great number of patients, but they did not understand them nor develop helpful treatments. A very different picture was presented by Victor Tausk, a member of the Vienna Psychoanalytic Society, who spent the war years as a physician with the Austrian army. He wrote several papers that revealed his empathy and understanding. He had considerable experience with men who attempted to desert from the army, and, based on careful observation, distinguished eight different types of deserters. His classification ranged from peasants with no sense of national identity who were simply fleeing home to their villages to what he termed "chronic fugitives": men from society's lowest strata who had been running away from brutal authorities all their lives. Tausk, significantly, made no attempt to force all these individuals into a single category or theoretical mold.

Alfred Adler, completely separated from the psychoanalytic movement by this time, had been drafted as a military physician in 1916 and saw a number of psychiatric cases. Given his Socialist commitments and identification with workers and society's victims, it is no surprise that he found himself in deep conflict as an army doctor, sympathizing with the very men he was required to send back to a war he deplored. He published a pamphlet in 1919 titled *The Other Side,* which contained a number of perceptive comments on the war. He described the variety of motives that caused men to join the army, including the seeking of advantage, the lure of adventure, escape from intolerable home situations, and idealism. He attempted to discuss the social forces at play in the war: economic motives, power seeking, and deception. An original psychological contribution was his observation of the way soldiers, caught between bullets and a court-martial, took on the values of their generals. This was an anticipation of the concept of "identification with the aggressor," later elaborated by Ferenczi and Anna Freud. Despite such astute observations, Adler was, like Freud, too quick to move to large theoretical generalizations. He did not attend to the experience of individual soldiers, nor did he develop effective treatment methods.

In his theories about the war neuroses, Freud overextended his valuable discoveries about the role of childhood, which led him and analysts such as Abraham to ignore the role of adult trauma. In reality, the experience with shell-shock victims revealed a complex picture. The predisposition of each soldier—a result of his childhood experience—made him more or less liable to break down when confronted with the stress of battle. Some very vulnerable individuals, such as those with highly traumatic early lives, would fall apart with relatively little provocation. Just being in the army and having to follow orders might be enough. Others, with strong and resilient personalities, could go through a great deal before they reached their breaking points. But, given enough stress—and much of what occurred in the Great War went beyond anyone's idea of reasonable limits—even the strongest would suffer deep psychological damage. In his book on the history of mental breakdown in war, *No More Heroes,* Richard Gabriel concluded: "Fear and psychiatric debilitation are constant companions in any war. Engaging in battle is one of the most threatening, stressful, and horrifying experiences that man is expected to endure. . . . Severe emotional response to battle is neither a rare nor an isolated event."

The legacy of psychoanalysis, together with that of descriptive psychiatry, had a baneful influence for years after the First World War. The idea that combat breakdowns were due solely to preexisting personality weaknesses—that the actual stress of combat did not need to be considered—became embedded in military policy. Freudian assumptions about childhood predisposition continued to inform psychiatric thinking through the Vietnam War. The dossiers of emotionally disturbed soldiers were packed with carefully compiled details of their early lives, while information on their combat experiences was ignored. Adult trauma was considered irrelevant to their disturbance. The influence of Freud's ideas about the war neuroses was not set aside until 1978, when American psychiatry accepted the idea that traumatic events in adulthood could lead to symptoms that could become manifest months or years later. Post-traumatic stress disorder (PTSD) was finally recognized as a legitimate phenomenon.

The encounter between psychoanalysis and the war neuroses shows Freud confronting the survivors of trauma and, as he had with his hysterical patients of the 1890s, both seeing and turning away from what he saw. His need to affirm his sweeping theory of sexuality, to explain all in terms of internal-instinctual forces while ignoring complex social conditions, to prove that psychoanalysis already knew about these conditions—that he was right and his established technique beyond question—blinded him to the evidence before his eyes. These patients could have led him to question his doctrines, to reassess the role of trauma, anxiety, grief, loss, and catharsis, but he would only do so partially, in his self-analytic way.

In March of 1919, Freud began writing one of his most significant theoretical essays, *Beyond the Pleasure Principle.* In this work, he finally modified his commitment to the principle of sexuality—pleasure seeking—as the primary motivation for all human behavior. The essay itself was a characteristic mixture of astute observations and new ideas, along with obscure theoretical speculations. It was here that he finally took up the traumatic neuroses of the Great War and used them to modify his views, though his comments were confined to just a few paragraphs. He noted how traumatized soldiers continued to have nightmares that reproduced the frightening situations that brought about their symptoms. They were "fixated" on their trauma, and could not, in their unconscious, escape from it. Such repetitive nightmares were evidence for what he termed "a compulsion to repeat." These fixations contradicted his theory that dreams were driven by the pleasure principle, that their purpose was the gratification of wishes. To explain this contradiction, he argued that something more must be going on in states of extreme anxiety than could be accounted for by the pleasure principle.

Freud then left the neuroses of war aside and turned to the minor trauma suffered by an infant when his mother temporarily left him. He had observed his one-and-a-half-year-old grandson at play, and described a game in which the infant would repeatedly throw a toy wooden reel attached to a string into his curtained crib so that it disappeared, while uttering an "o-o-o-o" sound that proved to be the German word *fort*—"gone." He would then pull the reel back and greet the reappearance of his toy with a joyful *da*—"there." Freud deduced that this *fort-da* game symbolized disappearance and return, and that it was related to the infant's separation from his mother. When she would leave, he was in a passive or helpless position and could do nothing to bring her back. But by making a symbolic game of her leaving, he translated passive to active: he obtained a sense of mastery over his situation by playing it out with his toy. From this small but significant observation, Freud suggested a model for children's play and, beyond this, for repetitive dreams and symptoms. Young children, as any parent knows, are fond of the endless repetition of events that have impressed them. Such repetitious play, Freud suggested, was their way of making themselves master of situations; events that were passively suffered were turned into active games and stories. So it was with repetitive nightmares. Freud concluded that they contradicted the pleasure principle because they were attempts not at wishful gratifications, but at the symbolic mastery of anxiety-laden experiences.

In a few pages at the beginning of *Beyond the Pleasure Principle,* Freud sketched out a theory that brought together children's play—and the enjoyment adults obtain from drama and fiction, which also involve the vicarious experience of emotional events—dreams and repetitive nightmares, and the reliving of frightening traumas. It was his genius to outline this theory of mastery in general terms and show how it encompassed a wide range of significant phenomena. Although both Simmel and Ferenczi, in the *Psychoanalysis and the War Neuroses* monograph, had discussed the role of mastery in the dreams and symptoms of trauma survivors, Freud did not give them credit. He had to work out his theories in his own way, to go back into himself and select, from all possible examples of trauma, the maternal loss suffered by a one-and-a-half-year-old boy.

The theory of mastery, outlined at the beginning of *Beyond the Pleasure Principle,* provided a coherent explanation for the repetitions encountered in neuroses and dreams. People become stuck or fixated on traumas that were impossible to resolve when they first occurred; symptoms and nightmares were attempts at mastery gone awry because the person was originally overwhelmed with fear and pain. Those working with the combat survivors of the war discovered what lay beneath their symptoms: helplessness, terror, guilt, grief, and rage. This was not anger that could be explained by an aggressive instinct that they brought with them when they entered the army. The constant fear of one's own death, along with exposure to the horrifying deaths of others, was quite sufficient to account for their emotional breakdowns.

Freud outlined his new theory of mastery in two short chapters at the beginning of *Beyond the Pleasure Principle,* but this was as far as he could go. He made some attempts to relate the fixations and repetitions to the "repetition compulsion" seen in neuroses and transference, but did not carry this line of thought very far. In the remainder of the essay, he turned to what he admitted was "speculation, often far-fetched speculation, which the reader will consider or dismiss according to his individual predilection." He turned his mind to large-scale "biological" forces, and embarked on an intellectual journey that ranged across the animal kingdom from amoebas to human beings, contained his guesses about the way in which life arose from inorganic matter, and concluded with the themes of Life and Death. His reasoning, in outline, ran as follows: In the beginning there was no life; all was inorganic. Organic matter gradually emerged; this was the beginning of life, which he ascribed to a "life instinct." But, since everything that lives eventually dies—all organic matter eventually returns to an inorganic state—there was also an "instinct" or "urge inherent in organic life to restore an earlier state of things." The word "urge" bridged the immense gap between different life-forms; for in what sense do plants or trees or bacteria feel "urges" in the same way that dogs or monkeys or human beings do? This led to the conclusion that "the aim of all life is death," and this "aim"—like the "urge"—then became the "death instinct" or "death drive." With a further series of theoretical leaps, he argued that this death instinct was the motive for complex human behavior such as the behavior of men in war, or the repetitive acts of neurotics. Aggression was the death drive turned outward; rather than seeking one's own death, one attacked others. By the end—and in subsequent writings—he spoke of the great forces of Eros and Thanatos—of Life and Death—that battle within the mind.

While some have found these theoretical speculations deep and profound—Melanie Klein and her psychoanalytic school place the death instinct, and the aggression that purportedly comes from it, at the heart of their thinking—a careful reading reveals a host of logical and factual difficulties. Freud used terms such as "instinct" and "drive" in the loosest ways, at one point referring to biological force in the most general sense—the anabolic and catabolic tendencies in all living cells—and, at another, to very specific human activities and motives, such as transference, murder, sadism, and masochism. The fact that living organisms die does not mean that human beings have a motive to do so, far less that the death and aggression of the Great War—or any other form of violence—can be explained by such a drive.

If his theory explains little about the psychology of death, it sheds even less light on aggression. While it is generally agreed that *Beyond the Pleasure Principle* is the essay in which Freud moved to a "dual instinct theory"—one which included aggression as well as sexuality—the derivation of aggression from a death drive simply does not work. Aggression—along with greed, competition, sadism, and power seeking—are important aspects of human experience, but little light is shed on them by talk about the "forces" that compel organic matter to become inorganic or the eternal strife between Eros and Thanatos. Of course, as is typical of Freud, he had a number of insightful things to say about anger, destructive aggression, and other human evils, as one encounters them in real life. The motivation for many of the jokes in his *Jokes and Their Relation to the Unconscious,* for the slips and errors described in *The Psychopathology of Everyday Life,* as well as many of the dreams in the dream book, involved such motives. He could be most insightful in exposing the nasty, competitive, greedy, and self-centered intentions that lurk behind innocent-seeming facades. It is in this sense that he already knew about the savage instincts of mankind. But such observations found no place in his psychoanalytic theories, for that would have been too much of a concession to Adler, who, several years earlier, had pointed to an aggressive drive, competitiveness as a need to overcome a sense of inferiority, and sibling rivalry. Because Freud, intensely competitive and rivalrous with his former colleague, could not credit Adler with a theory of aggression, he needed to derive his theory from what had the appearance of "biological-scientific" principles.

The infant that Freud observed playing the *fort-da* game was his grandson Ernst, the first child of his daughter Sophie. Sophie, married to the photographer Max Halberstadt and living in Berlin, contracted the Spanish flu in 1920; within a few days, she was dead. Freud's sons Martin, Oli, and Ernst had come through the fighting without serious physical injuries, but now his beloved daughter fell victim to the epidemic that had spread with fearsome rapidity in the closing years of the war. There is some dispute over whether Freud's speculations about the death instinct were written in response to the loss of his daughter; he claimed not, that *Beyond the Pleasure Principle* was begun earlier, though the term "death drive" did enter his correspondence with some frequency after he lost her.

Freud did not need the specific stimulus of Sophie's death to touch off such personal reactions, however. He had long been preoccupied with his own death. During the years of friendship with Fliess he had been convinced that he would die at a particular age or on a special date. In 1921, well before his cancer appeared, he wrote to Ferenczi that he "took a step into old age. Since then the thought of death has not left me." In 1930, he confided to a patient, the American psychiatrist Smiley Blanton, that "I think about the possibility of death every day. It is good practice." It is a familiar story; Freud moved toward a consideration of real traumas—those suffered by hysterics and other neurotics, by veterans of the war, by infants when they lose their mothers—and a consideration of the reality of human aggression, and then turned away to an instinct theory that located everything within the isolated individual, and which reduced aggression to an abstract drive, far removed from the reality of human fighting, including his own. His speculations provided him with the solace he had sought since boyhood: the refuge of his intellectual life.

CHAPTER 19

Freud at Work:
The Postwar Years

Now, psychoanalysis. Ever read anything about that? Sure you have.
—Anthony Powell, *A Dance to the Music of Time*

THE GREAT WAR had shattered the belief in progress and rationality held by so many Europeans and Americans, its senseless barbarity validating Freud's vision of man as an irrational, emotion-driven, unconscious creature. Psychoanalysis as a movement, a method of treatment and, more than anything, an intellectual atmosphere became increasingly influential and continued its spread throughout the world, seeming to provide a language for the destructiveness unleashed by the war, as well as for the changes in sexual mores and for new forms in art and literature. In 1920, Freud could write to Karl Abraham that "even in Vienna, interest in psychoanalysis has grown livelier."

The psychoanalytic movement picked up where it had left off in 1914. With the Austrian political and economic situation settled down, and communications across national boundaries again open, Freud and his followers took up the promotion of their cause. From 1918 until the advent of Nazism in 1933, an international psychoanalytic congress was held every two years in the major cities of Europe. New training institutes were established; the Vienna Society, which had limped through the war, now came back to life, while Abraham's Berlin Institute became a major center as Hanns Sachs, one of the original members of the Committee, moved there to join Abraham and Max Eitingon. By the 1920s, the European institutes, along with their counterparts in the United States and England, were training more and more psychoanalysts. New journals were published in England, the United States, and, somewhat later, in France and Italy, while Freud's own works became available in languages other than German. The most important translation was the English version of his *Col-*

lected Papers, carried out with great skill by Freud's analysand Joan Riviere—with the assistance of James and Alix Strachey, also his former patients—in 1924–1925. *The Collected Papers* finally gave British and American readers an edition of Freud in their own language that captured the spirit of his prose, in contrast to Abraham Brill's earlier clumsy version.

Psychoanalysis more and more permeated the Western world; many educated persons took it up—in New York it became fashionable to be "psyched," to undergo an analysis—and Freudian concepts made their way into newspapers, novels, plays, and, eventually, the movies. There were counterreactions, to be sure, from those who continued to find Freud's ideas about sexuality and the unconscious—not to mention his attack on God and religion—shocking; but a great many serious thinkers were influenced, to one degree or another, by psychoanalysis.

While Freud had a powerful interest in the spread of his theories and the movement, he left the organizational and administrative tasks to others, spending his daytime hours with a full complement of patients—he saw nine to ten a day in 1919—concentrating the rest of his energy, as always, on writing. In the aftermath of the war, he continued to work in much the same way as he had during the preceding years; new psychoanalytic ideas germinated from inner sources. His work as a therapist also remained much as it had always been; neither the evidence of the war neuroses, which had made plain the effects of trauma, nor the new concepts of mastery and aggression, introduced in *Beyond the Pleasure Principle,* had any discernible effect on the way he treated his patients.

The major theoretical revisions of *Beyond the Pleasure Principle* (1920) were followed the next year by *Group Psychology and the Analysis of the Ego* and, in 1923, by *The Ego and the Id. Group Psychology* was Freud's attempt to conquer new territory for psychoanalysis by extending his theories, developed entirely with individuals, to social or group life, using the army and the Catholic Church as his principal examples. The German title of the essay was *Massenpsychologie und Ich-Analyse,* thus, "group" would have been more accurately translated as "crowd" or "mass." Freud was attempting to explain two things in this essay: what holds groups together, and why they sometimes turn into unruly, violent mobs. His answer to the first was "libido," based on the assumption that the army is held together by the soldiers' love for their generals and the church cemented by the members' love for Christ. Groups became violent mobs, in his view, when they were overtaken by a "group mind."

In discussing the power of group leaders such as army generals or Christ, Freud approached the perennial human desire for ideal figures. This was the need that played an enormous role in his own life, witnessed by his turn from his failed father to a series of male idols. It was also a powerful force within the psychoanalytic movement, where younger colleagues looked to him as their commander in chief. But while these motives were prominent in his own background and the movement, Freud now redefined them in terms of the Oedipus complex. He turned away from the human craving for ideal figures, and interpreted relations between leaders and followers almost entirely as power struggles driven by competition and jealousy. As was characteristic, his account also neglected mothers and the pervasive human need for close bonds and enduring relationships.

Freud's attempt to explain crowd violence, why peaceful groups sometimes turn into unruly mobs, rested on his image of the "mass." Like infants, primitives, and neurotics, the mass was supposedly made up of creatures who were driven by their selfish instincts; they required—indeed, in his view, they seemed to crave—a strong leader to keep them under control. This was essentially the same line of reasoning he had used in explaining the aggression of the war. In support of this notion, he relied on the idea of the "group mind" espoused by the French physician and sociologist Gustave Le Bon, a notorious misogynist and racist. Freud was taken with Le Bon; he spoke of his "brilliantly executed picture of the group mind," and found his belief in the unconscious congenial.

In addition to Le Bon, Freud drew on his own 1913 essay *Totem and Taboo*, in which he had spun out a "scientific myth," as he called it then, about the original form of human society. He imagined this original group as a "primal horde" ruled by a single powerful male or "primal father," who was eventually overthrown by a band of sons who killed him and took over his prerogatives. While Freud attempted to disarm the reader by calling *Totem and Taboo* a "myth," in later essays such as *Group Psychology* this myth became his truth, used to explain things such as the bonds between soldiers or the ties among religious believers.

History provides abundant examples of competition, jealousy, and group violence, but Freud and Le Bon's theories offer little that explains these phenomena. The soldiers in the First World War were certainly not a "mass" who loved their generals or a crowd controlled by a leader in the way the primal horde was supposedly ruled by the powerful father. Nor can all of religion be explained by the love of the blind masses for holy figures or God.

Overall, *Group Psychology* suffered from a lack of firsthand observations of the very military and religious groups that Freud was attempting to interpret. He did have intimate experience with a group that could have provided evidence for his speculations: the psychoanalytic movement. But using this as an example would have required an awareness of his own tactics as a leader, and this was impossible. He could not see how tremendously important he was as a hero to his younger colleagues since, after the Fliess affair, he had disowned his own struggles to find an ideal father; nor could he see how damaged they were when he rejected them. Lacking an awareness of these motives, he described himself as the primal father, menaced by rebellious sons, holding the group together with his strength and power.

The Ego and the Id picked up where Freud left off in *Beyond the Pleasure Principle.* This was the essay in which he introduced his well-known terminology of *id, ego,* and *superego*—in German these were the colloquial *es, Ich,* and *über Ich* ("it," "I," and "over-I")—along with the metaphors and images that have propelled these ideas to prominence. The it, or id, is the repository of instinctual power, the completely unconscious "unknown and uncontrollable force [by which] we are lived." Freud borrowed this idea from Georg Groddeck, a German physician and psychotherapist, whose *Book of the It* he had read in manuscript just before writing *The Ego and the Id.* As he described it elsewhere, the unconscious id is a "seething cauldron" of instincts—the definition conjures up savage emotions, sexual, selfish, aggressive, destructive—ever threatening to erupt. The ego, in contrast, is the conscious self, representing "what may be called reason and common sense, in contrast to the id, which contains the passions." The ego was likened to a man on horseback; the id, or horse, has the superior strength, it is the power, while the ego-rider guides it along socially acceptable paths.

Freud's concepts of the id and the ego have passed into the common domain; they capture the familiar conflicts between passion and reason, between selfish emotions and civilized control. He provided an evocative language for these ideas. In addition, his theory of the superego broke new ground. He began by returning to the idea of an "unconscious sense of guilt," first discussed in his 1915 essay *Mourning and Melancholia,* and attempted to explain why certain persons suffer from an overly severe conscience, why they were subjected to extreme and unrealistic self-criticism and self-attack. He explained this by describing an internal voice—the superego—which judges, condemns, rewards, and punishes, a part of the personality that is built up from one's actual experiences with childhood authority figures. Children identify with the important figures in their lives, with their father's power and authority, with their mother's love and care, and make these qualities part of their developing selves. In his words, "character" is created from these idealizations and identifications.

While *The Ego and the Id* contained several fruitful contributions, Freud also returned, as was his wont, to well-worn speculations. The child's important relations within the family were largely defined in terms of the Oedipus complex, the mother was neglected in favor of paternal authority, and his picture of the id as a repository of untrammeled passion, while evocative, only captured one side of human experience, leaving out all those emotions—attachment, love, anxiety, curiosity—that were not at war with reason or a civilized life. His guiding image of the ego as a poor creature, mediating between the antisocial instincts of the id and the harsh aggressiveness of the superego, was a projection of certain nineteenth-century European beliefs and, even more, of his personal demons. If ever there was a man driven to constant work by a harsh superego it was Freud, who also felt menaced by emotions—"id impulses"—that ever threatened to erupt. He did approach this personal source on the very last page of *The Ego and the Id,* where he returned to trauma and anxiety, missing throughout the essay, and spoke of "excessive real danger [in which the ego] sees itself deserted by all protecting forces and lets itself die [here is] . . . the infantile anxiety of longing—the anxiety due to separation from the protecting mother." In this touching passage, his personal struggle made a fleeting appearance, only to be buried as he returned to his theories of Eros and the death instinct.

The writing of theoretical essays like *Beyond the Pleasure Principle* and *The Ego and the Id* was the means by which Freud carried on his self-analysis in symbolic or disguised form. This was a continuous process throughout his life; his underlying fears and longings drove the work, and made their appearance—as in his remarks about anxiety, death, and maternal loss in the final pages of *The Ego and the Id*—and then went back underground, only to reappear in later essays. The German scholar Ilse Grubrich-Simitis did a careful analysis of Freud's writing habits, based on access to his manuscripts, drafts, notes, and letters. She showed how he would typically begin a project in a state of passivity, waiting for material to emerge from his unconscious and then experience "frightful labour pains" as the writing took shape. He could only write in a state of psychological, if not physical, pain—what he termed "a modicum of misery"—which originated, as she put it, in his "anxieties of being lost, of starvation and of death." The writing would temporarily allay these painful states, but once the project was completed, the emotions would return and the whole process would be repeated.

The psychoanalytic essays that originated in Freud's ongoing self-exploration contained his most creative and original contributions, but they contrasted with the static quality of his work as a therapist. There he continued to play the role of the all-knowing father; his technique changed very little over the years. Freud's work as a therapist is revealed in his own case studies—he published two during this period—and in the independent accounts of some of his patients. The young Russian aristocrat Sergei Pankejeff, who has come to be known as "the Wolf Man" because of a childhood dream of wolves, was seen by Freud between 1911 and 1914, though the case, *From the History of an Infantile Neurosis,* was not published until 1918. As was true of a number of his works, Freud wrote this to prove the superiority of his theories. To this end, he attempted to locate the cause of the Wolf Man's neurosis in infantile sexual events, and also tried to show that later experiences and adult traumas were of little significance. Sergei was an extremely disturbed young man at the time of his analysis, suffering from a variety of hypochondriacal and depressive symptoms, with a shaky hold on reality, including an unclear sense of who he was, along with obsessions, compulsions, and inability to function effectively in almost any area of his life.

In his analysis, Sergei reported the memory of a frightening dream that he recalled from the age of four in which his bedroom window opened to reveal six or seven wolves sitting in a tree, staring silently at him. He awoke in terror, afraid they were going to eat him. Freud reconstructed the events of Sergei's infancy, focusing on the wolf dream, which he interpreted as the patient, presumably at the age of one and a half, witnessing his parent's having sexual intercourse, with the father penetrating the mother from behind. It was here that Freud elaborated his theory of the traumatic effect of exposure to the "primal scene," tracing almost all of Sergei's symptoms and life problems to the "scene" and related infantile-sexual events. Several later accounts, including the patient's own, point to the improbable nature of these interpretive speculations. Sergei had malaria at the time of his supposed primal scene exposure, a much more traumatic experience for an infant than witnessing his parents having sexual intercourse, in whatever position. In addition, modern research on memory has shown that it is impossible for an adult to recall events from the age of one and a half, as Freud insisted his patient did; in fact, an examination of the case shows Freud "educating" and "inducing" Sergei, who "very soon came to share my conviction that the causes of his infantile neurosis lay concealed behind [the dream]." Finally, Freud decided to speed up the treatment by imposing a termination date, since his patient was not giving him the confirmation of his interpretations he wanted, and it was only after this "blackmailing device" was employed that Sergei agreed with the interpretations. As Freud put it, "Under the inexorable pressure of this fixed limit his resistance and fixation to the illness gave way."

Many factors that may have caused the Wolf Man's severe disturbance found no place in Freud's case study. While he assumed that Sergei's relationship with his father was a loving one, in fact Mr. Pankejeff, a wealthy Russian aristocrat, had only sporadic contact with his son and died shortly before the beginning of the analysis. Freud, as usual, ignored the mother, who was a severely depressed and hypochondriacal woman, largely unavailable to her child, only attending to him when he was sick, a fact that Sergei himself related to his reliance on illness to obtain love and attention. (In spite of all his psychoanalytic treatment, his physical symptoms persisted throughout his life.) His contact with both parents was inadequate and inconsistent, and he was raised by a shifting series of servants and nannies of variable quality. His older sister was a very important figure throughout his childhood—she cared for, but also tormented, him—and her suicide before the onset of his adult breakdown was, like the death of his father and the loss of his nannies, an additional trauma.

While Freud had an affectionate and supportive attitude toward Ernst Lanzer—the Rat Man—he saw the Wolf Man as a recalcitrant baby, holding on to his symptoms and gratifications, as someone who needed to be pushed, prodded, and coerced into giving them up. There was little feeling of cooperation or collaboration in the case, though there was, in the end, compliance. Sergei had several subsequent psychological breakdowns and was seen again by

Freud before being turned over to one of his analysands, the young Ruth Mack Brunswick. He continued to have contact with psychoanalysis in one way or another for the rest of his life. In later years he earned money selling paintings of his wolf dream, and would answer the telephone "Wolf Man here," revealing how his status as Freud's famous patient had given him an identity that helped him survive.

Freud's other case history from this period, the last that he published, was his 1920 *Psychogenesis of a Case of Homosexuality in a Woman*, which described his treatment of an eighteen-year-old girl brought to him by her parents following a suicide attempt, so he could cure her homosexuality. The young woman had attached herself to a "society lady" or "cocotte"—apparently a bisexual prostitute—ten years her senior, openly flaunting the relationship, much to her family's dismay. One day, her father came upon the two women in the street and gave his daughter "an angry glance which boded no good," whereupon she threw herself over an embankment onto a railroad track, barely escaping permanent injury. In Freud's view this suicide attempt, while serious, was a manipulation that enabled the young woman to get her way with both her parents and the society lady. At other places in his discussion, he described her as someone without much in the way of symptoms or anxiety; he was interested in her as "a case of homosexuality in a woman," but had little feeling for the suffering revealed by her very real attempt to kill herself.

Freud's case report was a mixture of insightful observations along with personal biases and impositions of theory. He could see that her homosexuality was driven by the search for mother love: "The analysis revealed beyond all shadow of doubt that the lady-love was a substitute for—her mother." In support of this interpretation, he described a pattern in which the patient had, a few years earlier, attached herself to young women with children, again searching for the love that was missing at home. Her own mother "treated her children in quite different ways, being decidedly harsh towards her daughter and over-indulgent to her three sons." The mother, "still quite youthful herself, saw in her rapidly developing daughter an inconvenient competitor; she favoured her sons at her expense, limited her independence as much as possible, and kept an especially strict watch against any close relation between the girl and her father." Freud described the father as "an earnest, worthy man, at bottom very tender-hearted, but he had to some extent estranged his children by the sternness he had adopted towards them." Learning of his daughter's homosexual tendencies, "he flew into a rage and tried to suppress them by threats [viewing her] as vicious, as degenerate, or as mentally afflicted . . . [Her] homosexuality aroused the deepest bitterness in him, and he was determined to combat it with all the means in his power." He may have been "worthy" and "tender-hearted" in Freud's eyes, but he was an enraged antagonist to his daughter. In fact, it was his angry glance that precipitated her suicide attempt.

These observations about this girl's family situation could have led to a straightforward interpretation: the patient, despised as a female, and desperately longing for love, adopted a male role and sought affection from a mother figure. Freud did present the evidence for this view, and gave it some credence, but he could not leave it at that; his long-standing antagonism toward young women, and his need to fit patients into his theories, took him away from this simple explanation. At one point he commented on her sense of injustice that girls were not granted the same freedom as boys, and said with disdain that "she was in fact a feminist," which he attributed to her "pronounced envy for the penis." He then put forward an interpretation about her penis envy and Oedipus complex, assuming that she sought revenge on her father because he had given her mother still another baby, her youngest brother. He supported this idea by interpreting her suicide attempt as a symbolic expression of the wish to have a child by her father: "falling" over the embankment was, in Freud's view, an enactment of the German word *niederkommen,* which means both "to fall" and "to be delivered of child."

Freud's two different understandings of this young woman—the straightforward one based on the discrimination and deprivation of love she experienced, and his oedipal-symbolic interpretation—led to radically different approaches to her treatment. In the beginning, Freud—in marked contrast to her parents—was compassionate. Far from labeling her vicious, degenerate, or mentally afflicted, as her father had done, he listened to her ideas, dreams, and feelings, and tried to help her make sense of her unhappiness. This led to what he called "a single piece of material . . . which I could regard as a positive transference." The young woman reported a series of dreams that anticipated her cure by the analytic treatment and "expressed her joy over the prospects in life that would then be opened before her, confessed her longing for a man's love and for children." In other words, she saw Freud as an accepting and loving parental figure and was moving toward a resolution of her conflicts. Unfortunately, he could not tolerate this: "Warned through some slight impression or other, I told her one day that I did not believe these dreams, that I regarded them as false and hypocritical, and that she intended to deceive me just as she habitually deceived her father. I was right; after I had made this clear, this kind of dream ceased."

Freud explained this interpretation with a lengthy rationalization for the idea of "dreams that lie," since this notion contradicted his own theory that dreams are the "royal road" to the unconscious, that unlike conscious thoughts, they reveal the truth. In fact, he needed to go against his own dream theory because he found it so difficult to play the role of loving parent in the transference, especially with a young woman. Nor could he see this girl's plight in terms of the real emotional abuse she suffered; his theories demanded that she be driven by her childish and feminine sexuality, her wish for revenge, her manipulativeness, and deceit. After he rejected her attempt to win his love and approval, tentatively expressed in her dreams, she pulled back and remained cool to his interpretations. He referred to her use of the "Russian defense" and commented, "The resistance . . . withdraws to a certain boundary line, beyond which it proves to be unconquerable. The resistance very often pursues similar tactics . . . Russian tactics, as they might be called." The patient, now labeled a function—"the resistance"—is seen as if she were General Kutuzov, attempting to out-maneuver Napoléon. In the end, he characterized her as motivated by her wish to hold onto her homosexuality; and, when he thought she was transferring her anger at her father and her "repudiation of men" onto him, he abruptly ended the analysis.

Freud's case study contained some interesting general ideas on the genesis of homosexuality, including a discussion of the mixture of hereditary and environmental factors that determine adult sexual orientation and choice of a love object, and an awareness of the limitations of psychoanalytic treatment in "curing" this condition. In his *Three Essays* of 1905 he had taken an enlightened view of male homosexuality, noting how it was a valued practice in the high civilization of ancient Greece. This was one side of his feeling, yet it coexisted with his sense that it would be better to live a "normal" heterosexual life. While he was, at times, open about his own "homosexual libido," as in the Fliess and Jung affairs, for the most part, he experienced his longing for a man's love as a menacing inner force. His treatment of this young woman did not differ, in the end, from his therapy with Dora twenty years earlier; both were struggling to find love and understanding, neither were compliant with the social roles demanded of women nor with Freud's attempts to force them into the mold of his theories, and, in both cases, they got little or no help from him.

While Freud was largely controlling and dismissive of the Wolf Man and the young homosexual woman, the American psychiatrist Abram Kardiner—like Albert Hirst, whom he saw over ten years earlier—aroused his sympathy, which led to work that was, on balance, much more therapeutic. Kardiner saw Freud in 1921 when he was thirty and the Professor sixty-five, a time when Freud was at the height of his powers. They formed a positive bond from the very first meeting, the younger man feeling an "immediate trust" in Freud's "air of authority and strength" and Freud finding the deferential Kardiner easy to work with.

Kardiner grew up in extremely traumatic conditions; his parents were Jewish immigrants in the slums of New York City, barely surviving amidst poverty and disease. His father, driven to distraction by his inability to care for his family, went into rages in which he would beat his wife. She, in turn, contracted tuberculosis and died when Abram was three. As he put it: "My early childhood was a ceaseless nightmare, with starvation, neglect, a sense of being of no account, and a bewildering depressive feeling." These experiences resulted in a profound sense of worthlessness, an inability to perform in school despite his superior intelligence and talent, and a number of phobias and depressive reactions. Kardiner described his tumultuous childhood in his first session with Freud, who declared it "a perfect presentation."

Freud seemed to identify with the events of Kardiner's childhood, which resonated with his own poverty, early maternal losses, and fear that his mother would die from tuberculosis. His ability to empathize with Kardiner led to an interpretation that the young man felt was the most convincing and brilliant of his analysis. Ever since he was a child, Kardiner had had a phobia of masks and wax figures that he was completely unable to understand. From a dream, Freud was able to guess that "the first mask you saw was your dead mother's face," an interpretation that sent shivers through his analysand. Kardiner later checked with his older sister and discovered that, at age three, he had been left alone with his mother when she died and had spent a terrifying day with her dead body. As Kardiner and others noted, Freud was always at his best when interpreting dreams; in addition, his patient's phobia resonated closely with his own anxiety, as seen in the dream of his dead mother that he recalled from age seven.

After Kardiner's mother died, the father remarried. His new stepmother, physically healthy and competent, was able to provide a stable home for the young boy, and the family's financial situation gradually improved. She also took Abram into her bed between the ages of four and seven and had him fondle her and suck on her breasts, sexual activity that he enjoyed but which also aroused his guilt and fear of his father. This material was ripe for Freud's oedipal interpretations, of course, though it was not a matter of oedipal *wishes* but of a seductive stepmother, and further endeared his analysand to him.

Interpretations such as that of the mask phobia and clarifications of the guilty relationship with his stepmother were among the positive sides of Kardiner's analysis. Also of great benefit was the relationship with Freud, a man of immense stature, who clearly liked Kardiner and preferred him to many of his other patients. Kardiner reported an amusing conversation with James Strachey and John Rickman—like Strachey, an Englishman who later became one of Freud's translators—who were also in analysis with the Professor at this time. They were amazed to learn that Freud talked to Kardiner since, in their analyses, he was almost always silent. Rickman reported, in fact, that Freud often fell asleep during his sessions. Helene Deutsch, another young psychiatrist who saw Freud in analysis in 1919, reported that she twice spotted his cigar on the floor where it had dropped when he became bored and dozed off during her sessions.

When Freud did not like a patient, the treatment was useless, at best. Clarence Oberndorf was an American physician who Freud saw at this time. Freud took a dislike to him, saying he was "too skeptical and refractory in accepting interpretations." Freud ended the analysis, and was adamant in his condemnation of his patient's character. Kardiner, who knew Oberndorf then, and later in America, thought he was a most agreeable person, if a bit dull, and could not understand what the problem had been. With Kardiner, Freud was openly encouraging and supportive, telling him, at one point, that though he had experienced a great deal of adversity, he had "a lot of fight in him and he would be down at times but he would never be out." This was enormously important to this young man who had, for most of his life, struggled with depression and a debased image of himself.

Kardiner, who had learned early from his violent father how to inhibit his aggression and get along with authority, found it easy to accommodate himself to Freud's requirements. Nevertheless, he was privately critical of a number of aspects of his analysis. For one, he saw Freud as brilliant in some of his interpretations but neglecting the ongoing analytic relationship. In interpreting Kardiner's submissive attitude towards authority, Freud had spoken only of fear of the father. As Kardiner noted: "The man who had invented the concept of transference did not recognize it when it occurred here. He overlooked one thing. *Yes, I was afraid of my father in childhood, but the one whom I feared now was Freud himself.* He could make me or break me, which my father no longer could. By his statement, he pushed the entire reaction into the past, thereby making the analysis a historical reconstruction."

Freud was also fixated on his pet interpretations, particularly unconscious homosexuality in men and the Oedipus complex, and Kardiner said that the stress on these put him "on a wild-goose chase for years for a problem that did not exist." He also commented that Freud's style of analysis did not include a working through of issues: "He thought that once you had uncovered the Oedipus complex and understood your unconscious homosexuality, that once you knew the origins and the sources of all these reactions, something would happen that would enable you to translate these insights into your current life and thereby alter it." Despite these reservations, Kardiner found his analysis extremely valuable and went on to a long and productive career as a psychoanalyst and researcher in New York.

If Kardiner's analysis with Freud was largely successful, and Oberndorf's useless, the Professor's treatment of another American psychiatrist, Horace Frink, seen during this same period, was a disaster. Frink was thirty-seven years old when he first saw Freud in 1921. He had suffered serious losses in childhood, including being permanently separated from both parents after his father's business failed when Horace was eight, and the death of his mother from tuberculosis when he was fifteen. He had periodic bouts of severe depression, along with bursts of hypomanic activity which, in his later life, became a clear manic-depressive or bipolar psychosis, with suicide attempts and periods of hospitalization. At the time he saw Freud, however, he was functioning at a high level; with Brill and Oberndorf, he had founded the New York Psychoanalytic Society and had been elected its president in 1913. He had also published a well-received book in 1918 based on psychoanalytic principles: *Morbid Fears and Compulsions.* Frink was a bright, talented psychoanalyst who was also a gentile. When he came to see Freud, he appeared to be a candidate for the role of Amer-

Freud with Horace Frink.

ican crown prince, on the model of what Jung had once been in Europe. This was Freud's fantasy, of course, and had little to do with the reality of Frink or his life.

When Frink came to Freud for help in 1921, he was married with two young children, but felt he was in love with a patient, a wealthy, married, American woman named Angie Bijur. While the situation was a complicated one, Freud was blind to the depth of Frink's disturbance and chose to focus the analysis on issues that were important to him and the psychoanalytic cause. Far from seeing Frink's depression, periodic incapacitation, and incipient psychosis, he framed his interpretations in purely sexual terms; if Frink were to divorce his wife and marry the woman he loved—the fact that she was a patient and already married to someone else never entered his calculations—he would obtain sexual satisfaction and all would be well. Freud encouraged Frink and Angie, whom he also saw a few times, to divorce their spouses and get married, even warning Angie that if she did not give Horace her love, he was in danger of becoming a homosexual. Freud also knew that her money could be used to support psychoanalysis—she was already paying for Frink's and another American's analysis with him—and, while he claimed he was not pressuring them, the power he had for a person like Frink gave his interpretation-recommendation enormous force.

Frink complied with Freud's advice, but the new marriage failed, and he subsequently had a psychotic breakdown and made several suicide attempts. Among other things, abandoning his first wife, who died of pneumonia a few years later, and young children set off more guilt and depression. Frink was later treated successfully by the American psychiatrist Adolf Meyer, lived without further psychosis for a number of years, and was a stable father to his two children. He succumbed to heart disease and a final psychotic break at age fifty-three. Asked about Freud shortly before his death, Frink ruefully remarked, "He was a great man even if he did invent psychoanalysis."

Freud's treatment of three Americans in the 1920s and '30s—Ruth Mack, and Mark and David Brunswick—illustrates his typical mixing of personal, professional, financial, and therapeutic needs. Ruth was an intelligent and intuitive woman who began her treatment in 1924, both for personal reasons and to become an analyst herself. Mark Brunswick, who had long been in love with her, was in Vienna studying music and began analysis about the same time, while his brother David joined him a few years later. All three were considered millionaires by the Viennese; they had their own splendid house, a car with a chauffeur, and Mark and David lived without working during all the years of their stay in Austria.

Ruth saw Freud off and on until 1938. She had a poor relationship with her cold and distant father, and Freud quickly became the ideal older man in her life. She also suffered from a number of painful physical symptoms, which seemed a combination of actual diseases and depression-related somatic complaints. While there is no direct record of her analysis, her own publications on the significance of the "pre-oedipal" mother-infant relationship as a source of psychological disturbance hint at her problems in this area. She became one of Freud's great favorites, coming to Berggasse 19 for dinner, visiting the family during their summer vacations, drawing close to Mathilde and her husband, as well as the other Freud children, and serving as the Professor's personal physician for a time. Freud referred patients to her, the best-known being the prize of the Wolf Man, about whom she published a follow-up report to his original case history. While she venerated his genius, he allowed her to challenge him in ways that many other followers could not. Psychoanalysis gave Ruth an identity and career, and through the 1930s she was part of the intimate circle surrounding Freud.

Freud took Mark Brunswick into analysis, in part to treat his persistent psychological problems, but also so he could be made into a suitable husband for Ruth. Mark and Ruth were, in fact, married in 1927, and Freud went to their wedding despite his dislike of public ceremonies. He did not, for example, attend the weddings of his three sons. Notwithstanding all her treatment by Freud, Ruth's painful symptoms did not improve, and she turned increasingly to narcotics. Even during the years when she was in analysis she was addicted to morphine, which, as a physician, she was able to prescribe for herself. Ruth kept returning to her analysis with Freud, trying to fulfill needs that were never quite satisfied. She died some years later, in what appeared to be an inadvertent suicide, still addicted to drugs.

Mark Brunswick was a musician and somewhat of a free spirit who also suffered from persistent personal difficulties, including compulsive masturbation. He initially saw Freud for three-and-a-half years, the treatment ending when he was pronounced cured and ready to marry Ruth. A few years later, he encountered Freud in a social setting and told him that he still had all his symptoms, whereupon he was taken into a second analysis. Mark told Freud that the breaches of confidentiality during the first treatment—his therapy had regularly been discussed with Ruth—made him uncomfortable, and Freud admitted that that had been a mistake. Mark remained, as he had been all along, intimidated by Freud, very much aware of the differences between the man he encountered socially and the analyst he knew in the office, but unable to speak of this. The Professor was apparently unaware of Mark's fear of him. While admiring Freud's genius, Mark found him irritatingly silent and sometimes moralistic, especially in his attitude toward masturbation.

Of the three Brunswicks, David had the worst experience. Freud found him dull and only took him into treatment because of his connection with Ruth and because he could pay in dollars. He was fairly hard on the young man, insisting that he speak in German, which he could barely manage, and that he enroll in medical school, so he would be in a better position to perform as a psychoanalyst when he returned to America. David complied with this requirement but then dropped out, having no interest in medical studies. In a later interview, he spoke with some bitterness about his analysis; interestingly, he attributed the failure to Freud's not following his own classical dictates. David did not give up on psychoanalysis, however, seeking treatment with several others in the following years, including Ernst Simmel, Otto Fenichel, and Anna Freud. He eventually became an orthodox psychoanalyst in Los Angeles.

Both Mark and David reported that they considered it a mistake for Freud to see both them and Ruth; he should have, in their view, referred each to another analyst, many of whom were available in Vienna at the time. In the early 1930s, when they were all in treatment at $25 an hour six times a week— a very high fee, the equivalent of more than $360 an hour now—they constituted 60 percent of his practice and income. The rest was made up of other wealthy patients such as Dorothy Tiffany Burlingham and the Princess Marie Bonaparte. Seeing all the Brunswicks was good for him financially, but not for them therapeutically.

As Freud continued to see patients after the war and into the 1930s, his actual behavior as an analyst continued to depart markedly from his published recommendations. Several patients from this period have published firsthand accounts of their treatment by him that give a flavor of Freud in action, as well as revealing what was helpful, and not helpful, to each of them.

Smiley Blanton first saw Freud in 1929, when he was forty-seven and the Professor seventy-three. Blanton made several additional trips to Europe in the ensuing years to continue his analysis, the last meeting taking place in London in 1938, the year before Freud died. Blanton was a very agreeable man who took great pains to be friendly, appreciative, and not cause trouble; he had read all of Freud's books and was full of praise for them. For the first session, he was late through no fault of his own, yet was overcome with fear that Freud would interpret this as a sign of resistance. His overly developed conscience and strong sense of guilt made him a most compliant patient; he idolized Freud, and felt it a privilege to be treated by the great man. It is clear that free association was a rule for Freud and the patients' task was to follow it in the face of their resistance. Yet, with a guilt-ridden person like Blanton, Freud was gentle, told him he was not responsible for his unconscious mind, and need not feel he was in the wrong if he had difficulty associating.

The course of Blanton's analysis revealed both the open-minded and opinionated sides of Freud. Some of his interpretations were directly related to Blanton's associations, while others came from his theoretical preoccupations, such as his focus on sexuality and his prejudicial view of America. With all of his American patients—and they made up a large part of his practice in the last fifteen years—Freud never considered how his openly voiced hatred of their native country might be affecting them. As evidence of Freud's imposition of theory, he interpreted one of Blanton's dreams as showing an unconscious wish that Freud, whose cancer was apparent, would die. Blanton himself felt that he was, indeed, afraid that Freud would die, not because of a competitive wish, but because he did not want to lose this man who had become so central in his life.

Blanton felt his analysis helped him tremendously and attributed the success to the strength of Freud's personality, his dedication to the work, how he listened intently, and how he took him seriously. It is also clear that Freud came to like Blanton; he gave him gifts of his books, arranged for a friendly meeting with his wife, and, in a touching moment, impulsively held out his hand with affection after Blanton told him that the analysis was the most personally helpful thing that ever happened to him. In a late session Blanton told Freud: "I feel that a lot of the benefit of psychoanalysis is due to the character of the analyst. . . . I think a great deal of the benefit I have had from my analysis is the association with you and the appreciation of your courage [these were years when Freud underwent numerous operations for his cancer], your scientific manner, and your sympathy. [Blanton commented] Freud did not reply to this."

The American poet H.D. (Hilda Doolittle) saw Freud in 1933, when she was forty-six and he seventy-six, and for a few weeks the following year. She later wrote an evocative account of her time with him titled *Tribute to Freud* (1956). She had been through a series of traumatic events a few years earlier, including the breakup of her marriage, a bout of the Spanish influenza when she was pregnant, and the deaths of her brother and her father. These precipitated a psychological breakdown in which she drifted out of reality, losing her ability to write. At the time she came to Freud, after an unsuccessful analysis with Hanns Sachs, she was involved in a lesbian relationship with a wealthy woman named Winnifred Ellerman, who supported her emotionally and financially. In fact, Ellerman paid for the analysis with Freud, corresponded with him, and gave money to the Vienna Psychoanalytic Society.

H.D. was a mystical and spiritual person, a dreamer who lived in her imagination and, at times of crisis and stress, lost her grip on reality. Despite their differences, she and Freud connected through their common love of ancient Greece, her interest in his collection of artifacts, and their focus on myths and dreams. At the best times in her analysis, she felt him to be a "magician." Freud did all his typical theory-based interpreting with her—using his ideas about female sexuality, for example—but he did not become angry if she disagreed; but H.D., who was privately terrified, kept her disagreements to herself most of the time. The overall situation was quite tangled. Ellerman wrote to Freud a great deal as well as to Anna, and there was much contact with other patients and members of the Freud family, not to mention his dog: at one point he pressed H.D. to accept a puppy that was soon to be born, putting her in a very conflicted position, since she did not want a dog, but was too frightened to say so. Through it all, he seemed to respect and admire her, and conveyed this with compliments about the quality of her mind. She found her analysis very helpful, was able to resume writing, and had genuine affection for "Papa," as she called him. In her own view, the benefits of her analysis came more from Freud's intense interest and involvement, her connection with a person of such stature, and the strength of his personality than on what he believed was the essence of the treatment: interpretations of her unconscious conflicts.

John Dorsey—like Frink, Oberndorf, Kardiner, and Blanton an American psychiatrist—saw Freud in 1935, when he was thirty-five and the Professor seventy-seven. At the time, Freud's cancer was well advanced, and the Nazis were on the verge of taking control of Vienna. Dorsey was the youngest of five children from a midwestern Protestant background who had difficulty standing on his own and becoming an adult; like Blanton, he deferred to authority, felt guilty, and worked hard to please the older Professor, all of which made it comfortable for Freud to work with him. Dorsey's powerful idealization of Freud was present from the very beginning, when he was in awe of this "mightiest of men." Freud said almost nothing in the analysis, which Dorsey took as the Professor's great wisdom in letting him discover himself through free association. By the end, he spoke of "my practice of free-association [which] led to my Great

Me Awakening." When Dorsey asked at the end of their work what was most important, Freud unhesitatingly reminded him of the interpretation of a dream that revealed Dorsey's oedipal conflict. Dorsey's own reflections made it clear that what was valuable to him was the relationship with this revered man who had become his hero. Dorsey felt the analysis with Freud was one of the highlights of his life and, like Blanton, was greatly taken with Freud as a person— his dedication and seriousness, and his courage in the face of illness and impending death.

While Kardiner, Hirst, Blanton, H.D., and Dorsey had, on balance, positive experiences, Joseph Wortis's analysis, like those of Frink and Oberndorf, can only be termed a disaster. Wortis saw Freud in 1934, when he was twenty-eight and the Professor seventy-eight. They immediately got off on the wrong foot because Wortis had been referred to Freud by his kindly mentor Havelock Ellis, whose reservations about psychoanalysis aroused Freud's characteristic ire. Ellis had also suggested that Wortis look up Wilhelm Stekel when he was in Vienna; when Freud heard of this, he could barely contain his rage. In the analysis itself, Wortis appeared as a fairly repressed man who thought he was "normal" and wanted to use his treatment to further his psychiatric education. Nevertheless, he did make attempts to expose his feelings of inadequacy and other difficulties, though Freud did not seem particularly interested. The central problem, however, was that Wortis, unlike many of the others, was not compliant. He raised critical questions about psychoanalytic theory and vacillated between trying to be a good analysand, follow the rule of free association, and taking a more independent position, voicing his critical thoughts. Freud dealt with him by forceful interpretations of his resistance, threatened to kick him out at one point, and made textbook interpretations of his unconscious homosexuality, oedipal wishes, and primal scene exposure. Reading Wortis's account, one is reminded of Freud's work with Dora over thirty years before. Neither of these patients conveyed an appreciation of the Professor's stature and genius, nor did they show sufficient deference to his authority, and he could barely tolerate them.

Other patients Freud saw during the postwar years included his daughter Anna, whom he analyzed from 1918 to 1921 and, again, in 1924. In addition to his patients, there were colleagues who wished to be treated by him, such as Victor Tausk and Herbert Silberer. Tausk was a brilliant, creative, deeply disturbed young man from Croatia who had tried various careers, first in law, then in literature, journalism, and music. His first marriage failed, leading to a severe depression for which he was briefly hospitalized. He had come to Vienna in 1908, hoping that Freud would provide a cure for his continuing depression and inner turmoil, and that he would find a profession in psychoanalysis. Toward these goals, he undertook medical and psychiatric training; because of his personal difficulties, he was drawn to work with manic-depressive and schizophrenic psychoses and later made significant contributions in these areas, and was active in the Vienna Society. Freud became his idol, as he did for many of the early followers, and psychoanalysis became the center of his life. It was a profession that gave him meaningful work, a venue for his intellect and creativity, and a treatment that promised personal salvation.

In 1912, Tausk had become involved in a short-lived affair with Lou Andreas-Salomé, who was, at the same time, a close confidant of Freud's: she reported back to the Professor what she heard from her lover. With the onset of the war, Tausk served as a psychiatrist for four years, being exposed to many of its horrors. In September of 1915 Freud wrote to Ferenczi, "Tausk is in the hospital in Rzeszow and writes me gloomy letters from there." As a medical officer in the Austrian army he worked with many different types of soldiers who were suffering the effects of the war and wrote several essays as a result of these experiences, including his paper on deserters and, in 1916, *Diagnostic Considerations Concerning the Symptomatology of the So-called War-psychoses,* a paper that had much in common with Simmel's work.

At the conclusion of the war, Tausk's struggle with depression continued as he attempted to make a go of things amidst the economic hardships of Vienna. Lonely and subject to fluctuating moods, he desperately wished to be accepted into analysis with Freud. But the Professor was suspicious of this young man who, despite his fierce loyalty in the wars with Adler and Jung, posed a threat because of his creativity and originality. His ideas about psychosis, with which he had firsthand experience, were at odds with Freud's speculations and, in fact, had more in common with Jung's views, though Tausk did not present them as such. Freud rejected his plea for treatment, sending him, instead, to Helene Deutsch, a much younger and less experienced psychiatrist who was just beginning her own psychoanalytic training and was, in addition, in analysis with Freud. The triangle of Tausk–Frau Lou–Freud was now re-created with Tausk–Deutsch–Freud. Tausk spent his analysis with her talking mainly about the Professor, and she reported what he said back to Freud in her own analysis. After three months of this Freud called a halt; he did not like continually hearing about Tausk's "genius," and had long harbored suspicions that the younger man was "anticipating" his ideas. He insisted that Deutsch break off Tausk's analysis, which she did with some reluctance.

With his attempt to be treated by Freud frustrated, and dropped from the substitute analysis with Deutsch, where he at least had the illusion of a connection with the man he worshiped, Tausk committed suicide by gunshot and hanging three months later in 1919. His final note to Freud absolved the Professor of responsibility for his death and expressed his good wishes for psychoanalysis. The suicide cannot be blamed entirely on Freud's rejection, since Tausk was a difficult personality with many other troubled relationships. His friend the psychoanalyst Paul Federn called him a "superior, talented and high meaning man," but also noted that he "always bit the hand that reached out to help him" and was vain and envious. Tausk had been through a long series of unsuccessful affairs with different women, and his exposure to the war had, no doubt, taken its toll. Still, being turned away by the man he desperately needed and revered, and then having his analysis with Deutsch abruptly cut off by this same man, were the final blows that led to his suicide, according to Federn and others who knew him.

Freud spoke well of Tausk in his published obituary, but in a letter to Ferenczi he wrote: "Tausk shot himself on July 4, a week before the date set for his wedding, leaving behind tender and conciliatory letters. Etiology obscure, probably psychological impotence and the last act of his infantile struggle with the ghost of the father. Despite appreciation of his talent, no real sympathy in me." Freud expressed similar sentiments to Lou Andreas-Salomé a few months later, saying: "I confess that I do not really miss him; I had long realized that he could be of no further service, indeed that he constituted a threat to the future. . . . I would have dropped him long ago if *you* hadn't raised him so in my estimation."

Herbert Silberer, though never in analysis with Freud, was another member of the early group who was seriously damaged by Freud's rejection. He had joined the Vienna Society in 1910 and made original contributions to the understanding of dreams that Freud duly credited. Like Tausk and a number of others, he had enormous respect and admiration for the Professor, while, at the same time, striving to develop his own ideas. After the war, Freud ejected him from the Psychoanalytic Society, writing him a terse letter in 1922:

Dear Sir:

I request that you do not make the intended visit with me. As the result of the observations and impression of recent years I no longer desire personal contact with you.

Freud's disaffection was based not only on the independent nature of Silberer's views but, perhaps more, on the fact that Silberer had edited a journal with Stekel, which, according to another member of the Vienna Society, set off Freud's rage. Silberer committed suicide some nine months after he was dismissed, and while one cannot know all the reasons behind this tragic act, it is clear that Freud's rejection was a painful blow.

In his *Autobiographical Study* of 1925, Freud gave his version of the breaks with his followers, those who left the movement on their own or were forced out by him:

The secession of former pupils has often been brought up against me as a sign of my intolerance or has been regarded as evidence of some special fatality that hangs over me. It is a sufficient answer to point out that, in contrast to those who have left me, like Jung, Adler, Stekel, and a few besides, there are a great number of men like Abraham, Eitingon, Ferenczi,

Rank, Jones, Brill, Sachs, Pfister, van Emden, Reik, and others, who have worked with me for some fifteen years in loyal collaboration and for the most part uninterrupted friendship.

This is Freud rewriting history to his own advantage, for there had been many more analysts who broke away than his remarks imply. Herbert Graf was just one of the members of the original Wednesday Society who left because he could not tolerate Freud's autocratic ways. When Adler resigned there were nine others who followed him out of the Vienna Society, and Jung took several Swiss analysts with him when he and Freud had their falling out. Tausk, Silberer, and others were either rejected or left when their differences could not be mediated. More to the point, Freud failed to note that the collaboration of such "pupils" as Abraham, Eitingon, Sachs, and Jones was predicated on their loyalty; his friendship with them remained "uninterrupted" only if they displayed an unwavering adherence to his doctrines. In fact, Rank and Ferenczi, whom he could still call loyal in 1924, were soon to ran afoul of him when they expressed their own ideas. Freud demanded submission from all his psychoanalytic children, and played very much the same patriarchal role in his actual family.

CHAPTER 20

Freud at Home

In my private life I am a petit bourgeois. . . . I would not like one of my
sons to get a divorce or one of my daughters to have a liaison.

—Freud to Marie Bonaparte

WITHIN THE intimate circle of his family, Freud displayed the most patriarchal, the most ordinary middle-class values and tastes. These predilections came, in part, from his need to put right the poverty and chaos of his early years, to create a stable home where his wife and children were well provided for, to maintain a respectable family where calmness prevailed, passion was muted, and relationships were predictable and controlled. But it also created an atmosphere in which emotional expression was tightly constrained. The Freuds were not an openly affectionate family and physical contact was rare.

At home, Freud was seen as a great man, principally occupied with his work, which consumed long hours and most of his energy. Martha, Minna, the children, nieces, nephews, and family servants all admired and respected him. When he spent time with his sons and daughters, they felt he cared about them, was concerned for their welfare, was generous with money, and, on those occasions when it was required, interceded on their behalf. The image of him as a figure of power and importance was pervasive at home and was reinforced over the years by the outside world.

Martha was ever the efficient manager, extremely reserved, punctual, and orderly, someone who stayed in the background and provided for her husband and the children. Freud's daily life remained one of extreme regularity. He arose at seven, ate breakfast, and then had his beard trimmed by a barber who appeared every morning for that purpose. As the historian Paul Roazen noted, Martha "laid out his clothes, chose everything for him down to his handkerchiefs, and even put toothpaste on his toothbrush." He followed the routine established during the early years of his practice: psychoanalytic patients from eight to one, then dinner punctually on the hour. This was the principal time each day to interact with his wife and family. His children remembered him as a kind and somewhat interested father, but clearly more the great man focused on his work than a parent involved in their lives. Even Jones, who tried to present an ideal picture, noted that "he enjoyed his food and would concentrate on it. He was very taciturn during meals, which would sometimes be a source of embarrassment to strange visitors who had to carry on a conversation alone with the family."

His nephew Harry, son of his younger brother Alexander, remembered that his uncle was "always on very friendly terms with his children [but not] expansive . . . always a bit *formal* and *reserved*. It rarely happened that he kissed any of them; I might almost say, really never. And even his mother, whom he loved very much, he only kissed perforce at parting." Jones described Freud's revealing "habit of bringing his latest purchase of an antiquity, usually a small statuette, to the dinner table and placing it in front of him as a companion during the meal. Afterwards it would be returned to his desk and then brought back again for a day or two."

Following the midday dinner, the main meal of the day, Freud would take a walk. The route and timing were so predictable that those who knew him and wanted an audience could always catch him on a particular street or corner. From three in the afternoon until nine at night there were consultations and more analytic patients. Then supper, perhaps a walk with Martha or one of his daughters or a card game with Minna, and then writing and related psychoanalytic work in his study until 1 A.M. or later. Lectures were given at the university on Saturdays, followed by a game of the popular Viennese card game Tarok with his old friends. This outward regularity, with all the details of daily life taken care of by others, provided a structure: inside it, he lived with his ideas, creations, theories, ancient artifacts, and correspondence. He was a compulsive letter writer; it is estimated that he wrote more than twenty thousand letters during his lifetime, typically answering each one he received within a day and expecting the same in return.

On Sundays the family all went to Freud's mother's apartment for a meal; Martin Freud's description is revealing of his father's relationship with Amalia.

> As the evening went on, an atmosphere of growing crisis was felt by all as Amalia became unsettled and anxious. There are people who, when they are unsettled and disturbed, will hide these feelings because they do not want to affect the peace of those around them; but Amalia was not one of these. My father always came to these gatherings—I know of no occasion when he disappointed her—but his working day was a long one and he always came much later than any one else. Amalia knew this, but perhaps it was a reality she could never accept. Soon she would be seen running anxiously to the door and out to the landing to stare down the staircase.

An older Amalia Freud.

Was he coming? Where was he? Was it not getting late? This running in and out might go on for an hour, but it was known that any attempt to stop her would produce an outburst of anger which it was better to avoid by taking as little notice as possible. And my father always came at very much his usual time, but never at a moment when Amalia was waiting for him on the landing.

These family meals, which Freud dutifully attended, were invariably preceded by gastric distress, which he put down to other causes. He was able to dominate his wife, but he never talked back to his mother; even when he was successful and famous, she still made his stomach churn.

The summers were a break from the routine of hard work. The family would go to a spa or hotel in the mountains, where Sigmund would later join them. There would be hikes, mushroom gathering, and time spent with Martha, Minna, and the six children. Still, the focus remained on work. Much time was given over to writing if he was in the midst of a project, as was often the case. Toward the latter part of the summer there would be trips—to Italy, once to Athens—almost always with a male companion such as his brother Alexander or Sándor Ferenczi. On these occasions he would write daily letters to Martha, returning to the pattern of their courtship.

Because Freud's fame rests on his psychological theories, including theories about infancy and childhood, there is a tendency to judge him as a parent, to evaluate how his children fared as adults. This is a complicated matter, since many factors enter into the shaping of a child's personality, including genetic predisposition, the influence of both parents, and the world in which they live. In examining the lives of the Freud children, it is important to maintain a balanced view, to neither idealize the family nor focus excessively on disturbance. The children were born between 1887 and 1895 in the pre–First World War Austro-Hungarian Empire. Men of this time and station did not change diapers, help with the dishes, or get down on the floor and play with their babies as fathers may do today. Freud was a professional man whose work made great demands on him, a busy doctor who needed to present a respectable image to the world.

Freud and Martha's lack of sexual and physical intimacy was part of the general family atmosphere of emotional constriction, an ambience that created difficulties for all the children. Martin reported how neither his mother nor his father ever explained anything about sex to him. Once, when the topic of the difference between a bull and a steer came up, Freud commented, "You must be told these things," but didn't say any more about it. He sent all his sons to the family pediatrician Oscar Rie to be told the facts of life. In this, he was probably not unlike many fathers, then or now. But his middle son Oliver reported a more harmful experience. When he was sixteen and concerned about masturbation, he consulted his father, who "warned" him against it, causing Oliver to become "quite upset for some time." He felt that as a result of his father's censure, a barrier was created that prevented further communication between them.

The conservative atmosphere of the family was not confined to sexual and emotional control but extended into the political arena as well. The Freuds were successful, assimilated Jews, with two paths open to them. They could remain in touch with their own history and sympathize with workers and the poor, or identify with the upper classes. Freud's reaction was complex; some of his remarks revealed an awareness of the hardships of the poverty of his youth and showed sympathy for society's lower strata. But such expressions were rare; for the most part, he distanced himself from what he frequently referred to as the *Gesindel*—the "mob," "mass," or "rabble"—and identified with those he saw as respectable and powerful. In 1917, he wrote to Lou Andreas-Salomé about *das blöde Volk*—"the stupid common folk."

In the years before the First World War, the family admired the Austrian emperor Franz Josef. Martin recalled that "we Freud children were all stout royalists, delighting to hear, or to see, all we could of the Imperial Court." The emperor had a long history of pro-Semitism—in the 1890s he attempted to block the election of the anti-Semitic Viennese mayor Karl Lueger, and, during the Great War, gave sanctuary in Vienna to Jewish refugees from Galicia—and many Jews, especially from the wealthy and professional classes, were grateful to him because of such actions. Still, one could admire the emperor and retain a connection with one's roots; many other men from backgrounds similar to Freud's identified with the plight of the lower classes. Heinrich Braun, the boy Freud admired during their Gymnasium days, became a leading figure among the Austrian Social Democrats, and his brother-in-law Victor Adler, also a former schoolmate, was one of the leading Socialists in Europe. In fact, many of the leaders of the Social Democratic Party came from Jewish backgrounds similar to Freud's, including Alfred Adler (no relation to Victor) and Otto Bauer, the older brother of Freud's patient Dora.

The family atmosphere was characterized by emotional and sexual control, political conservatism, and conventional attitudes toward masculinity and femininity, and all these factors played themselves out in the lives of the individual children. Mathilde, the Freuds' firstborn, had married Robert Hollitscher, a Viennese businessman twelve years her senior. While the aftereffects of surgery prevented her from having children of her own, in all other respects she lived a most ordinary bourgeois life. She seemed to completely accept her father's idea of what a woman should be; as he described her in a letter to Fliess when she was a child, she was "altogether feminine." As he wrote to Mathilde when she was young and unsure of finding a man, "The more intelligent among young men are sure to know what to look for in a wife—gentleness, cheerfulness, and the talent to make their life easier and more beautiful." These were much the same qualities he had praised in Martha during their courtship.

The Hollitschers lived near Sigmund and Martha, and, as a good daughter, Mathilde saw her parents almost every day, helping out with the social side of her father's profession, such as assisting psychoanalytic visitors with living arrangements. After the death of her sister Sophie, Mathilde and her husband took the two motherless Halberstadt boys into their home for a time. In later years she became very close friends with Ruth and Mark Brunswick, who were so fond of her that they gave her name to their daughter. In all this, Mathilde seems to have been much like her mother—involved as a provider but not directly part of psychoanalysis. Roazen, who interviewed her as a widow in her seventies, found her a gracious and charming woman.

Freud's relations with his sons were ruled by his belief in the Oedipus complex; it was a living reality in his mind. He thought that every son—and this belief extended to many of his psychoanalytic colleagues—was driven toward deadly competition with his father. There were three boys, Martin, Oliver and Ernst, and Freud made sure they did not enter the competitive arena; he prevented them from becoming oedipal rivals by letting them know they were not to become physicians, much less psychoanalysts. Martin reported that "medicine as a profession for any of his sons was strictly banned by father," while Oliver remembered a subtler communication. His father would say in passing that he

The Freud children: Sophie, Mathilde, Anna, Oliver, Martin, and Ernst.

did not think any of them would study to become physicians, which achieved the goal of keeping them out of the field; for if he had directly forbidden it, in Oliver's view, they might have rebelled and gone into medicine.

Many fathers welcome their sons into their profession; indeed, they take pride in having a child carry on their legacy. Josef Breuer's son became a physician, and Schnitzler's father insisted that both his sons follow him into medicine, even though Arthur had little interest in it. And this was not only true for sons. Oscar Rie had two daughters; the younger one, Marianne, was given encouragement and special tutoring by her parents so she could study medicine. The daughter of Ludwig Rosenberg—like Rie, a pediatrician friend of Freud's from the old days and a Saturday night card-playing companion—also became a physician. Freud's position was quite the opposite. He was convinced that every son unconsciously wished to compete with and defeat his father, a conviction that came together with his need to maintain his dominance within the family.

Martin described a memory of mushroom hunting during the family summer vacations in the mountains. Freud would scout out a suitable area and then "was ready to lead his small band of troops, each young soldier taking up a position and beginning the skirmish at proper intervals, like a well-trained infantry platoon attacking through the forest. We played that we were chasing some flighty and elusive game; and there was always a competition to decide on the best hunter. Father always won."

This was an enjoyable game for the children during those rare weeks when they spent time with their busy father, a game that seems harmless enough. Still, the imagery is significant, for it reveals the way Freud even structured play with his children in military terms. And he had to remain the commander of the troops, he had to win. This vignette shows him acting, albeit playfully, the same way at home as he did within the movement; and, just as none of his psychoanalytic children were allowed to surpass him, he did not allow any of his sons to mount a challenge to his preeminence.

A good picture of the family's life, as well as a sense of Freud's personality, comes from the memoir written by Freud's first son. Martin was imaginative as a child and composed poems that Freud sent to Fliess during the years of their correspondence. While displaying some literary talent, and later trying his hand at writing, he had trouble with school in the early years. Throughout his life he was a man of action, not much given to introspection. As a youth he was ardent about dueling over matters of honor and later took up skiing and mountaineering, but was only excited by these sports if his life was at risk. He almost lost his leg in a skiing accident. He seemed to enjoy all the action during his service in the Austrian army and was rewarded with medals for heroism.

After Martin returned from the war in 1919, he married a woman named Ernestine Drucker—nicknamed "Esti"—became a lawyer, and went to work for his father, helping to manage the psychoanalytic press in Vienna. Esti came from a well-to-do Viennese family and was attractive, artistic, and, in her own words, "not at all a home girl." Her father-in-law disapproved. "She's much too pretty for our family!" Freud remarked, loud enough for her to hear. He saw her as too much the liberated, independent woman, too sexual, too extravagant in her tastes and spending. Freud forever branded her a black sheep. He also had a negative reaction to Rank's wife Tola, when Otto first brought her to Vienna, but Tola was more compliant than Esti, more concerned about pleasing the Professor and fitting into the psychoanalytic world, and he eventually came to accept her.

When Martin and Esti had children, Freud dictated their names, as had been the case with his own offspring. The firstborn was to be called Anton, after the recently deceased Anton von Freund, a wealthy Hungarian patient who had given money to support psychoanalysis. The next was named Miriam Sophie, though she became known by the middle name that Freud had requested in honor of his daughter who died in 1920. When Anton was three or four months old, Freud criticized Esti for "cuddling him too much." He believed that "too much" physical affection from parents was harmful, because it speeded up sexual maturation. Anyone who has observed a three- or four-month-old infant will appreciate the extreme nature of this belief.

Oliver, the second son, was very bright and mathematically inclined as a child; as Freud wrote to Fliess from a vacation in the country, "Oli classifies mountains here, just as he does the city railroad and tram lines in Vienna . . . [he] is again practicing the exact recording of routes, distances, names and places of mountains." These talents led him to pursue a technical education, and he later became a mathematical engineer. He married for the first time in 1915, then served as an engineer with the Austrian army during the First World War; the marriage dissolved during the time he was away. He married a Berlin woman named Henny Fuchs in 1923 and had one daughter, named Eva.

Freud initially had high hopes for Oliver because of his intelligence, but as a young man his orderliness and interest in classifying took on obsessive-compulsive proportions. He went into analysis with Franz Alexander in Berlin in the early 1920s and seemed to find some relief. Freud's understanding of his son's psychological difficulties followed his theories, locating the source of Oliver's troubles in internal, instinctual sources. As he wrote to Arnold Zweig, Oliver had "extraordinary gifts. . . . His character is faultless. Then the neurosis came over him and stripped off all the blooms. Being unfortunately strongly inhibited neurotically he had bad luck in life." To his follower Max Eitingon, he wrote: "It is particularly hard for me to be objective in this case, for he was my pride and my secret hope for a long time, until his anal-masochistic organization appeared . . . clearly I suffer very much with my feelings of helplessness." Apparently unaware of the effects on his children of his own need for control, punctuality, and a tightly regulated life—not to mention Martha's compulsions—he saw no connection between these family characteristics and his son's "neurosis."

Oliver's memories of his father were more balanced than his brother Martin's. He remembered him as a great man and recalled a crucial time when Freud gave him helpful advice regarding his school examinations. But he also could not forget the hurtful exchange when his father warned him not to masturbate. Of the children who survived, he was most distant from the family in later years.

Ernst, born a year after Oliver, appears to have been the happiest and most independent of the boys. He was known in the family as the stable and charming one; his parents called him their "lucky child" and, in later years, Freud referred to him as a "brick" and his "tower of strength." He trained as an architect, served in the Austrian army, and married a woman named Lucie Brasch after the war. They settled in Berlin and had three sons whose names were *not* dictated by Freud. Despite a brief separation early on, the marriage was an enduring and happy one.

Anna and Sophie at about age four and six.

Of the daughters, Sophie, who died in the influenza epidemic, was valued in the family for her beauty, though in photographs she and her younger sister Anna are both pretty little girls. When she was three, and the family attended Freud's sister Rosa's wedding, he commented, "The loveliest part of the wedding, by the way, was our Sopherl—with curled hair and a wreath of forget-me-nots on her head." In later years, Martha spent weeks, and sometimes months, with her at spas. They called her their "Sunday child."

Like Mathilde, Sophie was raised to play the conventional role of wife and mother. She married the Hamburg photographer Max Halberstadt in 1913, and they had two sons, Ernst and Heinz. At the time of her impending wedding, Freud was noticeably upset and Ferenczi referred to his "Sophie-Complex," suggesting that he not take her loss so much to heart. His daughter Anna later said that during that summer he was visibly depressed, the only occasion she remembered seeing him in such a state. This was also the time when he was about to lose another important love object: Carl Jung. While he felt depressed over the impending marriage of the lovely Sophie, he did not interfere as he later would with Anna's attempts to find a man.

Looking at these five Freud children in the context of their time and society, it is fair to say that they suffered the effects of the constricted family atmosphere *and* found ways to overcome it. Sophie, by all accounts, was a happy young woman, though she died early. The others all lived long lives, were married, had children—in Mathilde's case, substitute children—and the sons had careers. Martin and Oliver took two different paths in dealing with their father's power and the family atmosphere. Martin lived a life that was much the opposite of Freud's; he was a "sportsman," and, in later years, unfaithful to his wife. As his daughter Sophie made clear in her memoir, he was someone who did not love himself and was limited in his ability to love others. Oliver, on the other hand, incorporated the compulsive constrictions seen in both his parents. Mathilde and Ernst seem to have had reasonably happy and productive lives.

Did Freud spend too little time with his children, or was his behavior as a father typical of his time and place? He was attached to his wife and children in his way, but his relations with his psychoanalytic sons were much more intense than with his biological sons which, on balance, may have worked to the advantage of Martin, Oliver, and Ernst. While they missed out on time and closeness with their father, they were spared the hatred he directed against his younger colleagues when they attempted to break free from his control. Anna, the last Freud child, followed a different path than her five older siblings. Several circumstances converged, and she became the only one to follow her father into psychoanalysis.

CHAPTER 21

Anna Freud:
The Perfect Disciple

Papa always makes it clear that he would like to know me as much more rational and lucid than the girls and women he gets to know during his analytic hours, with all their moods, dissatisfactions and passionate idiosyncrasies. Thus I, too, would really like to be as he sees fit, first out of love for him, and second because I myself know that it is the only chance that one has to be somewhat useful and not a burden and a concern for others.

—Anna Freud, 1925

MARTHA WAS singularly uninterested in her husband's work, Freud's own sons were not permitted to enter the field, and his two older daughters were expected to fulfill their appropriate "feminine" roles. His youngest daughter Anna, however, was the exception, the one in whom family life and psychoanalysis intersected. In the end, she became what Freud had hoped for in such psychoanalytic sons as Jung, Rank, and Ferenczi: the perfect disciple. He fondly called her his "Antigone," after the daughter of Oedipus who never married, staying with her father and tending to him when he was old and infirm.

Anna was born just short of two years after Sophie, but was not welcomed by Martha, who was worn out by the five pregnancies and births she had endured in rapid succession over the preceding years. Tante Minna moved in with the Freuds when Anna was one, but she, too, did not seem to form an attachment to the new baby girl. It is very clear, from a variety of sources, including her own later accounts, that Anna was an unwanted child and that early maternal deprivation had long-lasting effects on her emotional life. As Eva Rosenfeld, who knew Anna intimately, put it, Martha "never loved" her and this was "the tragedy of Anna's life."

Anna did have a reliable and loving substitute mother during her early years, a Catholic nursemaid named Josefine Cihlarz. Looking back, Anna remembered her warmth and sympathy. Unfortunately, Josefine left the Freuds to begin her own family when Anna started school, though she still referred to her years later as "my old nursemaid, the oldest relation and the most genuine of my childhood." The parallel with the Catholic nursemaid of Freud's own earliest years is interesting, though Anna was older than her father had been when she lost this important mother figure.

The effects of Martha's coolness and absence reverberated throughout Anna's childhood and continued, in different forms, for the rest of her life. As a young girl she spoke of her misery, of "being left out by the big ones, of being only a bore to them, and of feeling bored and left alone." She felt she was "dumb," unattractive, and of no interest to anyone, though from photographs she seems a nice-looking young girl, not much different in appearance than her sister Sophie. In her mind, however, Sophie, the one who was defined as pretty and loved by Martha, was attractive in ways Anna could not imagine herself to be. As might be expected, she directed much jealousy toward this favored older sister. Anna's depression and sense of inferiority were apparent in her view of her body: her ankles were too thick, her feet were like a boy's, she covered herself with large and loose-fitting clothes, developed a hunched posture, as if hiding herself, and, in family photographs, was almost always unsmiling, the least happy of the children.

In describing her early years, Anna spoke of herself as "whiny" and lacking in "diligence." There was an early period when her dissatisfaction with neglect, her anger over the preference shown for Sophie, and her sadness were more openly expressed. When she was three, Freud referred to her "cheekiness," and commented that she was "beatified by naughtiness"; he affectionately called her his "Black Devil," a nickname she prized. But these open expressions of feeling did not last, especially in this family, where there was great pressure to fit the role of what her father called normal femininity. Her unhappiness, anger, and attempts at assertion were buried; she became an extremely obedient young girl.

All of the Freud children were predisposed to associate cleanliness and neatness with approval and love, an outgrowth of Martha's cleaning compulsions and early toilet training. For Anna, as well as her brother Oliver, this took on obsessive-compulsive dimensions. In later childhood, she was very fastidious with her clothes and would become anxious if her dresses were the least bit disheveled or unstarched; indeed, for the remainder of her life she was extremely orderly and diligent. This cleanliness, along with efforts to be "good," were attempts to win the love she so desperately craved.

Anna's depression resurfaced in adolescence in the form of physical symptoms and unpleasant emotional states: backaches, low energy, and what she called "dumbness." In a letter to her father, written when she was eighteen, she referred to a mysterious "it" that was not an illness, yet kept breaking out and making her feel exhausted and stupid. In her loneliness, she learned to console herself with daydreams and masturbation. Her symptoms and moods expressed her depression and degraded self-image, though the members of her family did not define them as such—certainly not her mother or her aunt Minna, nor her father, who had to fit her into his theories.

It was during this adolescent period that Anna increasingly turned toward Freud in her search for love. On a trip at age sixteen, she signed her letters to "Papa" with "hugs and kisses" and passionate pleas for letters. She wrote that she missed him and longed to have him call her by her old pet name of Black Devil. In 1913, Sophie married while Anna, eighteen years old, was on a tour in Italy. Freud wrote that there was no need for her to return for the wedding. She felt quite bitter about being left out of this important family event, but was consoled, later that year, when he joined her and they traveled together.

In response to Anna's complaints about being left out when her sister got married, Freud told her that she was jealous of the new husband who now had Sophie's love. This was an interpretation of her disguised Oedipus complex: jealousy of the brother-in-law as father figure who wins the mother's love. This did not fit Anna's experience; she wrote back disagreeing with his interpretation and complaining of her unhappiness:

> I am not really sick. It irrupts in me, somehow, and then I am very tired and must worry about all kinds of things. . . . [She says she is not jealous of Max Halberstadt, who she hardly knows, but is] glad that Sophie is getting married, because the unending quarrel between us was horrible for me. It was no matter for her, because she did not care for me, but I liked her very much and I always admired her a bit. . . . I truly do not know why I am sometimes quite well and sometimes not, and . . . I would like very much to be reasonable like Mathilde. . . . If I have a stupid day, everything looks wrong to me; for instance, today I cannot understand how it can sometimes be so stupid . . . I want to be a reasonable person.

By this time in her life, Anna had come to accept the idea that all her emotions were "unreasonable," not surprising in view of the family atmosphere. Freud wrote to her that her reaction to Sophie's wedding was the result of her being "overzealous, restless and unsatisfied because you have run away like a child from many things of which a grown-up girl would not be afraid." In his view, she would get over her moods when she accepted her "normal feminine" place.

This early interchange is representative of what went on in Anna's psychoanalysis with her father a few years later. Both times she turned to him seeking love and an explanation for the misery that kept befalling her. The cause of her unhappiness is not hard to see, though Freud, as her father and Martha's husband, was hardly in a position to be objective. In addition, her symptoms and depression were not unlike those he himself suffered in the 1890s, symptoms that were also related to maternal neglect. Just as he could never connect his own unhappiness and misery to his mother, he also could not relate Anna's disturbed state to her experience with Martha. In both his own case and hers, he substituted an oedipal interpretation, and, for both himself and his daughter, the prescription was the same: stop expressing the unruly emotions, stop being "overzealous, restless and unsatisfied," become a reasonable person. Because of his powerful position and her great need for his love, it is not surprising that Anna eventually complied with his demands.

A poem that Anna wrote as an adolescent gives a good picture of her state of mind prior to her analysis with her father:

> For one hour, one day, I do so wish
> To be rid of my self, no longer to know
> My own face, my own poor hand,
> Just once not to feel my thoughts.
> That man, that drayman, would I be,
> His shoulder rubbed sore from the strap;
> That porter, his neck bent, burdened;
> Someone other, who has no need to cover up—
> As I have been doing for so very long,
> With satisfactions cleverly calculated,
> Yet so stingy, so pitiful, that the dog
> Sunning himself in the corner there
> Would never look up from his bone for them.

This self-lacerating poem gives condensed expression to Anna's experience in a way that hardly any of her later writing does. There was no pleasure available to her as a girl; even a dog or the poorest man is better off than she. The lowest man at least has work to give his life some meaning, and, if he is in pain, it need not be hidden: he has "no need to cover up," while she must suffer in silence. Her emptiness, self-hate, and despair are painfully clear.

The emergence of the emotions associated with maternal neglect, her guilty daydreams and masturbation, and her struggle to understand herself brought Anna to the crucial turning point in her life and into psychoanalytic treatment with her father. Her formal analysis began in the last year of the Great War, a time when Freud was worried about his sons, who were all in the army, when Austria was on the verge of collapse, and the future of psychoanalysis appeared uncertain. If she needed his love, he was also looking for someone who would satisfy his needs. Anna was a very young and inexperienced twenty-three-year-old when she began her analysis; it lasted four years, long by the standards of the time. She had later, briefer, analyses—one in 1924–1925, three hours in 1929, and perhaps others that have gone unrecorded.

There are no direct accounts of Anna's analysis; indeed the whole treatment was covered up for many years—Jones, who knew of it, failed to mention it in his biography—and only brought to public attention in the 1960s. In his 1919 essay *A Child Is Being Beaten,* Freud used a disguised version of his daughter as a case example, while Anna's own 1922 paper, *Beating Fantasies and Daydreams,* was based on her own analysis, though she presented the material as if it were a patient that she was treating. In fact, she used this "case" to gain entrance to the Psychoanalytic Society, though she and her father both knew that she did not have any clinical experience. For many years, she continued to hide the fact that she was analyzed by Freud, though it has now been established that her paper was autobiographical and was written before she ever saw any patients of her own.

In *Beating Fantasies and Daydreams,* Anna described herself, in disguised form, as a young woman patient who was preoccupied with two fantasies. In one, a boy was being beaten by a grown-up, or many boys were being beaten by many grown-ups. This fantasy was charged with sensual feeling and culminated in a pleasurable act of masturbation. She dated its origin to her fifth or sixth year, the period before beginning school. While she did not mention it, this was the time when she lost her nurse Josefine, probably the only person who gave her physical comfort as a child. The other fantasy she referred to as her "nice stories." These were elaborate tales set in the Middle Ages with a great many variations and a number of subsidiary characters and details, though the theme of all of them was the same: an innocent young boy was menaced by a knight who, at the last moment, spared him and granted him favors.

Anna had divergent attitudes toward her two fantasies. The beating fantasies, with their masturbatory pleasure, were "ugly" and accompanied by "violent self-reproaches, pangs of conscience, and temporary depressed moods." The "nice stories" were just that: *nice,* nonsexual, and free from guilt. In her paper, she noted the thematic similarity of the two: both involved a strong and a weak person, a situation of danger and mounting tension, and a pleasurable resolution. Her interpretation of these fantasies, undoubtedly taken from her analysis, was that the girl-Anna was motivated by her incestuous feelings for her father: "in early childhood all the sexual drives were concentrated on a first love object, the father." This Oedipus complex was repressed and reemerged "in the language of the anal-sadistic organization as an act of beating." The nice stories, in contrast, were seen as healthy "sublimation"; sensual love was replaced by tender friendship. Freud's interpretation defined the masturbation and the daydreaming as the primary causes of Anna's troubles. Rather than viewing her escapes into fantasy and self-stimulation as attempts to find some comfort and solace within herself, he saw them as neurotic reactions that she must give up if she was to become normal. Many contemporary therapists, in contrast, would see Anna's fantasies and masturbation as the result of unhappiness and lack of love, as signs that her emotional states were not recognized or responded to.

Like Freud's own oedipal reconstruction of his childhood, his interpretation of his daughter's troubles contained a partial truth. Anna was certainly seeking her father's love, and all her conflicts in the spheres of affection, sexuality, and a possible adult identity became focused on him, more strongly than ever after he became her analyst. She longed for his love and, eventually, won him, pushing all rivals aside, including her mother. Her fantasies involved a child and a father figure and her sexual pleasure was associated with intense guilt. Freud's interpretation, which she eventually made her own, was that the specific features of the beating fantasies were disguises for her forbidden incestuous desire for "the first love object": the father. These features can be taken as support for an oedipal interpretation, but it leaves so much unaccounted for. The father is not the child's "first love object." The Oedipus complex, in Freud's view, is universal, as are "anal-sadistic" impulses. Yet Anna's beating fantasy, in which gratification can only be obtained if she is a boy being beaten, is quite unusual for a young girl: few need to obtain their pleasure in this way. Freud's interpretation did not explain anything about Anna as an individual; it simply forced her into a universal formula.

Both before and after analysis, Anna seemed interested in several men and sought intimacy with a series of women. When she was eighteen, she took a trip to London, where the thirty-five-year-old Ernest Jones paid court to her. Freud heard about this and vigorously intervened. He wrote to Anna: "I know from the most reliable sources that Doctor Jones has serious intentions of wooing you. It is the first time in your young life, and I have no thought of granting you the freedom of choice your two sisters enjoyed. For it has so happened that you have lived more intimately with us than they, and I would like to believe that you would find it more difficult to make such a decision for life without our—in this case my—consent."

Jones might indeed have been too old for the inexperienced young girl, but Freud continued to interfere with later, more suitable, partners. Hans Lampl, six years older than Anna, was a friend of the Freud family who eventually became a physician and a psychoanalyst. Freud had been friendly toward him, but this cooled when he showed an interest in Anna, who was now over twenty-five. He was deemed unsuitable by Freud and Anna concurred with her father. As she wrote, "I am often together with Lampl in a friendly relationship, but I also have daily opportunities to confirm our judgment of him from last year and to rejoice that we judged correctly."

Freud needed to keep her with him. As he wrote to Lou Andreas-Salomé in 1922: "I too very much miss Daughter-Anna . . . I have long felt sorry for her for still being at home with us old folks . . . but on the other hand, if she really were to go away, I should feel myself as deprived as I do now, and as I should do if I had to give up smoking!"

Given the degree of maternal deprivation in Anna's life, it is not surprising that the search for intimacy with women—several of them older, married and with children—became more important than finding a husband. From late adolescence, she looked for closeness and acceptance with a series of women who were all, significantly, tied to her father, which allowed her to obtain some love without threatening her connection to him. One of the first was Loe Kann, a wealthy and vivacious woman from Holland, at one time Ernest Jones's mistress, and an analysand of Freud's. In a letter to her father, Anna wrote, "I dream of her very often . . . you know that I am extraordinarily fond of her."

When Anna had been in analysis for a year she spent a summer with the Rie family. At the time, Oscar Rie's daughter Margarethe was in analysis with Freud; Anna became close to her, and they discussed their common experiences in therapy. Another woman in this series was Kata Levy, a Hungarian with connections to Ferenczi, who was the sister of Anton von Freund. Both Kata and Anton were also in analysis with the Professor.

For a time, Anna was close to her father's confidant Lou Andreas-Salomé, a woman her mother's age. She was able to share her feelings, as when she wrote to Frau Lou in 1924: "In the last week my 'nice stories' all of a sudden surfaced again and rampaged for days as they have not for a long while. Now they are asleep again, but I was impressed by how unchangeable and forceful and alluring such a daydream is, even if it has been—like my poor one—pulled apart, analyzed, published, and in every way mishandled and mistreated. I know that it is really shameful—especially when I do it between patients—but it was again very beautiful and gave me great pleasure." This was one of those rare occasions when the other side of Anna broke though, but, for the most part, she remained fixed in her role as the dutiful disciple, a role that Frau Lou supported.

Freud and Lou wrote about their shared "Daughter-Anna," and the older woman encouraged Anna's closeness with him. According to Anna's biographer, Elisabeth Young-Bruehl, "Frau Lou was not the sort of woman to question Anna Freud's adoration of—or identification with—her father; on the contrary, she promoted Anna Freud's desire to stay at home and dedicate herself to her father and to psychoanalysis."

Anna's tie to her father—already strong, and reinforced by her analysis with him—was permanently cemented when his cancer appeared in 1923. Freud was just short of his sixty-seventh birthday in April of 1923 when his internist, Felix Deutsch—the husband of his analysand, the psychoanalyst Helene Deutsch—discovered a suspicious lump in his patient's mouth and suggested that it be removed and tested. Freud had been smoking his twenty cigars a day for years and, while the connection between smoking and lung cancer was not established in the 1920s, carcinomas of the mouth were thought to be caused by pipes and cigars; in fact, doctors referred to them as "the rich man's cancer" because cigars were expensive. For reasons that are not clear, Freud originally went to a relatively unskilled and inexperienced doctor named Hajek to have the growth removed. The surgery was done poorly as an outpatient procedure, resulting in such copious bleeding that Freud's life was in danger, and he was forced to remain in the hospital. Martha and Anna both came to see him; finding her father weak and spattered with blood, Anna refused to leave and spent the night at his bedside. While neither Deutsch nor Hajek told Freud he had cancer, it is likely that he suspected the truth.

A few months after Freud's first surgery, Heinz Halberstadt, Heinerle as he was affectionately known, the four-year-old orphaned son of Freud's daughter Sophie, contracted tuberculosis. The disease progressed rapidly and, by the end of June, he was dead. Freud wrote to friends in Hungary that his grandson was "an enchanting little fellow, and I myself was aware of never having loved a human being, certainly never a child, so much. [His death was] very hard to bear. I don't think I have ever experienced such grief; perhaps my own sickness contributes to the shock." He was as openly depressed as anyone had ever seen him; as he wrote to Heinerle's father, "I have spent some of the blackest days of my life in sorrowing about the child."

Freud then went on his annual summer vacation, which included some time meeting with the members of the Committee at an Italian resort—they knew about the Professor's cancer but attempted to cover up their knowledge—and vacationing in Rome with Anna. In the fall he was back in Vienna and was told of the full seriousness of his condition. This time he put himself in the hands of an excellent surgeon, Hans Pichler, who had extensive experience doing reconstructive surgery on the mouths of soldiers wounded in the war. Two operations were performed that October, the second one lasting more than seven hours, in which Freud's entire upper jaw and palate on the right side were removed. Some remaining cancerous tissue was discovered later that month and a third operation was carried out. This proved successful, and there were no serious recurrences for a number of years. The surgeries left his nasal cavity and mouth open to each other, so that he had to be fitted with a prosthesis that closed the gap in his palate to enable him to eat, speak, and smoke.

Freud struggled with his prosthesis, which he called "the monster," along with pain and fear that the cancer would recur, for the rest of his life. Pichler performed more than thirty minor operations to remove precancerous tissue and continued to fit and refit the prosthesis, which caused a good deal of discomfort. Freud bore all these travails with great stoicism, and many who saw him during these years were impressed with his courage in the face of the pain and incapacity caused by his disease. While he continued to see patients, he increasingly withdrew from the outside world. Eating was difficult, and he would not do it in front of anyone but family members. The once brilliant lecturer was forced to talk around the cumbersome contraption that filled his mouth. He never again did any public speaking.

Freud more and more relied on Anna as his intermediary with other analysts and the rest of the world; Martha became a pro forma wife. Anna had become the closest person to him throughout his terrible medical ordeals; she had seen him through his surgeries, gone on vacations with him following the operations, and was chosen by him as the only one to help change his prosthesis. Jones noted: "From the onset of this illness to the end of his life Freud refused to have any other nurse than his daughter Anna. He made a pact with her at the beginning that no sentiment was to be displayed; all that was necessary had to be performed in a cool matter-of-fact fashion with the absence of emotion characteristic of a surgeon." It seems odd that Freud would demand that only Anna take out and replace his prosthesis. She had no medical training, and he had many physician colleagues and friends who were more likely candidates for the job. But he insisted that his Antigone nurse him in this way.

Anna soon began to publish her own work—her first book, *An Introduction to the Technique of Child Analysis,* came out in 1927—opening still another channel for the propagation of her father's theories. His dependence on her was profound; in 1929, when she was away in England to deliver a paper, he wrote to Lou Andreas-Salomé that "like Wolf [Anna's dog] I can hardly wait for her return. I write and he spends half the day laying apathetically in his basket."

While Anna spent much of her time after the appearance of Freud's cancer tending to him and promoting the psychoanalytic movement, she also continued to seek out close friendships with women. In the mid 1920s, she got to know Eva Rosenfeld, forming an intimacy that continued for over ten years. Eva was a woman whose life was cursed with death. She was one of four children whose father died when she was fifteen. Her three brothers were unable to manage their lives and died early. In reaction to the tragedies in her family, she assumed the role of competent caretaker and selfless mother-to-all. She married at nineteen and had four children of her own, but her two young sons died of dysentery in the final days of the Great War. Her most painful loss was the death of her vigorous, outgoing, and much-loved only daughter, the fifteen-year-old Rosemarie (Madi), who was killed in a mountaineering accident in 1927. Eva felt at the time that she would never get over the grief of Madi's death and, while she lived a long, active, and productive life, she never did. Following her daughter's death, Eva threw herself ever more into caring for others, making her house a home for deprived, lost, or unhappy children.

Anna had become friendly with Eva shortly before Madi's death—she came to Eva's aid at the time—and was drawn to this open, emotional, and motherly woman who gave so much love to others. Anna's letters to Eva expressed the depth of her attachment; in a letter written in July of 1930, the anniversary of Madi's death, she told her friend that "I am always wholly with you, today even infinitely more so than on that day. . . . For we keep growing together and becoming more deeply intertwined so that today I can no longer imagine what life would be like without you."

With Anna's encouragement, Eva entered analysis with Freud in March of 1929. He saw her six times a week for over two months, with additional, sporadic, sessions over the next three years. Because Eva was a friend of Anna's, and a near-member of the family, he, very uncharacteristically, did not charge her. She later wrote that "Freud's great mind was the gift of those years . . . [which] changed my life . . . I can never *think* any more without searching for the knowledge of unconscious processes and motivations." While she felt her analysis with Freud was enormously important, it did not touch her emotional core: "My analysis of 1929 to 1931 revealed none of this mystery [her reaction to Madi's death] though it explained to me all other relationships, friendships, and motivating processes." Like so many others, she was much taken with Freud's personal force, being "awestruck by this seventy-two-year-old man in whose presence I felt the weight of his deadly illness oppressing me, while his undaunted courage filled me with amazement and his interest in me seemed uncanny."

In her letters to Eva, Anna revealed a great deal about her innermost thoughts and emotions. Her friend's awe of Freud was supported by Anna, who wrote regarding Eva's later decision to leave Vienna that "Papa was very much in favor . . . and, since, as we say, he is always right, he is surely right this time too." While there were some remnants of Anna's earlier struggle for independence, she was, by the 1930s, completely taken over by her father's program for her life. The psychoanalyst Max Eitingon was interested in her, apparently pushing for an affair—he was in an unsatisfactory marriage—and while Anna confided to Eva that she felt some love for him, she turned him away. Even though it was she who put an end to the relationship, she was subsequently hurt and depressed and wrote to Eva about feeling "so stupid" and how something in me [kept] gnawing at my drowned friendship with Dr. Eitingon." She continued, "What is hurting me so much is not that I lost him but that he got over losing me so easily." She was depressed over this loss and wrote, "In the last two weeks I have been living as I did before I was an analyst . . . with Rilke poems and daydreams and weaving. This is Anna too, but without an interpreter." Despite these occasional attempts to return to her earlier life, a dream that she reported to Eva showed what she had, in fact, become: "I murdered our cook, Anna. I chopped off her head and cut her into pieces and had no guilt feelings at all, which was very funny. Now I know why; her name is Anna and that's me." In other places in the correspondence, Anna commented on her lack of independence and her "altruistic surrender."

It was during these same years that both Anna and Eva became friends with the wealthy American Dorothy Burlingham—heir to the Tiffany fortune—who came to Vienna with her four children, seeking treatment for her oldest son. Dorothy also wished to escape—and keep her children away from—her manic-depressive husband, who eventually committed suicide. Dorothy was first in analysis with Theodor Reik while her children were treated by Anna, but she soon settled into a long analysis with Freud. A school was needed for the Burlingham children, so Eva's house, already serving as a home for disturbed children, was made over into the Rosenfeld-Burlingham School. All the children in attendance were in analysis, many with Anna herself, including her nephew Ernsti, son of her dead sister Sophie.

Eva needed to make a new life for herself after her marriage broke up. She left Vienna with her one remaining child, Victor, in 1932, first for Berlin, where she trained to be a psychoanalyst, and then, in 1936, for London, where she had a second analysis with Melanie Klein. Anna pulled back from their affectionate bond and became increasingly cold and critical of her former friend. As Eva went on with her own life, she was no longer available as the selfless one that Anna relied on; in fact, she was now a potential competitor as a psychoanalyst. In addition, seeing Melanie Klein in analysis was defined by Freud and Anna as an inexcusable betrayal. What is more, Anna was drawing ever closer to Dorothy Burlingham. After the Freuds emigrated to London, Eva, who was already living there, made many attempts to renew the old closeness with Anna, but she was turned away. With the passing years, Anna became ever more like her father, insisting that Eva destroy all the letters she had written in the days of their friendship. As Eva's son wrote later, "One can never be sure of anything except Anna's desire to cover her tracks, of leaving behind no quotable hostages to fortune, which became ever more marked in later life." It is reminiscent of Freud's wish to destroy his letters to Fliess.

With Eva gone from Vienna in 1932, Anna became increasingly intimate with Dorothy. Eventually, the Burlingham and Freud families became completely enmeshed. Dorothy, already in analysis with Freud, took training to become a psychoanalyst herself. At the same time, she and Anna took charge of raising her children, using what they believed were enlightened psychoanalytic methods, and keeping them away from their father, who made desperate trips to Europe to be near them. The Burlinghams moved into the apartment above the Freuds on Berggasse 19 in 1929, and Dorothy continued in analysis with Freud after the move to London in 1938. She and Anna remained coworkers, intimate friends, and companions for the rest of their lives.

In the years that followed, Anna achieved power, influence, and fame. As her niece Sophie Freud, who was intimate with her in her final months, put it, "[Anna] did pay a price for being her father's delegate. I have repeatedly expressed my disappointment about this limitation. This was wrong of me. We must respect the choices that people make. Tante Anna never regretted any aspect of her life. She had been a loyal daughter and she had led a creative and fulfilling life that had enriched innumerable people around the world. She died at peace with herself."

CHAPTER 22

Otto Rank: "I Was In Deepest of All"

> *One day a young man who had passed through a technical training*
> *college introduced himself with a manuscript which showed very unusual*
> *comprehension. We persuaded him to go through the* Gymnasium—*Secondary*
> *School—and the University and to devote himself to the non-medical side of*
> *psychoanalysis. The little society acquired in him a zealous and dependable*
> *secretary and I gained in Otto Rank a most loyal helper and co-worker.*
>
> —Freud, *On the History of the Psycho-Analytic Movement*

IN 1924, the topics of mother love, loss and anxiety again came to the fore, this
time in a personal-theoretical conflict between Freud and one of his oldest and
most devoted followers: Otto Rank. When Freud wrote his *On the History of the
Psycho-Analytic Movement* in 1914, he described Rank as "zealous . . . dependable . . . and . . . loyal," but this would all change ten years later. They had first
met in 1905, when Rank brought the Professor his manuscript, *The Artist:
Approach to a Sexual Psychology,* a long essay the young man had created from his
immersion in drama, literature, philosophy, and, most significantly, all the works
of Sigmund Freud. Despite his brilliance, Rank's impoverished background
offered him little in the way of opportunity; he was working in a factory when
his doctor, Alfred Adler, introduced him to Freud. The twenty-one-year-old
Rank, who had broken off with his alcoholic father and had no relations with
women, was terribly isolated; living with his mother and older brother, he
existed mainly in his mind. It is an understatement to say that Freud became his
ideal; Freud himself, along with the fledgling psychoanalytic movement, became
Rank's entire life. He threw himself into this new world with tremendous passion and energy.

Rank was born Otto Rosenfeld in Leopoldstadt, the same Jewish ghetto where Jacob Freud settled his family when they first arrived in Vienna. He was the third child of an artisan jeweler and his young wife; Paul, their first child, was followed by a sister who died at four months of age, and then Otto, born a year and a half after the sister's death. The father was a self-centered alcoholic, given to outbursts of violence when drunk. Paul fought with him while Otto and his mother tended to withdraw into silence.

From the age of eighteen and a half to twenty-one Rank kept *Daybooks*—personal journals in which he recorded his memories, thoughts, and plans—and these remain the principal source of information about his childhood. There are only hints about the nature of Otto's relationship with his mother; for instance, "she found her satisfaction in the fact that at least we lived, that is, had something to eat and went decently clothed." In other words, she provided the bare necessities and was not abusive like the father. Yet the young Rank suffered from terrible loneliness and death anxiety, suggesting the lack of a secure maternal attachment.

Rank was unhealthy throughout his childhood, then contracted rheumatic fever at the age of nineteen; its lingering effects would contribute to his early death. As he put it in the *Daybooks*: "I myself have been weak and no good from birth, and have perhaps no single part that was completely right." As a child and adolescent, he was preoccupied with fears, imagining that a variety of diseases would kill him. At one point in the *Daybooks* he wrote: "Today I confirmed slight symptoms in myself of BRAIN PARALYSIS." His account of his childhood continued: "As the second important occurrence, even today after thirteen years, stands my introduction to erotic experience in my seventh year through one of my friends, for which I still curse him even today, vividly remembering . . . the foundation stone of my later sufferings was laid at that time; it was at the same time the gravestone of my joy."

These remarks leave the specific events in doubt, and Rank never referred to them later, but they suggest a sexual molestation by an older boy or man. The autobiographical *Daybooks* conveyed the pain and sense of inferiority associated with his diseased body, the unhappiness and anxiety of his home, and the disappointment, guilt, and misery connected with his first encounter with sexuality, experiences that left him isolated and bereft. Rank felt himself to be damaged and physically endangered; he was anxious and preoccupied with death: "Death, the mysterious phenomenon that many thinking people have attempted to explain, became a problem to me above all. I still remember that I did not sleep for many nights and thought only about dying with terror and chattering teeth. Especially that never-never-never coming again, and the impossibility of thinking it through to the end, filled me with terrible fear."

This is the kind of fragmentation or annihilation anxiety that often occurs in someone whose very identity or self is in danger of crumbling. Such conditions are typically the result of serious traumas, early losses, or relationship failures. The fear of sexuality brought about by what sounds like a molestation experience, with its profound disappointment in his older friend, reinforced his isolation and mistrust of people and intimacy. Anxiety about sexual contact was, for Rank, fear of annihilation: "I have an aversion to every contact with people, I mean to every physical contact. It costs me an effort to extend my hand to anyone, and if I must do it, I first put on gloves. I couldn't kiss anyone. . . . Every coitus, the momentary pleasurable sinking into the unconscious feeling of eternity, into Nothingness, is compensated by a death . . . and the momentary painful sinking away into the selfsame unconscious nothingness."

Rank's older brother Paul was given what advanced education the family could afford, and he became a lawyer while Otto, despite his intellectual gifts, was enrolled in a technical school where he was trained to be a machinist, a job that he found uninspiring and depressing. Then, at age fifteen, Paul was able to provide him with student tickets to the theater, beginning what Rank called his "theater craze." He would escape from the family misery and immerse himself in plays. This opened up the world of culture and literature, and the young man became a voracious reader. The plays of Ibsen, the novels of Stendhal and Dostoevsky, Darwin's *Origin of Species,* the philosophy of Nietzsche and Schopenhauer, all made up a world where he came alive. He had found a safe, though isolated, space, along with a gallery of heroes and models.

The writing of the *Daybooks* was a form of self-analysis, a self-exploration that progressed from age eighteen and a half to twenty-one. Thoughts of suicide, present in the beginning, dropped away and his extreme aversion to women and sexuality began to soften. In these ways, there was a growth in understanding and self-creation via writing, a process that continued throughout Rank's life. It is also clear that he was attempting to fashion a new self from his identification with figures in literature and philosophy. He rid himself of his father's name of Rosenfeld and adopted "Rank" from a character in Ibsen's *A Doll's House.* At nineteen he changed his religious registration from Jewish to "unaffiliated," a further attempt to escape the unhappiness associated with his father's name and the family religion.

In addition to novelists, playwrights, and philosophers, Rank's anxieties and dread of sexuality drew him, above all, to psychoanalysis. In his first book, *The Artist,* he demonstrated his mastery of all Freud's publications through 1905. Of the many authors Rank read, Freud spoke most directly to his personal concerns, especially his sexual fears and preoccupations. Actually meeting the great psychoanalyst, and being accepted by him, was destined to have the most profound effect on this young man, so hungry for a male hero, and so much in need of a vocation where he could employ his talents.

Rank was twenty-one when he met the forty-nine-year-old Freud. The Professor already had a solid reputation based on his publications, along with a devoted band of followers; the younger man did not even have a high school degree. The other members of the Wednesday Society were established professionals, while all Rank brought with him were his unpublished writings. Yet, on the basis of *The Artist*, Freud recognized the young man's potential, discussed the manuscript with him, and offered critical suggestions that were incorporated into the version that was published. He hired Rank as secretary, and his minutes of what became the Vienna Psychoanalytic Society remain an invaluable record of the events from 1906 to 1915. After Rank gave a presentation to the society in 1906, he was invited to become a participating member, as well as secretary. Freud encouraged his protégé to complete his higher education, giving financial as well as personal support. Rank went to the Gymnasium and then the University of Vienna, where he received his doctorate in 1912 with a thesis on the Lohengrin saga, one of the first applications of psychoanalysis to literary interpretation.

Rank's relationship with Freud had its personal as well as professional side. Because of his work with the society, and the two psychoanalytic journals that he later edited—*Imago*, which he founded with Hanns Sachs in 1912, and the *Zeitschrift*, or *International Journal for Psychoanalysis*, founded in 1913—there was frequent contact between them. Because they were rarely separated during these years, correspondence was rare, a misfortune for future historians. As Rank's biographer E. James Lieberman wrote, "Rank was virtually adopted into Freud's family; he was constantly involved with his mentor . . . he and Freud analyzed one another's dreams; and Rank wrote letters on behalf of Freud and himself for years."

Rank had dinner with the Freud family every Wednesday before the meeting of the society and there was even a rumor that Freud wanted him to marry Anna. In his role as secretary, he would sit at the Professor's side during meetings, and he and Sachs would typically walk home with him afterward. As Sachs wrote, "On these promenades the subjects that had been debated at the meetings and many others, were discussed and reexamined. Freud communicated to us his new ideas and theories." All these are indications of the special relationship between Freud and his young secretary. While Freud often complained about his Viennese followers, he exempted Rank, whose intelligence and promise he continued to value. Clearly, he was a favored son; a fact that later gave rise to intense jealousy on the part of Jones, Abraham, and others.

The close relationship between Freud and Rank, however, was not one between equals. Rank remained the dutiful son and devoted disciple, Freud the master. As Jones observed, in the years before the First World War Rank's attitude toward Freud was "noticeably timid and even deferential . . . he was known for his servility, even in a culture where respect for fathers and superiors in general was routine. At meetings Rank would be there to fetch a glass of water for Freud or to light his cigar." On his side, Freud, while valuing his young assistant, referred to him in his correspondence as "little Rank." As he wrote to Jung: "None of these Viennese will ever amount to anything; the only one with a future is little Rank, who is both intelligent and decent. . . . Yesterday little Rank returned from the university tour of Greece in a state of bliss. I had given him the money for it in return for the work he had done on the third edition of *The Interpretation of Dreams*. It was hard-earned money, but that didn't prevent the poor boy from bringing me two—and not cheap at all—Greek vases in token of his gratitude. He is a fine man." These comments were written around the time of the battles with Adler: Jung was still the crown prince, and "little Rank"—the "poor boy" with his talent, deference, and gratitude—fine and decent. (Rank was five feet four inches, while Freud was five feet seven inches and Jung was over six feet, so he was, in fact, "little." Still, Freud's remarks have a condescending flavor.)

Despite the negative innuendos in such remarks, it was a mutually supportive and enriching relationship for both Rank and Freud. The much younger man was taken under the wing of the person he most admired and respected in the world, given a job—freeing him from hateful work in a factory—money, a career, time and space to pursue his broad scholarly interests, an advanced education, colleagues, a substitute family, and even a home; he eventually lived in an apartment in the building that housed the Psychoanalytic Press.

There were gratifications on Freud's side, too, as Rank gave him exactly what *he* needed and wanted. He had the deepest admiration for Freud and his creations, along with a mastery of psychoanalytic theory that enabled him to extend it into new areas with great skill. As Freud wrote to Jung, "As reporter on the Vienna literature I should like to propose little Rank rather than Abraham. You know from his *Artist* how well he can formulate my ideas." Formulate Freud's ideas is exactly what Rank did during those years. He also gave endless hours of work on behalf of the psychoanalytic movement, and his loyalty earned him a place on the Committee. In his role as secretary he was in charge of the circular letters by which the Committee members communicated. Although he participated in the expulsions of Adler, Stekel, and Jung, his exact role is not known. Overall, he possessed just those qualities that Freud most required: unquestioning acceptance of his central doctrines, admiration, devotion, and loyalty.

But Rank was not destined to remain a devoted son. The ten years of work with Freud before the First World War consolidated the young man's strength; at the end of this time, he was an accomplished scholar, writer, and editor, with six books and a number of articles to his credit, along with all his effective work on behalf of the psychoanalytic movement. In 1915 he was drafted into the Austrian army and, in 1916, sent to Kraków, Poland, where he served for three years as editor of the daily *Krakauer Zeitung*. Many who knew Rank noted the great difference in him before and after his time in Kraków. The man who returned from the army was, in Jones' words, "tough . . . with a masterful air."

The deferential and overly polite manner was gone. It was as if a dutiful boy had left home for the first time and returned a strong and independent adult.

In addition to finding independence and success in his job as newspaper editor, Rank fell in love with an attractive and cultured young woman, Beata Mincer. Whatever his sexual inhibitions during the prewar period, they were now overcome, and Otto and Beata were married late in 1918, shortly before the end of the war. Rank and his new wife—called "Tola" by her friends—returned to Vienna, where he was reunited with Freud and threw himself back into psychoanalytic activities. In 1920 he began seeing patients in analysis, mainly on referral from the Professor, providing added income to his salary as managing director of the International Psychoanalytic Press. The Ranks had their only child, a daughter Helene, shortly after their return. "Little Rank," the poor boy who had gone into the army, was now a husband, father, practicing psychoanalyst, and man of many responsibilities.

Freud's first reaction to Rank's wife was dismissive. He wrote to Abraham, "Rank really seems to have done himself a good deal of harm with his marriage, a little Polish-Jewish wife whom no one finds congenial and who betrays no higher interests. Pretty sad and not quite comprehensible." Freud's initial, critical assessment of Tola came from his fear that the marriage would interfere with his secretary's devotion to him—though, in fact, it did not. Tola was nothing like the person he originally imagined, and the Ranks were soon functioning smoothly within psychoanalytic circles. Tola was charming and socially skillful; Freud, and the rest of his family, became fond of her. She was welcomed by them, and played a role in organizing their social life. She was also interested in psychoanalysis, became a member of the Vienna Society, and developed a practice working with children.

The time from 1920, when Rank began his practice, to 1924, when the break with Freud occurred, was one of tremendous expansion within psychoanalysis. Budding analysts from England, the United States, and other countries came to Vienna to be trained by Freud, and some were referred to his young disciple. Rank had been close to his fellow editor Hanns Sachs but, when Sachs moved to Berlin, he became more and more friendly with Sándor Ferenczi, an intimacy that Freud encouraged. By 1923, when they coauthored their book on psychoanalytic technique, *The Development of Psychoanalysis*, Rank considered the sensitive Hungarian his best friend.

In their book, Rank and Ferenczi advocated a form of therapy that departed from Freud's classical method. They called it an "active therapy" (a term later associated with Ferenczi), an approach that focused on the ongoing experience in which the analyst, far from playing the stern father role that Freud advocated, was a "midwife" who assisted the patient in the creation of a new personality. To accomplish this, they saw the reliving of emotional relationships as more important than an intellectual reconstruction of the past. Ferenczi and Rank emphasized emotion over intellect, the new relationship with the analyst over insight, and the adaptive capacities of the patient, in contrast to the power of id impulses. Resistance was seen as arising from what Rank would later call the patient's "creative will." In Rank's view, the patient did not resist the analyst in order to cling to infantile gratifications; rather, what Freud called resistance was reconceptualized as an expression of positive striving, an attempt, however ineffective, at mastery and adaptation. All these emphases gave their approach to therapy a more optimistic flavor than Freud's. While their work was a real departure from the way Freud himself practiced, he at least partly accepted the contributions of these two young men who were his personal favorites.

As secretary and Freud's right-hand man in Vienna, Rank stood at the very heart of the psychoanalytic movement. Because of the social dislocation and economic havoc wrought by the war, it took enormous efforts on his part to keep psychoanalytic publications going. As director of the Psychoanalytic Press in Vienna, there was more and more dissension with Jones, who ran English-language psychoanalytic publications from London. Publishing matters were only one source of conflict; many others developed among the Committee members, particularly between Rank on one side and Jones and Abraham on the other. Things came to such a pitch at the Committee meeting in 1923—the time when Freud's cancer first became known—that Rank pressed for Jones's resignation. Freud was in the middle, defending Rank against charges raised by Jones and Abraham, and interpreting their motives as hostility redirected from him, since he was forever convinced that all his "sons," deep in their unconscious, wished to dethrone him.

These conflicts within the Committee did not disturb the close working relationship between Rank and Freud; however, the development of Rank's new theoretical ideas soon would. His marriage and the birth of his daughter were important influences on these new theories. In Tola, he had at last found intimacy and a woman's love. It is clear from his early writings about sexuality that he associated closeness with women, and specifically contact with their genitals, with deep anxiety. His book *The Trauma of Birth* contained many examples of which the following was typical: "The boy wants to deny the existence of the female genitals, because he wishes to avoid being reminded of the horror of passing this organ." This fear was probably a conflation of Rank's early traumas: maternal deprivation and sexual molestation. With Tola, he had confronted and overcome this terror and even had a baby, and his later remarks in *The Trauma of Birth* demonstrate the change in his attitude: "Sexual love, then, which reaches its climax in the mating of two beings, proves to be the most sublime attempt partially to re-establish the primal situation between mother and child, which only finds its complete realization in a new embryo."

The main thesis of *The Trauma of Birth,* published in 1924, held that life in the womb was the prototype of pleasure and security and that separation from the mother at birth was the primary source of anxiety. Rank traced many later conflicts and neurotic symptoms to this original trauma. His recognition of the importance of the mother went back at least to 1907 when, in a discussion of the Rat Man case in the Wednesday Society, he said, "All factors clearly point to the patient's love for his mother, even though there has not yet been any direct reference to this in the analytic material."

Read in the light of all that came later, *The Trauma of Birth* stands as a transition in Rank's journey from faithful follower to independent theorist. He dedicated the book to Freud—"Presented to the Explorer of the Unconscious and Creator of Psychoanalysis"—and said that his thesis originated with his mentor: "We shall take as our guiding principle Freud's statement that all anxiety goes back originally to the anxiety at birth." This referred to one of Freud's asides in *The Interpretation of Dreams,* though the idea had always been on the periphery of his own thinking about anxiety. Whenever possible, Rank cited Freud and praised him, and also trotted out the obligatory criticisms of Adler and Jung. He also presented his theory as grounded in "biology," since birth is, after all, a physiological event. In all these ways, he tried to situate his new ideas within existing psychoanalytic theory, to show that they were nothing more than additions to the structure that Freud had erected.

Despite Rank's presentation of the birth trauma theory as consistent with existing psychoanalysis, it was, in fact, a most radical departure. Rank saw the relationship with the mother as more important, more emotionally powerful, than that with the father. Separation from the mother at birth was the *primary* source of anxiety; the Oedipus complex, with its castration anxiety, was secondary, a derivative of this first cause. This view detracted from the power of the father, with the consequence that the treatment became centered on the analyst's motherly role. A related aspect of this shift from father to mother was Rank's sense of himself as a facilitating midwife, rather than an authoritative father. Rank had returned to a version of Breuer's cathartic therapy, and his comments showed he was aware of this.

Rank also differed from Freud in the importance he gave to trauma itself. Anxiety, as he saw it, arose from a real event and was not a consequence of fantasy or sexual cravings. As he said: "If finally we turn to the original 'traumatic' theory of neuroses, as it was formulated in the classical *Studies of Hysteria* more than twenty-five years ago, I think that neither we nor the originator of this theory need feel ashamed of it . . . none of us . . . has abandoned the certainty that there is still more in the 'trauma' than we trust ourselves to admit."

This was followed by a discussion of "traumatic neurosis," using observations of men suffering the effects of the recent war. Rank questioned what had become a basic pillar of psychoanalytic theory, a dogma that went back to Freud's abandonment of the seduction theory in the 1890s. The concept of the birth trauma, or any other trauma for that matter, posed a radical challenge to Freud's unwavering need to minimize trauma in favor of conflicts driven by sexuality.

Combining the trauma of birth with the importance of the mother-infant relationship led to a therapy focused on the patient's attachment and separation from the analyst. Ferenczi and Rank had already emphasized the ongoing patient-therapist relationship; attention was now specifically directed at those aspects of the treatment—the ending of sessions, vacations, and particularly the end of the analysis—that were living versions of the separation of "birth," instances of the original anxiety situation. Freud himself was relatively blind to the power of attachments and separations in his work as a therapist; he would drop patients, or threaten to do so, with little awareness of how this affected them. In fact, the traumatic separations he inflicted on those who were close to him—patients, friends, followers, and colleagues—run like a red thread though the history of psychoanalysis.

The Trauma of Birth was not without serious problems. Two stand out: the concrete nature of the birth trauma concept and Rank's creation of a sweeping, single-cause theory. If viewed as a transitional work, it is clear that he was working his way back to the origin of anxiety in a broad array of attachment and separation experiences. However, modern research makes clear that mother-infant attachment is a process that develops over time, particularly during the first six months of life, and that separations and disruptions of this developing relationship are the origins of anxiety. Birth can be taken as a metaphor for all these separation experiences; indeed, Rank moved in this direction in his later writings, as when he described separation from the analyst as a recapitulation of the birth trauma. Nevertheless, most of the discussion in the 1924 book conceived of the birth trauma as a single, concrete event, as when he said that patients fear women's genitals because they were the site of the original horror. This concretization was unfortunate: a number of perceptive critics at the time, including Freud himself, pointed out that taken literally, the birth trauma theory did not stand up; anxiety is not related in any simple way to whether one's birth was more or less difficult or painful. Taken as a metaphor for attachment and separation from the mother, the trauma of birth was a creative forerunner of current theories; taken literally, it was wrong.

The second problem with *The Trauma of Birth* was Rank's attempt to encompass an extremely wide range of events with a single principle. All the symptoms and fears of neurosis and psychosis were seen as manifestations of the birth trauma—as, for example, mood swings in manic-depression, sexual variations, perversions, homosexuality, and psychosomatic conditions. Asthma was purportedly the result of breathing difficulties at birth, migraine headaches resulted from having one's head squeezed in the birth canal. Curiosity in children, dream symbolism, artistic productions, fairy tales and myths were all interpreted as manifestations of the wish to return to the womb. It is clear that in this grand theorizing, Rank followed Freud: mother was substituted for father, birth trauma for Oedipus complex, but the explanation of almost everything was reduced to a single cause. It may be useful to stretch a new theory to its limits, and some of the applications of the theory—especially if taken metaphorically—were of real interest. But, on balance, the leap to grand theory undercut the value of Rank's contribution.

The Trauma of Birth set Rank on a collision course with Freud and the other Committee members. Warnings were sounded from London and Berlin about this new book, as well as the previous one coauthored with Ferenczi. Jones saw Rank and Ferenczi moving toward Jung, "replacing analysis of childhood by discussions of current situations only." Abraham, in a related way, worried about "ominous" developments, ideas not "obtained in a legitimate analytic manner." Where Freud had been partly open to Rank and Ferenczi's earlier book, he soon came to agree with Jones and Abraham regarding *The Trauma of Birth,* and the breach between the Professor and Rank began to grow.

It was not Rank's intention that his book should cause a break with Freud, nor was it what Freud wanted. Their many years of close association, Freud's tremendous importance to Rank, the younger man's devoted service to the cause—all these, along with a store of genuine affection, combined to make the break a most difficult experience for both of them. Despite their bond, it was clear that Rank, with his brilliance and originality, along with his need to understand himself and his patients, was not content with the psychoanalytic status quo. The Rank who came home from the war could no longer subordinate himself as the dutiful son and orthodox psychoanalyst.

Rank should have known that the ideas in *The Trauma of Birth* would lead to conflict with Freud, since he had been present when Adler and Jung were attacked and expelled from the movement for questioning the centrality of sexuality and the Oedipus complex. But, because of his idealization of the Professor, he believed that psychoanalysis was a science, advancing as new discoveries were made, and that belief led him to imagine that his book would be accepted in a friendly spirit. Freud's personal support and acceptance of his previous contributions, and the many ways in which he was *partly* open about himself, and *partly* encouraged his protégés, led Rank to believe that his new ideas would be evaluated on their merits. It was, after all, dedicated to Freud, with acknowledgment of the master's foresight into the idea of birth anxiety, and contained the obligatory criticisms of Adler and Jung. What Rank failed to understand—what the sycophantic Jones and Abraham knew only too well—was the degree to which the theory and the movement were the embodiment of Freud's very being, and that only he was allowed to make significant changes.

Before *The Trauma of Birth* was published, tensions and conflicts had been mounting within the Committee, with Freud defending Rank against the charges made by Abraham and Jones. Ferenczi had joined in the defense, for he, too, disliked Abraham. But while Freud felt greater personal closeness to Rank and Ferenczi, he was also aligned with Abraham and Jones as protectors of *his* theory and movement. Even before the break, when his relations with Rank were friendly, he sensed his disciple's growing strength and independence as a personal threat. Late in 1923, Rank had sent Freud an interpretation of one of the Professor's dreams, to which Freud responded:

> It is a long time since you have tried to interpret one of my dreams in such a powerful analytic way. Since then much has changed. You have grown enormously and you know so much more about me. . . . [Freud then suggests a different interpretation of the dream.] . . . attention here, the old one and the young one are interchanged, you [Freud] . . . are not David, you are the boasting giant Goliath, whom another one, the young David will slay. And now everything falls into place around this point that you—Rank—are the dreaded David who with his *Trauma of Birth* succeeds in depreciating my work.

While Freud's tone in the rest of this letter was light and friendly, his feeling that Rank was a murderous son was obvious.

By early 1924, the situation was tense. Rank and Freud had been extremely close for a number of years, yet the younger man had now published a book that challenged the central tenets of psychoanalysis. Animosity and rivalry within the Committee had left Abraham and Jones with a store of ill will toward Rank; they were primed to attack him and urged Freud to do the same. Abraham warned Freud that the book by Ferenczi and Rank, as well as *The Trauma of Birth,* showed "manifestations of a regression in the scientific field, the symptoms of which agree in every small detail with those of Jung's secession from psychoanalysis." When Rank made a trip to the United States, Jones wrote to Abraham of Rank's "Jung-like decision to go to America without letting any of us [the Committee] know." These comments were typical of the way a class of "enemies" was created—"Adlerians," "Jungians"—and others branded as guilty by association with the tabooed group. After all, it was hardly a crime for Rank to leave the economic chaos of Europe after the First World War for a trip to the United States.

In April, Rank continued the debate with Freud by letter from America. While Freud had initially been cautious in his evaluation of *The Trauma of Birth,* it was not long before he began to voice the familiar criticisms, more and more expressing his dislike for Rank's ideas. He objected to the power attributed to the mother over the father, was not sympathetic to the modifications in technique, and regretted the retreat from "libido theory" and "the Oedipus," which would give ammunition to the "enemies of psychoanalysis." He "tested" the ideas on his own patients by giving them Rank's book and asking for their reactions. He wrote to Rank:

In the months since our separation I am even further from agreeing with your innovations. I have seen nothing in two of my cases that have been completed that confirms your views and generally nothing that I did not know before; the final birth phantasy seems to me still to be the child that one gives, analytically, to the father. I am often much concerned about you. The exclusion of the father in your theory seems to reveal too much the result of personal influences in your life which I think I recognize and my suspicion grows that you would not have written this book had you gone through an analysis yourself.

Freud asking his patients what they thought of Rank's ideas was hardly an objective test because they were committed to him as their analyst. Rank was incredulous about this so-called test, writing, "I still cannot believe that such a thing is possible." Freud then began to interpret the "personal influences in your life." In other words, he paid some attention to the ideas in Rank's book, but soon moved to interpretations of the author's purported neurosis. Rank wrote a long letter back, defending his position and taking up the theoretical issues point by point. He also vigorously objected to Freud's reference to personal factors:

I have a strong impression that you do not want or are unable to see certain things, because sometimes your objections sound as if you had not read at all or had not heard what I really said. . . . You apparently bring in the personal relations between you and me, where they do not belong . . . you were saying I would never have defended this point of view had I been analyzed. This may be true. The question is only, whether that would not have been very regrettable. After all that I have seen of results with analyzed analysts, I can only call it fortunate. . . . the accusation that an insight is derived from a complex [Freud's reference to "personal influences"] means very little in general . . . and . . . says nothing of the value or truth of this insight . . . I do not know either how much your judgment or prejudice against my position has been influenced by some noisy ranters who from time to time feel the irresistible urge to set themselves up as saviors of the psychoanalytic movement or your person, without seeing that they only give full rein to their childish jealousy . . . the Berlin plans and plots of which I hear seem to me so foolish in their gesture and so unworthy of a scientific movement that I hope you also will have little use for it . . . The more light is thrown on them the more agreeable it will be for me, for the more distinctly the abysmal ignorance of people like Abraham will be revealed. . . . Do not let us forget that the psychoanalytic movement as such is a fiction and for the people who are now eager to work at a psychoanalytic movement, I confess, I have no sympathy.

When Rank called the psychoanalytic movement "a fiction," he was referring to the way followers such as Jones and Abraham consistently put considerations of loyalty and adherence to doctrine ahead of needed developments in theory and therapy. He was angry because he felt Freud had dismissed his contribution as neurotic, a reaction much like Jung's when he had written to Freud that "your technique of treating your pupils like patients is a *blunder.*" And Freud's counterreaction was the same as it was with his former crown prince: "There are ugly things in your letter. To impute to Abraham 'profound ignorance,' to call him 'a noisy ranter,' that presupposes a disturbance in judgment only to be explained by a boundless affectivity, and fits ill with the overcoming of complexes. An evil demon makes you say that this psychoanalytic movement is a fiction and puts in your mouth the very words of the enemy."

Rank returned to Vienna toward the end of the year, for it was much too painful for him to break completely with Freud, and they made a last attempt at reconciliation. He went into "analysis" with the Professor, confessed that his book came from neurotic motives, and, at Freud's urging, wrote a letter of contrition to the Committee members in which he said that his actions "stemmed from unconscious conflicts":

> From a state which I now recognize as neurotic, I have suddenly returned to myself. Not only have I recognized the actual cause of the crises in the trauma occasioned by the dangerous illness of the Professor, but I was able also to understand the type of reaction and its mechanism from my childhood and family history—the Oedipus and brother complexes . . . I can only hope, dear Abraham, that my painfully won insight into this whole matter and my sincere regret will make it possible for you to forgive and forget the wrong which came to you from my state of mind. . . . I also beg you, dear Jones, to excuse the personal wrong I have committed.

As the biographer Ronald Clark noted, Rank's letter to the Committee was "similar in an uncanny way to the statement by prisoners of the Communists who have been brainwashed into confession." While Freud was temporarily mollified by the confession, Abraham and Jones remained suspicious and demanded further compliance.

Freud wrote about Rank at length to Lou Andreas-Salomé toward the end of 1924, giving several reasons for his "defection," including Rank's reaction to his cancer, his "very severe father-complex," and his attraction to the American dollar. He explained that Rank "felt his livelihood to be threatened by my illness and its dangers, looked round for a place of refuge, and hit upon the idea of making his appearance in America. It is really a case of the rat leaving the sinking ship."

Freud's cancer had a profound impact on all his close followers, who felt threatened with the possible death of their revered leader. Rank, more than any of the others, faced the loss of the only decent father-figure he had ever known. In later years, a rumor was spread by Jones, Max Schur, and others in

which Rank's "revolt" and "defection" from the movement were said to be motivated by his unconscious reaction to Freud's cancer, though there was never any
evidence to support this idea. Rather, it was clear that Rank was becoming his
own man from his time in Kraków, and that his changing ideas about psychoanalytic theory and technique were well developed before Freud's cancer was
diagnosed.

Rank steadily moved away from his confession and humble stance toward
the Committee, and the break then became final. Freud dropped him completely, as he had done before with Breuer, Adler, Stekel, Jung, and others. He
wrote to Ferenczi: "So quits! On his final visit I saw no occasion for expressing
my special tenderness; I was honest and hard. But he is gone now and we have
to bury him. Abraham has proved right." To Sachs, he wrote, "Now, after I
have forgiven everything, I am through with him."

Not content with the expulsion of Rank, Freud pressed Ferenczi to break
off with his coauthor and close colleague; later, when the two friends encountered each other, Ferenczi walked past Rank without a word. In a rare personal
comment, Rank said, "He was my best friend and he refused to speak to me."

But that was not the end. Abraham died in 1925, but Jones had a good deal
of control over psychoanalytic publications and perpetuated the slander of Rank.
At the time of the break he was already spreading rumors about Rank's mental
disturbance; later, in his biography of Freud, he spoke of "psychotic manifestations that revealed themselves in, among other ways, a turning away from Freud
and his doctrines. [And of] . . . a manic phase of his cyclothymia." Freud himself vacillated between labeling Rank as disturbed and childishly rebellious:
"Since leaving me Rank has been having periodic fits of depression, and in
between, sort of manic phases . . . one could call him ill." Yet, at other times,
he referred to his former protégé as "a naughty boy." Neither he nor Jones had
any contact with Rank after the final break, and those who did saw no signs of
depression or mania. In 1930, Brill, a favorite of Jones and Abraham, and then
head of the American Psychoanalytic Association, slandered Rank before a large
audience, describing his theories as the product of mental illness. And so the
story was spread. Lionel Trilling, reviewing the Jones biography of Freud in
1957, even embellished it, saying that both Rank and Ferenczi died insane.
There was no evidence for this: Rank, in spite of the painful rejection by Freud
and his former colleagues, lived a very productive life, one filled with further
growth and development, as well as new love.

Rank's view of Freud in the years that followed was fair and balanced. He
did not feel the bitterness and hatred that his former mentor directed at him
and others and, once free of the confines of orthodoxy, formulated a perceptive
view of the movement and its leader. In *Modern Education*, written in 1932, he
said, "Psychoanalysis has become as conservative as it appeared revolutionary; for
its founder is a rebellious son who defends paternal authority, a revolutionary

who, from fear of his own rebellious son-ego, took refuge in the security of the father role."

As was the case with others who proposed new ideas, Rank's concepts found their way into Freud's own theories in modified form. To justify his practice of taking over the ideas of his colleagues, Freud wrote, "It is not easy for me to feel my way into another person's thinking; as a rule I have to wait until I have found a connection with it in my own devious ways." While this seemed like a charming confession in which he admitted his uncertainty and appeared open about his way of working, it was confession as half-truth. True, it was not easy for him to take up the ideas of others, but it was because he had to maintain his dominance, to present the ideas of others as if they were his own. And so he did in *Inhibitions, Symptoms and Anxiety*, published in 1926, immediately after the break with Rank. In this essay, he finally revised his theory of anxiety, a revision that had been anticipated by Rank's ideas on the centrality of mother-infant separation.

Beginning with the earliest work with patients, Freud had observed the widespread appearance of anxiety. It was also an emotional state that was prominent in his own life: intense in his earliest years, dissociated for long periods, and reaching a peak during the self-analysis in his forties. The place of anxiety in his theory went hand in hand with this vacillating personal course. In the 1890s, he had come close to his earliest experiences of traumatic loss and helplessness and then reorganized himself around his theory of sexuality and the Oedipus complex. In this theory, real traumas were minimized and anxiety seen as a secondary phenomena, an emotion that occurs when the discharge of sexuality is blocked. He clung to this view for a very long time: as late as 1920, in a footnote added to the *Three Essays,* he said: "One of the most important results of psycho-analytic research is this discovery that neurotic anxiety arises out of libido, that it is a transformation of it, and that it is thus related to it in the same kind of way as vinegar is to wine."

While he had made comments all along that suggested a different view of anxiety, these were always off to the side, while the theory of sexuality occupied center stage. Nevertheless, his own traumatic anxiety always hovered in the background. *Inhibitions, Symptoms and Anxiety* was the essay where he finally made the decisive turn from old theory to new. It was a long piece in which he worked his way through previous theoretical commitments to a new position. By the end, he stated that his earlier theory was wrong and presented his new view: anxiety was a *signal,* a signal of *danger,* the danger of repeating a *trauma,* the trauma being *loss of the love object or its love.* As he put it: "It was anxiety which produced repression and not, as I formerly believed, repression which produced anxiety. . . . It is always the ego's attitude of anxiety which is the primary thing and which sets repression going. Anxiety never arises from repressed libido." In the essay, he continued to waver between this new conception and old ideas, but eventually moved to a clear statement of the origins of danger in separations from the love object: "Anxiety arose originally as a reaction to a state of *danger* and it is reproduced whenever a state of that kind recurs . . . [What are the dangers?] . . . when a child is alone, or in the dark, or when it finds itself with an unknown person instead of one to whom it is used—such as its mother. These three instances can be reduced to a single condition—namely, that of missing someone who is loved and longed for."

In the discussion that followed, Freud stressed the "infant's mental helplessness" which was "conditioned by separation from the mother." He now saw castration anxiety and moral anxiety—fear of punishment by the superego—as transformations of this earlier separation fear. Moral anxiety was now fear of "separation and expulsion from the horde," or fear of losing the love of the internal parent: the superego.

Freud's revision of his theory of anxiety was an important final step in his self-analysis via theory construction, a remarkable sign of growth for someone who was seventy years old at the time of its composition. Still, he never connected these ideas to his own life, and the revision had almost no impact on his later writings, where he continued to stress the centrality of sexual drive, the Oedipus complex, and the power of the father. This also continued to be the case with his treatment of patients; his new ideas had little effect on his clinical work. Nor did this theoretical revision have much impact on his orthodox followers. As late as 1960, Anna Freud and Max Schur were attacking John Bowlby's ideas about maternal attachment and separation anxiety as "not psychoanalysis." It remained for workers outside the movement to further develop these crucial insights about the origins of anxiety.

As the political situation in Europe deteriorated in the early 1930s, Rank divided his time between Paris and the United States and moved permanently to the United States in 1934. Before the move, he had established himself as a theorist, therapist, teacher, and lecturer in New York. Most of his trips to the United States were made without Tola and his daughter; gradually, the marriage drew to an end, though he helped them escape from Europe as the Nazis came to power.

When Rank had first come to New York, in the period before his break with Freud, he had been received as an emissary from the master, and a number of American candidates in psychoanalytic training were pleased to come to him for their analyses. But as word of his "defection" spread, Brill and others turned on him, and his former trainees were forced to be reanalyzed if they wished to remain within the official psychoanalytic organization. Not only was Rank banished, but those associated with him were required to be cleansed of his ideas. He was blacklisted, denied publication in psychoanalytic journals, and his contributions ignored. Rank's innovative ideas and techniques were taken up by others, however; Jessie Taft established a Rankian program at the University of Pennsylvania School of Social Work, and he influenced several psychotherapists who later became prominent figures: Carl Rogers, Franz Alexander, Rollo May, Robert J. Lifton, and Irvin Yalom.

Otto Rank.

Rank continued to grow and develop as a person. His later critiques of Freud, and his belated recognition of the contributions of Adler and Jung, showed his freedom from the ideological constraints of the movement he had served for so many years. Among his rare comments on the past, two stand out. Referring to his years with Freud, he ruefully said to Taft, "I was in deepest of all," a remark that captured his regret over participating in a movement that eventually turned on him. Speaking of his former mentor, he noted that intellectual independence in Freud's circle was subordinated to orthodoxy and that, from 1911 on, most of Freud's writing was a reaction to his critics.

Unlike Freud, whose hatred of the United States, set off by the anxiety and discomfort of his 1909 visit, lasted for the rest of his life, Rank found much to admire and love in his adopted country. He became involved with an American woman named Estelle Buel and identified with Mark Twain's Huckleberry Finn, signing his letters to her and to Jessie Taft as "Huck." In his last book, *Beyond Psychology*, written in English, Rank made illuminating comments on the American humorist. Twain's work contains many references to doubles and identity confusions, themes central to Rank's own life and discussed in his early book *The Double*. In Twain's most famous character, Huckleberry Finn, Rank found a new model. Huck was a motherless boy with a violent, alcoholic father who was cast into the world, where he relied on his wits and practical intelligence to survive. He maintained his faith and a certain innocence in the face of the human follies and cruelty he encountered. So did Otto Rosenfeld, the poor Jewish boy from the slums of Vienna.

Huckleberry Finn ends with the famous lines, "But I reckon I got to light out for the Territory ahead of the rest, because Aunt Sally she's going to adopt me and sivilize me and I can't stand it. I been there before." Like his literary counterpart, Rank had every reason to distrust the civilization he lived in, for this was 1939, with Europe plunging into the Second World War and his own country overrun by the Nazis. His experience with Freud and the movement had ended in tragic disappointment. Like Huck, Rank planned to head west for the Territory. Estelle Buel, whom he married in 1939, had a ranch in California where they hoped to settle. Sadly, he died at the age of fifty-five, before they could move there.

CHAPTER 23

"What Does a Woman Want?"

Men have had every advantage of us in telling their own story. Education has been theirs in so much higher a degree; the pen had been in their hands.

—Jane Austen, *Persuasion*

FREUD'S CONTACTS with society had become constricted after the appearance of his cancer in 1923, but, in his self-contained psychoanalytic world, he remained vital through his seventies, keeping up his correspondence, seeing patients, and, in his last decade, writing several noteworthy essays. *Inhibitions, Symptoms and Anxiety,* written in 1926 in response to Rank's challenge, was followed the next year by his most extensive discussion of religion: *The Future of an Illusion.* The essay began with his typical criticisms of the "masses," whom he characterized with the same words he often applied to women: "lazy and unintelligent . . . [with] . . . no love for instinctual renunciation."

In the essay, Freud argued that ordinary people could only be induced to perform the work of civilization by strong leaders, and described religion—Austrian Catholicism was the unnamed referent—as a system that kept the masses in check with its rules and fear of a God who rewarded and punished. God, according to him, was a projection of the powerful father of childhood, while religious practices were likened to obsessional neuroses, an idea he had first broached in his 1907 paper *Obsessive Actions and Religious Practices.* Freud believed that religion was a group neurosis that paralleled the neurosis of the individual: both substituted wishful fantasies or illusions for reality, both relied on magical rituals—prayers, supplications, obsessions, and compulsions—and he contrasted both unfavorably with science and psychoanalysis. There was a valuable idea here; rituals, whether personal or religious, can serve to contain and relieve anxiety and other disruptive emotions. But Freud was claiming much more in *The Future of an Illusion;* the essay was his attempt to conquer all of religion with the weapon of psychoanalytic interpretation.

Civilization and Its Discontents (1930) picked up where *The Future of an Illusion* left off, though it was a much richer essay in which Freud's long-standing personal concerns were again worked over in the guise of a general theoretical discussion. The essay began with a dialogue with the pacifist-novelist Romain Rolland, who had questioned Freud's characterization of religion as nothing more than childish worship of a powerful father figure. Rolland argued that his own faith was not tied to any specific doctrine or church, but was something he experienced as an "oceanic feeling," a sense of being at one with the universe, which he believed was the energy behind deep religious belief. Freud took up this idea and argued that it was nothing more than the infantile wish for oneness with the mother. He was not comfortable with the idea of an oceanic feeling because it gave too much power to mothers, and he turned away from it with the assertion that "I cannot think of any need in childhood as strong as the need for a father's protection." But he did not leave it at that, embarking on a long discussion of man's search for happiness, with a focus on the question of why so many people—one must assume himself as well—remained unhappy in the midst of civilized progress.

Civilization and Its Discontents explored the possibilities and dangers of love as a road to happiness. He dismissed the oceanic feeling or pleasurable sense of oneness—the possibility of love between a mother and baby and, by extension, between a man and woman—as infantile and unrealistic. Such love was dangerous, Freud wrote, because, when one fell into it, the boundaries of one's ego could melt away, a condition he associated with psychosis. Love was also threatening because it entailed giving up control, which left one extremely vulnerable: "We are never so defenseless against suffering as when we love, never so helplessly unhappy as when we have lost our loved object or its love." He counterposed this intensely pleasurable, but dangerous, state of love with its tempered, socialized form: "sublimated" or "aim-inhibited libido," the way of reason and science.

While Freud had long been a champion of reason, in the remainder of *Civilization* he raised questions about a way of life in which intellectual control was predominant, wondering whether such a life could really bring happiness. This led to a discussion of aggression and the way it turns against the self in the form of a punishing conscience or superego. In exploring this theme, he wrote many heartfelt passages about the privations and suffering that resulted, presumably, from his own ruthless suppression of his longings for love and pleasure. Too much guilt, too much aggression turned against the self, he mused, creates its own form of misery: "The sense of guilt [is] the most important problem in the development of civilization and . . . the price we pay for our advance in civilization is a loss of happiness through the heightening of the sense of guilt." In the end, he turned back to love as a way to happiness, though he could only express this in abstract terms: "And now it is to be expected that the other of the two 'Heavenly Powers', eternal Eros, will make an effort to assert himself in the struggle with his equally immortal adversary [aggression]. But who can foresee with what success and with what result?"

In 1930, Freud was awarded the Goethe Prize by the city of Frankfurt. The award included a stipend of $2,500, of which he gave $250 to his aging friend Lou Andreas-Salomé. The award stirred up mixed feelings: he was pleased with the public recognition and the association with Goethe, who was one of his oldest idols, yet he complained that the prize was a small token, late in coming. His letters over the years had revealed his disappointment in not receiving the more prestigious Nobel Prize. He also feared that the public honor of the award would draw forth new attacks from the enemies of psychoanalysis. Nevertheless, he dispatched Anna to Frankfurt to read his acceptance speech and collect the prize.

Civilization and Its Discontents, with its complex exploration of maternal love as a potential source of happiness, was completed by the end of 1929. The next year Freud's own mother neared the end of her long life. His seventieth birthday had been celebrated in 1926, and Amalia, then ninety-one, insisted on attending, even though she had to be carried by hand down the stairs of her apartment and up the stairs of her son's. She demanded a new dress for the occasion and was proud to tell the guests, "I am the mother." Over the next years, she had begun to weaken. In 1930, at the age of ninety-five, she was spending the summer at her usual spa, attended, as always, by her daughter Dolphie, whose entire life had been given over to her care. When she began her final decline, she was brought back to Vienna and died in September. Freud wrote to Ferenczi: "It has affected me in a peculiar way, this great event. No pain, no grief, which probably can be explained by the special circumstances— her great age, my pity for her helplessness towards the end; at the same time a feeling of liberation, of release, which I think I also understand. I was not free to die as long as she was alive, and now I am."

Freud wrote to Jones about "the increase in personal freedom" he acquired with the death of his mother and continued, "Otherwise no mourning, as is displayed so painfully by my brother, who is ten years younger than I. I was not at the funeral; again, Anna represented me . . . Her [Anna's] importance to me can hardly be increased." While his remarks have an air of measured wisdom, the lack of grief, so prominent in his brother's reaction, is striking. Freud's dominant feeling was one of relief; at last, Amalia was out of his life. And, in Anna, he had acquired—or created—a woman who took care of all his needs, while posing no threat to his dominance.

If *Civilization and Its Discontents* approached, in its roundabout and hesitant fashion, the value of love associated with mothers and women, Freud's specific theories about female psychology never progressed very far from the prejudices of his adolescence. As a seventeen-year-old he had written to his friend Emil Fluss, "How wise our educators that they pester the beautiful sex so little with

Freud and his mother, 1925.

scientific knowledge! . . . Women have come into the world for something better than to become wise." Over the years, he expressed both bewilderment about women, on the one side, and theoretical certainty, on the other. Unfortunately, it was the latter that became psychoanalytic doctrine. As early as 1905, in his *Three Essays on the Theory of Sexuality,* he had written that while the sexual life of men had yielded to his research, "that of women—partly owing to the stunting effect of civilized conditions and partly owing to their conventional secretiveness and insincerity—is still veiled in an impenetrable obscurity." In his 1926 essay *Lay Analysis* he spoke of "the sexual life of adult women [as] a 'dark continent' for psychology." In the minds of many Europeans, the "dark continent" was Africa, primitive land of untrammeled passion. Finally, in a famous remark quoted by Jones, he said, "The great question . . . which I have not yet been able to answer, despite my thirty years of research into the feminine soul, is 'What does a woman want?'" He was speaking the truth; he never understood women. That he didn't is hardly surprising, since he almost never allowed himself any genuine intimacy with them.

As an adolescent and young man, Freud had been committed to a "morality" of sexual and emotional control that was extreme, even for the Victorian era. He was a prude who lectured his friends on the evils of premarital sex and love affairs, could not bear the emotions aroused by music, and scolded his sisters for reading books that were too risqué. He had little contact with women outside his family until he was twenty-six years old, with the exception of his brief adolescent longing for Frau Fluss, a woman his mother's age. He had fallen instantly in love with Martha Bernays, whose petite stature, girlishness, and malleability attracted him. The passion of the long engagement, conducted mainly via correspondence, faded once they were married and living together. For the more than fifty years of their marriage, he was much more emotionally involved with psychoanalysis and his male friends than with her; Wilhelm Fliess was the great love of his adult life.

In the face of his own lack of sexual experience, Freud made sexuality the centerpiece of his theory of neurosis. A virgin at the time of his marriage, his own comments indicated that sex with Martha was constricted and unsatisfactory. Colleagues who disagreed with his theories had much more sexual experience than he did. The emotionally volatile Jung, sexually experienced when he married, had at least two affairs thereafter; Otto Rank, terrified of sex as a young man, overcame his fear and married twice, and engaged in several affairs; and the sexually impulsive Ferenczi was involved in a number of amorous contacts and several love affairs. None of these psychoanalytic colleagues could go along with the overarching role that Freud gave to what he called "the most unruly of all the instincts." Even Jones, who, like the others, had a good deal of sexual experience, disagreed with the Professor's ideas about women.

Despite Freud's paucity of romantic experience, he did not hesitate to propound theories about the sexual life of women, ideas that took their final form in three papers: *Some Psychical Consequences of the Anatomical Distinction between the Sexes* (1925); *Female Sexuality* (1931); and the essay *Femininity* from *New Introductory Lectures on Psycho-Analysis* (1933). While he qualified his position—because everyone was "bi-sexual," the things he said about women were found to some degree in men as well—his central argument was stated with conviction. He asserted that the principal source of anxiety in childhood was the threat of castration. The little boy who was frequently told, in this society, that his penis would be cut off if he stimulated himself did not necessarily believe such threats until he saw the genitalia of a sister, mother, or nurse, at which point the threats became real for him. This accounted for the "horror" that the sight of the female genitals supposedly aroused in males. The little girl, for her part, was shocked when she discovered what she didn't have: "She makes her judgement in a flash. She has seen it and knows that she is without it and wants to have it." This produced "envy of the penis" and a "wound to her narcissism [and] she develops, like a scar, a sense of inferiority."

As Freud saw it, the little girl could not accept her castrated condition at first and "insists on being like a man," and "to an incredibly late age she clings to the hope of getting a penis some time. That hope becomes her life's aim."

Girls were supposed to turn against their mothers when they became aware that they, too, were inferior, penis-less beings. As he put it in his 1916 essay *The Exceptions*: "Women regard themselves as having been damaged in infancy, as having been undeservedly cut short of something and unfairly treated; and the embitterment of so many daughters against their mother derives, ultimately, from the reproach against her for having brought them into the world as women instead of men." Little females, Freud concluded, were, before they came to terms with their castrated state, little males; their sexuality was "of a wholly masculine character," and their clitoris, which they took to be a small penis, was their "leading sexual zone."

Freud assumed that the great struggle of the young girl was to renounce the wish to be a boy. In addition, he thought envy of the penis was the basis of what he took to be women's greater propensity for jealousy. The girl had to give up clitoral masturbation if she was to avoid neurosis, since this represented her refusal to accept the fact that she does not have a penis, which led him to assert that only vaginal orgasms were "normal." The girl, if she was not to become neurotic or homosexual, had to renounce her wish for a penis, take her father as her love object, and resolve her version of the Oedipus complex by substituting the wish for a baby for the desire to be a man.

Freud's view of basic feminine nature was also intertwined with his ideas about the different moral or ethical capacities of men and women. He held that all morality was based on the renunciation of instinctual gratification, and that a crucial step in this process involved the resolution of the Oedipus complex. The little boy, for example, had to give up his sexual wish for his mother and identify with his father, who would then be incorporated into his personality as a controlling, authoritative voice. This was what Freud meant when he said, "the super-ego is the heir to the Oedipus Complex." While there was never much evidence in support of this idea, he used it to explain other things, such as women's supposedly inferior moral capacity. As he put it: "I cannot evade the notion . . . that for women the level of what is ethically normal is different from what it is in men . . . they show less sense of justice than men . . . they are less ready to submit to the great exigencies of life . . . they are more often influenced in their judgements by feelings of affection or hostility—all these would be amply accounted for by the modification in the formation of their super-ego which we have inferred above."

Freud believed that women were failed men, that "anatomy is destiny," and that penis envy was at the root of it all. In his view, girls become neurotic or perverse when they refuse to give up their unrealistic wish to be boys; and females were at a lower ethical level than males. Many writers, both within and outside of psychoanalysis, have made thoroughgoing critiques of these theories. Karen Horney, at the time an analyst trained in Abraham's Berlin Psychoanalytic Institute, was one of the first to question Freud's theories in her 1926 paper *The*

Flight from Womanhood. Freud was aware of Horney's dissent, but dismissed it in *Female Sexuality* because it "does not tally with my impressions." To counter such criticisms, he turned to three other women psychoanalysts—Helene Deutsch, Jeanne Lampl-de Groot, and Ruth Mack Brunswick—who agreed with his theories about women. Since he had analyzed all three, and they remained within his orbit, their opinions can hardly be considered objective. This was the same ploy he used to "test" Rank's theory of the birth trauma.

Freud wrote as if his theories of female psychology were based on his work with patients, yet, with one significant exception, no such evidence was cited in the essays themselves. The exception was a reference to *A Child Is Being Beaten,* which was based, as has now been established, on his analysis of his daughter Anna. He used her case to argue that beating fantasies were common in girls, which supported his idea of basic female masochism. But Anna Freud's compli-cated beating and masturbatory fantasies, hardly common in little girls, provide scant evidence for her father's notions about the sexuality of all females.

Extensive research has now shown that anatomy is not destiny; that penis envy and the wish to be male are not the core problems for little girls; that girls experience a primary femininity that is every bit as valuable as masculinity; and that women are as capable of moral judgment and ethical behavior as men. The femininity of girls, even very small girls, is easy to observe; Freud, who grew up in apartments crowded with five younger sisters, and who had three daughters of his own, had to work hard not to see what was there before his eyes. Certainly, women living in a society in which they were defined and treated as second-rate beings might have come to feel inferior about their femininity, and for some, though by no means all, this socially imposed state could have been symbolized by the lack of a penis. This was essentially Adler's theory of the inferiority com-plex and the masculine protest, concepts that rooted these psychological reac-tions in their social context, but Freud brushed Adler's ideas aside in a footnote to his *Psychical Consequences* paper.

The belief in the moral, intellectual, and physical inferiority of women went back to antiquity, and these attitudes ebbed and flowed throughout Freud's life-time. During his formative years, a system of discriminatory practices was firmly in place in Austria-Hungary: women could not vote and higher education was denied to them, as was participation in the professions and most other forms of mean-ingful work outside the home. After 1867, women could not form organizations or belong to political parties. Misogynist views were strongest on the Continent; as a student in Leipzig, the American M. Carey Thomas, later the president of Bryn Mawr College, wrote to her mother in 1880, "I wish I could convey to thee an idea of the way women are mentioned by the profs and in the German books."

Freud was familiar with the prevailing attitudes toward women from his own family experience. His mother, though a more powerful personality than his father, took these beliefs and practices for granted; her two sons were encour-aged to pursue education and careers, while her daughters were not; he was her

Golden Sigi, Dolphie was her servant. He knew, from childhood on, that none of the girls would be able to shine in school as he had done, and he carried on this tradition with Martha and his own sons and daughters.

The dominant nineteenth-century ideas about women did not go unchallenged. In response to the revolutions that broke out in Europe in 1848, a group of women, heckled by men and members of the press, had founded the first Viennese Women's Democratic Association. At the Seneca Falls Convention in New York in this same year, women organized to protest their exclusion from voting and education, as well as their lack of legal rights. John Stuart Mill had argued for the complete equality of the sexes in his 1861 essay *The Subjection of Women,* pointing out that until women were no longer subordinated, the question of the natural differences between the sexes could not be answered: "What is now called the nature of women is an eminently artificial thing." Freud had translated Mill's essay into German in 1880, and expressed his profound disagreement with its thesis in a letter to his fiancée a few years later.

The long-standing belief in the inferiority of women assumed a new, more powerful form after the middle of the nineteenth century, framed in the language of science and supported by seemingly objective evidence. It was a quasi-scientific system cobbled together from popular Darwinism—Darwin himself was much more cautious in applying the theory of evolution and championed higher education for women—Lamarckian theories of inheritance, physiology, and physics. This set of ideas was widely supported by scientists and medical doctors throughout the second half of the nineteenth century, and almost no one from these fields was sympathetic to the feminist movement; the men who were came from literature, philosophy, and the arts.

The scientific consensus held that the anatomy of women was more child-like than that of men, that they had smaller brains and were less intelligent, that menstruation was a handicap that prevented them from working effectively, and that men were more vigorous. The theory of the conservation of energy, borrowed from physics, was applied, leading to the assumption that there was a constant amount of "vital" or "life energy" and that if it was drained away to a woman's brain, not enough would be left for reproduction and child care, which would debilitate the race. Overall, women were believed to be less-developed males; they were thought to be more emotional, less governed by reason, frailer, weaker, and liable to be overtaken by their sexual instincts, especially during menstruation, when they could become completely irrational. Female sexuality was seen as such a serious threat to civilization that some physicians—including Rudolf Chrobak, the head of gynecology at the University of Vienna during Freud's years there—performed clitorectomies on young women who were chronic masturbators.

This system of beliefs was imbued with the immense prestige of science, while the effects of social discrimination and prejudice, which Mill had noted, were branded "unscientific." Even though there was never much evidence to support these theories, they became widely accepted; Freud himself absorbed them during his years at the university and after. As late as 1906, his friend Wilhelm Fliess had written in his magnum opus, *The Course of Life:* "In the mental life of woman the law of indolence dominates; while the man is keen on the new, woman opposes change: she receives passively and adds nothing of her own . . . Feeling is her domain. Sympathy is her virtue." While Freud eventually was able to move somewhat beyond these beliefs, they formed an unacknowledged backdrop to his thinking, resistant to change and more powerful because they were unacknowledged. His theory of the constant quantity of libidinal energy—if it was employed in masturbation or other sexual "perversions," it was not available for sublimated, "higher," civilized purposes—was based on these old ideas, as were his theories of women.

Mill's was a minority view in 1861, but when Freud was a young doctor, the discussion of women's issues was lively, and a variety of suggestions for reform were in the air. Throughout the Western world, the debate on women was a familiar feature of public life, although opinions remained deeply divided. By 1900, the United States, England, and almost every country in Europe had a significant feminist movement. Bertha Pappenheim was actively combating the mistreatment of girls and working to support the rights of women in Germany during this time. In 1895, the newly formed Austrian Women's Association mounted a mass campaign to support the opening of the medical profession to women, which was finally granted in 1900. Women gained admission to the University of Vienna Medical School, and eleven of the first eighteen graduates were Jewish, following in the footsteps of their brothers from earlier years. Oscar Rie supported his daughter's plan to study medicine but Freud did not encourage Anna, a close friend of Rie's daughter, to take more than a two-year teacher-training course. During the First World War, many women took on responsible, independent positions, developing confidence in their newfound strength and abilities. By 1918, almost all Austrian women were able to vote and obtain higher education, though access to many professions was still blocked.

In addition to the lifting of discriminatory restrictions, and the opening up of new opportunities, the belief system used to justify inequality was increasingly undermined by advances in science. The rise of modern genetics—Mendel's work was rediscovered in 1900—and the discovery of male and female hormones paved the way for a truly scientific study of sex differences. The Lamarckian theory of inheritance was disproven. Studies of brain size and the new intelligence tests, available by 1905, proved that males were not inherently smarter than females. By 1910, strict biological determinism was giving way to an appreciation of the host of environmental and cultural factors involved in the differences between men and women, and, by the end of the First World War, the whole quasi-scientific structure that supported the inferiority of women had collapsed. Havelock Ellis had published *Man and Woman* in 1894, summarizing the prevalent "scientific" and medical consensus on women's inferiority. He revised his book in 1929, incorporating the new evidence, and putting to rest the idea of inherent female inferiority.

Freud's position in the great debate about women, a debate that occupied many important thinkers throughout his lifetime, is not always easy to discern. He was certainly aware of the women's movement and, in his case reports and letters, made deprecatory comments about it. There was a lively discussion of Fritz Wittels's paper *The Natural Position of Women* in the Vienna Psychoanalytic Society in 1908, a paper suffused with outmoded, pseudoscientific ideas. Freud was favorably disposed to the paper, noting that "a woman cannot earn a living and raise children at the same time," and that "women as a group profit nothing by the modern feminist movement; at best a few individuals profit." Stekel and Hitschmann were critical of Wittels's presentation, and Adler even more so. In line with his Socialist commitments, Adler said, "Just as, under the sway of private ownership, everything becomes private property, so does woman. First, she is her father's possession; then the husband's. That determines her fate. Therefore, first of all, the idea of owning a woman must be abandoned."

By the 1920s, Freud was not openly espousing his old beliefs about the physiological or intellectual inferiority of women, but the essence of these ideas persisted in his theories in a new guise. He did not keep up with developments in other scientific fields once he left physiological research for psychoanalysis, so that outmoded ideas such as Lamarckian inheritance or his mechanistic theory of the conservation of libido lived on in his theories, as if in a time capsule. Havelock Ellis had revised his ideas about women in 1929 in response to new evidence, but Freud simply cloaked his old prejudices in the new psychoanalytic garb of anatomical inferiority and penis envy.

While the persistence of antiquated ideas about women in Freud's work can partly be explained by the Victorian beliefs he absorbed in his youth, he was, over time, able to move beyond a number of other outmoded ideas. His anti-female bias resulted from the interaction of nineteenth-century prejudices with his unique personal history. Amalia, with her agitation, aggression, and dominating ways, provided firsthand experience of a woman who fit the stereotype of the emotionally out-of-control female. Perhaps the most important personal influence, however, came from his experience with his sisters: the five babies born after the death of his brother Julius. Throughout his childhood he witnessed them receiving the maternal nurturing he was denied, which led him to project his own frustrated and dangerous longings for maternal love and care onto them. They became the ones who received too much "gratification," living prototypes for his ideas about the female sex as a whole. Like his mother and sisters, women were forever the infantile ones who could not control their instinctual cravings, in contrast to the accomplished firstborn son and morally superior older brother and, by extension, men as a class.

Freud's distorted views of women have permeated many sides of psycho-analysis. He had to see fathers as more powerful than mothers, paternal strength as more important than maternal love. As a therapist, he functioned as a fatherly authority and rejected the ideas of Breuer, Jung, Rank, and Ferenczi, who, each in his own way, gave equal status to mothers, stressed the centrality of mother-infant attachment, and saw the therapist as one who served both paternal and maternal functions. Freud, in contrast, set up technical rules that defined mater-nal activity as harmful "gratification" and "collusion" with the patient's infantile-sexual wishes. The rumors he would later spread about Ferenczi trying to cure his patients by kissing them was a distortion with which he discredited the important therapeutic innovations of his Hungarian colleague. His fear of his own longings for tenderness and love became dangerous "homosexual libido": the greatest threat a man could experience. Women, in his view, could feel noth-ing of value about their femininity; at "bed-rock" they were driven by penis envy, longing for the maleness they did not have.

Some have argued that there was another side to Freud's attitudes toward women. They point out that he welcomed women into psychoanalysis at a time when related professions excluded them; in this, they believe, he was ahead of his time, showing an openness and tolerance that was lacking in other men who controlled access to careers in medicine, the sciences, law, politics, and business. It is true that several women played important roles in psychoanalysis: his sister-in-law Minna was an early confidante, and, later, there were the analysts Lou Andreas-Salomé, Ruth Mack Brunswick, Helene Deutsch, Marie Bonaparte, and, of course, his daughter Anna. But, the reality of these relationships is less straightforward.

Because the psychoanalytic movement was the overriding consideration for Freud, he could put his distrust of women aside if they were firm adherents. Like his daughter Anna, all the other women with whom he maintained friendly relations were absolutely loyal to him and the cause. Before he was certain of their devotion, they were suspect. When he first encountered Frau Lou, he wrote to Ferenczi that she was "a woman of dangerous intelligence" and warned that "all the tracks around her go into the Lion's den but none come out." When Rank returned from the war with his attractive new wife, Freud was initially cool; it was only after Tola showed her willingness to become a dutiful member of the family that his feelings toward her softened. Martin's beautiful and extrav-agant wife Esti, on the other hand, did not show sufficient reverence and was forever branded a black sheep.

CHAPTER 24

Sándor Ferenczi: The Wise Baby

I am looking forward to a friend and traveling companion between whom and myself not a hint of discord is possible.
—Freud to Ferenczi, 1910

I count those days among the most beautiful of my life and think in gratitude of the incomparable guide you were to me.
—Ferenczi to Freud, 1923

For three years already I have been observing his increasing alienation, his inaccessibility to warnings against his technical errors, and, what is probably most crucial, a personal hostility toward me for which I have certainly given even less cause than in earlier cases.
—Freud writing about Ferenczi to Jones, 1932

He [Freud] does not love anyone, only himself and his work—and does not allow anyone to be original. . . . Thus the antitraumatic in Freud is a protective device against insight into his own weaknesses.
—Ferenczi, *Clinical Diary,* 1932

THE RELATIONSHIP between Freud and Sándor Ferenczi followed what is by now a familiar trajectory. For twenty-five years they had been friends and companions, shared ideas about projects, worked together in the psychoanalytic movement, and discussed their personal affairs. Freud had hoped that Ferenczi might marry his oldest daughter Mathilde and, at a later time, was therapist and adviser in a love triangle between the younger man, his mistress, and her daughter. He wrote more letters to his colleague in Budapest than to any other correspondent.

As was the case with Jung and Rank, the closeness was predicated on Ferenczi's remaining the dutiful, admiring, even worshipful, son-disciple, a role for which he was ideally suited. He had a great need to be loved, and Freud became the paramount authority in his life, psychoanalysis his calling and belief system. But Ferenczi was also a man of originality and creativity who continually searched for better ways to understand and treat his patients. During the last years of his life he was engaged in experiments with psychoanalytic technique that took him far from Freud's classical method. His late papers, along with the private *Clinical Diary* that he wrote in 1932, contained many ideas and methods that anticipated modern developments in psychoanalysis, and it was these which set him on an inevitable collision course with the Professor.

Sándor Ferenczi, born in 1873, was the eighth of twelve children, one of whom, a sister, died when he was five. His father was a Polish Jew who settled in the Hungarian town of Miskolc and ran a bookstore, where his middle son grew up in an atmosphere suffused with literature, poetry, music, and culture. When he was fifteen, his father, to whom he seemed to be close, died, leaving his mother with eleven children and the family business. As Ferenczi later reported to his friend Georg Groddeck, he received "too little love and too much severity" from his mother; while to Freud he wrote: "My mother was, up to my father's death, strict and, according to the way I felt at the time and as I do now, often unjust. I have conscious recollections of 'fantasies of being abandoned.'"

Ferenczi took his medical training at the University of Vienna and returned to Budapest, where he worked in various hospitals and clinics and immersed himself in topics that foreshadowed his later involvement with psychoanalysis: hypnotism, telepathy, spiritualism, homosexuality, and hysteria. He also worked in a clinic for prostitutes and wrote a number of articles on the medical and social problems of the disadvantaged, work which paralleled Adler's pamphlet on the plight of Austrian tailors. Both of these early psychoanalysts showed a special compassion for the poor that was strikingly absent in Freud's own work.

Many people described Ferenczi as warm, affectionate, caring, enthusiastic, hopeful, empathic, and, above all, accepting and understanding of others. He was also boyish and childlike, with an endearing playfulness and naïveté. His emotionality went hand in hand with a great need for love and approval; for many years he struggled to become independent from Freud but, at times, could be slavishly obedient. It is probable that the loss of his father, his mother's harshness, along with the fear of abandonment by her, and the competition of his many siblings for emotional resources left him deprived and longing for love. There was an additional childhood trauma; in his self-analytic work, he recovered a memory of a sexual molestation by a servant girl, and this awareness enabled him to recognize the reality of the child abuse suffered by some of his patients. He often spoke of himself as a "wise baby," that is, a baby or child who, from his position of deprivation, adopted a premature caretaking role.

While Freud was critical of what seemed to him Ferenczi's excessive need for love, it was precisely this quality that allowed the younger analyst to make direct contact with the childhood experiences of his patients. In addition, like many who were drawn to the field, Ferenczi's traumas and sensitivities left him open to anxiety and other disruptive emotions, as seen in a variety of complaints about his health.

Ferenczi was seventeen years younger than Freud, an age difference similar to that between the Professor and Jung. Like Jung, he was an established psychiatrist at the time he met Freud in 1908, with some years of clinical work and a number of publications to his credit. He found both Freud and psychoanalysis enticing. In contrast to the descriptive psychiatry of the day, with its largely ineffective methods, psychoanalysis was a treasure trove. Many of the early adherents were attracted by Freud's innovative ideas: by the richness of both the theory and therapy. Moreover, for almost all of the early psychoanalysts who wished to understand themselves, Freud held out the promise not only of being their leader and guide, but of being their therapist. This was particularly true in the case of Ferenczi.

Freud, for his part, was instantly taken with the new convert from Budapest. At their first meeting, he suggested that Ferenczi present a paper at the next psychoanalytic meeting and also invited him to join the family on their summer vacation. There was clearly a strong attraction from Freud's side, and Ferenczi became the only one in the psychoanalytic circle to regularly accompany him on his vacations. Less than one year after their first meeting, he was invited to go with Freud and Jung on their trip to the United States for the Clark lectures. As Freud wrote later: "For many successive years we spent the autumn holidays together in Italy, and a number of papers that appeared later in the literature under his or my name took their first shape in our talks there."

Ferenczi became another in the line of intimate male friends of Freud's adult years, a man who promised a special closeness and something more, for he was the ideal mirror to Freud's greatness, able to sense and anticipate the Professor's needs and respond to them. He was, indeed, a wise baby.

Ferenczi's early work displayed the breadth of his clinical interests, yet remained clearly within the framework of established psychoanalysis. In 1910, following Freud's suggestion, he proposed the foundation of the International Psychoanalytic Association with Jung as president, provoking conflicts with the Viennese analysts, and, in 1911, went along with the expulsion of Adler and his supporters. In 1912, Ferenczi met with Jones to form the Committee in reaction to the split with Adler and in anticipation of differences with Jung. Ferenczi was a loyal member of the palace guard and, as proof of his fealty, published a highly critical review of *Symbols of Transformation,* the book central to Freud's break with Jung. When the conflict between Freud and Rank came to a head twelve years later, the Hungarian attempted to mediate; in the end, however, he was not able to take a stand against Freud and collaborated in the expulsion of his comrade. One must remember that Ferenczi had lived through the purges of Adler, Stekel, Jung, and Rank and knew, all too well, the fate of those who disagreed with Freud over the central doctrines of psychoanalysis. Despite his sympathy for some of the contributions of these dissidents—and his letters and papers reveal that he had some—he was not able to oppose the Professor until he was almost sixty years old.

In the fall of 1914, Ferenczi began an "analysis" with Freud. The formal therapy took place on three occasions: about two weeks in October of 1914 (interrupted when Ferenczi was called up for military duty), three weeks in June or July of 1916, and two weeks in September or October of 1916—a total of about seven weeks. While this was hardly enough time to accomplish much therapy, their entire relationship was, in fact, an analysis since, from the time of their first encounter, powerful emotions had been mobilized in each of them. Scarcely a year after they met, Freud and Ferenczi, along with Jung, were analyzing each other's dreams and personalities on the trip to the United States. A great deal of the correspondence, especially from Ferenczi's side, consisted of attempts to work through ideas and feelings about himself and his connection to Freud. He frequently spoke of his love and need for the Professor, his ambivalence, his insecurities and anxiety, and his complex feelings about his patients, all topics that one would reveal to a therapist.

Less than three years after their first meeting, Freud and Ferenczi went on vacation together to Palermo, on the island of Sicily. Ferenczi was longing for greater intimacy; his immersion in Freud's works had led him to hope that in his contact with the founder of psychoanalysis there would be meaningful and open communication between them. As he put it in a letter following the Palermo trip: "Don't forget that for years I have been occupied with nothing but the products of your intellect, and I have also always felt the man behind every sentence of your works and made him my confidant."

But Freud remained deeply divided about intimacy. In his relationships he would promise closeness, only to withdraw behind the fortress of his authority. Jung had described how Freud did this with him on the trip to the United States, and it was precisely what happened with Ferenczi during the vacation in Palermo. Freud was writing his case study of the paranoid psychotic judge Schreber, and Ferenczi thought they could collaborate. But for Freud, collaboration meant using Ferenczi as a secretary; when the younger man balked at this, the Professor said, "So that's the way you are? You perhaps wanted to take the whole thing?"

Ferenczi came back to this incident repeatedly, for it seemed to him representative of his difficulties with Freud. Ferenczi was continually striving for emotional honesty; if there were feelings between them—loving, sexual, dependent, competitive, rivalrous—he wanted to discuss them, but Freud preferred to avoid

Freud and Sándor Ferenczi.

such discussions and interpreted his friend's desire for intimacy as "infantile" and, worse, as "feminine" and "homosexual." If Ferenczi wanted to collaborate on an essay, this was interpreted as "wanting to take the whole thing," that is, the younger man was an Oedipus who wanted to kill the father and have everything for himself. Again and again, Freud perceived desires for intimacy in murderously competitive terms.

The entire affair at Palermo activated Freud's memories of his time with Wilhelm Fliess, which he discussed in his letters to Ferenczi, who said he understood Freud's "justified distrust of people—even friends, after the Fliess case." Freud responded:

> Not only have you noticed that I no *longer* have any need for that full opening of my personality, but you have also understood it correctly returned to its traumatic cause . . . This need has been extinguished in me since Fliess's

case, with the overcoming of which you just saw me occupied. A piece of homosexual investment has been withdrawn and utilized for the enlargement of my own ego. I have succeeded where the paranoiac fails. Add to this the fact that I was for the most part not very well; I suffered more from my intestinal troubles than I cared to admit.

These were highly revealing comments. Ferenczi's pressure for intimacy reactivated the Fliess trauma and Freud struggled against the memories and feelings that remained from that earlier affair. He was averse to that sort of closeness and chose, instead, to concentrate his energy inward—toward what he called the enlargement of his own ego—so that his longings and disappointments were taken into the private world of theory construction. In place of sharing with his friend, he wrote, on his own, his essay on Schreber, a case study in which he attributed delusions of persecution to eruptions of "latent homosexual" impulses, as repressed wishes for the father's love. Freud saw his own longings for love, whether from Fliess or Ferenczi, as "homosexual" impulses, so dangerous they could cause a psychosis, and he forcefully suppressed them: "I have succeeded where the paranoiac fails."

Running through the Freud-Ferenczi correspondence for more than ten years is the complicated tangle of the younger man's love life. In 1900, at the age of twenty-seven, eight years before he met Freud, Ferenczi began a love affair with a married woman named Gizella Palos. She was eight years his senior and the mother of two daughters, Elma and Magda. Gizella's family had been close to the Ferenczis in Miskolc, so he had known her since childhood. Around 1910, Ferenczi took Gizella into analysis; it is clear from his correspondence with Freud that she was sympathetic toward the field, and that he was able to discuss many of his psychoanalytic interests with her.

In 1911, Gizella's daughter Elma began to suffer from depression, and Ferenczi began seeing her, too, in analysis. A suitor whom she rejected committed suicide during the course of her treatment; in response to her deepening unhappiness, Ferenczi, always in tune with the pain of others, fell in love with the young woman and began to contemplate marriage. He broke off her treatment and sent her to Freud for analysis to clarify their convoluted relationship. Freud saw her for about four months, and it was obvious that he did not like her and believed that Ferenczi should stay with Gizella. Elma returned to Budapest, and there was a further period of "analysis" with Ferenczi. This ended with his decision to give her up; she subsequently left Budapest and married an American, from whom she was later separated though never divorced. This did not end things. Ferenczi remained deeply ambivalent about his commitment to Gizella, who had divorced her husband by this time, and was uncertain about whether he should choose the mother or the daughter. He vacillated endlessly, not marrying Gizella until 1919, when she was fifty-four and he forty-six. It is reported that her ex-husband committed suicide on the day of her marriage.

Ferenczi's conflicts with these women were completely entangled with his relationship with Freud. Freud's infatuation with Jung came to its explosive end in 1912 and, with his heir apparent gone, his Hungarian friend became the person in whom he "invested his libido." On his side, Ferenczi found it very difficult to have a mature connection with a woman unless she was pronounced suitable by the Professor. In his relationship with both Gizella and Freud, he was very much a dependent child.

Such convolutions were not unusual in these early days of psychoanalysis, as therapeutic, collegial, and personal relationships were mixed together. Freud analyzed several of those who worked with him in the movement, such as Eitingon and his own daughter Anna. In 1913, he sent Jones for an analysis with Ferenczi and they both gossiped about their English colleague in their letters. Even so, the blurring of boundaries in this case was extreme. Ferenczi analyzed his mistress, then her daughter, then was in love with both and trying to decide which to marry. He then sent the daughter to Freud, and later took the young woman, about whom he was still vacillating, back into analysis. Elma's analyses with both Freud and Ferenczi were, in their eyes, tests to see whether she would make a suitable wife for Sándor while, at the same time, she was continually pressed to tell the truth and not "resist" the treatment. On his side, Freud was hardly neutral or objective, since he always favored Gizella. This compromised set of relationships was infused with a striking lack of confidentiality, as all the parties told each other what the others were saying or feeling, including in the so-called analyses. And they compounded these broken confidences with cautions not to tell the others.

The damaging indiscretions of the Ferenczi-Freud-Gizella-Elma affair were typical of the way Freud practiced analysis. Since he was the founder, what he did tended to shape the practice of many of his followers, though not all of them were as indiscreet as he. Still, while some analysts during these years did not observe the boundaries of confidentiality that are now deemed necessary, even by the standards of the time this case was characterized by excessive violations of privacy. The welfare of the two patients, Gizella and Elma, was continually compromised and subordinated to the interests of the controlling analysts, Freud and Ferenczi.

Two things were most important to Freud in this affair: his personal connection to Ferenczi and the promotion of the psychoanalytic movement. He believed these interests would best be served if Ferenczi stayed with Gizella, for she venerated the Professor, was loyal to the cause, and was also a mother figure who would keep Sándor bound in his place as a son. Even before Ferenczi brought the mother-daughter conflict to him, Freud had met Gizella and written to Jung: "She is splendid, a woman who has only recently stepped down from the summit of feminine beauty, clear intelligence and the most appealing warmth. I needn't tell you that she is thoroughly versed in our lore and a staunch supporter."

Freud's appraisal of Elma was quite the opposite. On an earlier occasion he had diagnosed her with the words "dementia praecox" (schizophrenia), for which there does not seem to be any evidence. Later, meeting both mother and daughter, he wrote to Ferenczi: "Frau G.'s visit was very nice; her conversation is particularly charming. Her daughter is made of coarser material, participated little, and for the most part had a blank expression on her face. Otherwise, of course, there was not the slightest abnormality noticeable in her. The scar [Elma had undergone a recent operation on her face] is really inconspicuous and gives good opportunities for her undeniable vanity."

Freud's therapy with Elma revealed his characteristic way of working, particularly with women. About her feelings for Ferenczi he said: "Certainly her love for you is based on her attitude toward her father and the competition with her mother." Later he spoke of "succeeding in penetrating and breaking through the father identification, which, in the form of prudery, was the main obstacle to the work and also constitutes a large portion of the manifest narcissism." And still later, after assuring Ferenczi that he would keep secrets from Elma, he wrote: "We came to the main resistance, her desire for revenge—transferred from her father—and it has been hard going ever since. Today I was tough, and she went away with a very angry expression on her face. I knew about the letter to you. It is entirely dictated by the same desire for revenge, over which a thick veil is naturally still lying, as is the case with everything that comes up. I am making an effort to tear it."

The thick veil covering everything that came up meant that Elma herself reported none of these things; they were Freud's interpretations, supposedly based on what she spoke about in the analysis. The comment on her "vanity," for example, sounds like his remarks as a twenty-year-old to one of his sisters, warning her not to have her head turned by praise and of the dangers of "becoming vain, coquettish, and insufferable." His censorious attitude toward the sexuality of young women changed very little over thirty years. Finally, he wrote to Ferenczi, "I am very glad to hear that you have remained consistently firm against Elma and have thwarted her tricks." "Resistance," "revenge," "vanity," "narcissism," "tricks"—these words reveal Freud's attitude toward this depressed young woman who was torn between the two people she loved: her mother and her former analyst.

In contrast to her daughter, both Freud and Ferenczi saw Gizella as supremely self-sacrificing, a quality that they repeatedly noted with approval. Ferenczi spoke of her "behaving with nobility, kindness, and generosity," of her "almost unbelievable capacity to understand and forgive," and of "dear, good, Frau G. . . . is loving and suffering unspeakably." She stood by Sándor throughout all his vacillations and tried, at the same time, to support her daughter. Gizella, seen through the eyes of these two men, was the endlessly self-sacrificing mother. She seemed to have no self of her own, existing only to fulfill the needs of her lover, her daughter, and the psychoanalytic cause.

This selfless Gizella was exactly the kind of woman that Freud was comfortable with. In his mind, she was another Martha, a woman who subordinated her personality to the needs of the man. If Ferenczi must have a woman in his life, it was best that it be someone like this because a sexually exciting young woman like Elma posed a threat to Freud's claim on his friend: "When your express letter arrived, I naturally thought it would contain news of your engagement [to Elma], and I recapitulated in myself the intentions of showing no sensitivity now that you neglect the sullen old man in favor of the charming young woman . . . I am gradually getting used to the idea that you could take your summer trip with her instead of with me, although if it comes to that, you certainly won't have *me* to thank for it. On the contrary, I will put as many difficulties in her way as possible."

Ferenczi ultimately capitulated to Freud: "The case of Elma has been completely settled. I politely but firmly rejected her attempted advances. Even though I long for youth and beauty, I still see very clearly what kinds of dangers I have to look forward to with her. She also no longer attracts me personally. So, the fact remains: I will resign myself to an intellectual and emotional union with Frau G., on which I can always build—you and science will have to share the libido that is left over."

And so, Ferenczi eventually followed Freud's advice and married Gizella. While she may have been a Martha in Freud's eyes, she was clearly more than this to the younger man, and there were many indications of genuine love and mutuality between them; it is possible that Ferenczi would have resolved his ambivalence in her favor even without Freud's intervention. But it is also clear that the need to bow to Freud's will in the matter interfered with his free choice. All was not smooth between Sándor and Gizella after their marriage. With his commitment to honesty, he bared his thoughts and actions to her, confessing his attraction to Elma, contact with prostitutes, and even an affair with Gizella's sister. Ferenczi's open, emotional nature sometimes made it hard for him to contain himself, a quality that caused pain to those close to him.

For many years, Ferenczi struggled, with much vacillation and difficulty, to break free from the position of dutiful son, to become independent and express his own views. In his son role, he could sound like the doctrinaire Karl Abraham or follow Freud into the deep waters of theoretical speculation. At the same time, he was driven to find more effective ways of working with his patients and he continually pushed the limits of the classical approach to therapy. He was not satisfied with attributing stalemates or treatment failures to resistance; he tried to see things from the patient's point of view—how they experienced his silence, abstinence, neutrality, and interpretations. And he was never comfortable playing the role of analyst-as-all-knowing-authority. In his last years, he experimented with more active forms of therapy and eventually settled on what he termed "the principle of relaxation" and "neocatharsis." These methods involved the creation of a safe therapeutic environment in which patients would feel comfortable expressing as much of their experience as possible, including traumatic material and any and all reactions to the analyst.

The essential features of Ferenczi's therapeutic innovations were developed in a series of papers that he published between 1928 and his death in 1933, papers that give a clear picture of his evolution as a psychoanalyst. He came to recognize the importance of "tact" and "empathy" and the centrality of the analyst-patient relationship as a curative force in itself. The analyst must be open: "One must never be ashamed unreservedly to confess one's own mistakes." What is more, the analyst must be "indulgent"; he should not frustrate the patient, an idea that directly contradicted Freud's principles of "neutrality" and "abstinence." Ferenczi's understanding of the cause of neuroses stressed the importance of actual traumas and a variety of parental abuses, along with the way these were covered up and distorted within families. As he put it: "One gets the impression that children get over even severe shocks without amnesia or neurotic consequences, if the mother is at hand with understanding and tenderness and—what is most rare—with complete sincerity."

Ferenczi's final paper, *Confusion of Tongues between Adults and the Child: The Language of Tenderness and of Passion* (1933), is his best known. In his work up to this point he had attempted to reconcile the irreconcilable: to fit his ideas within Freud's framework. Now he finally abandoned this impossible task. The "confusion of tongues" of the title referred to the different meanings of love and physical contact for children and adults. Because children were looking for tenderness in physical and emotional forms, Ferenczi argued that trauma resulted when parents or others interpreted their overtures as adult sexuality and then imposed their "passion" on the child.

This was Ferenczi's solution to the oft-debated seduction versus fantasy question. As he made clear, no one becomes disturbed solely because of his drives or fantasies, but the trauma and abuse that children suffer take a variety of forms, from subtle to gross. He was aware of the very different mental capacities of children who are only too ready to comply and accept parental definitions of reality, which often makes it difficult for the analyst to discern what a patient had actually gone through as a child. And he called attention to the damage that results when parents cover up their abusive treatment of children with half-truths and lies.

Ferenczi was finally able to completely leave the classical analytic method behind. It was only when he opened himself to his patients' experience, created a safe atmosphere, and took their criticisms to heart that he was able to move beyond the dance of knowing-analyst-authority and compliant-child-patient: "I started to listen to my patients when, in their attacks, they called me insensitive, cold, even hard and cruel, when they reproached me with being selfish, heartless, conceited."

In the *Confusion of Tongues* paper, Ferenczi made the important bridge between the traumas patients suffered as children, so often accompanied by their compliance with parental versions of reality, and their compliance as adult patients with the authority of the classical analyst. When he was able to give up such authority and listen seriously to what his patients told him about the impact of his silence, abstinence, and frustration, their traumatic memories and emotions, heretofore held back, emerged with force in the analytic sessions. Ferenczi found that when he worked within the confines of Freud's method, this material did not appear. What he had seen before he developed his innovative techniques—what Freud and his classical followers continued to see—were compliant patients who were not free to reveal the full reality of their experience. This insight was Ferenczi's most radical and threatening challenge to Freud, for it showed how analysis, practiced in the classical manner, could be a retraumatization of the patient. Whereas Freud thought of himself as a strong and firm father, many patients experienced this treatment as hard and cold, even cruel.

It was also at this time that Ferenczi was personally able to break free from Freud's authority. He wrote his strongest criticism of classical psychoanalysis in the privacy of his *Clinical Diary*: "The analytic situation, but specifically its rigid technical rules, mostly produce in the patient unalleviated suffering and in the analyst an unjustifiable sense of superiority accompanied by a certain contempt for the patient. . . . Analysis offers to persons otherwise somewhat incapacitated and whose self-confidence and potency are disturbed an opportunity to feel like a sultan, thus compensating him for his defective ability to love."

Ferenczi came to his new ideas about analytic therapy because of his unique capacity for empathy, his ability to see things from the patient's point of view. His continually evolving work made him the most *scientific* of the early psychoanalysts, though Freud and the loyalists always characterized him as a *mere therapist*—a man driven by his need to help and cure—while promoting themselves as the true scientific theorists. This was brought out in a brief obituary that Freud wrote after Ferenczi's death in 1933, in which he praised his former colleague's most fanciful theoretical flights, such as his 1924 book *Thalassa: A Theory of Genitality,* while simultaneously derogating his clinical contributions:

> After this summit of achievement, it came about that our friend slowly drifted away from us. . . . The need to cure and to help had become paramount in him. He had probably set himself aims which, with our therapeutic means, are altogether out of reach to-day. From unexhausted springs of emotion the conviction was borne in upon him that one could effect far more with one's patients if one gave them enough of the love which they had longed for as children . . . Signs were slowly revealed in him of a grave organic destructive process which had probably overshadowed his life for

many years already. Shortly before completing his sixtieth year he succumbed to pernicious anaemia. It is impossible to believe that the history of our science will ever forget him.

This is Freud the propagandist: subtle yet insidious. The "need to cure" is presented as an unrealistic—by implication wishful and childish—hope while the "unexhausted springs of emotion" suggest the irrationality of Ferenczi's therapeutic efforts. Freud always interpreted the ideas of those who disagreed with him as derived from their emotions; they were driven by blind feeling in contrast to his calm rationality. The comment about giving patients the love they missed is a reference to the rumor—a serious distortion of the truth, though for many years the accepted psychoanalytic lore—that Ferenczi tried to cure his patients by hugging and kissing them. And, finally, there is the comment that the "organic destructive process . . . overshadowed his life for many years," a deliberate distortion, since Freud knew that Ferenczi's anemia only appeared in his last year.

Freud's position set off an attack on Ferenczi by the faithful and, eventually, led to the censorship of his contributions. For many years after his death, rumors were spread that he had sexual contact with his patients; he was caricatured as the foolish doctor who tried to cure with hugs and kisses. These accusations were serious distortions of Ferenczi's sincere efforts to open himself emotionally to his patients' experience. Ferenczi was a man easily carried away by his feelings; as Judith Dupont, editor of his *Clinical Diary,* noted, he "sometimes lost control of the situation." He admitted as much in a letter to Freud, when he described an incident in which he "gave way to a kiss" with an attractive young woman who was discussing treatment with him, though he assured Freud that he quickly "ceased further intimacies" and attempted to work therapeutically with her. It is not clear that he did more than kiss Elma Palos when she was his patient, though her therapy was filled with indiscretions and violations of therapeutic boundaries. He recognized these earlier acts as mistakes and, in his later work, said he had learned not to repeat them.

The best-known case of affectionate contact involved the American psychiatrist Clara Thompson, who saw Ferenczi in 1928–1929 and boasted that "I can kiss Papa Ferenczi as often as I like." This was reported to Freud, and Jones later passed along a story that Thompson was "the evil genius in Ferenczi's later days." Far from an evil genius, she was a serious psychoanalyst who became a prominent neo-Freudian, worked with Karen Horney, and made important contributions to the field over the succeeding years. In response to the general accusations of affectionate contact, Freud wrote to Ferenczi in 1931:

> "Why stop at a kiss?" Surely, one can go still further and include "a hug", which, after all, will not get a woman pregnant. Still others, more daring, might go so far as to peep and show [leading to] all manner of petting par-

ties and promiscuity . . . The godfather, Ferenczi, looking down upon the scene he had created, would say to himself: "Perhaps, after all, I should have stopped *before* the kiss in working out my motherly love technique". [Freud goes on] and then you are to hear from the brutal fatherly side an admonition . . . according to my recollection a tendency to sexual play with patients [a reference to the Gizella-Elma affair] was not completely alien to you in preanalytic times, so that the new technique could well be linked to an old error.

Ferenczi was hurt by these accusations, which were serious distortions of his new methods. At a time when he was pushing his "principle of indulgence" to its limits, he did allow certain of his patients to kiss him—Thompson was one of these—though he did so for what seemed to him sound therapeutic reasons. In his response to Freud's letter, he acknowledged earlier mistakes, took responsibility for his actions, but made clear that he was not using his patients for his own gratification—to satisfy his needs for affection or sex—but was working to create an atmosphere of maternal warmth. The truth of Ferenczi's claim was later supported by Arnold Rachman: "On the basis of more than ten years' research on Ferenczi's clinical behavior, as revealed in his own work and described by his analysands, his colleagues, his friends, and other researchers, I have concluded that *there is no evidence that he engaged in any direct sexual behavior with patients or encouraged any analytic candidate, supervisee, or colleague to do so.*"

The growing conflicts between Freud and Ferenczi came to a head in the last years of the younger man's life. Ferenczi wrote about them in his *Clinical Diary,* which contained many insightful observations, based on his years in the psychoanalytic movement, along with his final assessment of Freud as a person and a psychoanalyst. In the privacy of his *Diary,* Ferenczi was at last able to voice his feelings about the man he loved, revered, and followed for so many years:

> Freud no longer loves his patients. He has returned to the love of his well-ordered and cultivated superego—a further proof of this being his antipathy toward and deprecating remarks about psychotics, perverts, and everything in general that is "too abnormal" . . . he still remains attached to analysis intellectually, but not emotionally . . . his therapeutic method, like his theory, is becoming more and more influenced by his interest in order, character, the replacement of a bad superego by a better one; he is becoming pedagogical.
>
> He [Freud] must have felt very comfortable in this role; he could indulge in his theoretical fantasies undisturbed by any contradiction and use the enthusiastic agreement of his blinded pupil to boost his own self-esteem. In reality, his brilliant ideas were usually based on only a single case, like illuminations as it were which dazzled and amazed, for example,

me . . . The advantages of following blindly were: 1) membership in a distinguished group guaranteed by the king, indeed with the rank of field marshal for myself—crown-prince fantasy—2) One learned from him and from his kind of technique various things that made one's life and work more comfortable: the calm, unemotional reserve; the unruffled assurance that one knew better; and the theories, the seeking and finding of the causes of failure in the patient instead of partly in ourselves. The dishonesty of reserving the technique for one's own person; the advice not to let patients learn anything about the technique; and finally the pessimistic view, shared with only a trusted few, that neurotics are a rabble.

Ferenczi visited Freud for a final time in 1932 to read his *Confusion of Tongues* paper, hoping that the Professor would listen and try to understand the clinical innovations in which he had invested so much of himself. But Freud had already turned on his friend, branding him a heretic, as revealed in comments he made to others at the time. To Eitingon he wrote, "Isn't Ferenczi a cross to bear? Once again for months no news of him. He is insulted because we are not charmed by his playing mother and child with his female pupils." To Jones: "For three years now I have been observing his increasing alienation, his inaccessibility to warnings against his incorrect technical path, and . . . a personal hostility toward me." After listening to Ferenczi's paper, Freud telegrammed to Eitingon, "Ferenczi read paper out loud. Harmless, stupid, also inadequate. Impression unpleasant," while to his daughter Anna, he said the paper was "confused, obscure, artificial." At the end of this, their final meeting, Ferenczi held out his hand for an affectionate good-bye, but Freud turned his back on him and walked out of the room.

Shortly after this final rebuff by Freud, Ferenczi wrote, "In my case the blood-crisis [pernicious anemia] arose when I realized that not only can I not rely on the protection of a 'higher power' but *on the contrary* I shall be trampled under foot by this indifferent power as soon as I go my own way and not his." As Michael Balint—a student and colleague of Ferenczi in Hungary and, later, an innovative psychoanalyst in England—put it, "Ferenczi's condition, suffered a shattering blow during his last meeting with Freud—and by his subsequent illness which, one does not know, was a coincidence or a consequence."

After the final encounter with Freud, Ferenczi was permitted to read the *Confusion of Tongues* paper at the Psychoanalytic Congress of 1932, and it was published in German in the *Internationale Zeitschrift*. But Jones blocked its publication in the English language *International Journal*, which he edited. This crucial act of censorship kept Ferenczi's ideas hidden for many years because, with the rise of Hitler, psychoanalysis would be banned in Germany and Austria, and, until the war ended in 1945, new psychoanalytic publications would only be available in English. With Ferenczi's death, and the censorship of his work in English publications, it was easy to misrepresent his contributions and slander him personally. In his biography of Freud, Jones spoke of Ferenczi's "mental deterioration . . . latent psychotic trends . . . [and a] . . . final delusional state." As Jones elaborated, "Toward the end of his life [he] developed psychotic manifestations that revealed themselves in, among other things, a turning away from Freud and his doctrines. The seeds of a destructive psychosis, invisible for so long at last germinated . . . [there were] delusions about Freud's supposed hostility . . . [and] violent paranoic and even homicidal outbursts."

Peter Gay gave essentially the same account, picturing Ferenczi as the misguided, delusional child, and Freud the long-suffering, ill-treated parent. Significantly, Jones's diagnosis of psychosis did not originate with him, but came from Freud himself, who wrote to his English supporter, laying on the usual labels: "mental degeneration" and "paranoia." Freud was particularly incensed by Ferenczi's believing what his patients told him and by the resurrection of the theory of trauma. As he wrote to his daughter Anna at the time: "Ferenczi offered observations on the hostility of patients and the need to accept their criticism and to acknowledge one's mistakes *before* them . . . He has completely regressed to etiological views I believed in, and gave up, 35 years ago: that the regular cause of neuroses is sexual traumas of childhood, said it in virtually the same words as I had used then!"

While Ferenczi presented strong challenges to Freud's long-standing beliefs, the fact that these came from a colleague he respected, a man who was his closest coworker and friend for many years, might have given him pause. While it is not reasonable to expect that Freud would have changed his own views at this late stage in his life, he could at least have considered these new ideas rather than anathematizing them. Far from this, his reaction to Ferenczi's innovations was outrage and attack.

A number of people had direct contact with Ferenczi during his final days and all of them reported that there was absolutely no truth to the story that he underwent a mental deterioration. This was a slander by diagnosis set in motion by Freud and perpetuated by Jones, Gay, and others. Balint was in contact with his colleague in Budapest until the very end and reported that he remained clearminded and alert, though feeble and incapacitated. Balint published a rebuttal to Jones after the Freud biography came out, but it had little effect on dispelling the rumors. The Swiss psychoanalytic scholar André Haynal has reviewed the evidence supplied by many, including physicians and psychiatrists, who had contact with Ferenczi in his last days and found that they all agreed that though ill and weak, his mind was not affected. To imagine the insecure, gentle, and loving Ferenczi as a "violent paranoic" given to "homicidal outbursts" is absurd. Indeed, he was such a sensitive soul that Freud's harsh rejection, after their many years of closeness, probably hastened, if it did not actually cause, his death.

CHAPTER 25

The Final Years

FREUD'S BREAK with Ferenczi in 1932, and the death of the Hungarian the following year, marked the end of the original Committee. Abraham had died in 1925, Rank had been expelled and was residing in the United States, and Eitingon, Jones, and Sachs, while remaining loyal, were all living in other countries by 1933. Colleagues and friends from earlier years were also gone: Josef Breuer, with whom Freud had not spoken since the turn of the century, died in 1925, and Wilhelm Fliess, whom he had not seen since 1902, died in 1928. Three of his lifelong physician friends, all known from prepsychoanalytic days and partners in the regular Saturday night card games, had also died: Leopold Königstein in 1924, Ludwig Rosenberg in 1928, and, closest of all, Oscar Rie, in 1931. Many of the old psychoanalytic guard were gone or living elsewhere, but several of his original followers, such as Paul Federn and Eduard Hitschmann, remained in Vienna.

While psychoanalysis had grown and was flourishing in many countries, Freud's own life was more and more encumbered by age and his progressive illnesses. He had heart disease in addition to cancer, and was increasingly dependent on his doctors and Anna. Hans Pichler, who had performed the major surgeries on his jaw and palate in 1923, continued to remove precancerous tissue over the succeeding years, as well as making new prostheses in attempts to ease the discomfort, though none of them were particularly satisfactory. Max Schur, a young Viennese internist, became Freud's personal physician in 1927, and they made a pact: when things reached an unbearable state, Schur would help him die.

Along with Anna and such long-term correspondent-friends as Frau Lou, Oskar Pfister, and the German novelist Arnold Zweig, there were new recruits—Marie Bonaparte, Heinz Hartmann, Ernst Kris and his wife, Marianne, the daughter of Oscar Rie—who fueled his hopes for the future of the movement. Princess Bonaparte was a convert to the cause who would play an important role in Freud's final years. She was the great-granddaughter of Napoléon's brother

Lucien and was married to Prince George of Greece, a woman with wealth and connections who was also intelligent and personally effective. She was, as Freud once called her, an "energy devil." Not finding satisfaction in trivial social life with her fellow aristocrats or emotional gratification with her older husband, and suffering from obsessions and symptoms of sexual disturbance, she turned to psychoanalysis. She entered treatment with Freud in September 1925 and, over the succeeding years, threw her considerable resources into the organization of psychoanalysis in France, as well as giving money to the Psychoanalytic Press in Vienna. The Princess and the Professor became personally close. She was just the kind of woman he liked: a grateful analysand who never questioned psychoanalytic doctrines. She was, as he wrote to Eitingon, "a quite outstanding, more than just half masculine female."

Despite the promising new supporters, Freud felt so disappointed, betrayed, and let down by friends and followers that in his late years, he turned to more trustworthy companions: pet dogs. Anna had acquired her German shepherd, Wolf, and, in 1927, her companion Dorothy Burlingham gave Freud a chow, the first of a series of this breed—Jo-Fi, the last, was his favorite—with whom he became inseparable. When the pain in his mouth was bad and he had trouble eating, he would put his food on the floor for his pet, much to Martha's dismay. Analysands during the last decade reported how the Professor's dog would sit at the foot of the couch through their analytic sessions and then get up at the appointed time, signaling that the hour was over.

"Black Thursday," the stock market crash of October 29, 1929, ushered in the Great Depression of the 1930s, the final act of a financial catastrophe long in the making. Political and economic conditions had been unstable throughout Europe in the years after the Great War, waxing and waning in different countries. In Germany, violent conflicts between Socialists, Communists, and right-wing groups increased through the 1920s, leaving the democratic Weimar Republic in a precarious position. Chaotic economic conditions, including out-of-control inflation which wiped out the savings of many families and caused the loss of jobs, fueled the political turmoil, paving the way for the rise of totalitarian regimes. Mussolini, the first of the modern fascist dictators, had come to power in Italy in 1922. Now the stage was set in Germany.

Adolf Hitler's National Socialist (Nazi) Party had only 12 seats in the Reichstag or parliament in 1928, but by 1930 they were the second-largest party, with 111 seats. With the economy failing, and political extremists fighting in the streets, Paul von Hindenburg, the aging president of the German Republic, appointed Hitler chancellor in 1933 in the hope that order would be restored. Elections were held in early March, making the National Socialists the governing party, and the new Reichstag quickly gave their chancellor dictatorial powers. Order would indeed be restored, but the order the Nazis imposed was something the modern world had never seen before.

Hitler immediately disbanded all democratic institutions; there were no more elections, concentration camps were opened for political opponents—though not yet for Jews—newspapers and the radio were taken over for purposes of propaganda, and paramilitary gangs of Brown- and Blackshirts roamed the streets beating, arresting, and murdering anyone who did not openly support the regime. Jews and other "undesirables" were purged from the government, universities, newspapers, and the arts. Anti-Semitism, clearly enunciated in Hilter's *Mein Kampf,* was now the official policy of the government.

In May of 1933, the Propaganda Ministry organized book burnings in Berlin and other German cities; Freud's works were thrown on the pyre along with those of other Jews—Einstein, Marx, Kafka, Schnitzler, and Stefan Zweig—and non-Jews whose views were deemed dangerous by the Nazis: Thomas and Heinrich Mann, Émile Zola, and Havelock Ellis. Freud was in distinguished company.

Much of Austria was Catholic and conservative, with a history of anti-Semitism, yet Vienna remained divided, with Nazis who agitated for merger, or *Anschluss,* with Germany, and, opposing them, Socialists and workers who, in 1928, staged an antigovernment uprising. The conservative chancellor Engelbert Dollfuss put this rebellion down with military force—more than a thousand were killed—and, by 1932, he had dissolved the parliament and set up camps for political opponents; Socialists were imprisoned and some executed. The situation, while more and more dictatorial, had still not reached the level of Nazi Germany; persecution of Jews had yet to break loose in full fury.

With Hitler in control and anti-Semitism on the rise, a number of Jews saw the future danger and left Germany as quickly as they could. Freud's sons Ernst and Oliver were both living in Berlin in 1933, and when one of Ernst's boys was called "Jew Freud" at school, he moved his family to England. Oliver returned to Vienna with his wife and daughter, then moved to France—first to Paris, and then to Nice, where Freud gave him the money to open a small photography business. A number of psychoanalysts in Germany emigrated: Max Eitingon to Palestine, and Hanns Sachs, Otto Fenichel, Erich Fromm, Ernst Simmel, and some fifty others, including the non-Jewish Karen Horney, to the United States. While the danger of staying was clearest to those living in Germany, some in the surrounding countries saw the handwriting on the wall: Helene Deutsch and her husband Felix left Austria for the United States about this same time.

Freud, with his dour perceptivity, was aware of how bad things were going; he had no illusions about Hitler. Yet he could not bring himself to believe in the full extent of the coming horror, and it would take him the longest time to leave Vienna. Ferenczi, in May of 1933, in one of the last letters he wrote to the Professor, had urged him to get out, but Freud would not hear of it. While many in Austria lived in conditions of anxious uncertainty and terrible deprivation, he was relatively comfortable. Seeing patients five hours a day at his fee of $25 per session brought in enough money, supplemented by royalties from the sale of his books, to support himself, the immediate family, Mathilde (whose husband, Robert, could not find work), and his son-in-law Max Halberstadt, in Hamburg, with some left over for savings. In April of 1933, he wrote to Ernest Jones that he expected the Hitler movement to spread to Austria, but that it would not be as bad as it was in Germany, since the Austrians were not as brutish as their German cousins. If Germany tried to annex her southern neighbor, France and the League of Nations would not permit it, he imagined, concluding, "I am resolved not to budge an inch." To his nephew Samuel Freud in Manchester he wrote: "We are determined to stick it out here to the last. Perhaps it may not come out too bad."

Freud was seventy-seven years old in 1933, sick with cancer for a decade, and dependent on his doctors. He had lived in Vienna since he was four years old and was locked into his tightly structured life. Nor had his old travel phobia completely vanished. It would have been exceedingly difficult for anyone his age, and in his state of health, to move. Many other Jews, including those far younger and healthier than he, who had successful lives and thought of themselves primarily as Austrians or Germans, did not foresee the havoc that the Nazis would wreak. Anti-Semitism had been a part of European life for centuries; at the most, they thought there would be restrictions and some privations. Hardly anyone could imagine the gas chambers and the Holocaust. It is easy to say now that Freud should have known what was coming and left Vienna earlier, but this is with the wisdom of hindsight. While it is understandable why Freud could not bring himself to leave, his intransigence made it difficult for his Jewish followers in Vienna to get out, since he spoke of "rats deserting a sinking ship." They had to cross him if they wished to emigrate.

In July of 1934, Chancellor Dollfuss was assassinated by an Austrian Nazi in an attempted coup. The coup was blocked, and Hitler held at bay for a few more years, as Kurt von Schuschnigg took over as chancellor. Schuschnigg attempted accommodation with the Nazis while trying to maintain Austrian independence, and Freud pinned his hopes on this.

In May of 1936, Freud celebrated his eightieth birthday, receiving a congratulatory letter composed by the writers Thomas Mann and Stefan Zweig, and signed by many others. He wrote to Arnold Zweig that he was content with his family life, especially Anna, "who satisfies in rare measure all of a father's demands." To Marie Bonaparte, he wrote of Martha, "It was really not a bad solution of the marriage problem and she is still today tender, healthy and active." The surgeries to remove cancerous tissue from his mouth continued, sometimes with severe pain. His personal physician Max Schur made clear to him that the cancer was due to smoking—it had been scientifically established by this time—which also aggravated his heart condition, but he could only give up his habit for brief periods.

At the end of the year Wilhelm Fliess came back into his life. When Fliess had died in 1928, his widow had written to Freud, asking for the return of her husband's letters. He had written back saying he had thrown them away or could not find them, and, in fact, they have never surfaced. Ida Fliess, however, had Freud's letters to Wilhelm, and she sold them to a German book dealer who was prepared to put them on the market. When Marie Bonaparte learned of this, she bought the letters for about $500 with the hope of preserving them. Freud wrote to her, urging that she give him the letters so he could dispose of them: "Our correspondence was the most intimate you can imagine . . . I do not want any of them to become known to so-called posterity." The Princess demurred and was able to smuggle the letters out of Europe; eventually they came into Anna's possession. Freud had reason to destroy the letters, since they contained a good deal of information that contradicted the mythologized self-portrait he had labored so long to construct.

Three weeks after learning that his letters to Fliess were still in existence, Freud began writing his essay *Analysis Terminable and Interminable.* It was here that he once again returned to the danger posed by a man's "passive" or "feminine" longings for another male, echoing the feelings of his long past attachment to his Berlin friend. In the essay, he reprised the Emma Eckstein case, again exculpating himself and Fliess.

Alfred Adler, who had not seen Freud in years, died on a lecture tour in the summer of 1937 at the age of sixty-seven. Arnold Zweig wrote to Freud that the death saddened him, to which the Professor replied: "I don't understand your sympathy for Adler. For a little Jew from a Viennese suburb, a death in Aberdeen, Scotland, is an unprecedented career in itself and a proof of how far he had come. Truly, his contemporaries have richly rewarded him for his service in having contradicted psychoanalysis."

Lou Andreas-Salomé also died in 1937, at the age of seventy-five. Freud learned of her death from the newspapers and wrote to Zweig that he "was very fond of her . . . strange to say without a trace of sexual attraction."

With all the political and economic chaos, the deaths of friends and former colleagues, and the threats to family members, Freud remained absorbed in his writing. He was working on a book about Moses, with whom he had long identified, attempting to prove that the first Jewish leader was an Egyptian prince. The book, *Moses and Monotheism,* was not completed until after the move to London, but it reveals his mixed attitude towards his Jewishness, brought out strongly during these years when violence against Jews was more blatant than at any time in his life. Freud never hesitated to declare himself a Jew—he was proud to be a defiant member of a group of outsiders—yet he distanced himself from the religion, tried to make its founder a non-Jew, and enjoyed thinking about all the anger his new book would stir up among believers.

In 1938, Chancellor Schuschnigg was forced to resign under pressure from Hitler. The Nazi henchman Arthur Seyss-Inquart took over the government and invited the Germans into Austria. The Anschluss was accomplished; German troops poured over the border and Nazism broke out in full force in Vienna, releasing Austria's own considerable anti-Semitism. Jewish apartments, stores, and synagogues were ransacked; thugs roamed the neighborhoods searching for victims; men and women were beaten and humiliated in the streets.

Wilhelm Stekel fled Vienna on the day before the Nazi takeover, taking a train to Switzerland and leaving all his possessions behind; eventually he made his way to London. Another "defector" from the early days was heard from at this time: Carl Jung. After Hitler came to power in 1933, the International Psychotherapy Association and its journal were forced to adhere to the party line, purging psychoanalysts and Jews. Jung took over as president and editor of the journal, moving the base of the association to neutral Switzerland in order to protect Jewish members. In addition, he made some efforts to rescue Jewish psychotherapists from the Nazis. At the same time, he wrote articles extolling the superiority of the "Aryan" over the Jewish soul, and proclaiming that Jews were not capable of understanding the Germanic people. His attempts to encompass political events in his theory of archetypes—he explained the rise of Hitler and the Nazis as the return of the Nordic god Wotan from the collective unconscious—were a muddle, and his politics, if he can be said to have any, leaned to the right. While he and his followers attempted to explain all this away after the war, and while it is clear he was never a Nazi and pulled out of the association in 1940 when it was taken over by Hitler's men, this was not his finest hour.

Jung's derogation of Jewish psychotherapy can best be understood if "Freud" is substituted for "Jew" and "Freudian" for "Jewish." His anger at his former mentor and the Committee remained alive, and led him to publish statements that, given the political context, can only be seen as sympathetic to the Nazis. Despite this anger, he sensed the danger to which Freud was personally exposed, and he and his colleague Franz Riklin attempted to help. They sent the blond and Aryan-looking Franz Riklin Jr. to Vienna with $10,000 of their own money, with instructions that he give it to Freud and urge him to leave the city. Riklin Junior appeared at the door of Berggasse 19 and was met by a suspicious Anna, who was hesitant to let him enter. Then Freud appeared, listened to the proposal, and turned down the money, saying, "I refuse to be beholden to my enemies."

While the majority of Jews in Vienna were victimized by the Nazis after the Anschluss, the Freuds were spared for the most part, though a gang of storm troopers did come to the apartment and confiscated $500. Now, more than ever, friends and colleagues begged Freud to leave, yet he still could not make up his mind. Then the Nazis moved in on the Psychoanalytic Press and arrested

Martin for a day. A week later, the Gestapo took Anna in for a day of questioning. Now Freud was convinced it was time to get out, but he had waited too long; leaving would require papers and the payment of fees to the Nazi authorities, and this would be difficult. Fortunately, there were a number of friends who brought their influence to bear, including William Bullitt, the American ambassador in Paris, whose wife had been analyzed by Freud in 1930, and who had collaborated with Freud on a psychobiography of Woodrow Wilson. Bullitt used his position to get President Roosevelt and the U.S. State Department to intercede with Germany on Freud's behalf; Princess Bonaparte used her money and position from Paris, and Ernest Jones his contacts and influence in London, to secure entry visas to England.

After some anxious weeks, the Freud party was permitted to leave Austria. Martha, Minna, Mathilde and her husband, and the late Sophie's son Ernst all left for England. Martin and his son Anton Walter also left for London, while his wife, Esti, and their daughter Sophie went to Paris to stay with Esti's younger sister. Freud's younger brother Alexander, his wife, and his son Harry managed to get out to Switzerland, then to England, and finally to Canada. In addition to these family members, the party included Freud's pet chow, the housekeeper Paula Fichtl, and Max Schur, his wife, and their two children. Freud's sisters Rosa, Mitzi, Pauline, and Dolfi—the oldest, Anna, had been living in New York since the turn of the century—all in their seventies, were left behind in Vienna. Jones later wrote that Freud and Alexander left them with a considerable sum of money, though this proved useless when the Nazis confiscated Jewish bank accounts.

There is a widely circulated story that before finally allowing the party to leave, the German authorities made Freud sign a document stating that he had been treated with "respect and consideration." It is said that he asked if he could add something, and wrote, "I can heartily recommend the Gestapo to anyone." This sounds like a fine bit of Freudian irony, though it would have been foolhardy to endanger so many lives on the very point of departure. The document has subsequently been found and it contains no such comment. Perhaps it was what Freud imagined himself writing.

Freud went by train to Paris, stayed overnight with Marie Bonaparte, and then took the night train to England the next day. On this final leg of the journey, he imagined himself William the Conqueror, arriving in 1066. Jones was in London to welcome them, Freud's nephew Sam came down from Manchester for a visit, and others in England extended their hospitality and good wishes over the next weeks. He was even visited by three secretaries of the Royal Society, who asked that he add his signature to their official book, where it reposes along with those of Isaac Newton, Charles Darwin, and other illustrious scientists.

After their fearful last-minute escape, the Freud party was finally safe in London, where Ernst had procured them a temporary house while he renovated their new permanent home at 20 Maresfield Gardens, Hampstead. They were able to settle into this house in September of 1938. Freud's office furniture, including the famous couch and his collection of antiquities, was sent from Vienna, and Anna and Paula Fichtl arranged everything just as it had been in Berggasse 19.

Within two weeks after the arrival in England, Freud was back at work on *Moses and Monotheism*. In his much earlier *Totem and Taboo,* he had speculated that civilization originated from the conflict between a powerful father and his murderous sons. Now, he depicted Moses as the strong leader—the primal father of Judaism, just as he saw himself as the primal father of psychoanalysis—who imposed his control on a primitive tribe of Semites. The tribe, in Freud's account, eventually rebelled against his rule and killed him. The inherited memories of their oedipal guilt, in his view, accounted for the special ethical virtues of the Jewish people.

What is particularly interesting is that Freud was writing about Moses and ancient Egypt in the late 1930s as the Nazis crushed his homeland and visited the cruelest imaginable persecution on the Jews. Escape into a fantasied ancient world was one of Freud's oldest means of dealing with trauma; he did it in his reading as a boy, and throughout his adult life he spent hours in his office surrounded by ancient artifacts. Versions of this consoling activity can be found in many of his theoretical writings. Little wonder that he preferred to live in this imaginary world than amid the horrors of contemporary Europe. In addition, the situation of the Jews with the rise of Hitler probably aroused his long-submerged feelings of terror and helplessness. Anti-Semitism had come and gone throughout his years in Vienna, but it had now reached murderous proportions. To manage the potential danger, Freud had minimized the threat posed by the Nazis. A friend, the French analyst René LaForgue, visited him in 1937 and advised him to leave Austria, to which Freud responded: "The Nazis? I am not afraid of them. Help me rather to combat my true enemy." LaForgue was astonished and asked which enemy that was, and Freud replied: "Religion, the Roman Catholic Church." Would that it had been so.

In *Moses and Monotheism,* Freud argued that Moses was not a Jew, but an Egyptian prince who took over leadership of a Semitic tribe and forced on them a monotheistic religion, taken from the pharaoh Akhenaten. Freud, in his identification with a strong leader, was making a fantasied escape from his inferior and endangered Jewish identity, while simultaneously imagining all the stir his book would cause among the faithful. *Moses and Monotheism* was conceived, written, and published in defiance of what he frequently referred to as "the compact majority." As he wrote to Eitingon, "I am prepared for the Jewish assault on it." He was still the powerful Freud—in his mind an Egyptian prince, Moses himself—shaking up the world, and not just another Jew forced to flee from his persecutors.

Freud also wrote a review-summary of his theories at this time, along the lines of his *Introductory Lectures,* titled *An Outline of Psycho-Analysis,* and a few other short, mostly unfinished, pieces. While the *Moses* book showed his defensive side, a small paper titled *Splitting of the Ego in the Process of Defense,* which he was writing in January of 1938, revealed his continuing self-exploration. The paper, which used Mark Brunswick as a case example, emphasized real trauma and returned to the idea of dissociation—what Breuer, so many years earlier, had called a "hypnoid state." Close to the end of his life, Freud returned to the central issues that led to the break with his first psychoanalytic collaborator: trauma and a splitting of the self.

These were the last significant things Freud would write. In September of 1938, Schur had detected a large lump in his mouth and Pichler came to London to perform a two-hour surgery. This temporarily controlled the cancer, but, within a few months, another, more ominous, lump appeared. As 1939 wore on, with Nazi atrocities accelerating in Europe, Freud's cancer continued to spread. Now it was inoperable, and he was finally forced to give up writing. He was in a great deal of pain, for which he only took aspirin, had trouble sleeping at night, and was increasingly weak and tired. Friends and followers came to visit—Jones, Sachs from America—but it was the ever-present Anna who meant the most to him. Finally, the cancer ate a hole in his cheek and the odor of decaying tissue was such that even his beloved chow shied away from him. He spoke to Schur, reminding him of the pact they had made in 1929 when the young man first became his physician: "Talk it over with Anna and if she thinks it's right, then make an end of it." Anna wanted to put it off, but Schur was able to convince her that it was pointless for her father to go on. She agreed. Morphine was injected; Freud slipped into a coma and died on September 23, 1939. The man who had been plagued with fears of death since he was a small boy, who thought he would die at age fifty-one or sixty-two, in accord with Fliess's fixed periods, who said "how sweet it must be to die" when he fainted with Jung in his fifties, and who had written of the death instinct as an inexorable force that returns us all to an inorganic state, had now, at the age of eighty-three, come to the end of his life.

Tanta Minna died of natural causes during the war, while Martha continued to live on in her modest and fastidious way. When Schur examined her husband in the final months, she would object to his sitting on the bed, since this messed up the bedclothes. Of her late husband, she reminisced: "In the fifty-three years of our marriage, there was not a single angry word between us, and that I always tried as much as possible to remove the *misère* of everyday life from his path. [It was a privilege to have been able to look after] our dear chief." She survived in London until 1951. Freud's younger brother Alexander died in Toronto in 1943. The oldest sister, Anna Freud Bernays, lived to the age of ninety-seven in New York, while her son, Edward Bernays, became a famous—or infamous—innovator in American advertising and public relations. The four Freud sisters, left behind in Vienna when the family escaped from the Nazis, were all killed in concentration camps in 1942.

Mathilde's husband Robert died in 1959, while she lived on in London until 1978, an elegant and charming old-world lady to the end. Martin and his wife Esti separated at the time the family fled Vienna. Esti and her daughter Sophie eventually settled in the United States while Martin stayed in London, isolated from the rest of the family because of Anna's disapproval of his private life. He ran a small shop and was cared for in his declining years by a young woman who became his caretaker and life partner. He died in Sussex in 1967. His son Anton Walter served as a parachutist in the British Royal Air Force during the Second World War, became a chemical engineer after the war, and married and raised three children. Martin's daughter Sophie went on to a distinguished career in the United States as a social worker, professor, and author. Oliver and his wife, Henny, escaped from France in 1943, but their daughter Eva stayed on under a non-Jewish identity, only to die of the effects of a toxic abortion just after the war ended. Oliver worked for many years as an engineer in Philadelphia before he and Henny retired to the country. He died in 1969. Ernst pursued his profession as an architect and also worked closely with Anna, editing the early collections of their father's letters. He died in 1970. His oldest son, Stephen, ran a small store, while the two other boys went on to extremely successful careers in their adopted country: Lucian, the middle child, became a world-famous painter, and Clemens (anglicized to Clement), the youngest, a television personality and member of Parliament. Ernst, Sophie Halberstadt's surviving son, changed his name to W. Ernest Freud and became a psychoanalyst under Anna's wing.

Anna inherited Freud's empire, becoming the leading spokesperson in the world for classical psychoanalysis. With her father dead, her life and work followed two paths. She was able to give some expression to the deprived-child side of herself while also continuing to serve as his emissary. As the Second World War came to England, she and Dorothy Burlingham took over the care of a group of children who had been separated from their families by the war and devoted herself to them. A number of people who saw her there were impressed with her genuine concern and affection for children, especially unloved and abandoned children, as well as her skill at helping them. This was Anna Freud at her best.

To the outside world, Anna Freud was the official representative of Freudian psychoanalysis: fiercely protective of her father's image and reputation, a strict classical analyst with her adult patients, and, in her teaching and articles, a defender of her father's doctrines. With her followers in England—and such bastions of orthodoxy as Ernst Kris, Kurt Eissler, and others in the United States—she maintained a tight censorship over Freud's letters and other documents that might cast a less than holy glow on him. Maresfield Gardens became her clinic, the place where she conducted psychoanalyses, the home she shared with her companion Dorothy Burlingham, and the repository of Freudian artifacts, manuscripts, and lore. She died in 1982. The house is now the Freud Museum.

Psychoanalysis Interminable: Freud as a Therapist

I pass with relief from the tossing sea of Cause and Theory to the firm ground of Result and Fact.

—Winston Churchill, 1898

In 1937, very near the end of his long career, Freud wrote *Analysis Terminable and Interminable*, an essay in which he revisited his many years of psychoanalytic experience, asserted what his "science" had proven, and presented his final thoughts on the possibilities and limitations of therapeutic cure. At the time he wrote this essay, he had become an intellectual giant, achieved fame and a degree of fortune, and vanquished many of his enemies; he had come a very long way from his childhood of poverty and helplessness. Psychoanalysis was established in countries throughout the world; he had many committed followers and, in Anna, a disciple who would carry his work into the future in exactly the way he desired. Still, he remained discontented deep within himself.

Analysis Terminable was a pessimistic essay; the limitations of analysis clearly outweighed the possibilities. Freud was old, sick, and in pain in 1937, with all of Europe on the brink of an abyss. His pessimism would have been expected under the circumstances. Still, the tone did not differ very much from earlier works when he was free of cancer and at the height of his powers. The essay is a curious document; while it is presented as his final assessment of the prospects for psychoanalytic treatment, a careful reading reveals a recycling of a few of his old cases, restatements of his theoretical shibboleths, and a continuation of his arguments with Otto Rank and Sándor Ferenczi.

Analysis Terminable and Interminable began with a discussion of attempts to shorten the length of treatment, as first suggested by Rank. Freud dismissed Rank's work as "a child of its time . . . We have not heard much about what the implementation of Rank's plan has done for cases of sickness. Probably not more than if the fire brigade, called to deal with a house that had been set on fire by an overturned oil-lamp, contented themselves with removing the lamp from the room." The striking image of the misguided fire-brigade sticks in one's mind; it is a fine piece of Freudian rhetoric, but, in fact, he did not address the important differences between his work and Rank's.

The possibility of shortening analysis was next examined with reference to the case of the Wolf Man. After Freud imposed a forced termination on the treatment, he declared it a success, without, as Rank would have counseled, dealing with the patient's reaction to the separation. But the Wolf Man suffered several relapses in the following years for which he was referred to a colleague. In his discussion of the case, Freud pictured himself as a hero doing battle with an adversary: the analyst-as-lion combating the wolf-patient's recalcitrant neurosis, the surgeon cutting out dead tissue and bone. But he never let himself imagine what it might have felt like to have one's renowned analyst break off the relationship. If Freud had not so vehemently rejected Rank's ideas about separation anxiety, he might have considered that loss was a major concern for his patient, and that his "heroic measure" of ending the analysis was, in fact, a further trauma for this homeless young man whose life was satiated with death and emotional deprivation.

Freud next turned to his treatment of Ferenczi, who had been dead for several years by 1937. He carried on the argument about therapeutic innovations, justifying his classical technique and attempting to refute Ferenczi's complaint that his own analysis with Freud had been, at best, marginally helpful. Freud continued, "We can understand how such a master of analysis as Ferenczi came to devote the last years of his life to therapeutic experiments, which, unhappily, proved to be in vain." What is significant here, as in the case of Rank, is what Freud does not consider, especially the important ways in which Ferenczi redefined the work of the analyst. How did he know that Ferenczi's new approach to therapy was not successful? Once he had been expelled from the movement there was no possibility of communication; neither Freud, nor any of his supporters, ever contacted Ferenczi's patients—some of whom, such as Clara Thompson, went on to become significant figures in the field—to see how they felt about their analyses. The reports from later years indicate that Ferenczi was a far more effective therapist than Freud. His methods were the forerunners of many modern forms of psychoanalytic therapy; they contained the essential elements of effective treatment, as demonstrated by a great deal of later research.

Freud then took up the case of a woman whom he treated many years previously for a "hysterical" inability to walk, claiming that "an analysis lasting three-quarters of a year removed the trouble and restored to the patient, an excellent and worthy person, her right to a share in life." Some years later, "profuse hemorrhages" led to the discovery of cancer and a hysterectomy, following which, she "became ill once more . . . [and] remained abnormal to the end of her life." Historical detective work has revealed that this woman was none other than Emma Eckstein, the victim of Fliess's botched nasal surgery, from which she nearly bled to death in 1895. Contrary to the picture sketched by Freud in 1937, she recovered after her therapy, but eventually relapsed and spent the last years of her life as a bedridden recluse. Since he was close to her family, corresponded with her, and analyzed her nephew in 1910, he must have been aware that her treatment could hardly be called a success.

Rank, the Wolf Man, Ferenczi, and Emma Eckstein are the only examples that Freud used to examine the success of psychoanalytic therapy. The rest of *Analysis Terminable* was made up of arguments and theoretical speculations. He was at the peak of his fame in 1937, yet he remained preoccupied with these cases: Emma Eckstein, whom he saw before he even developed his mature psychoanalytic approach; Ferenczi, whose formal analysis lasted a scant seven weeks; and the Wolf Man. There were many other patients who felt their analyses had been successful, and who had expressed their appreciation and gratitude to him, but none of them seemed to be on his mind. Similarly, despite the many theoretical and therapeutic innovations made over the years by himself and other colleagues, he was still carrying on his debate about treatment with Rank and Ferenczi. These four, and what they represented, were like old wounds that refused to heal.

Of Freud's four published case studies, only two could be considered successful, and, of these, only the Wolf Man was still alive, the Rat Man having been killed in the Great War. Thus, this was *the* case that purportedly demonstrated the curative power of psychoanalysis. What is more, Freud had intended his interpretive solution of the Wolf Man's neurosis as proof of the superiority of his theories in comparison to Adler's and Jung's. But because the patient kept suffering relapses and was still in Vienna talking to people, Freud felt the need to go over the case once again and show that if there was not a complete recovery, it was not his fault. As in the case of Emma Eckstein, he was still impelled, all these years later, to justify himself.

Freud's continuing preoccupation with Rank and Ferenczi sprang from sources in their personal relationships as well as the theoretical differences that divided them. The innovations espoused by both these former colleagues challenged the preeminence of his theories and, even more, his classical treatment method. This was the sort of thing that always stimulated a counterattack, because these ideas threatened the defenses with which Freud warded off intolerable emotions. Rank located the primary source of anxiety in separation from the mother, coming close to the complex that Freud was always attempting to grasp but ultimately could not face. Freud did take up Rank's ideas in his 1926 *Inhibitions, Symptoms and Anxiety,* but the new theory of anxiety that he outlined there had almost no impact on subsequent publications and never affected the way he treated his patients.

Ferenczi's innovations posed an even greater challenge to Freud's long-standing definition of psychoanalytic technique. Freud found strength and power in his position as the all-knowing psychoanalyst. While he invented the concept of transference, the way he actually worked with it was extremely limited. The case with countertransference, another of his discoveries, was even more striking; there are almost no instances in which he examined the effects of his own reactions and emotions on the course of an analysis. Ferenczi's approach to psychoanalytic treatment turned this on its head. He was forever probing himself—his own needs, emotions, and actions—and attempting to discern what effects these had on his patients. He also continued to question accepted beliefs such as the necessity of the analyst's silence, neutrality, and abstinence, was dubious about the effectiveness of interpretations—noting that analysis had become an ever more intellectualized game—and came to stress the curative power of an empathic and caring relationship, in and of itself. His extensive redefinition of psychoanalytic treatment was accompanied by the resuscitation of Breuer's old concept of catharsis—the beneficial effect of free emotional expression—and the significance of actual traumas. All these innovations were serious challenges to Freud's system, and he still felt that he had to refute them, as he did at the time of his final rebuff of his friend in 1932.

Consequently, it was essential, in *Analysis Terminable,* that Freud describe Ferenczi's experiments as valueless, that he characterize his former colleague as weak and misguided. To believe otherwise would be to open up his own disavowed traumas, needs, and longings: to face the possibility that the way he had coped with them all his life—the escape into the half-truths of grand theories, the replacement of trauma with wish and instinct, the assumption of the role of heroic father, with the concomitant disavowal of his longings for love—were all misguided.

At the end of *Analysis Terminable,* Freud returned to his entrenched doctrines as he summed up more than forty years of experience with a discussion of the obstacles to analytic cure. Why is the process so difficult, why does it take so long, and why is the outcome so uncertain? He provided two answers to these essential questions. First, people were unrelenting in their pursuit of instinctual gratifications; they would not give up their claims to infantile satisfactions. Second, they were driven by aggression and the death instinct—"the instinct of aggression or of destruction . . . which we trace back to the original death instinct of living matter"—which presumably countered their ability to get well.

Freud's account of selfish, infantile, and aggressive motives is compelling because it resonates with familiar experiences. There are certainly people who refuse to give up their pleasures, who behave in lazy, cruel, and aggressive ways: dishonest politicians, military dictators, drug users, alcoholics, criminals, sexual predators, and those addicted to sadism, violence, lying, and manipulation. Human history provides abundant examples of such unsavory characters. The problem with Freud's argument is that people who are primarily driven in such ways, with a few rare exceptions, do not seek psychoanalytic treatment. They are certainly not to be found among Freud's cases. His account of greed, aggression, and destructiveness may be evocative, but it bears little relation to his actual patients.

Freud's discussion of the limits of psychoanalytic cure concluded with his consideration of two themes that "give the analyst an unusual amount of trouble . . . *envy for the penis*" in the woman and, in the man "a struggle against his passive or feminine attitude to another male." Freud was convinced that these posed the strongest resistances to analytic cure. As he put it at the end of *Analysis Terminable:*

> At no other point in one's analytic work does one suffer more from an oppressive feeling that all one's repeated efforts have been in vain . . . than when one is trying to persuade a woman to abandon her wish for a penis on the ground of its being unrealizable or when one is seeking to convince a man that a passive attitude to men does not always signify castration . . . The rebellious overcompensation of the male produces one of the strongest transference-resistances. He refuses to subject himself to a father-substitute, or to feel indebted to him for anything, and consequently he refuses to accept his recovery from the doctor . . . [When these areas are reached] we have penetrated through all the psychological strata and have reached bedrock, and that thus our activities are at an end.

Like so many of his other works, *Analysis Terminable and Interminable* was an interior monologue presented in the guise of general psychoanalytic reflections. It was Freud's self-analysis, carried on over the years in his theoretical essays, that remained "interminable" and that, close to the end of his life, had still not given satisfaction. When he asserted that men will not give up their passive longings, that they will not subject themselves to a father substitute, he was commenting both on the refusal of his "sons" Rank and Ferenczi to submit to his authority, as well as his inability to completely conquer his own yearnings for love and care.

Freud's assertions in *Analysis Terminable and Interminable* were so intertwined with his disguised self-analysis that one cannot take them as fair or objective assessments of the effectiveness of his psychoanalytic treatments. There is, however, a great deal of evidence from the many cases reviewed in the preceding chapters—some of it based on the independent reports of patients—that permits such an assessment. How did Freud actually work as a therapist? Were his patients cured of the symptoms that brought them into treatment? Did they change, feel better, overcome their inhibitions, and go on to more satisfying and productive lives? If they were helped, what helped them? Were some harmed and, if they were, why was this so?

In his papers on psychoanalytic technique, Freud defined the classical method in terms of abstinence, neutrality, anonymity, confidentiality, and the prohibition of personal relationships. As we have seen, a great many of his cases revealed the tremendous gap between the way he said an analyst should practice and the way he acted. Psychiatrists David Lynn and George Vaillant have recently published a survey of forty-three cases seen by Freud in which they compare his actual methods with his published recommendations concerning psychoanalytic technique. Their findings are quite striking. Whereas, in his published recommendations, Freud counseled the analyst to be neutral and anonymous and to respect the patient's confidentiality, in his practice he was never anonymous, was neutral only 14 percent of the time, and violated confidentiality over 50 percent of the time. In addition, there were significant contacts and personal interactions outside of treatment in 72 percent of the cases. The detailed review of many of these cases in previous chapters supports these conclusions.

The case material shows that Freud was quite variable in the way he treated his patients, depending on his personal response to them. Two factors were most important: how they could be used to promote his theoretical or political agendas—how they confirmed his ideas about infantile sexuality or allowed him to triumph over Adler or Jung—and their compliance with his demands. All the patients who had positive or partially positive experiences in their therapy were in awe of his stature, did not openly challenge him, and felt honored that he was seeing them. This was clearest in the case of Albert Hirst, and also true with Abram Kardiner, Eva Rosenfeld, Smiley Blanton, John Dorsey, H.D., and several others. With patients who idolized him and were compliant, Freud could be interested, humorous, charming, brilliant, and even self-deprecating. Hirst and Kardiner were special cases in which feelings from his own youth seemed to be aroused, causing him to be unusually supportive. Those who did not comply—who openly raised questions about his theory or methods such as Dora, the young homosexual woman, Joseph Wortis, or Clarence Oberndorf—were attacked with interpretations of their motives and resistance. Clearly, Freud's positive response to his patients stemmed from what they did for him, whether they touched on aspects of his own history, played to his need to be aggrandized, provided confirmation of his theories, paid high fees in dollars, or gave financial help to the movement.

Freud almost never followed his recommendation of confidentiality, certainly not when he had some personal or political interest at stake. His involvement with Ferenczi, his mistress Gizella, and her daughter Elma was fraught with breaches of boundaries and endless gossip. His correspondence shows him violating the private communications of many of his other patients. Even more striking was Freud's mixing of personal and analytic relationships, a practice that later classical analysts would view as strictly prohibited. His analysis of his daughter Anna is the most glaring instance in which boundaries were violated as personal, professional, and therapeutic relations were intertangled. He also took Anna's closest friends Eva Rosenfeld and Dorothy Burlingham into analysis. Kata Levy was another woman he treated, despite the fact that she was a friend of Anna's, and he was also seeing her brother Anton von Freund. He saw all three Brunswicks at the same time, a practice that they came to believe was a mistake.

For Freud, psychoanalytic therapy was an intellectual enterprise. The patient was set the task of obeying the rule of free association; he expected resistance, which he then interpreted. The goal was insight, an awareness of one's unconscious. While he knew about transference—the concept was his invention, after all—in practice, he treated the patient's emotional reactions to him as impediments to be removed, like any other resistance. Many aspects of what would today be seen as transference—his patients' idolization of his genius, their fear of the power he had over their careers, their reactions to his cancer and possible death, interruptions in their treatment, or his abrupt decisions to terminate therapy—he ignored, if he was even aware of them. There were important ways in which he was remarkably unempathic, unaware of the effect he had on his patients, especially their fear of his power. A full appreciation of the centrality of anxiety was not only missing from his theory, it was overlooked in the treatment. H.D. was terrified of him from the time of her first contact, when she could not even make eye contact, but Freud seemed unaware of this or saw it as a resistance. Mark Brunswick described how Freud intimidated him, though he did not talk about this in the analysis, and Kardiner noted how Freud interpreted his fear of authority as fear of the father in childhood and not, as it so clearly was, fear of Freud in the present.

Freud's therapeutic style left a great deal of the patient's emotional life untouched. He did not place any value on catharsis, which had been central to the method Breuer originally developed and which was rediscovered by Ferenczi. He was not unemotional with all his patients; a number of them stress the intensity of his focus, though with others, such as Helene Deutsch, David Brunswick, the Stracheys, and John Rickman, his attention lapsed and he sometimes fell asleep during their hours. But his involvement was with the task at hand, a devotion to psychoanalysis, which coexisted with a certain reserve, if not coldness, in relation to them personally.

Although Freud's theories changed over the years—*Mourning and Melancholia* (1915) and *Inhibitions, Symptoms and Anxiety* (1926) introduced important new ways of understanding depression, anxiety, loss of love, and an appreciation of the role of the mother and maternal functions—none of these theoretical innovations affected the way he practiced. He saw Eva Rosenfeld from 1929 to 1931 and, while she found her analysis of great value, she also said that it did not deal with the most painful loss of her life, the death of her daughter, nor with the earlier deaths of her two young sons. The failure to place losses at the center of treatment was a striking feature in a great number of his cases, from the women in the *Studies* through Little Hans, the Wolf Man, Horace Frink, H.D., and his daughter Anna.

Many of the patients whose accounts have been reviewed saw Freud in the 1930s, long after he modified his theory of anxiety and loss, yet his interpretations remained where they had been at the turn of the century: the father and the Oedipus complex, unconscious homosexuality in men, exposure to the primal scene, and penis envy in women remained his staples. He could not part with these ideas, since they served defensive functions for him. Still, when he was most at ease with a patient, his intuitive genius interpreting dreams and symbolic material shone through, as in the insight into Kardiner's mask phobia.

In almost none of the cases we have considered was a successful outcome due to what Freud believed was essential to psychoanalytic cure: interpretations of the unconscious, and, most particularly, interpretations derived from his theoretical doctrines. Sometimes, insights into the unconscious were of value in providing meaning for previously bewildering aspects of a patient's experience, though in none of the successful cases was this the major factor. Again and again, from the young Albert Hirst, seen in 1909–1910, to the middle-aged Smiley Blanton, seen in the 1930s, it was the relationship with Freud that was most important. A great many of these patients saw him as a genius, a heroic figure, and were impressed with his serious interest in their thoughts, memories, and fantasies, his honest and straightforward manner, his sense of humor, the concentrated attention he paid to them, the strength of his character, and his courage in the face of illness and adversity. He was, in their eyes, a new ideal, a man they could emulate in the search for truth, and the fact that he was working directly with them was itself of enormous significance.

In addition to Freud's personality and stature, the psychoanalytic process itself had a curative power, quite separate from interpretations and insight. The psychoanalytic setting was designed to facilitate free and open communication; patients were instructed to say everything that came to mind without censorship and were listened to seriously, often for the first time in their lives. While Freud often interfered with their communications by imposing his pet interpretations, for at least some of the time he was open and noncritical. For guilt-ridden persons like the Rat Man, Hirst, Kardiner, or Blanton, this was extremely valuable. The value of the process itself is implicit in the comments of many of these patients; for them, open self-exploration was, in and of itself, of great therapeutic value. Even the young homosexual woman began to have a positive therapeutic response, as Freud listened to her seriously, before he imposed his interpretations on her and spoiled the treatment.

Along with the personal connection to Freud as an ideal figure, and the power of the psychoanalytic process, were many interchanges in which he praised and supported his patients, spoke of their talents and good qualities, gave gifts and revealed confidences, all of which made them feel liked, valued, and appreciated. His daughter Anna became his closest companion and heir. Ruth Brunswick knew she was his great favorite, and the Rat Man, Hirst, Kardiner, H.D., and Blanton all sensed that he liked them. Patients whom he found uninteresting or who set off his anger had very different experiences. He thought David Brunswick was boring, and no good came of the analysis. Freud attempted to use Horace Frink to advance the psychoanalytic movement, and the result was a disaster for this promising young man's life. Those who aroused his dislike— Dora, Wortis, Oberndorf—were damaged by his treatment of them.

There is a great irony at work here. Freud's published papers on technique prohibit the very activities—personal support, praise, friendly interactions, the giving of gifts—that were involved in successful therapeutic outcomes, while recommending the methods—abstinence, anonymity, silence—that were unhelpful and damaging. Freud's publications on technique came to define classical psychoanalysis for many years; the effects of his actual behavior with patients is only known from their scattered memoirs, reports, and interviews, none of which ever had any effect on the rules for how a "proper analysis" was to be conducted. When commentators note that Freud did not practice analysis in accord with his published recommendations, they typically see this as a lapse, forgivable because he was a genius who was free to do as he pleased. They do not draw the obvious, and more radical, conclusion: that the classical psychoanalytic method was, at best, marginally helpful to those patients who were compliant enough to put up with it, and, of even greater significance, that it never produced findings or evidence in support of the theories that Freud and his orthodox followers claimed it did.

Background and Sources

Every interpretation of Freud is shaped by the point of view, background, training, and allegiances of the interpreter. Those who are part of the psychoanalytic movement see him through the lens of that experience, whether they are fiercely loyal combatants such as Jones, Abraham, Sachs, Anna Freud, or Kurt Eissler and other later defenders of orthodoxy, or those aligned with the analysts who broke away: the Adlerians, Jungians, Horneyians, and others. Within present-day psychoanalysis there is a wide range of views and positions, from the most devoted to the sharply critical. All these analysts have at least one thing in common: work with patients in analysis and psychotherapy. There is also a large group—philosophers, literary critics, historians, experimental psychologists—who have written about Freud with little or no clinical experience. Each of these commentators brings their strengths and limitations; no position guarantees that the author will arrive at a coherent interpretation of Freud and his work. It is important, however, for writers to be open about their perspectives and the sources that have influenced their particular interpretations. What I wish to do here is present my own background so that the reader can understand what has shaped my ideas, what experiences and evidence I draw on in reaching my conclusions.

Over the years, my professional career has followed two parallel tracks. I have been a practicing psychotherapist and psychoanalyst, working with a variety of patients and methods, ranging from brief therapy to lengthy, in-depth psychoanalyses. I took full training at a psychoanalytic institute, including a personal analysis, and eventually became a training and supervising analyst myself, serving on the governing committees of the institute. I am familiar with patients and the therapeutic process from many years of direct immersion, and also know psychoanalysis, including its organizational structure and politics, on a firsthand basis.

I have also been an academic psychologist, engaged in teaching and a variety of scholarly and research projects almost all of which were related to Freud and psychoanalysis in one way or another. In the late 1960s, my graduate students and I did research on dreams, using the newly available techniques for monitoring REM (rapid eye movement) sleep. Freud's dream theory was tested using both experimental methods and naturalistic observations. Two publications came from this work: "Function of Dreams," and, with my students Ian Hunter and Ron W. Lane, the *Psychological Issues* monograph *The Effect of Stress on Dreams*. A few years later, my colleagues and I established a research, training, and treatment program in brief psychotherapy. This work allowed me to become familiar with the large body of interesting research on psychotherapy process and outcome. It was also at this time that I published my book on personality development, *From Instinct to Identity: The Development of Personality*. This was an attempt to integrate theoretical ideas from Freud, Erik Erikson, the neo-Freudians, John Bowlby, and Jean Piaget, along with research findings on nonhuman primates, primitive cultures, dreams, and child development. During the later years of my academic life I taught in the Humanities and Social Science Division of the California Institute of Technology.

Here, my colleagues were primarily historians, philosophers, and members of the literature faculty. Several were interested in psychoanalysis and, out of seminars and joint teaching, along with continued work as a psychotherapist, came my book *Dostoevsky: The Author as Psychoanalyst.* Traditional psychoanalytic interpretations of literature have treated authors and characters as if they were patients in analysis; in my book, I tried to see what Dostoevsky, an extremely insightful psychological observer, had to teach us.

In all this therapeutic work and research, I attempted to maintain a critical stance toward Freud and psychoanalysis. I used my direct experience, as well as what I could glean from the literature, to sort out what was valid and what not. For example, the dream research demonstrated that dreams do not primarily serve to gratify wishes; they are not driven by libido or the pleasure principle, as Freud supposed, but, rather, function to integrate a variety of emotional experiences—anxiety and conflict being most frequent—into the structure of the personality. In a related way, psychotherapy research demonstrated that the insight derived from interpretations is one component, though typically not the most important one, of effective psychotherapy. More central is an empathic relationship that facilitates a climate of openness, trust, safety, acceptance, and support. Contemporary psychoanalytic approaches to treatment—self-psychological, intersubjective, relational, interpersonal—are generally supported by this research, while the kind of classical analysis that originated with Freud is not.

The publication of *Freud's Unfinished Journey: Conventional and Critical Perspectives in Psychoanalytic Theory* was a continuation of my earlier interests in understanding how theory was shaped. As I compare that book with the present one, I can see that while quite critical of Freud's theories, as well as his treatment of patients, I was still under the spell of his personal myth. That is, I still believed that the wrong turns in psychoanalysis could be explained by the frequently cited cultural and historical factors—the influence of outmoded nineteenth-century scientific assumptions, Victorian attitudes toward sexuality, social prejudices about masculinity and femininity—but that Freud's shortcomings did not originate in his own personality. He had gone as far as he could, given his starting place, I still believed, and should not be held personally responsible for the limitations and wrong turns in the field. I was familiar with the existing biographies and more or less accepted their versions of his life. Several influences converged in the last few years that led me to radically change these views.

Direct experience at the upper levels of the psychoanalytic world put me in contact with the men and women who represented the best the field has to offer: senior training analysts, directors of institutes, writers of influential papers, and leaders of the American Psychoanalytic Association. I came to know many of them, to know their patients, and to see the outcome of a great number of personal psychoanalyses. This exposure to the actual practice of a large number of psychoanalysts, the long-term effects of psychoanalytic treatment, and psychoanalytic politics was, all in all, a sobering experience. This was psychoanalysis in the real world, in contrast to the version encountered in Freud's evocative essays. The personal or training analyses were variable—some beneficial, some useless, and others harmful; the teaching was rigid and largely out of date; and the politics no more enlightened than elsewhere. All these experiences played a part in moving me to a new vision of Freud.

All these aspects of my training and career converged in the writing of the present book, beginning with many years of immersion in Freud's work and other psychoanalytic sources as a teacher, researcher, and psychoanalyst. Direct experience as a practicing therapist has, in my view, been invaluable. If one writes about "hysteria," "obsessional neurosis," "resistance," "transference," or the controversies over Freud's form of treatment versus Rank's or Ferenczi's, it makes an enormous difference whether one has had direct contact with the persons and treatment processes to which these labels are applied. The commentator who only knows these phenomena from books is likely to have a very different perspective. Further sources of influence include my research on dreams, psychotherapy, and Dostoevsky. Familiarity with important research in the areas of trauma, infant observation, memory, and feminism and women's studies all expanded my view beyond psychoanalysis itself.

In a sense, the book has been germinating for almost forty years. I began writing it over five years ago as what I thought would be an article dealing with Freud's early losses. A close reading of Freud's complete letters to Fliess gave crucial firsthand data, for here was Freud, in his own words, struggling with his childhood memories and feelings as he formulated his basic theories. As the writing progressed, the article took on a life of its own; the explanatory scheme developed in the chapters on infancy and early childhood led to an expanded biography. I felt like a scientist who stumbles on a theory and finds that it reorders a mass of data into a new and more coherent form. As I did more and more research I kept coming across additional pieces of information that fit into the puzzle and enriched the account.

Primary Sources

The many authors writing about Freud may be placed, roughly, in one of three categories. There are those who see him through the lens of the personal myth that he created; no matter what new evidence is found, what criticisms raised, what deficiencies in theory or treatment exposed, these authors explain them away. Kurt Eissler, Peter Gay, Ernest Jones, Ernst Kris, and a number of others, along with a good deal of what is published in the *International Journal of Psychoanalysis* and the *Journal of the American Psychoanalytic Association,* fall in this category. Many of these biographers and commentators feel the need to treat every word Freud wrote as precious and worthy of endless study. At the other extreme are those who see Freud as a charlatan, his ideas derivative, psychoanalysis a sham. Critics in this camp range from the completely dismissive to those who raise substantive objections. Frederick Crews is a vociferous critic at the dismissive end—see *The Memory Wars: Freud's Legacy in Dispute* (New York: New York Review, 1995). Other critical accounts can be found in a series of recent articles and books: Mikkel Borch-Jacobsen, *Remembering Anna O.: A Century of Mystification,* trans. Kirby Olson (New York: Routledge, 1996); Allen Esterson, *Seductive Mirage: An Exploration of the Work of Sigmund Freud* (Chicago: Open Court, 1993); John Farrell, *Freud's Paranoid Quest: Psychoanalysis and Modern Suspicion* (New York: New York University Press, 1996); Peter J. Swales, "Freud, His Teacher and the Birth of Psychoanalysis," in Paul E. Stepansky, ed., *Freud: Appraisals and Reappraisals: Contributions to Freud Studies,* vol. 1 (Hillsdale, N.J.: Analytic Press, 1986, pp. 3–82); Richard Webster, *Why Freud Was Wrong: Sin, Science and Psychoanalysis* (New York: Basic Books, 1995); and Robert Wilcocks, *Maelzel's Chess Player: Sigmund Freud and the Rhetoric of Deceit* (Boston: Rowman and Littlefield, 1994). A number of the points made by these authors are valuable; indeed, some of the criticisms overlap with those in the present work. But, all too frequently, these commentators jump from valid criticisms of some part of Freud's work to a condemnation of the whole.

The third group, within which I would locate myself, is made up of those who see the significance of many of Freud's contributions, while attempting a balanced and critical assessment of other aspects of psychoanalysis. Authors and publications in this category include George E. Atwood and Robert D. Stolorow, "Freud," in *Faces in a Cloud: Subjectivity in Personality Theory,* 2nd ed. (New York: Jason Aronson, 1993); Henri F. Ellenberger, *The Discovery of the Unconscious: The History and Evolution of Dynamic Psychiatry* (New York: Basic Books, 1970); Robert R. Holt, *Freud Reappraised: A Fresh Look at Psychoanalytic Theory* (New York: Guilford Press, 1989); Charles Rycroft, *The Innocence of Dreams* (New York: Pantheon, 1979); Madelon Sprengnether, *The Spectral Mother: Freud, Feminism and Psychoanalysis* (Ithaca, N.Y.: Cornell University Press, 1990); and Robert J. Stoller, *Perversion: The Erotic Form of Hatred* (New York: Pantheon, 1975).

Freud

I read Freud in the well-known English translation, the *Standard Edition of the Complete Psychological Works of Sigmund Freud,* translated and edited by James Strachey, with the assistance of Anna Freud, Alix Strachey, and Alan Tyson, vol. 1–24 (London: Hogarth Press, 1955–1975). The *Standard Edition* is a most valuable resource: Strachey's translation is far superior to A. A. Brill's early American edition of Freud; it is also enriched by introductions to the books and papers that place them in context. Several authors have raised questions about Strachey's translation from the German, the most popular of which is Bruno Bettelheim, *Freud and Man's Soul* (New York: Knopf, 1983). Detailed scholarly discussions of the problems of translation can be found in several excellent books: Darius Ornston, *Translating Freud* (New Haven, Conn.: Yale University Press, 1992); Ilse Grubrich-Simitis, *Back to Freud's Texts: Making Silent Documents Speak* (New Haven, Conn.: Yale University Press, 1996); and several close studies of Freud's cases by Patrick J. Mahony: *Cries of the Wolf Man* (New York: International Universities Press, 1984); *Freud and the Rat Man* (New Haven, Conn.: Yale University Press, 1986), and *Freud's Dora: A Psychoanalytic, Historical and Textual Study* (New Haven, Conn.: Yale University Press, 1996). Since I do not read German, and have been dependent on English translations, I have studied all these works carefully to see if the English versions contain serious distortions that might have led me astray. It is generally agreed that Strachey tends to scientize Freud, making his colloquial, poetic, and evocative German into a more distanced, impersonal, and seemingly precise English. For example, Strachey translates the word for slips or mistakes, central to *The Psychopathology of Everyday Life,* as "parapraxis" when the English "blunder" or "faulty action" would have been more accurate. He uses the Latinisms "id" and "ego" when the everyday "it" and "I" would have better captured Freud's German. Here is a typical example given by Ornston: a passage that should be translated as "a group of ideas which belong together and have a common emotive tone" is, in Strachey's translation, "a group of interdependent ideational elements cathected with affect" (Ornston, p. 15). In addition to this scientizing of Freud, Strachey, who seems to have been strongly influenced by Ernest Jones, tends to smooth things over, leaving out Freud's hesitancies and uncertainties, and, in some cases, distorting his translations to make the master appear in a more favorable light. Although these sorts of corrections must be considered when working from the *Standard Edition,* one can read Freud in English—supplemented by the information supplied by Ornston, Mahony, and others—and clearly discern Freud's basic theories, case materials, and the main lines of his arguments, because much of the criticism of Strachey deals with relatively minor points. Grubrich-Simitis, by the way, has had access to a number of the earlier drafts of Freud's essays and she dispels still another myth—put about by Jones and others—that Freud wrote out his papers in their near-final form; that psychoanalysis was so perfectly formed in his mind that he could write it down with hardly any revision. The truth is that he sometimes incorporated the suggestions of colleagues such as Rank and Ferenczi, and that he wrote, revised, and rewrote, struggling to find the best expression of his ideas, just as any author does.

Freud was an incessant letter writer and a good deal of his extensive correspondence is available in English translation. The earliest selection to appear was *The Letters of Sigmund Freud,* edited by his son Ernst Freud (New York: Basic Books, 1960), which spans the years 1873, when Freud was seventeen, to 1939, the year of his death. This volume contains a number of letters to Martha Bernays, written during the years of their engagement (but only one-tenth of the total of about nine hundred written to her during this period; the rest remain locked away), as well as letters to other family members, friends, and colleagues. Freud's letters to Wilhelm Fliess—Fliess's side of the correspondence does not exist—first appeared in *The Origins of Psycho-Analysis,* edited by Marie Bonaparte, Anna Freud, and Ernst Kris (New York: Basic Books, 1954). The complete Fliess letters are available in *The Complete Letters of Sigmund Freud to Wilhelm Fliess, 1887–1904,* translated and edited by Jeffrey M. Masson (Cambridge: Harvard University Press, 1985). A comparison of these two versions reveals what Bonaparte, Anna Freud, and Kris left out in order to present Freud in what they believed was a favorable light. A number of the letters were edited and cut, while many others were omitted entirely; *Origins* only printed 140, in full or in part, of the total of 290 letters. *The Complete Letters* also includes 3 late letters from Fliess to Freud.

A full comparison of the two versions of the Freud/Fliess letters would make a long essay itself; just a few examples will serve to demonstrate how the editing of *Origins* was used to create a one-sided picture of Freud. In the letter of August 20, 1893, Freud referred to Fliess as "my beloved friend" and said of his marriage that "we are now living in abstinence; and you know the reasons for this as well." In a letter of June 22, 1894, he revealed his fear that he might die of heart disease, his struggle to stop smoking, his hurt at what he took to be Breuer's rejection, and his need for Fliess's support. This continued in the letter of July 14, 1894, in which he told Fliess, "Your praise is nectar and ambrosia for me, because I know full well how difficult it is for you to bestow it." All three of these letters, which show Freud in a less than masterful light, were omitted from the Bonaparte-Anna Freud-Kris selection. Most of Freud's disparaging and vitriolic comments on Breuer were censored. The whole episode of Fliess's botched operation on Emma Eckstein's nose, the bleeding and the postsurgical complications, as well as Freud's exoneration of Fliess and blaming of Eckstein (reported in letters of March 4, 8, 13, 28 and April 11, 26, 1895) was not included. *Origins* does contain most of the important letters dealing with the abandonment of the trauma theory (letters of September 21 and October 3, 15, and 27, 1897) that contain vital material on the early memories of the death of Julius, the nurse, the *Kasten* incident, and the "discovery" of his Oedipus complex. Yet, even with this material, there was censoring. For example, they reprinted a letter of February 11, 1897, but cut the following obviously significant passage: "Unfortunately, my own father was one of these perverts and is responsible for the hysteria of my brother—all of whose symptoms are identifications—and those of several younger sisters."

The correspondence between Freud and Karl Abraham, edited by Freud's son Ernst and Abraham's daughter Hilda, appeared in *A Psychoanalytic Dialogue: The Letters of Sigmund Freud and Karl Abraham, 1907–1926,* translated by Bernard Marsh and Hilda C. Abraham (London: Hogarth Press and the Institute of Psycho-Analysis, 1965). Like the version of the Fliess letters edited by Bonaparte, Anna Freud and Kris, this is a censored version that gives a distorted picture of the two men. Ernst Falzeder is currently working on a complete version of this correspondence and, in a telling article, "Whose Freud Is It? Some Reflections on Editing Freud's Correspondence" (*International Forum of Psychoanalysis* 5, 1996, pp. 77–86), he revealed the sort of censoring that has been typical of the editing practices of the faithful. He described "overt censorship and the cultivation of certain myths," noted Anna Freud's "far-reaching influence on *The Origins*," and the way she ordered cuts and omissions. Overall, Falzeder showed how the censored version of the Freud/Abraham letters left in discussions of theory while eliminating intimate personal material, particularly hostile comments about other people.

The complete correspondence between Freud and Jung is available in *The Freud/Jung Letters: The Correspondence Between Sigmund Freud and C. G. Jung,* edited by William McGuire, translated by Ralph Manheim and R. F. C. Hull (Princeton, N.J.: Princeton University Press, 1974). This is an uncensored version of a most significant correspondence. All of the existing letters from Freud to his adolescent friend Eduard Silberstein have been published in 1990—Silberstein's half of the correspondence has not survived—in *The Letters of Sigmund Freud to Eduard Silberstein: 1871–1881,* edited by Walter Broehlich, translated by Arnold J. Pomerans (Cambridge, Mass.: Harvard University Press, 1990). These letters give a revealing picture of the mind of the young Freud. All of the letters between Freud and Ernest Jones appeared in a version edited by R. Andrew Paskauskas, *The Complete Correspondence of Sigmund Freud and Ernest Jones: 1908–1939* (Cambridge, Mass.: Harvard University Press, 1993). Of great interest are the letters between Freud and Sándor Ferenczi, two volumes of which have appeared: Eva Brabant, Ernst Falzeder, and Patrizia Giampieri-Deutsch, eds., *The Correspondence of Sigmund Freud and Sándor Ferenczi,* vol. 1, 1908–1914, and Ernst Falzeder and Eva Brabant, eds., with the collaboration of Patrizia Giampieri-Deutsch, *The Correspondence of Sigmund Freud and Sándor Ferenczi,* vol. 2, *1914–1919* (Cambridge, Mass.: Harvard University Press, 1993 and 1996). The third and final volume apparently will not be published. Other collections include an incomplete selection of the correspondence with the Swiss pastor Oskar Pfister, *Psychoanalysis and Faith: The Letters of Sigmund Freud and Oskar Pfister,* edited by Heinrich Meng and Ernst L. Freud, translated by Eric Mosbacher (New York: Basic Books, 1963); a selection of correspondence with the writer Arnold Zweig edited by Ernst L.

Freud, *The Letters of Sigmund Freud and Arnold Zweig* (New York: Harcourt, Brace and World, 1970); and the correspondence with his friend and supporter Lou Andreas-Salomé, in Ernst Pfeiffer, ed., *Sigmund Freud and Lou Andreas-Salomé: Letters,* translated by William Robson-Scott and Elaine Robson-Scott (New York: Harcourt Brace Jovanovich, 1972).

Biographies

Fritz Wittels's, *Sigmund Freud: His Personality, His Teaching and His School* (London: Allen and Unwin, 1924) was the first published biography of Freud. Wittels heard Freud lecture around the turn of the century and joined the Wednesday Society in 1905, where he was a participant until 1910. The strengths of this book come from his firsthand observations during the years when he was in the Vienna group, and attended the international congresses, its limitations from Wittels's biases and the unavailability of much information in 1924 that later became public. Wittels's attitude toward Freud was mixed; he saw him as the greatest psychological genius of the age, thought *The Three Essays* was his most important book, and accepted the theories of sexuality and the Oedipus complex without question. He also shared Freud's retrograde ideas about women. On the other hand, he was aware that Freud could not accept the contributions of others and referred to him as "a despot who will not tolerate the slightest deviation from his doctrine" (p. 18). It was this, apparently, that led to his own resignation from the Vienna Society in 1910. Wittels accepted Freud's own version of his childhood, family life, and the breaks with Breuer, Adler, and Jung, though he was a coworker of Stekel's and valued his work because it was based on extensive clinical evidence. He believed that the conflicts within the psychoanalytic movement were driven by quests for political power more than theoretical differences, and saw Freud's increasing interest in metapsychology—which he characterized as an unfortunate move from science to philosophy—as a result of his inability to absorb the contributions of Adler, Stekel, and others.

Ernest Jones's three-volume biography, *The Life and Work of Sigmund Freud,* vol. 1, *The Formative Years and the Great Discoveries, 1856–1900,* vol. 2, *The Years of Maturity, 1901–1919;* and vol. 3, *The Last Phase, 1919–1939* (New York: Basic Books, 1953, 1955, 1957), is the officially sanctioned biography—Jones's dedication reads, "To Anna Freud, True Daughter of an Immortal Sire"—and Anna allowed him access to many unpublished materials. Jones was an active participant in the psychoanalytic movement almost from the beginning; he was a member of the Committee, knew most of the other early analysts, and was a loyal combatant through the psychoanalytic wars. He did not question Freud's stature as hero and saw almost everything through the lens of classical theory; in fact, in his later years he moved toward the ideas of Melanie Klein, thus becoming even more prone than Freud to interpretations in terms of infantile instinctual drives. His own relations with a number of the early analysts were less than friendly—Rank and Ferenczi were the objects of particular hostility—so his accounts of their conflicts with Freud are not to be trusted. Nevertheless, if one keeps these biases in mind, there remains a wealth of detailed, firsthand material in Jones.

Max Schur's *Freud: Living and Dying* (New York: International Universities Press, 1972) is an important resource. Schur was Freud's personal physician during his last years; it was he who gave Freud the morphine to end his life when the cancer had reached an unbearable stage. The book contains much valuable information, particularly about Freud's medical history; for example, it has the most detailed account of Freud's cardiac problems of the 1890s, as well as a discussion of the themes of death in Freud's writing. Schur was also the first person to publish an account of the Emma Eckstein episode—omitted from the Bonaparte-Anna Freud-Kris version of the Fliess letters—in a 1966 article. Like Jones, Schur, who later became a classical analyst in America, was unwavering in his loyalty to Freud, and his book should be read with that in mind.

Roland Clark's *Freud: The Man and the Cause* (New York: Random House, 1980) is a readable account with much useful information, perhaps the best of the existing biographies. Clark was not a psychoanalyst or therapist, which has its advantages and limitations. He was not held back by ties of loyalty, as Jones was, yet he had no way of understanding psychoanalytic ideas and therapy outside of the Freudian framework. The book was published before the complete Fliess letters, and other vital primary materials, were available, which is a serious limitation.

Peter Gay's *Freud: A Life for Our Time* (New York: Norton, 1988) is the best-known modern biography. Gay had access to almost all of the new scholarly material, including Masson's version of the complete Fliess letters. He presents his work as fair, scrupulously documented, and objective—though, in my view, it is not. He amassed a great deal of scholarly and archival material, including sources in German that were not available in English, and interviewed a number of people. The book also contains much of the evidence surrounding the various psychoanalytic controversies. The problem is that none of this evidence seems to have had any effect on Gay's view of Freud, which remains as worshipful as that of Jones. One comes away from this biography believing that Freud was on the right side of all the controversies, that he was the hero and the others cowards, petty, or mentally disturbed. This can be seen most clearly in Gay's version of the relationships with Breuer, Stekel, Adler, Jung, Rank, and Ferenczi. Like Freud, he rarely dealt with these controversies with an evenhanded consideration of evidence, but preferred to interpret the motives of the participants and slanted his account with rhetorical language. For example, he presented Freud's version of Breuer's supposed flight from Bertha Pappenheim (pp. 66–67) when she revealed her erotic transference as fact, even though he cited Henri F. Ellenberger, *The Discovery of the Unconscious,* and Albert Hirschmüller, *The Life and Work of Josef Breuer: Physiology and Psychoanalysis* (New York: New York University Press, 1989) in the original 1979 German edition, in a footnote (p. 664), both of whom demonstrated that Breuer continued to treat Bertha for some years after his supposed flight (see chapter 9 of this volume for a full account).

Gay's version of the end of the Freud-Ferenczi relationship, including Freud's report that Ferenczi became psychotic in his final days, contained the same kind of distortion as his account of Breuer's treatment of Bertha Pappenheim. He perpetuated the rumors about Ferenczi's mental instability, describing his "virtual merging with his analysands [in a] . . . mystical sense of union with the universe, a kind of self-made pantheism" (pp. 576–586). A review of Ferenczi's late papers—see chapter 24—revealed that there is no substance to this characterization. Gay went on to quote Freud with approval when he said that Ferenczi suffered a "grave delusional outbreak . . . a mental degeneration which took the form of a paranoia." Michael Balint was with Ferenczi in Budapest during his final days and published a letter (Michael Balint, "Sándor Ferenczi's Last Years" [letter to the editor], *International Journal of Psychoanalysis* 39, 1958, pp. 68–71) correcting these rumors after they appeared in Jones's biography. Gay did not cite this source, and the same kind of treatment was accorded the other dissidents.

Gay argued that his biography differed from Jones's in the picture he presented of Freud's mother. It is true that in the chapter on Freud's childhood, he referred to Amalia as "doting, energetic, and domineering," whereas Jones left out the "domineering." And Gay did describe the losses of the early years. However, he buried the more complete version of Amalia's difficult personality five hundred pages into the text (pp. 504–505) and, more to the point, none of this information had any effect on Gay's understanding of Freud's early life, which is conceptualized in the standard terms: that he was motivated by curiosity aroused by the complex family network, and that his conflicts were oedipal and sexual. Gay did not seriously consider theories other than Freud's; for example, John Bowlby, whose work on attachment, loss, and grief appeared in psychoanalytic journals as early as 1960, did not even appear in this book. Heinz Kohut, whose ideas about the powerfully motivating need for ideal figures fit Freud very closely, was dismissed by Gay as follows: "[His ideas] are still experimental and tentative, having been written before Kohut turned his particular reading of narcissism into an ideology" (p. 766). In sum, Gay and I consider much of the same evidence but come to very different conclusions because he can only see Freud as he presented himself.

In the "Bibliographic Essay" at the back of *Freud: A Life for Our Time* (pp. 741–779), Gay sorted through much of the vast literature on Freud and the movement. It is here that he engaged other authors who line up on various sides of the psychoanalytic controversies. Jones's biography, Gay wrote, while not without faults, "contains many astute judgements"; a biographical sketch by Eissler and Schur is "dependable"; Schur's book, *Freud: Living and Dying*, contains "judicious, well-informed judgments"; Hanns Sachs's *Freud: Master and Friend* is "admiring but not sycophantic, it 'feels' right" (it is hard to imagine a more adoring picture; Sachs calls Freud "a good hater" and thinks this is a virtue); Lionel Trilling's 1955 Freud lecture is "a brilliant, civilized ruminative defense"; and Heinz Hartmann's 1960 Freud lecture "repays close reading" (see pp. 743–745). All of these men are adherents of orthodox analysis. In discussing Freud's theories of aggression and the death instinct, Gay selected "some outstanding contributions"; all the authors he cited are members of the orthodox fold: Otto Fenichel, Anna Freud, Beata Rank, Heinz Hartmann, Ernst Kris, Rudolph Loewenstein, and Kurt Eissler. There is no consideration of critical views of this most problematic aspect of psychoanalytic theory. Overall, most of the main areas of controversy are not spelled out and alternative positions are not given a fair hearing.

While the commentators that Gay approved were described as "dependable," "reliable," "astute," "well-informed," and "judicious," those who expressed differing views were denigrated with a different set of adjectives and innuendos. Gay quoted a damning review of Paul Roazen's *Freud and His Followers* (New York: Knopf, 1975) by Richard Wollheim, which concluded, "Freud has as good a friend in Professor Roazen as ever Brutus found in Mark Antony," and added, "Precisely." In fact, Roazen's book contains a wealth of information about the psychoanalytic movement based on firsthand interviews with many of the participants; it is a most valuable source of primary data, dismissed by Gay without consideration of the evidence. In a similar vein, he labeled Roazen's book on Freud and Victor Tausk a "tendentious study." Helen Puner's early biography—about which more later—"is fairly hostile and neither very scholarly nor very reliable." In another instance, the book by Joseph Wortis, a psychiatrist who wrote about his experience being analyzed by Freud (see chapter 19), was dismissed as "ultimately unsatisfactory, since Wortis was not really interested in being analyzed" (p. 771). When one reads the book, it is clear that whenever Wortis raised legitimate questions, Freud attacked him with interpretations of his resistance, a tactic that Gay perpetuated.

Gay handled the many critiques of Freud's views about women in the same way, writing: "Much, indeed most, of the literature that has gathered round Freud's views on female development, specifically sexuality, is polemical; the issue has been almost completely politicized. Fortunately, analysts, male and female, have kept their heads. There are two responsible surveys . . ." He approved of several articles from psychoanalytic journals that presented minor modifications of Freud's views that were, to Gay, "clear-headed" and "rational" (see pp. 773–774). The extensive, well-documented, and persuasive literature by other authors—presumably, not "responsible," "rational," or "clear-headed"—was omitted. (See Gloria Steinem, "What if Freud Were Phyllis?" in *Moving beyond Words* [New York: Simon and Schuster, 1994, pp. 19–90], which includes extensive references to this critical literature.)

Finally, Gay dealt with that crucial issue, Freud's shift from the seduction theory to his focus on sexual instinct and fantasy, and, as might be expected, did not question Freud's version. In the "Bibliographical Essay" he commented on the criticisms raised by Jeffrey M. Masson, in his book *The Assault on Truth,* as follows:

The discussion over Freud's so-called seduction theory has been muddied by Jeffrey Moussaieff Masson [who] argues—preposterously—that Freud abandoned that theory because he could not tolerate the isolation from the Vienna medical establishment to which his radical ideas had condemned him. [Gay goes on to say that Freud never denied that seduction and rape occurred in some cases, and concluded] . . . the standard accounts of Freud's attitude toward his seduction theory, given in Jones, Vol I, 263–67, and by other writers, stand up (p. 751).

It is true that Freud never completely gave up the idea that some, presumably small, number of patients suffered sexual traumas, but, in his practice, he almost never framed his interpretations along these lines. What Gay did, overall, was to attack Masson's guesses about *why* Freud abandoned the theory—which are clearly presented by Masson as speculations—while avoiding the main question: were Freud's patients subject to sexual abuse and other forms of trauma or were their neuroses caused by their sexual impulses and fantasies? There is much evidence today that documents the widespread and extremely harmful effects of sexual abuse in childhood. See David Finkelhor, ed., *A Sourcebook on Child Sexual Abuse* (Beverly Hills, Calif.: Sage Publications, 1986); Judith L. Herman, *Trauma and Recovery* (New York: Basic Books, 1992); and Jennifer J. Freyd, *Betrayal Trauma: The Logic of Forgetting Childhood Abuse* (Cambridge, Mass.: Harvard University Press, 1996), for overviews, as well as the discussion in chapter 8. There is also overwhelming clinical evidence that real disturbing experiences of a variety of kinds lie at the root of anxiety, depression, and symptoms, and not sexual drives and fantasies. But this kind of evidence, falling outside the psychoanalytic mainstream, is not the sort of thing that Gay considered.

A large number of books containing biographical material have been published since Gay. Lisa Appignanesi and John Forrester's *Freud's Women* (London: Virago Press, 1992) has a brief biographical sketch focused on Freud's relationships with the women in his life. A search of the literature reveals, however, only two recent books that qualify as full biographies. The first is Peter M. Newton's *Freud: From Youthful Dream to Mid-Life Crisis* (New York: Guilford Press, 1995). This is an interpretation of Freud's life in terms of the stages of adult development; Newton employed a theoretical scheme of stages that run from childhood to adolescence, young adulthood, age-thirty transition, midlife transition, midlife crisis, and so forth. He then attempted to fit the major events of Freud's life within this explanatory scheme. Although he has relied on much of the new data used in the present book, in almost every instance he reached conclusions opposite to mine. Despite his use of adult-development theory, his overall conception of Freud did not depart from Jones, Gay, and other loyal followers. In his account, Amalia was an ideal mother, the Oedipus complex the major event of childhood, Freud's love for Gisela Fluss persisted for ten years, Freud's real ambition was to be a great healer, and Breuer caused the break in their relationship.

The other recent biography is Paul Ferris's *Dr. Freud: A Life* (Washington, D.C.: Counterpoint, 1997). Ferris is a novelist, journalist, and author of several other biographies. He blended both old and new material together in a book that mixes scholarship with rumor, all done in a chatty, offhand style. While there are some important pieces of new information, Ferris does not, in my view, have any understanding of what patients in therapy are struggling with—he characterizes the early "hysterics" as manipulative malingerers—and has no way of understanding the psychological dynamics of Freud or others. He cannot tell the difference between the central controversies that had long-lasting effects on Freud's life and work, and minor bits of gossip. For example, Adler and his ideas are covered in three pages, despite the fact that Freud remained obsessed with this controversy to the end of his life, while seven pages were devoted to Peter Swales's speculations about whether Freud had an affair with his sister-in-law Minna. At his worst, Ferris relied on crude language to create caricatures, as when he wrote of Freud and Jones, "If it suited both men to agree that mind-fucking was the

Father's speciality, what was there to complain about?" (p. 269). All in all, it is hard to imagine what the reader would get from this biography; certainly not a coherent sense of Freud the man, nor much understanding of the complexities of psychoanalysis.

I did not read Helen W. Puner's *Freud: His Life and His Mind* (New York: Howell, Soskin, 1947) until I was almost finished writing this book. It had been attacked by both Jones and Gay, and when I read that Anna Freud was incensed at her brother Oliver for giving information to Puner, I decided it was worth a look. Given the time when it was published, it turned out to be a most perceptive work. None of Freud's correspondence had been published in 1947—Puner did not know that there was a baby Julius who died, or anything about the actual circumstances of the family's life in Freiberg, and her picture of Freud's parents and childhood was limited to what he himself wrote. Nor did she know of the existence of someone named Wilhelm Fliess. Nevertheless, she constructed a balanced account, which includes an appreciation of his accomplishments, along with his autocratic behavior within the movement, his drive to be a hero and create a grand theory, his treatment of Martha, and the bitterness and unhappiness of his later years. Her version seems more fully human than what one finds in Jones and Gay, as seen in this insightful passage: "He came in time to act as if he *were* a Messiah. He was a kind, a benevolent, a good man, but he was kind without softness, benevolent without compassion, and good without mercy. He behaved always on the assumption that his word could not be questioned, his authority could not be opposed" (p. 253).

In addition to Freud's own publications, letters, and the biographies discussed above, I have made use of a number of other sources. Herman Nunberg and Ernst Federn, eds., *Minutes of the Vienna Psychoanalytic Society* vol. 1, 1906–1908; vol. 2, 1908–1910; vol. 3, 1910–1911; vol. 4, 1912–1918 (New York: International Universities Press, 1962, 1967, 1974, 1975) is an important source for the early days of the movement. These minutes were recorded by Otto Rank, then secretary of the society, and they provide a most informative account of the discussions and debates between Freud and the first psychoanalysts. Here one can read the early contributions of Adler, Rank, Stekel, Tausk, Sabina Speilrein, and others in their own words.

Henri F. Ellenberger's *The Discovery of the Unconscious* is an extremely valuable book. He placed Freud and his work in a broad context, showing what was original and what derivative. His chapters on Adler, Jung, and the French psychotherapist Pierre Janet are illuminating. He gave a clear sense of the ways in which Janet's work as a therapist predated Freud's, and also why Janet did not have the influence that Freud did. Ellenberger carried out research on primary sources and was the first to dispel several myths, including that surrounding Breuer's treatment of Bertha Pappenheim, and the supposed hostile reception that Freud's paper on "male hysteria" received from his Viennese medical colleagues. He showed how Freud's version of his isolation and ill-treatment by his colleagues in the early years was not supported by the facts. Ellenberger also had interesting things to say about Freud's creation of a heroic myth, and the psychological disturbance he suffered in the 1890s, which he explained as a "creative illness," though he did not cite the traumas and losses that I feel are central, in part because important source materials were not available in 1970. He also shows, with a scrupulous sifting of the evidence, how Freud exaggerated the extent of anti-Semitism, the opposition of the academic world, and Victorian prejudices in order to picture himself as a hero, struggling alone against hostile forces, and how, along with this, he denigrated the achievements of predecessors, disciples, rivals, and others so that his absolute originality could be highlighted. Clark drew on Ellenberger, particularly in his discussion of the Breuer–Bertha Pappenheim affair, but Gay, whose biography appeared eighteen years after *The Discovery of the Unconscious,* devoted but a few lines to Ellenberger in his "Bibliographic Essay."

Paul Roazen's *Freud and His Followers* is based on well over one hundred interviews, carried out between 1964 and 1967, with persons who knew Freud: disciples, members of the movement, other psychoanalysts, twenty-five of Freud's patients, some of his in-laws, and three of his children. The accounts of family members and patients were published later in *Meeting Freud's Family* (Amherst: University of Massachusetts Press, 1993), and *How Freud Worked: First-Hand Accounts of Patients* (Northvale, N.J.: Jason Aronson, 1995). All these books are rich storehouses of information, based, as they are, on firsthand information. As just one example, in the course of his interviews, Roazen uncovered the fact that Anna Freud was analyzed by her father, something that she and many others had covered up for many years. *Freud and His Followers* contains chapters on the movement and loyalists, as well as on most of the major figures who broke with the Professor. While I do not agree with all of Roazen's interpretations of his material, his biographical sketch of Freud is, in my view, much more balanced than what one finds in Jones, Shur, or Gay, and the primary source material in these three books is invaluable.

Hendrik M. Ruitenbeek's *Freud as We Knew Him* (Detroit: Wayne State University Press, 1973) contains a series of short pieces by a variety of authors, many of whom knew Freud directly or had personal contact with him. This is where one finds the vignettes by Freud's sister Anna and his niece Judith Bernays Heller. Like the material provided by Roazen, one needs to read these accounts with an awareness of the allegiances of the reporter; nevertheless, they contain much valuable material.

George E. Atwood and Robert D. Stolorow published a very insightful biographical sketch of Freud in *Faces in a Cloud: Subjectivity in Personality Theory,* 2nd ed. (Northvale, N.J.: Jason Aronson, 1993). They were among the first authors to detail the pervasive effects of Freud's early maternal losses, showing how his experiences with his mother produced an intense ambivalence, and how he defended against this by maintaining an idealized image of her, with the hatred split off and finding expression toward a series of other targets. They traced the course of this pattern through his relationships with Martha and Fliess, and demonstrated its influence on his theories.

E. James Lieberman's *Acts of Will: The Life and Work of Otto Rank* (New York: The Free Press, 1985; paperback ed. with new preface, Amherst: University of Massachusetts Press, 1993) has insightful sections on Freud, the Vienna Society, and the psychoanalytic movement, as well as excellent critical discussions of Jones and Gay that parallel, and antedate, mine.

Patrick J. Mahony has carried out a series of studies of Freud as a writer, and published books covering several of the major case studies, all of which are noteworthy for the care of their scholarship, detail, and perceptivity. See Patrick J. Mahony, *Freud as a Writer* (New Haven, Conn.: Yale University Press, 1987); *Cries of the Wolf Man; Freud and the Rat Man;* and *Freud's Dora: A Psychoanalytic, Historical and Textual Study.* Mahony's remarks in the "Conclusions" of the *Dora* book are worth quoting: "Impeding the progress of psychoanalysis alone, the erroneous, idealizing, and hagiographical reactions to Freud constitute a boring yet pitiful story. It is my firm conviction, however, that despite his foibles and despite his diverse misdeeds (which must be recognized and addressed), Freud does not need idealizing protection: he is great enough to stand on his own" (p. 149).

Frank Sulloway's *Freud: Biologist of the Mind: Beyond the Psychoanalytic Legend* (New York: Basic Books, 1979) followed Ellenberger in exposing the myths that have surrounded Freud and the history of psychoanalysis, providing a good deal of additional detail. That part of his book is quite valuable. However, when Sulloway moved beyond this recasting of history, he presented his theory that Freud was a "crypto-biologist," many of whose key ideas were taken from Fliess, an interpretation which has very little to recommend it, as I argue in my 1981 essay-review of Sulloway's book.

All who work with psychoanalytic historical material owe a debt to Jeffrey M. Masson, who was able to break through the fortress of orthodoxy and publish the complete Freud/Fliess correspondence. Also of interest is Masson's *The Assault on Truth: Freud and Child Sexual Abuse* (New York: Farrar, Straus and Giroux, 1984). Here he questions—correctly in my opinion—the orthodox account of the abandonment of the seduction theory, though his speculations about why Freud made this shift are not persuasive. The book also contains valuable information on the later life of Emma Eckstein, including an important letter to her from Freud. Many in the psychoanalytic establishment turned on Masson, treating his work in the same way Freud did those who questioned his theories, and Masson himself became a critic of all forms of psychotherapy in *Against Therapy: Emotional Tyranny and the Myth of Psychological Healing* (New York: Fontana, 1990). Few have commented on what, in my view, is one of his most interesting publications, *Final Analysis: The Making and Unmaking of a Psychoanalyst* (New York: Fontana, 1992). This book recounted the analysis that he underwent as part of his training at the Toronto Psychoanalytic Institute with a senior analyst who was autocratic, arbitrary, and abusive. Some may think the picture is extreme, but I am familiar, both from descriptions of psychoanalytic trainees as well as from observing a number of such analysts, that Masson's account is entirely believable.

When this book was near completion, I came upon Madelon Sprengnether's *The Spectral Mother: Freud, Feminism and Psychoanalysis* (Ithaca, N.Y.: Cornell University Press, 1990), along with two of her later essays: "Mourning Freud," in Anthony Elliott and Stephen Frosh, eds., *Psychoanalysis in Contexts* (New York: Routledge, 1995, pp. 142–165), and "Reading Freud's Life" (*American Imago* 52, no. 1, 1995, pp. 9–54). Of all the works I have read, Sprengnether's ideas resonate most closely with my own. Her interpretation of Freud was based on a close reading of his texts along with a critical use of the feminist literature. She astutely described his self-creation as a hero, accompanied by the denigration of the contributions of forerunners such as Janet. At the core of her analysis was his neglect of the role of the mother, both in his own life and that of his patients. She sees his creation of the Oedipus complex as an escape from the grief and mourning related to maternal loss; that is, as a defense against these emotions. She and I arrived at our closely related interpretations from partly overlapping and partly different sources. *The Spectral Mother* also contains detailed readings of a number of Freud's principal essays and cases that repay careful study, as do the two later papers that further developed her position.

As in the case of Sprengnether's work, I found Gloria Steinem's "What if Freud Were Phyllis?" when my book was almost finished. The essay is written in the form of a Swiftian satire in which Freud's anti-feminine biases are highlighted by imagining him as a woman expressing a reverse set of views about men: penis envy becomes womb envy, hysteria becomes testyria, and so on. The satire is accompanied by an extensive set of footnotes, which shows that Steinem has mastered a great deal of the current literature and makes many of the points, in starker form, that are elaborated in this book. While the effect is almost entirely critical of Freud, perhaps inevitable in a satire, the essay is well worth reading.

Phyllis Grosskurth's *The Secret Ring: Freud's Inner Circle and the Politics of Psychoanalysis* (Reading, Mass.: Addison-Wesley, 1991) is an account of the formation of "the Committee"— the palace guard created by the small group of Freud's most loyal followers in 1912—that contains portraits of its members and many of the peripheral players. It is a scholarly and well-documented work that draws on all the sources available as of 1990 and gives a good picture of Freud's tactics as a politician, his need to control and dominate the psychoanalytic movement, and his cold treatment of all those who did not put "the cause" above all else.

Notes

Abbreviations Used in Notes

Freud, *[Title]*: All of Freud's publications, identified by title only, are taken from *The Standard Edition of the Complete Psychological Works of Sigmund Freud*, vol. 1–24, ed. and trans. by James Strachey, in collaboration with Anna Freud, assisted by Alix Strachey and Alan Tyson (London: Hogarth Press, 1953–1974).

Freud, *Letters*: E. L. Freud, ed., *The Letters of Sigmund Freud.*

Freud/Abraham: H. Abraham and E. L. Freud, eds., *A Psychoanalytic Dialogue.*

Freud/Ferenczi: E. Brabent and E. Falzeder, eds., *The Correspondence*, vols. 1 and 2.

Freud/Fliess: J. M. Masson, ed., *The Complete Letters.*

Freud/Jones: R. A. Paskauskas, ed., *The Complete Correspondence.*

Freud/Jung: W. McGuire, ed., *The Freud/Jung Letters.*

Freud/Pfister: H. Meng and E. L. Freud, eds., *Psychoanalysis and Faith.*

Freud/Salomé: E. Pfister, ed., *Freud–Andreas-Salomé: Letters.*

Freud/Silberstein: W. Broehlich, ed., *The Letters.*

Freud/Zweig: E. L. Freud, ed., *The Letters.*

Introduction

1 *"I have destroyed all"* Freud to Martha, Freud, *Letters,* pp. 140–141.

Chapter 1. A Traumatic Infancy

Freud's own recollections of his infancy and childhood, like anyone else's, are a combination of fact, fantasy, reconstruction, memories of what his parents told him later, and things he wanted to believe. While his writings abound in personal reference, both direct and symbolic, he only published two more or less direct accounts; one, his paper *Screen Memories,* of 1899, and the other, the *Autobiographical Study* of 1925, though the second contains the briefest mention of the earliest years. The richest personal material can be found in the letters Freud wrote to Fliess during the time of his self-analysis, which contain the memories that he was able to recover of his infancy. There are also his own dreams, reported in *The Interpretation of Dreams,* and *On Dreams,* and various slips, errors, and associations in *The Psychopathology of Everyday Life.* To this material can be added those indirect or symbolic references that appear throughout his writings: things he "sees" in other people and in works of literature, history, and other sources. Such comments provide evidence for the recurrent patterns of Freud's personality, laid down by his early experiences, as these are revealed in his discussion of certain issues—infancy and childhood, sexuality and pleasure, anxiety and loss—that he works and reworks throughout his life. In addition to these indirect sources are those emotional-relational configurations—for example, his way of relating to women and his love-hate relations with his male intimates—that occur repeatedly over the years.

The existing biographies of Jones, Clark, and Gay all contain accounts of Freud's infancy but, in each case, they are brief and do not move beyond his own reconstructed version. Schur provides more detail though he, too, does not question Freud's own interpretation. The best and most detailed account is Marianne Krüll's *Freud and His Father,* translated by Arnold J. Pomerans (New York: Norton, 1986; original German edition, 1979). Krüll presents a full picture of the Jewish shtetl background of Jacob Freud's family as well as the most detailed description of the years in Freiberg, drawing on many original German sources, some of which, such as the papers by Gicklhorn and Sajner, are not available in English. Krüll is an independent thinker whose research is not constrained by psychoanalytic orthodoxy. However, when she comes to interpreting her carefully amassed data, she turns to speculations that are not very persuasive. Her thesis is that Jacob Freud felt guilty for moving away from the Orthodox Judaism of his father and that he passed on an unconscious "mandate" to his first-born son to expunge this guilt, a theory that is then used to account for many aspects of Freud's life and thought.

In addition to the personal and biographical information about Freud, the present version of his infancy relies on the large and impressive amount of research on infancy and mother-infant interaction that has appeared in recent years. A complete listing of all these sources would be too cumbersome; a selection must begin with John Bowlby's *Attachment and Loss* (New York: Basic Books, 1969–1973). There are many later elaborations of his ideas: see Mary Ainsworth, M. C. Blehar, E. Waters, and S. Wall, *Patterns of Attachment* (Hillsdale, N.J.: Erlbaum, 1978), and Mary Main and N. Kaplan, "Security in Infancy, Childhood and Adulthood: A Move to the Level of Representation," in I. Bretherton and E. Waterns, eds., *Monographs of the Society for Research in Child Development* (1986). Daniel Stern, in *The Interpersonal World of the Infant: A View from Psychoanalysis and Developmental Psychology* (New York: Basic Books, 1985), presents a clear integration of infant research and psychoanalysis. Mother-infant interaction is documented in Beatrice Beebe and Frank M. Lachmann, "Mother-Infant Mutual Influence and Precursors of Psychic Structure," in Arnold Goldberg, ed., *Progress in Self-psychology,* vol. 3 (Hillsdale, N.J.: Analytic Press, 1988), pp. 3–25. An excellent article by Beatrice Beebe, Frank Lachmann, and Joseph Jaffe, "Mother-Infant Interaction Structures and Presymbolic Self—and Object Representations" (*Psychoanalytic Dialogues* 7, 1997, pp. 133–182), contains an extensive and up-to-date bibliography. See also Edward Tronick, "Emotions and Emotional Communication in Infants" (*American Psychologist* 44, 1989, pp. 112–119). Work on infant memory can be found in Michael Moscovitch, *Infant Memory* (New York: Plenum Press, 1984), and infant emotional development is described in the excellent book by L. Alan Sroufe, *Emotional Development: The Organization of Emotional Life in the Early Years* (Cambridge, U.K.: Cambridge University Press, 1995), which contains references to many other sources.

The research on infant development will permit us to clarify the effects of trauma and losses as well as the capacities—such as dissociation—that children have for dealing with such events. An excellent review of the distinctions between "dissociation" and "repression," as well as the issue of memory and amnesia in early childhood, can be found in Jennifer J. Freyd, *Betrayal Trauma: The Logic of Forgetting Childhood Abuse* (Cambridge, Mass.: Harvard University Press, 1996). Early traumas are stored as "procedural memories," which produce "implicit knowledge" that is typically not represented with language. Relatively recent research on memory will also allow us to review Freud's claims about what infants and very young children can remember with what has now been established about their psychological capacities. As one example, in his *Screen Memories* paper, Freud reports a "memory" of his years in

Freiberg in which he "was never free from a longing for the beautiful woods near our home, in which—as one of my memories from those days tells me—I used to run off from my father, almost before I had learnt to walk" (p. 312). Babies learn to walk around the age of one and they don't "run off" from their fathers, but venture gingerly away from their caretakers and, if they lose contact, become anxious. Nor are two-year-olds capable of being in love with "the beautiful woods"; they are primarily attached to the adults who care for them. Freud's "memory," like his oedipal reconstruction, gives him more independent capacities than he had at the age described. In addition, a love of nature is a later achievement; Freud's longing for the woods is an idealized picture that he created at a later time to shield himself from the very painful events he experienced in Freiberg. (See also Freud's reference to a happy time in Freiberg in his "Letter to the Burgomaster of Příbor," in the *Standard Edition,* vol. 21, p. 259.)

7   *Freud has emerged*   Charles Rycroft, "Freud, Sigmund: 1856–1939," in Justin Wintle, ed., *Makers of Modern Culture* (New York: Facts on File, 1981), p. 177.

7   The information on Freiberg, the situation of Jews, the preceding years of Jewish history, the specific situation of Jacob Freud and Amalia, and the extended family are taken primarily from Krüll, *Freud and His Father,* and the additional sources she cites, supplemented by Jones, Gay, Clark, and Schur.

10   *"I have also long"*   Freud/Fliess, p. 268. See also Freud, *The Interpretation of Dreams,* p. 483.

10   *In a rare published*   See Freud, *Screen Memories.*

11   *The losses began*   The most detailed account of this period is in Krüll, who provides the information about the death of Amalia's brother Julius, not cited in other sources.

12   *"The expression on my mother's"*   Freud, *The Interpretation of Dreams,* p. 583.

12   *"the three fates who"*   Ibid., pp. 204–205.

13   *"I greeted my"*   Freud/Fliess, p. 268.

13   *"The turning away from"*   Freud, "Femininity," in *The New Introductory Lectures,* pp. 121–123.

14   *dislike of this sister*   Jones, *The Life and Work,* vol. 1, p. 10, says that Freud never liked his sister Anna. Freud later wrote to Fliess in 1900 that "my eldest sister Anna and her four children have just arrived there from New York. I do not know what this means and suspect nothing good. I have never had any special relationship with her." Freud/Fliess, p. 406.

14   *Freud was cared for*   Information on Freud's nursemaid can be found in the biographies; the most detailed account is in Krüll, *Freud and His Father,* pp. 119–122.

14   *"Told me a great"*   Freud/Fliess, p. 268.

15   *"I shall be grateful"*   Freud/Fliess, p. 269.

15   *"my mother was nowhere"*   Ibid., p. 271. The *Kasten* memory is retold in *The Psychopathology of Everyday Life* (pp. 49–51), with a footnote added in 1924 giving it a sexual interpretation that was missing from the version in the Fliess letters. The fact that the nursemaid is made into a witch-like figure fit with the way the omnipresent servants of Freud's society became targets on which to vent anger that was too threatening to direct toward parents. This gave a concrete reality to the division of women into idealized— loving, slender, beautiful—and devalued types. The infant Freud's desperate need for his mother's love made it far too dangerous to express his frustration and rage toward her. It was much safer to attack the servants, who were viewed by others as inferior beings.

16   *Jacob Freud's business collapsed*   The account of the collapse of Jacob's business is attributed by Jones to a Moravian economic downturn and anti-Semitism, an account repeated in all the other biographies. Krüll, *Freud and His Father,* corrects these versions; see pp. 143–145.

16   *the "original catastrophe"*   Freud, *Screen Memories,* p. 314.

16   *On the departure*   References to Freud's travel phobia can be found in Freud/Fliess, pp. 268–269, 392. See also Jones, *The Life and Work*, vol. I, p. 13. Eva Rosenfeld, who was analyzed by Freud, and was a close friend of Anna's and the entire family, remembered how "terribly nervous" Freud was on a train ride until his luggage had been assembled, which she traced to the "trauma" of leaving home as a small boy. See the interview with Eva Rosenfeld in Roazen, *How Freud Worked*, p. 215.

16   *"you yourself have seen"*   Freud/Fliess, p. 268.

17   *The traumatic experiences*   Discussions of the dissociation of traumatic memories, both in children and adults, can be found in many sources. Overviews with many references are available in Judith L. Herman, *Trauma and Recovery* (New York: Basic Books, 1992), and Freyd, *Betrayal Trauma*. Other useful sources include David Finkelhor, ed., *A Sourcebook on Child Sexual Abuse* (Beverly Hills, Calif.: Sage Publications, 1986); Jody M. Davies and Mary G. Frawley, *Treating the Adult Survivor of Childhood Sexual Abuse* (New York: Basic Books, 1994); Richard P. Kluft, ed., *Incest-Related Syndromes of Adult Psychopathology* (Washington, D.C.: American Psychiatric Press, 1990); Lenore C. Terr, *Unchained Memories: True Stories of Traumatic Memories, Lost and Found* (New York: Basic Books, 1994); and Basil A. van der Kolk, *Psychological Trauma* (Washington, D.C.: American Psychiatric Press, 1987).

18   *"A single idea"*   Freud/Fliess, p. 268.

19   *"A mother is only"*   Freud, "Femininity," in *New Introductory Lectures*, p. 133.

19   *"I was not anxious"*   Freud, *The Interpretation of Dreams*, p. 584.

20   *"An intimate friend"*   Ibid., p. 483.

20   *Freud's attribution of guilt*   Freud's claim that his feelings of guilt began with the death of Julius when he was under two years old is not consistent with studies of the emotional development of children. Infants can feel shame as early as two, but it is externally based; it requires an adult presence. Guilt, along with pride, does not appear until the third year, with greater differentiation of the self and the internalization of standards. The same applies to Freud's retrospective account of his "sexual" play with John and Pauline. The best discussion of these issues, including additional references, can be found in Sroufe, *Emotional Development*; see, especially, pp. 72, 194, 198–200.

21   *"In the self-confessions"*   Siegfried Bernfeld, "Sigmund Freud, M.D., 1882–1885," *International Journal of Psycho-Analysis* 32: 204–217 (1951), p. 208.

Chapter 2. *Childhood and Adolescence*

The details of Freud's childhood are found in all the biographies; Krüll, as usual, provides the fullest and best documented account. The descriptions of Freud's father and mother come, primarily, from his son Martin's memoir, *Sigmund Freud: Man and Father* (New York: Vanguard Press, 1958; later editions titled *Glory Reflected*). The brief reminiscences of Freud's sister Anna and his niece Judith Bernays Heller appear in Ruitenbeek, *Freud as We Knew Him*. The most detailed picture of Freud as an adolescent is revealed in the letters he wrote to his close friend Eduard Silberstein.

22   *"When I was three"*   Freud, *Screen Memories*, p. 312.

24   *"It was in the seventh"*   Quoted in Ernst Freud, Lucie Freud, and Ilse Grubrich-Simitis, eds., *Sigmund Freud, His Life in Pictures and Words*, trans. Christine Trollope (New York: Harcourt, Brace, Jovanovich, 1976), p. 134.

24   *"Reading and studying"*   Jones, *The Life and Work*, vol. 1, p. 21.

24   *When Sigmund was nine*   The most detailed account of the scandal involving Josef Freud and counterfeit money can be found in Nicholas Rand and Maria Torok, *Questions for Freud: The Secret History of Psychoanalysis* (Cambridge, Mass.: Harvard University Press, 1997). See also Krüll, *Freud and His Father*, pp. 164–166. Rand and Torok,

in my opinion, give far too much importance to the counterfeit money scandal as an influence on Freud's life, though their book contains several other useful historical explorations, including a comparison of Freud's literary analysis of Jensen's *Gradiva* with the text of the original novel, which again demonstrates his avoidance of death and loss.

25 *Emanuel, his family* Information on the later lives of Emanuel, Philipp, and their families can be found in Krüll, *Freud and His Father,* pp. 172–176, and Michael Molnar, "Sigmund Freud's Notes on Faces and Men," in Michael S. Roth, ed., *Freud: Conflict and Culture* (New York: Knopf, 1998), pp. 42–44.

25 *"Yesterday I met"* Freud to Martha, in Freud, *Letters,* p. 86.

25 *"I know from my youth"* Freud/Fliess, p. 374.

25 *"Every member of my family"* Martin Freud, *Sigmund Freud: Man and Father,* p. 10.

26 *"tall and broad"* Judith Bernays Heller, "Freud's Mother and Father," in Ruitenbeek, *Freud as We Knew Him,* p. 335.

26 *"When he isn't exactly grouchy"* Freud to Martha, in Freud, *Letters,* p. 22.

26 *"I cannot think of any need"* Freud, *Civilization and Its Discontents,* p. 72.

27 *"When I was a young man"* Freud, *The Interpretation of Dreams,* p. 197.

27 *identify with powerful, dominating men* Freud referred to his idolization of Hannibal and also characterized himself as a "conquistador" in the Fliess correspondence (see Freud/Fliess, p. 398). The Hamburg educator Joachim Heinrich Campe published his book *The Discovery of America* between 1786 and 1813, and it was widely used as a text in German-speaking schools; it is likely that Freud read it as a boy. The Native Americans were described as poor and ignorant and Cortés, the great conquistador, as a man of "unusual courage and indefatigable endurance of all discomfort, a restless hard pushing mind [with] a burning desire to excel." Campe encouraged German children to emulate Cortés and become, like him, a "great man." See Susanne Zantop, *Colonial Fantasies: Family and Nation in Precolonial Germany, 1770–1870* (Durham, N.C.: Duke University Press, 1997, p. 116).

28 *"From his nursery"* Freud, *Some Reflections on Schoolboy Psychology,* p. 244.

28 *"They were highly emotional"* Martin Freud, *Sigmund Freud: Man and Father,* p. 11.

29 *"[Jacob] remained quiet"* Judith Bernays Heller, "Freud's Mother and Father," pp. 336–339. Additional information about Amalia's character is supplied by Alexander Freud's wife in Roazen, *Meeting Freud's Family,* p. 195, and Robert Jokl, a Viennese psychoanalyst and former patient of Freud's, in Roazen, *How Freud Worked.* Jokl "thought that Freud was 'very dependent' on his mother, and that much of Freud's tendency to anxiety could be traced to his inner reliance on her. Freud's mother was 'very small, nice and dominating'; she had a family 'court' around her" (p. 140).

30 *"When I was a child"* Freud, *An Autobiographical Study,* p. 8.

30 *At the* Gymnasium For evidence that Freud was not rebellious as a schoolboy, see Ellenberger, *The Discovery of the Unconscious.* Ellenberger cites the original research of Gicklhorn, based on a study of the school archives, and concludes, that Freud "was not among the misdemeanants, but one of those who cooperated with the authorities by giving information" (p. 458).

30 *Significantly, with all his* For Freud's claim that he forgot the little Hebrew he once knew, see Gay, *Freud,* pp. 599–600. Clark, *Freud* (p. 12), states that Freud refused to accept royalties from Hebrew and Yiddish translations of his works. Krüll, *Freud and His Father* (p. 138), reports that Amalia spoke Yiddish, even in old age, so that, in the earliest years in Freiberg, Freud was probably immersed in this language. Research has shown how early memories are encoded in the language that the child grows up with and that such memories are less available to adult consciousness in a second language acquired later in life. Thus, another reason for Freud's wish to avoid Yiddish; not only were they the sounds associated with poor shtetl Jews, but they were connected to his

own early traumas. See RoseMarie Perez Foster, *The Power of Language in the Clinical Process* (Hillsdale, N.J.: Jason Aronson, 1997).

31 *"I used to find"* Freud, *Some Reflections on Schoolboy Psychology*, p. 241.

31 *"When I was a boy"* Alexander Freud, quoted in Ernst Freud, Lucie Freud, and Ilse Grubrich-Simitis, *Sigmund Freud: His Life in Pictures and Words*, p. 59.

32 *"Not only did he read"* Anna Freud Bernays, "My Brother, Sigmund Freud," in Ruitenbeek, *Freud as We Knew Him*, p. 142. Freud's sister wrote her impressions of family life when she was close to eighty years old and some of her memories are no doubt inaccurate. She tends to remember things as better than they were, calling her father "brilliant" and describing the living quarters as less impoverished then they were. Still, certain specific memories have the ring of truth and fit with other information about Freud's childhood.

32 *"becoming vain, coquettish"* Freud, quoted in Jones, *The Life and Work*, vol. 1, p. 21.

33 *"In spite of his youth"* Ibid., p. 142. Martin Freud, in *Sigmund Freud: Man and Father*, p. 19, reports that his father prohibited a piano in the apartment of his own family.

33 *"the pained expression"* Jones, *The Life and Work*, vol. 1, pp. 17–18. Freud's aversion to music is remarked on by his later analysand Mark Brunswick, in Roazen, *How Freud Worked*. V. I. Lenin, who used to love music as a boy, would not listen to it later in order to harden himself as a revolutionary.

34 *The life of the writer* Schnitzler's autobiography, *My Youth in Vienna*, trans. Catherine Hutter (New York: Holt, Rinehart and Winston, 1970), gives an excellent picture of life in Vienna during these years, as do a number of his plays and novels.

35 *"We soon became"* Freud to Julie Braun-Vogelstein, in Freud, *Letters*, p. 379.

35 *"We used to be"* Freud to Martha, in Freud, *Letters*, p. 96.

36 *"I was seventeen"* Freud, *Screen Memories*, p. 34.

36 *"It would seem that"* Freud/Silberstein, pp. 17–18.

37 *"She asked me how"* Ibid., p. 18.

37 *"A thinking man is"* Ibid., pp. 92–93.

Chapter 3. The Early Adult Years: Searching for an Identity

39 The information on Vienna in the latter half of the nineteenth century, the situation of Jews, the percentages of Jews in different professions, and related facts are taken from Steven Beller, *Vienna and the Jews: 1867–1938* (Cambridge, U.K.: Cambridge University Press, 1989); George E. Berkley, *Vienna and Its Jews: The Tragedy of Success, 1880s–1980s* (Cambridge, Mass.: Abt Books, 1988); Josef Fraenkel, ed., *The Jews of Austria: Essays on Their Life, History and Destruction* (London: Vallentine, Mitchell, 1970); and Marsha L. Rozenblit, *The Jews of Vienna, 1867–1914: Assimilation and Identity* (Albany: State University of New York Press, 1983). Specific information on Freud's experience can be found in the biographies by Jones, Clark, and Gay. Freud continued to write to his friend Silberstein during his time in the university and these letters provide valuable information in his own voice.

40 *An important difference* The situation of assimilated Jews in Freud's Vienna was complex. While they cut themselves off from outward signs of their past, there were ways in which they could not escape their Jewishness. Their very success—financial, professional, social—made them the objects of hatred to the many small tradesmen and shopkeepers, almost all Catholic, whose lives were disrupted by the Industrial Revolution. The members of these groups blamed their plight on the upper classes and, since many bankers and industrialists were Jewish, it was a situation ripe for the return of anti-Semitism. Looking back in the light of later events, one can see that the success of the Viennese Jews was an interlude between centuries of discrimination and oppression and

the new racial anti-Semitism soon to befall them. They could not know what was coming, of course, and most of them lived comfortably. They did not dwell on the travails suffered by previous generations, nor did they identify with the new immigrants who were living reminders of shame and poverty. Nevertheless, their heritage lived on in corners of their minds. Stories they heard from their parents or grandparents made clear that persecution was but a generation or two in the past. And there were continuing signs; in spite of their success and the many opportunities open to them, they still encountered instances of prejudice. Children would be taunted, called names, and occasionally beaten up in certain neighborhoods, and there were, as the century drew to a close, growing anti-Semitic movements at the university.

In 1885, Karl Lueger was elected mayor of Vienna on an anti-Semitic platform. It was sheer opportunism on his part: he had no personal animus toward Jews and, once elected, he did nothing to restrict their freedom. In fact, they flourished during his thirteen-year administration as never before. He also proved to be a very effective mayor, instituting many public projects that benefited the city. Nevertheless, the election of a mayor on an openly anti-Semitic platform legitimized these beliefs and helped prepare the way for the more violent anti-Semitism of the twentieth century.

41   *The father, he wrote*   Freud to Emil Fluss, quoted in Gay, *Freud*, p. 19.
42   *"There is the pleasant"*   Freud/Silberstein, p. 78.
43   *"Braun is here but"*   Ibid., p. 166.
43   *Eduard Silberstein came from*   The most detailed description of Silberstein and his life is found in ibid., which includes a memoir by Silberstein's granddaughter.
44   *"He was an intellectual"*   Rosita Braunstein Vieyra, "Biographical Notes on Dr. Eduard Silberstein," in ibid., pp. 193–194.
44   *"Come to Vienna"*   Ibid., pp. 27, 36, 45.
44   *"I have your melancholy"*   Ibid., p. 77.
45   *"My mother would"*   Ibid., pp. 21, 24.
45   *"feminine creatures whose"*   Ibid., p. 83.
45   *"deleterious effect flattery"*   Ibid., p. 93.
45   *"Young ladies are boring"*   Ibid., p. 40.
46   *"I am going to continue"*   Ibid., p. 83.
46   *"Italian goddesses . . . specimens"*   Ibid., p. 153.
46   *"treated unsuccessfully by Freud"*   Rosita Braunstein Vieyra, "Biographical Notes on Dr. Eduard Silberstein," in ibid., p. 192.
46   *"threw herself to"*   Walter Boehlich, in ibid., p. xv. The other biographies, somewhat surprisingly, do not report anything about the suicide of Silberstein's wife at Freud's office.
47   *"semi-nocturnal"*   Ibid., p. 87.
47   *"Under the powerful"*   Freud, *An Autobiographical Study*, p. 8.
48   *"no particular partiality"*   Ibid., p. 8.
48   *"Of the next, my first"*   Freud/Silberstein, p. 24.
48   *"whom I revere"*   Ibid., p. 96.
48   *"godless medical man"*   Ibid., p. 70.
49   *When he began*   The most detailed account of the University of Vienna and its medical faculty is in Gay, *Freud*, pp. 29–31.
49   *In 1875 the family*   Freud speaks of his trip to Manchester in Freud/Silberstein, p. 174.
50   *"At length, in"*   Freud, *An Autobiographical Study*, p. 9.
51   *"Brücke and I"*   Emil Du Bois-Reymond, quoted in David Shakow, "Psychoanalysis and American Psychology," in Louis Breger, ed., *Clinical-Cognitive Psychology: Models and Integrations* (Englewood Cliffs, N.J.: Prentice-Hall, 1969), p. 60.
52   *"He was a small man"*   Jones, *The Life and Work*, vol. 1, p. 44.
54   *"Biology is truly"*   Freud, *Beyond the Pleasure Principle*, p. 73.

Chapter 4. Opening Up: Martha, Cocaine, Fleischl

56   *"One would have imagined"*   Anna Freud Bernays, in Ruitenbeek, *Freud as We Knew Him,* p. 145.

56   *"When making a decision"*   Freud, quoted in Theodor Reik, *Listening with the Third Ear: The Inner Experience of a Psychoanalyst* (New York: Farrar, Straus, 1948), p. 7.

57   *Eli Bernays and Freud*   Eli and Anna's daughter Judith wrote about her grandparents in the memoir already cited. Their son Edward Bernays invented "public relations" and had a long career in advertising in New York.

58   *"Today is the sixteenth"*   Freud to Martha, in Freud, *Letters,* p. 69.

58   *"Heavens above"*   Ibid., p. 101.

58   *"Do you still remember"*   Ibid., p. 190.

59   *"He [Mill] lacked"*   Ibid., pp. 75–76.

60   *"Freud was throughout"*   Jones, *The Life and Work,* vol. 1, p. 102.

60   *"Freud had been disturbed"*   Ibid., p. 120.

61   *"most dangerous rival . . . unbearable"*   Ibid., p. 117.

61   *"she was not to write"*   Ibid., p. 137.

61   *"She is fascinating"*   Freud to Martha, quoted in ibid., p. 116.

62   *"taking a line"*   Freud to Martha, Freud, *Letters,* p. 38.

62   *"was fusion rather"*   Jones, *The Life and Work,* vol. 1, p. 110.

63   *"The turning-point came"*   Freud, *An Autobiographical Study,* p. 10.

64   *severe psychological symptoms*   Jones reports that Freud suffered all his life from "incapacitating spells of migraine, quite refractory to any treatment" (*The Life and Work,* vol. 1, p. 169).

64   *"I could achieve more"*   Freud to Martha, in Freud, *Letters,* p. 202.

64   *"Freud's intellect is"*   Breuer in a letter to Wilhelm Fliess, July 5, 1895, quoted in Hirschmüller, *The Life and Work of Josef Breuer.*

65   *"You know what Breuer"*   Freud in an unpublished letter to Martha, quoted in Jones, *The Life and Work,* vol. 1, p. 197.

65   *"Realizing that I was"*   Freud to Martha in Freud, *Letters,* pp. 40–41.

66   *"like sitting in the sun"*   Freud to Martha, quoted in Jones, *The Life and Work,* vol. 1, p. 167.

66   *"again behaved magnificently"*   Ibid., p. 167.

67   *Freud's papers on cocaine*   All of Freud's papers on cocaine, along with related material, are collected in Robert Byck, ed., *Cocaine Papers by Sigmund Freud* (New York: New American Library, 1974).

67   *"this divine plant"*   *Über Coca,* in ibid., p. 50.

67   *"dined well so"*   Freud, quoted in Jones, *The Life and Work,* vol. 1, p. 80.

67   *"Woe to you"*   Freud to Martha, in ibid., p. 84.

68   *It seems clear that*   While Freud eventually gave up the use of cocaine after 1900, his powerful addiction to nicotine lasted all his life. Modern research has shown that the effects of nicotine and cocaine are similar; both elevate mood, enhance cognition, and decrease appetite. See Stephen M. Stahl, *Essential Psychopharmacology: Neuroscientific Basis and Clinical Applications* (Cambridge, U.K.: Cambridge University Press, 1996, pp. 359–363).

68   *"I may here go"*   Freud, *An Autobiographical Study,* pp. 14–15. One wonders why Freud blamed Martha for his failure to become famous—who, by the way, remembers Koller today?—and, of greater importance, why he wrote as if he stopped using cocaine. Why didn't he continue to investigate medication as a means of treating his patient's symptoms, since cocaine had worked so well for him? On a related note, Freud claimed, regarding Fleischl's addiction to cocaine, that it happened because he injected the drug rather that taking it orally as Freud did. This left out the fact that Freud had

recommended and given injections to other patients for some years. (See Jones, *The Life and Work,* vol. 1, pp. 95–96.)

68   *"The subjective phenomena"* Freud, "On the General Effect of Cocaine," in Byck, *Cocaine Papers,* p. 115.

69   *"He is a thoroughly"* Freud to Martha, in Freud, *Letters,* p. 11.

69   *"I admire and love"* Freud to Martha, quoted in Jones, *The Life and Work,* vol. 1, p. 90. The question can be raised whether Freud's feelings for Fleischl were "homosexual." Certainly there are elements of physical attraction: his awareness of Fleischl's "manly features" and the connection of his friend with ancient Greece, where homosexuality between older men and boys was valued. And the nights together which Freud found so "agitating and exciting . . . [making] an ensemble that cannot be described," with Fleischl in his bath, point to an intimacy that was physical, intellectual, and emotional. On the other hand, it can be argued that it was difficult for men at this time to find women who shared their interests; the worlds of science and medicine were almost completely male. Can these cultural factors explain the closeness that Freud found with Fleischl? Not entirely. More was involved, for Freud would become intimate with Wilhelm Fliess a few years later in much the same way he was with Fleischl, even though, at this later time, he was married and had a wife and children as potential sources of love and closeness.

There is no evidence that the two men engaged in overt homosexual activity. Later in his life, Freud would refer to his homosexual attraction to several of his male colleagues, but considered such feelings extremely threatening; he had to control them, drawing close and then retreating, and continually fighting to rid himself of the impulses. Since these desires were expressions of his longings for early love, I think his own later term "bisexuality" is a better fit. At base, he was looking for the same thing from both men and women, and while it was somewhat less dangerous to seek it with his male friends, there was still a good deal of threat.

69   *Fleischl bore a striking* The pictures of Fleischl and Braun are found in E. Freud, L. Freud, and I. Grubrich-Simitis, *Freud: His Life in Pictures and Words,* pp. 66, 88. The picture of Fleischl over Freud's couch is from the book of photographs taken of Bergasse 19 when the family left Vienna; see Edmund Engelman, *Bergasse 19: Sigmund Freud's Home and Offices, Vienna 1938* (Chicago: University of Chicago Press, 1976), plate 10.

69   *"His life became"* Jones, *The Life and Work,* vol. 1, p. 44.

70   *"I believe he"* Freud to Martha, in Freud, *Letters,* p. 11.

70   *"[Freud] asked him"* Freud, quoted in Jones, *The Life and Work,* vol. 1, p. 90.

73   *"Every note of the"* Ibid., p. 91.

Chapter 5. Jean-Martin Charcot: "The Napoléon of Neuroses"

Sources for this chapter include Ellenberger, *The Discovery of the Unconscious;* Sulloway, *Freud: Biologist of the Mind;* Georges Guillain, *J. M. Charcot, His Life, His Work* (London: Pitman Medical Publishing, 1959); and Guy Williams, *The Age of Miracles: Medicine and Surgery in the Nineteenth Century* (Chicago: Academy Press, 1987). In addition, there is the obituary Freud wrote about Charcot in 1893, his letters to Martha, and some material from *An Autobiographical Study.*

74   *"very honorable but"* Freud to Martha, quoted in Gay, *Freud,* p. 47.

74   *"downright championship"* Fleischl to Freud, in ibid., p. 47.

75   *"An incredible number"* Freud to Martha, in Freud, *Letters,* p. 173.

75   *"intimate, endearing voice"* Ibid., p. 181.

75   *"a vast overdressed"* Ibid., p. 187.

75   *"arrogant . . . inaccessible"* Freud to Martha, quoted in Jones, *The Life and Work,* vol. 1, p. 183.

75   *"strike me as uncanny"* Freud to Martha, in Freud, *Letters,* pp. 187–188.

75   *"The ugliness of"* Freud to Martha, quoted in Jones, *The Life and Work,* vol. 1, p. 184.

76   *"I had to pay"* Freud to Martha, in Freud, *Letters,* pp. 174, 176.

76   *"The idea that you"* Ibid., pp. 197, 199.

76   *"You write so"* Ibid., p. 200.

77   *"began to feel"* Ibid., p. 177.

77   *"drank beer . . . a little cocaine . . . quite calm"* Ibid., pp. 195–196.

77   *"The bit of cocaine . . . it was so"* Ibid., pp. 201, 203.

77   *"Charcot lets fall"* Ibid., p. 176.

77   *"I think I am"* Ibid., p. 185.

78   *"Charcot arrived, a tall"* Ibid., p. 175.

79   *"A more authoritarian man"* Leon Daudet, quoted in Ellenberger, *The Discovery of the Unconscious,* p. 92.

79   *"an ambitious man"* From the *Diary* of the Goncourt brothers, quoted in ibid., p. 92.

80   *"He was not"* Freud, *Charcot (Obituary),* p. 12.

80   *"He was almost uncanny"* Axel Munthe, quoted in Williams, *The Age of Miracles,* p. 164.

81   *"What impressed me"* Freud, *An Autobiographical Study,* p. 13.

82   *Alongside of Charcot* The accounts of Charcot's hypnotic demonstrations and the distortions involved in his work with hysteria are well documented in Ellenberger, *The Discovery of the Unconscious,* pp. 98–101, and Sulloway, *Freud: Biologist of the Mind,* pp. 39–41.

83   *"He put forward"* Freud, *Charcot,* p. 21.

84   *"we enter into the history"* Ibid., p. 19.

84   *Freud left Paris early* Freud spent a month studying with Adolf Baginsky in Berlin and then worked part-time for ten years at the Kassowitz Institute in Vienna. In both of these settings he saw numbers of children suffering from "nervous diseases." Baginsky was a well-known spokesman for the role of masturbation as a cause of "hysteria" and a host of other diseases in children, beliefs that were used to justify various operations in which the genitalia of children—mainly female—were surgically mutilated. A number of these children were probably survivors of abuse of various kinds, yet Freud never mentioned his contact with infants and children in these settings, or the influence of these experiences on his own work. Two recent papers by the Italian psychoanalyst Carlo Bonomi deal with this topic: "Why Have We Ignored Freud the 'Pediatrician'?" (*Cahiers Psychiatriques Genevois,* Special Issue, 1994, pp. 55–99), and "'Sexuality and Death' in Freud's Discovery of Sexual Aetiology" (*International Forum of Psychoanalysis* 3, 1994, pp. 63–87).

84   *"I met with a bad"* Freud, *An Autobiographical Study,* pp. 15–16. Ellenberger, *The Discovery of the Unconscious,* pp. 437–438, provides documentation that casts serious doubt on Freud's version of the hostile reception of his paper on male hysteria. Freud's recasting of the history of this event is an early instance of what became a persistent tactic; the way he characterized himself as a lonely innovator, struggling for recognition against a hostile world.

85   *"contradicts the . . . Theory is good"* Freud, *Charcot,* p. 13.

85   *"If I find someone"* Ibid., p. 19.

Chapter 6. Martha: "The Loss of an Illusion"

86   *"Dr. Sigmund Freud, Docent"* Gay, *Freud,* p. 53.

87   *"the first day of what"* Freud to Emmeline Bernays, quoted in Jones, *The Life and Work,* vol. 1, p. 150.

87 *"how not being allowed"* Martha to a cousin, quoted in Clark, *Freud*, p. 89.

87 *"terribly ugly . . . looks strikingly like me"* Freud to Emmeline and Minna Bernays, quoted in Gay, *Freud*, p. 54.

88 *"He suddenly felt"* Clark, *Freud*, p. 112.

89 *Martha's younger sister* Peter Swales has argued that Freud had an affair with his sister-in-law Minna in "Freud, Minna Bernays, and the Conquest of Rome: New Light on the Origins of Psychoanalysis" (*New American Review* 1 (2/3), 1982, pp. 1–23). The story originated with some remarks Jung made after his visit to the Freuds in Vienna, which were later reported by John Bilinsky in his article "Jung and Freud: The End of a Romance" (*Andover Newton Quarterly* 10, 1969, 39–43). See also the comments of the Harvard psychologist Henry Murray, quoted in Roazen, *How Freud Worked*, p. 208. Swales develops a very complex scenario in which he places Freud and Minna in an Italian spa at the same time and, by reinterpreting some of Freud's dreams and slips, concludes that they had an affair from which Minna became pregnant, with Freud subsequently paying for her abortion. Swales's story depends on a number of guesses and suppositions about events that may or may not have occurred and that cannot be verified at this remove in time. Among other problems, an affair would be completely out of character for both Freud and Minna, who were extremely sexually and emotionally constricted. Freud, as we have seen, was more strongly attracted to men, in any case, though he needed to keep these "affairs" on an intellectual level. One must also ask, what difference would it make if Swales's story was true? It changes nothing about the validity, or lack of validity, of psychoanalysis. Jung did have affairs—which is probably why he assumed that the intellectual compatibility he observed between Freud and Minna was accompanied by physical intimacy—as did Ferenczi, but this tells us nothing about the truth or value of their theories or approaches to therapy.

89 *"I knew Aunt Minna"* Martin Freud, *Sigmund Freud: Man and Father*, p. 60.

90 *"This brings us to"* Freud, *"Civilized" Sexual Morality and Modern Nervous Illness*, pp. 194–195.

91 *"Sexual excitement, too"* Freud/Fliess, p. 276.

91 *"My Indian summer"* Freud/Jung, p. 292.

91 *"I stand for an"* Freud to James J. Putnam, in Freud, *Letters*, p. 308.

91 *"I always think"* Freud to Martha, quoted in Jones, *The Life and Work*, vol. 1, p. 140.

92 *"became his tyrant"* Freud/Fliess, p. 129.

92 *"Do you really think"* Martha, quoted in Rene Laforgue, "Personal Memories of Freud," in Ruitenbeek, *Freud as We Knew Him*, p. 342.

92 *"So far as psychoanalysis"* Anna Freud in a letter to Kurt Eissler, quoted in Elisabeth Young-Bruehl, *Anna Freud: A Biography* (New York: Summit Books, 1988), p. 30.

92 *"It is bold . . . Contact with such"* Freud to Martha, quoted in Jones, *The Life and Work*, vol. 1, p. 128.

92 *"did not think it"* Ibid., p. 174.

92 *"The mob gives vent"* Freud to Martha, in Freud, *Letters*, pp. 50–51.

93 *"diversion . . . however, only"* Martha, quoted in Gay, *Freud*, p. 60.

93 *The most striking* Information on contraception in the nineteenth century is taken from Janet F. Brodie, *Contraception and Abortion in Nineteenth-Century America* (Ithaca, N.Y.: Cornell University Press, 1994), which also cites a number of other sources. Regarding the availability of condoms in Vienna, see Frederic Morton, *A Nervous Splendor: Vienna, 1888–1889* (London: Penguin, 1979), p. 195. He describes Sigi Ernst, whose trade was so well known that his advertisements for condoms did not need to mention what he sold. In 1888, two years after Freud and Martha were married, he opened an additional, more discreet entrance to his establishment for his estimable clientele.

93 *his patient Albert Hirst* Freud's analysis of Albert Hirst is detailed in David J. Lynn, "Sigmund Freud's Psychoanalysis of Albert Hirst" (*Bulletin of the History of Medicine* 71, 1997, pp. 69–93). See also Roazen, *How Freud Worked*, pp. 1–30.

96 *he effaced Martha's individuality* Martha and her friend and contemporary Bertha Pappenheim (Anna O.), who will be discussed in the next chapter, present a striking contrast. Bertha, also raised in an Orthodox Jewish home, could not tolerate the stifling female role that was imposed on her and her rebellion was an important element in her emotional breakdown.

Some interesting comments on the Freud family are provided by their maid Paula Fichtl. Minna was "hard," while Martha was "quiet and gentle. She was shy, she did everything for the Professor, but she was always serious. She never joked, and she never talked much at all. . . . Nobody ever made a fuss over her. It was as if she were pushed aside. Not even the children made a fuss over her. *They* loved the father, Miss Freud [Anna] loved the father, Auntie Minna—they all, all of them loved the father." Interview with Paula Fichtl, reported in Linda Donn, *Freud and Jung: Years of Friendship, Years of Loss* (New York: Scribners, 1988), p. 12.

Chapter 7. Josef Breuer and the Invention of Psychotherapy

Information on Josef Breuer's life and scientific accomplishments, as well as a more detailed account of his work with Bertha Pappenheim, can be found in the thorough and scholarly biography by Albrecht Hirschmüller, *The Life and Work of Josef Breuer: Physiology and Psychoanalysis.*

99 *"Each individual hysterical"* Breuer and Freud, *Studies on Hysteria,* p. 6.
100 *In his search* Freud had Breuer describe his treatment of Bertha Pappenheim "again and again" according to Jones, *The Life and Work,* vol. 1, p. 226.
100 *"If it is a merit"* Freud, *Five Lectures on Psychoanalysis,* p. 9.
101 *"[Mother, age 22] died"* Ibid., p. 11.
101 *"None of you realizes"* Ibid., p. 28.
103 *Breuer was probably* A great deal has been written about the case of Bertha Pappenheim (Anna O.). See Henri F. Ellenberger, "The Story of Anna O.: A Critical Review of New Data" (*Journal of the History of the Behavioral Sciences* 8, 1972, 267–279). Hirschmüller, in *The Life and Work of Josef Breuer,* pp. 95–132 and 276–308, presents Breuer's full, original notes on the case, along with correspondence and other relevant data. Lucy Freeman's *The Story of Anna O.* (New York: Walker, 1972) is a readable account. And Marianne Tolpin, "The Unmirrored Self, Compensatory Structure, and Cure: The Exemplary Case of Anna O.," in Barry Magid, ed., *Freud's Case Studies: Self-Psychological Perspectives* (Hillsdale, N.J.: Analytic Press, 1993, pp. 9–29), discusses the case from the point of view of self-psychology. Mikkel Borch-Jacobsen, *Remembering Anna O.: A Century of Mystification,* presents a largely unsympathetic account, though the book contains some valuable references.
103 *"Breuer had a very"* Hirschmüller, *The Life and Work of Josef Breuer,* p. 129. The connection between Bertha Pappenheim and Breuer's mother is discussed in a paper by George H. Pollock, "The Possible Significance of Childhood Object Loss in the Josef Breuer-Bertha Pappenheim (Anna O.)-Sigmund Freud Relationship. I. Josef Breuer" (*Journal of the American Psychoanalytic Association* 16, 1968, pp. 711–739).
103 *"markedly intelligent . . . passionately fond of"* Breuer, *Studies on Hysteria,* pp. 21–22.
104 *"Two entirely distinct . . . having two selves"* Ibid., p. 24.
105 *"There were extremely"* Ibid., p. 24.
105 *"she was completely"* Ibid., p. 25.
105 *"Her right arm"* Ibid., pp. 38–39.
106 *"this girl, who"* Ibid., p. 22.

107   *Breuer ended his*   Data on Breuer's continuing work with Bertha is in Hirschmüller, *The Life and Work of Josef Breuer*, p. 137, who also notes that he continued to see patients in therapy as late as 1912.

107   *"Love did not come"*   Poem by Bertha Pappenheim, quoted in ibid., p. 308.

108   *"Her excessively regimented"*   Breuer, quoted in ibid., p. 277.

108   *"gaiety had displeased"*   Ibid., p. 278.

110   *"When cases now"*   Ibid., p. 145.

Chapter 8. Breuer, Freud, and the Studies on Hysteria: 1886–1895

111   *four of Freud's cases*   Data on the real names and life circumstances of Freud's four cases, along with references to other discussions of this material, can be found in Appignanesi and Forrester, *Freud's Women*, pp. 91–120.

112   *Freud's first case*   An insightful discussion of the case of Emmy von N. can be found in Philip M. Bromberg, "Hysteria, Dissociation, and Cure: Emmy von N Revisited" (*Psychoanalytic Dialogues* 6, 1996, pp. 55–71). For an expanded discussion of trauma and dissociation, see Bromberg's excellent book, *Standing in the Spaces: Essays on Clinical Process, Trauma and Dissociation* (Hillsdale, N.J.: Analytic Press, 1998).

112   *"Keep still!"*   Freud, *Studies on Hysteria*, p. 49.

112   *"carefully, but under"*   Ibid., p. 49.

112   *"When I was five"*   Ibid., pp. 52, 55.

112   *"got up all at once"*   Ibid., p. 60.

113   *"living for years"*   Ibid., pp. 88, 103.

113   *In this passage*   While Freud clearly connects Frau Emmy's traumas with her symptoms, he also recasts his observations in abstract theoretical terms. He does this in two ways; first, with the concepts of force and energy, and second, with an emphasis on the primary role of sexuality: "We regard hysterical symptoms as the effects and residues of excitations which have acted upon the nervous system as traumas. Residues of this kind are not left behind if the original excitation has been discharged by abreaction or thought-activity. . . . We must regard the process as though a sum of excitation imping-ing on the nervous system is transformed into chronic symptoms in so far as it has not been employed for external action in proportion to its amount" (ibid., p. 86).

     What Freud is doing here is translating threatening experience into the impersonal terms of neurology. In other words, the emotions and relationships observed in the patient are recast in the language from his days in Brücke's laboratory, a time and place where he felt calm and safe. Anxiety, terror, death, and grief—which abound in Frau Emmy's case—become the more distant "excitations"; strangulated affect becomes undischarged neural energy.

114   *"Were you ashamed"*   Ibid., p. 117.

114   *"senseless rage against"*   Ibid., p. 132.

114   *"a mere suspicion"*   Ibid., p. 134.

115   *"first the patient's"*   Ibid., p. 135.

115   *"jokingly called her"*   Ibid., p. 140.

115   *"felt acutely her"*   Ibid., p. 141.

115   *"Now he is free"*   Ibid., pp. 156–157.

115   *As was true*   In a later interview, Elisabeth described Freud as "a young, bearded nerve specialist they sent me to," and commented that he had tried "to persuade me that I was in love with my brother-in-law, but that wasn't really so." Quoted in Gay, *Freud*, p. 72.

116   *"outbursts of weeping . . . nervous cough"*   Freud, *Studies on Hysteria*, pp. 162–169.

116 *The case material* In addition to the five long case histories and the six vignettes, there
is the case of Cäcilie M.—in reality, the wealthy Anna von Lieben—treated first by
Breuer and then by Freud, who saw her intensively, sometimes twice a day, for almost
three years, ending in 1893. A full account of her treatment in not presented in the
Studies, perhaps because, despite the length of the treatment, there was no cure, but
fragments are used to illustrate the somatic representation of psychological conflicts, as
when a violent facial pain is traced to a bitter insult that she experienced as a "slap in
the face." See Peter J. Swales, "Freud, His Teacher and the Birth of Psychoanalysis," in
Paul E. Stepansky, ed., *Freud: Appraisals and Reappraisals: Contributions to Freud Studies,* vol. 1 (Hillsdale, N.J.: Analytic Press, 1986, pp. 3–82), for a lengthy, speculative
account of Freud's treatment of Cäcilie M. Appignanesi and Forrester, *Freud's Women,*
also discuss the case (pp. 72, 86–91).

117 *"Exhaustive researches"* Freud, *Sexuality in the Aetiology of the Neurosis,* pp. 263, 269.

117 *This statement shows* It comes as a surprise to learn what "sexual factors" Freud posits
in the *Aetiology* paper: masturbation, coitus interruptus, abstinence, what he calls "detri-
mental forms of sexual intercourse" that involve birth control—indeed, anything other
than what he refers to as "normal" sexuality, by which he apparently means intercourse
to orgasm between adults without the interference of contraception. Current knowledge
of sexual function makes clear that there is no factual basis for these claims: masturbation does not lead to exhaustion, contraception does not produce neurotic symptoms,
abstinence does not cause anxiety. These presumed effects were interpretive speculations
on Freud's part that had no basis in the data he observed. The thrust of the 1898 paper
is to label all forms of sexual expression as pathological that fall outside a narrow definition of "normal."

Chapter 9. The Break with Breuer

118 *"You know what Breuer"* Freud to Martha, February 2, 1886, quoted in Jones, *The
Life and Work,* vol. 1, p. 197.

118 *"I think of the"* Freud/Fliess, pp. 304–305.

118 *"Painful emotion"* Breuer and Freud, *Studies on Hysteria,* pp. 5–6.

119 *A "number of brutal"* Ibid., p. 213.

119 *"Along side sexual"* Ibid., p. 247.

119 *"One point on which"* Breuer, lecture of 1895, reported in Freud/Fliess, p. 151 n.

120 *"Breuer has put"* Freud, *Studies on Hysteria,* pp. 285–286.

120 *"I decided to"* Ibid., p. 110.

120 *"penetrating into"* Ibid., p. 139.

120 *"the weapons in the"* Ibid., p. 266.

120 *"surgical intervention"* Ibid., p. 305.

121 *"We shall in the"* Freud, *Sexuality in the Aetiology of the Neuroses,* p. 269.

122 *Freud's dire view* Schur, *Freud: Living and Dying,* pp. 40–62, has carefully reviewed
the cardiac episode, using modern medical knowledge, as well as what was known in
the 1890s. He concludes that Freud almost certainly had a coronary blockage, with the
typical symptoms: pain in the region of the heart (angina), rapid and irregular heart
beats (tachycardia), pain radiating down the left arm, and shortness of breath (dyspnea).
All these are well-established symptoms of heart disease, and were known to be so at the
time. Schur concludes that the most likely diagnosis is that Freud had a blockage
(thrombus) in a small coronary artery, and that it either passed, or caused a minor heart
attack from which he subsequently recovered. Freud's positive response to the drug dig-
italis, a cardiac stimulant, further supports this diagnosis.

Fliess proposed that Freud's heart symptoms, like so much else in his view, could
have a nasal origin, in which case surgery on the nose would be helpful, and, some

months later, Freud had Fliess operate on his nose. Freud reported his various physical reactions, both on his nose and heart symptoms, commenting: "Though not designed to make one feel at ease, this information affords some pleasure because it emphasizes once again that the condition of the heart depends upon the condition of the nose" (Freud/Fliess, p. 67). More than a month later, he again expressed both his hopes and doubts about Fliess's treatment of his heart condition: "With regard to my own ailment, I would like you to continue to be right—that the nose may have a large share in it and the heart a small one. Only a very strict judge will take it amiss that in view of the pulse and the insufficiency [his actual coronary symptoms] I frequently believe the opposite" (Freud/Fliess, p. 125).

123   *"Now I have"*   Freud, *On the History of the Psycho-Analytic Movement,* p. 12.

123   *Nor does the evidence*   Ellenberger, "The Story of Anna O.," was the first to uncover evidence that contradicts the tale of Breuer's flight from Bertha Pappenheim. Accounts can also be found in Ellenberger, *The Discovery of the Unconscious,* pp. 481–484, and Hirschmüller, *The Life and Work of Josef Breuer,* pp. 112–116, 136–141.

124   *"I learned many"*   Breuer in a letter to August Forel, November 21, 1907, quoted in Paul F. Cranefield, "Josef Breuer's Evaluation of His Contribution to Psychoanalysis" (*International Journal of Psycho-Analysis* 39, 1958, pp. 319–322). See also Andre E. Haynal, *The Technique at Issue: Controversies in Psychoanalysis from Freud and Ferenczi to Michael Balint,* trans. Elizabeth Holder (London: Karnac Books, 1988), p. 31.

125   *Freud also needed*   The fact that Breuer did not aspire to fame via the construction of grand theories is illustrated by the following comments from his concluding chapter in the *Studies:*

> The attempt that has been made here to make a synthetic construction of hysteria out of what we know of it today is open to the reproach of eclecticism, if such a reproach can be justified at all. There were so many formulations of hysteria . . . But it can scarcely be otherwise; for so many excellent observers and acute minds have concerned themselves with hysteria. It is unlikely that any of their formulations was without a portion of the truth. A future exposition of the true state of affairs will certainly include them all and will merely combine all the one-sided views of the subject into a corporate reality. Eclecticism, therefore, seems to me nothing to be ashamed of [p. 250].

125   *"May I mention"*   Hanna Breuer, in a letter to Jones, April 21, 1954, quoted in Clark, *Freud,* pp. 138–139.

Chapter 10. *Self-analysis and the Invention of the Oedipus Complex*

126   *"A single idea"*   Freud/Fliess, p. 272.

127   *Some historians have*   The fact that Freud was almost completely out of touch with modern life is revealed in the way his apartment and office were furnished, his inability to listen to music, and his taste in literature. In 1907, his publisher Hugo Heller sent him a questionnaire asking for a list of ten good authors. Freud listed the Swiss Gottfried Keller and Conrad Ferdinand Meyer, the Frenchmen Anatole France and Emile Zola, the Englishmen Rudyard Kipling and Lord Macaulay, the Russian Dmitry Merezhkovsky (whose *Romance of Leonardo da Vinci* he was to draw on), the Dutchman "Multatuli" (the essayist and novelist Eduard Douwes Dekker), and the American Mark Twain. An odd list, and only Zola, Kipling, and Twain—and possibly Anatole France—have stood the test of time. Freud's eating habits were quite conventional: his favorite dish was *Rindfleisch* —roast beef with onions—and he had no taste for French cuisine.

127   *"Of the world"*   Freud/Fliess, p. 152. Freud had a love-hate relationship with Vienna that lasted all his life. Jones quotes from unpublished letters to Martha: Vienna "disgusts" him, and is "physically repulsive" to him, Jones, *The Life and Work*, vol. 1, p. 293. He wrote to Fliess in 1900 that "I hate Vienna almost personally" (Freud/Fliess, p. 403). Yet he had great difficulty leaving and was obviously bound to the city.

127   *"Annerl produced her"*   Freud/Fliess, p. 184.

127   *"Much joy could"*   Ibid., p. 236.

128   *"Esteemed friend"*   Ibid., p. 15.

128   *"Your cordial letter"*   Ibid., p. 16.

129   *"I am looking forward"*   Ibid., pp. 193, 238–239.

129   *"I have had no"*   Ibid., p. 31.

129   *"You altogether ruin"*   Ibid., p. 56.

129   *"And you are the"*   Ibid., p. 73.

129   *"Altogether I miss"*   Ibid., p. 123.

129   *"Your kind should"*   Ibid., p. 158.

130   *"we are now living"*   Ibid., p. 54.

130   *"[The children] and wife"*   Ibid., p. 68.

132   *"There still was"*   Ibid., p. 117.

132   *"You did it as well"*   Ibid., p. 118.

132   *"For me you remain"*   Ibid., p. 125.

133   *"First of all Eckstein"*   Ibid., p. 183.

133   *The Eckstein episode*   What scanty evidence exists on the later life of Emma Eckstein is summarized in Masson, *The Assault on Truth*, pp. 241–258. Emma apparently recovered from her "hysteria" as a result of Freud's treatment, and, for a time, saw patients in psychoanalysis and did a small amount of writing about childhood sexuality. She eventually relapsed and spent her later years as a recluse, unable to get off her couch. Freud wrote to her in November of 1905 blaming her for wanting to see him without payment and, especially, for believing that another doctor had successfully treated her condition as if it were organic. This, in his mind, ruined her for analysis. In the view of her nephew Albert Hirst, "Freud was not unhappy to be rid of a burdensome charity case" (Masson, *The Assault on Truth*, p. 258). Freud wrote about Emma in one of his last publications—*Analysis Terminable and Interminable,* in 1937—justifying his treatment of her, with no mention of the trauma inflicted on her by him and Fliess, and blaming her relapse on a hysterectomy.

134   *"mystical nonsense"*   The review of Fliess's 1897 book is quoted in Freud/Fliess, p. 310 n. Freud did sever his connection to the journal but, as he revealed in an analysis of one his dreams, "in my letter of resignation [to the editor] expressed a hope that *our personal relations would not be affected by the event"*; Freud, *On Dreams*, p. 663. That is, even as he was publicly supporting his friend, he was looking out for his future self-interest.

134   *"With regard to"*   Freud/Fliess, p. 193.

134   *"I hope the path"*   Ibid., p. 356.

134   *Fliess's theoretical imperialism*   In the throes of his attraction to Fliess's biological theories, Freud wrote his *Project for a Scientific Psychology*, an attempt at a neurological model of the mind. He wrote to his friend with enthusiasm:

> The barriers suddenly lifted, the veils dropped, and everything became transparent—from the details of the neuroses to the determinants of consciousness. Everything seemed to fall into place, the cogs meshed, I had the impression that the thing now really was a machine that shortly would function on its own. The three systems of neurones; the free and bound states of quantity; the primary and secondary processes; the main tendency and the compromise tendency of the nervous

system; the two biological rules of attention and defense; the characteristics of quality, reality, and thought; the state of the psychosexual group; the sexual determination of repression; finally, the factors determining consciousness as a function of perception—all that was correct and still is today! Naturally, I can scarcely manage to contain my delight [ibid., p. 146].

Freud attempted to force the central concepts of psychoanalysis into the neurological mold of the *Project*. But they did not fit, and he abandoned the effort; the *Project* was done as a draft, sent to Fliess, but never published. In his next major work, *The Interpretation of Dreams*, he moved onto psychological ground. But the physicalist assumptions of the *Project* did not entirely disappear; they intrude into the later "metapsychology" and other of his speculative works. As James Strachey put it: "The *Project*, or rather its invisible ghost, haunts the whole series of Freud's theoretical writings to the very end." (Introduction to the *Project for a Scientific Psychology, Standard Edition*, vol. 1, p. 290.)

Freud began a long tradition in psychoanalysis in which "scientific" is equated with "biological"; psychological contributions are viewed as less valuable than biological speculations. The following is typical: "Perhaps with your [Fliess's] help I shall find the solid ground on which I can cease to give psychological explanations and begin to find a physiological foundation!" (Freud/Fliess, p. 193). In fact, this has things backward. What is most often termed "biological" in psychoanalysis are speculations that have little or no basis in observation; they are the counterparts of Fliess's numerological, pseudobiological theories. Biology is not inherently scientific, nor is psychology inherently speculative. One can approach any subject scientifically, be it cells, diseases, emotions, sexuality, neuroses, or family relationships. One works carefully from observations, stays close to the data, and attempts to make generalizations that are internally coherent and consistent with known facts. Freud was quite familiar with this method; he was trained in it in the physiology laboratory, and had done careful scientific research in the areas of neuroanatomy and aphasia.

135 *"By the time he"* Freud/Fliess, p. 202.

135 *"the most important event"* Freud, *The Interpretation of Dreams*, p. 317.

135 *The years immediately preceding* Otto Rank, who knew Freud intimately for many years and worked with him revising *The Interpretation of Dreams*, believed that the loss of Breuer was more important than the death of Jacob Freud in setting the self-analysis in motion. As he put it: "There is scarcely any doubt which event in the life of the 40-year-old Freud was more significant: the death of his father or the *simultaneous* separation from Breuer, to whom he owed the key to understanding the neurotic and the basis of his own success, and from whom he was compelled to break in order to go the way of his own development." (Rank, quoted in Lieberman, *Acts of Will*, p. 323.)

135 *"There is ample"* Jones, *The Life and Work*, vol. 1, pp. 304–305.

136 *"I no longer believe"* Freud/Fliess, pp. 264–265.

136 *"A single idea"* Ibid., p. 272.

137 *"The expectation of"* Ibid., p. 266.

137 *In November of 1899* The accounts of the Hummel and Kutschera trials and their widespread coverage in the daily press can be found in Larry Wolff, *Postcards from the End of the World: Child Abuse in Freud's Vienna* (New York: Atheneum, 1988).

138 *"If hysterical subjects"* Freud, *On the History of the Psycho-Analytic Movement*, pp. 17–18.

138 *"I had gone to"* Freud, *The Interpretation of Dreams*, p. 421.

139 *"emotional storm"* Ibid., p. 422.

140 *association with Wilhelm Fliess* There is very little information about Fliess from other sources. Freud's analysand and translator Alix Strachey met him in 1924 and wrote to

her husband James, "Yes, he is the great Fliess. He's very charming and old-fashioned; almost a dwarf with a huge stomach." Quoted in Edward Shorter, *From Paralysis to Fatigue: A History of Psychosomatic Illness in the Modern Era* (New York: Free Press, 1992), p. 67. More troubling is the claim that Fliess sexually molested his son Robert, who is often mentioned as a child in the Freud/Fliess letters. Masson, in *The Assault on Truth,* pp. 138–142, makes the case that Fliess did molest his son. As an adult, Robert Fliess had a long career as a psychoanalyst and, in one of his final publications—*Symbol, Dream and Psychosis* (New York: International Universities Press, 1973)—argued strongly that Freud had been wrong to abandon the seduction theory. Against the tide of the psychoanalytic establishment, he claimed that his clinical work had revealed widespread physical and sexual abuse in most of his neurotic patients. He described a particular type of parent who he labeled an "ambulatory psychotic"—someone who appears normal in the outside world, and may even be a great scientist, but who abuses his children within the privacy of his home. Fliess's remarks fit his father, though he does not specifically state this in the book. Masson cites a personal communication from Robert Fliess's widow, Elenore, which confirms that her husband had been abused by his father. See Masson, *The Assault on Truth,* p. 231.

Chapter 11. The Interpretation of Dreams *and the End of the Fliess Affair*

142 *"felt impelled to start"* Freud/Fliess, p. 243.

142 *"deep in the dream book"* Ibid., p. 298.

142 *"I shall change"* Ibid., p. 313.

142 *analyzed and reinterpreted* Max Schur was the first to link the Irma dream to Fliess's operation on the nose of Emma Eckstein. See Max Schur, "Some Additional 'Day Residues' of 'the Specimen Dream of Psychoanalysis,'" in Rudolph M. Loewenstein, Lotte M. Newman, Max Schur, and Albert J. Solnit, eds., *Psychoanalysis: A General Psychology—Essays in Honor of Heinz Hartmann* (New York: International Universities Press, 1966, pp. 45–85). Erik Erikson, "The Dream Specimen of Psychoanalysis" (*Journal of the American Psychoanalytic Association* 2, 1950, pp. 5–56), presents a sensitive discussion that places the dream in both personal and social contexts. The "Irma" of the dream was a composite of Emma Eckstein and Anna Hammerschlag-Leichtheim, daughter of Freud's old Hebrew teacher, who was also a patient and the woman after whom he would name his daughter Anna. Martha was, in fact, pregnant with Anna at the time the dream occurred. It is clear, however, that the events surrounding the operation on Emma Eckstein's nose provided the main emotional stimulus for the dream.

142 *family pediatrician Oscar Rie* Oscar Rie was an old friend of Freud's as well as pediatrician to all the children. Yet, in his dreams, Freud is always taking his revenge on him. In addition to the Irma dream, there is another—see *The Interpretation of Dreams,* pp. 269–271—in which he speaks of Rie, "whose fate it seems to be to be ill-treated in my dreams" (p. 271). By Freud's own account, Rie was wonderful with the Freud children, saved them from illnesses, and also gave them presents. He was, in other words, a giving parental figure like Breuer who, because of this, became the recipient of love and hate. In further associations to the Irma dream, he speaks of his "thirst for revenge" directed at both Rie and Breuer (ibid., p. 124).

143 *"better, but not quite well"* Freud, *The Interpretation of Dreams,* p. 106.

143 *"a big white patch"* Ibid., p. 107.

143 *"was the fulfillment"* Ibid., p. 119.

143 *"a dream is the (disguised)"* Ibid., p. 160.

143 *"Do you suppose"* Freud/Fliess, p. 417.

144 *"In the pages"* Freud, *The Interpretation of Dreams,* p. 1.

146 *"My procedure is"* Ibid., p. 105. An example from the Irma dream will illustrate the wordplay found in dreams, and also cast further light on Freud's penchant for concealing things about himself just when he seems to be most open. The unclean "syringe" with which Rie injects Emma is, in German, *Spritze*—"squirter"—the colloquial word for penis, for which the English "prick" would be equivalent. Thus, Emma is made ill by having a dirty prick stuck into her. Freud's wife, Martha, is alluded to in his associations, but he leaves out the fact that at the time of the dream, she was more than five months pregnant with their last child—her sixth in eight years—a pregnancy that she did not want. Thus, Freud was guilty of sticking his penis into Martha and causing distressing swelling, just as Fliess intruded into Emma Eckstein's nose with disastrous consequences, both sources of real guilt that Freud attempts to disavow in the dream.

146 *"All elongated objects"* Ibid., p. 354.

146 *"I should like to"* Ibid., pp. 359–360.

146 *"Symbols allow us"* Ibid., p. 151.

146 *"Moreover, symbolism"* Freud, *Moses and Monotheism,* pp. 98–99. See Rand and Torok, *Questions for Freud,* pp. 9–23, for a discussion of Freud's interpretation of dream symbols as universal or individualized. They note how he revised *The Interpretation of Dreams* a number of times over the years; 185 new pages were added by the 1923 edition. The movement in these new additions was in the direction of universal symbolism and away from individualized meaning. Interpretations in terms of universal symbols don't require the participation of the dreamer-patient, so that the analyst becomes ever more the knowing authority. A review of Freud's work with a number of patients over many years shows him moving between individual and standardized interpretations. When he is analyzing his own dreams in *Interpretation* he typically does not force their meaning into fixed categories. The same tends to be true with patients he likes. However, when he has a "resistant" patient—one who does not comply or agree with him—he can become very insistent about the truth of his interpretations.

147 *"Oddly enough, something"* Freud/Fliess, p. 379.

147 *"The psychologists will"* Ibid., pp. 368–369.

148 *"The reception it"* Ibid., p. 405.

148 *"My writings were not"* Freud, *On the History of the Psycho-Analytic Movement,* pp. 22–23.

148 *"For more than ten"* Freud, *An Autobiographical Study,* p. 48.

148 *"for some years"* Jones, *The Life and Work,* vol. 1, p. 361.

149 *"Epoch making . . . The book is* Näcke, quoted in Sulloway, *Freud: Biologist of the Mind,* pp. 450–451.

149 *"No other work"* Freud/Fliess, p. 353.

149 *"scornful or pitying superiority"* Is Freud's version of the reception of his work true? He did experience himself as a lonely and heroic pioneer, battling against a world of enemies, but this was his idiosyncratic construction of reality, as revealed by the fact that he continued to feel misunderstood and badly treated in later years when he was famous throughout the world. In other words, the actual response to his publications had little effect on his perception of how others were treating him. He felt ill-used unless his work met with complete acceptance and admiration. See, for example, Hannah S. Decker, "The Medical Reception of Psychoanalysis in Germany, 1894–1907: Three Brief Studies" (*Bulletin of History of Medicine,* 45, 1971, pp. 461–481), who notes that Freud's attitude "was based on the illogical expectation that the entire medical world would immediately recognize the truths he had uncovered. Because it did not do so, he felt 'isolated' and wrote about it in all his accounts of psychoanalysis; his version has often been accepted without further investigation" (p. 480).

There is a good deal of relatively recent, careful research that suggests a very different picture. The truth is that while some in the medical community were hostile, others thought well of Freud's work, referred him patients, and reviewed his books with care and respect. This more balanced version of the initial reception of psychoanalysis is elaborated by Roazen in *Freud and His Followers,* and, especially, in Ellenberger's well-documented *The Discovery of the Unconscious.* The historian of science Sulloway, in *Freud: Biologist of the Mind,* presents the most detailed account of the reception accorded Freud's early work. *The Interpretation of Dreams* and the 1901 essay *On Dreams* received at least thirty reviews, many of them recognizing their importance and originality. A review of the *Three Essays on the Theory of Sexuality* in 1906 said, "No other work . . . treats important sexual problems in so brief, so ingenious, and so brilliant a manner." There were criticisms, to be sure, but many of these, from today's vantage point, were legitimate. As Sulloway puts it:

> Strong opposition was not the initial reaction to Freud's theories; nor was any opposition premised upon the purported triumvirate of sexual prudery, hostility to innovation, and anti-Semitism that dominates the traditional historical scenario on this subject. Furthermore, it is important to distinguish Freud's theories of dreams and sexual development, which were both well received at first, from his theories of the neuroses, which provoked increasingly lively opposition owing to his predominately single-factor—sexual—explanation. Opposition to Freud's etiological theories dates from the mid-1890's, but even here the objections raised by Freud's contemporaries were far more rational—and justified—than psychoanalyst-historians have been willing to admit [p. 453].

It is important to keep in mind that Freud's version of the early history of psychoanalysis was by far the most influential one for over fifty years. The new historical evidence did not appear until after 1970 and was not widely known until the late 1980s. Freud's story of his years of splendid isolation and, of even greater significance, his belief that he and his theories were greeted with hostility, justified the siege mentality with which he shaped organized psychoanalysis. All those who worked with him during his lifetime only had the version they heard from the Professor; indeed, many loyal psychoanalysts still do not credit the newer historical evidence.

149   *"Thus we are becoming"*   Freud/Fliess, p. 398.
150   *"Remember that I"*   Ibid., p. 398.
150   *"There has never"*   Ibid., p. 405.
150   *"On that occasion"*   Comments made by Fliess in 1906, reprinted in Bonaparte, Anna Freud, and Kris, *The Origins of Psycho-Analysis,* p. 324.
151   *"There is no concealing"*   Freud/Fliess, p. 447.
151   *"share [Fliess's] contempt"*   Ibid., p. 426.
151   *"no one can replace"*   Ibid., p. 412.
151   *"I particularly warn"*   Letter from Freud to Abraham, February 13, 1911, quoted in Gay, *Freud,* p. 182; see also footnote, p. 676. This, like a number of Freud's other hostile comments, was omitted from the original version of the Freud/Abraham letters. A complete version of the correspondence is currently being prepared by Ernst Falzeder.
152   *"the large conception"*   Freud, *Beyond the Pleasure Principle,* p. 45.

Chapter 12. The Great Freud Emerges: 1899–1905

153   *"You known how"*   Freud/Fliess, p. 324.
153   *"Julius had not"*   Ibid., p. 324.
154   *"I am slowly"*   Ibid., p. 425.
154   *"By mistakes I"*   Freud, *The Claims of Psychoanalysis to Scientific Interest,* p. 166.
154   *"antipathy to his"*   Freud, *The Psychopathology of Everyday Life,* p. 25.
154   *"like any other"*   Ibid., p. 41.

154 *"Gentlemen: I take"* Ibid., p. 59.
154 *"without patriotic feelings"* Ibid., p. 90.
155 *"launched some very"* Ibid., p. 93.
155 *"It is painful"* Ibid., p. 144.
155 *long* Signorelli *example* Freud discusses his forgetting of the name *Signorelli* in *The Psychopathology of Everyday Life*, pp. 2–7. All quotes are found in those pages.
156 *"egoistic, jealous and"* Ibid., p. 276.
157 *"it has been a"* Freud/Fliess, p. 427.
157 *"It is a hysteria"* Ibid., p. 434.
157 *"in the first bloom"* Freud, *Fragment of an Analysis of a Case of Hysteria*, p. 23.
157 *"A violent feeling"* Ibid., p. 28.
158 *"indications . . . seemed to"* Ibid., p. 92.
158 *"What are transferences"* Ibid., p. 116. Working with the transference eventually became the feature that distinguished psychoanalytic treatment from almost all other methods. It gives it great power as a therapy, a power that the analyst can use for good or ill. Freud saw transference as a resistance because it interfered with the work of analysis as he defined it: the uncovering of unconscious material. Similarly with countertransference, the analyst's unconscious reactions to the patient, which he discovered later. He saw this, too, as something that needed to be removed or overcome so the work of the analysis could proceed. Later psychoanalysts have greatly broadened the concepts of both transference and countertransference. Transference is no longer seen as a resistance to be removed; it has become the very medium in which the analysis takes place.
159 *"I withdrew my"* Freud/Fliess, p. 456.
159 *Freud completed his write-up* There is a large secondary literature on the Dora case, including articles by analysts who elaborate one or another minor points, and criticisms by a variety of individuals: feminists, child and adolescent therapists, and contemporary theorists. Many of these commentaries point to more satisfactory explanations for Dora's neurosis than that offered by Freud. She was an adolescent girl, only thirteen at the time of the first attempted seduction by Herr K., caught up in a family pattern of manipulation, deceit, and mystification. All the adults most important to her lied about the way she was being exploited. Her mother, a woman whose cleaning obsessions were of near psychotic proportions, was unavailable to her, while her father, whom she loved, handed her over to Herr K. in exchange for the favors of his wife, while, at the same time, denying that anything was going on between himself and Frau K.
    Early critical commentaries can be found in Erik Erikson's book *Insight and Responsibility* (New York: W. W. Norton, 1964), and Steven Marcus's "Freud and Dora: Story, History, Case History" (*Psychoanalysis and Contemporary Thought* 5, 1976, pp. 389–442). I present a discussion of the case in *Freud's Unfinished Journey*, pp. 75–79. Hannah Decker's *Freud, Dora, Vienna 1900* (New York: Free Press, 1991) locates the case in its social-historical context. Charles Bernheimer and Claire Kahane's edited volume, *In Dora's Case: Freud-Hysteria-Feminism* (New York: Columbia University Press, 1985) contains several valuable essays; see, particularly, Madalon Sprengnether, "Enforcing Oedipus: Freud and Dora," pp. 254–276. Paul H. Ornstein's "Did Freud Understand Dora?" in Barry Magid, ed., *Freud's Case Studies: Self-Psychological Perspectives* (pp. 31–85), presents an evaluation of the case from a self-psychological perspective. Patrick J. Mahony's *Freud's Dora* is the most recent and comprehensive overview of the case. It contains an excellent review of the historical and background material, Freud's literary strategies and treatment issues, concurrent concerns from Freud's life, and many useful references. His conclusion is worth quoting: "Freud built gratuitous reconstructions, projecting onto the young Dora his own excitability and wishes for her excitation and corralling her desires within the orbit of his knowledge and ambitions.

Failing in common sense and common decency, he dismissed much of the victim's complaint but praised the attacker. Freud had neither respect nor sympathy for Dora" (p. 143).

159   *"he brought with"*   Freud/Fliess, p. 417.

159   *"yearning . . . which"*   Ibid., p. 332.

160   *"My longing for Rome"*   Ibid., p. 285.

160   *"the favourite hero"*   Freud, *The Interpretation of Dreams,* pp. 196–197.

160   *"a high point"*   Freud/Fliess, p. 449.

160   *"divine city"*   All of the quotations from Freud about his trip to Rome are from Gay, *Freud,* p. 135, who cites postcards available in the Freud Museum.

160   *"conquered those"*   Jones, *The Life and Work,* vol. 2, p. 19.

160   *"conquest of Rome"*   Gay, *Freud,* p. 136.

161   *"those discoverers"*   Freud, *Fragment of an Analysis of a Case of Hysteria,* p. 12.

162   *call himself* Herr Professor   Freud reported the details of how he finally secured his promotion to *Professor Extraordinarious* to Fliess in a letter of March 11, 1902; see Freud/Fliess, pp. 456–457. See also Jones, *The Life and Work,* vol. 1, p. 340, and Gay, *Freud,* pp. 136–137.

162   "Sexual Theory and Anxiety"   Freud/Fliess, p. 389.

163   *"In its disclosure"*   Steven Marcus, introduction to Sigmund Freud, *Three Essays on the Theory of Sexuality* (New York: Basic Books, 1962), p. xx. Late-nineteenth-century Europe, England, and the United States were gripped by a kind of sexual mania in which masturbation, thumb sucking, and the other pleasurable-sensual activities of childhood were believed to cause a host of illnesses, both physical and psychological. Parents were counseled about the dangers of these sexual evils; children had their hands tied down in bed to keep them from "touching" themselves and were told that their thumbs or penises would be cut off if they used them for pleasure. In extreme cases, the genitalia of girls and women were surgically attacked. These ideas and practices, which appear barbarous today, had their origins in religion and were then given a "scientific" cloak by some medical authorities, including the pediatrician Adolf Baginsky, with whom Freud had studied briefly in Berlin on his way back from Paris in 1885. This was the cultural background out of which Freud developed his theories of sexuality. His work, along with that of others, played a crucial role in society's liberation from these old beliefs and practices. Sexual fantasies of a variety of kinds, masturbation, and hostile-rivalrous wishes directed at siblings and parents could now be seen as normal aspects of human development.

164   *"Child psychology"*   Freud, *The Interpretation of Dreams,* p. 127.

164   *"It often happens"*   Freud, *Three Essays on the Theory of Sexuality,* p. 228. As is so often the case, the quotation also contains a personal referent. When he states that "jealousy in a lover is never without an infantile root," one thinks of his own intense jealousy during his courtship of Martha, and its connection with his infancy and childhood.

165   *The* Three Essays *began*   Freud's theories of homosexuality were modern for their time, but they also had their limitations. Here is an illustrative passage, one that also contains veiled self-references:

> In all the cases we have examined we have established the fact that the future inverts [he is speaking of male homosexuals], in the earliest years of their childhood, pass through a phase of very intense but short-lived fixation to a woman—usually their mother—and that, after leaving this behind, they identify themselves with a woman and take *themselves* as their sexual object. That is to say, they . . . look for a young man who resembles themselves and whom *they* may love as their mother loved *them* . . . They have thus repeated all through their lives the mechanism by which their inversion arose. Their compulsive longing for men has turned out to be determined by their ceaseless flight from women [ibid., p. 145].

Present evidence does not support this as an explanation for all male homosexuality—Freud did not say it was—indeed, there are probably as many types of homosexuality as there are of heterosexuality. And, certainly, biological predisposition plays a role, as he would also agree. What is significant is the explanatory model that underpins this account, a model that points to emotional prototypes: choice of the adult love object is shaped by early relations of love or their failure. The account is enormously suggestive: why would connection to the mother be short-lived? What conditions would predispose someone to use themselves as a love object rather than other people? Where are fathers in all this? Freud says, "We have observed that the presence of both parents plays an important part. The absence of a strong father in childhood not infrequently favours the occurrence of inversion." In addition, one can take some of his comments as indirect references to his own history. While his own "bisexuality" drew him to idealized men and not young boys, he had a "short-lived" connection with his mother, missed a "strong father," and was, for many years—until the end of the relationship with Fliess—"compulsively longing" for a man and in "flight from women."

166   *"It has justly"*   Ibid., p. 226.
166   *"Anxiety in children"*   Ibid., p. 224.
166   *"It is only children"*   Ibid., p. 224.
167   *"It is easy to"*   Ibid., p. 203.
167   *"It is an instructive"*   Ibid., p. 191.
168   *"Left to himself"*   Ibid., pp. 275–276. One of Freud's early sexual theories posited masturbation as the cause of "neurasthenia," a neurotic condition characterized by fatigue, lack of energy, and difficulty working—in other words, what today would be termed mild to moderate depression. Freud frequently referred to his own neurasthenia in his correspondence with Martha. The belief that masturbation was the cause of a variety of diseases had its origin in nineteenth-century religious and pseudomedical views on the depleting effects of spending one's "sexual substance," views with no basis in reality. Masturbation, by itself, does not cause depression, fatigue or anything like it, and there is nothing in Freud's own case material to support this idea. So we are left with the puzzle of why he clung to this outmoded notion. Again, substituting *early longing* for *sexuality* provides an answer. We can imagine the structure of his own beliefs as something like this: "If I give in to my longings—my wish to be cared for, for sensual pleasure, for closeness and intimacy—I will be in danger of feeling the great sadness of my early losses: I will be depressed, neurasthenic. So I had better fight against these longings, against these dangerous sexual instincts."

Chapter 13. The Psychoanalytic Movement: Images of War

173   *Freud invited two*   Not much information is available about Rudolf Reitler and Max Kahane. Reitler apparently died young after a long and severe illness, while Kahane, according to Stekel, was a friend from Freud's youth who later "had a bitter break up with Freud"; quoted in Bernhard Handlbauer, *The Freud-Adler Controversy* (Oxford, U.K.: Oneworld, 1998), p. 15.
173   *"These first evenings"*   *The Autobiography of Wilhelm Stekel* (New York: Liveright, 1950), p. 116. Stekel's autobiography gives a good picture of him as a person and his later work as a therapist, as well as his version of the relationship with Freud.
173   *He even gave*   Stekel's article from the *Prager Tagblatt* is reprinted, in translation, in Handlbauer, *The Freud-Adler Controversy*, p. 18.
174   *"The gatherings followed"*   Max Graf, "Reminiscences of Professor Sigmund Freud" (*Psychoanalytic Quarterly* 11, 1942, pp. 471, 474–475). While Freud was hard and demanding with his followers and required compliance of his patients, he also had a generous and playful side, as illustrated by his treatment of a young man named Bruno

Goetz, who consulted him about headaches and eye trouble in 1905. Freud read his poems, gave him a prescription for his eyes—how he knew what was needed remains a mystery—told him he did not need analysis, and sent him on his way with an envelope that contained 200 crowns, which Freud had given "for the pleasure you have given me with your verses and the story of your youth." See Goetz, "Some Memories of Sigmund Freud," in Ruitenbeek, *Freud as We Knew Him,* pp. 266–268.

174   *"[His] pupils were"* Helene Deutsch, "Freud and His Pupils: A Footnote to the History of the Psychoanalytic Movement" (*Psychoanalytic Quarterly* 9, 1940, pp. 188–189). Minutes of Vienna Psycho-Analytical Society were not taken until 1906, when Rank became the secretary, so there are no written records for the period 1902–1906. What occurred during these first years must be reconstructed from the scattered accounts of the participants.

175   *"the ingenious conceptions"* C. G. Jung, *The Psychology of Dementia Praecox,* quoted in William McGuire, "Introduction," Freud/Jung, p. xvii.

175   *must be Welsh* recounted in Jones, *The Life and Work,* vol. 2, p. 43. The Freud/Jones letters give a good picture of the relationship from both sides. Jones published widely in the psychoanalytic literature and was at work on an autobiography, after completing his *Life and Work* of Freud, at the time of his death: see Jones, *Free Associations: Memories of a Psychoanalyst* (New York: Basic Books, 1959).

176   *Karl Abraham* The published version of the Freud/Abraham letters are a selectively edited version of the correspondence; the complete letters are currently being prepared for publication by Ernst Falzeder. A good sense of Abraham's approach to psychoanalysis can be gleaned from his collected papers: Karl Abraham, *Selected Papers of Karl Abraham, M.D.,* trans. Douglas Bryan and Alix Strachey (London: Hogarth Press, 1949).

176   *The majority of Freud's* A good sense of Sachs' personality comes through in his autobiographical *Freud: Master and Friend* (Cambridge, Mass.: Harvard University Press, 1944).

176   *Oskar Pfister* The Freud/Pfister correspondence gives a sense of their relationship.

177   *"a sort of catacomb"* Karl Furtmüller, quoted in Handlbauer, *The Freud-Adler Controversy,* p. 24.

177   *"I was the apostle"* Stekel, *Autobiography,* p. 106.

177   *"His simplicity and"* Emma Goldman, *Living My Life* (New York: Knopf, 1931), p. 173.

178   *"He was dominated"* Sachs, *Freud: Master and Friend,* p. 70.

178   *"brown and lustrous"* Wittels, *Sigmund Freud,* p. 129, quoted in Gay, *Freud,* p. 156.

178   *"critical exploring gaze"* Joan Riviere, "An Intimate Impression," in Ruitenbeek, *Freud as We Knew Him,* p. 129.

178   *"deep-set and piercing"* Sachs, *Freud: Master and Friend,* p. 43.

178   *"almost melodramatic"* Mark Brunswick, in an interview quoted in Roazen, *How Freud Worked,* p. 88.

178   *"at the meetings"* Nunberg and Federn, *Minutes of the Vienna Psychoanalytic Society,* vol. 1, p. xxi.

179   *"The whole clique"* Stekel, quoted in Handlbauer, *The Freud-Adler Controversy,* p. 26.

180   *"led to the complete"* Freud, *Notes upon a Case of Obsessional Neurosis,* pp. 207–208, 249. Elizabeth Zetzel, "Additional Notes upon a Case of Obsessional Neurosis" (*International Journal of Psychoanalysis* 47, 1966, pp. 123–129), was one of the first to use Freud's original notes in a reappraisal of the Rat Man case. I discuss the role of the patient's anxiety as fear of death in *Freud's Unfinished Journey,* pp. 65–67. Sandra Kiersky and James L. Fosshage, "The Two Analyses of Dr. L: A Self-Psychological Perspective on Freud's Treatment of the Rat Man," in Magid, *Freud's Case Studies,* pp. 107–133, present a valuable reinterpretation of the case from a self-psychological point of view. Patrick J. Mahony, in *Freud and the Rat Man,* presents a comprehensive overview,

with most of the relevant references. Mahony, in a very detailed discussion, notes that Freud's claim that there was "a complete restoration of the patient's personality, and . . . removal of his inhibitions" was exaggerated for purposes of impressing his followers and promoting the psychoanalytic movement.

181 *"clear-headed and shrewd"* Freud, *Notes upon a Case of Obsessional Neurosis*, p. 158.

181 *"By all accounts"* Ibid., pp. 200–201.

182 *"When he was very"* Ibid., pp. 205–206.

182 *"the greatest fright"* Ibid., p. 309. This material is from the "original record of the case," but is not included in Freud's published version.

183 *Freud's famous* Analysis Critical discussions of the case of Little Hans can be found in Erich Fromm, "The Oedipus Complex: Comments on the Case of Little Hans" (*Contemporary Psychoanalysis* 4, 1968), pp. 178–188; E. J. Anthony, "The Reactions of Parents to the Oedipal Child," in E. J. Anthony and Theresa Benedek, eds., *Parenthood* (Boston: Little, Brown, 1970), pp. 275–288; and Anna Ornstein, "Little Hans: His Phobia and His Oedipus Complex," in Magid, *Freud's Case Studies,* pp. 87–106. Ornstein presents a discussion from a self-psychological point of view, along with an up-to-date set of references.

184 *"If you do that"* Freud, *Analysis of a Phobia in a Five-Year-Old Boy,* p. 8.

184 *"And have I"* Ibid., pp. 44–45.

184 *published six papers* Freud's papers on technique are *The Handling of Dream-Interpretation in Psycho-Analysis* (1911); *The Dynamics of the Transference* (1912); *Recommendations to Physicians Practising Psycho-Analysis* (1912); *On Beginning the Treatment (Further Recommendations on the Technique of Psycho-Analysis I)* (1913); *Remembering, Repeating and Working-Through (Further Recommendations on the Technique of Psycho-Analysis, II)* (1914); and *Observations on Transference-Love (Further Recommendations on the Technique of Psycho-Analysis, III)* (1915).

185 *"Analytic Treatment should"* Freud, *Lines of Advance in Psycho-Analytic Therapy,* p. 162.

185 *Bruno Walter* Walter's treatment by Freud, including the quoted dialogue, is reported in Bruno Walter, *Theme and Variations: An Autobiography* (London: Hamish Hamilton, 1947), p. 184. Quoted in Clark, *Freud,* p. 193.

185 *man named Albert Hirst* The analysis of Hirst, drawing on an unpublished autobiographical manuscript and other sources, is reported in detail in David J. Lynn, "Sigmund Freud's Psychoanalysis of Albert Hirst" (*Bulletin of the History of Medicine* 71, 1997, pp. 69–93). Roazen interviewed Hirst and has a chapter on his treatment in *How Freud Worked,* pp. 1–30.

186 *equivalent to $190 per session* Information on the equivalent value of Freud's fees in today's dollars was supplied by Dr. Rod Kiewiet, professor of economics at the California Institute of Technology. The 1910 dollar would be equal to $18.86 today, while the 1932 dollar, when Freud was charging $25.00 per session, would be worth $14.54, making his fee during the 1930 depression years the equivalent of $363.00 per session.

186 *"You aren't a weak"* Freud to Hirst, quoted in Roazen, *How Freud Worked,* p. 20.

187 *"I could choke"* Lynn, "Sigmund Freud's Psychoanalysis," p. 82.

187 *While one cannot* Hirst's father broke off the analysis after ten months, and Albert emigrated to New York the next year. There was a flare-up of his old feelings of incompetence and failure in the early 1920s, which he successfully overcame by using the insights he remembered from his analysis and thinking of Freud. He went on to a long and successful career and died in 1974, writing that he was grateful for the mercy of God, the generosity of America, and his analysis with Sigmund Freud. Kurt Eissler interviewed Hirst for the Freud Archives and pressed him to say that the analysis followed the classical method, but Hirst stuck with his memory of what had helped him. The mere fact that he was talking with Freud, in his opinion, had more effect than anything else.

188   *"pure gold of analysis"*   Freud, *Lines of Advance in Psycho-Analytic Therapy,* p. 168.
188   *"Why are you so"*   C. G. Jung, *Memories, Dreams, Reflections,* ed. Aniela Jaffe, trans. Richard Winston and Clara Winston (New York: Random House, 1961; reprinted, Vintage Books, 1989), p. 156.
188   *"The trip to the"*   Ibid., p. 158.
189   *"colitis earned in"*   Gay, *Freud,* p. 567.
190   *"so different than"*   Jones, *The Life and Work,* vol. 2, pp. 59–60.
190   *a form of "savagery"*   Edward Bernays, quoted in Roazen, *Meeting Freud's Family,* p. 170. Freud's nephew, as well as his son Oliver, gave information to Roazen regarding Freud's reaction to America.
190   *"America is gigantic"*   This, and the following remarks about the United States, are cited in Gay, *Freud,* pp. 563–566. Even the loyal Jones could see that Freud's feelings about America were unreasonable:

> Freud did not go away with a very favorable impression of America. Such prejudices were very apt to last with him, and this one never entirely disappeared. . . . Freud himself attributed his dislike of America to a lasting intestinal trouble brought on, so he very unconvincingly asserted, by American cooking, so different from what he was accustomed to. But this ignores the important fact that he had suffered from this complaint most of his life, many years before he went to America and many years after . . . He even went so far as to tell me that his handwriting had deteriorated since the visit to America (*The Life and Work,* vol. 2, pp. 59–60).

191   *"There is a difference"*   Eugen Bleuler in a letter to Freud, October 19, 1910, quoted in Clark, *Freud,* p. 294. Bleuler was the first real psychological psychiatrist and his careful descriptive work on schizophrenia, a term he coined, set the standard for the field at the time. He originated the terms *depth psychology, ambivalence,* and *autism.* His description of schizophrenia stressed the lack of unity of the personality, the schism between thought and affect, "double book-keeping," and the coexistence of love and hate. While Freud was eager to get him as a member and supporter of the psychoanalytic movement, and while Bleuler read and was impressed with a number of psychoanalytic ideas, Freud never seems to have read Bleuler's work and certainly made no use of it in his major case study of the paranoid schizophrenic judge, Schreber, which he published in 1911.
191   *"Most of you are"*   Wittels, *Sigmund Freud,* p. 140.
192   *"I shall be very happy"*   Freud/Jung, p. 388.
192   *"We can say with"*   Stekel, in the announcement for the Third International Psycho-Analytical Congress, quoted in Clark, *Freud,* p. 218.
192   *"This continual arming"*   Eduard Bernstein, quoted in James Joll, *The Origins of the First World War,* 2nd ed. (London: Longman, 1984), p. 79.
193   *"A vast array of"*   Alfred Vagts, *A History of Militarism* (Westport, Conn.: Greenwood Press, 1981), p. 13.

Chapter 14. Alfred Adler: The First Dissident

There is no really satisfactory biography of Adler, though information on his life can be found in a number of sources. Phyllis Bottome describes her husband as Adler's closest English friend and her book *Alfred Adler: Apostle of Freedom* (London: Faber and Faber, 1939) was written in response to Adler's request. It is, not surprisingly, a worshipful work, though it does contain useful information. Carl Furtmüller's 1946 *A Biographical Essay* can be found in Heinz L. Ansbacher and Rowena R. Ansbacher, eds., *Superiority and Social Interest: A Collection of Later Writings* (London: Routledge and Kegan Paul, 1965, pp. 330–393). Furtmüller was a friend and colleague of Adler's and his essay reports events from the Vienna days. Manes Sperber, *Masks of Loneliness: Alfred Adler in Perspective,* trans. by Krishna Winston

(New York: Macmillan, 1974), was written by one of Adler's coworkers and is focused more on his contributions than his life. Ellenberger's chapter on Adler in *The Discovery of the Unconscious* (pp. 571–656) has an excellent summary of biographical information, along with an extensive discussion of Adler's contributions. Roazen's *Freud and His Followers* has an informative chapter on Adler, Stekel, and their differences with Freud. Another contribution is Paul E. Stepansky, *In Freud's Shadow: Adler in Context* (Hillsdale, N.J.: Analytic Press, 1983), which primarily deals with Adler's work and his relationship with Freud and others in his circle. The most recent source is Handlbauer's *The Freud-Adler Controversy,* which contains important information not found elsewhere.

Adler's theories and methods, as presented in his own publications, are not always easy to follow, but Heinz L. Ansbacher and Rowena Ansbacher, in *The Individual Psychology of Alfred Adler* (New York: Basic Books, 1956), have done an excellent job of organizing and presenting his work. As they put it: "His style was extremely terse, so that a number of important ideas may occasionally be found in a single sentence. He generally introduced his concepts only in bare outline, one might say almost as hints."

194   *his brother Alexander's*   Noted in Roazen, *Freud and His Followers,* pp. 178, 569.
196   *economics of their*   The relative social-class background of Freud and Adler's patients comes from a study by Isidor Wasserman, "A Letter to the Editor" (*American Journal of Psychotherapy* 12, 1958, pp. 623–627), cited in Handlbauer, *The Freud-Adler Controversy,* p. 148.
197   *Adler looked to the future*   Freud's hatred of the telephone, as well as other implements of the modern age such as bicycles, is reported in Martin Freud, *Sigmund Freud: Man and Father,* pp. 38, 106, 121.
197   *Child Guidance Clinics*   Information on the clinics comes from Sheldon T. Selesnick, "Alfred Adler, 1870–1937: The Psychology of the Inferiority Complex," in Franz Alexander, Samuel Eisenstein, and Martin Grotjahn, eds., *Psychoanalytic Pioneers* (New York: Basic Books, 1966), p. 84.
197   *"the long and deep"*   Bottome, *Alfred Adler,* p. 117.
198   *"a neurotic symptom"*   Reitler, quoted in Nunberg and Federn, *Minutes of the Vienna Psycho-Analytic Society,* vol. 1, p. 71.
198   *"the speaker has"*   Stekel, quoted in ibid., p. 162.
198   *"disapprove[d] of the"*   Hitschmann, quoted in ibid., p. 163.
198   *"denounce[d] the . . . arrogance"*   Wittels, quoted in ibid., p. 241.
198   *"horrified and fears"*   Stekel, quoted in ibid., pp. 255–256.
198   *"takes exception to"*   Wittels, quoted in ibid., p. 257.
198   *Freud typically stayed*   Ibid., pp. 315–317. The most detailed discussion of the conflicts within the Vienna Society meetings can be found in Handlbauer, *The Freud-Adler Controversy,* pp. 38–66. See also Stepansky, *In Freud's Shadow,* pp. 81–149.
198   *"The assembly is"*   Handlbauer, *The Freud-Adler Controversy,* pp. 62–63.
199   *"demonstrate the existence"*   Adler, quoted in Nunberg and Federn, *Minutes of the Vienna Psycho-Analytic Society,* vol. 1, p. 41.
199   *"cooks very frequently"*   Freud, quoted in ibid., pp. 46–47.
199   *"aggressive drive"*   Both aggression and the need for affection were later redefined. Aggression was subsumed under the more general idea of "striving to overcome," to reach a higher level of integration or wholeness. This is a forerunner of the concept of mastery, central to many modern theories. The need for affection was later defined as a specific manifestation of "community feeling," the orientation toward caring and cooperative relations with others. Aggression was then seen as a pathological form of the striving to overcome, as when the child is "pampered," meets with excessive frustration, lack of understanding, or cruelty. In other words, neurosis arises out of a conflict between aggression and community feeling when the former prevails. The following quote from Ansbacher and Ansbacher, *The Individual Psychology* (p. 48), in which

aggression is defined as "masculine protest," gives a good idea of how Adler saw these motives in operation:

> Every form of inner compulsion in normal and neurotic individuals may be derived from this attempt at the masculine protest. Where it succeeds, it naturally strengthens the masculine tendencies enormously, posits for itself the highest and often unattainable goals, develops a craving for satisfaction and triumph, intensifies all abilities and egotistical drives, increases envy, avarice and ambition, and brings about an inner restlessness which makes any external compulsion, lack of satisfaction, disparagement, and injury unbearable. Defiance, vengeance, and resentment are its steady accompaniments. Through a boundless increase in sensitivity, it leads to continuous conflicts.

This is a good description of what today would be called pathological narcissism with characteristic narcissistic rage.

199   *"Fighting, wrestling"*   Ibid., p. 35.
199   *"Children want to be"*   Ibid., p. 40.
200   *"To this is added"*   Ibid., p. 55.
200   *"All neurotics have"*   Ibid., p. 47.
201   *"For our consideration"*   Ibid., p. 64.
201   *"The sexual references"*   Ibid., p. 72.
201   *"I have seen many"*   Ibid., p. 69.
201   *"difficult to understand"*   Freud, quoted in ibid., p. 70. They draw on an early paper by Kenneth M. Colby, "On the Disagreement between Freud and Adler" (*American Imago* 8, pp. 229–238), which made use of the *Minutes* before they were made public.
201   *"Two traits are"*   Freud, quoted in Ansbacher and Ansbacher, *The Individual Psychology*, pp. 70–71.
202   *"I may even speak"*   Freud, *On the History of the Psychoanalytic Movement*, p. 51.
202   *"a morose and cantankerous"*   Jones, *The Life and Work*, vol. 2, p. 130.
203   *The last point*   Adler's theories may be summed up as follows: his observations and concepts are stated in a language close to human experience; aggression, the seeking of power, and competitive striving are central (the concept of "sibling rivalry" is his); and libido is defined as a need for affection and love. The theory is a psychology of the ego: it is one's self that feels inferior or competent, unmanly or strong, weak or powerful. Freud criticized this emphasis on the ego, but it is a feature that places Adler close to many contemporary psychoanalytic theorists. Adler's stress on a drive to overcome, to seek wholeness, anticipates current views that speak of the need for an integrated identity, a coherent self. Finally, his concept of a "life plan" or "personal myth" anticipates modern ideas about internal structures of belief.
203   *"Freud took a"*   Sachs, *Freud: Master and Friend*, p. 53.
203   *"Freud had a sheaf"*   Wittels, quoted in Clark, *Freud*, p. 308.
203   *"misconceived and dangerous"*   Handlbauer, *The Freud-Adler Controversy*, p. 131.
203   *Nine members*   Before resigning, the group supporting Adler issued a statement protesting the actions of the society: "Whereas it is our opinion that the Society and the *Zentralblatt* should be levers of power in the face of opponents of psychoanalysis . . . these actions [the attack on Adler and his removal as editor] show ever more conspicuously the attempts to create levers of power within the framework of psychoanalysis, and to uphold them with all the ruthlessness typical of power struggles. Our feelings rise up against such actions." Quoted in Handlbauer, *The Freud-Adler Controversy*, p. 140.
204   *"Rather tired after"*   Freud/Jung, p. 273.
204   *"morbid sensitivity"*   Freud/Jones, pp. 93, 112.
204   *"If we focus on"*   Ansbacher and Ansbacher, *The Individual Psychology*, p. 115.
204   *"Difficult questions in"*   Ibid., p. 117.

205 *"All masturbatory"* Stekel, quoted in Nunberg and Federn, *Minutes of the Vienna Psycho-Analytic Society,* vol. 3, p. 345.

206 *"injuriousness of masturbation"* Freud, quoted in ibid., vol. 4, pp. 38–39, 41. Freud summarized his views on pp. 92–94. The discussions of masturbation in the Vienna Society revealed that most of the members accepted Freud's view that it was directly linked to neurosis (see vol. 3, p. 320). Stekel paid more attention to the observable evidence, seeing the conflicts of masturbation as socially determined; that is, Catholics are more guilty. But his was a minority view, since Adler and the other nine had already been driven out. In a discussion of January 24, 1912, Josef Karl Friedjung discussed an empirical study in which he surveyed a number of nannies, who reported that all (male and female) infants masturbate; hence, it could not be much of an explanation for who becomes neurotic and who does not. Freud was not receptive to such evidence, stating that psychoanalysis reaches back to the first and second year and proves otherwise.

206 *Most of the other* Discussion of Freud forcing Stekel out of the editorship is in Roazen, *Freud and His Followers,* pp. 211–222. See also Handlbauer, *The Freud-Adler Controversy,* pp. 138–139.

206 *"partly through the"* Freud, *On the History of the Psycho-Analytic Movement,* p. 19.

206 *"treason"* Freud/Abraham, p. 127.

206 *"that pig, Stekel"* Freud/Jones, p. 264.

207 *Like Josef Breuer* The references to Stekel still making friendly overtures to Freud are in Roazen, *Freud and His Followers,* p. 220, and Roazen, *How Freud Worked,* p. 126. Krüll has an appreciation for the forward-looking nature of Stekel's ideas and the way in which he posed a threat to Freud's defenses; see *Freud and His Father,* pp. 190, 265 n.

Chapter 15. The King and His Knights: The Committee

Phyllis Grosskurth's *The Secret Ring: Freud's Inner Circle and the Politics of Psychoanalysis* presents a detailed history of the Committee, portraits of the major players, and a comprehensive, fair-minded account. Christine Gallant, *Tabooed Jung: Marginality as Power* (New York: New York University Press, 1996), locates the political machinations represented by the Committee in the context of a broader social analysis, bringing in many useful references.

208 *"a tight, small"* Gay, *Freud,* pp. 229–230.

208 *"What took hold of"* Freud/Jones, p. 147.

209 *"a boyish perhaps"* Ibid., p. 148.

209 *"the idea of a small"* Ibid., p. 149.

210 *"a fiery little man"* Roazen, *Freud and His Followers,* p. 342.

210 *"the l.b." for little beast* The complete quote is from a letter from James to Alix Strachey: "I had a very tiresome hour with Jones . . . the little beast—if I may venture so to describe him—is really most irritating." Perry Meisel and Walter Kendrick, eds., *Bloomsbury/Freud: The Letters of James and Alix Strachey* (New York: Basic Books, 1985), p. 83.

212 *"I simply could not"* Sachs, *Freud: Master and Friend,* p. 128.

212 *"fighter . . . [who] stood within"* Ibid., pp. 112, 117, 122–123.

213 *"happy, tranquil, perfect"* Hilda Abraham, as reported by Martin Grotjahn in "Karl Abraham: The First German Psychoanalyst," in Alexander, Eisenstein, and Grotjahn, *Psychoanalytic Pioneers,* p. 2.

213 *"perhaps a little cool"* Gay, *Freud,* p. 180.

213 *"orderly, methodical"* Sachs and Theodor Reik, quoted in Roazen, *Freud and His Followers,* p. 331.

213 *"was . . . at times curiously"* Jones, "Introductory Memoir," in Karl Abraham, *Selected Papers of Karl Abraham, M.D.,* trans. Douglas Bryan and Alix Strachey (London: Hogarth Press and the Institute of Psycho-Analysis, 1949), p. 39.

214 *"He had watched"* Grotjahn, "Karl Abraham," p. 11.

214 *"I shall more particularly"* Abraham, "The Experiencing of Sexual Traumas as a Form of Sexual Experience," in *Selected Papers,* p. 48.

214 *"If there is an"* Ibid., p. 54.

215 *"infantile sexual traumas"* Ibid. Abraham's other papers reveal the extremely doctrinaire nature of his views. In "A Particular Form of Neurotic Resistance Against the Psycho-Analytic Method," *Selected Papers,* pp. 303–311, patients who do not agree with his interpretations are said to have "an unusual degree of defiance, which has its prototype in the child's conduct towards its father." Patients who do not comply, who think they may know more about themselves than he does, are displaying their "envy." This paper makes clear that Abraham has complete confidence in the analyst's rules and authority, and if things do not proceed as required, if the patient does not wish to lie on the couch or follow the basic rule of free association, this is evidence of an unconscious motive—sexual, sadistic, envious—on their part. In "Manifestations of the Female Castration Complex," *Selected Papers,* pp. 338–369, he takes the position that the societal treatment of women has little importance:

> It is said that girls even in childhood are at a disadvantage in comparison to boys because boys are allowed greater freedom; or that in later life men are permitted to choose their profession and can extend their sphere of activity in many directions, and in especial are subjected to far fewer restrictions in their sexual life. Psychoanalysis, however, shows that conscious arguments of this sort are of limited value, and are the result of rationalization—a process which veils the underlying motives. Direct observation of young girls shows unequivocally that at a certain stage of their development they feel at a disadvantage as regards the male sex on account of the inferiority of their sexual genitals. The results obtained from the psycho-analysis of adults fully agree with this observation. We find that a large proportion of women have not overcome this disadvantage, or, expressed psycho-analytically, that they have not successfully repressed and sublimated it [p. 339].

> The remainder of the paper traces a variety of neurotic and symptomatic states— frigidity, homosexuality, a sadistic-hostile or "anal" attitude toward men—to the woman's penis envy, to her inability to accept her anatomical inferiority.

215 *"He was entirely devoted"* Jones, *The Life and Work,* vol. 2, p. 161.

216 *"Our Congress this year"* Eitingon, "Bulletin of the International Psychoanalytical Association" (*International Journal of Psychoanalysis* 9, 1928, p. 133).

Chapter 16. Carl Gustav Jung: The Favorite Son Expelled

The major source of information about Jung's childhood, as well as his version of the break with Freud, is C. G. Jung, *Memories, Dreams, Reflections,* ed. Aniela Jaffe, trans. Richard Winston and Clara Winston (New York: Vintage Books, 1989). This is an autobiographical work that he dictated between 1956 and 1959 when he was over eighty years old. Jung's many essays and books can be found in the twenty volumes of his *Collected Works,* trans. R. F. C. Hull (New York: Pantheon 1953–1983). The fourth volume, *Freud and Psychoanalysis* (1961), contains Jung's papers from the years when he was in the psychoanalytic movement, as well as later essays dealing with Freud and psychoanalysis. The complete Freud/Jung letters are, of course, an invaluable resource.

Many biographies and other works containing biographical information have been written about Jung, though there is no recent, full-scale biography that is really satisfactory. Victor Brome, *Jung* (New York: Atheneum, 1981), is a readable earlier account. Frank McLynn, *Carl Gustav Jung* (New York: St. Martin's Press, 1996), is the most recent biography but it is, in my view, unsatisfactory due to the author's lack of sympathy and understanding for his subject. Deirdre Bair is currently working on a new biography of Jung which, judging from her previous books, should be just what is needed. Other useful works include the chapter on Jung in Ellenberger, *The Discovery of the Unconscious* (pp. 657–748), which contains both a survey of the life and a thorough consideration of the contributions. Roazen, *Freud and His Followers*, has a chapter on Jung (pp. 223–295), focused on the relationship and the break with Freud. Atwood and Stolorow have an insightful chapter on Jung in their *Faces in a Cloud* (pp. 73–109), in which they relate core aspects of his theories to his early experiences. Other useful books include Linda Donn, *Freud and Jung: Years of Friendship, Years of Loss;* Robert C. Smith, *The Wounded Jung: Effects of Jung's Relationships on His Life and Work* (Evanston, Ill.: Northwestern University Press, 1996); and Christine Gallant, *Tabooed Jung: Marginality as Power.*

217 *"a fine, warm summer"* Jung, *Memories, Dreams, Reflections*, p. 6.

218 *"I also had vague"* Ibid., p. 9.

218 *"was deeply troubled"* Ibid., p. 8. Smith, *The Wounded Jung*, reports that the uncensored version of *Memories, Dreams, Reflections* contains many more details of the mother's mental aberrations; that she "was hysterical from disappointment with her husband, whose life took a turn for the worse after he . . . left the University" (p. 17), and that she only recovered after he died, when Carl was twenty-one. From his college days on, Freud turned to science and rationality and was, throughout his life, vehemently antireligious: God was nothing more than the projection of a childish wish for an all-powerful father; religion was to be dethroned by superior psychoanalytic interpretation. Jung, while rejecting the conventional Christianity of his pastor-father, continued to search for meaning in the world's myths and spiritual belief systems.

218 *"first conscious trauma"* Ibid. p. 17.

219 *"I had never come across"* Albert Oeri, quoted in John Kerr, *A Most Dangerous Method: The Story of Jung, Freud and Sabina Spielrein* (New York: Knopf, 1994), p. 46.

219 *"It was as if I"* Jung, *Memories, Dreams, Reflections*, p. 19.

219 *"Somewhere deep in the"* Ibid., pp. 44–45.

219 *Both extremes, inferiority* Jung's discussion of his "No. 1" and "No. 2" personalities is in ibid., pp. 68–69.

220 *"a man I once worshiped"* Jung, in Freud/Jung, p. 95.

220 *a study of "occult" phenomena* See Jung, *On the Psychology and Pathology of So-Called Occult Phenomena*, in Jung, *Collected Works*, vol. 1, pp. 3–88.

221 *Diagnostic Association Studies* See Jung, *Studies in Word Association* (New York: Moffat Yard, 1919).

221 *"I am confident that"* Freud, in Freud/Jung, p. 3.

222 *"Your therapy seems"* This, and the previous comments on Bleuler, are from ibid., pp. 4–5.

222 *"especially gratified to"* Freud, in ibid., p. 5.

222 *"You see that you"* Freud, in ibid., p. 8.

222 *"My material is totally"* Jung, in ibid., p. 14.

222 *"You are quite mistaken"* Freud, in ibid., p. 17.

223 *"exceedingly friendly and"* Jung, in ibid., p. 20.

223 *colleague Ludwig Binswanger* Binswanger, who had a long career in psychiatry, describes the initial visit that he and Jung made to Freud, as well as his own relationship with Freud over the many succeeding years. See *Sigmund Freud: Reminiscences of a Friendship* (New York: Grune and Stratton, 1957).

223 *"the first man of real"* Jung, *Memories, Dreams, Reflections*, p. 149.

223 *"At the moment I"* Jung, in Freud/Jung, p. 45.

223   *"In your six-year-old"*   Freud, in ibid., p. 48.

224   *"I have a boundless"*   Jung, in ibid., p. 95.

224   *"The day after our"*   Binswanger, *Sigmund Freud,* p. 2.

224   *"I am suffering all"*   Jung, in Freud/Jung, pp. 95–96.

224   *"also the reason why"*   Jung to Jolande Jacobi, quoted in Donn, *Freud and Jung,* p. 151.

225   *"Heartiest thanks for"*   Jung, in Freud/Jung, p. 96.

225   *Jung was solidly in*   For Jung's publications during the years when he worked closely with Freud, see *Freud and Psychoanalysis (Collected Works,* vol. 4).

225   *"winning the Swiss"*   Kerr, in *A Most Dangerous Method,* argues that in 1907–1908, it was not at all clear whether Freud's psychoanalytic movement in Vienna, or the work centered around Bleuler and Jung in Zurich, would become more prominent in the world at large.

225   *"I evidently still have"*   Freud, in Freud/Jung, p. 209.

225   *"You may rest assured"*   Jung, in ibid., p. 212.

225   *"when I formally adopted"*   Freud, in ibid., p. 218.

225   *"Jung was to be the"*   Jones, *The Life and Work,* vol. 2, p. 33.

225   *He would lash out*   Jung's reports on colleagues, patients, and his work as a therapist reveal his emotional volatility, along with his original and critical mind. Abraham was at the Burghölzli during these years and Jung never liked or trusted him, suspecting him of stealing the ideas of others. As he put it in an early letter to Freud: "Of all our assistants he is the one who always holds a little aloof from the main work and then suddenly steps into the limelight with a publication, as a loner. Not only I but the other assistants too have found this rather unpleasant. He is intelligent but not original, highly adaptable, but totally lacking in psychological empathy, for which reason he is usually very unpopular with the patients" (Jung, in Freud/Jung, p. 78).

These remarks, like others—he referred to Max Eitingon as "a totally impotent gasbag" (see Freud/Jung, p. 90)—were in part motivated by rivalry for Freud's favor, a fact which Jung admitted. Nevertheless, the comments on Abraham seem prescient in the light of the German analyst's later career. Freud, while not disagreeing with the substance of Jung's remarks, urged cooperation for the sake of the cause. When Jung eventually began to take a position that departed from the Professor's, Abraham was quick to attack, branding him a heretic.

225   *woman named Sabina Spielrein*   Jung's work with Spielrein, as well as her later life and career, are chronicled in Aldo Carotenuto, *A Secret Symmetry: Sabina Spielrein between Jung and Freud,* trans. Arno Pomerans, John Shepley, and Krishna Winston (New York: Pantheon, 1982), and Kerr, *A Most Dangerous Method.*

226   *"When Freud visited me"*   Jung, *Memories, Dreams, Reflections,* p. 128. The American psychiatrist Irmarita Putnam first saw Jung and then Freud in therapy in the 1920s and remarked that "one could not have imagined any two people more different." Quoted in Roazen, *How Freud Worked,* p. 172.

226   *"whenever I got stuck"*   Jung, in Freud/Jung, p. 153.

227   *Symbols of Transformations*   See Jung, *Symbols of Transformation,* in the *Collected Works,* vol. 5.

227   *"I am afraid there is"*   Freud, in Freud/Jung, p 469.

227   *"all the difficulties that"*   Jung, in ibid., p. 471.

227   *"very similar to what"*   Freud, in ibid., p. 507.

227   *"I am reading fat books"*   Freud/Ferenczi, vol. 1, p. 316.

228   *"I awaited your letters"*   Freud, in Freud/Jung, p. 488.

228   *"One repays a teacher"*   Jung, in ibid., p. 491.

228   *"I spared him nothing"*   Freud in Freud/Ferenczi, vol. 1, p. 434.

228   *"How sweet it must be"*   Jones, *The Life and Work,* vol. 2, p. 317.

228   *"The dining-room of"*   Freud in Freud/Jones, p. 524.

228   *"Repressed feelings, this time"* Freud in a letter to Ludwig Binswanger, quoted in Binswanger, *Sigmund Freud,* p. 49.
229   *"I saw Munich first"* Freud/Jones, p. 182.
229   *"I . . . have settled well"* Freud in Freud/Ferenczi, vol. 1, p. 440.
229   *"This is just"* Jung in Freud/Jung, p. 526.
229   *"May I say a few words"* Ibid., pp. 534–535.
230   *"One who while behaving"* Freud, in ibid., p. 539.
230   *"I accede to your wish"* Jung, in ibid., p. 540.
230   *"not at all too early"* Jones in Freud/Jones, p. 199.
230   *"Jung is crazy, but"* Freud in Freud/Abraham, p. 141. There is an interesting contrast between Jung's account of the time with Freud—written many years later in *Memories, Dreams, Reflections*—and Freud's 1914 *History* essay. When both are compared with the letters the two men wrote at the time, it is clear that Jung's version is far less distorted. In the account in *Memories,* he is open about his admiration for Freud, describes their differences more or less fairly, and does not attack or slander his former mentor. In Freud's *History,* he presents himself as the tolerant but mistreated father of his angry ungrateful sons, Adler and Jung.
230   *"So we are at last"* Ibid., p. 186. The editors of the Freud/Abraham letters changed "pious parrots" to the milder "disciples." (See Ferris, *Dr. Freud,* p. 435 n.)
231   *"After the break with"* Jung, *Memories, Dreams, Reflections,* pp. 167, 170.
231   *"I was menaced by"* Ibid., pp. 176, 179.
231   *"the myth in which"* Ibid., p. 171.
232   *"confrontation with the"* Ibid., p. 170.
232   *Toni Wolff, a woman* Antonia "Toni" Wolff, was, like Sabina Spielrein, a hospitalized psychotic patient when Jung first began treating her. She benefited from her therapy and was later helpful to him when he descended into a near-psychotic state himself after the break with Freud. Jung later made her his mistress and insisted that she be accepted by his wife, which, over the years, became an extremely difficult situation for the two women. Emma, from an important Zurich family, was socially compromised by her husband's affair, while Toni suffered the plight of the other woman. While she recovered from her psychosis and was active as a Jungian therapist, she was bitter about her position, became an alcoholic, and died young from the effects of her drinking. See Brome, *Jung,* pp. 129–132; McLynn, *Carl Gustav Jung,* pp. 182–184; Donn, *Freud and Jung,* pp. 178–181; and Polly Young-Eisendrath, letter to the author, 1998.

Chapter 17. The First World War

233   *"the bombshell has burst"* Freud, in Freud/Abraham, p. 181.
234   *"a frenzy of delight"* James Joll, *The Origins of the First World War,* 2nd ed. (London: Longman, 1984), p. 131.
234   *"a new Austrianness"* Holger H. Herwig, *The First World War: Germany and Austria-Hungary, 1914–1918* (New York: St. Martin's Press, 1998), p. 273.
234   *"people are very dejected"* Alexander Freud, quoted in Gay, *Freud,* p. 346.
234   *"These simple, starving"* Oscar Kokoschka, quoted in Martin Gilbert, *The First World War: A Complete History* (New York: Henry Holt, 1994), p. 46.
234   *"For the first time"* Freud in Freud/Abraham, pp. 185–186.
234   *"Freud's immediate"* Jones, *The Life and Work,* vol. 2, p. 171.
235   *"I have felt like"* Ferenczi in Freud/Ferenczi, vol. 2, p. 11.
235   *"hoped to get a"* Freud in Freud/Ferenczi, p. 13.
235   *as a ten-year-old* Gay, *Freud,* p. 26.

235 *war of movement* George L. Mosse, *Fallen Soldiers: Reshaping the Memory of the World Wars* (New York: Oxford University Press, 1990), p. 4.

235 *the Austro-Hungarian army* Joll, *The Origins of the First World War,* p. 165.

236 *The bloody realities* Mosse, *Fallen Soldiers,* p. 19.

236 *"We must embrace it"* Abel Bonnard, quoted in Joll, *The Origins of the First World War,* p. 217.

236 *"Just as storms"* Karl von Stengel, quoted in Roger Chickering, *Imperial Germany and a World Without War: The Peace Movement and German Society, 1892–1914* (Princeton, N.J.: Princeton University Press, 1975), p. 394.

236 *"Europe, in her insanity"* Albert Einstein, quoted in Gilbert, *The First World War,* p. 40.

236 *Einstein was among* Roland N. Stromberg, *Redemption by War: The Intellectuals and 1914* (Lawrence: Regents Press of Kansas, 1982), p. 190.

237 *"Woe to him"* General Helmuth von Moltke (the elder), quoted in Niall Ferguson, *The Pity of War* (New York: Basic Books, 1999), p. 8. The "short war illusion" was not shared by all European military thinkers. In 1895, the quartermaster of the German Staff, Major General Köpke, warned of a future war of "tedious and bloody crawling" (ibid., p. 88). In 1912, this view was echoed by Moltke (the younger) and General Erich Ludendorff in a letter to the War Ministry (ibid., p. 97). In Russia, at the end of the century, Lieutenant Colonel A. A. Gulevich of the General Staff Academy predicted that the next European war would be long and exhausting. It is thought that Gulevich might have contributed to Ivan Bloch's work; see Walter Pintner, "Russian Military Thought: The Western Model and the Shadow of Suvorov," in Peter Paret, ed., with the collaboration of Gordon A. Craig and Felix Gilbert, *Makers of Modern Strategy: From Machiavelli to the Nuclear Age* (Princeton, N.J.: Princeton University Press, 1986), p. 365. Lord Kitchener, the newly appointed British secretary for war, forecast at the first cabinet meeting that the war would last three years and require an army of several million men; see Anthony Babington, *Shell-Shock: A History of the Changing Attitudes to War Neurosis* (London: Leo Cooper, 1997), p. 42.

237 *"H. G. Wells"* Paul Crook, *Darwinism, War and History* (Cambridge, U.K.: Cambridge University Press, 1994), p. 101.

237 *"Eight to ten million"* Friedrich Engels, quoted in Joll, *The Origins of the First World War,* p. 207.

237 *"Jones, is of course"* Freud, in Freud/Abraham, p. 195.

237 *"living from one"* Ibid., p. 193.

238 *"I have thought up"* Freud, in Freud/Ferenczi, vol. 2, p. 13.

238 *"A chill of horror"* Captain Spears, quoted in Gilbert, *The First World War,* pp. 51–52.

238 *"Terror overcomes"* General Helmuth von Moltke (the younger), quoted in ibid., p. 73.

238 *"One finds"* Henry James, quoted in Alan Price, *The End of the Age of Innocence: Edith Wharton and the First World War* (New York: St. Martin's Press, 1998), p. xii.

238 *"by catastrophic strokes"* Freud, in Freud/Abraham, p. 195.

238 *unleashed brutality* Ibid., p. 197.

238 *"It is like remembering"* Ibid., 197.

238 *"In the spring"* Freud, in Freud/Ferenczi, vol. 2, p. 37.

239 *"First and most impressive"* Victor Fleming, quoted in Gilbert, *The First World War,* p. 112.

239 *Germany had suffered* Herwig, *The First World War,* p. 119.

239 *In the first five months* Gilbert, *The First World War,* p. 123.

239 *The Austro-Hungarian army* Herwig, *The First World War,* p. 120.

239 *food shortages* Ibid., p. 274.

239 *"The work is again going well"* Freud, in Freud/Ferenczi, vol. 2, p. 36.

240 *"I may say"* Ibid., p. 37.

240 *"Impotence and penury"* Freud, in Freud/Abraham, p. 208.

240 *"I thought in all clarity"* Ibid., p. 210.

240   *On February 16 . . . he gave a lecture*   According to Ernst Falzeder and Eva Brabant, the editors of the correspondence between Freud and Ferenczi, the lecture to the B'nai B'rith was given on February 16, 1915. Slightly altered, it was published as the second part of *Thoughts on War and Death;* see Freud/Ferenczi, p. 56 n. In the *Standard Edition,* Strachey states that *Our Attitude towards Death* was written in April, after *The Disillusionment of the War.* Because the contents of the two parts of the essay correspond to the order given by Falzeder and Brabant, I accepted their chronology. Freud had joined the B'nai B'rith lodge—his Jewish brethren—in 1897, when he was feeling isolated without Breuer and with Fliess in Berlin. He gave a few lectures, but his participation faded once the psychoanalytic movement began after 1902. Isolated from colleagues by the war, he again turned to this group.

240   *"saucy . . . gallows humor"*   Freud, in Freud/Ferenczi, vol. 2, p. 56.

241   *"We are paralyzed"*   Freud, *Our Attitude towards Death,* p. 291.

241   *"strips us of the"*   Ibid., p. 299. With the success of the Central Powers, Abraham compared psychoanalysis with a military campaign, writing that the Entente was like a patient resisting an interpretation: "In principle, the war has already been won, though the other side do not want to admit it yet. This is similar to what we see in some difficult cases. We are used to these resistances and to seeing them yield in the end." Abraham, in Freud/Abraham, p. 231.

241   *"at bottom"*   Freud, *Our Attitude towards Death,* p. 289.

241   *"a gang of murderers"*   Ibid., p. 297.

242   *"we will not be consoled"*   Ibid., p. 290.

242   *"when the highest stake"*   Ibid., p. 290.

242   *"dare not contemplate"*   Ibid., p. 291.

242   *"interesting . . . its full content"*   Ibid.

242   *"war cannot be abolished"*   Ibid., p. 299.

242   *"If you want to preserve"*   Ibid., p. 300.

242   *"relished the excitement"*   For sources of this feeling see Samuel Hynes, *The Soldiers' Tale: Bearing Witness to Modern War* (New York: Penguin Books, 1997), p. 39, and Ferguson, *The Pity of War,* pp. 361–362.

242   *"a Paleolithic savage"*   Richard Tawney, quoted in Alfredo Bonadeo, *Mark of the Beast: Death and Degradation in the Literature of the Great War* (Lexington: University Press of Kentucky, 1989), p. 20.

242   *"the beast that is inside man"*   Pierre Drieu La Rochelle, quoted in ibid., p. 55.

242   *"workers of war"*   Stephan Máday, quoted in Herwig, *The First World War,* p. 204.

242   *"we are all screws in a machine"*   Ernst Toller, quoted in ibid., p. 204.

242   *"the tense excitement"*   Ernst Jünger, quoted in Bonadeo, *Mark of the Beast,* p. 36

242   *no one believed in their own death*   Freud, *Our Attitude towards Death,* p. 297.

243   *"kept alive by brandy"*   Wilfred Owen, quoted in Bonadeo, *Mark of the Beast,* p. 96.

243   *"death is no longer a chance"*   Freud, *Our Attitude towards Death,* p. 291.

243   *"nearly every soldier"*   C. R. M. F. Cruttwell, quoted in Hynes, *The Soldiers' Tale,* pp. 56–57.

243   *the epidemic of mental illness*   Gilbert, *The First World War,* p. 61; Babington, *Shell-Shock,* p. 43.

244   *"We cannot help but feel"*   Freud, *The Disillusionment of the War,* p. 275.

244   *"a cog in the gigantic"*   Ibid., p. 275. Freud referred solely to the emotions of civilians; he did not extend the idea of helplessness to the soldiers in the trenches.

244   *"We had expected"*   Ibid., p. 276. Here, Freud's discussion of European disillusionment provides a clear example of what Edward Said calls the culture of imperialism: world domination has "fallen" to the nations "of white race" because of their higher civilization, not their military conquests. Freud had long enjoyed referring to himself as a "conquistador." The plans of the Austro-Hungarian Empire to crush the Serbs at the start of the war did not trouble him; Ernest Jones, having read a history of Croatia,

was sympathetic to the Serbs, and he also was aware in 1912 that Freud was inclined to narrow views of other nations when he remarked: "The Serbs are so impudent." Jones, *The Life and Work*, vol. 2, p. 168. The widespread and unquestioned nature of such rhetoric in Europe is discussed in Said, *Culture and Imperialism* (New York: Knopf, 1993).

244   *"We pictured"*   Freud, *The Disillusionment of the War*, p. 278.

244   *"stand helpless"*   Ibid., p. 280.

245   *a general human failing*   Freud had a long-standing habit of expressing derogatory national stereotypes in his correspondence. Even in these essays, he could not resist taking a poke at Americans: " . . . as shallow and empty as, let us say, an American flirtation . . . as contrasted with a Continental love affair . . . " Freud, *Our Attitude towards Death*, p. 290. While studying in Paris, in a letter to Minna Bernays, he described the French as "the people of psychological epidemics, of hysterical mass convulsions." Gay, *Freud*, p. 48. Before the war, Freud had been an Anglophile, but he reflected the chauvinism stimulated by the war in a letter to Lou Andreas-Salomé, written in November 1914: "It is a consolation that our German people have behaved best in all this; perhaps because it is certain of victory. The tradesman faced with bankruptcy is always a swindler." Freud/Salomé, p. 21. He was, however, quite indignant when, after the invasion of Belgium, Germany was called barbaric. Freud, *The Disillusionment of the War*, p. 279.

245   *As late as 1917*   Gilbert, *The First World War*, p. 318.

245   *"suggest that the motives"*   Joll, *The Origins of the First World War*, p. 142.

245   *Ideologies such as*   See ibid., chapter 8, pp. 199–229, for a detailed discussion of prewar culture.

246   *"Much evidence belies"*   Stromberg, *Redemption by War*, pp. 190–191. See Eric J. Leed, *No Man's Land: Combat and Identity in World War I* (Cambridge, U.K.: Cambridge University Press, 1979), for a longer discussion of the craving for some higher purpose in life among the volunteers for the war.

246   *"Some of the assaults"*   Lloyd George, quoted in Gilbert, *The First World War*, p. 537.

246   *"We may anticipate"*   Freud, *The Disillusionment of the War*, p. 286.

246   *in the winter of 1914*   Writing to Lou Andreas-Salomé in November 1914, he was profoundly gloomy about the postwar world: "The world will never again be a happy place. It is too hideous. And the saddest thing about it is that it is exactly the way we should have expected people to behave from our knowledge of psychoanalysis." Freud/Salomé, p. 21.

246   *"This . . . is the one"*   Jules Romain, quoted in Bonadeo, *Mark of the Beast*, p. 123.

246   *Twelve essays were planned*   Only five of the planned essays were eventually published, though a sixth, "A Phylogenetic Fantasy," has recently been unearthed in manuscript form. His letters to Ferenczi concerning this last paper show his enthusiasm for Lamarckian ideas on the inheritance of acquired characteristics. The "fantasy" expanded the theory he had earlier presented in *Totem and Taboo*; here he would show how anxiety and neurosis were passed down through the history of the species, how the "childhood" of mankind paralleled the childhood of individuals, and how this "phylogenetic inheritance" was the breeding ground for psychological disturbance. He guessed that certain anxieties originated when men were threatened with extinction in the Ice Age, and how primitive methods of birth control might be implicated in hysteria. Ilse Grubrich-Simitis, ed., *A Phylogenetic Fantasy: Overview of the Transference Neuroses*, trans. Axel Hoffer and Peter T. Hoffer (Cambridge, Mass.: Harvard University Press, 1987).

247   *"my ideal and woebegone child"*   Freud, in Freud/Fliess, p. 216.

247   *"one part of the ego"*   Freud, *Mourning and Melancholia*, p. 247.

247   *By April, ration cards*   Herwig, *The First World War*, p. 275.

248   *"My second warrior"*   Freud, in Freud/Salomé, p. 35.

248 *"For had I known"* Ibid., p. 43.
248 *funeral wreaths* Freud in Freud/Abraham, p. 235.
248 *"for two weeks"* Freud in Freud/Ferenczi, vol. 2, p. 182.
248 *The poor harvest* Herwig, *The First World War,* p. 277.
248 *"her grief surpassed"* Freud in Freud/Abraham, p. 255.
248 *"The Hungarians"* Ibid., p. 255.
248 *"people in the suburbs"* J. M. Roberts, *Europe, 1880–1945* (London: Longman, 1970), p. 285.
249 *"strings of poorly dressed"* Herwig, *The First World War,* p. 274.
249 *necessitated the recall* Gilbert, *The First World War,* p. 391.
249 *"Yesterday, I smoked"* Freud in Freud/Ferenczi, vol. 2, p. 245.
249 *"like a doctor's family"* Freud in Freud/Abraham, p. 276.
249 *"mood is powerless"* Ibid., p. 275.
249 *"this time I felt"* Freud in Freud/Ferenczi, vol. 2, p. 291.
249 *"Analysis then showed"* Ibid., p. 291.
250 *the epidemic* Ibid., p. 291.
250 *"Annerl's analysis"* Ibid., p. 302.
250 *he had lost* Celia Bertin, *Marie Bonaparte: A Life* (New York: Harcourt, Brace, Jovanovich, 1982), p. 156.
250 *"The Hapsburgs"* Freud in Freud/Ferenczi, vol. 2, p. 311.
250 *"I expect"* Ibid., p. 310.
250 *"Our analysis"* Ibid., p. 311.
250 *More soldiers were killed* Gilbert, *The First World War,* p. 540.
250 *The devastation* Béla K. Királyi, "Elements of Limited and Total Warfare," in Robert A. Kann, Béla K. Királyi, and Paula S. Fichtner, eds., *The Hapsburg Empire in World War I* (Boulder, Colo.: East European Monographs, 1975), p. 137.
251 *"One can say"* Paul Valery, quoted in Hans Kohn, "The Crisis in European Thought and Culture," in Jack Roth, ed., *World War I: A Turning Point in Modern History* (New York: Knopf, 1967), p. 29.
251 *Many experienced* Arthur Marwick, *War and Social Change in the Twentieth Century: A Comparative Study of Britain, France, Germany, Russia, and the United States* (London: Macmillan, 1974), p. 84.
251 *Before the war* Martin Stone, "Shell Shock and the Psychologists," in W. F. Bynum, Roy Porter, and Michael Shepherd, eds., *The Anatomy of Madness: Essays in the History of Psychiatry* (London: Tavistock Publications, 1985), vol. 2, p. 243.
251 *After the war* Andrew Scull, Charlotte Mackenzie, and Nicholas Hervey, *Masters of Bedlam: The Transformation of the Mad-Doctoring Trade* (Princeton, N.J.: Princeton University Press, 1996), p. 273.
251 *"what had been considered"* Cyril Burt, quoted in Stone, "Shell-Shock and the Psychologists," p. 245.
251 *Increased sexual freedom* Marwick, *War and Social Change,* p. 93.

Chapter 18. Trauma Revisited: The Neuroses of War

252 *"Most of the neurotic diseases"* Freud in Sándor Ferenczi, Karl Abraham, Ernst Simmel, and Ernest Jones, *Psychoanalysis and the War Neuroses,* with an introduction by Sigmund Freud (London: International Psycho-Analytical Library, 1921), p. 1.
252 *"The older I get"* World War I veteran quoted in Richard A. Gabriel, *No More Heroes: Madness and Psychiatry in War* (New York: Hill and Wang, 1987), frontispiece.
253 *There was no medical* Ibid., p. 113.
253 *"trivial bullet and shell wounds"* Lieutenant Colonel Gordon Holmes, quoted in Gilbert, *The First World War,* p. 61.

253   *None of the armies had*   Gabriel, *No More Heroes*, p. 113, on the Allied armies; Babington, *Shell-Shock*, p. 47 on the Germans. Mental breakdown in war, however, was not new to the First World War, even though the numbers were higher. Observers of battle had noted the phenomenon throughout the history of warfare. The Spanish Army of Flanders, during the Thirty Years War, reported soldiers being discharged for emotional disability; seventeenth-century military physicians saw that the source of the symptoms was not physical wounds, noting "imagination alone can cause all this," Gabriel, *No More Heroes*, p. 57. In the Boer War of 1899, a high insanity rate was recorded, and an authoritative study was made by the British army, Babington, *Shell-Shock*, pp. 35–37. Just prior to World War I, in 1905, Russia had been the first nation to post psychiatrists to the front lines during the Russo-Japanese War, and casualties due to mental breakdowns had been documented, Gabriel, *No More Heroes*, p. 61. Immobility was also a feature of that war, and Captain R. L. Richards, an observer from the United States Medical Corps, was "astonished" at the huge numbers of mentally disabled and predicted large numbers of such cases in future wars, Babington, *Shell-Shock*, pp. 39–40, and Leed, *No Man's Land*, p. 165. The surprise with which war neuroses and psychoses was greeted in the Great War had more to do with a "need not to know" linked to the emphasis on offensive doctrine in which morale was seen as the key to victory.

253   *"Captain Spencer . . . babbling"*   Hynes, *The Soldiers' Tale*, p. 62.
253   *"infinitely small, running"*   Leed, *No Man's Land*, p. 8.
254   *Men who broke down*   Ibid., p. 171. See also Hans Binneveld, *From Shell-Shock to Combat Stress: A Comparative History of Military Psychiatry*, trans. John O'Kane (Amsterdam: Amsterdam University Press, 1997), pp. 84, 87–102. As late as 1920, Sir Robert Armstrong, a British psychiatrist, speaking at a meeting of the Medico-Psychological Society, rejected Freudian ideas: psychoanalysis was "probably applicable to people on the Austrian and German frontiers, but not to virile, sport-loving, open-air people like the British." Cited in Stone, "Shell-Shock and the Psychologists," p. 247.
254   *"Are you freezing?"*   quoted in Herwig, *The First World War*, p. 193.
254   *he was sentenced to execution*   Gilbert, *The First World War*, p. 275. Examining the records of military trials, Babington has documented a number of cases in which soldiers in the British army with records of mental disability were executed throughout the war. Babington, *Shell-Shock*, pp. 1–6, 56, 70, 92. At Question Time in the House of Commons in December 1917, the under-secretary of state for war stated "that in all the cases which had been brought to his notice the courts had given most careful attention to the reports on the prisoners." In fact, during the previous four months, General Sir Douglas Haig had confirmed death sentences on soldiers whose records showed hospital treatment for shell-shock, pp. 101–103. General Luigi Cadorna, chief of the Italian General Staff, ordered a regime of discipline through terror with summary executions. Not until 1917 did the Italian government revoke his absolute power and restore civilian authority over wholesale executions; see Bonadeo, *Mark of the Beast*, pp. 81–84.
254   *a cult or ideology of the offensive*   The success of highly motivated Japanese troops in the Russo-Japanese War had convinced European observers that morale could overcome the problems of modern weaponry. See Michael Howard, "Men against Fire: Expectations of War in 1914," and Stephen Van Evera, "The Cult of the Offensive and the Origins of the First World War," in Steven Miller, ed., *Military Strategy and the Origins of the First World War* (Princeton, N.J.: Princeton University Press, 1985); and Michael Howard, "Men Against Fire: The Doctrine of the Offensive in 1914," in Paret, *Makers of Modern Strategy*, pp. 510–527. Russian strategists were more divided on the eve of the Great War; a long-standing "national school" was opposed by modernizers who stressed the importance of firepower; see Pintner, "Russian Military Thought," in Paret, *Makers of Modern Strategy*, pp. 359, 367–369. Military strategy was intermingled with nationalistic projections: "The defensive is never an acceptable role to the Briton, and he makes little or no study of it" (Major General Sir W. G. Knox, quoted in Howard,

"Men Against Fire: Expectations of War in 1914," p. 55). In 1913, the new regulations of the French army stated: "The French Army, returning to its traditions, recognizes no law save that of the offensive" (quoted in Howard, "Men Against Fire: The Doctrine of the Offensive in 1914," p. 520). General Cadorna, chief of the Italian General Staff, was convinced that the doctrine would restore greatness to Italy; see Bonadeo, *Mark of the Beast*, pp. 83–86.

254 *where doctors used painful electric* Binneveld, *From Shell-Shock to Combat Stress*, p. 107.

255 *"neurotics, like the delinquents"* Paul Dubois, cited in Ruth Leys, "Traumatic Cures: Shell-Shock, Janet and the Question of Memory" (*Critical Inquiry* 20, 1994, pp. 621–662, p. 628).

255 *"The great merit of Freud"* W. H. R. Rivers, quoted in Clark, *Freud*, pp. 386, 598 n.

256 *William Brown, a British physician* Leys, "Traumatic Cures," pp. 621–625.

256 *Simmel summarized* Simmel's book has not been translated into English, but his article in *Psychoanalysis and the War Neuroses* gives a good summary of his position.

257 *"Shutting the door"* Siegfried Sassoon, quoted in Babington, *Shell-Shock*, p. 112. The work of W. H. R. Rivers with Sassoon and other British soldiers is vividly brought to life in Pat Barker's novel *Regeneration* (New York: Viking, 1991). Rivers' own life, including his work as a therapist during the Great War, is chronicled in Richard Slobodin, *W. H. R. Rivers* (New York: Columbia University Press, 1978).

258 *"This is the first time"* Abraham, in Freud/Abraham, p. 271.

258 *"he has not yet in any way"* Ibid., p. 280.

258 *"German war medicine"* Freud in Freud/Ferenczi, vol. 2, p. 265.

258 *"I am swimming in satisfaction"* Ibid., p. 296.

259 *"It is a question of aggressive"* Abraham, quoted in Binneveld, *From Shell-Shock to Combat Stress*, p. 120.

259 *"War neurotics already before the trauma"* This and the following quotes are taken from Abraham's paper in *Psychoanalysis and the War Neuroses*, pp. 23–28. Freud continued to feel that Abraham's position, not only on the war neuroses, but on the broader issue of drive/fantasy versus actual trauma, was most closely aligned with his own. To Abram Kardiner in 1921 he said, "He [Abraham] is the most accurate and honest worker that I have among my followers." (See Kardiner, *My Analysis with Freud: Reminiscences* [New York: W. W. Norton, 1977] p. 83.) John Dorsey, in 1935, asked Freud who was his "best pupil" and the prompt reply was "Karl Abraham." (Dorsey, *An American Psychiatrist in Vienna, 1935–1937, and His Sigmund Freud* [Detroit: Center for Health Education, 1976] p. 52.)

259 *"the driving forces . . . opponents of psychoanalysis . . . has shown what results"* Freud, Introduction to *Psychoanalysis and the War Neuroses*, pp. 1–2.

260 *Josef Breuer, seventy-two years old* The account of Breuer's work during the war is found in George H. Pollock, "The Possible Significance of Childhood Object Loss in the Josef Breuer-Bertha Pappenheim (Anna O.)-Sigmund Freud Relationship. I. Josef Breuer."

260 *"great dangers escaped"* Freud, in Freud/Pfister, p. 64.

260 *"It would be interesting, no doubt"* Freud, *Our Attitude towards Death*, p. 291.

260 *"We have over and over again"* W. H. R. Rivers, quoted in Binneveld, *From Shell-Shock to Combat Stress*, p. 117.

260 *"When the furious struggle"* Freud, *Our Attitude towards Death*, p. 295.

261 *"Do you see"* Leed, *No Man's Land*, p. 107.

261 *"most of the neurotic diseases"* Freud, introduction to *Psychoanalysis and the War Neuroses*, p. 1.

261 *officially declared mentally disabled* Leed, *No Man's Land*, p. 189.

261 *"These are the men whose minds"* Wilfred Owen, quoted in Gilbert, *The First World War*, p. 318.

261 *For ten years after the war* Hynes, *The Soldiers' Tale*, p. 99.

262 *"My experiences in the First World War"* Edmund Blunden, quoted in Paul Fussell, *The Great War and Modern Memory* (Oxford, U.K.: Oxford University Press, 1977), p. 256.
262 *segments of "before" and "after"* Leed, *No Man's Land,* pp. 2–3.
262 *"Hard to believe"* Stuart Cloete, quoted in ibid., p. 2.
262 *relationships of unusual intensity* Hynes, *The Soldiers' Tale,* p. 9.
262 *how many a brief bombardment* Sassoon, quoted in Herman, *Trauma and Recovery,* p. 23.
262 *a young woman patient* Freud/Salomé, pp. 91–92.
263 *treated cases of war neuroses* On Dr. Fritz Kaufmann and the "surprise attack method" in the German army, see Binneveld, *From Shell-Shock to Combat Stress,* pp. 107–109; on Dr. Lewis Yealland in the British army, ibid., pp. 111, 113.
263 *He had considerable experience* Victor Tausk, "On the Psychology of the War Deserter," trans. Eric Mosbacher and Marius Tausk (*Psychoanalytic Quarterly* 38, 1969), pp. 354–381.
263 *He published a pamphlet* Adler's writing on the First World War has not been translated into English. For a summary of his views, see Ansbacher and Ansbacher, *The Individual Psychology,* pp. 457–459.
264 *Fear and psychiatric debilitation* Gabriel, *No More Heroes,* p. 62.
264 *through the Vietnam War* Binneveld, *From Shell-Shock to Combat Stress,* p. 195.
264 *Post-traumatic stress disorder* Ibid., p. 195. In 1971, the Vietnam Veterans against the War contacted the psychiatrists Robert Lifton and Chaim Shaton in order to organize psychological help for veterans that would be under their own control. Lifton and Shaton began to organize "rap groups," informal and democratic group therapy. By 1973, Lifton published *Home from the War: Learning from Vietnam War Veterans* (Boston: Beacon Press, 1973), a study of the specific problems of the Vietnam veteran. These findings were part of the effort to change the American Psychiatric Association's *Diagnostic and Statistical Manual* (DSM-I) definition of trauma when the editorial committee, in 1976, began to prepare a revised edition, DSM-II. Together with records of traumatic reactions to civilian disasters, the findings of Lifton and his associates were accepted by the committee in 1978: PTSD became an official diagnostic term. Ibid., pp. 184–189.
266 *"speculation, often far-fetched"* Freud, *Beyond the Pleasure Principle,* p. 24.
266 *there was also an "instinct"* Ibid., p. 36.
267 *"took a step into old age"* Freud, in a letter to Ferenczi in May of 1921, cited in Ferris, *Dr. Freud,* p. 338.
268 *"I think about the possibility"* Freud, quoted by Smiley Blanton, *Diary of My Analysis with Sigmund Freud* (New York: Hawthorn Books, 1971), p. 48.

Chapter 19. Freud at Work: The Postwar Years

269 *"even in Vienna"* Freud in Freud/Abraham, p. 306.
270 *analysand Joan Riviere* Riviere, who suffered a nervous breakdown at the age of twenty-seven after the death of her father, entered a five-year analysis with Ernest Jones in 1916 in which he violated almost all professional boundaries short of having sex with her. He gave her no regular appointment, told her about his own troubles, lent her his summer cottage, and worked with her on the English translations of Freud's works. By his own account, the "analysis" was, not surprisingly, a failure. He sent her to Freud in 1922, writing that she was "torturing me without intermission . . . being a fiendish sadist" (Jones, in Freud/Jones, p. 454). Freud began seeing her and wrote back to Jones that she "does not appear to me half as black as you had painted her" (Freud, in Freud/Jones, p. 464).
271 *sociologist Gustave Le Bon* Phillip Rieff—a sociologist friendly to psychoanalysis—has characterized Le Bon as a "notorious racist, political anti-Semite and intellectual servi-

tor of the French military class." Phillip Rieff, "Origins of Freud's Political Psychology" (*Journal of the History of Ideas* 17, 1956), p. 238. Quoted in Clark, *Freud*, p. 433.

272 *idea from Georg Groddeck* His book is available in English: Georg Groddeck, *The Book of the It* (New York: Random House, 1961).

272 *"what may be called reason"* Freud, *The Ego and the Id*, p. 25.

273 *"excessive real danger"* Ibid., p. 58.

273 *"anxieties of being lost"* This, and the preceding quotations, are taken from Ilse Grubrich-Simitis, "Nothing about the Totem Meal! On Freud's Notes," trans. Veronica Mächtlinger, in Michael S. Roth, ed., *Freud: Conflict and Culture* (New York: Knopf, 1998), p. 18.

274 *"very soon came to share"* Freud, *From the History of an Infantile Neurosis*, p. 33.

274 *"Under the inexorable pressure"* Ibid., p. 11.

274 *Many factors that may* Publications by others who had contact with the Wolf Man provide important supplemental evidence, as does his own later account of his life and treatment. The case can be viewed from a variety of perspectives: Freud's, Sergei's, and others who knew him. A good deal of this additional material is collected in Muriel Gardiner, ed., *The Wolf-Man by the Wolf-Man* (New York: Basic Books, 1971). This volume contains Sergei's own "Recollections of My Childhood," Ruth Mack Brunswick's "Supplement," describing her treatment of him, which, since she was herself a patient of Freud's, does not question the Professor's formulations, and Gardiner's own memoirs based on her many years of association with the Wolf Man. Interviews from later in Sergei's life can be found in Karen Oberholzer, *The Wolf-Man Sixty Years Later* (New York: Continuum, 1982). Other accounts include Patrick Mahony, *Cries of the Wolf-Man;* and Barry Magid, "Self Psychology Meets the Wolf Man," in Magid, *Freud's Case Studies*, pp. 157–187. The fact that the Wolf Man case was written to counter Adler and Jung is reported in Strachey's introduction to the case in the *Standard Edition*, vol. 14, p. 5.

275 *"Wolf Man here"* Mentioned in Oberholzer, *The Wolf-Man Sixty Years Later*.

275 *"an angry glance"* Freud, *The Psychogenesis of a Case of Homosexuality in a Woman*, p. 148.

275 *"The analysis revealed"* Ibid., p. 156.

275 *"treated her children"* Ibid., p. 149.

275 *"still quite youthful"* Ibid., p. 157.

275 *"an earnest, worthy . . . he flew into"* Ibid., p. 149.

276 *"she was in fact"* Ibid., p. 169.

276 *"falling" over the embankment* Ibid., p. 162.

276 *"a single piece of"* Ibid., p. 164.

276 *"Warned through some"* Ibid., p. 165.

277 *"the resistance . . . withdraws"* Ibid., p. 163.

277 *Freud's case study* Compared to Freud's other published case studies, there is very little secondary literature on the homosexual woman. See Barry Magid, "The Homosexual Identity of a Nameless Woman," in Magid, *Freud's Case Studies*, pp. 189–200, and Adrienne Harris, "Gender as Contradiction" (*Psychoanalytic Dialogues* 1, 1991), p. 197–224.

277 *"immediate trust . . . air of"* Abram Kardiner, *My Analysis with Freud*, p. 17.

277 *"My early childhood"* Ibid., p. 27.

278 *"a perfect presentation"* Freud, in ibid., p. 37.

278 *"the first mask you saw"* Freud, in ibid., p. 61.

278 *Kardiner reported an amusing* Ibid. pp. 77–78.

278 *Helene Deutsch, another* Reported in Paul Roazen, *Brother Animal: The Story of Freud and Tausk* (New York: Random House, 1969), p. 94.

278 *"too skeptical and"* Freud, quoted in Kardiner, *My Analysis with Freud*, p. 70. Kardiner reports that Oberndorf got off on the wrong foot with Freud during the very first session. He reported a dream of riding in a carriage pulled by two horses, one white and

the other black, going to an unknown destination. Freud told him he would never marry because he didn't know whether to choose a white or a black woman. Oberndorf was a southerner raised by a black "mammy," so that, earlier in his life, he had both white and black mothers. He never did marry, so Freud's interpretation was an inspired insight. Forcefully stated in the first session, however, it was not something that Oberndorf could hear or work with, and he haggled about the dream for months until Freud kicked him out of the analysis. Ibid., pp. 75–76.

279   *"a lot of fight in"*   Freud, in ibid., p. 51.

279   *"The man who had"*   Kardiner in ibid., p. 58.

279   *"on a wild-goose chase"*   Ibid., p. 98.

279   *"He thought that once"*   Ibid., pp. 62–63. Overall, Kardiner found his analysis with Freud an extremely valuable experience. He did not adapt to the orthodox mold, however; those aspects of his own life experience—the influence of his early social milieu and the traumas he suffered—led to work integrating psychoanalysis with anthropology and research on the traumas of war. See Abram Kardiner and Herbert Spiegel, *War, Stress and Neurotic Illness* (1941; rev. ed., New York: P. Hoeber, 1947). The final sections of *My Analysis with Freud* contain trenchant criticisms of the psychoanalytic movement, which Kardiner likens to a dogmatic religion.

279   *American psychiatrist, Horace Frink*   The principal sources on Freud's treatment of Frink are Silas L. Warner, "Freud's Analysis of Horace Frink, M.D.: A Previously Unexplained Therapeutic Disaster" (*Journal of the American Academy of Psychoanalysis* 22, 1994, pp. 137–152), which draws on an unpublished biographical manuscript by Frink's daughter, Helen Frink Kraft. See also Lavinia Edmunds, "His Master's Choice" (*Johns Hopkins Magazine,* April 1988, pp. 40–49), reprinted in Fredrick C. Crews, ed., *Unauthorized Freud: Doubters Confront a Legend* (New York: Viking, 1998, pp. 261–276). Freud's comments on Frink in his letters to Jones are revealing. At first Frink is "very good" and "a very nice boy"—Freud/Jones, pp. 418, 434. Once he is overtaken by psychosis, however, his condition is blamed on his inability to tolerate the frustration of the "free satisfaction of his infantile desires." Ibid., p. 552.

280   *Freud encouraged Frink*   Freud wrote to Jones that he "had to assure her [Angie] of the intensity and genuineness of his [Frink's] affection and to convince him of the presence of those feelings in himself, which he did not dare to confess to himself." Ibid., p. 443.

281   *"He was a great man"*   Frink, quoted in Warner, "Freud's Analysis of Horace Frink," p. 148.

281   *Freud's treatment of three Americans*   Information on Freud's analyses of the Brunswicks is drawn from Roazen, *How Freud Worked,* pp. 31–114, who interviewed both Mark and David Brunswick in the 1960s. Additional information on Ruth Mack Brunswick is from Roazen, *Freud and His Followers,* pp. 420–436. Freud relied on Ruth as his delegate, mediating between the New York and Vienna Psychoanalytic Societies. As one of the earliest American analysts to be directly trained by him, she analyzed several people who became prominent in the next generation, including Max Schur and his wife, Muriel Gardiner, Karl Menninger, and Wilhelm Fliess's son Robert.

283   *Smiley Blanton first saw*   Blanton's first-person account is in Blanton, *Diary of My Analysis with Sigmund Freud.*

283   *"I feel that a lot"*   Ibid., p. 112.

283   *The American poet H.D.*   H.D.'s account of her analysis is published as H.D., *Tribute to Freud* (New York: New Directions, 1956).

284   *John Dorsey—like Frink*   See Dorsey, *An American Psychiatrist in Vienna, 1935–1937, and His Sigmund Freud.*

284   *"mightiest of men"*   Ibid., p. xvi.

284   *"my practice of"*   Ibid., p. 196.

285   *Joseph Wortis's analysis*   See Joseph Wortis, *Fragments of an Analysis with Freud* (New York: Simon and Schuster, 1954).

285 *Tausk was a brilliant* A detailed account of Freud's relationship with Tausk can be found in Roazen, *Brother Animal.* Roazen's book prompted Kurt Eissler to write a thousand-plus page book in rebuttal: Kurt Eissler, *Talent and Genius: The Fictitious Case of Tausk contra Freud* (New York: Quadrangle Books, 1971). Roazen's work is the more convincing, since Freud's treatment of Tausk is consistent with his rejection of so many of his other colleagues.

286 *"Tausk is in the hospital"* Freud, in Freud/Ferenczi, vol. 2, p. 78.

286 *As a medical officer* See Tausk, "On the Psychology of the War Deserter," pp. 354–381.

286 *"superior, talented"* Paul Federn, quoted in Roazen, *Brother Animal,* p. 153.

287 *"Tausk shot himself"* Freud, in Freud/Ferenczi, vol. 2, p. 361.

287 *"I confess that I"* Freud in Freud/Salomé, p. 98.

287 *"Dear Sir: I request"* Freud, quoted in Roazen, *Freud and His Followers,* p. 339. See also the interview with Robert Jokl, who knew Silberer well, in Roazen, *How Freud Worked,* p. 117. Jokl described Silberer as "a little feminine," which may have been an additional reason for Freud's rejection. (Jokl, quoted in Roazen, *How Freud Worked,* p. 138.)

287 *"The secession of former"* Freud, *An Autobiographical Study,* p. 53.

Chapter 20. Freud at Home

In addition to the major biographies and letters, this chapter draws on the following sources: Martin Freud, *Sigmund Freud: Man and Father;* Roazen, *Meeting Freud's Family,* which is based on firsthand interviews with some family members and others who knew the Freuds (see also the chapter on family life in Roazen's *Freud and His Followers,* pp. 55–63); Sophie Freud, *My Three Mothers and Other Passions* (New York: New York University Press, 1988), a book of essays by the daughter of Freud's oldest son, Martin. Erich Fromm, *Sigmund Freud's Mission: An Analysis of His Personality and Influence* (New York: Grove Press, 1959), has some important insights into Freud and his family relationships.

289 *"In my private life"* Freud to Marie Bonaparte, quoted in Bertin, *Marie Bonaparte: A Life,* p. 155.

289 *"laid out his clothes"* Roazen, *Freud and His Followers,* pp. 56–57. See also Jones, *The Life and Work,* vol. 2, p. 382.

290 *"he enjoyed his food"* Jones, ibid., p. 382.

290 *"always on very friendly"* Harry Freud, "My Uncle Sigmund," in Ruitenbeek, *Freud as We Knew Him,* p. 312.

290 *"habit of bringing"* Jones, *The Life and Work,* vol. 2, p. 393.

290 *"As the evening went on"* Martin Freud, *Sigmund Freud: Man and Father,* p. 12. After Amalia's death, the Sunday family gatherings continued at Sigmund and Martha's; the four sisters, Alexander, and sometimes some of the children and grandchildren attended. Freud himself would make a brief appearance, and Alexander was allowed in his study, but the sisters were not. (Sophie Freud, interview.)

292 *"You must be told"* Martin Freud, *Sigmund Freud, Man and Father,* p. 80.

292 *"warned . . . quite upset"* Oliver Freud, quoted in Roazen, *Meeting Freud's Family,* p. 180.

292 *"the stupid common folk"* Freud, in a letter to Lou Andreas-Salomé, November 22, 1917, quoted in Gay, *Freud,* p. 405, who has a more accurate translation than that in the Freud/Salomé letters.

292 *"we Freud children"* Martin Freud, *Sigmund Freud: Man and Father,* p. 29.

293 *Mathilde, the Freuds' firstborn* Roazen, *Meeting Freud's Family,* pp. 119–134, reports an interview with Mathilde.

293   *"The more intelligent among"* Freud to Mathilde, in Freud, *Letters,* p. 272.

293   *"medicine as a profession"* Martin Freud, *Sigmund Freud: Man and Father,* p. 160.

293   *His father would say* Oliver Freud, in an interview with Roazen, *Meeting Freud's Family,* p. 179.

295   *"was ready to lead"* Martin Freud, *Sigmund Freud: Man and Father,* p. 58.

295   *excited by these sports* Martin reports that he "indulged in plenty of escapades . . . duels, student brawls . . . mountain rescues . . . to my mind in those days any sport in which you could not kill yourself had no moral value." Ibid., p. 157. Martin carried on affairs with a number of women throughout the years of his marriage, and, when the Freuds were all forced to flee the Nazis in 1938, his secret apartment was discovered, along with photographs of his many attractive lovers. Interestingly, the pictures were secreted inside a volume of his father's *Four Case Studies.* Once his sexual escapades came to light, he was divorced, and the family—principally Anna, who was now in charge—viewed him with scorn and, with her control of the family money, made sure that he was cut off financially. According to Martin's daughter Sophie, in the later years of his life in London, when he ran a small shop, he hired a much younger woman who eventually became his life companion. See Sophie Freud, *My Three Mothers,* pp. 291–297. Mark Brunswick commented that in the 1930s, Martin had the reputation of being a Don Juan: see Roazen, *How Freud Worked,* p. 94. All of these activities—the seeking of danger, heroism in the war, sexual affairs—may have been attempts at enlivenment to counter the control and emotional deadness that he experienced as a child. They were also, obviously, ways in which he could differentiate from, if not surpass, his powerful, but bookish and sexually inhibited, father.

295   *"not at all . . . She's much too pretty"* Reported by Esti Freud in Roazen, *Meeting Freud's Family,* pp. 137, 138.

295   *in her tastes and spending* The family was decidedly nonostentatious and extremely frugal, even in the years of Freud's fame and financial success. (Sophie Freud, interview.)

296   *"cuddling him too much"* Roazen, *Meeting Freud's Family,* p. 154.

296   *"Oli classifies mountains"* Freud/Fliess, pp. 358, 364.

296   *Franz Alexander in Berlin* See Roazen, *Meeting Freud's Family,* p. 186, and Young-Bruehl, *Anna Freud,* p. 115.

296   *"extraordinary gifts . . ."* Freud in a letter to Arnold Zweig on January 28, 1934, quoted in Gay, *Freud,* pp. 429–430. This comment was apparently cut from the published Freud/Zweig correspondence. Freud also wrote to Zweig that Oli "will never achieve anything in Paris." Freud/Zweig, p. 54. Zweig, however, met with Oli and they discussed their common experiences in the Great War. He wrote Freud that Oliver was "too decent to find it easy to adapt himself to life. It was shattering to observe how he too talked most vividly and warmly when speaking about his wartime service." Zweig, who had extensive combat experience, had sympathy for Oliver's difficulties which Freud, with no sense of what the war had inflicted on his sons, apparently did not. Ibid., pp. 56–57.

296   *"It is particularly hard"* Freud to Max Eitingon, December 13, 1920, quoted in Young-Bruehl, *Anna Freud,* p. 115. Other family members reported that however repressed Oliver had been earlier, he became even more inhibited and withdrawn after the death of his only child. By 1943, Oliver and his wife settled in the United States, where he worked for many years as an engineer. Roazen, who interviewed him as a retiree of seventy-five, found him "an exceptionally nice man, conscientious and truthful." He also observed the same traits of precision that were present in Oli as a child. While all the other Freuds settled in London after the flight from Vienna in 1938, Oliver had moved to the country his father hated. In 1947 he cooperated with the American journalist Helen Puner on her not altogether flattering biography of Freud, incurring the wrath of Anna.

297 *"The loveliest part"* Freud/Fliess, p. 187.
297 *"Sophie-Complex"* Ferenczi, in Freud/Ferenczi, vol. 1, p. 462.

Chapter 21. Anna Freud: The Perfect Disciple

Elisabeth Young-Bruehl's, *Anna Freud: A Biography* is a major source for this chapter, though I do not share her overall sense of Anna, nor her assessment of her contributions. She calls Anna ". . . her generation's most scientifically exact and wide-ranging theoretical and clinical contributor" (p. 18), a view that finds scant support in Anna's publications, which contain few original ideas and are, for the most part, a slavish application of her father's theories. Sophie Freud, *My Three Mothers and Other Passions,* has a discussion of her aunt (see, particularly, chapters 1, 2, and 20) that is very perceptive. Peter Heller, ed., *Anna Freud's Letters to Eva Rosenfeld,* trans. Mary Weigand (Madison, Conn.: International Universities Press, 1992), is an excellent source, with discussions by Heller, Victor Ross (Eva Rosenfeld's son), and the psychoanalytic scholar Gunther Bittner. Several individuals who were analyzed by Anna have written about their experience. The best, in my view, is Peter Heller, "Reflections on a Child Analysis with Anna Freud and an Adult Analysis with Ernst Kris" (*Journal of the American Academy of Psychoanalysis* 20, 1992, pp. 48–74). See, also, Esther Menaker, *Appointment in Vienna* (New York: St. Martin's Press, 1989), and Arthur S. Couch, "Anna Freud's Adult Psychoanalytic Technique: A Defense of Classical Analysis" (*International Journal of Psychoanalysis* 76, 1995, pp. 153–171).

299 *"Papa always makes"* Anna Freud to Max Eitingon, quoted in Young-Bruehl, *Anna Freud,* p. 156.
299 *"never loved . . . the tragedy"* Eva Rosenfeld, quoted in Roazen, *Meeting Freud's Family,* p. 208. Eva, who knew Anna and the whole family very well, wrote to Anna in 1947 about the way Anna excluded her: "Surely you realize to what extent you are repeating together with Dorothy [Burlingham] the 'impregnable fortress' which your mother and aunt once represented for you." Heller, *Anna Freud's Letters,* p. 182. Martha and Minna were known as "the Siamese twins," and one assumes that the information about the way they excluded Anna during her childhood was conveyed to Eva during the years of their intimacy.
300 *"my old nursemaid"* Anna Freud to Max Eitingon, quoted in Young-Bruehl, *Anna Freud,* p. 35.
300 *"being left out"* Anna Freud to Murial Gardiner, quoted in ibid., p. 37.
300 *"cheekiness . . . beatified by"* Anna Freud, in ibid., 43.
300 *Anna's depression* Young-Bruehl speculates about "psychasthenia," a "mild eating disorder," and "conversion symptoms"; different words for the depressive reactions of someone whose unhappiness, blocked from open expression, could only emerge as mysterious symptoms.
301 *"I am not really sick"* Anna Freud, letter to her father, quoted in ibid., pp. 57–58.
301 *"overzealous, restless and unsatisfied"* Freud to Anna, February 2, 1913, quoted in ibid., p. 59.
302 *"For one hour, one day"* Poem by Anna Freud, quoted in ibid., p. 88.
303 *Anna's . . . 1922 paper* Anna Freud, "Beating Fantasies and Daydreams" (*International Journal of Psychoanalysis* 4, 1923, pp. 89–102).
303 *"nice stories . . . violent self-reproaches"* These and the other quotations are from ibid.
303 *"in early childhood"* Ibid., 153.
304 *Like Freud's own oedipal* Freud's oedipal interpretation did not explain Anna's need to make herself a boy in her imagination, or her heavy reliance on fantasy as opposed to real relationships. Nor did it explain the self-punishing quality of her daydreams, along

with the misery and self-hate of her waking state. In Freud's theory, all these factors were explained by the strength of her sexual instincts. But this is a completely circular explanation. If one has extreme guilt or a powerful oedipal fixation, this is caused by strong instincts, yet the only evidence for this strength are the guilt and the Oedipus complex themselves. What is more, this interpretation leaves out almost everything that is implicated in Anna's depression: the lack of her mother's love, the loss of her nurse, the favoritism shown Sophie and the other children, the suppressive, emotionally constricted family atmosphere, and the preference given to boys in nineteenth-century European society.

Anna clearly felt unattractive and incapable of being loved as a woman. Mathilde and Sophie, not she, were defined as the feminine ones in the family. And Martha, along with Aunt Minna, was not available as an object of love or a female role model. As a girl, she was a failure; she could not imagine herself successfully competing with the pretty Sophie, or with the reasonable Mathilde. She believed that if she were a boy—her society clearly favored males—she would have a chance at love and acceptance. Men, as her adolescent poem revealed, also had the possibility of meaningful work. Given her unloved and depressed state, she did not believe that she could find much satisfaction in the world; no one would love her, she had to comfort and soothe herself. And so she turned to the gratifications of self-stimulation and a private fantasy life. As Stekel put it in 1911, "Women . . . have masturbated because, in their case, access to an adequate source of gratification was closed off" (Stekel, in debates on masturbation in the Vienna Psychoanalytic Society, Nunberg and Federn, *Minutes*, vol. 4, p. 42). Masturbation, so central to Anna's guilt-filled struggle to find some pleasure, will serve as a key illustration of the way in which Freud's sexual theory shaped his analysis of his daughter. As the comparison of Freud's and Stekel's views in the debate on masturbation revealed, Freud believed that masturbation was a "vehicle of pathogenic effects," that it was itself a cause of neurosis, especially when coupled with fantasy. These beliefs were no doubt communicated to his daughter during her analysis, reinforcing her sense of guilt about gratifying herself while, at the same time, pushing her toward the resolution of her emotional conflicts through compliance.

304   "*I know from the most*"   Freud, in a letter to Anna, quoted in Young-Bruehl, *Anna Freud*, p. 67.

304   "*I am often together*"   Anna Freud, in a letter to her father, quoted in ibid., p. 96.

304   "*I too very much miss Daughter-Anna*"   Freud to Andreas-Salomé, in Freud/Salomé, p. 113.

305   "*I dream of her*"   Anna, in a letter to her father, quoted in Young-Bruehl, *Anna Freud*, p. 68.

305   *When Anna had been*   Margarethe Rie married Hermann Nunberg, a member of the Vienna Psychoanalytic Society, and emigrated to Philadelphia in 1932. Her younger sister Marianne married Ernst Kris and both became psychoanalysts in America, as well as close collaborators with Anna Freud, who, just to further complicate matters, was Kris's analyst.

305   "*In the last week*"   Anna Freud to Andreas-Salomé, quoted in ibid., p. 121.

305   *Frau Lou was not*   Ibid., p. 113.

305   *His [Freud's] cancer appeared*   Freud's cancer is discussed, in the general context of his overall health, in Schur, *Freud: Living and Dying*, chapters 13–15.

306   "*an enchanting little fellow*"   Freud to Kata and Lajos Levy, in Freud, *Letters*, p. 344.

306   "*I have spent some*"   Freud to Max Halberstadt, letter of July 7, 1923, quoted in Clark, *Freud*, p. 441.

307   "*From the onset*"   Jones, *The Life and Work*, vol. 3, p. 96.

307   *her first book*   See Anna Freud, "An Introduction to the Technique of Child Analysis," in *The Writings of Anna Freud*, vol. 1 (New York: International Universities Press, 1973).

307   "*like Wolf [Anna's dog]*"   Freud, in Freud/Salomé, p. 182.

307   *got to know Eva Rosenfeld*   Information about Eva and her life is in Heller, *Anna Freud's Letters,* and Roazen, *How Freud Worked,* pp. 195–230.

307   *"I am always wholly"*   Anna to Eva, in Heller, *Anna Freud's Letters,* p. 145.

308   *"Freud's great mind"*   Eva Rosenfeld, in ibid., pp. 36, 69.

308   *"My analysis of 1929"*   Ibid., p. 69.

308   *"awestruck by this"*   Ibid., p. 71.

308   *"Papa was very much"*   Anna, in ibid., p. 177.

308   *"so stupid"*   Ibid., p. 138.

308   *"In the last two weeks"*   Ibid., p. 149.

308   *"I murdered our cook"*   Ibid., p. 169. Leo Tolstoy took over the life of his youngest daughter Sasha, making her his disciple in much the same way that Freud did with Anna. Like Anna, Sasha was a late child, neglected by her mother and desperate for love. See Anne Edwards, *Sonia: The Life of Countess Tolstoy* (New York: Simon and Schuster, 1981).

308   *wealthy American Dorothy Burlingham*   See Michael J. Burlingham, *The Last Tiffany: A Biography of Dorothy Tiffany Burlingham* (New York: Atheneum, 1989). This is a full biography that covers Dorothy's life, her analysis with Freud—or what is known of it—and her relationship with Anna.

309   *Rosenfeld-Burlingham School*   Many individuals who later made significant contributions to psychoanalysis worked at the Rosenfeld-Burlingham School. Erik Erikson was a teacher there, as well as an analysand of Anna's. Peter Heller was a student there as well as a patient of Anna's. He also later married—and, still later, divorced—Dorothy's youngest daughter, "Tinky." He has made some trenchant comments about his former mother-in-law in Heller, "Reflections on a Child Analysis," p. 78.

309   *"One can never be sure"*   Eva Rosenfeld's son Victor Ross, in Heller, *Anna Freud's Letters,* p. 38. Information about Anna as a therapist is provided in several sources. Esther Menaker commented:

> It was this giving up of a personal sexual and erotic life of her own that was particularly difficult for me as her analysand. I was a recently married young woman, in love with a somewhat older husband, away from home for the first time, making adaptations to the culture of a foreign country and to a new, intimate relationship, who needed to feel in her analyst an understanding of erotic feelings and of the adjustments that are required in the context of sexual interactions. Anna Freud provided almost none of this. Instead, she came across as an ascetic, virtuous, and conscientious schoolgirl—comely and with a certain charm and grace, but asexual. I had to project onto her person fantasies of a sex life in which I could scarcely believe. I must say that it is a tribute to the human imagination that I was able to grow on this rather restricted diet.

Esther Menaker, "On Anna Freud: A Discussion of Personal Analytic Reactions in the Early Days of Psychoanalysis" (*Journal of the American Academy of Psychoanalysis* 19, 1991), p. 608.

A view of Anna as an analyst at a much later time is provided by Arthur Couch in "Anna Freud's Adult Psychoanalytic Technique." He was originally trained in Boston, and then went to London and had a six-year analysis with Anna, beginning in October of 1967. This was the mature Anna, practicing in the classical fashion. Couch was, overall, pleased with his analysis. He was struck by her relaxed manner and naturalness, though, within the therapy itself, she was a strict Freudian. While not seeming cold, she kept her distance and the work was focused on interpretations of unconscious material, particularly from dreams, childhood memories, and transference reactions. Couch notes that while there was a good deal of reconstruction of childhood, she never dealt with the mother-infant relationship. And, while there was much work done on the transference, it was not about the emotional relationship in the room; she would never say something like "you mean me." In these last two respects, she worked very much like her father, avoiding the deepest areas of her own pain and working more on an intellectual than an emotional level.

Two examples from Anna's later life illustrate her need to protect her father's theories and the movement, as well as the lack of self-awareness that resulted from her training by him. John Bowlby, first trained as a psychoanalyst in the British Institute, formulated his own extremely influential theories about mother-infant attachment and the effects of maternal separation and loss, and published one of his earliest papers— "Grief and Mourning in Infancy and Early Childhood" (*Psychoanalytic Study of the Child* 15, 1960, pp. 9–94), a paper that Anna Freud discussed. Bowlby's work, well documented with research and clinical evidence, eventually became enormously influential in calling attention to the role of the mother-infant bond in the creation of the child's sense of security, as well as separation and loss as causes of anxiety and depression. In her comments on Bowlby's paper, Anna was unable to take up the evidence, nor could she seriously consider his ideas when they are at odds with her father's. Her criticisms were the usual ones: Bowlby's findings were not "what psychoanalysis has shown," nor what "psychoanalysis knows."

In 1967, Heinz Kohut, the founder of psychoanalytic self-psychology, sent Anna a paper in which emphasis was given to the real traumas of childhood, just as Bowlby's work called attention to the effects of real disruptions of mother-child attachment. Anna wrote back:

> Loss of object in early times, traumatic disappointment in the maternal or parental object: I have to add here that recently I acquired a mistrust of the concepts which are in such wide use now. The terms seem to imply that there were real events in the external world and I think only too often that this is not true. That what exerts an influence are purely internal fluctuations of cathexis. There are, of course, no undisturbed relationships, especially not in childhood where the demands on the object are so unrealistic. I am thinking here of two of my own patients, both homosexual before their analysis, both narcissistic personalities, one of them besides an addict, the other an obsessional neurosis. Both of them had devoted mothers who never wavered in their attention to them. Both had siblings, and were themselves the youngest, which means that the presence of the sibling was a given, an immutable fact from the beginning, not a traumatic event. In spite of this, they acted as if they had been deserted at some time by the mother, and the addiction quite obviously had to make up for this. What the analysis showed was an inordinate jealousy of the siblings, which turned every attention paid to them by the mother into a traumatic experience. Would you call this a disappointment or loss of the object? In reality it is an inordinate demand with disastrous consequences. Is it a special oversensitiveness and shakiness of object-relationship, i.e., a failure of frustration tolerance in this respect? Whatever it is, I believe it should not be confused with a real life experience, such as death, separation, neglect, etc.

Quoted in George Cocks, ed., *The Curve of Life: The Correspondence of Heinz Kohut* (Chicago: University of Chicago Press, 1994), p. 184.

Given what is now known about Anna's own childhood, this dismissal of Kohut's ideas, like her attack on Bowlby, is most revealing. The thrust of her argument was that her patients' obsessions, addictions, and homosexuality could not be explained by actual problems in the maternal relationship because they were youngest children, not replaced by siblings, and, hence, not traumatized. Yet she herself was a youngest child and, due to the particular constellation in her family, was not loved by her mother. Her own sibling rivalry was strengthened by the favoritism shown her brothers and sisters. These real experiences played a role in the sexual inhibitions and ambiguous gender of her adult self. It was also significant that she continued to espouse the classical psychoanalytic line that defined homosexuality as pathology; both of her patients were presumably cured of their "sexual perversion." She also claimed to have cured her patients of their obsessions and addictions, yet the obsessional neatness of her own childhood persisted for the rest of her life; she was an inveterate knitter, and kept every letter and note that came her way, which were systematically filed away. The "addiction" to fantasy and masturbation that she struggled so hard against has been well documented.

In her analysis with her father, Anna's symptoms, fantasies, and masturbation were not related to loss of mother or lack of love; rather, they were interpreted as the result of her unruly sexual instincts. Her comments to Kohut show that she had made this interpretation her own; it appeared in her letter in the references to "purely internal fluctuations of cathexis," "demands on the object [mother,] [that] are so unrealistic," and "inordinate jealousy of the siblings." The result of her analysis—like her father's self-analysis—was to disavow the painful traumas of maternal loss, and to enshrine this disavowal in a theory and interpretive method that was forced on patients.

309 *"[Anna] did pay a price"* Sophie Freud, *My Three Mothers and Other Passions*, p. 325.

Chapter 22. Otto Rank: "I Was in Deepest of All"

The major source for this chapter was E. James Lieberman, *Acts of Will: The Life and Work of Otto Rank*. Lieberman's biography is comprehensive, balanced, and insightful, both in its treatment of Rank and in its account of Freud and the psychoanalytic movement. Also valuable was Jessie Taft, *Otto Rank: A Biographical Study Based on Notebooks, Letters, Collected Writings, Therapeutic Achievements and Personal Associations* (New York: Julian Press, 1958). Taft was a patient, student, and, later, colleague and close friend of Rank in the United States. As the title of her book indicates, it contains many primary documents, including the *Daybooks* Rank kept from age eighteen to twenty-one. Esther Menaker, *Otto Rank: A Rediscovered Legacy* (New York: Columbia University Press, 1982), contains additional biographical information. An excellent summary article is Robert Kramer, "'The Bad Mother Freud Has Never Seen': Otto Rank and the Birth of Object-Relations Theory" (*Journal of the American Academy of Psychoanalysis* 23, 1995, pp. 293–321). Robert Kramer, ed., *Otto Rank: A Psychology of Difference: The American Lectures* (Princeton, N.J.: Princeton University Press, 1996), is a valuable source, containing an introductory overview by Kramer and a series of lectures by Rank, given between 1924 and 1938, that provide a clear exposition of his views. Lecture Eight, "The Anxiety Problem," contains Rank's response to Freud's *Inhibitions, Symptoms and Anxiety*. Rank's own extensive works, from his first book, *The Artist*, to his final book, *Beyond Psychology*, provide invaluable material.

310 *"One day a young"* Freud, *On the History of the Psycho-Analytic Movement*, p. 25.
310 *manuscript [for] The Artist* Otto Rank, *Der Künstler* (in English, *The Artist*), 2nd ed. Vienna: Internationaler Psycholanalytischer Verlag, 1925.
311 *Rank kept Daybooks* The *Daybooks* contain poems, observations, philosophical speculations, and references to novels he was working on, in addition to autobiographical material.
311 *"she found her satisfaction"* *Daybooks*, quoted in, Taft, *Otto Rank*, p. 10. Lieberman characterizes Rank's mother as "sensitive" and "caring" (p. 22). In the "Epilogue" to *Acts of Will*, he quotes a letter from Isidor Sax, a Vienna friend of Rank's, who said "he was very fond of his mother, with an abiding love" (p. 395). This may have been visible in the adolescent and adult Rank, but so much in Rank's *Daybooks* and writing, even before he began seeing patients, points to profound anxiety centered on the mother-infant relationship that one suspects it arises from his own earliest experience.
311 *"I myself have been"* Ibid., p. 16.
311 *"Today I confirmed"* Ibid., p. 16.
311 *"As the second important"* Ibid., pp. 10–11.

311   *"Death, the mysterious"*   Ibid., p. 11.

312   *"I have an aversion"*   Ibid., pp. 22–23.

313   *"Rank was virtually adopted"*   Lieberman, *Acts of Will*, p. 134. During the years that Rank was completing his advanced education he continued to work as secretary to Freud and the society. The minutes of the meetings show him as an active participant in the discussions, as well as someone who contributed original papers. At the same time, he pursued his scholarly work and expanded his knowledge of mythology, art, anthropology, history, and literature. His second publication, *The Myth of the Birth of the Hero,* published in 1909, to which Freud contributed original material, was a widely read book. Other works during this period included *The Double,* an exploration of the theme of dual or split personality in the works of Poe, Dostoevsky, E. T. A. Hoffmann, and R. L. Stevenson. His third book, *The Incest Motif in Poetry and Legend,* was published in 1912. All these works display Rank's mastery of psychoanalytic theory, his encyclopedic knowledge—particularly of mythology—and his skill at integrating the two fields. Freud was extremely pleased to see his ideas extended to these new areas. He had pointed the way as early as *The Interpretation of Dreams,* with references to *Oedipus Rex* and *Hamlet.* Now Rank had greatly expanded these early forays.

313   *"On these promenades"*   Sachs, *Freud: Master and Friend,* pp. 62–63. With Sachs, Rank founded the journal *Imago* for the purpose of applying psychoanalysis to literature and the arts. He added chapters and edited later editions of Freud's *Interpretation of Dreams.* Given Rank's background and life situation, his accomplishments are truly remarkable. The early work that culminated in *The Artist* was done completely on his own; he had no teachers, no fellow students, only what he was able to take from books and the theater. Yet he laid out a program of self-study and psychological exploration that he would pursue for the rest of his life.

313   *"noticeably timid"*   Jones, *The Life and Work,* vol. 2, p. 160.

314   *"None of these Viennese"*   Freud, in Freud/Jung, p. 403.

314   *"As reporter on the"*   Ibid., p. 150.

314   *"tough . . . with a masterful"*   Jones, *The Life and Work,* vol. 3, p. 12.

315   *"Rank really seems to"*   Freud, in a letter to Abraham, December 25, 1918, quoted in Gay, *Freud,* p. 471.

315   *Tola was charming*   Robert Jokl, a member of the Vienna Society who was analyzed by Freud, commented on how "Mrs. Rank had not 'diverged' from the psychoanalytic viewpoint . . . how she had been 'very clever' and 'never really broke' with Freud." Quoted and paraphrased in Roazen, *How Freud Worked,* p. 124.

315   *book on psychoanalytic technique*   Sándor Ferenczi and Otto Rank, *The Development of Psychoanalysis,* trans. Caroline Newton (1924; reprint, New York: Dover, 1956).

316   *"The boy wants to deny"*   Otto Rank, *The Trauma of Birth* (1924; reprint, New York: Robert Brunner, 1952), p. 38.

316   *"Sexual love, then"*   Ibid., p. 43.

317   *"All factors clearly point"*   Rank, in Nunberg and Federn, *Minutes,* vol. 1, p. 233.

317   *"We shall take as our"*   Rank, *The Trauma of Birth,* p. 11.

317   *Despite Rank's presentation*   The emphasis on separation from the mother as a real trauma led to additional ideas at variance with received theory. Rank had a concept of the child's image of a "good" and "bad" mother, the first associated with the pleasure and security of life in the womb, and the second with the trauma of birth and all later separations and frustrations. These ideas are the precursors of later theories that describe a "splitting" of the mother into good and bad versions. What is significant about Rank's theory is that he ties the good and bad images to actual experiences of pleasure and pain associated with the mother-infant relationship, rather than to innate drives, as Melanie Klein was to do later.

317   *"If finally we turn"*   Ibid., p. 46.

318 *Birth can be taken*   Rank later said that in *The Trauma of Birth,* he had gone too far. At the time, there were those who took his thesis literally, and were recommending routine cesarean sections for all deliveries so infants would not have to suffer the trauma of birth!

319 *"replacing analysis of childhood"*   Jones, quoted in Lieberman, *Acts of Will,* p. 210.

319 *"ominous . . . obtained in a legitimate"*   Abraham, in Freud/Abraham, p. 349.

320 *"It is a long time"*   Freud, in a letter to Rank, quoted in Taft, *Otto Rank,* pp. 78–79.

320 *"manifestations of a regression"*   Abraham, in Freud/Abraham, p. 351.

320 *"Jung-like decision"*   Jones to Abraham, quoted in Lieberman, *Acts of Will,* p. 223.

321 *"In the months since"*   Freud to Rank, quoted in Taft, *Otto Rank,* p. 99.

321 *"I still cannot believe"*   Rank to Freud, quoted in Lieberman, *Acts of Will,* p. 219.

321 *"I have a strong impression"*   Rank to Freud, quoted in Taft, *Otto Rank,* pp. 101–103.

322 *"your technique of treating"*   Jung, in Freud/Jung, p. 534.

322 *"There are ugly things"*   Freud to Rank, quoted in Taft, *Otto Rank,* p. 108.

322 *"From a state which I"*   Rank to the Committee, ibid., p. 110, and Lieberman, *Acts of Will,* p. 249.

322 *"similar in an uncanny way"*   Clark, *Freud,* p. 456.

322 *"defection . . . very severe . . . felt his"*   Freud in Freud/Salomé, p. 143.

323 *Rank steadily moved away*   After the break with Freud, and before moving to America, Rank spent time in Paris where, among other activities, he treated Anaïs Nin. At the conclusion of the analysis, they had an affair—as she was wont to do with many of the men in her life. See Lieberman, *Acts of Will,* pp. xviii–xix, and Deirdre Bair, *Anaïs Nin: A Biography* (New York: Penguin Books, 1995), pp. 186–193.

323 *"So quits! On his final"*   Freud in a letter to Ferenczi, April 26, 1925, quoted in Lieberman, *Acts of Will,* p. 260.

323 *"Now, after I have forgiven"*   Sachs, *Freud: Master and Friend,* p. 150.

323 *"He was my best friend"*   Rank, quoted in Taft, *Otto Rank,* p. xvi.

323 *"psychotic manifestations"*   Jones, *The Life and Work,* vol. 3, p. 45. Lieberman provides a comprehensive discussion of the libel of Rank set in motion by Jones. See *Acts of Will,* pp. xxxix–xlii.

323 *"Since leaving me"*   Freud, quoted in Lieberman, *Acts of Will,* p. 321. Freud was still at it in 1935, writing to Arnold Zweig that Rank was "a mountebank . . . who travels around maintaining that he can cure a severe obsessional neurosis in four months!" Freud, in Freud/Zweig, pp. 107–108.

323 *Lionel Trilling, reviewing   New York Times Book Review,* October 13, 1957, p. 7.

323 *"Psychoanalysis has become"*   Otto Rank, *Modern Education,* trans. Mabel Moxon (New York: Knopf, 1932), pp. 193–194.

324 *"It is not easy for me"*   Freud, in a letter to Rank, quoted in Taft, *Otto Rank,* p. 87.

324 *"One of the most important"*   Freud, *Three Essays on the Theory of Sexuality,* p. 224.

324 *"It was anxiety which"*   Freud, *Inhibitions, Symptoms and Anxiety,* p. 32.

325 *"Anxiety arose originally"*   Ibid., p. 134.

325 *Anna Freud and Max Schur*   Discussion of John Bowlby, "Grief and Mourning," pp. 53–84.

326 *"I was in deepest"*   Rank, quoted in Taft, *Otto Rank,* p. xvi.

Chapter 23. *"What Does a Woman Want?"*

328 *"lazy and unintelligent"*   Freud, *The Future of an Illusion,* p. 7. For an interesting discussion of *The Future of an Illusion,* see the Freud/Pfister correspondence, pp. 115–116. Pfister raises many good points that move beyond Freud's attempt to reduce all of religion to his rational, "scientific" point of view.

329 *"I cannot think of any"*   Freud, *Civilization and Its Discontents,* p. 72.

329 *"We are never so"* Ibid., p. 82.

329 *"The sense of guilt"* Ibid., p. 134.

329 *"And now it is"* Ibid., 145.

330 *"I am the mother"* Quoted in Roazen, *Freud and His Followers,* p. 46, from an interview with Otto Isakower.

330 *"It has affected me"* Freud, *Letters,* p. 400.

330 *"Otherwise no mourning"* Freud, in Freud/Jones, p. 677.

330 *"How wise our educators"* Freud, in a letter to Emil Fluss, February 7, 1873, quoted in Gay, *Freud,* p. 522.

331 *"that of women"* Freud, *Three Essays on the Theory of Sexuality,* p. 151.

331 *"the sexual life of adult women"* Freud, *The Question of Lay Analysis,* p. 212.

331 *"The great question . . . which"* Freud, quoted in Jones, *The Life and Work,* vol. 2, p. 468.

332 *"the most unruly of"* Freud, *Three Essays,* p. 22.

332 *"She makes her . . . envy of . . . wound to"* Freud, *Some Psychical Consequences,* pp. 252–253.

332 *"insists on . . . to an incredibly"* Freud, *Female Sexuality,* pp. 229–230.

333 *"Women regard themselves"* Freud, *The Exceptions,* p. 315.

333 *"I cannot evade the"* Freud, *Some Psychical Consequences,* pp. 257–258. In *Civilization and Its Discontents,* he states: "Women soon come into opposition to civilization and display their retarding and restraining influence—those very women who, in the beginning, laid the foundations of civilization by the claims of their love. Women represent the interests of the family and of sexual life. The work of civilization has become increasingly the business of men, it confronts them with ever more difficult tasks and compels them to carry out instinctual sublimations of which women are little capable" (pp. 103–104).

333 *Question Freud's theories* Karen Horney, "The Flight from Womanhood: The Masculinity Complex in Women as Viewed by Men and Women," in Harold Kelman, ed., *Feminine Psychology* (1926; reprint, New York: W. W. Norton, 1967, pp. 54–70). Horney was originally trained in Abraham's Berlin Institute before moving to America in the 1930s. She was subsequently expelled from the New York Psychoanalytic Institute and the American Psychoanalytic Association for challenging orthodox doctrines, particularly the theory of femininity. See Bernard J. Paris, *Karen Horney: A Psychoanalyst's Search for Self-Understanding* (New Haven, Conn.: Yale University Press, 1994).

334 *"does not tally with"* Freud, *Female Sexuality,* p. 243.

334 *"I wish I could convey"* Cynthia E. Russett, *Sexual Science: The Victorian Construction of Womanhood* (Cambridge, Mass.: Harvard University Press, 1989), p. 190.

335 *dominant nineteenth-century ideas* See Peiter M. Judson, "The Gendered Politics of German Nationalism in Austria: 1800–1900," in David F. Good, Margarete Grandner, and Mary Jo Maynes, eds., *Austrian Women in the Nineteenth and Twentieth Centuries* (Providence, R.I.: Berghahn Books, 1996,) pp. 1–18.

335 *"What is now called"* John Stuart Mill, quoted in Russett, *Sexual Science,* p. 1.

335 *The scientific consensus* See ibid. for an excellent overview of this area. Good et al., *Austrian Women,* also presents a number of papers bearing on this topic.

335 *performed clitorectomies on* See Marie-Luise Angerer, "The Discourse on Female Sexuality in Nineteenth Century Austria," in Good et al., *Austrian Women,* pp. 179–196.

336 *"In the mental life of"* Wilhelm Fliess, *The Course of Life,* quoted in Gay, *Freud,* p. 513.

336 *Mill's was a minority view* See Judson, "The Gendered Politics," p. 8.

336 *Women gained admission* See James C. Albisetti, "Female Education in German-Speaking Austria, Germany, and Switzerland, 1866–1914," in Good et al., *Austrian Women,* p. 50.

337 *Havelock Ellis had published* Russett, *Sexual Science,* pp. 28 and 169.

337 *"a woman cannot . . . women as a group"* Freud, in Nunberg and Federn, *Minutes,* vol. 1, p. 351.

337 *"Just as, under the sway"* Adler, in ibid., p. 352.

338 *Because the psychoanalytic movement* Yet women turned to psychoanalysis because there were few other places to express their troubled emotions. In analytic therapy, they could freely explore their confusions, conflicts, disturbances—even their sexuality. For a woman, the question was, "What do I want from psychoanalysis?" As they discovered its potential to expand their personal freedom, they found, paradoxically, that it was infused with pernicious and outmoded beliefs about female inferiority.

338 *"a woman of dangerous"* Freud, in Freud/Ferenczi, vol. 1, p. 423, 476.

Chapter 24. Sándor Ferenczi: The Wise Baby

There is no full-scale biography of Ferenczi. Useful sources for this chapter include the edited collection by Lewis Aron and Adrienne Harris, eds., *The Legacy of Sándor Ferenczi* (Hillsdale, N.J.: Analytic Press, 1993), which contains many useful papers; Andre E. Haynal, *The Technique at Issue: Controversies in Psychoanalysis from Freud and Ferenczi to Michael Balint;* Martin Stanton, *Sándor Ferenczi: Reconsidering Active Intervention* (Northvale, N.J.: Jason Aronson, 1991); and Arnold W. Rachman, ed., "Psychoanalysis' Favorite Son: The Legacy of Sándor Ferenczi" (*Psychoanalytic Inquiry* 17, 1997), a collection of papers. Roazen has a chapter on Ferenczi in *Freud and His Followers,* pp. 363–371. Ferenczi's papers are available in a two-volume set: *First Contributions to Psycho-Analysis* and *Final Contributions to the Problems and Methods of Psycho-Analysis* (London: Hogarth Press, 1955). An invaluable source is *The Clinical Diary of Sándor Ferenczi,* ed. Judith Dupont, trans. Michael Balint and Nicola Z. Jackson (Cambridge, Mass.: Harvard University Press, 1995), and, of course, the two-volume Freud/Ferenczi *Letters.*

339 *"I am looking forward"* Freud, in Freud/Ferenczi, vol. 1, p. 202.

339 *"I count those days"* Ferenczi, in a letter to Freud, September 3, 1923, quoted in Gay, *Freud,* p. 576.

339 *"For three years already"* Freud, in Freud/Jones, pp. 708–709.

339 *"He [Freud] does not"* Ferenczi, *The Clinical Diary,* pp. 160, 186.

340 *"too little love"* Ferenczi, in a letter to Georg Groddeck, quoted in Stanton, *Sándor Ferenczi,* p. 7.

340 *"My mother was, up to"* Ferenczi, in Freud/Ferenczi, vol. 1, p. 383.

341 *"For many successive years"* Freud, *Sándor Ferenczi (Obituary),* pp. 227–228.

342 *"Don't forget that"* Ferenczi, in Freud/Ferenczi, vol. 1, p. 219.

342 *"So that's the way"* Reported by Ferenczi in a letter to Groddeck of December 24, 1921, quoted in a footnote in Freud/Ferenczi, vol. 1, p. 215.

343 *"justified distrust of people"* Ferenczi, in Freud/Ferenczi, p. 219.

343 *"Not only have you"* Freud, in ibid., p. 221. An extended discussion of the Palermo incident is presented by Lewis Aron, "'Yours, Thirsty for Honesty, Ferenczi': Some Background to Sándor Ferenczi's Pursuit of Mutuality," *American Journal of Psychoanalysis* 58, 1998, pp. 5–20.

345 *Such convolutions were not unusual* As the psychoanalyst-historian Andre Haynal notes:

> Elma's psychoanalysis [contained] many indiscretions between the two men . . . All the people involved committed indiscretions: Ferenczi sent Freud copies of Elma's letters, in which she 'wants to know *positively* what you have written to me about her;' Freud wrote confidentially to Gizella about Ferenczi—and the letter fell into Ferenczi's hands . . . Ferenczi likewise asked Freud to say certain things to Gizella for him . . . Ferenczi visited Freud in Vienna to speak with him about Elma. This meeting was kept secret from Elma herself, who was living in Vienna at the time.

Haynal, introduction to Freud/Ferenczi, vol. 1, p. xxiii.

345 *"She is splendid"* Freud, in Freud/Jung, pp. 270–271.

346 *"Frau G.'s visit"* Freud, in Freud/Ferenczi, vol. 1, p. 254.

346 *"Certainly her love for you"* Ibid., p. 327.

346 *"succeeding in penetrating"* Ibid., p. 340.

346 *"We came to the main"* Ibid., p. 349.

346 *"I am very glad to"* Ibid., p. 395.

346 *"behaving with . . . almost unbelievable . . . dear, good"* Ferenczi, in ibid., pp. 336, 343, 375.

347 *"When your express letter"* Freud, in ibid., p. 324.

347 *"The case of Elma has"* Ferenczi, in ibid., p. 413. A detailed discussion of the Ferenczi-Freud-Gizella-Elma episode can be found in Andre Haynal and Ernst Falzeder, "'Healing Through Love'? A Unique Dialogue in the History of Psychoanalysis" (*Free Associations* 2, 1991, pp. 1–20).

347 *deep waters of theoretical* See Ferenczi's *Thalassa: A Theory of Genitality*, trans. Henry A. Bunker (1924; reprint, London: Karnac Books, 1989). Here, Ferenczi engages in the same kind of speculation about a "death instinct" and a "nirvana principle" that one finds in Freud's *Beyond the Pleasure Principle*. Freud, in Ferenczi's obituary, calls *Thalassa* "his most brilliant and most fertile achievement . . . " (p. 228), but goes on to criticize Ferenczi's later work as dominated by an unrealistic "need to cure."

348 *The essential features of* The clinical innovations of Ferenczi's last years are outlined in five papers that are reprinted in his *Final Contributions to the Problems and Methods of Psycho-Analysis*: "The Problem of the Termination of the Analysis" (1927), pp. 77–85; "The Elasticity of Psycho-Analytic Technique" (1928), pp. 87–101; "The Principle of Relaxation and Neocatharsis" (1929), pp. 108–125; "Child Analysis in the Analysis of Adults" (1931), pp. 126–141; and "Confusion of Tongues between Adults and the Child" (1933), pp. 156–167.

348 *"One must never be"* Ferenczi, "Elasticity of Technique," p. 95.

348 *"One gets the impression"* Ferenczi, "Child Analysis," p. 138.

348 *Ferenczi's final paper* A detailed discussion of the *Confusion of Tongues* paper, including the history of its treatment by the psychoanalytic establishment, is in Arnold W. Rachman, "The Confusion of Tongues Theory: Ferenczi's Legacy to Psychoanalysis" (*Cahiers Psychiatriques Genevois* [Special Issue], 1994, pp. 235–255).

348 *"I started to listen"* Ferenczi, "Confusion of Tongues," p. 157. The argument has been made, by Freud himself among others, that Ferenczi's understanding of neurosis, and his treatment approach, were only applicable to the special population of "difficult cases" that he saw. Freud wrote that he did not encounter the same clinical phenomena because he worked with "healthier" individuals—primarily analysts in training. It is questionable whether Freud's cases were as free from trauma as he liked to believe; Dora, the Rat Man, the Wolf Man, Horace Frink, H.D., and several others were severely disturbed. The point is that Ferenczi's cases were, in fact, very much like the patients described in the *Studies on Hysteria*, and it was on this population that Freud erected the foundation of psychoanalysis. The argument that the difference between Freud and Ferenczi can be explained as due to their work with different kinds of patients does not hold up. Ferenczi had, like Rank, rediscovered what Breuer had found in the 1890s: the role of trauma, dissociation, fragmentation of the self, and the value of a "friendly" and collaborative approach, ideas long dismissed by Freud. In *The Clinical Diary* (p. 58), Ferenczi says: "My model for this process is probably that of Dr. Breuer, who did not shrink from seeking and finding the truth in the most nonsensical statements of a hysteric, whereby he had to rely both theoretically and technically on the hints and suggestions of the patient."

349 *"The analytic situation"* Ferenczi, *The Clinical Diary*, p. 194.

349 *"After this summit"* Freud, *Sándor Ferenczi (Obituary)*, p. 229.

350 *"sometimes lost control"* Judith Dupont, "Michael Balint: Analysand, Pupil, Friend and Successor to Sándor Ferenczi," in Aron and Harris, *The Legacy of Sándor Ferenczi*, p. 156.

350 *"gave way . . . ceased further"* Ferenczi, in Freud/Ferenczi, vol. 2, pp. 252–254. The case is complicated, as Ferenczi's letter makes clear. The young woman was suicidal when she came for treatment, and Ferenczi followed a vacillating course with her, drawing her in and pushing her away. He encouraged her to write her life story, then disapproved of her attempt to publish it. He seemed stuck between his empathy for her, on the one hand, and his attempts to follow Freud's dictates, on the other. His great ambivalence toward women, which he is open about in his letter, is partly played out with this young woman, to her detriment.

350 *"I can kiss Papa"* Clara Thompson, quoted in Haynal, *The Technique at Issue*, p. 30.

350 *"the evil genius in"* Jones, in Freud/Jones, p. 729.

350 *"Why stop at a kiss?"* Freud, quoted in Haynal, *The Technique at Issue*, p. 30, and Dupont, in a footnote in Ferenczi, *The Clinical Diary*, pp. 3–4.

351 *"On the basis of more"* Arnold W. Rachman, "Ferenczi and Sexuality," in Aron and Harris, *The Legacy of Sándor Ferenczi*, pp. 84–85.

351 *"Freud no longer loves"* Ferenczi, *The Clinical Diary*, pp. 93, 185–186. Ferenczi's quote of Freud saying that "neurotics are a rabble" is supported by several other sources. To his Italian follower Edoardo Weiss, Freud said, "Regretfully, only a few patients are worth the trouble we spend on them." See Weiss's *Sigmund Freud as a Consultant: Recollections of a Pioneer in Psychoanalysis* (New York: Intercontinental Medical Book Corp., 1970), p. 37. To Oskar Pfister, he wrote, "I have found little that is 'good' about human beings on the whole. In my experience most of them are trash." Freud/Pfister, p. 61. In April 1928, he told the Hungarian psychoanalyst Istvan Hollos: "Finally I confessed to myself that I do not like these sick people, that I am angry at them to feel them so far from me and all that is human . . . [It might be] the consequence of an ever more evident partisanship for the primacy of the intellect, a hostility toward the id? Or what else?" Quoted in Gay, *Freud*, p. 537.

352 *"Isn't Ferenczi a cross"* Freud to Eitingon, quoted in Gay, *Freud*, p. 582

352 *"For three years now"* Freud, in Freud/Jones, pp. 708–709.

352 *"Ferenczi read paper"* Freud to Eitingon, quoted in Gay, *Freud*, p. 583.

352 *"confused, obscure, artificial"* Freud to Anna, in ibid., p. 584.

352 *At the end of this* Freud's rebuff is reported in Fromm, *Sigmund Freud's Mission*, pp. 69–70, who heard it from Izette de Forest, a student and friend of Ferenczi's. See also Haynal, *The Technique at Issue*, p. 52.

352 *"In my case the blood-crisis"* Ferenczi, *The Clinical Diary*, p. 212.

352 *"Ferenczi's condition, suffered"* Michael Balint, quoted in ibid., p. 222.

353 *"mental deterioration . . . Toward the end"* Jones, *The Life and Work*, vol. 3, p. 45. For additional comments, see pp. 127, 166, 176, 178.

353 *"Ferenczi offered observations"* Freud to Anna, quoted in Gay, *Freud*, pp. 583–584.

353 *Balint published a rebuttal* Michael Balint, "Sándor Ferenczi's Last Years," letter to the editor (*International Journal of Psychoanalysis* 39, 1958, pp. 68–71).

353 *Andre Haynal has reviewed* Haynal, *The Technique at Issue*, pp. 53–54. See also Sandor Lorand, "Sándor Ferenczi: Pioneer of Pioneers," in Alexander, Eisenstein, and Grotjahn, *Psychoanalytic Pioneers*, pp. 14–35. Haynal and Ernst Falzeder, in "The Psychoanalytic Movement: 'Healing Through Love?' A Unique Dialogue in the History of Psychoanalysis," state that "after Ferenczi's death, analysts, impressed by the fact that even such an intimate friendship could be heavily disturbed by these problems, became circumspect in their discussions of technique" (p. 17).

Chapter 25. The Final Years

355 *an "energy devil"* Freud to Ferenczi, October 23, 1927, quoted in Gay, *Freud,* p. 541. For an account of Bonaparte's life, including her analysis with Freud, see Bertin, *Marie Bonaparte.*

355 *"a quite outstanding"* Freud to Eitingon, October 30, 1925, quoted in Gay, *Freud,* p. 542.

355 *The Professor's dog would* The American psychiatrist Roy Grinker saw Freud in analysis in 1933 and reports that the dog would scratch at the door to be let out of the consulting room and Freud would say, "Jo-Fi doesn't approve of what you're talking about." When she would come back in he would say, "Jo-Fi wants to give you another chance." Once, when Grinker was "emoting with a good deal of vigor, the damn dog jumped on top of me, and Freud said, 'You see, Jo-Fi is so excited for you that you've been able to discover the source of your anxiety.'" Quoted in "Reminiscences of Dr. Roy Grinker" (*Journal of the American Academy of Psychoanalysis* 3, 1975), p. 216.

356 *his fee of $25* Freud's fee would be the equivalent of approximately $363 per hour in present dollars.

357 *"I am resolved"* Freud, in Freud/Jones, p. 716.

357 *"We are determined"* Freud to Sam Freud, quoted in Gay, *Freud,* p. 593.

357 *"who satisfies in rare"* Freud to Arnold Zweig, June 17, 1936, quoted in Gay, *Freud,* p. 613. The quote, which was edited out of Freud/Zweig, continues " . . . when a passionate woman almost wholly sublimates her sexuality!"

357 *"It was really not"* Freud to Marie Bonaparte, September 27, 1936, quoted in Jones, *The Life and Work,* vol. 3, p. 209.

358 *"Our correspondence was"* Freud to Marie Bonaparte, January 3, 1937, quoted by Masson in introduction to Freud/Fliess, p. 7. See Mahony, *Freud's Dora,* p. 23. Mahony has also written a long paper on the Freud/Fliess relationship, "Friendship and Its Discontents" (*Contemporary Psychoanalysis* 15, 1979, pp. 55–109).

358 *"I don't understand your"* Freud to Arnold Zweig, June 22, 1937, quoted in Gay, *Freud,* p. 615. The letter is omitted from Freud/Zweig. There is some dispute over how to translate Freud's term *Judenbube.* Jones originally had it "Jew boy"; Gay made it "Jewish boy"; "little Jew" seems a compromise. Gay notes that Freud's reference to Adler is "callous and snide"; it is clear that his hatred toward Adler never softened.

358 *"was very fond of her"* February 10, 1937, quoted in ibid., p. 616; omitted from Freud/Zweig.

359 *"I refuse to be beholden"* See Gay, *Freud,* p. 779, for a more detailed account. Gay was initially dubious about the story but became convinced after consulting Robert McCully, who wrote of it. See Robert S. McCully, "Remarks on the Last Contact between Freud and Jung" (*Quadrant: Journal of the C. G. Jung Foundation* 20, 1987, pp. 73–74). See also McLynn, *Jung,* pp. 416–417.

360 *William Bullitt, the American ambassador* For a longer account of the Freud-Bullitt relationship and their collaboration on the Wilson psychobiography, see Gay, *Freud,* pp. 555–562. Clark, *Freud,* pp. 474–478, in contrast to Gay, does not try to reinterpret this inept book in terms favorable to Freud.

360 *"respect . . . I can heartily"* The original story is in Jones, *The Life and Work,* vol. 3, p. 226. The report on the actual document is in Roazen, *Meeting Freud's Family,* p. 47, who cites an article in the *Journal of the International Association for the History of Psychoanalysis,* English ed., 8, 1989, pp. 13–14.

360 *imagined himself William the Conqueror* See Jones, *The Life and Work,* vol. 3, p. 228.

361 *"The Nazis? I am not"* Freud, quoted by LaForgue in Ruitenbeek, *Freud as We Knew Him,* p. 344.

361 *"I am prepared for"* Freud to Eitingon, March 5, 1939, quoted in Gay, *Freud,* p. 646.

362   *"Talk it over with Anna"*   See Schur, *Freud: Living and Dying*, p. 529. Gay describes the final days, drawing on unpublished materials by Schur, in *Freud*, pp. 651, 739.

362   *"In the fifty-three years"*   Martha to Ludwig Binswanger, November 7, 1939, quoted in Gay, *Freud*, p. 60.

363   *her son, Edward Bernays*   For an interesting account of Edward Bernays, see Malcolm Gladwell, "The Spin Myth," *New Yorker*, July 6, 1998, pp. 66–74.

Appendix. Psychoanalysis Interminable: Freud as a Therapist

365   *"a child of its time"*   Freud, *Analysis Terminable and Interminable*, p. 216.

366   *"We can understand"*   Ibid., p. 230.

366   *"an analysis lasting"*   Ibid., p. 222.

367   *Historical detective work*   See Masson, *The Assault on Truth*, pp. 241–258.

368   *"the instinct of aggression"*   Freud, *Analysis Terminable*, p. 243.

369   *"give the analyst . . . a struggle"*   Ibid., p. 250.

369   *"At no other point"*   Ibid., p. 252.

370   *Psychiatrists David Lynn and George Vaillant*   See David J. Lynn and George E. Vaillant, "Anonymity, Neutrality, and Confidentiality in the Actual Methods of Sigmund Freud: A Review of Forty-Three Cases, 1907–1939" (*American Journal of Psychiatry*, 155:2, 1998, pp. 163–171).

Bibliography

Abraham, Hilda C., and Freud, Ernst L., eds. *A Psychoanalytic Dialogue: The Letters of Sigmund Freud and Karl Abraham, 1907–1926.* Trans. Bernard Marsh and Hilda C. Abraham. London: Hogarth Press and the Institute of Psycho-Analysis, 1965.

Abraham, Karl. *Selected Papers of Karl Abraham, M.D.* Trans. Douglas Bryan and Alix Strachey. London: Hogarth Press and the Institute of Psycho-Analysis, 1949.

Ainsworth, Mary, Blehar, M. C., Waters, E., and Wall, S. *Patterns of Attachment.* Hillsdale, N.J.: Erlbaum, 1978.

Albisetti, James C. "Female Education in German-Speaking Austria, Germany, and Switzerland, 1866–1914." In David F. Good, Margarete Grandner, and Mary Jo Maynes, eds., *Austrian Women in the Nineteenth and Twentieth Centuries: Cross-disciplinary Perspectives.* Providence, R.I.: Berghahn Books, 1996, pp. 39–58.

Alexander, Franz, Eisenstein, Samuel, and Grotjahn, Martin, eds. *Psychoanalytic Pioneers.* New York: Basic Books, 1966.

Angerer, Marie-Luise. "The Discourse on Female Sexuality in Nineteenth Century Austria." In David F. Good, Margarete Grandner, and Mary Jo Maynes, eds., *Austrian Women in the Nineteenth and Twentieth Centuries: Cross-disciplinary Perspectives.* Providence, R.I.: Berghahn Books, 1996, pp. 179–196.

Ansbacher, Heinz L., and Ansbacher, Rowena R., eds. *The Individual Psychology of Alfred Adler.* New York: Basic Books, 1956.

Anthony, E. J. "The Reactions of Parents to the Oedipal Child." In E. J. Anthony and Thresa Benedek, eds., *Parenthood.* Boston: Little, Brown, 1970, pp. 275–288.

Appignanesi, Lisa, and Forrester, John. *Freud's Women.* London: Virago Press, 1992.

Aron, Lewis. "'Yours, Thirsty for Honesty, Ferenczi': Some Background to Sándor Ferenczi's Pursuit of Mutuality." *American Journal of Psychoanalysis* 58, 1998, pp. 5–20.

Aron, Lewis, and Harris, Adrienne, eds. *The Legacy of Sándor Ferenczi.* Hillsdale, N.J.: Analytic Press, 1993.

Atwood, George E., and Stolorow, Robert D. "Freud." In *Faces in a Cloud: Subjectivity in Personality Theory.* 2nd ed. New York: Jason Aronson, 1993.

———. "C. G. Jung. "In *Faces in a Cloud: Subjectivity in Personality Theory.* 2nd ed. New York: Jason Aronson, 1993.

Babington, Anthony. *Shell-Shock: A History of the Changing Attitudes to War Neurosis.* London: Leo Cooper, 1997.

Bair, Deirdre. *Anaïs Nin: A Biography.* New York: Penguin Books, 1995.

Balint, Michael. "Sándor Ferenczi's Last Years." Letter to the editor. *International Journal of Psychoanalysis* 39, 1958, pp. 68–71.

Barker, Pat. *Regeneration.* New York: Viking, 1991.

Beebe, Beatrice, and Lachmann, Frank M. "Mother-Infant Mutual Influence and Precursors of Psychic Structure." In Arnold Goldberg, ed., *Progress in Self-psychology,* vol. 3. Hillsdale, N.J.: Analytic Press, 1988, pp. 3–25.

Beebe, Beatrice, Lachmann, Frank, and Jaffe, Joseph. "Mother-Infant Interaction Structures and Presymbolic Self and Object Representations." *Psychoanalytic Dialogues* 7, 1997, pp. 133–182.

Beller, Steven. *Vienna and the Jews: 1867–1938.* Cambridge, U.K.: Cambridge University Press, 1989.

Bergahn, Volker R. *Militarism: The History of an International Debate, 1861–1979.* Cambridge, U.K.: Cambridge University Press, 1981.

Berkley, George E. *Vienna and Its Jews: The Tragedy of Success, 1880s–1980s.* Cambridge, Mass.: Abt Books, 1988.

Bernheimer, Charles, and Kahane, Claire, eds. *In Dora's Case: Freud-Hysteria-Feminism.* New York: Columbia University Press, 1985.

Bertin, Celia. *Marie Bonaparte: A Life.* New York: Harcourt, Brace, Jovanovich, 1982.

Bettelheim, Bruno. *Freud and Man's Soul.* New York: Knopf, 1983.

Bilinsky, John M. "Jung and Freud: The End of a Romance." *Andover Newton Quarterly* 10, 1969, 39–43.

Binneveld, Hans. *From Shell Shock to Combat Stress: A Comparative History of Military Psychiatry.* Trans. John O'Kane. Amsterdam: Amsterdam University Press, 1997.

Binswanger, Ludwig. *Sigmund Freud: Reminiscences of a Friendship.* New York: Grune and Stratton, 1957.

Blanton, Smiley. *Diary of My Analysis with Sigmund Freud.* New York: Hawthorn Books, 1971.

Bonadeo, Alfredo. *Mark of the Beast: Death and Degradation in the Literature of the Great War.* Lexington: University Press of Kentucky, 1989.

Bonaparte, Marie, Freud, Anna, and Kris, Ernst, eds. *The Origins of Psycho-Analysis: Letters to Wilhelm Fliess: Drafts and Notes: 1887–1902.* New York: Basic Books, 1954.

Bonomi, Carlo. "'Sexuality and Death' in Freud's Discovery of Sexual Aetiology." *International Forum of Psychoanalysis* 3, 1994, pp. 63–87.

———. "Why Have We Ignored Freud the 'Pediatrician'?" *Cahiers Psychiatriques Genevois,* Special Issue, 1994, pp. 55–99.

Borch-Jacobson, Mikkel. *Remembering Anna O.: A Century of Mystification.* Trans. Kirby Olson. New York: Routledge, 1996.

Bottome, Phyllis. *Alfred Adler: Apostle of Freedom.* London: Faber and Faber, 1939.

Bowlby, John. "Grief and Mourning in Infancy and Early Childhood." *Psychoanalytic Study of the Child* 15, 1960, pp. 9–94.

———. *Attachment and Loss.* Vol. 1: *Attachment.* New York: Basic Books, 1969.

———. *Attachment and Loss.* Vol. 2. *Separation.* New York: Basic Books, 1973.

Brabent, Eva, Falzeder, Ernst, and Giampieri-Deutsch, Patrizia, eds. *The Correspondence of Sigmund Freud and Sándor Ferenczi.* Vol. 1, *1908–1914.* Cambridge, Mass.: Harvard University Press, 1993.

Breger, Louis. "Function of Dreams." *Journal of Abnormal Psychology Monograph* 72, pp. 1–28, 1967.

———. *From Instinct to Identity: The Development of Personality.* Englewood Cliffs, N.J.: Prentice-Hall, 1974.

———. *Freud's Unfinished Journey: Conventional and Critical Perspectives in Psychoanalytic Theory.* London: Routledge and Kegan Paul, 1981.

———. "Freud Conventionalized: Review of Frank J. Sulloway, *Freud: Biologist of the Mind.*" *Journal of the American Academy of Psychoanalysis* 9, 1981, pp. 459–472.

———. *Dostoevsky: The Author as Psychoanalyst.* New York: New York University Press, 1989.

Breger, Louis, ed. *Clinical-Cognitive Psychology: Models and Integrations.* Englewood Cliffs, N.J.: Prentice-Hall, 1969.

Breger, Louis, Hunter, Ian, and Lane, Ron W. "The Effect of Stress on Dreams." *Psychological Issues,* monograph 27. New York: International Universities Press, 1971.

Bridenthal, Renate, and Koonz, Claudia, eds. *Becoming Visible: Women in European History.* Boston: Houghton Mifflin Company, 1977.

Brodie, Janet F. *Contraception and Abortion in Nineteenth-Century America.* Ithaca, N.Y.: Cornell University Press, 1994.

Broehlich, Walter, ed. *The Letters of Sigmund Freud to Eduard Silberstein: 1871–1881.* Trans. Arnold J. Pomerans. Cambridge, Mass.: Harvard University Press, 1990.

Bromberg, Philip M. "Hysteria, Dissociation, and Cure: Emmy von N Revisited." *Psychoanalytic Dialogues* 6, 1996, pp. 55–71.

———. *Standing in the Spaces: Essays on Clinical Process, Trauma and Dissociation.* Hillsdale, N.J.: Analytic Press, 1998.

Brome, Victor. *Jung.* New York: Atheneum, 1981.

Burlingham, Michael J. *The Last Tiffany: A Biography of Dorothy Tiffany Burlingham.* New York: Atheneum, 1989.

Byck, Robert, ed. *Cocaine Papers by Sigmund Freud.* New York: New American Library, 1974.

Bynum, W. F., Porter, Roy, and Shepherd, Michael, eds. *The Anatomy of Madness: Essays in the History of Psychiatry,* vols. 1–2. London: Tavistock Publications, 1985.

Carotenuto, Aldo. *A Secret Symmetry: Sabina Spielrein between Jung and Freud.* Trans. Arno Pomerans, John Shepley, and Krishna Winston. New York: Pantheon, 1982.

Carr, William. *The Origins of the War of German Unification.* London: Longman, 1991.

Chickering, Roger. *Imperial Germany and a World Without War: The Peace Movement and German Society, 1892–1914.* Princeton, N.J.: Princeton University Press, 1975.

Clark, Ronald W. *Freud: The Man and the Cause.* New York: Random House, 1980.

Cocks, George, ed. *The Curve of Life: Correspondence of Heinz Kohut.* Chicago: University of Chicago Press, 1994.

Cohen, Gary B. *Education and Middle-class Society in Imperial Austria, 1848–1918.* West Lafayette, Ind.: Purdue University Press, 1996.

Colby, Kenneth M. "On the Disagreement between Freud and Adler." *American Imago* 8, 1951, pp. 229–238.

Couch, Arthur S. "Anna Freud's Adult Psychoanalytic Technique: A Defense of Classical Analysis." *International Journal of Psychoanalysis* 76, 1995, pp. 153–171.

Cranefield, Paul F. "Josef Breuer's Evaluation of His Contribution to Psychoanalysis." *International Journal of Psycho-Analysis* 39, 1958, pp. 319–322.

Crews, Frederick C. *The Memory Wars: Freud's Legacy in Dispute.* New York: New York Review, 1995.

Crews, Frederick C., ed. *Unauthorized Freud: Doubters Confront a Legend.* New York: Viking, 1998.

Crook, Paul. *Darwinism, War and History.* Cambridge, U.K.: Cambridge University Press, 1994.

Davies, Jody M., and Frawley, Mary G. *Treating the Adult Survivor of Childhood Sexual Abuse.* New York: Basic Books, 1994.

Decker, Hannah S. "The Medical Reception of Psychoanalysis in Germany, 1894–1907: Three Brief Studies." *Bulletin of History of Medicine* 45, 1971, pp. 461–481.

———. *Freud, Dora, Vienna, 1900.* New York: Free Press, 1991.

Deutsch, Helene. "Freud and His Pupils: A Footnote to the History of the Psychoanalytic Movement." *Psychoanalytic Quarterly* 9, 1940, pp. 184–194.

Donn, Linda. *Freud and Jung: Years of Friendship, Years of Loss.* New York: Scribner's, 1988.

Dorsey, John M. *An American Psychiatrist in Vienna, 1935–1937, and His Sigmund Freud.* Detroit: Center for Health Education, 1976.

Dupont, Judith. "Michael Balint: Analysand, Pupil, Friend and Successor to Sándor Ferenczi." In Lewis Aron and Adrienne Harris, eds., *The Legacy of Sándor Ferenczi*. Hillsdale, N.J.: Analytic Press, 1993.

Edmunds, Lavinia. "His Master's Choice." *Johns Hopkins Magazine,* April 1988, pp. 40–49. Reprinted in Fredrick C. Crews, ed., *Unauthorized Freud: Doubters Confront a Legend.* New York: Viking, 1998, pp. 261–276.

Edwards, Anne. *Sonia: The Life of Countess Tolstoy.* New York: Simon and Schuster, 1981.

Eissler, Kurt. *Talent and Genius: The Fictitious Case of Tausk contra Freud.* New York: Quadrangle Books, 1971.

Eitingon, Max. "Bulletin of the International Psychoanalytical Association." *International Journal of Psychoanalysis* 9, 1928.

Ellenberger, Henri F. *The Discovery of the Unconscious: The History and Evolution of Dynamic Psychiatry.* New York: Basic Books, 1970.

———. "The Story of Anna O.: A Critical Review of New Data." *Journal of the History of the Behavioral Sciences* 8, 1972, 267–279.

Engelman, Edmund. *Bergasse 19: Sigmund Freud's Home and Offices, Vienna 1938.* Chicago: University of Chicago Press, 1976.

Erikson, Erik. "The Dream Specimen of Psychoanalysis." *Journal of the American Psychoanalytic Association* 2, 1950, pp. 5–56.

———. *Insight and Responsibility.* New York: W. W. Norton, 1964.

Esterson, Allen. *Seductive Mirage: An Exploration of the Work of Sigmund Freud.* Chicago: Open Court, 1993.

Evans, Richard J. *Comrades and Sisters: Feminism, Socialism, and Pacifism in Europe, 1870–1975.* New York: St. Martin's Press, 1987.

Falzeder, Ernst. "Whose Freud Is It? Some Reflections on Editing Freud's Correspondence." *International Forum of Psychoanalysis* 5, 1996, pp. 77–86.

Falzeder, Ernst, and Brabant, Eva, with the collaboration of Giampieri-Deutsch, Patrizia. *The Correspondence of Sigmund Freud and Sándor Ferenczi.* Vol. 2, *1914–1919.* Cambridge, Mass.: Harvard University Press, 1996.

Farrell, John. *Freud's Paranoid Quest: Psychoanalysis and Modern Suspicion.* New York: New York University Press, 1996.

Ferenczi, Sándor. *First Contributions to Psycho-Analysis,* and *Final Contributions to the Problems and Methods of Psycho-Analysis.* London: Hogarth Press, 1955.

———. *Thalassa: A Theory of Genitality.* Trans. Henry A. Bunker. 1924. Reprint, London: Karnac Books, 1989.

———. *The Clinical Diary of Sándor Ferenczi.* Ed. Judith Dupont. Trans. Michael Balint and Nicola Z. Jackson. Cambridge, Mass.: Harvard University Press, 1995.

Ferenczi, Sándor, and Rank, Otto. *The Development of Psychoanalysis.* Trans. Caroline Newton. 1924. Reprint, New York: Dover, 1956.

Ferguson, Niall. *The Pity of War.* New York: Basic Books, 1999.

Ferris, Paul. *Dr. Freud: A Life.* Washington, D.C.: Counterpoint, 1997.

Finkelhor, David. *Sexually Victimized Children.* New York: Free Press, 1979.

Finkelhor, David, ed. *A Sourcebook on Child Sexual Abuse.* Beverly Hills, Calif.: Sage Publications, 1986.

Fliess, Robert. *Symbol, Dream and Psychosis.* New York: International Universities Press, 1973.

Fraenkel, Josef, ed. *The Jews of Austria: Essays on Their Life, History and Destruction.* London: Vallentine, Mitchell, 1970.

Freeman, Lucy. *The Story of Anna O.* New York: Walker, 1972.

Freud, Anna. "Beating Fantasies and Daydreams." *International Journal of Psychoanalysis* 4, 1923, pp. 89–102.

———. "An Introduction to the Technique of Child Analysis." In *The Writings of Anna Freud,* vol. 1. New York: International Universities Press, 1973.

Freud, Ernst L., ed. *The Letters of Sigmund Freud.* Trans. Tania Stern and James Stern. New York: Basic Books, 1960.

——. *The Letters of Sigmund Freud and Arnold Zweig.* New York: Harcourt, Brace and World, 1970.

Freud, Ernst, Freud, Lucie, and Grubrich-Simitis, Ilse, eds. *Sigmund Freud, His Life in Pictures and Words.* Trans. Christine Trollope. New York: Harcourt, Brace, Jovanovich, 1976.

Freud, Harry. "My Uncle Sigmund." In Hendrik M. Ruitenbeek, ed., *Freud as We Knew Him.* Detroit: Wayne State University Press, 1973, pp. 312–313.

Freud, Martin. *Sigmund Freud: Man and Father.* New York: Vanguard Press, 1958.

Freud, Sigmund. All titles are from *The Standard Edition of the Complete Psychological Works of Sigmund Freud,* ed. and trans. James Strachey, in collaboration with Anna Freud, assisted by Alix Strachey and Alan Tyson. London: Hogarth Press. Works will be cited by title, volume, date, and page number.

——. *Studies on Hysteria* (with Josef Breuer), 2, 1893–1895, pp. 1–335.

——. *Charcot (Obituary),* 3, 1893, pp. 9–23.

——. *The Aetiology of Hysteria,* 3, 1896, pp. 189–221.

——. *Sexuality in the Aetiology of the Neuroses,* 3, 1898, pp. 261–285.

——. *Screen Memories,* 3, 1899, pp. 301–322.

——. *The Interpretation of Dreams,* 4 and 5, 1900, pp. 1–627.

——. *On Dreams,* 4, 1901, pp. 631–686.

——. *The Psychopathology of Everyday Life,* 6, 1901, pp. 1–310.

——. *Fragment of an Analysis of a Case of Hysteria,* 7, 1905, pp. 3–122.

——. *Three Essays on the Theory of Sexuality,* 7, 1905, pp. 125–243.

——. *Jokes and Their Relation to the Unconscious,* 8, 1905, pp. 3–258.

——. *Obsessive Actions and Religious Practices,* 9, 1907, pp. 115–127.

——. *'Civilized' Sexual Morality and Modern Nervous Illness,* 9, 1908, pp. 177–204.

——. *Analysis of a Phobia in a Five-Year-Old Boy,* 10, 1909, pp. 3–149.

——. *Notes Upon a Case of Obessional Neurosis,* 10, 1909, pp. 153–326.

——. *Five Lectures on Psychoanalysis,* 11, 1910, pp. 3–36.

——. *The Handling of Dream-Interpretation in Psychoanalysis,* 12, 1911, pp. 85–96.

——. *The Dynamics of the Transference,* 12, 1912, pp. 97–108.

——. *Recommendations to Physicians Practising Psycho-Analysis,* 12, 1912, pp. 109–120.

——. *On Beginning the Treatment (Further Recommendations on the Technique of Psycho-Analysis, I),* 12, 1913, pp. 121–144.

——. *Remembering, Repeating and Working-Through (Further Recommendations on the Technique of Psycho-Analysis, II),* 12, 1914, pp. 145–156.

——. *Observations on Transference-Love (Further Recommendations on the Technique of Psychoanalysis, III),* 12, 1914, pp. 157–171.

——. *Totem and Taboo,* 13, 1912, pp. 1–161.

——. *Some Reflections on Schoolboy Psychology,* 13, 1914, pp. 241–244.

——. *On the History of the Psycho-Analytic Movement,* 14, 1914, pp. 3–66.

——. *Instincts and Their Vicissitudes,* 14, 1915, pp. 105–140.

——. *Repression,* 14, 1915, pp. 141–158.

——. *The Unconscious,* 14, 1915, pp. 161–215.

——. *A Metapsychological Supplement to the Theory of Dreams,* 14, 1917, pp. 217–235.

——. *Mourning and Melancholia,* 14, 1917, pp. 237–258.

——. *Thoughts for the Times on War and Death,* 14, 1915, pp. 273–302.

——. *Some Character Types Met with in Psycho-Analytic Work,* 14, 1916, pp. 309–333.

——. *Introductory Lectures on Psychoanalysis,* 15 and 16, 1916–1917, pp. 15–496.

——. *From the History of an Infantile Neurosis,* 17, 1918, pp. 3–122.

——. *Lines of Advance in Psycho-Analytic Therapy,* 17, 1919, pp. 157–168.

———. *'A Child Is Being Beaten': A Contribution to the Study of the Origin of Sexual Perversions,* 17, 1919, pp. 177–204.

———. *"Introduction" to Psycho-Analysis and the War Neuroses,* 17, 1919, pp. 206–210.

———. *Beyond the Pleasure Principle,* 18, 1920, pp. 3–64.

———. *Group Psychology and the Analysis of the Ego,* 18, 1921, pp. 67–143.

———. *The Psychogenesis of a Case of Homosexuality in a Woman,* 18, 1920, pp. 145–172.

———. *The Ego and the Id,* 19, 1923, pp. 3–66.

———. *Some Psychical Consequences of the Anatomical Distinction between the Sexes,* 19, 1925, pp. 243–258.

———. *An Autobiographical Study,* 20, 1925, pp. 3–74.

———. *Inhibitions, Symptoms, and Anxiety,* 20, 1926, pp. 77–174.

———. *The Question of Lay Analysis,* 20, 1926, pp. 179–258.

———. *The Future of an Illusion,* 21, 1927, pp. 3–56.

———. *Civilization and Its Discontents,* 21, 1930, pp. 59–145.

———. *Female Sexuality,* 21, 1931, pp. 223–243.

———. *New Introductory Lectures on Psycho-Analysis,* 22, 1933, pp. 3–182.

———. *Sándor Ferenczi (Obituary),* 22, 1933, pp. 227–229.

———. *Moses and Monotheism: Three Essays,* 23, 1939, pp. 3–137.

———. *An Outline of Psycho-Analysis,* 23, 1940, pp. 141–207.

———. *Analysis Terminable and Interminable,* 23, 1937, pp. 211–253.

———. *Splitting of the Ego in the Process of Defence,* 23, 1940, pp. 273–278.

Freud, Sophie. *My Three Mothers and Other Passions.* New York: New York University Press, 1988.

Freyd, Jennifer J. *Betrayal Trauma: The Logic of Forgetting Childhood Abuse.* Cambridge, Mass.: Harvard University Press, 1996.

Fromm, Erich. *Sigmund Freud's Mission: An Analysis of His Personality and Influence.* New York: Grove Press, 1959.

Furtmüller, Carl. *A Biographical Essay.* In Heinz Ansbacher and Rowena R. Ansbacher, eds., *Superiority and Social Interest: A Collection of Later Writings.* London: Routledge and Kegan Paul, 1965, pp. 330–393.

Fussell, Paul. *The Great War and Modern Memory.* Oxford, U.K.: Oxford University Press, 1977.

Gabriel, Richard A. *No More Heroes: Madness and Psychiatry in War.* New York: Hill and Wang, 1987.

Gallant, Christine. *Tabooed Jung: Marginality as Power.* New York: New York University Press, 1996.

Gardiner, Murial, ed. *The Wolf-Man by the Wolf-Man.* New York: Basic Books, 1971.

Gay, Peter. *Freud: A Life for Our Time.* New York: W. W. Norton, 1988.

———. *The Cultivation of Hatred.* New York: W. W. Norton, 1993.

Gicklhorn, Renee. "The Freiberg Period of the Freud Family." *Journal of the History of Medicine* 24, 1969, pp. 37–43.

Gilbert, Martin. *The First World War: A Complete History.* New York: Henry Holt, 1994.

Gillis, John R., ed. *The Militarization of the Western World.* New Brunswick, N.J.: Rutgers University Press, 1989.

Gladwell, Malcolm. "The Spin Myth." *New Yorker,* July 6, 1998, pp. 66–74.

Goldman, Emma. *Living My Life.* New York: Knopf, 1931.

Good, David F., Margarete Grandner, and Mary Jo Maynes, eds. *Austrian Women in the Nineteenth and Twentieth Centuries: Cross-disciplinary Perspectives.* Providence, R.I.: Berghahn Books, 1996.

Graf, Max. "Reminiscences of Professor Sigmund Freud." *Psychoanalytic Quarterly* 11, 1942, pp. 465–476.

Grinker, Roy R., Sr. "Reminiscences of Dr. Roy Grinker." *Journal of the American Academy of Psychoanalysis* 3, 1975, pp. 211–221.

Groddeck, Georg. *The Book of the It.* New York: Random House, 1961.

Grosskurth, Phyllis. *The Secret Ring: Freud's Inner Circle and the Politics of Psychoanalysis.* Reading, Mass.: Addison-Wesley, 1991.

Grotjahn, Martin. "Karl Abraham: The First German Psychoanalyst." In Franz Alexander, Samuel Eisenstein, and Martin Grotjahn, eds., *Psychoanalytic Pioneers.* New York: Basic Books, 1966, pp. 1–13.

Grubrich-Simitis, Ilse. *Back to Freud's Texts: Making Silent Documents Speak.* Trans. Philip Slotkin. New Haven, Conn.: Yale University Press, 1996.

———. "Nothing about the Totem Meal! On Freud's Notes." Trans. Veronica Mächtlinger. In Michael S. Roth, ed., *Freud: Conflict and Culture.* New York: Knopf, 1998, pp. 15–31.

Grubrich-Simitis, Ilse, ed. *A Phylogenetic Fantasy: Overview of the Transference Neuroses* (Sigmund Freud). Trans. Axel Hoffer and Peter T. Hoffer. Cambridge, Mass.: Harvard University Press, 1987.

Guillain, Georges. *J. M. Charcot, His Life, His Work.* London: Pitman Medical Publishing, 1959.

Handlbauer, Bernhard. *The Freud-Adler Controversy.* Trans. Laurie Cohen. Oxford, U.K.: Oneworld, 1998.

Harris, Adrienne. "Gender as Contradiction." *Psychoanalytic Dialogues* 1, 1991, pp. 197–224.

Haynal, Andre E. *The Technique at Issue: Controversies in Psychoanalysis from Freud and Ferenczi to Michael Balint.* Trans. Elizabeth Holder, London: Karnac Books, 1988.

Haynal, Andre, and Falzeder, Ernst. "The Psychoanalytic Movement: 'Healing Through Love'? A Unique Dialogue in the History of Psychoanalysis." *Free Associations* 2, 1991, pp. 1–20.

H.D. (Hilda Doolittle). *Tribute to Freud.* New York: New Directions, 1956.

Heller, Judith Bernays. "Freud's Mother and Father." In Hendrik M. Ruitenbeek, ed. *Freud as We Knew Him.* Detroit: Wayne State University Press, 1973, pp. 334–340.

Heller, Peter. "Reflections on a Child Analysis with Anna Freud and an Adult Analysis with Ernst Kris." *Journal of the American Academy of Psychoanalysis* 20, 1992, pp. 48–74.

Heller, Peter, ed. *Anna Freud's Letters to Eva Rosenfeld.* Trans. Mary Weigand. Madison, Conn.: International Universities Press, 1992.

Herman, Judith L. *Trauma and Recovery.* New York: Basic Books, 1992.

Herwig, Holger H. *The First World War: Germany and Austria-Hungary, 1914–1918.* New York: St. Martin's Press, 1998.

Hirschmüller, Albrecht. *The Life and Work of Josef Breuer: Physiology and Psychoanalysis.* New York: New York University Press, 1989.

Holt, Robert R. *Freud Reappraised: A Fresh Look at Psychoanalytic Theory.* New York: Guilford Press, 1989.

Horney, Karen. "The Flight from Womanhood: The Masculinity Complex in Women as Viewed by Men and Women." In Harold Kelman, ed., *Feminine Psychology,* 1926. Reprint, New York: W. W. Norton, 1967, pp. 54–70.

Hynes, Samuel. *The Soldiers' Tale: Bearing Witness to Modern War.* New York: Penguin Books, 1997.

Jannen, William Jr. *The Lions of July: Prelude to War, 1914.* Novato, Calif.: Presidio Press, 1997.

Joll, James. *The Origins of the First World War.* 2nd ed. London: Longman, 1984.

Jones, Ernest. *The Life and Work of Sigmund Freud.* Vol. 1: *The Formative Years and the Great Discoveries, 1856–1900.* New York: Basic Books, 1953.

———. *The Life and Work of Sigmund Freud.* Vol. 2: *The Years of Maturity, 1901–1919.* New York: Basic Books, 1955.

———. *The Life and Work of Sigmund Freud.* Vol. 3: *The Last Phase, 1919–1939.* New York: Basic Books, 1957.

———. *Free Associations: Memories of a Psychoanalyst.* New York: Basic Books, 1959.

Judson, Peiter M. "The Gendered Politics of German Nationalism in Austria: 1800–1900." In David F. Good, Margarete Grandner, and Mary Jo Maynes, eds., *Austrian Women in the Nineteenth and Twentieth Centuries.* Providence, R.I.: Berghahn Books, 1996, pp. 1–18.

Jung, C. G. *Studies in Word Association.* New York: Moffat Yard, 1919.

———. *Symbols of Transformation.* In *The Collected Works of C. G. Jung.* Vol. 5. Trans. by R. F. C. Hull. New York: Pantheon, 1956.

———. *On the Psychology and Pathology of So-Called Occult Phenomena.* In *The Collected Works of C. G. Jung.* Vol. 1. New York: Pantheon, 1957, pp. 3–88.

———. *Freud and Psychoanalysis.* In *The Collected Works of C. G. Jung.* Vol. 4. Trans. by R. F. C. Hull. New York: Pantheon Books, 1961.

———. *Memories, Dreams, Reflections.* Ed. Aniela Jaffe, trans. Richard Winston and Clara Winston. New York: Vintage Books, 1989.

Kann, Robert A., Béla K. Királyi, and Paula S. Fichtner, eds. *The Hapsburg Empire in World War I.* Boulder, Colo.: East European Monographs, 1977.

Kardiner, Abram. *My Analysis with Freud: Reminiscences.* New York: W. W. Norton, 1977.

Kardiner, Abram, and Herbert Spiegel. *War, Stress and Neurotic Illness.* 1941. Rev. ed., New York: P. Hoeber, 1947.

Keegan, John. *The First World War.* New York: Knopf, 1999.

Kerr, John. *A Most Dangerous Method: The Story of Jung, Freud and Sabina Spielrein.* New York: Knopf, 1994.

Kiersky, Sandra, and Fosshage, James L. "The Two Analyses of Dr. L: A Self-Psychological Perspective on Freud's Treatment of the Rat Man." In Barry Magid, ed., *Freud's Case Studies: Self-Psychological Perspectives.* Hillsdale, N.J.: Analytic Press, 1993, pp. 107–133.

Klein, George S. *Psychoanalytic Theory: An Exploration of Essentials.* New York: International Universities Press, 1976.

Kluft, Richard P., ed. *Incest-Related Syndromes of Adult Psychopathology.* Washington, D.C.: American Psychiatric Press, 1990.

Kohn, Hans. "The Crisis in European Thought and Culture." In Jack Roth, ed., *World War I: A Turning Point in Modern History.* New York: Knopf, 1967.

Korchin, Sheldon, and Sands, Susan H. "Principles Common to All Psychotherapies." In Charles E. Walker, ed., *Handbook of Clinical Psychology.* Homewood, Ill.: Dow-Jones, Irwin, 1982.

Kramer, Robert. "'The Bad Mother Freud Has Never Seen': Otto Rank and the Birth of Object-Relations Theory." *Journal of the American Academy of Psychoanalysis* 23, 1995, pp. 293–321.

Kramer, Robert, ed. *Otto Rank: A Psychology of Difference: The American Lectures.* Princeton, N.J.: Princeton University Press, 1996.

Krüll, Marianne. *Freud and His Father.* Trans. Arnold J. Pomerans. New York: W. W. Norton, 1986.

Laforgue, Rene. "Personal Memories of Freud." In Hendrik M. Ruitenbeek, ed., *Freud as We Knew Him.* Detroit: Wayne State University Press, 1973, pp. 341–349.

Leed, Eric J. *No Man's Land: Combat and Identity in World War I.* Cambridge, U.K.: Cambridge University Press, 1979.

Leys, Ruth. "Traumatic Cures: Shell-Shock, Janet and the Question of Memory." *Critical Inquiry* 20, 1994, pp. 621–662.

Lieberman, E. James. *Acts of Will: The Life and Work of Otto Rank.* New York: The Free press, 1985; paperback ed. with new preface, Amherst: University of Massachusetts Press, 1993.

Lifton, Robert J. *Thought Reform and the Psychology of Totalism.* New York: W. W. Norton, 1961.

————. *Home from the War: Learning from Vietnam War Veterans.* Boston: Beacon Press, 1973.

————. *The Life of the Self.* New York: Simon and Schuster, 1976.

————. *The Protean Self: Human Resilience in an Age of Fragmentation.* New York: Basic Books, 1993.

Lorand, Sandor. "Sándor Ferenczi: Pioneer of Pioneers." In Franz Alexander, Samuel Eisenstein, and Martin Grotjahn, eds., *Psychoanalytic Pioneers.* New York: Basic Books, 1966, pp. 14–35.

Luborsky, Lester, Crits-Christoph, Paul, Mintz, John, and Auerbach, Alice. *Who Will Benefit from Psychotherapy? Predicting Therapeutic Outcomes.* New York: Basic Books, 1988.

Lynn, David J. "Freud's Analysis of A.B., a Psychotic Man, 1925–1930." *Journal of the American Academy of Psychoanalysis* 21, 1993, pp. 63–78.

————. "Sigmund Freud's Psychoanalysis of Albert Hirst." *Bulletin of the History of Medicine* 71, 1997, pp. 69–93.

Lynn, David J., and Vaillant, George E. "Anonymity, Neutrality, and Confidentiality in the Actual Methods of Sigmund Freud: A Review of Forty-Three Cases, 1907–1939." *American Journal of Psychiatry* 155:2, 1998, pp. 163–171.

Magid, Barry. "The Homosexual Identity of a Nameless Woman," In Barry Magid, ed., *Freud's Case Studies: Self-Psychological Perspectives.* Hillsdale, N.J.: Analytic Press, 1993, pp. 189–200.

————. "Self Psychology Meets the Wolf Man." In Barry Magid, ed., *Freud's Case Studies: Self-Psychological Perspectives.* Hillsdale, N.J.: Analytic Press, 1993, pp. 157–187.

Magid, Barry, ed. *Freud's Case Studies: Self-Psychological Perspectives.* Hillsdale, N.J.: Analytic Press, 1993.

Mahony, Patrick J. "Friendship and Its Discontents." *Contemporary Psychoanalysis* 15, 1979, pp. 55–109.

————. *Cries of the Wolf Man.* New York: International Universities Press, 1984.

————. *Freud and the Rat Man.* New Haven, Conn.: Yale University Press, 1986.

————. *Freud as a Writer.* New Haven, Conn.: Yale University Press, 1987.

————. *Freud's Dora: A Psychoanalytic, Historical and Textual Study.* New Haven, Conn.: Yale University Press, 1996.

Main, Mary, and Kaplan, N. "Security in Infancy, Childhood and Adulthood: A Move to the Level of Representation." In I. Bretherton and E. Waterns, eds., *Monographs of the Society for Research in Child Development.* N.p.: 1986.

Marcus, Steven. Introduction to Sigmund Freud, *Three Essays on the Theory of Sexuality.* New York: Basic Books, 1962, p. xx.

————. "Freud and Dora: Story, History, Case History." *Psychoanalysis and Contemporary Thought* 5, 1976, pp. 389–442.

Margolis, Deborah P. *Freud and His Mother: Preoedipal Aspects of Freud's Personality.* Northvale, N.J.: Jason Aronson, 1996.

Marwick, Arthur. *War and Social Change in the Twentieth Century: A Comparative Study of Britain, France, Germany, Russia, and the United States.* London: Macmillan, 1974.

Masson, Jeffrey M. *The Assault on Truth: Freud and Child Sexual Abuse.* New York: Farrar, Straus and Giroux, 1984.

————. *Against Therapy: Emotional Tyranny and the Myth of Psychological Healing.* New York: Fontana, 1990.

————. *Final Analysis: The Making and Unmaking of a Psychoanalyst.* New York: Fontana, 1992.

Masson, Jeffrey M., ed. and trans. *The Complete Letters of Sigmund Freud to Wilhelm Fliess: 1887–1904.* Cambridge, Mass.: Harvard University Press, 1985.

McCully, Robert S. "Remarks on the Last Contact between Freud and Jung." *Quadrant: Journal of the C. G. Jung Foundation* 20, 1987, pp. 73–74.

McGuire, William, ed. *The Freud/Jung Letters: The Correspondence between Sigmund Freud and C. G. Jung.* Trans. Ralph Manheim and R. F. C. Hull. Princeton, N.J.: Princeton University Press, 1974.

McLynn, Frank. *Carl Gustav Jung.* New York: St. Martin's Press, 1996.

Meisel, Perry, and Kendrick, Walter, eds. *Bloomsbury/Freud: The Letters of James and Alix Strachey.* New York: Basic Books, 1985.

Menaker, Esther. *Otto Rank: A Rediscovered Legacy.* New York: Columbia University Press, 1982.

———. *Appointment in Vienna.* New York: St. Martin's Press, 1989.

———. "On Anna Freud: A Discussion of Personal Analytic Reactions in the Early Days of Psychoanalysis." *Journal of the American Academy of Psychoanalysis* 19, 1991, pp, 606–611.

Meng, Heinrich, and Freud, Ernst L., eds. *Psychoanalysis and Faith: The Letters of Sigmund Freud and Oskar Pfister.* Trans. Eric Mosbacher. New York: Basic Books, 1963.

Miller, Steven E., ed. *Military Strategy and the Origins of the First World War.* Princeton, N.J.: Princeton University Press, 1985.

Molnar, Michael. "Sigmund Freud's Notes on Faces and Men." In Michael S. Roth, ed., *Freud: Conflict and Culture.* New York: Knopf, 1998, pp. 42–44.

Morton, Frederic. *A Nervous Splendor: Vienna, 1888–1889.* London: Penguin, 1979.

Moscovitch, Michael. *Infant Memory.* New York: Plenum Press, 1984.

Mosse, George L. *Fallen Soldiers: Reshaping the Memory of the World Wars.* New York: Oxford University Press, 1990

Newton, Peter M. *Freud: From Youthful Dream to Mid-Life Crisis.* New York: Guilford Press, 1995.

Nunberg, Herman, and Federn, Ernst, eds. *Minutes of the Vienna Psycho-Analytic Society.* Vol. I, *1906–1908.* Vol. 2, *1908–1910.* Vol. 3, *1910–1911.* Vol. 4, *1912–1918.* New York: International Universities Press, 1962, 1967, 1974, 1975.

Oberholzer, Karen. *The Wolf-Man Sixty Years Later.* New York: Continuum, 1982.

Ornstein, Anna. "Little Hans: His Phobia and His Oedipus Complex." In Barry Magid, ed., *Freud's Case Studies: Self-Psychological Perspectives.* Hillsdale, N.J.: Analytic Press, 1993, pp. 87–106.

Ornstein, Paul H. "Did Freud Understand Dora?" In Barry Magid, ed., *Freud's Case Studies: Self-Psychological Perspectives.* Hillsdale, N.J.: Analytic Press, 1993, pp. 31–85.

Ornston, Darius G., ed. *Translating Freud.* New Haven, Conn.: Yale University Press, 1992.

Paret, Peter, ed., with the collaboration of Craig, Gordon A., and Gilbert, Felix. *Makers of Modern Strategy from Machiavelli to the Nuclear Age.* Princeton, N.J.: Princeton University Press, 1986.

Paris, Bernard J. *Karen Horney: A Psychoanalyst's Search for Self-Understanding.* New Haven, Conn.: Yale University Press, 1994.

Paskauskas, R. Andrew. *The Complete Correspondence of Sigmund Freud and Ernest Jones: 1908–1939.* Cambridge, Mass.: Harvard University Press, 1993.

Perez Foster, RoseMarie. *The Power of Language in the Clinical Process.* Hillsdale, N.J.: Jason Aronson, 1997.

Pfeiffer, Ernst, ed. *Sigmund Freud and Lou Andreas-Salomé: Letters.* Trans. William Robson-Scott and Elaine Robson-Scott. New York: Harcourt Brace Jovanovich, 1972.

Pick, Robert. *The Last Days of Imperial Vienna.* London: Weidenfeld and Nicolson, 1975.

Pollock, George H. "The Possible Significance of Childhood Object Loss in the Josef Breuer-Bertha Pappenheim (Anna O.)-Sigmund Freud Relationship. I. Josef Breuer." *Journal of the American Psychoanalytic Association* 16, 1968, pp. 711–739.

Price, Alan. *The End of the Age of Innocence: Edith Wharton and the First World War.* New York: St. Martin's Press, 1998.

Puner, Helen W. *Freud: His Life and His Mind.* New York: Howell, Soskin, 1947.

Rachman, Arnold W. "Ferenczi and Sexuality." In Lewis Aron and Adrienne Harris, eds., *The Legacy of Sándor Ferenczi.* Hillsdale, N.J.: Analytic Press, 1993, pp. 81–100.

———. "The Confusion of Tongues Theory: Ferenczi's Legacy to Psychoanalysis." *Cahiers Psychiatriques Genevois* (Special Issue), 1994, pp. 235–255.

Rachman, Arnold W., ed. "Psychoanalysis' Favorite Son: The Legacy of Sándor Ferenczi." *Psychoanalytic Inquiry* 17, 1997, pp. 393–572.

Rand, Nicholas, and Torok, Maria. *Questions for Freud: The Secret History of Psychoanalysis.* Cambridge, Mass.: Harvard University Press, 1997.

Rank, Otto. *Modern Education.* Trans. Mabel Moxon. New York: Knopf, 1932.

———. *Beyond Psychology.* Camden, N.J.: Haddon Craftsmen, 1941.

———. *The Myth of the Birth of the Hero.* Trans. by Fred Robbins and Smith Ely Jelliffe. 1909. Reprint, New York: Brunner, 1952.

———. *The Trauma of Birth.* 1924. Reprint, New York: Robert Brunner, 1952.

———. *The Double.* Trans. by Harry Tucker. 1914. Reprint, Chapel Hill: University of North Carolina Press, 1971.

Reik, Theodor. *Listening with the Third Ear: The Inner Experience of a Psychoanalyst.* New York: Farrar, Straus, 1948.

Rieff, Phillip. "Origins of Freud's Political Psychology." *Journal of the History of Ideas* 17, 1956, pp. 235–249.

Roazen, Paul. *Brother Animal: The Story of Freud and Tausk.* New York: Knopf, 1969.

———. *Freud and His Followers.* New York: Knopf, 1975.

———. *Meeting Freud's Family.* Amherst: University of Massachusetts Press, 1993.

———. *How Freud Worked: First-Hand Accounts of Patients.* Northvale, N.J.: 1995.

Roberts, J. M. *Europe, 1880–1945.* London: Longman, 1970.

Robertson, Priscilla S. *An Experience of Women: Pattern and Change in Nineteenth Century Europe.* Philadelphia: Temple University Press, 1982.

Ropp, Theodore. *War in the Modern World.* New York: Macmillan, 1962.

Rosenbaum, Max, and Muroff, Melvin, eds. *Anna O.: Fourteen Contemporary Reinterpretations.* New York: Free Press, 1984.

Roth, Michael S., ed. *Freud: Conflict and Culture.* New York: Knopf, 1998.

Rozenblit, Marsha L. *The Jews of Vienna, 1867–1914: Assimilation and Identity.* Albany: State University of New York Press, 1983.

Rubin, Jeffrey B. *A Psychoanalysis for Our Time: Exploring the Blindness of the Seeing I.* New York: New York University Press, 1998.

Ruitenbeek, Hendrik M., ed. *Freud as We Knew Him.* Detroit: Wayne State University Press, 1973.

Russett, Cynthia E. *Sexual Science: The Victorian Construction of Womanhood.* Cambridge, Mass.: Harvard University Press, 1989.

Rycroft, Charles. *Psychoanalysis Observed.* New York: Coward-McCann, 1967.

———. *The Innocence of Dreams.* New York: Pantheon, 1979.

———. "Freud, Sigmund: 1856–1939." In Justin Wintle, ed., *Makers of Modern Culture.* New York: Facts on File, 1981, pp. 174–177.

Sachs, Hanns. *Freud: Master and Friend.* Cambridge, Mass.: Harvard University Press, 1944.

Said, Edward W. *Culture and Imperialism.* New York: Knopf, 1993.

Schnitzler, Arthur. *My Youth in Vienna.* Trans. Catherine Hutter. New York: Holt, Rinehart and Winston, 1970.

Schorske, Carl E. *Fin-de-Siècle Vienna: Politics and Culture.* New York: Vintage Books, 1981.

Schreiner, George A. *The Iron Ration: Three Years in Warring Central Europe.* New York: Harper and Brothers, 1918.

Schur, Max. "Some Additional 'Day Residues' of the Specimen Dream of Psychoanalysis." In Rudolph M. Loewenstein, Lotte M. Newman, Max Schur, and Albert J. Solnit, eds., *Psychoanalysis: A General Psychology—Essays in Honor of Heinz Hartmann.* New York: International Universities Press, 1966, pp. 45–85.

———. *Freud: Living and Dying.* New York: International Universities Press, 1972.

Scull, Andrew, Mackenzie, Charlotte, and Hervey, Nicholas. *Masters of Bedlam: The Transformation of the Mad-Doctoring Trade.* Princeton, N.J.: Princeton University Press, 1996.

Selesnick, Sheldon T. "Alfred Adler, 1870–1937: The Psychology of the Inferiority Complex." In Franz Alexander, Samuel Eisenstein, and Martin Grotjahn, eds., *Psychoanalytic Pioneers.* New York: Basic Books, 1966, pp. 78–86.

Shapiro, Ester R. "Grief in Freud's Life: Reconceptualizing Bereavement in Psychoanalytic Theory." *Psychoanalytic Psychology* 13, 1996, pp. 547–566.

Shay, Jonathan. *Achilles in Vietnam: Combat Trauma and the Undoing of Character.* New York: Atheneum, 1994.

Shorter, Edward. *From Paralysis to Fatigue: A History of Psychosomatic Illness in the Modern Era.* New York: Free Press, 1992.

Slobodin, Richard. *W. H. R. Rivers.* New York: Columbia University Press, 1978.

Smith, Robert C. *The Wounded Jung: Effects of Jung's Relationships on His Life and Work,* Evanston, Ill.: Northwestern University Press, 1996.

Snyder, Jack. *The Ideology of the Offensive: Military Decision Making and the Disasters of 1914.* Ithaca, N.Y.: Cornell University Press, 1984.

Sperber, Manes. *Masks of Loneliness: Alfred Adler in Perspective.* Trans. by Krishna Winston. New York: Macmillan, 1974.

Sprengnether, Madelon. "Enforcing Oedipus: Freud and Dora." In Charles Bernheimer and Claire Kahane, eds., *In Dora's Case: Freud-Hysteria-Feminism.* New York: Columbia University Press, 1985, pp. 254–276.

———. *The Spectral Mother: Freud, Feminism and Psychoanalysis.* Ithaca, N.Y.: Cornell University Press, 1990.

———. "Mourning Freud." In Anthony Elliott and Stephen Frosh, eds., *Psychoanalysis in Contexts.* New York: Routledge, 1995, pp.142–165.

———. "Reading Freud's Life." *American Imago* 52, no. 1, 1995, pp. 9–54.

Sroufe, L. Alan. *Emotional Development: The Organization of Emotional Life in the Early Years.* Cambridge, U.K.: Cambridge University Press, 1995.

Stahl, Stephen M. *Essential Psychopharmacology: Neuroscientific Basis and Clinical Applications.* Cambridge, U.K.: Cambridge University Press, 1996.

Stanton, Martin. *Sándor Ferenczi: Reconsidering Active Intervention.* Northvale, N.J.: Jason Aronson, 1991.

Stargardt, Nicholas. *The German Idea of Militarism: Radical and Socialist Critics, 1866–1914.* Cambridge, U.K.: Cambridge University Press, 1994.

Steinem, Gloria. "What if Freud Were Phyllis?" In *Moving beyond Words.* New York: Simon and Schuster, 1994, pp. 19–90.

Stekel, Wilhelm. *The Autobiography of Wilhelm Stekel.* New York: Liveright, 1950.

Stepansky, Paul E. *In Freud's Shadow: Adler in Context.* Hillsdale, N.J.: Analytic Press, 1983.

Stern, Daniel. *The Interpersonal World of the Infant: A View from Psychoanalysis and Developmental Psychology.* New York: Basic Books, 1985.

Stoller, Robert J. *Sex and Gender.* Vol. 1. New York: Science House, 1968.

———. *Perversion: The Erotic Form of Hatred.* New York: Pantheon, 1975.

Stolorow, Robert D., Brandchaft, Bernard, and Atwood, George E. *Psychoanalytic Treatment: An Intersubjective Approach.* Hillsdale, N.J.: Analytic Press, 1987.

Stromberg, Roland N. *Redemption by War: The Intellectuals and 1914.* Lawrence: Regents Press of Kansas, 1982.

Strupp, Hans H. "Can the Practitioner Learn from the Researcher?" *American Psychologist* 44, 1989, pp. 717–724.

Sulloway, Frank J. *Freud: Biologist of the Mind: Beyond the Psychoanalytic Legend.* New York: Basic Books, 1979.

Swales, Peter J. "Freud, Minna Bernays, and the Conquest of Rome: New Light on the Origins of Psychoanalysis." *New American Review* 1 (2/3), 1982, pp. 1–23.

———. "Freud, His Teacher and the Birth of Psychoanalysis." In Paul E. Stepansky, ed., *Freud: Appraisals and Reappraisals: Contributions to Freud Studies.* Vol. 1. Hillsdale, N.J.: Analytic Press, 1986, pp. 3–82.

Swenson, Carol R. "Freud's 'Anna O.': Social Work's Bertha Pappenheim." *Clinical Social Work Journal* 22, 1994, pp. 149–163.

Taft, Jessie. *Otto Rank: A Biographical Study Based on Notebooks, Letters, Collected Writings, Therapeutic Achievements and Personal Associations.* New York: Julian Press, 1958.

Tausk, Victor. "On the Psychology of the War Deserter." Trans. Eric Mosbacher and Marius Tausk. *Psychoanalytic Quarterly* 38, 1969, pp. 354–381.

Terr, Lenore C. *Unchained Memories: True Stories of Traumatic Memories, Lost and Found.* New York: Basic Books, 1994.

Tronick, Edward. "Emotions and Emotional Communication in Infants." *American Psychologist* 44, 1989, pp. 112–119.

Vagts, Alfred. *A History of Militarism.* Westport, Conn.: Greenwood Press, 1981.

van der Kolk, Basil A. *Psychological Trauma.* Washington, D.C.: American Psychiatric Press, 1987.

Walter, Bruno. *Theme and Variations: An Autobiography.* London: Hamish Hamilton, 1947.

Warner, Silas L. "Freud's Analysis of Horace Frink, M.D.: A Previously Unexplained Therapeutic Disaster." *Journal of the American Academy of Psychoanalysis* 22, 1994, pp. 137–152.

Wasserman, Isidor. "A Letter to the Editor." *American Journal of Psychotherapy* 12, 1958, pp. 623–627.

Webster, Richard. *Why Freud Was Wrong: Sin, Science and Psychoanalysis.* New York: Basic Books, 1995.

Weiss, Edoardo. *Sigmund Freud as a Consultant: Recollections of a Pioneer in Psychoanalysis.* New York: Intercontinental Medical Book Corp., 1970.

Wilcocks, Robert. *Maelzel's Chess Player: Sigmund Freud and the Rhetoric of Deceit.* Boston: Rowman and Littlefield, 1994.

Williams, Guy. *The Age of Miracles: Medicine and Surgery in the Nineteenth Century.* Chicago: Academy Press, 1987.

Williamson, Samuel R. Jr. *Austria and the Origins of the First World War.* New York: St. Martin's Press, 1991.

Wittels, Fritz. *Sigmund Freud: His Personality, His Teaching and His School.* London: Allen and Unwin, 1924.

Wolff, Larry. *Postcards from the End of the World: Child Abuse in Freud's Vienna.* New York: Atheneum, 1988.

Wollheim, Richard, ed. *Freud: A Collection of Critical Essays.* New York: Anchor, 1974.

Wortis, Joseph. *Fragments of an Analysis with Freud.* New York: Simon and Schuster, 1954.

Young-Bruehl, Elisabeth. *Anna Freud: A Biography.* New York: Summit Books, 1988.

Zantop, Susanne. *Colonial Fantasies: Conquest, Family, and Nation in Precolonial Germany, 1770–1870.* Durham, N.C.: Duke University Press, 1997.

Zetzel, Elizabeth. "Additional Notes upon a Case of Obsessional Neurosis." *International Journal of Psychoanalysis* 47, 1966, pp. 123–129.

Credits

I wish to thank Mr. Tom Roberts of Sigmund Freud Copyrights/Mark Paterson & Associates for his assistance and generosity. The publisher and author are grateful to the following for permission to reprint copyrighted materials:

Published Works

From *Freud: The Man and the Cause* by Ronald Clark, copyright © 1980 by E. M. Partners A. G., reprinted by permission of Random House, Inc. From *Freud: A Life for Our Time* by Peter Gay, copyright © 1988 by Peter Gay, used by permission of W. W. Norton & Company, Inc. From *The Individual Psychology of Alfred Adler* by Heinz L. Ansbacher and Rowena R. Ansbacher, copyright © 1956 by Basic Books, Inc., copyright © renewed 1984 by Heinz L. and Rowena R. Ansbacher, reprinted by permission of Basic Books, a member of Perseus Books, L.L.C. From *The Life and Work of Sigmund Freud* (3 vols.) by Ernest Jones, copyright © 1953, 1955, 1957 by Ernest Jones, copyright © renewed 1981, 1983, 1985 by Mervyn Jones, reprinted by permission of Basic Books, a member of Perseus Books, L.L.C. From *The Letters of Sigmund Freud and Karl Abraham* by Hilda C. Abraham, copyright © 1964 by Sigmund Freud Copyrights Ltd., and Dr. Hilda Abraham, reprinted by permission of Basic Books, a member of Perseus Books, L.L.C., and A. W. Freud et al./Mark Paterson & Associates. From *The Letters of Sigmund Freud*, edited by Ernst L. Freud, copyright © 1960 by Sigmund Freud Copyrights Ltd., copyright © renewed, reprinted by permission of Basic Books, a member of Perseus Books, L.L.C., and A. W. Freud/Mark Paterson & Associates. From the *Standard Edition of the Complete Psychological Works of Sigmund Freud* (24 vols.), translated and edited by James Strachey in collaboration with Anna Freud, assisted by Alix Strachey and Alan Tyson, reprinted by permission of A. W. Freud et al./Mark Paterson & Associates. From *The Complete Letters of Sigmund Freud to Wilhelm Fliess, 1887–1904*, translated and edited by Jeffrey Moussaieff Masson 1985, reprinted by permission of A. W. Freud et al./Mark Paterson & Associates. From *The Correspondence of Sigmund Freud and Sándor Ferenczi*, vol. 1 (1991), edited by E. Falzeder and P. Giamperi-Deutsch, translated by P. T. Hoffer; vol. 2 (1993), edited by E. Brabant, E. Falzeder, and P. Giamperi-Deutsch, reprinted by permission of A. W. Freud et al./Mark Paterson & Associates. From *The Complete Correspondence of Sigmund Freud and Ernest Jones, 1908–1939*, edited by R. Andrew Paskaukas, introduction by Ricardo Steiner, reprinted by permission of A. W. Freud et al./Mark Paterson & Associates. From *The Letters of Sigmund Freud to Eduard Silberstein, 1871–1881*, edited by Walter Boehlich, translated by Arnold J. Pomerans, reprinted by permission of A. W. Freud et al./Mark Paterson & Associates. From *The Clinical Diary of Sándor Ferenczi*, edited by Judith

458   *Credits*

Dupont, translated by Michael Balint and Nicola Zarday Jackson, reprinted by permission of the estate of Sándor Ferenczi by arrangement with Mark Paterson & Associates. From *The Freud/Jung Letters: The Correspondence between Sigmund Freud and C. G. Jung,* edited by William McGuire, translated by Ralph Manheim and R. F. C. Hull, copyright © 1974 by Princeton University Press. Reprinted by permission of Princeton University Press and Mr. Leo La Rosa of the Estate of C. G. Jung. From *Memories, Dreams, Reflections* by C. G. Jung, recorded and edited by Aniela Jaffe, translated by Richard and Clara Winston, copyright © 1961, 1962, 1963 by Random House, Inc., copyright © renewed 1989, 1990, 1991 by Random House, Inc., reprinted by permission of Pantheon Books, a division of Random House, Inc., and Mr. Leo La Rosa of the Estate of C. G. Jung. From *Anna Freud: A Biography* by Elisabeth Young-Bruehl, reprinted by permission of Georges Borchardt Inc., Literary Agency.

Photographs

Figure on page 2 copyright © by W. E. Freud, by arrangement with Mark Paterson & Associates.

Figures on pages 24, 26, 43, 50, 53, 63, 67, 70, 71, 79, 83, 90, 104, 131, 133, 189, 195, 210, 241, 280, 291, 294, 297, 331, and 343, reprinted by permission of A. W. Freud et al./ Mark Paterson & Associates.

Figures on pages 32 and 72 copyright © by Edmund Engelman, from *Sigmund Freud Photographs, Vienna, 1938* by Thomas Engelman. Reprinted by permission.

Figure on page 221 reprinted by permission of Mr. Leo La Rosa, the Estate of C. G. Jung.

Figure on page 326 reprinted by permission of Rupert Pole/Anaïs Nin Foundation.

Index